Executive Compensation

An
Introduction
to Practice
& Theory

Steven Balsam, Ph.D.

WorldatWork. Press

About WorldatWork®

WorldatWork (www.worldatwork.org) is the association for human resources professionals focused on attracting, motivating and retaining employees. Founded in 1955, WorldatWork provides practitioners with knowledge leadership to effectively implement total rewards—compensation, benefits, work-life, performance and recognition, development and career opportunities—by connecting employee engagement to business performance. WorldatWork supports its 30,000 members and customers in 30 countries with thought leadership, education, publications, research and certification.

The WorldatWork group of registered marks includes: WorldatWork®, workspan®, Certified Compensation Professional or CCP®, Certified Benefits Professional® or CBP, Global Remuneration Professional or GRP®, Work-Life Certified Professional or WLCP™, WorldatWork Society of Certified Professionals®, and Alliance for Work-Life Progress® or AWLP®.

WorldatWork Journal, WorldatWork Press and Telework Advisory Group are part of the WorldatWork family.

WorldatWork.
The Total Rewards Association
www.worldatwork.org

Editor: Christina Fuoco-Karasinski
Cover Design: Jamie Hernandez
Production Manager: Rebecca Williams Ficker

Dedication

To my loving wife Lori and my wonderful daughters Gabby and Ally, and in honor of my parents, who dedicated their lives to raising me.

Acknowledgements

I would like to thank Erica Harris and Yong Fang for their invaluable assistance in helping me prepare this book, as well as Robert Jones, Terry Adamson, Arun Upadhyay and Richard Gifford for reading earlier versions of the manuscript. I would also like to thank Dan Cafaro and Larry Fleischman for helping me initiate this project, and Andrea Ozias and Christina Fuoco-Karasinski for their help in producing a polished final version. Finally, I would also like to thank my wife Lori, who not only put up with me during the writing of the book, but who also contributed her time as a research assistant and editor.

Table of Contents

Part II: The Components of the Compensation Package

Part I
Introduction

Chapter 1

Executive Compensation: How Much Is Too Much?

A Tale of Two Men

At the beginning of 2001, James Kiltz was hired to engineer a turnaround at Gillette, a once high-flying conglomerate with a stagnated stock price. In January 2005, Kiltz agreed to sell Gillette to Procter & Gamble, earning himself an estimated $185 million and widespread scorn across the state of Massachusetts (Forelle 2005). This is despite the fact that during his tenure, the share price of Gillette increased 76 percent (versus a slight decline in the S&P 500 index), increasing shareholder value by more than $20 billion.

The controversy surrounding Kiltz's compensation package stands in stark contrast to the near silence from the media in response to an even richer contract involving radio personality (that is, shock jock) Howard Stern. In January 2006, just before he started his show for Sirius satellite radio, Stern received 34 million shares of Sirius common stock worth $220 million (McBride 2006). Stern was also promised cash payments estimated to be $80 million per year from 2006-2010, making the total value of his contract more than $600 million (Murray 2006). Yet other than envy, nary a peep was heard from the media.

As illustrated by the above example, compensation paid to the top executives of publicly traded corporations is a politically sensitive area, with critics claiming that amounts paid to executives are too high[1] (for example, Crystal 1991, Bebchuk and Fried 2004a), and corporations arguing they need to pay to attract, retain and motivate quality people (for example, Kay 1998).[2] Opponents of current levels of executive pay such as the AFL-CIO, have resorted to publicizing what they think are excessive amounts via Web sites such as Executive PayWatch (www.aflcio.org/corporatewatch/paywatch/), and introducing legislation in Congress (see Appendices 11-1 through 11-3). Others have argued (for example, Jensen and Murphy 1990) that it's not how much you pay but how you pay that matters. Regardless, executive compensation, in particular that of the chief executive officer or CEO, is well followed in academic journals and the popular press. Annual surveys of executive compensation are a fixture in most business publications and major newspapers, for example, *Forbes*, *BusinessWeek*, *Fortune* and *The Wall Street Journal*.

Executive compensation is important. A well-designed compensation plan can reward executives and shareholders, whereas a poorly designed plan can waste corporate resources without motivating the executive. At the extreme, a poorly designed incentive system can cause the executive to take actions that reduce shareholder value—for example, cutting back on long-term profitable investments to increase current compensation. Research has shown that when the corporation is performing poorly, shareholder proposals on executive compensation are likely to be made (Thomas and Martin 1999), with most of these proposals calling for limits on amounts paid to executives, although more recently, shareholder proposals have sought to tie executive pay to performance (Favole 2007). Other research has shown that stock prices react positively to initiation and/or amendment of compensation plans (Morgan and Poulsen 2000, Brickley et al. 1985, Tehranian and Waegelein 1985), indicating that shareholders believe the plans will motivate executives to increase shareholder value.[3] Executive compensation is also important because it affects compensation levels and composition throughout the organization (Gomez-Mejia 1994). It affects the level of compensation throughout the organization because lower-management compensation is often a function of upper-management compensation, and affects the composition of their compensation package because the same goals, for example increased equity incentives, may be applied as well. This book will examine the components of the compensation plan, identifying the effects and consequences of its various aspects, as well as discuss how to design an optimal plan for a set of circumstances.

Underlying the need for, and importance of, executive compensation plans is the separation of ownership from the control of the modern corporation (Berle and Means 1932, Jensen and Meckling 1976). Thus, the goal of the executive compensation plan is to align the interests of executives and stakeholders, commonly assumed to be shareholders. Issues to be discussed in this book include the components of the plan, the allocation of compensation among the components, and the role of the individual components in motivating and retaining employees, and mitigating the owner-manager conflict. This discussion will draw upon the practitioner and academic literature, as well as the popular press, and will include descriptive statistics, as well as examples from well-known companies.

A basic assumption of this book, and of much of the academic literature, is that individuals are work averse, that is, they prefer to work as little, and consume as much leisure, as possible. One way, but not the only, or even most efficient, way to overcome this tendency is with economic incentives. Without incentives, employees will slack off, providing the minimal effort necessary to retain their jobs. In fact, while this book focuses on the executive suite, much of the discussion is readily applicable to lower-level employees. Most companies already know that and are providing incentives, from commissions to bonuses to stock options to more employees. Examples include paying salespeople by commission, authors with royalties, etc. In the executive compensation arena, a large percentage of compensation is tied to firm performance via equity compensation, i.e., stock options and grants.

Proper compensation is necessary to recruit and retain employees. If compensation is too low, relative to the employee's best alternative opportunity, he or she will leave. For example, a survey conducted by Watson Wyatt Worldwide and WorldatWork (2006) found that compensation is the reason most frequently cited (71 percent of the time) by top performers when they leave an organization. The following two examples involving Microsoft illustrate the importance compensation plays in employee morale and retention, and the continual need to fine-tune compensation to meet the demands of the marketplace. Bank (1999) reports that Microsoft "increased base pay and stock options for most of its 30,000 employees," stating it was "an essential part of Microsoft staying competitive and successful." Later, in response to a flat stock price in 2003, Microsoft shifted its equity compensation from stock options to restricted stock.

A company must be careful in making these changes. How does one determine what is too low? If it is determined that compensation is too low, what form should the increases take? Across-the-board pay raises may be insufficient to keep stellar performers, and simply end up rewarding those who would have stayed otherwise, that is, those not valued by the marketplace. And should the bull market in tech stocks resume, Microsoft might regret cancelling its option program.

Owner-Manager Conflict: Agency Theory

Understanding the executive compensation package and its role in the modern corporation requires a basic understanding of corporate governance, a topic that will be discussed in more detail in Chapter 10. In the modern, and sometimes not so modern, corporation, the ownership and management functions are separated. This separation can arise from two situations. In the first situation, there are individuals with pre-existing businesses who either do not have the desire and/or skills required to manage the business. In the second, there are individuals with good ideas/products that may not have the funds necessary to bring those products to market and/or sustain themselves through the startup period and thus must seek outside investors. Our capital markets, public and private, allow these individuals to meet and transact business in a way favorable to both. Public capital markets include domestic and international stock and bond markets (for example, the New York and Tokyo Stock exchanges). Private capital markets include venture capitalists, banks, friends, neighbors and relatives. Given the freedom to contract, or not to contract, it is generally assumed that contracts are entered into only when both parties expect to be better off.

This separation of the ownership and management functions can lead to conflicts. For example, while the owner(s) are concerned with the maximization of the value of their stake in the corporation, the executive(s) are concerned with the maximization of their well-being, which involves a trade-off between maximizing their wealth and minimizing their effort. At the extreme, owners bear the risk that executives will transfer the assets of the company to themselves, which is to say, they will steal the assets. While not a major risk in countries with well-developed legal systems, the risk does exist.[4,5] A more likely scenario is that executives, while not stealing the assets, may not manage them in a value-maximizing way. That is, they might pass up profitable investments because taking those investments would require increased effort on their part. They might also overconsume the perquisites of their position, for example, purchase a corporate jet rather than fly commercial airlines.

Academics refer to the costs arising from the separation of the ownership from the management of the corporation as agency costs (see Jensen and Meckling 1976). If these costs can be reduced, the gains can be shared between the owners and executives. Therefore, owners and executives have the incentive to minimize these costs.

The mechanisms for controlling the incentive conflicts arising from the separation of the ownership and control of the corporation include, but are not limited to, monitoring by large shareholders and the board of directors, equity ownership by executives, the market for corporate control, the managerial labor market and compensation contracts that provide incentives to increase shareholder value. In publicly held corporations, shareholders elect a board of directors, which in turn has the power to hire and fire executives. It also has the responsibility of setting executive compensation. Most boards now have a committee devoted to compensation issues, a committee normally referred to as the "compensation committee."

Monitoring by the board of directors has its limitations. For example, the board cannot review every decision the executive makes, and even if it could, it may lack the firm and/or industry-specific expertise to evaluate those decisions.[6] Further, given most directors have limited investment in the corporations on whose boards they sit, directors' incentives may not be aligned with those of shareholders. The existence of a large shareholder, be it an individual or institution, can mitigate this problem, as the large shareholder has the incentives and the financial resources to monitor management.

Ownership by executives, which will be discussed in more detail in chapter nine, mitigates the incentive conflicts by aligning the interests of executives with those of shareholders. It does so by making the executives shareholders in the corporation. As such, they, like other shareholders, are interested in seeing the corporation's share price increase. Unfortunately, given most executives have rather limited resources when compared to the market values of their employer, executives own rather small amounts of their employer. Further, as elaborated on in Chapter 9, when the executive wealth constraint is combined with risk aversion, it may not be in the best interests of other shareholders for an executive to have a large amount of his or her wealth tied up in the corporation's stock.

The market for corporate control, in theory, provides executives with incentives to increase shareholder value. The reason is that if executives manage the corporation in a suboptimal way, the value of the corporation's shares will be low, and if a group of individuals or another corporation believes it could manage the corporation more efficiently, it has the incentive to purchase the corporation to obtain the increase in value from the improved management. If such a purchase were to occur, it is highly likely that the new owners would fire the executives it believed were managing the corporation suboptimally in the first place.

The managerial labor market, or market for a particular executive's services, mitigates the incentive conflicts by providing executives with the incentive to perform well, thereby increasing their market value, that is, their value to other potential employers. Unfortunately, some of the techniques used to retain executives, such as noncompete agreements, which will be discussed in Chapter 3, also reduce the incentives provided by the managerial labor market. That is, an executive with a noncompete agreement is contractually prohibited from working for some potential employers, normally companies in the same industry, for a period of time after he or she leaves his or her current employer. Thus, executives with noncompete clauses have less motivation to be concerned about their value to other employers.

The compensation package can also be used to align the interests of owners and executives. Properly designed, the compensation package can be a tool for mitigating the conflict between owners and executives. It does so by rewarding executives for taking actions that increase shareholder value. Unfortunately, owners (and directors) have incomplete information about the actions of executives. Further, they may not have the expertise to evaluate those actions, even if the actions are observable. Thus it is difficult to base compensation on actions alone. Rather, compensation is often tied to measures that are positively correlated with managerial effort, for example accounting income, share price or market share.

Other Theories that Explain and Influence Executive Compensation

Under agency theory, the compensation package is important because it is used to provide the proper incentives to executives, and hence, mitigate the conflict between owners and executives. While the majority of this book, and many of the academic studies cited herein, is grounded in agency theory, other theories, competing and complementary, exist to explain the composition and importance of the executive compensation package and will be (implicitly) drawn upon throughout the book. These theories include *class hegemony, efficiency wage, figurehead, human capital theory, marginal productivity, prospect, social comparison* and *tournament theory*.

Class hegemony theory argues that executives share a common bond, and that through board of directors composed primarily of CEOs, executives are able to pursue their own goals and interests (and not those of shareholders). In particular, Gomez-Mejia (1994) notes, "board input is primarily used to legitimize high executive pay, reflecting a shared commitment to protect the privileges and wealth of the managerial class." *Efficiency wage* theory (Prendergast 1999) suggests executives are paid a premium to provide them with the incentive to exert effort to avoid being fired. This premium leads them to put forth effort because of the consequences of being fired, which include having to accept another position at a lower wage. In theory, this effort increases executive productivity and reduces turnover. Ungson and Steers (1984) argue the CEO, unlike an operational manager, should not be paid based upon operating results, but rather for his or her role as leader or political figurehead *(figurehead theory)*. As such, the CEO is a symbol and representative of the corporation, representing the organization at ceremonial events and political functions, and managing interactions with owners, employees, government and the general public. Under *human capital theory*, the value of the executive, and hence, his or her compensation, is based upon his or her accumulated knowledge and skills. Agarwal (1981, p. 39) explains the logic behind human capital theory:

The amount of human capital a worker possesses influences his or her productivity, which in turn influences his or her earnings. The same general reason should hold for executives as well. Other things being equal, an executive with a greater amount of human capital would be better able to perform his or her job and thus be paid more.

Managerialism theory argues "that the separation of ownership and control in modern corporations gives top managers almost absolute power to use the firm to pursue their personal objectives" (Gomez-Mejia 1994). They could then use this power to increase the level and reduce the risk of their compensation. Under *marginal productivity theory*, in equilibrium, the executive should receive, as compensation, his or her value to the corporation. Gomez-Mejia (1994) defines this as the "observed performance of the firm minus what performance would be if the next best alternative executive was at the helm, plus the pay that would be necessary to acquire the latter's services." In contrast to agency theory, which assumes risk aversion, *prospect theory* focuses on the executive's loss aversion (Wiseman and Gomez-Mejia 1998). That is, in certain circumstances, for example to avoid losses or missing goals and/or targets, the executive is actually willing to take risks. In contrast, the executive is unwilling to take risks once he or she has achieved his or her performance goals, as the benefit (to the executive) of increasing performance is more than offset by the possibility of falling below target. Under *social comparison theory*, board members use their pay as a reference point when setting pay of executives (O'Reilly et al. 1988). Under *tournament theory* (Lazear and Rosen 1981, Rosen 1986), executive compensation is set to provide incentives, not to the executives, but rather to their subordinates. The executive may in fact receive no incentives from the package, and may be over-paid relative to his or her marginal product or value to the corporation. The incentive is for lower-level executives to work hard, win the tournament and be promoted, whereby they will receive that higher level of compensation. Rosen (1986, page 714) claims, "Payments at the top have indirect effects of increasing productivity of competitors further down the ladder."

External Influences on the Compensation Package

A number of items external to the corporation and the executive influence the amount and composition of the compensation package. For example, different components of the compensation package have different financial reporting treatments. That is, while items like salary and bonus reduce reported accounting income when earned by the executive, prior to 2006, most stock options did not reduce reported accounting income. Given the desire of executives to report a higher level of income, this differential accounting treatment may have caused them to design compensation packages that included more stock options, and less other compensation, than would otherwise be optimal. Starting with fiscal years beginning after June 15, 2005, Statement of Financial Accounting Standards No.

123(revised) requires the expensing of all option grants, thereby eliminating the accounting incentive to issue stock options. Consistent with this leveling of the accounting treatment, during the past few years we have seen a decrease in the use of stock options.[7]

Similarly, components of the compensation package are not treated equally for tax purposes. For example, Section 162(m) of the Internal Revenue Code limits the deductibility of compensation to the CEO and the next four highest-paid executives to $1 million per individual, with an exception allowed if compensation is "performance based." Whereas salary can never be performance based, bonus plans can be modified to meet the exception, and in most cases, stock option plans are performance based by definition. Thus, the tax code provides incentives for corporations subject to this constraint to shift compensation from salary to bonus and stock option plans. Consistent with these incentives, research discussed later in this book has found these shifts have occurred.

Finally, the political environment surrounding executive compensation has the potential to influence the level and composition of the compensation package because of the potential "political costs" that may be imposed upon the executive and the corporation. Narrowly defined, political costs are the costs imposed upon the executive and the corporation by the government's ability to tax and regulate. An example would be Section 162(m) of the Internal Revenue Code, which limited tax deductions and, hence, increased the after-tax cost of executive compensation. Political costs also include actions taken by nongovernment regulators, for example, the Financial Accounting Standards Board, which after multiple attempts, finally passed a standard requiring that corporations recognize an expense for the stock options granted to employees. Broadly defined, political costs include the costs imposed upon the executive and the corporation by interested parties, which include, but are not limited to, politicians, regulators, unions, suppliers and customers. These parties have made periodic accusations that executive compensation is excessive and unrelated to corporate performance. In theory, the pressure and costs imposed by these parties could reduce the level of executive compensation and/or cause a shift from the components of compensation that are not based upon corporate performance, for example salaries and pensions, toward components of compensation that are based upon corporate performance, for example bonuses and stock options. In practice, political pressure may lead firms to attempt to hide compensation, for example shifting compensation from items that are clearly reported in the proxy statement, like salary and bonus, to items that are harder to value, like pensions.[8] Further political costs provide incentive to shift away from performance-based compensation, such as stock options, to avoid the political costs associated with large payouts.[9]

Sources of Data on Executive Compensation

Data on executive compensation are contained in proxy statements mailed to shareholders and filed with the Securities and Exchange Commission (SEC). The SEC then makes these statements publicly available, in its offices and online, via its Electronic Data Gathering, Analysis and Retrieval system (EDGAR) at *www.sec.gov/edaux*. Section §229.402. Item 402, of SEC Regulation S-K, which has been reproduced in the Appendix to this chapter, requires and governs the disclosures. It requires disclosure of compensation for the CEO, chief financial officer (CFO), the next three highest-paid executives and potentially two additional individuals for whom disclosure would have been required but for the fact that the individual was not serving as an executive officer of the registrant at the end of the last completed fiscal year.

The SEC requires disclosure of the following information in a summary table for the most recent three-year period: salary, bonus, stock awards, option awards, nonequity plan incentive compensation, change in pension value and nonqualified deferred compensation earnings and all other compensation.

Compared to the prior requirements, this new table, which went into effect for filings after Dec. 15, 2006, provides several items not previously required. First, each public company is now required to incorporate the value of the change in pension value and nonqualified deferred compensation earnings, which as illustrated by the Richard Grasso (former New York Stock Exchange CEO) case, can be quite large, and as discussed by Bebchuk and Fried (2004b), can be used to obscure the true value of the compensation package. Additionally, the company now must provide a summary number for total compensation in the last column of the table, which, as noted in Murphy (1996), some companies may have had the incentive to obscure previously.

In addition to the summary compensation table, the SEC requires a series of additional tables, with three focusing on equity compensation. The first table requires disclosure of grants of plan-based awards, in particular the estimated future payouts, including threshold, target and maximum payouts for plans where the payouts depend upon future outcomes, and the number of fixed share and option awards (and the exercise price of those options). The second table will disclose the status (i.e., vested versus unvested), amount and value of share awards outstanding at year-end, while a third table discloses options exercised and shares vested, including the value recognized for each.

Whereas previously, firms provided one or more tables that in theory allowed investors and others to estimate the amount of pension payouts, the revised regulations require a table where the firm needs to disclose the present value of each of the named executives' accumulated benefits. The firm also needs to provide a table detailing nonqualified deferred compensation, including executive contributions, firm contributions, earnings and withdrawals during the last fiscal year, and the accumulated balance at the end of the year. Both of these tables, in addition to the summary compensation table, make it easier for interested individuals to identify the true compensation earned in the current year, as well as the firm's future obligation.

An additional tabular disclosure is required for director compensation. Akin to that required for executives, the firm must disclose a summary number for total compensation, including cash earned, the value of options and stock granted during that year, and changes in the present value of pensions and other nonqualified deferred compensation plans.

In addition to the tables discussed above, the new disclosure regulations require a substantial amount of qualitative disclosure about compensation arrangements, e.g., employment contracts. A central location, but not the only location, for these disclosures is Compensation Discussion and Analysis, during which the compensation committee of the board of directors discusses the corporation's compensation policies applicable to executive officers, the specific relationship of corporate performance to executive compensation and the criteria upon which the CEO's pay was based, etc. The specific rules regarding this report are reproduced below.

(b) *Compensation discussion and analysis.*

    (1) Discuss the compensation awarded to, earned by or paid to the named executive officers. The discussion shall explain all material elements of the registrant's compensation of the named executive officers. The discussion shall describe the following:

        (i)   The objectives of the registrant's compensation programs;

        (ii) What the compensation program is designed to reward;

        (iii) Each element of compensation;

        (iv) Why the registrant chooses to pay each element;

        (v) How the registrant determines the amount (and, where applicable, the formula) for each element to pay; and

        (vi) How each compensation element and the registrant's decisions regarding that element fit into the registrant's overall compensation objectives and affect decisions regarding other elements.

A big weakness of these disclosures, according to this author (among others), is the failure of the SEC to require disclosure of targets as discussed in the paragraph below:

4. Registrants are not required to disclose target levels with respect to specific quantitative or qualitative performance related-factors considered by the compensation committee or the board of directors, or any other factors or criteria involving confidential trade secrets or confidential commercial or financial information, the disclosure of which would result in competitive harm for the registrant. The standard to use when determining whether disclosure would cause competitive harm for the registrant is the same standard that would apply when a registrant requests confidential treatment of confidential trade secrets or confidential commercial or financial information pursuant to Securities Act Rule 406 (17 CFR 230.406) and Exchange Act Rule 24b–2 (17 CFR 240.24b–2), each of which incorporates the criteria for nondisclosure when relying upon Exemption 4 of the Freedom of Information Act (5 U.S.C. 552(b)(4)) and Rule 80(b)(4) (17 CFR 200.80(b)(4)) thereunder. A registrant is not required to seek confidential treatment under the procedures in Securities Act Rule 406 and Exchange Act Rule 24b-2 if it determines that the disclosure would cause competitive harm in reliance on this instruction; however, in that case, the registrant must discuss how difficult it will be for the executive or how likely it will be for the registrant to achieve the undisclosed target levels or other factors.

The weakness is that investors and other interested parties have no way to determine whether the thresholds set require sufficiently high performance for the amounts involved.

The information disclosed in these proxy statements are then compiled and disseminated in a number of ways. News organizations, for example, *Forbes*, *BusinessWeek* and *The Wall Street Journal*, all publish annual surveys of executive compensation, in effect making the information freely available to the public in a more accessible form. Data intermediaries, such as *The Corporate Library*, *Equilar* and *Executive Compensation Advisory Services*, compile and maintain databases of this information, which they then use to provide customized reports to clients. The database utilized in this book is Standard & Poor's *ExecuComp*, which contains information about executive compensation in the 1,500 companies that form the S&P 500, S&P MidCap 400 and S&P SmallCap 600 indices.

Footnotes

1 A more thorough discussion of whether executive compensation is too high is contained in part IV of this book.

2 This controversy extends to not-for-profit institutions as well. In 1992, an uproar resulted from the disclosure that United Way of America President William Aramony had received an annual compensation package worth $463,000. Even though Aramony resigned his position shortly after this disclosure, it was estimated that United Way collections would be down 10 percent in 1992 from the year earlier, with the implication that some, if not all, of the drop was caused by the scandal (Stodghill et al. 1992).

3 An alternative view is that executives, who possess inside information, introduce/revise these plans when they believe the corporation is under-valued. Thus, the increased price reaction is a response to the information released, rather than the initiation/revision of the plan itself.

4 While not a major risk, executive theft or malfeasance does happen, for example Tyco International (see Maremont and Cohen 2002 for details). Another example that is unfolding is the scandal involving the backdating of options, which will be discussed in detail in Chapter 6.

5 See Leggett (2000) and Latour and Delaney (2002) for examples of these risks outside the United States.

6 One reason the board cannot review every decision is the limited amount of time it has to spend on corporate matters, especially if the corporation is not its primary employer. For example, Silverman (2000b) reports that directors work an average of 173 hours annually. This information has reportedly increased over the past few years.

7 The decrease in the use of stock options prior to the date for expensing mandated under SFAS 123(revised) can be explained by the fact that mandatory expensing was widely anticipated.

8 Bebchuk and Fried 2004b refer to pensions as "stealth compensation."

9 To elaborate, as risk-averse individuals, most executives prefer fixed to conditional compensation. Exacerbating the desire for fixed compensation, if the executive does take conditional compensation, for example stock options, and the share price goes up significantly, he or she will earn what appears to be a windfall profit and will be widely criticized for doing so—especially if he or she has the misfortune to exercise those options in a year where the share price did not do so well.

Appendix 1-1

13. Revise § 229.402 to read as follows:

§ 229.402 (Item 402) Executive Compensation

(a) General—

(1) Treatment of foreign private issuers. A foreign private issuer will be deemed to comply with this Item if it provides the information required by Items 6.B and 6.E.2 of Form 20–F (17 CFR 249.220f), with more detailed information provided if otherwise made publicly available or required to be disclosed by the issuer's home jurisdiction or a market in which its securities are listed or traded.

(2) All compensation covered. This Item requires clear, concise and understandable disclosure of all plan and non-plan compensation awarded to, earned by, or paid to the named executive officers designated under paragraph (a)(3) of this Item, and directors covered by paragraph (k) of this Item, by any person for all services rendered in all capacities to the registrant and its subsidiaries, unless otherwise specifically excluded from disclosure in this Item. All such compensation shall be reported pursuant to this Item, even if also called for by another requirement, including transactions between the registrant and a third party where a purpose of the transaction is to furnish compensation to any such named executive officer or director. No amount reported as compensation for one fiscal year need be reported in the same manner as compensation for a subsequent fiscal year; amounts reported as compensation for one fiscal year may be required to be reported in a different manner pursuant to this Item.

(3) Persons covered. Disclosure shall be provided pursuant to this Item for each of the following (the "named executive officers"):

(i) All individuals serving as the registrant's principal executive officer or acting in a similar capacity during the last completed fiscal year ("PEO"), regardless of compensation level;

(ii) All individuals serving as the registrant's principal financial officer or acting in a similar capacity during the last completed fiscal year ("PFO"), regardless of compensation level;

(iii) The registrant's three most highly compensated executive officers other than the PEO and PFO who were serving as executive officers at the end of the last completed fiscal year; and

(iv) Up to two additional individuals for whom disclosure would have been provided pursuant to paragraph (a)(3)(iii) of this Item but for the fact that the individual was not serving as an executive officer of the registrant at the end of the last completed fiscal year.

Instructions to Item 402(a)(3)

1. Determination of most highly compensated executive officers. The determination as to which executive officers are most highly compensated shall be made by reference to total compensation for the last completed fiscal year (as required to be disclosed pursuant to paragraph (c)(2)(x) of this Item) reduced by the amount required to be disclosed pursuant to paragraph (c)(2)(viii) of this Item, provided, however, that no disclosure need be provided for any executive officer, other than the PEO and PFO, whose total compensation, as so reduced, does not exceed $100,000.

2. Inclusion of executive officer of subsidiary. It may be appropriate for a registrant to include as named executive officers one or more executive officers or other employees of subsidiaries in the disclosure required by this Item. See Rule3b–7 under the Exchange Act (17 CFR 240.3b– 7).

3. Exclusion of executive officer due to overseas compensation. It may be appropriate in limited circumstances for a registrant not to include in the disclosure required by this Item an individual, other than its PEO or PFO, who is one of the registrant's most highly compensated executive officers due to the payment of amounts of cash compensation relating to overseas assignments attributed predominantly to such assignments.

(4) Information for full fiscal year. If the PEO or PFO served in that capacity during any part of a fiscal year with respect to which information is required, information should be provided as to all of his or her compensation for the full fiscal year. If a named executive officer (other than the PEO or PFO) served as an executive officer of the registrant (whether or not in the same position) during any part of the fiscal year with respect to which information is required, information shall be provided as to all compensation of that individual for the full fiscal year.

(5) Omission of table or column. A table or column may be omitted if there has been no compensation awarded to, earned by, or paid to any of the named executive officers or directors required to be reported in that table or column in any fiscal year covered by that table.

(6) Definitions. For purposes of this Item:

    (i) The term stock means instruments such as common stock, restricted stock, restricted stock units, phantom stock, phantom stock units, common stock equivalent units or any similar instruments that do not have option-like features, and the term option means instruments such as stock options, stock appreciation rights and similar instruments with option-like features. The term stock appreciation rights ("SARs") refers to SARs payable in cash or stock, including SARs payable in cash or stock at the election of the registrant or a named executive officer. The term equity is used to refer generally to stock and/or options.

    (ii) The term plan includes, but is not limited to, the following: Any plan, contract, authorization or arrangement, whether or not set forth in any formal document, pursuant to which cash, securities, similar instruments, or any other property may be received. A plan may be applicable to one person. Registrants may omit information regarding group life, health, hospitalization, or medical reimbursement plans that do not discriminate in scope, terms or operation, in favor of executive officers or directors of the registrant and that are available generally to all salaried employees.

    (iii) The term incentive plan means any plan providing compensation intended to serve as incentive for performance to occur over a specified period, whether such performance is measured by reference to financial performance of the registrant or an affiliate, the registrant's stock price, or any other performance measure. An equity incentive plan is an incentive plan or portion of an incentive plan under which awards are granted that fall within the scope of Financial Accounting Standards Board Statement of Financial Accounting Standards No. 123 (revised 2004), Share-Based Payment, as modified or supplemented ("FAS 123R"). A non-equity incentive plan is an incentive plan or portion of an incentive plan that is not an equity incentive plan. The term incentive plan award means an award provided under an incentive plan.

    (iv) The terms date of grant or grant date refer to the grant date determined for financial statement reporting purposes pursuant to FAS 123R.

    (v) Closing market price is defined as the price at which the registrant's security was last sold in the principal United States market for such security as of the date for which the closing market price is determined.

    (b) Compensation discussion and analysis.

(1) Discuss the compensation awarded to, earned by, or paid to the named executive officers. The discussion shall explain all material elements of the registrant's compensation of the named executive officers. The discussion shall describe the following:
   (i)   The objectives of the registrant's compensation programs;
   (ii) What the compensation program is designed to reward;
   (iii) Each element of compensation;
   (iv) Why the registrant chooses to pay each element;
   (v)   How the registrant determines the amount (and, where applicable, the formula) for each element to pay; and
   (vi) How each compensation element and the registrant's decisions regarding that element fit into the registrant's overall compensation objectives and affect decisions regarding other elements.

(2) While the material information to be disclosed under Compensation Discussion and Analysis will vary depending upon the facts and circumstances, examples of such information may include, in a given case, among other things, the following:
   (i)   The policies for allocating between long-term and currently paid out compensation;
   (ii) The policies for allocating between cash and non-cash compensation, and among different forms of non-cash compensation;
   (iii) For long-term compensation, the basis for allocating compensation to each different form of award (such as relationship of the award to the achievement of the registrant's long-term goals, management's exposure to downside equity performance risk, correlation between cost to registrant and expected benefits to the registrant);
   (iv) How the determination is made as to when awards are granted, including awards of equity-based compensation such as options;
   (v)   What specific items of corporate performance are taken into account in setting compensation policies and making compensation decisions;
   (vi) How specific forms of compensation are structured and implemented to reflect these items of the registrant's performance, including whether discretion can be or has been exercised (either to award compensation absent attainment of the relevant performance goal(s) or to reduce or increase the size of any award or payout), identifying any particular exercise of discretion, and stating whether it applied to one or more specified named executive officers or to all compensation

subject to the relevant performance goal(s);

(vii) How specific forms of compensation are structured and implemented to reflect the named executive officer's individual performance and/or individual contribution to these items of the registrant's performance, describing the elements of individual performance and/or contribution that are taken into account;

(viii) Registrant policies and decisions regarding the adjustment or recovery of awards or payments if the relevant registrant performance measures upon which they are based are restated or otherwise adjusted in a manner that would reduce the size of an award or payment;

(ix) The factors considered in decisions to increase or decrease compensation materially;

(x) How compensation or amounts realizable from prior compensation are considered in setting other elements of compensation (e.g., how gains from prior option or stock awards are considered in setting retirement benefits);

(xi) With respect to any contract, agreement, plan or arrangement, whether written or unwritten, that provides for payment(s) at, following, or in connection with any termination or change-in-control, the basis for selecting particular events as triggering payment (e.g., the rationale for providing a single trigger for payment in the event of a change-in-control);

(xii) The impact of the accounting and tax treatments of the particular form of compensation;

(xiii) The registrant's equity or other security ownership requirements or guidelines (specifying applicable amounts and forms of ownership), and any registrant policies regarding hedging the economic risk of such ownership;

(xiv) Whether the registrant engaged in any benchmarking of total compensation, or any material element of compensation, identifying the benchmark and, if applicable, its components (including component companies); and

(xv) The role of executive officers in determining executive compensation.

Instructions to Item 402(b)

1. The purpose of the Compensation Discussion and Analysis is to provide to investors material information that is necessary to an understanding of the registrant's compensation policies and decisions regarding the named executive officers.

2. The Compensation Discussion and Analysis should be of the information contained in the tables and otherwise disclosed pursuant to this Item. The Compensation Discussion and Analysis should also cover actions regarding executive compensation that were taken after the registrant's last fiscal year's end. Actions that should be addressed might include, as examples only, the adoption or implementation of new or modified programs and policies or specific decisions that were made or steps that were taken that could affect a fair understanding of the named executive officer's compensation for the last fiscal year. Moreover, in some situations it may be necessary to discuss prior years in order to give context to the disclosure provided.

3. The Compensation Discussion and Analysis should focus on the material principles underlying the registrant's executive compensation policies and decisions and the most important factors relevant to analysis of those policies and decisions. The Compensation Discussion and Analysis shall reflect the individual circumstances of the registrant and shall avoid boilerplate language and repetition of the more detailed information set forth in the tables and narrative disclosures that follow.

4. Registrants are not required to disclose target levels with respect to specific quantitative or qualitative performance-related factors considered by the compensation committee or the board of directors, or any other factors or criteria involving confidential trade secrets or confidential commercial or financial information, the disclosure of which would result in competitive harm for the registrant. The standard to use when determining whether disclosure would cause competitive harm for the registrant is the same standard that would apply when a registrant requests confidential treatment of confidential trade secrets or confidential commercial or financial information pursuant to Securities Act Rule 406 (17 CFR 230.406) and Exchange Act Rule 24b–2 (17 CFR 240.24b–2), each of which incorporates the criteria for nondisclosure when relying upon Exemption 4 of the Freedom of Information Act (5 U.S.C. 552(b)(4)) and Rule 80(b)(4) (17 CFR 200.80(b)(4)) thereunder. A registrant is not

required to seek confidential treatment under the procedures in Securities Act Rule 406 and Exchange Act Rule 24b-2 if it determines that the disclosure would cause competitive harm in reliance on this instruction; however, in that case, the registrant must discuss how difficult it will be for the executive or how likely it will be for the registrant to achieve the undisclosed target levels or other factors.

5. Disclosure of target levels that are non-GAAP financial measures will not be subject to Regulation G (17 CFR 244.100—102) and Item 10(e) (§ 229.10(e)); however, disclosure must be provided as to how the number is calculated from the registrant's audited financial statements.

(c) Summary compensation table—(1) General. Provide the information specified in paragraph (c)(2) of this Item, concerning the compensation of the named executive officers for each of the registrant's last three completed fiscal years, in a Summary Compensation Table in the tabular format specified below.

Summary Compensation Table

Name and principal position	Year	Salary ($)	Bonus ($)	Stock awards ($)	Option awards ($)	Nonequity incentive plan compensation ($)	Change in pension value and qualified deferred compensation earnings ($)	All other compensation ($)	Total ($)
(a)	(b)	(c)	(d)	(e)	(f)	(g)	(h)	(i)	(j)
PEO.									
PFO.									
A.									
B.									
C.									

(2) The Table shall include:
  (i) The name and principal position of the named executive officer (column (a));
  (ii) The fiscal year covered (column (b));
  (iii) The dollar value of base salary (cash and non-cash) earned by the named executive officer during the fiscal year covered (column (c));
  (iv) The dollar value of bonus (cash and non-cash) earned by the named executive officer during the fiscal year covered (column (d)).

Instructions to Item 402(c)(2)(iii) and (iv)

1. If the amount of salary or bonus earned in a given fiscal year is not calculable through the latest practicable date, a footnote shall be included disclosing that the amount of salary or bonus is not calculable through the latest practicable date and providing the date that the amount of salary or bonus is expected to be determined, and such amount must then be disclosed in a filing under Item 5.02(f) of Form 8–K (17 CFR 249.308).

2. Registrants need not include in the salary column (column (c)) or bonus column (column (d)) any amount of salary or bonus forgone at the election of a named executive officer pursuant to a registrant's program under which stock, equity-based or other forms of non-cash compensation may be received by a named executive officer instead of a portion of annual compensation earned in a covered fiscal year. However, the receipt of any such form of non-cash compensation instead of salary or bonus earned for a covered fiscal year must be disclosed in the appropriate column of the Summary Compensation Table corresponding to that fiscal year (e.g., stock awards (column (e)); option awards (column (f)); all other compensation (column (i))), or, if made pursuant to a non-equity incentive plan and therefore not reportable in the Summary Compensation Table when granted, a footnote must be added to the salary or bonus column so disclosing and referring to the Grants of Plan-Based Awards Table (required by paragraph (d) of this Item) where the award is reported.

  (v) For awards of stock, the aggregate grant date fair value computed in accordance with FAS 123R (column (e));
  (vi) For awards of options, with or without tandem SARs (including awards that subsequently have been transferred), the aggregate grant date fair-value computed in accordance with FAS 123R (column (f)).

Instructions to Item 402(c)(2)(v) and (vi)

1. For awards reported in columns (e) and (f), include a footnote disclosing all assumptions made in the valuation by reference to a discussion of those assumptions in the registrant's financial statements, footnotes to the financial statements, or discussion in the Management's Discussion and Analysis. The sections so referenced are deemed part of the disclosure provided pursuant to this Item.

2. If at any time during the last completed fiscal year, the registrant has adjusted or amended the exercise price of options or SARs previously awarded to a named executive officer, whether through amendment, cancellation or replacement grants, or any other means ("repriced"), or otherwise has materially modified such awards, the registrant shall include, as awards required to be reported in column (f), the incremental fair value, computed as of the repricing or modification date in accordance with FAS 123R, with respect to that repriced or modified award.

   (vii) The dollar value of all earnings for services performed during the fiscal year pursuant to awards under nonequity incentive plans as defined in paragraph (a)(6)(iii) of this Item, and all earnings on any outstanding awards (column (g))

Instructions to Item 402(c)(2)(vii)

1. If the relevant performance measure is satisfied during the fiscal year (including for a single year in a plan with a multi-year performance measure), the earnings are reportable for that fiscal year, even if not payable until a later date, and are not reportable again in the fiscal year when amounts are paid to the named executive officer.

2. All earnings on non-equity incentive plan compensation must be identified and quantified in a footnote to column (g), whether the earnings were paid during the fiscal year, payable during the period but deferred at the election of the named executive officer, or payable by their terms at a later date.

   (viii) The sum of the amounts specified in paragraphs (c)(2)(viii)(A) and (B) of this Item (column (h)) as follows:

(A) The aggregate change in the actuarial present value of the named executive officer's accumulated benefit under all defined benefit and actuarial pension plans (including supplemental plans) from the pension plan measurement date used for financial statement reporting purposes with respect to the registrant's audited financial statements for the prior completed

fiscal year to the pension plan measurement date used for financial statement reporting purposes with respect to the registrant's audited financial
statements for the covered fiscal year; and

(B) Above-market or preferential earnings on compensation that is deferred on
a basis that is not taxqualified, including such earnings on nonqualified
defined contribution plans.

Instructions to Item 402(c)(2)(viii)

1. The disclosure required pursuant to paragraph (c)(2)(viii)(A) of this Item
    applies to each plan that provides for the payment of retirement benefits,
    or benefits that will be paid primarily following retirement, including but
    not limited to tax-qualified defined benefit plans and supplemental execu-
    tive retirement plans, but excluding tax-qualified defined contribution plans
    and nonqualified defined contribution plans. For purposes of this disclo-
    sure, the registrant should use the same amounts required to be disclosed
    pursuant to paragraph (h)(2)(iv) of this Item for the covered fiscal year and
    the amounts that were or would have been required to be reported for the
    executive officer pursuant to paragraph (h)(2)(iv) of this Item for the prior
    completed fiscal year.

2. Regarding paragraph (c)(2)(viii)(B) of this Item, interest on deferred
    compensation is above-market only if the rate of interest exceeds 120% of
    the applicable federal longterm rate, with compounding (as prescribed
    under section 1274(d) of the Internal Revenue Code, (26 U.S.C. 1274(d)))
    at the rate that corresponds most closely to the rate under the registrant's
    plan at the time the interest rate or formula is set. In the event of a discre-
    tionary reset of the interest rate, the requisite calculation must be made on
    the basis of the interest rate at the time of such reset, rather than when
    originally established. Only the above-market portion of the interest must
    be included. If the applicable interest rates vary depending upon conditions
    such as a minimum period of continued service, the reported amount
    should be calculated assuming satisfaction of all conditions to receiving
    interest at the highest rate. Dividends (and dividend equivalents) on
    deferred compensation denominated in the registrant's stock ("deferred
    stock") are preferential only if earned at a rate higher than dividends on the
    registrant's common stock. Only the preferential portion of the dividends
    or equivalents must be included. Footnote or narrative disclosure may be
    provided explaining the registrant's criteria for determining any portion

considered to be above-market.

3. The registrant shall identify and quantify by footnote the separate amounts attributable to each of paragraphs (c)(2)(viii)(A) and (B) of this Item. Where such amount pursuant to paragraph (c)(2)(viii)(A) is negative, it should be disclosed by footnote but should not be reflected in the sum reported in column (h).

(ix) All other compensation for the covered fiscal year that the registrant could not properly report in any other column of the Summary Compensation Table (column (i)). Each compensation item that is not properly reportable in columns (c)-(h), regardless of the amount of the compensation item, must be included in column (i). Such compensation must include, but is not limited to:

(A) Perquisites and other personal benefits, or property, unless the aggregate amount of such compensation is less than $10,000;

(B) All "gross-ups" or other amounts reimbursed during the fiscal year for the payment of taxes;

(C) For any security of the registrant or its subsidiaries purchased from the registrant or its subsidiaries (through deferral of salary or bonus, or otherwise) at a discount from the market price of such security at the date of purchase, unless that discount is available generally, either to all security holders or to all salaried employees of the registrant, the compensation cost, if any, computed in accordance with FAS 123R;

(D) The amount paid or accrued to any named executive officer pursuant to a plan or arrangement in connection with:

(1) Any termination, including without limitation through retirement, resignation, severance or constructive termination (including a change in responsibilities) of such executive officer's employment with the registrant and its subsidiaries; or

(2) A change in control of the registrant.

(E) Registrant contributions or other allocations to vested and unvested defined contribution plans;

(F) The dollar value of any insurance premiums paid by, or on behalf of, the registrant during the covered fiscal year with respect to life insurance for the benefit of a named executive officer; and

(G) The dollar value of any dividends or other earnings paid on stock or option awards, when those amounts were not factored into the grant date fair value required to be reported for the stock or option award in columns (e) or (f); and

Instructions to Item 402(c)(2)(ix)

1. Non-equity incentive plan awards and earnings and earnings on stock and options, except as specified in paragraph (c)(2)(ix)(G) of this Item, are required to be reported elsewhere as provided in this Item and are not reportable as All Other Compensation in column (i).

2. Benefits paid pursuant to defined benefit and actuarial plans are not reportable as All Other Compensation in column (i) unless accelerated pursuant to a change in control; information concerning these plans is reportable pursuant to paragraphs (c)(2)(viii)(A) and (h) of this Item.

3. Any item reported for a named executive officer pursuant to paragraph (c)(2)(ix) of this Item that is not a perquisite or personal benefit and whose value exceeds $10,000 must be identified and quantified in a footnote to column (i). This requirement applies only to compensation for the last fiscal year. All items of compensation are required to be included in the Summary Compensation Table without regard to whether such items are required to be identified other than as specifically noted in this Item.

4. Perquisites and personal benefits may be excluded as long as the total value of all perquisites and personal benefits for a named executive officer is less than $10,000. If the total value of all perquisites and personal benefits is $10,000 or more for any named executive officer, then each perquisite or personal benefit, regardless of its amount, must be identified by type. If perquisites and personal benefits are required to be reported for a named executive officer pursuant to this rule, then each perquisite or personal benefit that exceeds the greater of $25,000 or 10% of the total amount of perquisites and personal benefits for that officer must be quantified and disclosed in a footnote. The requirements for identification and quantification apply only to compensation for the last fiscal year. Perquisites and other personal benefits shall be valued on the basis of the aggregate incremental cost to the registrant. With respect to the perquisite or other personal benefit for which footnote quantification is required, the registrant shall describe in the footnote its methodology for computing the aggregate incremental cost. Reimbursements of taxes owed with respect to perquisites or other personal benefits must be included in column (i) and are subject to separate quantification and identification as tax reimbursements (paragraph (c)(2)(ix)(B) of this Item) even if the associated perquisites or other personal benefits are not required to be included because the total amount of all perquisites or personal benefits for an indi-

vidual named executive officer is less than $10,000 or are required to be identified but are not required to be separately quantified.

5. For purposes of paragraph (c)(2)(ix)(D) of this Item, an accrued amount is an amount for which payment has become due.

  (x) The dollar value of total compensation for the covered fiscal year (column (j)). With respect to each named executive officer, disclose the sum of all amounts reported in columns (c) through (i).

Instructions to Item 402(c)

1. Information with respect to fiscal years prior to the last completed fiscal year will not be required if the registrant was not a reporting company pursuant to section 13(a) or 15(d) of the Exchange Act (15 U.S.C. 78m(a) or 78o(d)) at any time during that year, except that the registrant will be required to provide information for any such year if that information previously was required to be provided in response to a Commission filing requirement.

2. All compensation values reported in the Summary Compensation Table must be reported in dollars and rounded to the nearest dollar. Reported compensation values must be reported numerically, providing a single numerical value for each grid in the table. Where compensation was paid to or received by a named executive officer in a different currency, a footnote must be provided to identify that currency and describe the rate and methodology used to convert the payment amounts to dollars.

3. If a named executive officer is also a director who receives compensation for his or her services as a director, reflect that compensation in the Summary Compensation Table and provide a footnote identifying and itemizing such compensation and amounts. Use the categories in the Director Compensation Table required pursuant to paragraph (k) of this Item.

4. Any amounts deferred, whether pursuant to a plan established under section 401(k) of the Internal Revenue Code (26 U.S.C. 401(k)), or otherwise, shall be included in the appropriate column for the fiscal year in which earned.

(d) *Grants of plan-based awards table.*

(1) Provide the information specified in paragraph (d)(2) of this Item, concerning each grant of an award made to a named executive officer in the last completed fiscal year under any plan, including awards that subsequently have been transferred, in the following tabular format (on page 28):

Grants of Plan-Based Awards

Name	Grant date	Estimated future payout under nonequity incentive plan awards			Estimated future payout under equity incentive plan awards			All other stock awards; number of shares of stock or units (#)	All other option awards; number of securities underlying options (#)	Executive or base price of option awards ($/SH)
		Threshold ($)	Target ($)	Maximum ($)	Threshold (#)	Target (#)	Maximum (#)			
(a)	(b)	(c)	(d)	(e)	(f)	(g)	(h)	(i)	(j)	(k)
PEO										
PFO										
A										
B										
C										

(2) The Table shall include:

(i) The name of the named executive officer (column (a));

(ii) The grant date for equity-based awards reported in the table (column (b)). If such grant date is different than the date on which the compensation committee (or a committee of the board of directors performing a similar function or the full board of directors) takes action or is deemed to take action to grant such awards, a separate, adjoining column shall be added between columns (b) and (c) showing such date;

(iii) The dollar value of the estimated future payout upon satisfaction of the conditions in question under non-equity incentive plan awards granted in the fiscal year, or the applicable range of estimated payouts denominated in dollars (threshold, target and maximum amount) (columns (c) through (e)).

(iv) The number of shares of stock, or the number of shares underlying options to be paid out or vested upon satisfaction of the conditions in question under equity incentive plan awards granted in the fiscal year, or the applicable range of estimated payouts denominated in the number of shares of stock, or the number of shares underlying options under the award (threshold, target and maximum amount) (columns (f) through (h)).

(v)   The number of shares of stock granted in the fiscal year that are not required to be disclosed in columns (f) through (h) (column (i));

(vi) The number of securities underlying options granted in the fiscal year that are not required to be disclosed in columns (f) through (h) (column (j)); and

(vii) The per-share exercise or base price of the options granted in the fiscal year (column (k)). If such exercise or base price is less than the closing market price of the underlying security on the date of the grant, a separate, adjoining column showing the closing market price on the date of the grant shall be added after column (k).

Instructions to Item 402(d)

1. Disclosure on a separate line shall be provided in the Table for each grant of an award made to a named executive officer during the fiscal year. If grants of awards were made to a named executive officer during the fiscal year under more than one plan, identify the particular plan under which each such grant was made.

2. For grants of incentive plan awards, provide the information called for by columns (c), (d) and (e), or (f), (g) and (h), as applicable. For columns (c) and (f), threshold refers to the minimum amount payable for a certain level of performance under the plan. For columns (d) and (g), target refers to the amount payable if the specified performance target(s) are reached. For columns (e) and (h), maximum refers to the maximum payout possible under the plan. If the award provides only for a single estimated payout, that amount must be reported as the target in columns (d) and (g). In columns (d) and (g), registrants must provide a representative amount based on the previous fiscal year's performance if the target amount is not determinable.

3. In determining if the exercise or base price of an option is less than the closing market price of the underlying security on the date of the grant, the registrant may use either the closing market price as specified in paragraph (a)(6)(v) of this Item, or if no market exists, any other formula prescribed for the security. Whenever the exercise or base price reported in column (k) is not the closing market price, describe the methodology for determining the exercise or base price either by a footnote or accompanying textual narrative.

4. A tandem grant of two instruments, only one of which is granted under an incentive plan, such as an option granted in tandem with a performance share, need be reported only in column (i) or (j), as applicable. For example, an option granted in tandem with a performance share would be reported only as an option grant in column (j), with the tandem feature noted either by a footnote or accompanying textual narrative.

5. Disclose the dollar amount of consideration, if any, paid by the executive officer for the award in a footnote to the appropriate column.

6. If non-equity incentive plan awards are denominated in units or other rights, a separate, adjoining column between columns (b) and (c) shall be added quantifying the units or other rights awarded.

(e) *Narrative disclosure to summary compensation table and grants of planbased awards table.* (1) Provide a narrative description of any material factors necessary to an understanding of the information disclosed in the tables required by paragraphs (c) and (d) of this Item. Examples of such factors may include, in given cases, among other things:

(i) The material terms of each named executive officer's employment agreement or arrangement, whether written or unwritten;

(ii) If at any time during the last fiscal year, any outstanding option or other equity-based award was repriced or otherwise materially modified (such as by extension of exercise periods, the change of vesting or forfeiture conditions, the change or elimination of applicable performance criteria, or the change of the bases upon which returns are determined), a description of each such repricing or other material modification;

(iii) The material terms of any award reported in response to paragraph (d) of this Item, including a general description of the formula or criteria to be applied in determining the amounts payable, and the vesting schedule. For example, state where applicable that dividends will be paid on stock, and if so, the applicable dividend rate and whether that rate is preferential. Describe any performance-based conditions, and any other material conditions, that are applicable to the award. For purposes of the Table required by paragraph (d) of this Item and the narrative disclosure required by paragraph (e) of this Item, performancebased conditions include both performance conditions and market conditions, as those terms are defined in FAS 123R; and

(iv) An explanation of the amount of salary and bonus in proportion to total compensation.

Instructions to Item 402(e)(1)

1. The disclosure required by paragraph (e)(1)(ii) of this Item would not apply to any repricing that occurs through a pre-existing formula or mechanism in the plan or award that results in the periodic adjustment of the option or SAR exercise or base price, an antidilution provision in a plan or award, or a recapitalization or similar transaction equally affecting all holders of the class of securities underlying the options or SARs.

2. Instructions 4 and 5 to Item 402(b) apply regarding disclosure pursuant to paragraph (e)(1) of this Item of target levels with respect to specific quantitative or qualitative performance-related factors considered by the compensation committee or the board of directors, or any other factors or criteria involving confidential trade secrets or confidential commercial or financial information, the disclosure of which would result in competitive harm for the registrant.

(2) [Reserved]

Outstanding Equity Awards At Fiscal Year-End

	Option Awards					Stock Awards			
Name	Number of securities underlying unexercised options (#) exercisable	Number of securities underlying unexercised options (#) unexer-cisable	Equity incentive plan awards: number of securities underlying unexercised unearned options (#)	Option exercise price (#)	Option expiration date	Number of shares or units of stock that have not vested (#)	Market value of shares or units of stock that have not vested (#)	Equity incentive plan awards: number of unearned shares, units or other rights that have not vested (#)	Equity incentive plan awards: market or payout value of unearned shares, units or other rights that have not vested ($)
(a)	(b)	(c)	(d)	(e)	(f)	(g)	(h)	(i)	(j)
PEO									
PFO									
A									
B									
C									

(f) Outstanding equity awards at fiscal year-end table. (1) Provide the information specified in paragraph (f)(2) of this Item, concerning unexercised options; stock that has not vested; and equity incentive plan awards for each named executive officer outstanding as of the end of the registrant's last completed fiscal year in the following tabular format:

(2) The Table shall include:

(i) The name of the named executive officer (column (a));

(ii) On an award-by-award basis, the number of securities underlying unexercised options, including awards that have been transferred other than for value, that are exercisable and that are not reported in column (d) (column (b));

(iii) On an award-by-award basis, the number of securities underlying unexercised options, including awards that have been transferred other than for value, that are unexercisable and that are not reported in column (d) (column (c));

(iv) On an award-by-award basis, the total number of shares underlying unexercised options awarded under any equity incentive plan that have not been earned (column (d));

(v) For each instrument reported in columns (b), (c) and (d), as applicable, the exercise or base price (column (e));

(vi) For each instrument reported in columns (b), (c) and (d), as applicable, the expiration date (column (f));

(vii) The total number of shares of stock that have not vested and that are not reported in column (i) (column (g));

(viii) The aggregate market value of shares of stock that have not vested and that are not reported in column (j) (column (h));

(ix) The total number of shares of stock, units or other rights awarded under any equity incentive plan that have not vested and that have not been earned, and, if applicable the number of shares underlying any such unit or right (column (i)); and

(x) The aggregate market or payout value of shares of stock, units or other rights awarded under any equity incentive plan that have not vested and that have not been earned (column (j)).

Instructions to Item 402(f)(2)

1. Identify by footnote any award that has been transferred other than for value, disclosing the nature of the transfer.

2. The vesting dates of options, shares of stock and equity incentive plan awards held at fiscal-year end must be disclosed by footnote to the applicable column where the outstanding award is reported.

3. Compute the market value of stock reported in column (h) and equity incentive plan awards of stock reported in column (j) by multiplying the closing market price of the registrant's stock at the end of the last completed fiscal year by the number of shares or units of stock or the amount of equity incentive plan awards, respectively. The number of shares or units reported in columns (d) or (i), and the payout value reported in column (j), shall be based on achieving threshold performance goals, except that if the previous fiscal year's performance has exceeded the threshold, the disclosure shall be based on the next higher performance measure (target or maximum) that exceeds the previous fiscal year's performance. If the award provides only for a single estimated payout, that amount should be reported. If the target amount is not determinable, registrants must provide a representative amount based on the previous fiscal year's performance.

4. Multiple awards may be aggregated where the expiration date and the exercise and/or base price of the instruments is identical. A single award consisting of a combination of options, SARs and/or similar option-like instruments shall be reported as separate awards with respect to each tranche with a different exercise and/or base price or expiration date.

5. Options or stock awarded under an equity incentive plan are reported in columns (d) or (i) and (j), respectively, until the relevant performance condition has been satisfied. Once the relevant performance condition has been satisfied, even if the option or stock award is subject to forfeiture conditions, options are reported in column (b) or (c), as appropriate, until they are exercised or expire, or stock is reported in columns (g) and (h) until it vests.

(g) Option exercises and stock vested table. (1) Provide the information specified in paragraph (g)(2) of this Item, concerning each exercise of stock options, SARs and similar instruments, and each vesting of stock, including restricted stock, restricted stock units and similar instruments, during the last completed fiscal year for each of the named executive officers on an aggregated basis in the following tabular format (on page 34):

Option Exercises and Stock Vested

Name	Option Awards		Stock Awards	
	Number of shares acquired on exercise (#)	Value realized on exercise ($)	Number of shares acquired on vested (#)	Value realized on vested ($)
(a)	(b)	(c)	(d)	(e)
PEO				
PFO				
A				
B				
C				

(2) The Table shall include:

   (i) The name of the executive officer (column (a));

   (ii) The number of securities for which the options were exercised (column (b));

   (iii) The aggregate dollar value realized upon exercise of options, or upon the transfer of an award for value (column (c));

   (iv) The number of shares of stock that have vested (column (d)); and

   (v) The aggregate dollar value realized upon vesting of stock, or upon the transfer of an award for value (column (e)).

Instruction to Item 402(g)(2)

Report in column (c) the aggregate dollar amount realized by the named executive officer upon exercise of the options or upon the transfer of such instruments for value. Compute the dollar amount realized upon exercise by determining the difference between the market price of the underlying securities at exercise and the exercise or base price of the options. Do not include the value of any related payment or other consideration provided (or to be provided) by the registrant to or on behalf of a named executive officer, whether in payment of the exercise price or related taxes. (Any such payment or other consideration provided by the registrant is required to be disclosed in accordance with paragraph (c)(2)(ix) of this Item.) Report in column (e) the aggregate dollar amount realized by the named executive officer upon the vesting of stock or the transfer of such instruments for value. Compute the aggregate dollar amount realized upon vesting by multiplying the number of shares of stock or units by the market value of the underlying shares on the vesting date. For any amount realized upon exercise or vesting for which receipt has been deferred, provide a footnote quantifying the amount and disclosing the terms of the deferral.

(h) Pension benefits. (1) Provide the information specified in paragraph (h)(2) of this Item with respect to each plan that provides for payments or other benefits at, following, or in connection with retirement, in the following tabular format:

Pension Benefits

Name	Plan name	Number of years credited service (#)	Present value of accumulated benefit ($)	Payments during last fiscal year ($)
(a)	(b)	(c)	(d)	(e)
PEO				
PFO				
A				
B				
C				

(2) The Table shall include:
(i) The name of the executive officer (column (a));
(ii) The name of the plan (column (b));
(iii) The number of years of service credited to the named executive officer under the plan, computed as of the same pension plan measurement date used for financial statement reporting purposes with respect to the registrant's audited financial statements for the last completed fiscal year (column (c));
(iv) The actuarial present value of the named executive officer's accumulated benefit under the plan, computed as of the same pension plan measurement date used for financial statement reporting purposes

with respect to the registrant's audited financial statements for the last completed fiscal year (column (d)); and

(v) The dollar amount of any payments and benefits paid to the named executive officer during the registrant's last completed fiscal year (column (e)).

Instructions to Item 402(h)(2)

1. The disclosure required pursuant to this Table applies to each plan that provides for specified retirement payments and benefits, or payments and benefits that will be provided primarily following retirement, including but not limited to tax-qualified defined benefit plans and supplemental executive retirement plans, but excluding tax-qualified defined contribution plans and nonqualified defined contribution plans. Provide a separate row for each such plan in which the named executive officer participates.

2. For purposes of the amount(s) reported in column (d), the registrant must use the same assumptions used for financial reporting purposes under generally accepted accounting principles, except that retirement age shall be assumed to be the normal retirement age as defined in the plan, or if not so defined, the earliest time at which a participant may retire under the plan without any benefit reduction due to age. The registrant must disclose in the accompanying textual narrative the valuation method and all material assumptions applied in quantifying the present value of the current accrued benefit. A benefit specified in the plan document or the executive's contract itself is not an assumption. Registrants may satisfy all or part of this disclosure by reference to a discussion of those assumptions in the registrant's financial statements, footnotes to the financial statements, or discussion in the Management's Discussion and Analysis. The sections so referenced are deemed part of the disclosure provided pursuant to this Item.

3. For purposes of allocating the current accrued benefit between tax qualified defined benefit plans and related supplemental plans, apply the limitations applicable to tax qualified defined benefit plans established by the Internal Revenue Code and the regulations thereunder that applied as of the pension plan measurement date.

4. If a named executive officer's number of years of credited service with respect to any plan is different from the named executive officer's number of actual years of service with the registrant, provide footnote disclosure quantifying the difference and any resulting benefit augmentation.

(3) Provide a succinct narrative description of any material factors necessary to an understanding of each plan covered by the tabular disclosure required by this paragraph. While material factors will vary depending upon the facts, examples of such factors may include, in given cases, among other things:

(i) The material terms and conditions of payments and benefits available under the plan, including the plan's normal retirement payment and benefit formula and eligibility standards, and the effect of the form of benefit elected on the amount of annual benefits. For this purpose, normal retirement means retirement at the normal retirement age as defined in the plan, or if not so defined, the earliest time at which a participant may retire under the plan without any benefit reduction due to age;

(ii) If any named executive officer is currently eligible for early retirement under any plan, identify that named executive officer and the plan, and describe the plan's early retirement payment and benefit formula and eligibility standards. For this purpose, early retirement means retirement at the early retirement age as defined in the plan, or otherwise available to the executive under the plan;

(iii) The specific elements of compensation (e.g., salary, bonus, etc.) included in applying the payment and benefit formula, identifying each such element;

(iv) With respect to named executive officers' participation in multiple plans, the different purposes for each plan; and

(v) Registrant policies with regard to such matters as granting extra years of credited service.

(i) Nonqualified defined contribution and other nonqualified deferred compensation plans. (1) Provide the information specified in paragraph (i)(2) of this Item with respect to each defined contribution or other plan that provides for the deferral of compensation on a basis that is not tax-qualified in the following tabular format (on page 38):

Nonqualified Deferred Compensation

Name	Executive contributions in last FY ($)	Registrant contributions in last FY ($)	Aggregate earnings in last FY ($)	Aggregate withdrawals/ distributions ($)	Aggregate balance at last FYE ($)
(a)	(b)	(c)	(d)	(e)	(f)
PEO					
PFO					
A					
B					
C					

(2) The Table shall include:

    (i) The name of the executive officer (column (a));

    (ii) The dollar amount of aggregate executive contributions during the registrant's last fiscal year (column (b));

    (iii) The dollar amount of aggregate registrant contributions during the registrant's last fiscal year (column (c));

    (iv) The dollar amount of aggregate interest or other earnings accrued during the registrant's last fiscal year (column (d));

    (v) The aggregate dollar amount of all withdrawals by and distributions to the executive during the registrant's last fiscal year (column (e)); and

    (vi) The dollar amount of total balance of the executive's account as of the end of the registrant's last fiscal year (column (f)).

Instruction to Item 402(i)(2)

Provide a footnote quantifying the extent to which amounts reported in the contributions and earnings columns are reported as compensation in the last completed fiscal year in the registrant's Summary Compensation Table and amounts reported in the aggregate balance at last fiscal year end (column (f)) previously were reported as compensation to the named executive officer in the registrant's Summary Compensation Table for previous years.

(3) Provide a succinct narrative description of any material factors necessary to an understanding of each plan covered by tabular disclosure required by this paragraph. While material factors will vary depending upon the facts, examples of such factors may include, in given cases, among other things:

(i) The type(s) of compensation permitted to be deferred, and any limitations (by percentage of compensation or otherwise) on the extent to which deferral is permitted;

(ii) The measures for calculating interest or other plan earnings (including whether such measure(s) are selected by the executive or the registrant and the frequency and manner in which selections may be changed), quantifying interest rates and other earnings measures applicable during the registrant's last fiscal year; and

(iii) Material terms with respect to payouts, withdrawals and other distributions.

(j) Potential payments upon termination or change-in-control. Regarding each contract, agreement, plan or arrangement, whether written or unwritten, that provides for payment(s) to a named executive officer at, following, or in connection with any termination, including without limitation resignation, severance, retirement or a constructive termination of a named executive officer, or a change in control of the registrant or a change in the named executive officer's responsibilities, with respect to each named executive officer:

(1) Describe and explain the specific circumstances that would trigger payment(s) or the provision of other benefits, including perquisites and health care benefits;

(2) Describe and quantify the estimated payments and benefits that would be provided in each covered circumstance, whether they would or could be lump sum, or annual, disclosing the duration, and by whom they would be provided;

(3) Describe and explain how the appropriate payment and benefit levels are determined under the various circumstances that trigger payments or provision of benefits;

(4) Describe and explain any material conditions or obligations applicable to the receipt of payments or benefits, including but not limited to noncompete, non-solicitation, nondisparagement or confidentiality agreements, including the duration of such agreements and provisions regarding waiver of breach of such agreements; and

(5) Describe any other material factors regarding each such contract, agreement, plan or arrangement.

Instructions to Item 402(j)

1. The registrant must provide quantitative disclosure under these require-
    ments, applying the assumptions that the triggering event took place on the
    last business day of the registrant's last completed fiscal year, and the price
    per share of the registrant's securities is the closing market price as of that
    date. In the event that uncertainties exist as to the provision of payments
    and benefits or the amounts involved, the registrant is required to make a
    reasonable estimate (or a reasonable estimated range of amounts) applicable
    to the payment or benefit and disclose material assumptions underlying
    such estimates or estimated ranges in its disclosure. In such event, the
    disclosure would require forward-looking information as appropriate.

2. Perquisites and other personal benefits or property may be excluded only if
    the aggregate amount of such compensation will be less than $10,000.
    Individual perquisites and personal benefits shall be identified and quanti-
    fied as required by Instruction 4 to paragraph (c)(2)(ix) of this Item. For
    purposes of quantifying health care benefits, the registrant must use the
    assumptions used for financial reporting purposes under generally accepted
    accounting principles.

3. To the extent that the form and amount of any payment or benefit that
    would be provided in connection with any triggering event is fully disclosed
    pursuant to paragraph (h) or (i) of this Item, reference may be made to that
    disclosure. However, to the extent that the form or amount of any such
    payment or benefit would be enhanced or its vesting or other provisions
    accelerated in connection with any triggering event, such enhancement or
    acceleration must be disclosed pursuant to this paragraph.

4. Where a triggering event has actually occurred for a named executive
    officer and that individual was not serving as a named executive officer
    of the registrant at the end of the last completed fiscal year, the disclosure
    required by this paragraph for that named executive officer shall apply
    only to that triggering event.

5. The registrant need not provide information with respect to contracts,
    agreements, plans or arrangements to the extent they do not discriminate
    in scope, terms or operation, in favor of executive officers of the registrant
    and that are available generally to all salaried employees.

    (k) *Compensation of directors.* (1) Provide the information specified in para-
        graph (k)(2) of this Item, concerning the compensation of the directors for
        the registrant's last completed fiscal year, in the following tabular format:

Director Compensation

Name	Fees earned or paid in cash ($)	Stock awards ($)	Option awards ($)	Nonequity incentive plan compensation ($)	Change in pension value and nonqualified deferred compensation earnings	All other compensation ($)	Total ($)
(a)	(b)	(c)	(d)	(e)	(f)	(g)	(h)
A							
B							

(2) The Table shall include:

    (i) The name of each director unless such director is also a named executive officer under paragraph (a) of this Item and his or her compensation for service as a director is fully reflected in the Summary Compensation Table pursuant to paragraph (c) of this Item and otherwise as required pursuant to paragraphs (d) through (j) of this Item (column (a));

    (ii) The aggregate dollar amount of all fees earned or paid in cash for services as a director, including annual retainer fees, committee and/or chairmanship fees, and meeting fees (column (b));

    (iii) For awards of stock, the aggregate grant date fair value computed in accordance with FAS 123R (column (c));

    (iv) For awards of stock options, with or without tandem SARs (including awards that subsequently have been transferred), the aggregate grant date fair value computed in accordance with FAS 123R (column (d)).

Instruction to Item 402(k)(2)(iii) and (iv)

For each director, disclose by footnote to the appropriate column, the aggregate number of stock awards and the aggregate number of option awards outstanding at fiscal year end.

    (v) The dollar value of all earnings for services performed during the fiscal year pursuant to non-equity incentive plans as defined in paragraph (a)(6)(iii) of this Item, and all earnings on any outstanding awards (column (e));

(vi) The sum of the amounts specified in paragraphs (k)(2)(vi)(A) and (B) of this Item (column (f)) as follows:

(A) The aggregate change in the actuarial present value of the director's accumulated benefit under all defined benefit and actuarial pension plans (including supplemental plans) from the pension plan measurement date used for financial statement reporting purposes with respect to the registrant's audited financial statements for the prior completed fiscal year to the pension plan measurement date used for financial statement reporting purposes with respect to the registrant's audited financial statements for the covered fiscal year; and

(B) Above-market or preferential earnings on compensation that is deferred on a basis that is not tax-qualified, including such earnings on nonqualified defined contribution plans;

(vii) All other compensation for the covered fiscal year that the registrant could not properly report in any other column of the Director Compensation Table (column (g)). Each compensation item that is not properly reportable in columns (b)–(f), regardless of the amount of the compensation item, must be included in column (g). Such compensation must include, but is not limited to:

(A) Perquisites and other personal benefits, or property, unless the aggregate amount of such compensation is less than $10,000;

(B) All "gross-ups" or other amounts reimbursed during the fiscal year for the payment of taxes;

(C) For any security of the registrant or its subsidiaries purchased from the registrant or its subsidiaries (through deferral of salary or bonus, or otherwise) at a discount from the market price of such security at the date of purchase, unless that discount is available generally, either to all security holders or to all salaried employees of the registrant, the compensation cost, if any, computed in accordance with FAS 123R;

(D) The amount paid or accrued to any director pursuant to a plan or arrangement in connection with:

(1) The resignation, retirement or any other termination of such director; or

(2) A change in control of the registrant;

(E) Registrant contributions or other allocations to vested and unvested defined contribution plans;

(F) Consulting fees earned from, or paid or payable by the registrant and/or its subsidiaries (including joint ventures);

(G) The annual costs of payments and promises of payments pursuant to director legacy programs and similar charitable award programs;

(H) The dollar value of any insurance premiums paid by, or on behalf of, the registrant during the covered fiscal year with respect to life insurance for the benefit of a director; and

(I) The dollar value of any dividends or other earnings paid on stock or optionawards, when those amounts were not factored into the grant date fair value required to be reported for the stock or option award in column (c) or (d); and

Instructions to Item 402(k)(2)(vii)

1. Programs in which registrants agree to make donations to one or more charitable institutions in a director's name, payable by the registrant currently or upon a designated event, such as the retirement or death of the director, are charitable awards programs or director legacy programs for purposes of the disclosure required by paragraph (k)(2)(vii)(G) of this Item. Provide footnote disclosure of the total dollar amount payable under the program and other material terms of each such program for which tabular disclosure is provided.

2. Any item reported for a director pursuant to paragraph (k)(2)(vii) of this Item that is not a perquisite or personal benefit and whose value exceeds $10,000 must be identified and quantified in a footnote to column (g). All items of compensation are required to be included in the Director Compensation Table without regard to whether such items are required to be identified other than as specifically noted in this Item.

3. Perquisites and personal benefits may be excluded as long as the total value of all perquisites and personal benefits for a director is less than $10,000. If the total value of all perquisites and personal benefits is $10,000 or more for any director, then each perquisite or personal benefit, regardless of its amount, must be identified by type. If perquisites and personal benefits are required to be reported for a director pursuant to this rule, then each perquisite or personal benefit that exceeds the greater of $25,000 or 10% of the total amount of perquisites and personal benefits for that director must be quantified and disclosed in a footnote. Perquisites and other personal benefits shall be valued on the basis of the aggregate incremental cost to

the registrant. With respect to the perquisite or other personal benefit for which footnote quantification is required, the registrant shall describe in the footnote its methodology for computing the aggregate incremental cost. Reimbursements of taxes owed with respect to perquisites or other personal benefits must be included in column (g) and are subject to separate quantification and identification as tax reimbursements (paragraph (k)(2)(vii)(B) of this Item) even if the associated perquisites or other personal benefits are not required to be included because the total amount of all perquisites or personal benefits for an individual director is less than $10,000 or are required to be identified but are not required to be separately quantified. (viii)The dollar value of total compensation for the covered fiscal year (column (h)). With respect to each director, disclose the sum of all amounts reported in columns (b) through (g).

Instruction to Item 402(k)(2)

Two or more directors may be grouped in a single row in the Table if all elements of their compensation are identical. The names of the directors for whom disclosure is presented on a group basis should be clear from the Table.

(3) Narrative to director compensation table.

Provide a narrative description of any material factors necessary to an understanding of the director compensation disclosed in this Table.

While material factors will vary depending upon the facts, examples of such factors may include, in given cases, among other things:

(i) A description of standard compensation arrangements (such as fees for retainer, committee service, service as chairman of the board or a committee, and meeting attendance); and

(ii) Whether any director has a different compensation arrangement, identifying that director and describing the terms of that arrangement.

Instruction to Item 402(k)

In addition to the Instructions to paragraph (k)(2)(vii) of this Item, the following apply equally to paragraph (k) of this Item: Instructions 2 and 4 to paragraph (c) of this Item; Instructions to paragraphs (c)(2)(iii) and (iv) of this Item; Instructions to paragraphs (c)(2)(v) and (vi) of this Item; Instructions to paragraph (c)(2)(vii) of this Item; and Instructions to paragraph (c)(2)(viii) of this Item. These Instructions apply to the columns in the Director Compensation Table that are analogous to the columns in the Summary

Compensation Table to which they refer and to disclosures under paragraph (k) of this Item that correspond to analogous disclosures provided for in paragraph (c) of this Item to which they refer.

Instruction to Item 402

Specify the applicable fiscal year in the title to each table required under this Item which calls for disclosure as of or for a completed fiscal year.

Chapter 2

Overview of the Compensation Package

Introduction

This chapter will introduce the basic components of the compensation package, as well as provide some descriptive information about the usage of those components in executive compensation during the past 14 years.[1] As noted in Chapter 1, it is important that companies continually fine-tune their executive compensation programs, and the shifts in use of compensation components during the years provide descriptive information showing that compensation plans have changed over the years. By examining the components of these executive compensation packages, one can start to understand the importance of the total package, and the implications in the hiring, motivation and retention of executives.

Compensation Package

The executive compensation package can, and most often does, contain many components. These components have differing effects on employee motivation and risk, as well as different costs for the corporation. A well-constructed compensation package must make trade-offs between these components to maximize the net benefit[2] to the corporation and the executive. The major and most common components of compensation, which will be discussed in detail later in this book, are salary, bonus, stock options and stock grants, pensions, benefits, perquisites and severance. To start, let's define these components:

Salary

Salary is the fixed contractual amount of compensation that does not explicitly vary with performance. However, it can be affected by performance, as good performance can lead to higher salary in future periods. For example, the employment agreement between Boeing and James McNerney, its chairman, president and chief executive officer, entered into on June 29, 2005, explicitly states,

> Mr. McNerney will receive an annual base salary of $1,750,000. The base salary may be increased, but not decreased, from time to time by the Board.[3]

Bonus

Bonus is a form of compensation that may be conditioned upon individual, group or corporate performance. For most executives, their bonus is based upon individual performance and is determined as part of a plan covering a larger group of employees. Thus, their employment contract may only specify their participation in the plan or a minimum bonus they are guaranteed. For example, the following passage is from the contract of Mark Hurd, president and CEO of Hewlett Packard, which guarantees him a minimum bonus of $2.8 million:

> At least $2,800,000 (target at 200% of base), pro-rated for mid-year entry with a maximum target opportunity of $8,400,000 (600% of base) assuming performance goals are achieved under the Company's executive pay-for-results plan. The applicable targets for the second six months of 2005 and the first six months of 2006 will be deemed to have been met and any incentive earned during the first half of fiscal year 2005 will be pro-rated based on the hire date.[4]

The performance conditions used to determine a bonus may be implicit or explicit, objective or subjective, and financial or nonfinancial. In some cases bonuses can be based upon one factor, for example, net income or sales, whereas in other cases they can be based upon a combination of factors. In addition, bonuses can be based upon short-term or long-term measures. For example, in discussing its 2006 long-term incentive plan, Duke Energy lists the following criteria that may be used in determining performance awards:

> shall be limited to total shareholder return; stock price increase; return on equity; return on capital; earnings per share; EBIT (earnings before interest and taxes); EBITDA (earnings before interest, taxes, depreciation and amortization); ongoing earnings; cash flow (including operating cash flow, free cash flow, discounted cash flow return on investment, and cash flow in excess of costs of capital); EVA (economic value added); economic profit (net operating profit after tax, less a cost of capital charge); SVA (shareholder value added); revenues; net income; operating income; pretax profit margin; performance against business plan; customer service; corporate governance quotient or rating; market share; employee satisfaction; safety; employee engagement; supplier diversity; workforce diversity; operating margins; credit rating; dividend payments; expenses; fuel cost per million

BTU; costs per kilowatt hour; retained earnings; completion of acquisitions, divestitures and corporate restructurings; and individual goals based on objective business criteria underlying the goals listed above and which pertain to individual effort as to achievement of those goals or to one or more business criteria in the areas of litigation, human resources, information services, production, inventory, support services, site development, plant development, building development, facility development, government relations, product market share or management.[5]

It is worth noting that Duke Energy uses traditional financial measures like revenues and net income, as well as nonfinancial measures like customer service and employee satisfaction, in determining executive performance awards, which are long-term bonuses.

Stock Options

Stock options allow their holder to purchase one or more shares of stock at a fixed "exercise" price over a fixed period of time. They have value if the corporation's share price is greater than the exercise price. Because the exercise price is normally set at the share price on the date of grant,[6] the ultimate value of the option depends upon the performance of a corporation's share price subsequent to the date of grant. That is, they can be extremely valuable when the share price rises dramatically, but can also expire worthless if the share price declines.[7] As with bonuses, in most cases the executive participates in a stock option plan along with other employees. Thus, the employment contract only specifies that the executive will participate in the plan and does not provide the amount of the executives' grant. An exception to that rule is the employment agreement between the Walt Disney Co. and Michael D. Eisner, its CEO, entered into Jan. 8, 1997, which states:

5. Stock Options

(a) In connection with this Agreement Executive has been granted stock options on Sept. 30, 1996, to purchase (i) 5,000,000 shares of Company common stock having an exercise price equal to the per share fair market value determined in accordance with the applicable provisions of the Company's 1995 Stock Incentive Plan (the "Plan") of Company common stock on Sept. 30, 1996, (the "A Options") and (ii) 3,000,000 shares of Company common stock of which 1,000,000 shall have an exercise price equal to 125 percent of the per share fair market value of the Company common stock on such date ("Group 1"), 1,000,000 shall have an exercise price equal to 150% of the per share fair market value of the Company common stock on such date ("Group 2"), and 1,000,000 shall have an exercise price equal to 200% of the per share fair market value of the Company common stock on such date ("Group 3") ("Groups 1, 2 and 3 are collectively referred to herein as the B Options"). The A Option shall vest on Sept. 30, 2003. Group 1 of the B Options shall vest on Sept. 30, 2004. Group 2 of the B Options shall vest on Sept. 30, 2005. Group 3 of the B Options shall vest on Sept. 30, 2006. The A Option shall expire on Sept. 30, 2008, and the B Options shall expire on Sept. 30, 2011. Such options shall be subject to, and governed by, the terms and provisions of the Plan except to the extent of modifications of such options which are permitted by the Plan and which are expressly provided for in this Agreement.

There are several details of Eisner's grant that are worth discussing. First is the large amount of options granted (8 million) that were valued by Disney at $195,583,281 on the date of grant.[8] As will be shown later in this chapter and book, the grant size and value far exceed that of the average option grant. Second, some of the options ("A" options) have an exercise price equal to the current market value, whereas others ("B" options) have exercise prices greater than the current market value. While the former is most common, the latter, which is referred to as a premium option, does occur with some frequency and will be discussed in more detail in Chapters 6 and 15. Third, the options do not vest until Sept. 30, 2003 ("A" options), or Sept 30, 2004 ("B" options). By vest, it means that the options cannot be exercised until that date has passed. In other words, Eisner cannot exercise his options until either seven or eight years have passed from the date of grant. While most option grants have vesting periods (occasionally corporations grant options that vest or are exercisable immediately), this is an exceptionally long vesting period. In most cases the executive must also continue to be employed by his or her company to be allowed to exercise the options. Consequently, if Eisner leaves prior to vesting, he will forfeit the options and the ensuing profits. Thus, the extended vesting period provides Eisner with incentive to remain with Disney. Finally, the options expire on (can no longer be exercised after) either Sept. 30, 2008, or Sept. 30, 2011, giving them a 12- or 15-year life. While all options have expiration dates, the norm is 10 years. As will be noted in Appendix 6-3, the longer the life, the more valuable the option.

Stock Grants

Stock grants occur when corporations give shares to their employees. They differ from stock options in that they have no exercise price. Whereas a stock option only has value if the corporation's share price is above the exercise price, a stock grant has value as long as the share price is above zero. Consequently, a stock grant is always worth more than a stock "option" grant for the same number of shares.

Stock grants can be unrestricted or restricted. An example of a restriction imposed upon a stock grant might be that the employee cannot sell the shares until he or she has worked for the corporation for a period of time. For example, Comerica awards restricted stock to key employees, and the shares are:

> forfeitable if such individuals do not remain employees for the period Comerica requires (typically between three and five years).[9]

Another example of a restriction is one based upon performance. Performance-based restrictions have become more common in recent years, and will probably become even more common in the future. Consider the following discussion, which is contained in the Pepsico Performance-Based Long-Term Incentive Award plan, of forfeiture of restricted stock units if performance conditions are not met.

3. Forfeiture of Restricted Stock Units. The number of Restricted Stock Units that are payable shall be determined based on the achievement of performance targets. Subject to the terms and conditions set forth herein, the Restricted Stock Units shall be subject to forfeiture as follows:

    (a) The payment of one-third of the Restricted Stock Units shall be determined based on the achievement of specific {Year} performance targets. The specific performance targets and the percentage of the one-third of the Restricted Stock Units that shall be forfeited if such targets are not achieved shall be established by the Committee in the first ninety (90) days of {Year}.

    (b) The payment of one-third of the Restricted Stock Units shall be determined based on the achievement of specific {Year+1} performance targets. The specific performance targets and the percentage of the one-third of the Restricted Stock Units that shall be forfeited if such targets are not achieved shall be established by the Committee in the first ninety (90) days of {Year+1}.

    (c) The payment of one-third of the Restricted Stock Units shall be determined based on the achievement of specific {Year+2} performance targets. The specific performance targets and the percentage of the one-third of the Restricted Stock Units that shall be forfeited if such targets are not achieved shall be established by the Committee in the first ninety (90) days of {Year+2}.[10]

These restrictions can be binding. In a series of form 4s[11] filed with the Securities and Exchange Commission on Feb. 3, 2006, executives at the Pepsi Bottling Group including John T. Cahill, chairman and CEO, reported the forfeiture of restricted stock due to failure to meet performance targets. For Cahill, the number of shares forfeited was 63,830,[12] which valued at that day's closing price of $56.81 was worth $3,626,182.

Other Stock-Based Forms of Compensation

While not as popular as stock options and grants, some companies grant *stock appreciation rights, phantom stock* and/or *equity units*. Stock appreciation rights, sometimes called SARs, are the right to receive the increase in the value of a specified number of shares of common stock over a defined period of time. Economically, they are equivalent to stock options with one exception. With a stock option, the executive has to purchase and then sell the shares to receive his or her profit.[13] With a stock appreciation right, the corporation simply pays the executive, in cash or common stock, the excess of the current market price of the shares over the exercise price.[14] Thus, the executive is able to realize the benefits of a stock option without having to purchase the stock. In most cases, stock appreciation rights are granted in tandem with stock options where the executive, at the time of exercise, can choose to exercise either the stock option or stock appreciation right.

Phantom stock acts like common stock, but does not constitute claims for ownership of the corporation. It entitles the executive to receive the increase in common stock prices *and* any dividends declared on common stock. It is often used in privately or publicly held corporations, where the owners do not want to dilute existing ownership.

Equity units entitle the holder to purchase common stock at its book value and then resell the stock to the corporation at their its book value at a later date. The owner also gets the dividend payments on the stock. Like phantom stock, equity units are often used in privately or publicly held corporations, where the owners do not want to dilute existing ownership.

Pensions

Pensions are a form of deferred compensation, whereby after retirement from the corporation, the employee receives a payment or series of payments. These payments may be defined by the pension plan,[15] or based upon the amounts accumulated in the employee's personal retirement account.[16] If the payments are defined by the plan, they can be based upon a number of factors including, but not limited to, number of years with the corporation, earnings while working and level within the corporation. Pensions can be structured in many ways. For example, the payments can be fixed in amount or they can be adjusted for inflation. Due to Internal Revenue Code limitations, in most cases, executives are covered by more than one plan. That is, they participate in a primary "tax-qualified" plan along with other employees, and have at least one "supplemental" nonqualified plan. The second plan is necessitated by Internal Revenue Code limitations on payments from a qualified plan. That is, to qualify for favorable tax treatment, the plan must be nondiscriminatory, that is, the benefits cannot be skewed in favor of highly paid employees, *and* the corporation cannot consider compensation in excess of a threshold, which was $220,000 for the year 2006 (section 401(a)(17)), in determining pension benefits, nor make payments in excess of $175,000 (section 415(b)). As noted throughout this book, most top executives make substantially larger sums. Thus, the supplemental plan or plans provide additional benefits without limitation.[17]

Benefits and Perquisites

In addition to receiving salary, bonuses, stock-based compensation and pensions, executives receive a variety of benefits and perquisites, whose value must be reported in the proxy statement.[18] These items include corporate cars; the use of corporate airplanes and apartments; special dining facilities; country club memberships; health, dental, medical, life and disability insurance; and the ability to defer compensation at above-market rates of interest. The following disclosures from the Wachovia Corp. illustrate that the value of these benefits can be substantial.[19]

(2) Represents the personal benefits outlined in the table below, valued at the incremental cost to Wachovia of providing such benefits, as well as tax reimbursements for each of the Named Officers in 2005:

Table 2-1

	Thompson	Jenkins	Carroll	Kelly	Cummings	Malone
Supplemental life insurance benefits (a)	$56,850	—	—	99,348	36,587	—
Financial planning and tax preparation services	6,000	15,000	6,060	15,000	15,000	9,665
Taxes on behalf of Named Officer (b)	17,321	—	—	—	—	10,254
Personal use of corporate aircraft (c)	27,602	2,555	2,907	—	—	1,674
Personal use of automobile	—	—	—	—	—	4,066
Membership dues (d)	1,595	1,345	455	—	—	—
Totals	109,368	18,900	9,422	114,348	51,587	25,659

(a) In 2003, Wachovia terminated split-dollar life insurance agreements with its executive officers. Following such terminations, Wachovia received its interest in the related life insurance policies under those agreements. These amounts reflect payments made by Wachovia in 2005 to compensate the applicable executive for the cost of obtaining and maintaining personal supplemental life insurance benefits in lieu of those split-dollar life insurance arrangements.

(b) Reflects amounts paid by Wachovia on behalf of the applicable executive to offset taxes. The $17,321 paid on behalf of Mr. Thompson in 2005 was for payment to offset tax associated with income imputed for personal use of corporate aircraft as discussed in note (c). The $10,254 paid on behalf of Malone was payment to offset Internal Revenue Code Section 280(G) excise tax estimates in 2005.

(c) The value of personal use of corporate aircraft reflects the calculated incremental cost to Wachovia of personal use of corporate aircraft. Incremental costs have been calculated based on the variable operating costs to Wachovia. Variable costs consist of trip-specific costs including fuel, catering, mileage, maintenance, universal weather monitoring, landing/ramp fees and other miscellaneous variable costs. Incremental cost calculations do not include fixed costs associated with owning our aircraft. Corporate aircraft are used primarily for business travel. Our board of directors has required Wachovia's CEO to use corporate aircraft for all travel whenever practical for security reasons. In 2005, Thompson was reimbursed $17,321 for taxes associated with personal use of corporate aircraft as noted in

(b) above. On certain occasions, an executive's spouse or other family member may accompany the executive on a flight. Calculations exclude spouse or other family member when such travel is necessary for business purposes. The amounts reported reflect a change in valuation methodology in 2005 from prior years in which the cost of the personal use of corporate aircraft had been calculated using the Standard Industrial Fare Level tables found in the applicable federal income tax regulations. The 2004 and 2003 amounts set forth in "Other Annual Compensation" have been recalculated so that amounts are reported consistently.

(d) Amounts represent reimbursement for social club memberships paid in 2005 for 2004 membership periods. Wachovia ceased reimbursements for social club memberships for the Named Officers in January 2005.

Wachovia is not the only company to provide its executives with significant perks. American Financial Group provided Carl Linder III, co-CEO, with insurance benefits worth $205,700, aircraft usage valued at $160,500, meals and personal use of company tickets to sporting events worth $28,500, and automotive, security and administrative services valued at $68,000, for a total of $462,700.[20] Perhaps the most interesting was Joseph Steinberg, Leucadia National president, who racked up $743,556 in personal use of corporate aircraft; it exceeded his salary of $630,429.[21] Rajan and Wulf (2006) report that 66 percent of the employers in their sample offer their CEO access to the company plane, 38 percent offer chauffeur service, 56 percent a company car, 47 percent country club membership, 48 percent lunch club membership, 17 percent health club membership, 70 percent financial counseling, 65 percent tax preparation and 59 percent estate planning. In the past, many corporations (Sessa and Egodigwe 1999) would offer their executives interest-free loans to finance their purchases of corporate stock, however, section 402(a) of the Sarbanes-Oxley Act of 2002 generally prohibits loans to executives and directors.

Section 402(a): Prohibition on Personal Loans to Executives

Generally, it will be unlawful for an issuer to extend credit to any director or executive officer. Consumer credit companies may make home improvement and consumer credit loans and issue credit cards to their directors and executive officers if it is done in the ordinary course of business on the same terms and conditions made to the general public.

Severance

Severance payments are fairly common and have become very controversial (this will be explored in Chapter 8). Severance payments occur when an executive leaves the company under pressure or is fired without cause. While they are sometimes provided for in the executive's employment contract, severance payments at most, occur once at the end of the executive's tenure with the company. Below is the excerpt discussing termination of employment, the types of termination/resignation and severance payable under each of the alternatives from the employment agreement of William Leonard, Aramark's president and CEO, dated Oct. 27, 2003:

9. Termination of Employment.

(a) Termination for Cause; Resignation Without Good Reason.

(i) ARAMARK may terminate Mr. Leonard's employment hereunder for Cause in accordance with the provisions of Section 9(a)(ii), and the Term shall end on the date of any such termination. Mr. Leonard may voluntarily terminate his employment hereunder without Good Reason. In such event, the Term will end on the date of any such termination. In the event Mr. Leonard's employment is terminated by ARAMARK for Cause or Mr. Leonard resigns from his employment without Good Reason, Mr. Leonard shall receive the following amounts:

(A) Any Base Salary accrued but unpaid, and any accrued vacation as of the effective date of termination (the "Accrued Amounts");

(B) A prorated Target Bonus with respect to ARAMARK's fiscal year in which termination occurs equal to the Target Bonus multiplied by the number of days employed over total days in the year in which Mr. Leonard's employment terminated (a "Pro-Rata Bonus");

(C) Supplemental Retirement Benefits payable pursuant to Exhibit A;

(D) All amounts otherwise payable or coverages otherwise afforded pursuant to the terms of any employee benefit plan maintained by ARAMARK (the "Plan Amounts"); and

(E) Mr. Leonard may elect to continue at his sole expense the Executive Health Plan (to the extent Mr. Leonard and members of his family are eligible for such benefit and, for this purpose, Mr. Leonard shall be deemed to be employed by ARAMARK) for a period not to exceed three years.

In addition, all of the options and Installment Stock Purchase Opportunities ("ISPOs") held by Mr. Leonard shall remain subject to the terms and conditions of the applicable plans.

    (ii) Termination for "Cause" shall mean termination by action of the Board because of: (A) Mr. Leonard's repeated and willful failure to perform his duties hereunder in any material respect; (B) a felony conviction of Mr. Leonard; or (C) any willful misconduct by Mr. Leonard that is materially injurious to the financial condition or business reputation of ARAMARK and its affiliates and subsidiaries taken as a whole, provided, however, that no event or circumstance shall be considered to constitute Cause within the meaning of clause (A) or (C) unless Mr. Leonard has been given written notice of the events or circumstances constituting Cause and has failed to effect a cure thereof within 30 calendar days after his receipt of such notice.

    (iii) Resignation for "Good Reason" shall mean the resignation of Mr. Leonard after (x) ARAMARK, without the express written consent of Mr. Leonard, materially breaches this Agreement or Mr. Leonard is not serving on the Board (other than with the express written consent of Mr. Leonard); (y) Mr. Leonard notifies ARAMARK in writing of the nature of such material breach or failure to be a member of the Board and (z) ARAMARK does not correct such material breach or failure within 30 calendar days after its receipt of such notice. ARAMARK acknowledges and agrees that a material breach for purposes of this Section 9 shall include, but not be limited to, any material reduction in Mr. Leonard's duties or authority (whether or not accompanied by a change in title), any diminution in Mr. Leonard's title, any failure to pay Mr. Leonard's Base Salary and any relocation of Mr. Leonard's principal place of business outside of Philadelphia, Pennsylvania.

    (b) Termination Without Cause; Resignation for Good Reason.

ARAMARK may terminate Mr. Leonard's employment hereunder without Cause, in which case the Term will end on the date of any such termination. Mr. Leonard may terminate his employment hereunder for Good Reason, and the Term shall end upon such termination of employment.

In the event Mr. Leonard's employment is terminated by ARAMARK without Cause or if Mr. Leonard should resign for Good Reason, Mr. Leonard shall receive the following amounts, and ARAMARK shall have no further obligation to Mr. Leonard under this Agreement, except as specifically set forth in this Agreement:

(i)   The Accrued Amounts;

(ii) The Pro-Rata Bonus;

(iii) A lump sum payment equal to two times Mr. Leonard's Base Salary, payable within 10 business days after the effective date of termination of employment;

(iv) A lump sum payment equal to two times Mr. Leonard's Target Bonus payable within 10 business days after the effective date of termination of employment;

(v)   Supplemental Retirement Benefits shall be payable pursuant to Exhibit A;

(vi) Health and welfare plan participation shall continue for three years from the effective date of termination, as if Mr. Leonard had remained an active employee.

(vii) Mr. Leonard may elect to continue at ARAMARK's expense the Executive Health Plan (to the extent Mr. Leonard and members of his family are eligible for such benefit and, for this purpose, Mr. Leonard shall be deemed to be employed by ARAMARK) for a period not to exceed three years; and

(viii)The Plan Amounts.

In addition, all of the options and ISPOs to purchase shares of Stock of ARAMARK held by Mr. Leonard shall become vested and immediately exercisable but will in all respects otherwise remain subject to the terms and conditions of the applicable plans.[22]

Change-in-Control Payments

Change-in-control clauses are also standard in the executive compensation contract. A change-in-control payment occurs when the company is acquired by another company and provides the executive with some insurance should he or she lose his or her job as a result of the merger, which often happens. As will be discussed in Chapter 8, this insurance is necessary to provide the executive with the incentives not to oppose a takeover, as otherwise an executive who is worried about losing his or her position will oppose the takeover. The following illustration of a change-in-control clause is from the employment contract of James Kiltz, former CEO of Gillette, whose controversial change-in-control payment was discussed in the introduction to chapter one.

15. Change of Control.

    (a) Notwithstanding any other provision of this Agreement, the provisions of this Section 15 shall apply if there occurs a Change of Control during the Term of Employment and the Executive's employment is terminated (i) during the period from the Change of Control Effective Date through the second anniversary thereof by the Company, other than for Cause or as a result of the Executive's Disability or death, or by the Executive for Good Reason, (ii) by the Executive for any reason during the 30-day period immediately following the first anniversary of a Change of Control, or (iii) by the Company prior to a Change of Control, if, in accordance with the definition of Change of Control Effective Date, it is reasonably demonstrated by the Executive that such termination of employment (A) was at the request of a third party that has taken steps reasonably calculated to effect a Change of Control or (B) otherwise arose in connection with or anticipation of a Change of Control.

    (b) In the event of a termination of the Executive's employment described in Section 15(a), then the Executive shall be entitled to the benefits set forth in Section 14(d), as modified by this Section 15. In lieu of the lump sum payments provided for in clauses (i), (ii), (iii) and (iv) of Section 14(d), the Company shall pay to the Executive, in a lump sum in cash within 30 days after the date of termination, an amount equal to the aggregate of the following amounts:

        (i) the sum of (A) the Executive's Base Salary through the date of termination to the extent not theretofore paid, (B) the product of (x) the Highest Annual Bonus and (y) a fraction, the numerator of which is the number of days in the current fiscal year through the date of termination and the denominator of which is 365, reduced (but not below zero), if the date of termination occurs in the same fiscal year as the Change of Control, by the Executive's Bonus Payment Amount, (C) if elected by the Executive, any compensation previously deferred by the Executive under the Company's Supplemental Savings Plan, Incentive Bonus Plan and/or

Stock Equivalent Unit Plan or any other plan, agreement or arrangement of the Company (together with any accrued interest or earnings thereon), and (D) any accrued vacation pay, in each case to the extent not theretofore paid;

(ii) the amount equal to the product of (A) three and (B) the sum of (x) the Executive's Base Salary and (y) the Executive's Highest Annual Bonus; and

(iii) if elected by the Executive within 60 days following execution of this Agreement and prior to the Change of Control Effective Date, in lieu of and in substitution for the monthly benefit represented thereby, an amount equal to the lump sum actuarial equivalent (utilizing the interest rate and mortality table in effect for lump sum distributions under the Company's tax-qualified pension plan immediately prior to the Change of Control Effective Date, and determined assuming benefit commencement as of the date of termination) of that portion (if any) of the Executive's monthly supplemental pension benefit otherwise payable under Section 10, that accrues as a result of the application of the first sentence of Section 15(c).

(c) In addition, in the event of a termination of the Executive's employment described in Section 15(a), in lieu of the benefit provided in clause (vi) of Section 14(d), the Executive shall be entitled to three (3) additional years of service for the purpose of determining the supplemental pension benefit pursuant to Section 10; provided, however, that the total number of years of service taken into account in determining such benefit shall in no event exceed ten (10).

(d) Finally, in the event of a termination of the Executive's employment described in Section 15(a), the following additional benefits shall be provided to the Executive:

(i) for purposes of determining the Executive's eligibility for retiree benefits pursuant to the Company's welfare plans, practices, programs and policies, the Executive shall be considered to have remained employed until three years after the date of termination, provided, however, that the Executive's commencement of such retiree benefits shall not be any sooner than the Executive's earliest retirement date under the Company's Retirement Plan and

Supplemental Retirement Plan;

(ii) the Company shall, at its sole expense as incurred, provide the Executive with outplacement services the scope and provider of which shall be selected by the Executive in the Executive's sole discretion; and

(iii) clause (vii) of Section 14(d) shall be amended by changing the phrase "24 months" to "36 months."[23]

While the payments to Kiltz were controversial, the provisions in his contract are fairly standard in the contracts of top executives of major corporations.

Usage of Major Components of Compensation

Tables 2-2 through 2-4 (beginning on page 62) show the frequency with which salary, bonus, long-term incentive payments, stock options and stock grants are included in the CEO compensation package of large corporations.[24] Table 2-2 (page 62) shows the frequency with which these components are used by year, whereas Table 2-3 (page 63) shows the frequency across industry and Table 2-4 (page 64) shows the frequency by the size of the corporation. With few exceptions, salary is paid to the CEO every year. Between 72 percent and 85 percent of CEOs receive bonus payments in a given year. A smaller proportion of CEOs (between 12 percent to 25 percent) receives payments from a long-term incentive plan (sometimes referred to as a performance plan) in a given year. Stock options are granted to between 58 percent and 77 percent of CEOs each year, whereas restricted stock is granted to between 18 percent and 45 percent of CEOs in a given year.

But even these relatively high proportions understate the true percentage of CEOs with bonus plans and those receiving stock options. First, with respect to bonuses, the data in the tables reflects bonuses actually paid. A greater percentage of CEOs may have bonus plans, but performance may have not reached the threshold necessary for payout. For example, Anheuser-Busch's 2006 proxy statement contained the following, explaining why no bonuses were paid for 2005:

The Officer Bonus Plan authorizes the Committee to establish programs that allow payment of cash bonuses to participants based on pre-established minimum performance goals for designated performance periods. Pursuant to the Plan, in February 2005 the Committee adopted the 2005 Officer Bonus Program, which established a minimum performance goal and a formula for determining a maximum bonus pool, both of which

Table 2-2:

Percentage of Firms Providing Salary, Bonus, Long-Term Incentive Payments, Stock Options or Stock Grants to Their CEO by Year

Year	Salary	Bonus	Long-Term Incentive Payments	Stock Options	Stock Grants
1992	99.48	82.38	24.61	57.51	20.47
1993	99.62	81.25	17.79	66.73	18.75
1994	99.66	81.35	13.68	65.66	17.84
1995	99.56	81.54	16.62	66.62	18.20
1996	99.27	79.77	16.66	70.93	20.29
1997	99.41	82.51	17.07	71.39	19.63
1998	99.54	80.10	15.89	73.43	20.30
1999	99.12	78.77	14.76	75.12	18.74
2000	99.11	79.41	13.67	74.16	19.59
2001	98.82	72.04	12.32	77.19	20.56
2002	98.86	75.39	12.25	76.11	23.42
2003	98.93	79.62	12.68	72.39	29.98
2004	99.29	83.27	13.71	70.09	37.06
2005	99.25	84.91	16.04	68.66	45.21

Note: Calculations in this table are based upon data contained in the July 2006 version of Standard & Poor's Compustat.

were based on pretax earnings of the Company for 2005 after adjustments for certain items. The Committee also determined a bonus formula for allocating the pool among the participants in which maximum payouts for participants were expressed as a percentage of the total pool.

In February 2006 the Committee certified that the 2005 performance goal was not met. Therefore, no bonuses for 2005 were paid to the plan participants, including Mr. Stokes, the 17 other executive officers, and the 38 other officers of the Company and Anheuser-Busch Inc.[25]

With long-term plans, corporations may skip years by definition, for example a target is set in 2008 for the three-year period 2009 through 2011. By definition, no long-term bonus payment will be made in either 2009 or 2010 regardless of how well the corporation is doing. Of course, corporations can, and do, use overlapping performance periods. That is, the corporation in the example above may also award bonuses for the three-year periods ending in 2009 and 2010 also.

With respect to stock options and stock grants, the percentages in the table repre-

Table 2-3:

Percentage of Firms Providing Salary, Bonus, Long-Term Incentive Payments, Stock Options or Stock Grants to Their CEO in 2005, by Industry

Industry	Standard Industrial Classification Codes	Salary	Bonus	Long-Term Incentive Payments	Stock Options	Stock Grants
Mining and Construction	1000-1999	100.00	96.10	16.88	64.94	67.53
Manufacturing	2000-3999	99.22	83.46	17.0	73.48	42.12
Transportation, Communications, Electric, Gas and Sanitary Services	4000-4999	98.65	85.14	36.49	53.38	46.62
Wholesale and Retail Trade	5000-5999	100.00	81.71	5.71	67.43	35.43
Finance, Insurance and Real Estate	6000-6999	99.07	86.92	18.22	66.36	52.34
Services	7000-8999	99.04	85.65	4.78	69.86	45.93

Note: Calculations in this table are based upon data contained in the April 2006 version of Standard & Poor's ExecuComp.

sent the grants in a given year. Sometimes corporations do not make grants annually, but make large grants in one year intended to represent a longer period. For example, as discussed earlier in this chapter, the Walt Disney Co. in 1996 awarded its CEO, Michael Eisner, options on 8 million shares with a grant date value of $195,583,281.[26] Prior to that, Disney had not granted Eisner any options since 1989, nor has it since granted him any.[27]

Substantial variation in the composition of the compensation package is observed over time (Table 2-2), with the biggest change involving the percentage of CEOs receiving stock compensation. Or more recently, the percentage of CEOs receiving stock grants. As noted in Table 2-2, the percentage of CEOs receiving stock option grants increased from 58 percent in 1992 to 77 percent in 2001, before declining to 69 percent in 2005. Similarly, the percentage of CEOs receiving stock grants increased from 18 percent in 1994 to 45 percent in 2005, with a sharp increase occurring since 2002. Both of these increases are consistent with evidence presented later in this book indicating that stock-based compensation has become a more important component of the executive compensation package. Further, the dramatic jump in the percentage of CEOs receiving stock grants from 2002 to 2005, at a time when the percentage of CEOs receiving stock options declined, is consistent with the recent changes in accounting for share-based payments influencing the form of compensation.

Table 2-4:

Percentage of Firms Providing Salary, Bonus, Long-Term Incentive Payments, Stock Options or Stock Grants to Their CEO in 2005, by Firm Size
(firms divided into deciles by market value of equity)

	Size Decile	Salary	Annual Bonus	Long-Term Incentive Payments	Stock Options	Stock Grants
Smallest	1	98.63	64.38	4.79	53.42	31.51
	2	100.00	75.51	4.76	65.99	33.33
	3	98.64	88.44	10.20	67.35	39.46
	4	99.32	87.67	11.64	68.49	48.63
	5	99.32	83.67	12.24	63.95	47.62
	6	99.32	90.48	23.13	70.75	51.70
	7	100.00	87.67	15.75	69.18	52.74
	8	99.32	91.16	24.49	72.11	44.22
	9	99.32	89.12	22.45	77.55	47.62
Largest	10	98.64	90.48	30.61	78.91	55.10

Note: Calculations in this table are based upon data contained in the April 2006 version of Standard & Poor's ExecuComp.

Variation is also observed across industries (Table 2-3). Compensation is likely to be similar within an industry, because corporate characteristics (see Chapter 14) influence compensation package design, and because these corporations are competing to hire and retain the same individuals. In contrast, the amount, as well as the components, of the compensation package will vary across industries, as industries offer different opportunities and challenges, and compete for executives with different skill sets. Hambrick and Abrahamson (1995) document differences in managerial discretion across industries. Take, for example, regulated companies. It has been argued that the level of compensation, as well as the composition of the compensation package, varies with the complexity and growth of the corporation. Palia (2000), among others, finds regulated companies pay less than that of the nonregulated companies, a finding that can in part be attributed to the limited growth opportunities these companies had (until recently), and in part to the regulated environment in which they operate.

In 2005, the percentage of CEOs receiving a bonus ranged from a low of 82 percent in wholesale and retail trade to a high of 96 percent in mining and construction.[28] The percentage of CEOs receiving long-term incentive payments ranged from a low of 5 percent in services to a high of 36 percent, in transportation, communications, electric, gas and sanitary services; whereas the percentage of CEOs receiving stock options ranged from 53 percent in transportation, communications, electric, gas and sanitary services to 73 percent in manufacturing; and the percentage receiving stock grants ranged from 35 percent in wholesale and retail trade to 68 percent in mining and construction. As noted above, these differences arise from differences in corporate characteristics across industries that lead to differences in compensation contract design. These differences also arise from firm performance realizations that are similar within an industry. Consider, for example, a scenario where a worldwide oversupply depresses steel prices and causes most steel companies to report losses. As a consequence, companies in the steel industry would be less likely to pay bonuses.

Finally, and perhaps most strikingly, variation is observed by the size of the corporation (Table 2-4). Compensation is likely to be similar within similar-sized corporations because these corporations are competing to hire and retain the same individuals. Moreover, CEO compensation has long been shown, in academic research dating back to Taussig and Barker (1925), to vary/increase with the size of the corporation. In 2005, the percentage of corporations paying bonuses increased from 64 percent for corporations in the smallest decile to 90 percent for corporations in the highest decile. Similarly, the percentage of corporations making long-term incentive payments, granting stock options and providing stock grant increased from five percent to 31 percent, 53 percent to 79 percent and 32 percent to 55 percent, respectively, as we move from the smallest to the largest corporations in the ExecuComp database. Thus, Table 2-4 shows that the frequency of the use of the various types of compensation increases with the size of the corporation.

Relative Importance of Components of Compensation Package

As observed above, corporations normally include multiple forms of fixed and variable compensation in the compensation package. They do so because each component has a different effect on employee motivation and risk, as well as different costs to the corporation.[29] That is, executives have bonus plans based, to some extent, on controllable variables to offset the risk of stock-based compensation, which is in part driven by uncontrollable market forces. The corporation weighs the cost of using potentially controllable variables against the benefit of reducing executive risk and, hence, the wages demanded. Tables 2-2 through 2-4 showed the fraction of corporations including salary, bonus, long-term incentive payments, stock options and stock grants in their CEO's compensation package. In contrast, Figure 2-1 and Tables 2-5 through 2-7 starting on page 66, show the relative importance of these components, that is, the percentage these components represent in the CEO compensation package of large corporations.

Three things should be noted about Table 2-5 on page 67 and the remaining tables in this chapter. The first thing to note about Table 2-5 is that, while we examine salary, bonus, long-term incentive payments, stock options and stock grants, the totals do not add up to 100 percent because of the omission of other compensation, for example the perks previously discussed. While small relative to the other components of the compensation package, for some companies—see previous Wachovia example—other compensation can be material. The second item that should be explained is how the variables are valued. Companies report salaries and bonuses earned, whether paid in the current period or not, as well as the value of stock grants, other annual and all other compensation. These amounts are picked up by ExecuComp and used in this study. The valuation of stock option grants, however, is more subjective. Under prior standards, companies have been allowed to report in their proxy statement either their estimate of the grant date value of the options using an option-pricing model, or the potential realizable value of the options assuming the share price grows at a rate of 5 percent or 10 percent per year until the option expires. Thus, some companies report grant date values and others potentially realizable values. However, using information available about the corporation, ExecuComp estimates the value of all option grants using option-pricing models (the appendix to Chapter 6 provides a brief introduction to option-pricing models). For consistency across companies, the ExecuComp estimate is used in these tables and throughout this book. The last difference between Tables 2-5 through 2-7 and the earlier tables is the addition of a second row for each year (industry, size decile), where the first row represents the mean for that compo-

Figure 2-1:

Mean Percentage of Compensation Package Represented by Components

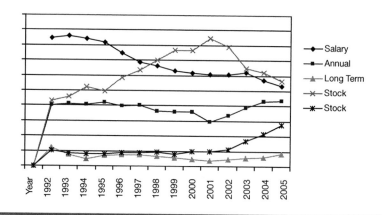

Table 2-5:

Percentage of CEO Compensation Package Represented by Components, By Year
(Means on top, medians below)

Year	Salary	Bonus	Long-Term Incentive Payments	Stock Options	Stock Grants
1992	42.40	20.03	5.96	21.41	5.06
	37.26	19.16	0.00	17.89	0.00
1993	42.99	20.57	3.76	22.83	4.21
	39.16	19.63	0.00	17.73	0.00
1994	42.16	20.33	2.42	26.13	3.93
	37.84	18.65	0.00	20.95	0.00
1995	41.00	20.96	3.40	24.79	4.07
	36.20	19.58	0.00	19.20	0.00
1996	37.46	19.85	3.74	29.13	4.50
	32.58	17.80	0.00	25.27	0.00
1997	34.24	20.03	3.85	31.81	4.51
	27.54	18.07	0.00	27.16	0.00
1998	33.29	18.33	3.21	35.14	4.67
	26.46	15.77	0.00	34.32	0.00
1999	31.50	18.03	2.72	38.25	3.96
	25.31	14.84	0.00	38.60	0.00
2000	30.80	18.03	2.41	38.36	4.84
	23.53	14.27	0.00	37.09	0.00
2001	30.46	14.73	1.94	42.19	4.96
	22.41	10.66	0.00	43.08	0.00
2002	30.39	16.86	2.30	39.37	5.66
	22.83	13.60	0.00	39.66	0.00
2003	31.12	19.39	2.85	32.53	8.44
	24.58	16.74	0.00	29.73	0.00
2004	28.39	21.48	3.09	30.96	10.77
	21.61	18.67	0.00	28.35	0.00
2005	26.75	21.76	4.19	28.27	13.77
	20.82	19.31	0.00	24.19	0.00

Calculations in this table are based upon data contained in the April 2006 version of Standard & Poor's ExecuComp.

nent for that year, and the second row represents the median.[30] Medians are presented beginning in Table 2-5 to demonstrate that the trends observed are not being caused by outliers, but rather are representative of the population being examined.

Table 2-6

Percentage of 2005 CEO Compensation Package Represented by Components, by Industry

(Means on top, medians below)

Industry	Standard Industrial Classification Code	Salary	Bonus	Long-Term Incentive Payments	Stock Options	Stock Grants
Mining and Construction	1000-1999	18.11	29.95	4.16	22.43	20.91
		16.65	24.40	0.00	20.07	17.68
Manufacturing	2000-3999	27.49	20.00	4.19	31.30	11.81
		21.17	17.84	0.00	29.56	0.00
Transportation, Communications, Electric, Gas and Sanitary Services	4000-4999	28.41	23.89	10.38	16.73	14.56
		23.43	21.14	0.00	9.00	0.00
Wholesale and Retail Trade	5000-5999	30.80	20.48	1.36	30.91	10.59
		24.08	18.14	0.00	33.78	0.00
Finance, Insurance and Real Estate	6000-6999	23.36	26.31	5.36	21.48	17.97
		18.73	24.83	0.00	18.24	4.01
Services	7000-8999	26.69	18.91	0.80	34.28	14.98
		18.16	17.07	0.00	33.39	0.00

Note: Calculations in this table are based upon data contained in the April 2006 version of Standard & Poors ExecuComp.

Substantial changes in the composition of the compensation package are observed over time (Figure 2-1 and Table 2-5). For example, the mean (median) percentage of the CEO compensation package represented by salary is dropping in a linear manner over time, from a high of 43 (39) percent in 1993 to 27 (21) percent in 2005. In contrast, while the percentage of the CEO compensation package represented by bonus has varied over time, that variation has been both down and up. That is, the mean (median) percentage of the compensation package represented by the bonus dropped from 20 (19) percent in 1992 to 15 (11) percent in 2001, before increasing to 22 (19) percent in 2005. Similarly, the percentage of the CEO compensation package comprised of stock options first went up, and then down, during the period under observation. From a mean (median) percentage of 21 (18) percent in 1992, stock options increased to 42(43) percent of the CEO compensation package in 2001 before declining precipitously to 28(24) percent in 2005.

Table 2-7

Percentage of 2005 CEO Compensation Package Represented by Components, by Firm Size
(Firms Divided into Deciles by Market Value of Equity)
(Means on top, medians below)

	Size Decile	Salary	Bonus	Long-Term Incentive Payments	Stock Options	Stock Grants
Smallest	1	48.59	14.66	0.56	19.25	9.34
		44.50	11.05	0.00	10.84	0.00
	2	39.43	17.66	1.19	26.83	9.18
		35.15	14.05	0.00	19.83	0.00
	3	30.17	24.16	2.22	28.56	11.04
		25.87	20.46	0.00	24.30	0.00
	4	28.84	22.27	2.35	29.87	12.57
		24.60	20.22	0.00	24.44	0.00
	5	27.77	21.76	3.12	27.06	13.94
		21.68	19.81	0.00	19.98	0.00
	6	22.34	23.00	6.66	26.30	17.20
		18.73	19.69	0.00	21.00	5.45
	7	22.48	24.75	4.18	27.57	15.78
		19.86	22.90	0.00	24.78	2.18
	8	19.22	24.38	6.55	30.20	14.95
		15.28	21.99	0.00	27.05	0.00
	9	17.34	23.08	6.80	33.84	15.48
		12.80	20.40	0.00	29.86	0.00
Largest	10	12.15	21.61	8.22	33.36	17.93
		9.99	19.19	0.00	31.80	13.35

Note: Calculations in this table are based upon data contained in the April 2006 version of Standard & Poor's ExecuComp.

Finally, stock grants, while still less frequently observed than either salary, bonus or stock option grants, and used by less than half of the firms (consequently the median is zero), have increased rather dramatically in the past few years. While fairly constant as a percentage of total compensation, with the mean ranging from 4 percent to 5 percent from 1992 to 2001, since that time the mean has nearly tripled to 14 percent of total compensation. My belief is that this recent shift has been caused by a substitution from stock options to stock grants. The reasons, which to some extent are speculation on my part, include the change in accounting for share-based payments, which removed the favorable treatment for fixed stock options; the lesser dilution associated with full-value stock grants, that is, fewer shares need to be granted to employees than options to achieve the same intended value; and the lower risk associated with stock grants, that is, as long as the company does not go bankrupt they always retain some value, whereas it is not uncommon for options to expire worthless.

Even more variation is observed looking across industries. For example, in 2005, the mean (median) percentage of CEO compensation represented by salary ranged from a low of 18 (17) percent in mining and construction to a high of 31 (24) percent in wholesale and retail trade. Similarly, the percentage of CEO compensation represented by the bonus ranged from a low of 19 (17) percent, in services, to a high of 30 (24) percent, in mining and construction. Transportation, communications, electric, gas and sanitary services had the lowest mean and median percentages represented by stock options, 17 percent and 9 percent, and services the highest, at 34 percent and 33 percent, respectively. The usage of stock grants also varied across industries, with the percentage ranging from a mean (median) of 11 (0) percent in wholesale and retail trade to 21 (18) percent in mining and construction.

Finally, and perhaps most interestingly, variation is observed by the size of the corporation. In 2005, the mean (median) percentage of the CEO compensation package represented by salary declines from 49 (44) percent for the smallest decile of corporations to 12 (10) percent in the largest. In contrast, the percentage of the compensation package represented by stock options and stock grants generally increase with the size of the corporation. The percentage of the CEO

Figure 2-2:
Mean CEO Compensation

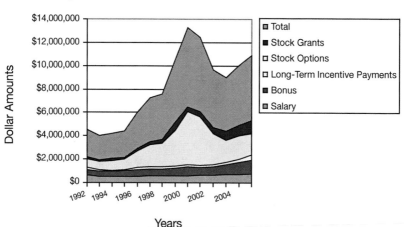

compensation package represented by stock options increases from a mean (median) of 19 (11) percent in the smallest decile of corporations to a mean (median) of 33 (32) percent in the largest decile of corporations. The proportion of the compensation package represented by stock grants increases from a mean (median) of 9 (0) percent in the smallest decile of corporations to a mean (median) of 18(13) percent in the largest decile of corporations.

As will be shown in Chapter 9, CEO percentage ownership decreases with increases in the size of the corporation. As noted in Chapter 1, executive ownership and the executive compensation package are two of the mechanisms for minimizing the agency costs arising from the separation of the ownership and management of the corporation. Consequently, the trends observed in the composition of the compensation package, that is, the increased use of stock-based compensation as the size of the corporation increases, may be an optimal response to the lower level of incentives provided by equity ownership in larger corporations.

The evidence in Tables 2-2 through 2-7 shows there is considerable variation in the items included in the CEO compensation package, and the relative importance of those items. These differences occur over time, across industry and across the size of the corporation.

Magnitude of Compensation Package

Figure 2-2 and Tables 2-8 through 2-10 show the dollar amounts of CEO compensation. Table 2-8 (on page 72) and Figure 2-2 show that the dollar amounts of salary, bonus, stock options and stock grants, as well as total compensation, have increased over time. For example, mean (median) total compensation increased from $2,333,037 ($1,733,573) in 1992 to $5,578,289 ($3,346,766) in 2005, an increase of 139 (93) percent. Interestingly, and contrary to much of what is observed in the popular press, the table illustrates that CEO compensation can go down. That is, mean total compensation was greatest in 2000, at $6,798,501, dropping in 2001, 2002 and 2003, before increasing in 2004 and 2005.

As can be observed from Table 2-8, much of this variation is driven by the variation in the value of stock option grants. That is, the mean (median) value of stock option grants increased from $703,729 ($304,110) in 1992 to $4,541,631 ($787,070) in 2000, before decreasing to $1,870,255 ($685,749) in 2005. While the long-term trend is positive, that is, the mean (median) increase from 1992 to 2005 is 165 (125) percent respectively, just looking at the first and last year obscures the sharp increase in the use of stock options from 1992 to 2000, followed by the decrease from 2001 to 2005.

In contrast, the other major components of the compensation package increased fairly linearly from 1992 to 2005. Mean (median) salary increased from

Table 2-8

Average of CEO Compensation Package by Components, by Year
(Means on top, medians below)

Year	Salary	Bonus	Long-Term Incentive Payments	Stock Options	Stock Grants	Total
1992	$634,985	$492,553	$151,298	$703,729	$215,168	$2,333,037
	$606,731	$348,620	$0	$304,110	$0	$1,733,573
1993	$546,874	$441,671	$108,781	$695,825	$140,987	$2,069,518
	$500,000	$253,405	$0	$212,411	$0	$1,286,968
1994	$516,424	$445,190	$80,764	$865,193	$136,716	$2,165,706
	$460,000	$250,000	$0	$244,969	$0	$1,256,749
1995	$528,130	$491,271	$110,178	$851,137	$144,064	$2,255,157
	$468,941	$259,918	$0	$234,493	$0	$1,283,191
1996	$545,858	$580,879	$175,121	$1,433,953	$205,362	$3,085,245
	$500,000	$281,664	$0	$360,293	$0	$1,553,564
1997	$558,574	$609,246	$184,213	$1,889,510	$250,917	$3,739,953
	$508,269	$330,472	$0	$455,804	$0	$1,841,877
1998	$578,714	$602,348	$165,293	$2,025,985	$305,280	$3,886,906
	$525,000	$315,000	$0	$603,409	$0	$1,974,109
1999	$581,250	$681,843	$189,021	$3,043,341	$665,992	$5,433,456
	$525,000	$335,000	$0	$721,281	$0	$2,128,109
2000	$604,363	$748,715	$173,894	$4,541,631	$431,939	$6,798,501
	$550,000	$349,918	$0	$787,070	$0	$2,383,935
2001	$640,637	$667,486	$159,138	$4,182,563	$432,724	$6,363,233
	$575,952	$299,471	$0	$999,902	$0	$2,555,272
2002	$657,880	$699,480	$171,019	$2,666,515	$521,392	$4,958,512
	$600,001	$350,000	$0	$956,216	$0	$2,650,720
2003	$685,181	$872,487	$219,186	$1,879,651	$719,983	$4,625,956
	$635,114	$420,000	$0	$671,136	$0	$2,501,804
2004	$707,813	$1,041,247	$247,054	$2,051,080	$865,841	$5,159,517
	$650,000	$559,075	$0	$755,922	$0	$2,968,837
2005	$745,962	$1,200,417	$425,516	$1,870,255	$1,054,171	$5,578,289
	$697,115	$650,000	$0	$685,749	$0	$3,346,766

Note: Calculations in this table are based upon data contained in the April 2006 version of Standard & Poor's ExecuComp.

$634,985 ($606,731) in 1992 to $745,962 ($697,115) in 2005, an increase of 17 (15) percent, and mean (median) bonus increased from $492,553 ($348,620) to $1,200,417 ($650,000), an increase of 143 (86) percent. Mean long-term incentive payments increased from $151,298 in 1992 to $425,516 in 2005, an increase of 181 percent. The largest percentage increase was in the value of stock grants, whose mean increased from $215,168 in 1992 to $1,054,171 in 2005, an increase of 390 percent. As a measure of comparison, the cumulative inflation rate over that time period was slightly more than 39 percent. Thus, while average CEO salary lagged the consumer price index during the 1992-2005 period, total compensation, and the variable components of the CEO compensation package, have increased at rates in excess of inflation during those years.

Table 2-9 (on page 74) shows the differences across industry groupings. In 2005, mean (median) total CEO compensation ranged from a low of $4,864,539 ($3,078,679) in wholesale and retail trade to a high of $10,174,142 ($4,605,399) in mining and construction. When comparing these two industries, it becomes readily apparent that these differences are driven almost entirely by conditional compensation, as mean salary is actually greater in wholesale and retail trade. In contrast, the mean (median) annual bonus received by CEOs in mining and construction, $3,295,610 ($901,230), is significantly higher than the amount received by CEOs in wholesale and retail trade, $882,217 ($600,464), as is the mean (median) value of stock option grants, $2,621,029 ($782,695) versus $1,820,982 ($961,199), and stock grants, $2,506,729 ($480,000) versus $1,010,853 (0).

Table 2-10 on page 75 shows the differences across the size of the corporation. As would be expected, the average dollar amounts of salary, bonus, stock options, stock grants and total compensation all increase with the size of the corporation. In 2005 the mean (median) total compensation for a CEO of a corporation in the smallest size decile was $1,331,332 ($926,136), whereas the comparable amounts for a CEO of a corporation in the largest size decile were $14,938,239 ($12,488,782), roughly 10 times as much.[31] This pattern, while consistent across all components of the compensation package, is most pronounced for conditional compensation, that is, bonuses, stock options and stock grants. It reflects what some consider the added skills needed to run a larger corporation, and to some extent, the added effect on profitability a CEO can have in a larger corporation, that is, the dollar gains from his or her actions will be greater the larger the corporation.

Relative Pay of CEO to Other Top Executives

The CEO is the leader of the modern corporation. As such, the CEO normally receives higher compensation than his or her subordinates. The amount of this differential can be a source of friction, however. As noted elsewhere in this book, the popular press has noted that CEO pay is out of line compared with that of the

Table 2-9:

Average of 2005 CEO Compensation Package by Components, by Industry; (Means on top, medians below)

Industry	Standard Industrial Classification Code	Salary	Bonus	Long-Term Incentive Payments	Stock Options	Stock Grants	Total
Mining and Construction	1000-1999	$747,028	$3,295,610	$582,898	$2,621,029	$2,506,729	$10,174,142
		$750,000	$901,230	$0	$782,695	$480,000	$4,605,399
Manufacturing	2000-3999	$731,125	$909,824	$412,725	$1,872,101	$802,220	$4,966,378
		$686,802	$592,524	$0	$791,776	$0	$3,120,895
Transportation, Communications, Electric, Gas and Sanitary Services	4000-4999	$809,135	$1,156,551	$779,969	$955,708	$933,060	$4,884,841
		$695,158	$633,982	$0	$172,524	$0	$3,014,274
Wholesale and Retail Trade	5000-5999	$787,362	$882,217	$85,447	$1,820,982	$1,010,853	$4,864,539
		$720,231	$600,464	$0	$961,199	$0	$3,078,679
Finance, Insurance and Real Estate	6000-6999	$772,507	$1,970,031	$746,259	$1,817,513	$1,536,149	$7,245,712
		$749,360	$950,000	$0	$508,647	$126,625	$3,776,006
Services	7000-8999	$670,356	$836,826	$70,426	$2,311,247	$918,316	$5,061,391
		$600,000	$504,438	$0	$1,066,043	$0	$3,356,119

Note: Calculations in this table are based upon data contained in the April 2006 version of Standard & Poor's ExecuComp.

average worker. As an illustration, several years ago *Time* magazine contained the following note: 476:1 Ratio of the average salary of an American CEO to that of an American blue-collar worker. [32]

Tables 2-11 through 2-13 beginning on page 76 provide some descriptive statistics on the variation of the compensation package throughout the executive suite for the 2005 fiscal year. The difference, while not as pronounced as the *Time* magazine quote, is substantial. Looking at Table 2-11, which controls for corporate characteristics, as pay for the second- to fifth-highest executive is calculated as a fraction of CEO pay, in terms of total compensation, the second highest-paid executive makes a median 50 percent of what the CEO makes, whereas the fifth highest paid-executive makes a median of 29 percent of the CEO.[33] Viewed from the bottom

Table 2-10:

Average of 2005 CEO Compensation Package by Components, by Firm Size (Firms Divided into Deciles by Market Value of Equity)

	Size Decile	Salary	Bonus	Long-Term Incentive Payments	Stock Options	Stock Grants	Total
Smallest	1	$459,288	$221,127	$14,743	$286,616	$205,112	$1,331,332
		$430,500	$102,400	$0	$78,519	$0	$926,136
	2	$546,886	$316,531	$27,576	$617,712	$299,575	$2,024,425
		$522,115	$225,000	$0	$312,430	$0	$1,517,297
	3	$588,486	$649,415	$84,780	$1,148,194	$528,444	$3,145,755
		$540,383	$481,250	$0	$484,305	$0	$2,227,969
	4	$604,697	$547,121	$83,800	$1,003,686	$442,396	$2,795,930
		$600,000	$447,463	$0	$575,891	$0	$2,289,259
	5	$668,145	$783,568	$356,669	$1,210,588	$638,675	$3,810,741
		$678,058	$635,654	$0	$578,121	$0	$3,079,348
	6	$716,594	$1,273,445	$364,014	$1,450,717	$1,143,917	$5,177,757
		$725,000	$737,900	$0	$748,446	$105,744	$3,592,950
	7	$820,232	$1,196,115	$397,437	$1,543,810	$933,331	$5,246,714
		$806,376	$980,875	$0	$925,125	$183,385	$4,172,151
	8	$829,553	$1,684,088	$513,067	$2,122,074	$1,431,910	$6,873,563
		$852,232	$1,160,027	$0	$1,432,944	$0	$5,250,596
	9	$1,002,514	$2,193,647	$878,640	$4,075,088	$1,685,618	$10,178,806
		$1,000,000	$1,500,000	$0	$2,239,169	$0	$7,862,208
Largest	10	$1,186,063	$3,089,783	$1,534,174	$5,202,049	$3,212,403	$14,938,239
		$1,090,000	$2,237,700	$0	$3,343,835	$1,201,850	$12,488,782

Note: Calculations in this table are based upon data contained in the April 2006 version of Standard & Poor's ExecuComp.

up, the CEO makes about twice the next highest-paid executive, and more than three times the fifth-highest-paid executive. This differential is consistent with tournament theory, see for example Lazear and Rosen (1981), whereby CEO pay is not necessarily based upon the CEO's value or marginal product, but rather held out as an incentive or reward to lower-level executives to strive to become CEO. Rosen (1986, page 714) claims, "Payments at the top have indirect effects of increasing productivity of competitors further down the ladder." Hence, the differential is necessary. This differential is greatest for conditional, in particular long-term, compensation, consistent with risk aversion playing a role in the setting of the compensation package allowing for the possibility of a large payoff if the

Table 2-11:

Median Ratio of 2005 Highest-Paid Executive's Compensation to Compensation Earned by Next Four Highest-Paid Employees

Rank	Salary	Bonus	Long-Term Incentive Payments	Stock Options	Stock Grants	Total
1	1.00	1.00	1.00	1.00	1.00	1.00
2	0.62	0.50	0.36	0.40	0.39	0.50
3	0.53	0.36	0.27	0.30	0.30	0.39
4	0.47	0.29	0.24	0.25	0.24	0.33
5	0.43	0.24	0.18	0.22	0.21	0.29

Note: Calculations in this table are based upon data contained in the April 2006 version of Standard & Poor's ExecuComp.

Table 2-12:

Percentage of 2005 Compensation Package Represented by Components, by Executive Rank

(Means on top, medians below)

Rank	Salary	Bonus	Long-Term Incentive Payments	Stock Options	Stock Grants
1	26.83	23.84	4.15	27.01	13.16
	21.06	20.34	0.00	22.61	0.00
2	31.08	23.16	3.80	25.11	12.10
	26.54	21.01	0.00	20.29	0.00
3	33.51	21.63	3.65	24.41	11.91
	28.93	20.01	0.00	19.75	0.00
4	35.52	20.83	3.57	23.60	11.58
	30.88	19.41	0.00	19.32	0.00
5	35.58	19.46	3.46	24.11	12.07
	31.87	17.79	0.00	19.29	0.00

Calculations in this table are based upon data contained in the April 2006 version of Standard & Poor's ExecuComp.

Table 2-13:

Average of 2005 Compensation Components, by Executive Rank
(Means on top, medians below)

Rank	Salary	Bonus	Long-Term Incentive Payments	Stock Options	Stock Grants	Total
CEO	$745,962	$1,200,417	$425,516	$1,870,255	$1,054,171	$5,578,289
	$697,115	$650,000	$0	$685,749	$0	$3,346,766
2	$479,345	$679,499	$173,813	$881,018	$459,597	$2,825,846
	$417,635	$350,000	$0	$263,408	$0	$1,612,556
3	$400,528	$450,018	$133,875	$597,915	$358,481	$2,067,780
	$350,777	$250,000	$0	$221,673	$0	$1,245,646
4	$360,182	$366,062	$107,302	$505,004	$296,691	$1,722,821
	$317,500	$201,448	$0	$184,904	$0	$1,067,344
5	$330,162	$300,906	$93,569	$486,218	$297,249	$1,604,787
	$298,094	$170,000	$0	$170,983	$0	$956,075

Note: Calculations in this table are based upon data contained in the April 2006 version of Standard & Poor's ExecuComp.

corporation does well and recognizing, perhaps, that the CEO is the individual with the largest effect on corporationwide payoffs. Table 2-12 provides support for this theory, as salary, while making up a mean (median) 27 (21) percent of the CEO compensation package, increases monotonically until it makes up 36 (32) percent of the compensation package of the fifth highest-paid individual. Conversely, the proportion of stock options in the compensation package drops from a mean (median) of 27 (23) percent for the CEO to a still substantial 24 (19) percent for the fifth highest-paid executive. Table 2-13 provides the actual dollar amounts, which for total compensation range from a mean (median) $1,604,787 ($956,075) for the fifth highest-paid executive to $5,578,289 ($3,346,766) for the CEO.

Summary
This chapter provided an overview of the executive compensation package. It began by explaining the major components of the compensation package, which are salary, bonus, stock options and grants, pensions and benefits, and provided examples from publicly held corporations of the use of each component in the executive compensation package. The chapter then provided descriptive statistics of the use of these components in the compensation packages of the corporations forming the S&P 500, S&P MidCap 400 and S&P SmallCap 600 indices for the years 1992-2005.

In terms of usage, salary is observed in the compensation packages of almost all CEOs across time, industry and corporate size, whereas other components of the compensation package, for example, stock option grants, have become more prevalent over the period under examination, and vary by industry and with the size of the corporation. While salary is observed in almost all compensation packages, its importance varies over time and across industry and corporate size. For example, the mean (median) percentage of the CEO compensation package represented by salary dropped from 49 (44) percent in 1992 to 12 (10) percent in 2005. Similar variation was observed with respect to the other components of the compensation package.

Examining the amounts involved, CEO compensation appears rather large, at least in nominal terms, with the amounts growing over the years examined. That is, mean (median) total compensation increased from $2,333,037 ($1,733,573) in 1992 to $5,578,289 ($3,346,766) in 2005, an increase of 139 (93) percent. While high, this does not provide evidence one way or the other as to whether CEOs are overpaid. That issue will be taken up in Chapter 11.

Footnotes

1 For the most part the data is limited to the period from 1992-2005. This period coincides with the increased proxy-statement disclosures that began in 1992.

2 Benefit less related costs.

3 Page 3, Boeing 8-K filed with the Securities and Exchange Commission, July 6, 2005.

4 Exhibit 99-2, Hewlett Packard 8-K filed with the Securities and Exchange Commission, March 29, 2005.

5 Page 23, Duke Energy proxy statement filed with the Securities and Exchange Commission, Sept. 15, 2006.

6 This has traditionally been the case, driven in part by the favorable accounting treatment allowed fixed options granted at or above the market price. For example, Matsunaga (1995, note 6) finds only 5 percent of his sample firms issued options with an exercise price below the fair market value at the grant date. Given that fixed stock options no longer have favorable accounting treatment, their use may wane relative to other forms of compensation.

7 As will be discussed later in this book (in particular Chapter 6), when share prices fall after the date of grant, resulting in the exercise price of the option being greater than the share price, companies sometimes grant additional options at the lower price and/or reduce the exercise price on the existing option.

8 Page 16, Walt Disney Co. proxy statement filed with the Securities and Exchange Commission, Jan. 9, 1997.

9 Page 23, Comerica proxy statement filed with the Securities and Exchange Commission, April 10, 2006.

10 Exhibit 99.2 of Pepsico form 8-K filed with the Securities and Exchange Commission, Feb. 2, 2006.

11 A form 4 is a Statement of Changes in Beneficial Ownership.

12 John T. Cahill, form 4 filed with Securities and Exchange Commission, Feb. 3, 2006.

13 In some cases, companies have set up programs with investment bankers that allow (for a commission) the executive to engage in a simultaneous exercise of his/her options and sale of the shares acquired upon exercise. This allows the executive to avoid having to pay the exercise price on the shares being acquired, and as a result, lowers the costs of the two transactions.

14 To the executive, a stock appreciation right is preferred to a stock option, as it allows the executive to avoid transaction costs associated with the exercise of the

option and the subsequent sale of the shares acquired upon exercise. The corporation, on the other hand, prefers stock options, which are a source, rather than a use, of cash. In addition, in the past (pre-SFAS 123(revised)) the financial reporting treatment for stock options was more favorable than that for stock appreciation rights (see Balsam and Paek 2001 for a discussion of these issues).

15 These plans are known as defined benefit plans.

16 These plans are known as defined contribution plans, the most common of which would be 401(k)s.

17 As will be discussed in more detail in Chapter 7, there are costs to these supplemental plans that do not exist for tax-qualified plans. With a tax-qualified plan, the corporation funds the plan and takes an immediate deduction at the time of funding, whereas the employee does not recognize income until the time he or she receives the pension. In contrast, supplemental plans cannot be funded, or the employee would have to immediately recognize taxable income. Consequently, because the plan is not funded, the corporation cannot take an immediate deduction.

18 The corporation need not disclose the value of the benefits if the "aggregate amount of such compensation is less than $10,000" (Securities and Exchange Commission regulation S-K 229.402 (c)(2)(ix)(A)).

19 Pages 22-24, First Union Corporation Proxy statement filed with Securities and Exchange Commission, March 13, 2006.

20 Pages 11 and 12, American Financial Group Proxy statement filed with Securities and Exchange Commission, April 12, 2006.

21 Page 12, Leucadia National proxy statement filed with Securities and Exchange Commission, April 22, 2005.

22 Pages 3-5 of Exhibit 10-28, Aramark form 10-K filed with Securities and Exchange Commission, Dec. 19, 2003.

23 Pages 9-21 of Exhibit 10-g, Gillette form 10-K filed with the Securities and Exchange Commission, March 14, 2005.

24 Tables 2-2 through 2-4, and most of the other tables in the book, are prepared using data from Standard and Poor's Market Insights. The executive compensation component of Market Insights, also known as ExecuComp, includes data for approximately 1,500 firms, the S&P 500, S&P MidCap 400 and S&P SmallCap 600.

25 Page 20, Anheuser-Busch proxy statement filed with the Securities and Exchange Commission, March 9, 2006.

26 Page 16, Walt Disney Co. proxy statement filed with the Securities and Exchange Commission, Jan. 9, 1997.

27 While Eisner has not received any additional options on Disney stock since 1996, in 2000 he did receive a grant of 2 million options on Disney Internet Group stock valued at $37,740,000 (pages 20 and 21, Walt Disney proxy statement, filed with the Securities and Exchange Commission Jan. 12, 2001).

28 The industry partitions used in these tables are admittedly not very precise, and thus each classification includes a wide variety of firms. Had a finer partition been used, the variation across industries would have been greater.

29 Those benefits and costs will be discussed in detail in Section II of this book.

30 For ease of presentation, the figures will be based upon the means.

31 As a frame of reference, in 2005 the mean (median) market value of a corporation in the largest decile was $57 ($37) billion, while that of a corporation in the smallest decile was $202 ($209) million, an order of magnitude much greater than the 10 observed for CEO compensation. Consequently, CEO compensation is a much smaller percentage of market value for larger firms.

32 Hambly (2000).

33 Because small denominators have the ability to create extremely large ratios, and consequently disproportionately affect the means, only medians are presented in this table.

Chapter 3

An Introduction to Designing the Executive Compensation Contract

Introduction

This chapter will introduce, in general terms, some of the issues involved in designing an executive compensation contract. The issues to be discussed are, (1) making the offer attractive, (2) providing incentives to increase shareholder value, (3) providing incentives to remain with the corporation, (4) minimizing the costs to shareholders and (5) minimizing risk to shareholders. While the discussion that follows will focus on designing a contract to attract a new executive from outside the corporation, much of the discussion applies to internal promotions, as well as to designing a contract to retain existing executives.

Making the Offer Attractive

To illustrate the decisions a corporation must make in designing a compensation package, consider the corporation that wishes to hire an executive from outside. First, the corporation must make the compensation package lucrative enough to entice the targeted executive to take the position. That is, the value of the compensation package offered to the executive should exceed his or her next best opportunity, or "opportunity cost." This may be his or her current compensation package, or the compensation package being offered by another potential employer. However, simply exceeding the executives' current compensation package may not be enough. Changing jobs is a gamble and executives, as risk-averse individuals, need to be compensated for taking chances. To induce them to take that chance, a substantial premium may be involved. To reduce that premium and to combat the natural risk aversion of the executive, the firm may have or choose to include a severance provision in the contract to minimize the financial risk to the executive.

As an illustration, consider what Citigroup offered, in October 1999, to Robert E. Rubin to become chairman of its executive committee. Rubin just resigned his position as U.S. Secretary of the Treasury, making approximately $150,000 a year. Citigroup, in addition to giving him options on 1.5 million shares, which it valued at $18.5 million,[1] promised him an additional 1.5 million options in 2000, and at least $1 million in salary and $14 million in bonus in each 2000 and 2001.[2] While substantially above his salary as secretary of the Treasury, the amount did not seem unreasonable (to Citigroup at least), given what he had earned prior to his government service or what he could earn if he returned to Wall Street. Prior to entering governmental service, Rubin was co-senior partner and co-chairman of Goldman, Sachs & Co. Thus, an estimate of his opportunity cost would be the earnings of the current chairman of Goldman Sachs and other Wall Street companies. In 1999, Henry M. Paulson Jr., chairman and CEO of Goldman Sachs, received a $300,000 salary, a bonus of $16,062,153 and restricted stock valued at $8,828,701.[3] The chairman and CEO of Merrill Lynch, David H. Komansky, received a compensation package of $25.8 million;[4] and the chairman and CEO of Morgan Stanley Dean Witter, Philip J. Purcell, received a $775,000 salary, a bonus of $12,112,500, restricted stock worth $8,184,303 and stock options valued at $5,556,250.[5]

It should be noted that the value of the compensation package to the executive includes both pecuniary and nonpecuniary factors. An executive may be willing to accept a lesser-paying position if the corporation's headquarters is in a preferred location. Alternatively, an executive might be willing to accept less compensation to work for corporation A than for corporation B because corporation A is viewed as more prestigious and/or has more growth potential. For example, in September 1999 George Shaheen left his position as head of Andersen Consulting making a "secure seven-figure annual income"[6] to become chief executive officer and president of Webvan for a base salary of $500,000, subject to annual adjustment, and a target bonus of $250,000. In connection with this agreement, Shaheen was granted 1.25 million shares of fully vested common stock and was granted an option to purchase an additional 15 million shares of common stock at an exercise price of $8 per share.[7]

To Illustrate that Upside Potential

At the high point of the first day of Webvan's November 1999 IPO, Shaheen's 15 million stock options were worth $390 million. Along with the 1.25 million shares he was granted, he was worth some $815 million.[8]

Providing the Proper Incentives

The corporation wants to design the contract to encourage the CEO to act in a way consistent with its objective, presumably value maximization. In doing so, the corporation recognizes that the different components of the compensation package have different effects on CEO incentives, risk, political costs and tax payments, and on its own financial reporting, political costs and tax payments.

To make things simple, and minimize contracting costs, the corporation could offer to pay the CEO a salary, which would fix compensation regardless of performance. However, in that situation, the CEO has little financial incentive to maximize shareholder value because he or she does not benefit from doing so.[9] And considering that economists view most individuals as work averse (although there are many who would argue that individuals who make it to the executive suite are not work averse, but rather workaholics), the CEO would have incentive to shirk and/or overconsume perquisites. Alternatively, the corporation could offer the CEO a contract whereby his or her compensation is solely based upon corporate performance. While this would provide the CEO with incentive to maximize shareholder value, it would impose substantial risk on the CEO.[10] As most economists assume individuals are risk averse, the CEO would be unwilling to take the contract unless there was a substantial premium built into it to compensate for the risk involved. For example, the CEO might be willing to accept $1 million if compensation was fixed, but require an expected payout of $3 million if compensation were totally based upon performance. The corporation would then have to decide if the increased performance that could be expected under the performance-based contract would warrant the extra costs of the contract.

In practice, we observe few contracts that are either totally fixed or variable. One famous example that comes to mind is that between Lee Iacocca and the Chrysler Corp. When Iacocca joined Chrysler in 1978, he took all of his compensation in the form of stock options, which are completely variable in the sense that they only have value if the underlying stock increases in value—so if the stock price did not increase Iacocca would have nothing. Another example is Steve Jobs of Apple Computer. Taking over as interim CEO on Sept. 10, 1997,[11] Jobs received no compensation in 1997, other than 30,000 options granted to all directors[12], salary of $1 in 1998[13] and salary of $1 in 1999.[14] However, upon formally accepting the position of CEO in January 2000, Apple granted Jobs options to purchase 10 million shares.[15] While no valuation was disclosed by Apple at the time (under Securities and Exchange Commission requirements they will not have to disclose a value for the options until they file their proxy statement for the 2000 fiscal year), according to Menn (2000),

The options were priced at $87.188 each. Apple shares closed at $111.31 in Nasdaq trading on Friday. That means the marketing whiz has already earned more than $240 million on paper from the stock's appreciation.

Perhaps the most profitable example of an executive forgoing all other options in exchange for stock options is that of Lawrence Ellison, chief executive officer of Oracle, who in 1999 agreed to take no salary and bonus for fiscal 2000 through fiscal 2003, in exchange for options on 10 million shares.[16] *The Wall Street Journal* (2000e) reports that this "arrangement has netted Mr. Ellison a paper windfall of about $1.3 billion." Other examples of executives forgoing salary, along with brief explanations as to why they elected to forgo salary, are included in Table 3-1 on page 88. It is interesting to note, that of the eight examples in that table, three of the executives who have elected to forgo salary are controlling shareholders, and even the others, while not reported, have (or had in the case of now retired executives) substantially greater than average equity stakes in their employers.

At the other extreme are Warren Buffett and Jeff Bezos. Buffett is the famed investor and CEO of Berkshire Hathaway, a company with a compensation package that primarily consists of salary, a salary that has been fixed at $100,000 per year for each of the last 25 years.[17] And yet Berkshire Hathaway has done extremely well over that period. The secret: Buffett owns approximately 40 percent of Berkshire Hathaway stock,[18] which provides sufficient incentive by itself for him to want to increase shareholder value. Bezos, chairman and CEO of Amazon.com, also receives compensation consisting solely of salary, which has been fixed at $81,840 since 1998.[19] Like Buffett, Bezos owns about almost 25 percent of the outstanding shares of Amazon.com.[20] While the ownership of corporate shares by Buffett and Bezos is not the norm, in considering the effect of compensation on incentives, ownership is a factor that always has to be considered. Academic researchers (for example, Jensen and Murphy 1990a & b, Hall and Liebman 1998, Murphy 1998) have noted that the relationship between pay and performance is driven primarily by ownership, broadly defined as holdings of stock and stock options.

More commonly, compensation packages include fixed and variable components. Fixed components are included to reduce the risk to the CEO and guarantee a standard of living, whereas variable components are included to provide incentives and align the interests of management and shareholders. Assuming that the compensation package the corporation designs will include fixed and variable components, the corporation then has to decide how much of each to include, and what forms they should take. Fixed components might include salary and benefits, such as employer-paid life insurance, health care and pensions. Variable components might include bonuses, where the payout may be based on reported accounting numbers, market share or customer satisfaction, and stock compensation, where the payout is based on stock prices. Each has differing effects on CEO incentives and has differing costs to the corporation.

Referring to the incentives, consider salary and the pension benefit, both nominally fixed in amount. While nominally fixed in amount, both provide certain incentives and can influence the decisions the CEO makes, personally and for the corporation. For example, while salary is nominally fixed in amount, it can be renegotiated *upward or downward*, although the latter is less frequent than the former. And a defined benefit pension plan can be structured so that it does not vest immediately and/or so the benefit increases with the individual's tenure with the corporation. Both give the CEO incentive to remain with the corporation. However, if the pension is not fully funded the CEO has the incentive to reduce the risk of the corporation, which could involve forgoing otherwise profitable projects.[21] Why? Because if the corporation goes bankrupt, not only does the CEO lose his or her job, but also to the extent his or her pension is not fully funded, he or she becomes an unsecured creditor of the corporation. Why not then simply make the fixed component all salary? One reason is that our tax code provides incentives for employers to provide things like life insurance, health care and pensions.[22] Sometimes the tax incentives even exist for the employee to defer salary to future periods.[23] To the extent that the compensation package can be structured to minimize taxes, or more formally, the joint tax burden of the corporation and CEO, both parties can be made better off.

When a corporation is determining the variable components of its compensation plan, that is, determining whether variable compensation should include bonuses, stock compensation or both, it must also realize that different forms of variable compensation provide different incentives. The corporation should also realize that the structure of an incentive plan can yield very specific orientation and behaviors. A bonus plan based upon accounting numbers may lead to higher reported accounting income, but not necessarily higher shareholder value, as management may make cosmetic changes to its financial statements to increase its bonuses (see discussion in Chapter 5, Section 2). Similarly, if managers are rewarded for increasing market share, the corporation may get increased market share, but at the cost of reduced profits and reduced shareholder value. In contrast, stock compensation only increases in value when value (narrowly defined as share price) increases, but subjects the manager to market risks, for which he or she will

Table 3-1:

Additional Examples of Executives Foregoing Salary

Corporation, Executive, Title	Explanation
Capital One Financial • Richard D. Fairbank, chairman of the board and chief executive officer	"Since 1997, Mr. Fairbank has elected to forego all of his annual cash compensation (base salary or annual cash incentive) and annual retirement plan contributions and instead receive grants equity compensation."[1]
Univision Communications • A. Jerrold Perenchio, chairman, chief executive officer and controlling shareholder	"Mr. Perenchio, Univision's Chairman and Chief Executive Officer, serves without salary, bonus or equity-based compensation. As a significant stockholder and holder of majority voting power, Mr. Perenchio remains highly motivated to increase Univision's stockholder value and to incentivize management to do the same."[2]
USANA • Dr. Myron W. Wentz, chairman of the board, chief executive officer and controlling shareholder	"The Company's Founder and Chairman of the Board of Directors, Dr. Myron W. Wentz, has served with the title of Chief Executive Officer of USANA since its inception. During 2005, we paid no salary and no cash bonus to Dr. Wentz. At the end of 2005, however, the Compensation Committee made a stock option grant to Dr. Wentz, which was fully vested as of the date of grant."[3]
Duke Energy • Paul M. Anderson, chairman of the board.	"The employment agreement between Duke Energy and Mr. Anderson (as described in "Employment Contracts and Termination of Employment and Change-in-Control Arrangements" under "Executive Compensation" below) establishes that Mr. Anderson's compensation will be provided in the form of stock-based compensation in lieu of base salary, annual cash incentives and certain employee benefits. The purpose of the structure of this compensation package is to directly align Mr. Anderson's compensation with shareholders by making his compensation contingent upon stock price, Duke Energy performance and dividend yield."[4]
El Paso Energy • William A. Wise, chairman of the board, chief executive officer and president	"base salary was eliminated in 1996 and replaced with long-term awards of stock options and restricted stock, the majority of which vest only after the expiration of specified time periods and only if certain performance targets are met within those periods."[5]

Table 3-1:

Additional Examples of Executives Foregoing Salary (Continued)

Corporation, Executive, Title	Explanation
Viacom • Summer Redstone, chairman of the board, chief executive officer and controlling stockholder	"has waived payment of any salary or bonus compensation for his services as Chief Executive Officer of the Company."[6]
Pepsico • Roger Enrico, chairman of the board and chief executive officer	"At Mr. Enrico's request, the Committee again approved a reduction in Mr. Enrico's annual salary from $900,000 to $1, and recommended to the Board of Directors that it consider using the savings to support front line employees. In January 1999, the Board approved annual charitable contributions of approximately $1,000,000 to fund additional scholarships for children of PepsiCo's front line employees."[7]
Borders Group • Robert DiRomualdo, chairman • George Mrkonic, vice chairman	Messrs. DiRomualdo and Mrkonic were granted options in lieu of cash for 100% of their fiscal 1999 salary and bonus. The options grants to Messrs. DiRomualdo and Mrkonic covered 194,826 and 94,322 shares, respectively. The salary and bonus to which the named officers were entitled for fiscal 1999 is as follows: Mr. DiRomualdo, $474,553 salary, $474,553 bonus; Mr. Mrkonic, $257,500 salary, $257,500 bonus."[8]

[1] Page 31, Capital One Financial proxy statement filed with Securities and Exchange Commission, March 23, 2006.
[2] Page 17, Univision Communications proxy statement filed with Securities and Exchange Commission, March 17, 2006.
[3] Page 27, USANA proxy statement filed with Securities and Exchange Commission, March 14, 2006.
[4] Page 39, Duke Energy proxy statement filed with Securities and Exchange Commission, Sept. 15, 2006.
[5] Page 7, El Paso Energy proxy statement filed with Securities and Exchange Commission, March 11, 1999.
[6] Page 12, Viacom proxy statement filed with Securities and Exchange Commission, April 16, 1999.
[7] Page 9, Pepsico proxy statement filed with Securities and Exchange Commission, March 24, 2000.
[8] Page 5, Borders Group proxy statement filed with Securities and Exchange Commission, April 21, 2000.

want to be compensated for. Theoretically, this market risk can be controlled for with a market-adjusted option whereby the exercise price of the option can be adjusted up or down depending on market movements. However, corporations do not seem to grant market-adjusted options.[24] Separately, as discussed in Chapter 6, recent research has shown that tying compensation to stock prices may lead to some unethical behavior, for example, the backdating of stock option grant dates.

If stock compensation is used, the corporation must decide if it should take the form of stock grants or stock options. Stock grants are valuable as long as the share price is above zero, whereas stock options are only valuable if the share price is greater than the exercise price (the price at which the option allows the holder to purchase shares). In general, stock options will provide the CEO with more incentives to take risks than stock grants. Yet certain companies, such as Philip Morris, grant restricted stock "in an effort to retain its executives in the face of a steep drop in the company's share price," arguing that options do not "work well for tobacco companies, whose share prices now are influenced more by what happens in courtrooms than by whether management is meeting its goals."[25]

In practice (see Tables 2-2 through 2-4), we see corporations including both bonuses and stock-based compensation in the compensation package, as a way of reducing the risks to the executive (Sloan 1993). Alternatively, the bonus might be used as a way to reward the executive regardless of performance. For example, in 1999 Eastman Kodak gave its retiring CEO a $2.5 million bonus "in recognition of the company's financial performance" even though in a bull market the corporation's shares declined 8 percent in value.[26]

Designing the Contract to Retain the Executive

To minimize recruiting and training costs and avoid the downtime associated with an open position, corporations would like to ensure that the executive being recruited stays with the corporation. There are two nonmutually exclusive tracks the company can take. The first approach would be to provide monetary incentives to stay, for example, compensation that vests over a period of time and hence is forfeited if the executive leaves before the end of the vesting period. This track, which involves long-term components of compensation such as restricted stock, stock options and pensions, could be referred to as the "golden handcuff" approach. An example would be the Special Equity Grant given to Richard A. McGinn, Lucent Technologies' board chairman and CEO.

> SPECIAL EQUITY GRANT:
> As an incentive for Mr. McGinn to continue providing the company with first-class leadership and to guide the company toward its goal of becoming the pre-eminent supplier of next-generation communications networks, we granted Mr. McGinn an additional stock option in fiscal 1999 covering 1 million shares. This option will vest only if Mr. McGinn stays with the company for five years from the grant date.[27]

This grant is in addition to his annual grant of 400,000 options (which vest after three years), and was valued by the corporation at the time of grant at

$11,180,000.[28] The intrinsic value of the additional grant at Dec. 31, 1999, was $45,640,600. Being that the grant is not yet exercisable, if McGinn were to leave Lucent he would forego that entire amount, providing him with the incentive to stay.[29]

However if the new employer is willing to reimburse the executive for amounts forfeited when leaving the old employer, the employment contract loses its retentive effect. An example of a corporation compensating an executive for items forfeited at a prior employer is found in the employment contract of Jim McNerney, the newly hired CEO of Boeing. McNerney, at the time CEO of 3M, forfeited significant amounts of unvested equity compensation in moving to Boeing. However, the package he received at Boeing made provisions for equity that Mr. McNerney left behind.

> As compensation to replace unvested 3M equity awards that Mr. McNerney will forfeit, he was granted, effective July 1, 2005, the following Buy-Out Restricted Stock Awards: (i) for forfeited 3M stock options, 159,000 shares of restricted Boeing stock with vesting and restrictions lapsing in five equal annual installments beginning on May 10, 2006; (ii) for forfeited 3M restricted stock awards, 162,000 shares of restricted Boeing stock with vesting and restrictions lapsing in six equal annual installments beginning on Jan. 1, 2006; and (iii) for forfeited 3M restricted stock awards, 70,000 shares of restricted Boeing stock with vesting and restrictions lapsing in three equal annual installments beginning July 1, 2006. The aggregate value of the Buy-Out Restricted Stock Awards as of July 1, 2005, was $25,289,880.[30]

The second approach is to limit the executive's alternative employment opportunities with noncompete, nondisclosure and nonsolicitation provisions. These provisions are fairly standard in executive contracts. An example of each of these provisions was found in the employment agreement between James McNerney and Boeing dated June 29, 2005.

11. (a) **CONFIDENTIALITY.** The Executive agrees that he shall not, directly or indirectly, use, make available, sell, disclose or otherwise communicate to any person, other than in the course of the Executive's employment and for the benefit of the Company (as determined by the Executive in good faith), either during the period of the Executive's

employment or at any time thereafter, any nonpublic, proprietary or confidential information, knowledge or data relating to the Company, any of its subsidiaries, affiliated companies or businesses, which shall have been obtained by the Executive during the Executive's employment by the Company. The foregoing shall not apply to information that (i) was known to the public prior to its disclosure to the Executive; (ii) becomes known to the public subsequent to disclosure to the Executive through no wrongful act of the Executive or any representative of the Executive; or (iii) the Executive is required to disclose by applicable law, regulation or legal process (provided that the Executive provides the Company with prior notice of the contemplated disclosure and reasonably cooperates with the Company at its expense in seeking a protective order or other appropriate protection of such information). Notwithstanding clauses (i) and (ii) of the preceding sentence, the Executive's obligation to maintain such disclosed information in confidence shall not terminate where only portions of the information are in the public domain.

(b) **NONSOLICITATION**. During the Executive's employment with the Company and for the one-(1) year period thereafter, the Executive agrees that he will not, directly or indirectly, individually or on behalf of any other person, firm, corporation or other entity, knowingly solicit, aid or induce (i) any managerial level employee of the Company or any of its subsidiaries or affiliates to leave such employment in order to accept employment with or render services to or with any other person, firm, corporation or other entity unaffiliated with the Company or knowingly take any action to materially assist or aid any other person, firm, corporation or other entity in identifying or hiring any such employee (provided, that the foregoing shall not be violated by general advertising not targeted at Company employees nor by serving as a reference for an employee with regard to an entity with which the Executive is not affiliated), or (ii) any customer of the Company or any of its subsidiaries or affiliates to purchase goods or services then sold by the Company or any of its subsidiaries or affiliates from another person, firm, corporation or other entity or assist or aid any other persons or entity in identifying or soliciting any such customer (provided, that the foregoing shall not apply to any product or service which is not covered by the noncompetition provision set forth in Section 11(c), below).

(c) **NONCOMPETITION**. The Executive acknowledges that he performs services of a unique nature for the Company that are irreplaceable, and that his performance of such services to a competing business (other than respecting a product or service of the Company involving less than one percent (1%) of the Company's revenues in the prior fiscal year ("De Minimis")) will result in irreparable harm to the Company. Accordingly, during the Executive's employment hereunder and for the one-(1) year period thereafter, the Executive agrees that the Executive will not, directly or indirectly, own, manage, operate, control, be employed by (whether as an employee, consultant, independent contractor or otherwise, and whether or not for compensation) or render services to any person, firm, corporation or other entity, in whatever form, engaged in any business of the same type as any business in which the Company or any of its subsidiaries or affiliates is engaged on the date of termination or in which they have proposed, on or prior to such date, to be engaged in on or after such date and in which the Executive has been involved to any extent (other than De Minimis) at any time during the twelve (12)-month period ending with the date of termination, in any locale of any country in which the Company conducts business. This Section 11(c) shall not prevent the Executive from owning not more than one percent (1%) of the total shares of all classes of stock outstanding of any publicly held entity engaged in such business, nor will it restrict the Executive from rendering services to charitable organizations, as such term is defined in Section 501(c) of the Code.[31]

Employees in general, and high-level executives in particular, build up a certain level of corporation- and industry-specific knowledge. Hence, a manufacturing executive at an automaker would be more valuable to a rival automaker than to a computer manufacturer. Thus, preventing executives from taking positions (through the noncompete provision) at rival corporations makes them less likely to leave. Further, even if the executive were willing to take a position not in competition with his former employer, he or she would be prohibited, through the nonsolicitation provision, from hiring any of his or her former colleagues. While the above example pertains to a chief executive officer, similar provisions can be designed for a broad base of executives. For example, as shown below, American Express has restrictions on about 520 employees, requiring they forfeit certain components of their compensation package if they act in a way detrimental to the best interests of the corporation, including but not limited to working for competitors, soliciting customers and/or employees, and disclosure of confidential information.

> *Detrimental Conduct.* To help protect the Company's competitive position, approximately 520 executives, including the executive officers, have signed agreements that include a provision that requires them to forfeit the proceeds from some or all of their long-term incentive awards received up to two years prior to employment termination, if they engage in conduct that is detrimental to the Company. Detrimental conduct includes working for certain competitors, soliciting the Company's customers or employees after employment ends and disclosing the Company's confidential information.[32]

Of course, if a corporation wants an executive badly enough, it can negotiate with the executive's former employer to release the executive from the above restrictions. Such a case arose when Conseco hired Gary C. Wendt to be its chairman and CEO. Wendt, although no longer employed by General Electric, was bound by a noncompete provision. To get General Electric to waive that provision and allow it to hire Wendt, Conseco gave General Electric a warrant to purchase 10.5 million shares of its common stock as described below:

> On June 28, 2000, Conseco Inc. ("Conseco" or the "Company") elected Mr. Gary C. Wendt its Chairman of the Board and Chief Executive Officer. Mr. Wendt served as the Chairman of the Board and Chief Executive Officer of General Electric Capital Services, Inc. until 1998 and, in connection with his departure, entered into an agreement with General Electric Company ("GE") containing, among other things, obligations of Mr. Wendt not to compete with GE with respect to financial services businesses and non-hire obligations. In connection with his employment by the Company, it was necessary to receive a waiver from GE of the noncompetition obligations. As part of receiving the waiver, a number of benefits Mr. Wendt would have otherwise retained or received from GE were terminated. Conseco also issued a warrant for 10.5 million shares of its common stock to a subsidiary of GE in connection with the waiver. This warrant has an exercise price of $5.75 per share and is exercisable at any time prior to its scheduled expiration on June 28, 2005.[33]

As alluded to in the paragraph above, Wendt also forfeited certain benefits by taking the position with Conseco. He estimated that if he had fulfilled the remaining 21 months of his noncompete agreement he would have received $65 million.34

A third approach, if the first two do not work, is to use the legal system to deter potential competitors from hiring your executives. Thurm (2001) discusses some of the legal steps companies have taken to prevent employees from working for competitors, including forcing former employees already working for competitors to leave their new positions. A particularly well-publicized case involved the 1993 hiring by Volkswagon of José Ignacio López de Arriortúa. While the case was a bit more complicated than normal because of the allegations of theft of confidential documents, it is an example of how multiple legal systems can be used to deter would-be employers. The hiring of López, who was at the time employed by General Motors, led to Volkswagon being entangled in both the United States and German court systems for four years, and ultimately led it to pay General Motors $100 million as a settlement.35 More recently, Microsoft fought, and lost, a battle to prevent Kai-Fu Lee, a former Microsoft vice president hired by Google to be president of its China operations (Delaney 2005, Waters 2005).

Minimize Costs to the Corporation

In addition to making the package attractive enough to entice/retain the individual under consideration and structuring the package so that the individual has the appropriate incentives, the corporation has to take into consideration a multitude of costs, some of which are not generally thought of as costs. First, consider the financial costs of different forms of variable compensation. Bonuses normally require the payment of cash, whereas stock compensation only requires the issuance of previously unissued shares, a trade-off that may be important for cash-strapped corporations. Also, the accounting and tax treatments differ between bonuses and stock compensation, and different types of stock compensation. For example, while bonuses are normally recognized as an expense for financial reporting purposes in the period earned, stock compensation is normally recognized as an expense over the vesting period. Furthermore, under the Internal Revenue Code, bonuses are both taxable to the employee and deductible by the employer in the period paid. However, if stock option grants meet certain conditions (see Chapter 6, Section 8), they are not taxable to the employee until they are exercised, and certain options are not even taxable then.

While stock options are treated favorably under the Internal Revenue Code, other forms of compensation are not looked upon as favorably. In particular, subject to certain exceptions, which will be discussed later in this book, Section 162(m) of the code limits tax deductions for compensation paid to the top five executives of the corporation to $1 million per executive per year. Thus, while not limiting the amount of compensation a corporation can pay its executives, Section 162(m) affects the after-tax cost to the corporation. In the example previously cited, Robert E. Rubin being hired by Citigroup, Citigroup may only be able to deduct $1 million of the $15 million it has promised to pay him in 2000 and 2001. However, it appears Citigroup has taken steps to preserve that deductibility. Citigroup, in its proxy statement dated March 17, 2000 (page 26), notes that Rubin is promised a minimum bonus of $14 million for each of 2000 and 2001, adding "which bonus amounts are being deferred." While not explicitly mentioning Section 162(m), this action is consistent with it, as if the amount is deferred until Rubin is no longer subject to Section 162(m), Citigroup will be able to fully deduct it on its tax return. As with other financial decisions, the corporation must take into account the after-tax cost when designing the compensation package.

Nonfinancial costs have to be considered, too. One such cost would be equity. For example, it would be somewhat insulting to the outgoing CEO if the new CEO were to make more than he or she did. Not only would this be somewhat insulting, it would tend to breed some resentment and not bode well for a working relationship between the two, with the latter possibly retaining the chairmen position, or at least a position on the board of directors. Dechow and Sloan (1991) report that 57 percent of their sample CEOs stay on as chairman after retirement, while Brickley et al. (1999, Table 3) report that 18 percent of departed CEOs are still chairmen two years after retirement. Including those that relinquish the chair position, Dechow and Sloan (1991) find 84 percent initially remain on the board, while Brickley et al. (1999) find almost 50 percent are still on the board two years later.

Similarly, the existence of a large gap between the newly hired CEO and the remainder of the executive group would add insult to injury, as not only were the existing executives passed over in favor of an outsider, but that new CEO is being paid significantly more than they are. While in many cases those passed over for the top slot leave the corporation, it is also true that in many cases the corporation, while not wanting to make them CEO, would like to retain them.36 These concluding points illustrate that while explicitly a contract is being designed for one person, there are ramifications beyond that person that must be taken into consideration. This issue will be further discussed in the next chapter.

Summary

This chapter was a brief introduction into the design of an executive compensation contract. It was an introduction, as many of the details needed to design a compensation contract will be discussed in subsequent chapters.

While most of the discussion can be applied to designing contracts to motivate and retain existing executives, the context of the chapter was designing a compensation contract to attract a new executive to an existing corporation. Five broad areas were discussed: (1) making the offer attractive, (2) providing incentives to increase shareholder value, (3) providing incentives to remain with the corporation, (4) minimizing the costs to shareholders and (5) minimizing the risk to the executive.

In general, for the offer to be attractive to the executive, its magnitude must exceed the executive's opportunity cost, which is either his or her current compensation or the compensation being offered by another competitor for his or her services. While a large compensation package may attract an executive, it may not provide the proper incentives to increase shareholder value. The corporation must provide these incentives in the compensation package, which it normally does through the use of conditional compensation. However, the corporation must take into account the executive's risk aversion, which can have two adverse effects on the corporation. First, a risk-averse individual will demand a higher level of compensation the greater the risk of that compensation. Second, a risk-averse executive may modify his or her behavior in a manner not consistent with maximizing shareholder value if his or her compensation is at risk. Thus, compensation packages normally include fixed components to reduce the executive's risk and conditional components to provide incentives to increase shareholder value.

Assuming the corporation is successful in attracting the executive, it wants to make sure that he or she remains with the corporation. The compensation contract can be designed to provide monetary incentives for the executive to remain with the corporation. One approach is to provide the executive with compensation that vests over a period of time, and hence is forfeited if the executive leaves before the end of the vesting period. A second approach is to limit the executive's alternative employment opportunities with noncompete, nondisclosure and nonsolicitation provisions. By limiting the executive's alternative employment opportunities, the corporation can make it more likely the executive will remain with the corporation.

The corporation also wants to minimize the cost to shareholders, with the goal of maximizing shareholder value. It must consider both financial and nonfinancial costs. It must consider that each component of the compensation package can have a differing impact on the cash flow, financial reporting and tax status of the corporation and executive. It must also consider whether the new executive's contract will have an adverse effect on the morale and motivation of existing executives. That is, attracting a star executive may not be worthwhile if the result will be a poor working relationship between the new executive and the current occupants of the executive suite.

Footnotes

1 Page 22, Citigroup proxy statement filed with the Securities and Exchange Commission, March 17, 2000.

2 Page 26, Citigroup proxy statement filed with Securities and Exchange Commission, March 17, 2000.

3 Page 8, Goldman Sachs Group proxy statement filed with the Securities and Exchange Commission, Feb. 14, 2000.

4 Page 19, Merrill Lynch proxy statement filed with the Securities and Exchange Commission, March 9, 2000.

5 Pages 10 and 12, Morgan Stanley Dean Witter proxy statement filed with the Securities and Exchange Commission on Feb. 23, 2000.

6 Whitford (1999), page 44.

7 Employment contract, dated Sept. 21, 1999, between George Shaheen and Webvan Group.

8 Reingold (2000), page 112.

9 Some financial incentive does exist. If the corporation performs well as a result of his or her actions, the CEO could get a raise from his or her current employer, and/or increase his or her reputation/value in the managerial labor market.

10 As an example of the risk involved, Reingold (2000) reports that starting in 1997, the top five executives of the Borders Group elected to take options in lieu of salaries. Reingold states that, "With his options under water, Vice Chairman Bruce A. Quinnell had to borrow to pay his living expenses."

11 Page 6, Apple Computer proxy statement filed with Securities and Exchange Commission, March 16, 1998.

12 Page 8, Apple Computer proxy statement filed with Securities and Exchange Commission, March 16, 1998.

13 Page 7, Apple Computer proxy statement filed with Securities and Exchange Commission, Feb. 9, 1999.

14 Page 7, Apple Computer proxy statement filed with Securities and Exchange Commission, March 6, 2000.

15 Page 19, Apple Computer proxy statement filed with Securities and Exchange Commission, March 6, 2000.

16 Page 12, Oracle proxy statement filed with Securities and Exchange Commission, Sept. 11, 2000.

[17] Page 5, Berkshire Hathaway proxy statement filed with Securities and Exchange Commission, March 13, 2006.

[18] Page 8, Berkshire Hathaway proxy statement filed with Securities and Exchange Commission, March 13, 2000.

[19] Page 8, Amazon.com proxy statement filed with Securities and Exchange Commission, April 20, 2006, page 7, Amazon.com proxy statement filed with Securities and Exchange Commission, April 11, 2003, and page 7 Amazon.com proxy statement filed with Securities and Exchange Commission, March 29, 2000.

[20] Page 7, Amazon.com proxy statement filed with Securities and Exchange Commission, April 20, 2006.

[21] Most CEOs are covered by two defined benefit pension plans. The basic plan is at least partially funded, governed by ERISA (Employee Retirement Income Security Act) and guaranteed somewhat by the PBGC (Pension Benefit Guaranty Corp.). However, limits imposed by ERISA and the Internal Revenue Code limit the payouts from these plans. Thus, most corporations have a supplemental plan for their top executives. Given that the supplemental plan is not tax qualified, if it were funded the executive would be taxed immediately. Thus, these plans are generally unfunded.

[22] For example, assuming the requirements set by the Internal Revenue Code are met, payments for employee life insurance and health-care benefits are deductible by the employer but not recognized as income by the employee. Thus, the employee is better off having the employer purchase these items on his or her behalf, than if the employer would have paid those amounts as salary, with the employee purchasing those benefits with his or her after-tax salary.

[23] Miller and Scholes (1982) show this occurs when the corporate tax rate is less than that of the individual.

[24] A plethora of possible explanations exist. One is that under prior accounting standards, an expense would have to be recognized for market-adjusted options (whereas none is recognized for most options currently granted), hence accounting treatment has kept corporations from granting these options. The other is that managers want the upside potential associated with unadjusted options, and may have other mechanisms, e.g., repricing, to control downside risk. These issues are more fully discussed in Chapter 6.

[25] Fairclough (2000).

[26] *The Wall Street Journal* (2000b).

[27] Page 28 of Lucent Technologies proxy statement filed with the Securities

and Exchange Commission, Dec. 21, 1999.

28 Page 32 of Lucent Technologies proxy statement filed with the Securities and Exchange Commission, Dec. 21, 1999.

29 Soon thereafter Lucent hit some hard times, and McGinn left the company Oct. 22, 2001 (page 33 of Lucent Technologies proxy statement filed with the Securities and Exchange Commission, Dec. 28, 2001).

30 Page 3, Boeing 8-K filed with the Securities and Exchange Commission, July 6, 2005.

31 Pages 15 and 16, Exhibit 99.1 to Boeing 8-K filed with the Securities and Exchange Commission, July 6, 2005.

32 Page 23, American Express proxy statement filed with Securities and Exchange Commission, March 22, 2006.

33 Conseco 8-K filed with the Securities and Exchange Commission, July 10, 2000.

34 Hallinan (2000).

35 Puri (1997).

36 Corporations are not always successful in this retention and many acknowledge that when multiple candidates are competing for the same position, the losers in the competition are likely to depart. For example, when Jeffrey R. Immelt was named to be John F. Welch's successor as CEO of General Electric, it took the two other internal candidates, Robert L. Nardelli and W. James McNerney, only nine days to secure positions as CEOs of Home Depot and Minnesota Mining & Manufacturing, respectively, leaving positions to be filled at GE Power Systems and GE Aircraft Engines (Lublin et al. 2000).

Part II
The Components of the Compensation Package

Chapter 4

Salary

Introduction

Salary is the most basic part of the compensation package. It is normally fixed in amount, although it is variable in the sense that it can be renegotiated. That is, an individual can get raises for good performance, or take a pay cut for poor performance. It provides riskless compensation to almost all employees, except for employees working solely on commission and the occasional CEO who elects not to take a salary (see Chapter 3). At a minimum, salary (along with the other parts of the compensation package) must be competitive with an individual's other opportunities, that is his or her opportunity cost. This is necessary to recruit new employees and retain those that the corporation already employs. Examples exist of executives leaving their positions for more lucrative opportunities and of executive contracts being negotiated upward because of competing offers.

While salary needs to be competitive, because it is only one component of the compensation package, it need not always be greater than the salaries offered by competitors for the executives' services. Consider the following example: Joseph Galli, executive vice president at Black & Decker, takes the position of president at Amazon.com. His salary declines from $475,000 at Black & Decker[1] to $200,000 at Amazon.com.[2] Why did he take the job? Amazon gave him a signing bonus of $7.9 million payable over a three-year period, and options to purchase almost 4 million shares over a 20-year period.[3] The intrinsic value (excess of market over exercise price) of those options, all of which were unexercisable, at Dec. 31, 1999, was $71,233,260.[4, 5] By comparison, on Dec. 31, 1998, Galli held Black & Decker options with an intrinsic value of $13,331,542.[6]

Another example is Frank Newman, president and CEO of More.com. In accepting his position at More.com, Newman accepted a salary of $500,000[7], whereas in the previous year he had earned $668,307[8] as chairman, president and CEO of the Eckerd Corp., a subsidiary of JCPenney. Why did he take the cut in salary? More.com also guaranteed a first-year bonus of $250,000, a $500,000 relocation grant, a $1 million signing bonus and options to acquire 1,633,752 shares.[9]

On the other hand, Boeing persuaded Alan R. Mulally (who later left Boeing to become CEO at Ford) to remain with the corporation rather than take a position at Raytheon by giving him $5.2 million in restricted stock and 200,000 in stock options.[10]

> ... a senior Boeing official said Mulally, 53, received the options and restricted stock before he was installed as head of the jetliner division to keep him from joining another company. Mulally had been offered a job as chief executive of Raytheon.[11]

As shown in Chapter 2, salary is a major component of the CEO compensation package, a component that is used in almost all compensation packages (see Tables 2-2 through 2-4), one that makes up a significant proportion of compensation (see Tables 2-5 through 2-7) and is substantial in amount (see Tables 2-8 through 2-10). While shrinking over time as a proportion of the total compensation package (see Table 2-5), salary is increasing in amount (see Table 2-8), in most years, at a rate in excess of inflation. Table 4-1 shows the percentage change in salary for

Table 4-1:

Percentage Change in Salary for CEOs with Same Company for Consecutive Years

Year	Mean Percentage Change In Salary	Median Percentage Change In Salary	Average Change in Consumer Price Index CPI-U
1993	4.08	-5.17	2.99%
1994	-9.05	0.00	2.56%
1995	-3.75	3.04	2.83%
1996	1.97	4.72	2.95%
1997	4.54	4.85	2.29%
1998	5.10	5.18	1.56%
1999	3.70	4.21	2.21%
2000	4.09	4.93	3.36%
2001	5.05	4.76	2.85%
2002	4.22	3.15	1.58%
2003	6.69	3.89	2.28%
2004	6.33	3.89	2.66%
2005	5.13	3.89	3.39%

Note: Calculations in this table are based upon data contained in the April 2006 version of Standard & Poor's ExecuComp and the Consumer Price Index, All Urban Consumers, as found on the Bureau of Labor Statistics Web site.

CEOs that have been with the same corporation (and in the same position) for at least two years. In the early 1990s, the rate of increase of salary was actually negative. That is, from 1992 to 1993, the median salary decreased, while from 1993 to 1994 and again from 1994 to 1995, mean salary decreased, and in 1996, while positive, the mean increase in salary was less than the mean increase in inflation.

Consequently, while salary is increasing, and generally at a rate faster than inflation, because of faster increases in the other components of the compensation package, salary is a declining part of the average compensation package. In particular, as shown in Chapter 2, the pattern is driven by disproportionate increases in the value of stock and option grants. Whether that pattern continues or reverts is uncertain, and is partially, if not primarily, dependent on future stock market performance.

Incentives

As discussed in Chapter 3, salary has limited incentive effects, as it does not increase with shareholder value. If that were truly the case, in the absence of other forms of compensation, a work-averse individual would merely expend the minimal effort necessary not to get fired. However, there is always the possibility of salary

Figure 4-1:
Growth in Salary Versus Growth in CPI

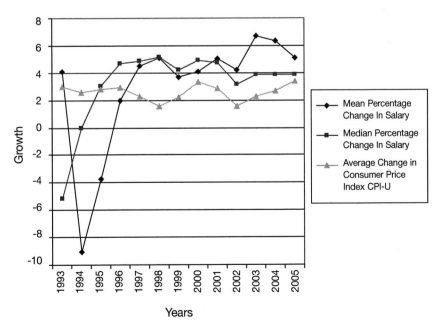

renegotiation. That is, if the corporation does well the executive can get a raise, which provides some incentive to work hard to increase shareholder value.

Table 4-2 investigates the possibility that CEOs' salaries are adjusted for corporate performance during the years 1993 through 2005. In the table, corporations are divided into 10 portfolios depending upon their percentage change in income. To the right of the performance decile are mean and median increases in CEO salary for the subsequent year, for that portfolio. Viewing the table, it appears there is a relationship between salary and performance. That is, the mean (median) increase in next-period salary is 3 (2) percent for the lowest performers and 7 (5) percent for the highest performers.

Further analysis shows the percentage of CEOs receiving a raise in their salary increases from 58 percent for the lowest performers to 75 percent for the highest performers, while the percentage of CEOs seeing their salary go down drops from 17 percent for the lowest performers to 7 percent for the highest. So even CEOs in the lowest-performing corporations are more likely to get a raise than not, and few CEOs in any corporation take salary cuts.

An alternative source of incentives is the "managerial labor market" whereby executives who do well will be sought after by other corporations.[12] Gibbons and Murphy (1992), in discussing the implicit incentives associated with career concerns, note that "for young workers it can be optimal for current pay to be completely independent of current performance." For older workers, the post-retirement market may provide some incentives. That is, Brickley et al. (1999) document that CEOs whose corporations perform well hold more post-retirement directorships than CEOs whose corporations perform poorly.

Finally, research (for example, Warner et al. 1988) has shown that turnover is inversely related to corporate performance. That is, CEOs in poorly performing corporations are more likely to be replaced. So it is true that an executive receiving only salary does have some incentives to perform well.

Effect on Willingness to Take Risks

While the executive may have the incentive to perform well, he or she may not have the same risk preferences as shareholders. For example, shareholders are assumed to be well diversified, in that losses in one part of their portfolio are expected to be offset by gains in another part of their portfolio. Executives are less diversified in that their human capital, which may be defined as the present value of their future earnings, is largely tied to the prospects of their employer. Poor performance and/or bankruptcy could then have a two-fold effect on the

Table 4-2:

Relation Between Changes in Performance and Changes in Next-Period Salary

Performance Decile	Mean Increase in Next-Period Salary	Median Increase in Next-Period Salary	Percentage of CEOs with Increase in Salary	Percentage of CEOs with Decrease in Salary
Lowest	3.21	2.15	58.39	17.03
2	5.87	4.73	71.35	9.03
3	5.63	3.96	68.31	8.46
4	5.35	4.36	76.03	6.08
5	5.49	5.00	75.78	5.83
6	7.04	5.45	78.98	4.35
7	6.69	5.43	76.19	6.32
8	6.28	5.00	71.26	8.62
9	7.17	5.02	75.37	6.98
Highest	6.95	5.20	75.06	7.14

Note: Calculations in this table are based upon data contained in the April 2006 version of Standard & Poor's ExecuComp.

executive. First, he or she would lose his or her job. Then, he or she would have to enter the job market, a market that would then penalize him or her for past failures. And this is without considering any shareholdings the executive may have in his or her employer. As is noted in Chapter 9, executives in general, and CEOs in particular, are under pressure, political and otherwise, to own shares in their employer. Some companies (for example, American Express[13], Tribune[14]) even have formal requirements that executives own shares worth a multiple of their annual compensation. Thus, if the corporation fails, they would not only lose their job, but also their investments and possibly their pensions, or at least the unfunded supplemental part. For these reasons, executives prefer to take less risk than shareholders. The possibility then exists that executives will elect to pass on projects that increase corporate value because they are risky.

The nonsalary portion of the compensation package can be structured to provide the executive with incentives to take risk. For example, because their payoff increases with share prices, stock options and stock grants, under certain circumstances (to be discussed in Chapter 6), will provide incentives for executives to undertake risky, but profitable projects. In contrast, an executive compensated solely with salary will have the incentive to forgo any projects that increase risk, regardless of how profitable they may be.

How Much?

The major question with salary, as well as with the other components of the compensation package, is how much to pay. How does the employer determine what to offer a new employee? And how much should the company pay an existing one? Factors to be considered include, but are not limited to, the size of the corporation (recall from Chapter 2 that there is a positive relationship between size and executive compensation), individual characteristics (for example, education and experience) and the responsibilities of the executive (for example, is the executive going to be the CEO or the CEO and chairman).

In Chapter 3, the situation where a corporation is looking to hire a new CEO was discussed. If the corporation has been operating for several years, it usually has the option to choose between an internal and external candidate. In either case it has been noted that the promotion carries with it a significant raise. This raise should be high enough to attract the outside candidate or to reward the internal candidate, but not so high as to breed resentment within the corporation[15]. The issue then becomes one of equity. At what point will the amount paid to the CEO become a problem with other executives and/or employees? From Table 2-11 we can see that the second in command, or the second highest-paid executive, receives a salary that is, on average, 62 percent of the salary paid to the CEO.

Hiring an external candidate complicates matters even more. To attract a new employee, the corporation must design the compensation package to entice the targeted executive to take the position. Normally, but not always, this requires a raise. For example, a survey by Watson Wyatt Worldwide and WorldatWork (2006) found employees require a median increase of 20 percent to change employers. This increase may not take the form of salary. There are examples, some of which are cited above, of individuals taking new positions with a lower salary but more of other forms of compensation. The fact that much of the compensation is conditional may make it easier to sell to existing executives, that is, the new CEO will only receive that compensation if the stock price increases, and if that happens we will all be better off. It should also be noted that part of this increase could be the result of the employer compensating its new CEO for compensation forfeited at his or her old employer.

Some of the complications of hiring an external candidate involve the potential animosity between the newly hired CEO and the passed-over internal candidates, who possess valuable firm-specific knowledge not held by the new CEO. Those individuals will be upset not only because they were passed over for the job, but also because the new individual will be making more than they are. But, they need to be retained and encouraged to remain productive because their firm-specific knowledge cannot easily be replaced.

Equity Issues

This discussion leads to a more generic set of problems involving equity. Vertical equity refers to equity across levels of the organization. That is, equity between upper-level management and lower-level employees. While most employees are willing to accept the fact that top executives receive higher compensation, too large a spread in compensation levels can lead to conflict, which can result in employee demands for reductions in executive pay, or increases in their own compensation. It can also lead to other negative consequences for the corporation. Research has shown, for example, O'Reilly et al. (1996) Pfeffer and Davis-Blake (1992), that vertical inequity is associated with higher turnover. Cowherd and Levine (1992) show that inequity between top managers and lower-level employees may diminish product quality. To mitigate this issue, some companies, for example Whole Foods, have instituted policies that limit the disparity between top executive compensation and that of the average worker.

> We have a policy that limits the cash compensation paid to any Team Member in each calendar year, as follows:
> A compensation cap is calculated each year by reference to a particular multiple of the average cash compensation of all full-time Team Members employed during such year. For its fiscal year 2005, the Company continues to use 14 times the above described average.[16]
> Note however, this limit does not apply to all compensation:
> Employee benefits, stock options and any other form of non-cash compensation, such as 401(k) match, are not counted in determining and applying the salary cap.[17]

Horizontal equity refers to equity within a level of the organization. Baker et al. (1988) note, "Personal executives often espouse the virtues of horizontal equity systems which treat employees at the same level in an organization fairly and equally." In an academic context, Pfeffer and Langton (1993, page 382) "show that the greater the degree of wage dispersion within academic departments, the lower is individual faculty members' satisfaction and research productivity and the less likely it is that faculty members will collaborate on research." Supporting this view, Siegel and Hambrick (2005) show that "collaboration is diminished when large pay disparities exist."

Yet no two individuals are identical, and problems will exist if you try to compensate them either identically or differentially. If the corporation pays individuals identically it has several effects. First, it removes the implicit promise of reward for performance. As noted above, salary, while fixed, can be renegotiated upward or downward. If salary is fixed within a level, it would be harder to reward an individual for outstanding performance. The corporation could still reward the individual via promotion, but that may not always be possible, as there may not be openings. Thus, at a minimum, fixing salary within a level removes one tool with which to reward performance. Consequently, it would reduce employees' motivation to work hard and excel. It would also make it difficult to recruit talented individuals. As noted by Murphy et al. (1991), "the most talented people will not go into activities where horizontal equity and other ethical considerations prevent them from capturing the quasi rents on their ability." Shaw et al. (2002) consider the trade-off between the equity and incentive effects, finding that "dispersion can foster competition and lack of cooperation." Consequently "use of individual incentives and dispersed wages" works better in a situation with low interdependence. They add that dispersion will be more likely to be accepted when it is viewed as legitimate, less likely when it is viewed as favoritism. Legitimacy is always an issue, as those receiving lesser salaries and/or raises may not agree that they are less valuable to the corporation. An interesting example of this is contained in research conducted by Cross (1977). Cross conducted a survey of college professors, finding that 94 percent rated their own research above average in quality.

Internal equity, the comparison of one's compensation against the compensation of other positions in the organization, encompasses vertical and horizontal equity. External equity is the comparison of one's compensation to that of peers outside the corporation. That is, a comparison of compensation with peers in similar jobs, but in different organizations. Employees/executives who see their peers making more than they do are less likely to be satisfied and more likely to seek employment elsewhere, which could lead to "brain drain." It could also lead to a form of "adverse selection," a situation in which those who leave (because they were underpaid relative to their skill set) are the most valuable, whereas those who stay (because they are overpaid relative to their skill set) are least valuable. Using matching offers to retain the most valuable employees has its own problems, in that it seems to reward and encourage disloyalty. First, by selectively giving out raises, it creates internal equity problems for the corporation. The person who received the matching offer now earns more than his or her peers. Second, once it becomes known that the employer will match job offers from outside the corporation, employees increase the amount of time they spend looking for such an offer. For these employees, there are three potential outcomes, none of which are optimal from the corporate point of view. The first possibility is that the employee receives and accepts an offer from a new employer. The second possibility is that the employee receives an offer from a new employer and uses it to extract concessions from his or her current employer. The final possibility is that the employee does not receive any offers and thus remains with his or her current employer, but becomes demoralized and, hence, unmotivated.

Political Costs

Whenever discussing the executive suite of major corporations it would be remiss to ignore the potential political considerations, which have also been referred to as political costs.[18] Participants in the political process are made aware of high executive compensation through public disclosures in proxy statements filed with the Securities and Exchange Commission and reports in the business press.[19] These politicians, regulators, shareholders and employees have the ability to impose costs on the executive and corporation. An example of how politicians impose costs on corporations and their executives for paying "excessive compensation" is Section 162(m) of the Internal Revenue Code that limits the deductibility of executive compensation.

Particularly visible is high compensation at a time when the corporation is losing money and/or laying off workers. An example was the resignation under duress of Leo Mullin, former CEO and chairman of Delta Air Lines. As the airline industry suffered in the aftermath of the Sept. 11, 2001, terrorist attacks, Delta "created the retention program and a separate program of bankruptcy-proof retirement trusts for 35 executives in early 2002" (Perez 2003). However at a time when Delta was asking for concessions and laying off 16,000 employees, an uproar ensued, causing Mullin to resign (Adams and Reed 2003). While retaining top executives is necessary in times of financial distress, executives need to show that they are sharing the pain and not profiting from it. Empirically, Hallock (1998) concludes that layoffs do not increase CEO compensation, while DeAngelo and DeAngelo (1991) find the "average CEO salary plus bonus declining 18 percent" during a period where the steel industry was losing money and asking for union concessions.

Among the components of the compensation package, salary is uniquely vulnerable to political criticism because it is not based on, and therefore cannot be justified by, reference to performance.

Financial Consequences
Cash flows
Each component of the executive compensation package impacts the corporation's cash flows, directly via the actual payment and indirectly via the corporation's tax returns. Normally the payment of salary is a cash outflow, whereas the benefit from the tax deduction is a cash inflow (alternatively, it can be viewed as a reduction of another cash outflow, income taxes). Sometimes the executive defers part or all of the salary earned. In those cases, there is no immediate cash outflow (or inflow). Also, while compensation is normally deductible as an ordinary business expense under Section 162 of the Internal Revenue Code, if the executive is subject to the limitations of Section 162(m), the corporation may not be able to fully deduct salary payments. Core and Guay (2001) provide evidence consistent with cash-constrained corporations using stock options in lieu of cash compensation to conserve cash.

Tax deductibility
Specifically, Section 162(m), which is reproduced in Appendix 4.1, limits the deductibility of compensation to $1 million per covered individual, where covered individual is defined as the CEO plus the next four highest-paid executives. The $1-million limitation is not binding if the amounts involved are specified in a contract executed prior to Feb. 17, 1993 (Section 162(m)(4)(D)). Further, amounts meeting the performance-based criteria set forth in Section 162(m)(4)(B) & (C) are not subject to the limitation. Salary, by definition, is not performance based, thus absent stipulation in a pre-existing (Feb. 17, 1993) contract, amounts in excess of $1 million will not be deductible. A few corporations, for example IBP, restructured their compensation packages, including cutting salary, to meet the requirement of Section 162(m):

> The Chairman and Chief Executive Officer's salary and performance-based bonus for 1994 were established by the Compensation Committee in December of 1993. Mr. Peterson's base salary was decreased to $1,000,000 from $1,240,000. His performance-based bonus was established at 1.3% of the first $100,000,000 of operating income, after adjustments and consistent with the bonus calculations for management generally, and 1% of any operating income that exceeded $100,000,000, this bonus formula was approved by stockholders at the annual meeting. These actions were based on the changes to Section 162(m) of the Internal Revenue Code which requires that any compensation over $1,000,000 be performance-based (or

meet other exceptions provided by the Section) to be deductible by the Company. The salary and performance-based bonus were determined pursuant to the changes to Section 162(m) and in order to retain Mr. Peterson as Chairman and Chief Executive Officer. The bonus method was designed to incentivize Mr. Peterson with a performance-based bonus that was competitive with the industry and also allows the Company to take a deduction for federal income tax purposes.[20]

Still, as illustrated by Table 4-3 on page 116, many corporations pay at least one executive more than $1 million in salary, and this number has been increasing over time. Corporations paying more than $1 million thus have two choices, the first being to forfeit the deductions, the latter being to defer compensation. Leonhardt (2000) notes:

> A growing number of companies seem no longer to care about the effects of a 1993 law—the one pay initiative that grew out of the Bill Clinton's 1992 presidential campaign—that limits the maximum amount of base pay they can deduct from taxes for their top five executives to $1 million each. (The law exempts any amount above $1 million that is tied to performance, or that is deferred.)

An example of a company electing to forfeit deductions is Archer Daniels Midland:

> Section 162(m) of the Internal Revenue Code generally disallows a tax deduction to public corporations for compensation paid in excess of $1,000,000 annually to each of the Company's Chief Executive and four other most highly-compensated executive officers except for qualifying "performance-based" compensation. A portion of the compensation paid to certain of the Company's executive officers will be subject to the deduction limitation. In order to retain the flexibility to compensate its executive officers in a competitive environment in accordance with the principles discussed above, the Committee believes that it would be inadvisable to adopt a strict policy of compliance with the performance-based compensation exception to Section 162(m).[21]

The corporation can preserve the tax deduction if the executive defers compensation to a period in which he or she is no longer subject to the provisions of Section 162(m), that is, a period in which he or she is no longer the CEO or one of the next four highest-paid individuals. Estee Lauder includes such a provision in its compensation agreements with its executives as follows:

> Each agreement described above provides that the Company may require the executive to defer certain amounts to be received by him to the extent such amounts may not be deductible by reason of Section 162(m) of the Internal Revenue Code.[22]

Corporations can minimize the impact of Section 162(m) by shifting compensation from salary to forms of compensation that meet the performance-based criteria set forth in Section 162(m). Table 2-5 shows that in recent years the proportion of the CEO compensation package comprised of salary decreased, while the proportion of the compensation package comprised of stock option grants (which are generally considered performance based) increased. However, in the most recent years, the percentage of stock options has fallen while that of restricted stock, which is less likely to be performance based, has increased.

Table 4-3:
Number of Firms Where Salary Exceeds $1 Million, By Executive Rank

Year	CEO	2nd Highest Paid	3rd Highest Paid	4th Highest Paid	5th Highest Paid
1992	14	0	0	0	0
1993	18	4	1	1	0
1994	21	4	1	1	0
1995	22	4	1	0	1
1996	31	6	1	1	0
1997	34	10	2	1	0
1998	43	11	4	2	0
1999	48	14	6	2	1
2000	62	15	6	6	0
2001	88	18	8	6	3
2002	119	17	11	5	4
2003	151	24	14	6	6
2004	211	32	17	9	9
2005	235	38	16	10	5

Note: Calculations in this table are based upon data contained in the April 2006 version of Standard & Poor's ExecuComp.

Financial Reporting

Beyond the cash flow effects, there is the financial reporting, or accounting costs, involved. Each component of the compensation package has an impact on reported profitability. Salary is recorded as an expense in the period earned, whether deferred or paid currently, and whether deductible for tax purposes or not. In contrast, the expense associated with stock-based compensation, options and restricted stock is normally recognized over the vesting period.

Summary

The focus of this chapter was on salary, the most basic part of the compensation package. While normally fixed in amount, it is variable in the sense that it can be renegotiated, as an individual can get raises for good performance, or take a pay cut for poor performance. As shown in Chapter 2, salary is a decreasing portion of an increasingly large compensation package. This chapter showed that, even though salary is a decreasing portion of the compensation package, it is still increasing, and in most years, at a rate faster than the consumer price index.

Salary, as a fixed component of the compensation package, has little effect on incentives. For example, it appears that regardless of performance, most CEOs get a raise in salary and few take pay cuts. Similarly, as a fixed component, salary provides executives with no incentive to take risks.

The amount of salary paid to an executive can cause problems inside and outside the organization. Inside the corporation, concerns about equity and, consequently, disgruntled employees and a potential decrease in productivity arise. Outside the corporation, regulators, politicians, unions and the press have the ability to scrutinize large amounts paid as salary, amounts that cannot be justified based upon performance, and impose political costs on the corporation and executive.

Footnotes

1 Page 12, Black & Decker proxy statement filed with the Securities and Exchange Commission, March 15, 1999.

2 Page 12, Amazon.com proxy statement filed with the Securities and Exchange Commission, March 29, 2000.

3 Page 12, Amazon.com proxy statement filed with the Securities and Exchange Commission, March 29, 2000.

4 Page 9, Amazon.com proxy statement filed with the Securities and Exchange Commission, March 29, 2000.

5 To illustrate the risks involved, when Galli left Amazon.com to become CEO of VerticalNet, those same options had an intrinsic value of zero.

6 Page 14, Black & Decker proxy statement filed with the Securities and Exchange Commission, March 15, 1999.

7 Silverman (2000).

8 Page 16, JCPenney proxy statement filed with the Securities and Exchange Commission, April 14, 2000.

9 Silverman (2000).

10 Page 16, Boeing proxy statement filed with the Securities and Exchange Commission, March 19, 1999.

11 Holmes (1999). See also Zuckerman (1999).

12 See, for example, Fama (1980).

13 Page 23, American Express proxy statement filed with the Securities and Exchange Commission, March 22, 2006.

14 Page 23, Tribune proxy statement filed with the Securities and Exchange Commission, March 24, 2006.

15 Tournament theory suggests that compensation should be significantly higher for the CEO. That higher amount provides incentives for lower-level executives to strive for the CEO position.

16 Page 10, Whole Foods proxy statement filed with the Securities and Exchange Commission, Jan. 30, 2006.

17 Page 10, Whole Foods proxy statement filed with the Securities and Exchange Commission, Jan. 30, 2006.

18 Watts and Zimmerman (1986) discuss political costs extensively, although Balsam and Ryan (1996) are the first to apply it to executive compensation.

[19] As noted earlier, *BusinessWeek*, *Forbes* and *The Wall Street Journal*, as well as regional newspapers such as the *Philadelphia Inquirer*, all publish annual CEO compensation surveys.

[20] IBP proxy statement filed with Securities and Exchange Commission, March 17, 1995.

[21] Page 13, Archer Daniels Midland proxy statement filed with Securities and Exchange Commission, Sept. 22, 2005.

[22] Page 30, Estee Lauder proxy statement filed with Securities and Exchange Commission, Sept. 29, 2006.

Appendix 4-1

Section 162(m) Certain Excessive Employee Remuneration

(1) In general.

In the case of any publicly held corporation, no deduction shall be allowed under this chapter for applicable employee remuneration with respect to any covered employee to the extent that the amount of such remuneration for the taxable year with respect to such employee exceeds $1,000,000.

(2) Publicly held corporation.

For purposes of this subsection, the term "publicly held corporation" means any corporation issuing any class of common equity securities required to be registered under section 12 of the Securities Exchange Act of 1934.

(3) Covered employee.

For purposes of this subsection, the term "covered employee" means any employee of the taxpayer if—

(A) as of the close of the taxable year, such employee is the chief executive officer of the taxpayer or an individual acting in such a capacity, or

(B) the total compensation of such employee for the taxable year is required to be reported to shareholders under the Securities Exchange Act of 1934 by reason of such employee being among the 4 highest compensated officers for the taxable year (other than the chief executive officer).

(4) Applicable employee remuneration.

For purposes of this subsection—

(A) In general. Except as otherwise provided in this paragraph, the term "applicable employee remuneration" means, with respect to any covered employee for any taxable year, the aggregate amount allowable as a deduction under this chapter for such taxable year (determined without regard to this subsection) for remuneration for services performed by such employee (whether or not during the taxable year).

(B) Exception for remuneration payable on commission basis. The term "applicable employee remuneration" shall not include any remuneration payable on a commission basis solely on account of income generated directly by the individual performance of the individual to whom such remuneration is payable.

(C) Other performance-based compensation. The term "applicable employee remuneration" shall not include any remuneration payable solely on account of the attainment of one or more performance goals, but only if—

      (i)   the performance goals are determined by a compensation committee of the board of directors of the taxpayer which is comprised solely of 2 or more outside directors,

      (ii) the material terms under which the remuneration is to be paid, including the performance goals, are disclosed to shareholders and approved by a majority of the vote in a separate shareholder vote before the payment of such remuneration, and

      (iii) before any payment of such remuneration, the compensation committee referred to in clause (i) certifies that the performance goals and any other material terms were in fact satisfied.

(D) Exception for existing binding contracts. The term "applicable employee remuneration" shall not include any remuneration payable under a written binding contract which was in effect on February 17, 1993, and which was not modified thereafter in any material respect before such remuneration is paid.

(E) Remuneration. For purposes of this paragraph, the term "remuneration" includes any remuneration (including benefits) in any medium other than cash, but shall not include—

      (i)   any payment referred to in so much of section 3121(a)(5) as precedes subparagraph (E) thereof, and

      (ii) any benefit provided to or on behalf of an employee if at the time such benefit is provided it is reasonable to believe that the employee will be able to exclude such benefit from gross income under this chapter.

For purposes of clause (i), section 3121(a)(5) shall be applied without regard to section 3121(v)(1).

(F) Coordination with disallowed golden parachute payments. The dollar limitation contained in paragraph (1) shall be reduced (but not below zero) by the amount (if any) which would have been included in the applicable employee remuneration of the covered employee for the taxable year but for being disallowed under section 280G.

Chapter 5

Short- and Long-Term Bonuses

As a way of managing fixed costs, more companies are relying on variable pay. White (2006) reports, "Employers are making more workers eligible for bonuses and have increased the share of their payroll devoted to variable pay in the past few years."

Introduction

Bonuses are traditionally considered to be a variable, or at-risk, form of compensation, although the amount of risk the executive is subject to depends upon the plan's parameters. The payment can be subjective or based upon objective criteria. It can be based upon one or more performance measures, including, but not limited to, accounting earnings, stock price performance, sales, market share and customer satisfaction. The plan's parameters should include the performance measure or measures, the targets or thresholds for payouts, and the form and timing of payout. One of the more interesting measures, and one used to achieve very specific goals, is the bonus plan adopted by Coca-Cola, which bases pay, in part, on the achievement of goals "related to diversity, quality and the environment."[1]

Some bonus plans utilize totally quantitative formulas based solely on accounting performance. Appendix 5-1 provides an example of a bonus provision, from the contract signed by Dennis R. Glass, CEO of the Jefferson-Pilot Corp., Dec. 6, 2003. The contract provides for the payment of an annual or short-term bonus, denominated as a percentage of base salary, based solely upon one financial factor, growth in operating earnings per share. The contract has a threshold, which is also known as a lower bound, below which no bonus will be paid. That threshold is 5 percent. That is, if growth in operating earnings per share is less than 5 percent, no bonus will be paid pursuant to the contract. It also has an upper bound, beyond which increases in growth will not increase the bonus amount. That upper bound is 15 percent. When growth in operating earnings per share equals 5 percent, Glass will receive a bonus of 50 percent of base salary. The bonus will increase with growth, reaching a maximum of 200 percent of base salary when growth in operating earnings per share is 15 percent (or more).

In contrast, as described in the report of its compensation and benefits committee (see Appendix 5-2), American Express utilizes multiple financial and nonfinancial factors in determining annual and long-term incentive awards. These include measures ranging from shareholder return and earnings growth to customer and employee survey results.

The parameters can be set so that the executive bears little or no risk, for example, by basing the bonus on sales rather than profits, or by setting the performance threshold low. Alternatively, executives can be guaranteed "minimum" bonuses. As discussed in Chapter 3, when Citigroup hired Robert E. Rubin as chairman of its executive committee it guaranteed him a bonus of at least $14 million per year for 2000 and 2001.[2] Another example, see paragraph (d) below, occurred when George W. Buckley was hired as 3M's president, CEO and chairman of the board:

4.2 Annual Bonus.

(a) The Company shall pay to Executive an annual bonus ("Annual Bonus") for each Fiscal Year which begins during the Employment Period. Executive shall be eligible for an Annual Bonus ranging from zero to the Maximum Annual Bonus. Except as noted below, the Annual Bonus shall be paid and otherwise subject to the terms of the Company's Executive Profit Sharing Plan, as may be amended, and any successor to such plan.

(b) If Executive achieves his target performance goals (the "Target Annual Goals"), as determined by the Committee on an annual basis after consulting with Executive, such Annual Bonus shall be designed to realize a target amount (the "Target Annual Bonus") of not less than the greater of (i) $2,600,000 and (ii) 150% of Base Salary. If Executive achieves his maximum performance goals (the "Maximum Annual Goals") as determined by the Committee on an annual basis after consulting with Executive, such Annual Bonus shall be designed to not exceed 150% (or such greater amount as may be determined by the Board in its sole discretion) of the Target Annual Bonus (the "Maximum Annual Bonus"). Such performance goals shall be set by the Committee within 90 days after the first day of the applicable Fiscal Year. The actual amount of any Annual Bonus may fluctuate with the Company's performance.

(c) The Company shall pay the Annual Bonus in a payment of cash, Common Shares (including restricted shares), or a combination thereof determined by the Committee at such times and in such manner as is consistent with the treatment of other senior executives of the Company and with the provisions of the Company's Executive Profit Sharing Plan or its successor plan.

(d) Notwithstanding the above provisions of this Section 4.2, the minimum Annual Bonus for the 2006 Fiscal Year shall be $2,600,000, and shall be paid in cash.[3]

Both of these examples of guaranteed bonuses involve newly hired executives. For two reasons, it may be reasonable to guarantee a bonus for the first year or two of an executive's tenure. First, it reduces the executive's risk, thereby reducing the level of compensation that needs to be paid to attract the executive. Second, given that performance in the early years of an executive's tenure may reflect the actions of his or her predecessor more than his or her own, it would be unfair to penalize the executive for that performance.

Bonuses can be based upon short-term performance, normally one year or annually, or long-term performance, normally from three to five years, with many companies, such as American Express, having both. Long-term bonus plans are sometimes referred to as performance plans. Among the types of long-term plans are performance unit and performance share plans. With both types of plans, the executive is awarded a number of units or shares at the beginning of the performance period, with the number earned based upon performance during the period. The major difference between the plans is that with performance units, the value of those units is usually predetermined, whereas with performance shares, the value of those shares is based upon share price at the end of the period. Appendix 5-3 contains the Lucent Technologies 1996 Long Term Incentive Program, which allows for performance units and performance shares (see section nine). In contrast to the detailed description of plan parameters in Glass' contract in Appendix 5-1, the Lucent Technologies plan is rather vague about the performance measures, thresholds and amount of payment. For example, the plan notes, "Performance Awards in the form of Performance Units or Performance Shares may be issued …". That is, they do not have to be used. Recall from Table 2-2, less than 20 percent of corporations make long-term incentive payments in any given year. Second, the plan does not define the measures or thresholds, merely noting, "The performance criteria to be achieved during any Performance Period and the length of the Performance Period shall be determined by the Committee upon the grant of each Performance Award or at any time thereafter."

As shown in Chapter 2, bonuses are a major component of the CEO compensation package. Tables 2-2 through 2-4 show (annual) bonuses are paid about 80 percent of the time, while long-term incentive payments or bonuses are paid about 15 percent of the time. Tables 2-5 through 2-7 show the proportion of compensation comprised of short- (approximately 20 percent) and long-term (less than 5 percent) bonuses, while Tables 2-8 through 2-10 show the amounts involved. While roughly stable over time as a percentage of the total compensation package (see Table 2-5), bonuses are increasing in amount (see Table 2-8), and in most years, at a rate in excess of salaries and inflation (see Table 5-1). Table 5-1 shows the percentage change in bonus for CEOs who have been with the same corporation (and in the same position) for at least two years, whereas Table 5-2 on page 129 shows the same percentage changes in long-term incentive payments for the subset of firms which make those payments. Table 5-1 and Figure 5-1 on page 128 show that, for continuing CEOs, the mean (median) change in bonus ranges from -7.47 (-18.10) to 24.31 (23.44) percent. Table 5-2 and Figure 5-2 on page 130 show an even more pronounced pattern for long term incentive payments, with the mean (median) increase ranging from -8.59 (-9.75) to 30.82 (100) percent. When compared to the change in salary in Table 4-1, we see that the variation in bonuses is much greater, as would be expected if bonuses are more likely to be tied to performance. Consistent with this, Table 5-3 on page 131 shows the relationship between bonus and corporate performance. As in Table 4-2, the corporations are divided into 10 portfolios depending upon their percentage change in income. To the right of the performance decile are mean and median increases in CEO bonus for the current year, for that portfolio[4]. Viewing the table, it appears the relationship between bonus and performance is much stronger than the relationship between salary and performance. That is, the mean (median) decrease in bonus for firms in the lowest performance decile is -31.77 (-50) percent, while the mean (median) increase in bonus for firms in the highest-performance decile is 43.39 (50.38) percent, a range of 75.16 (100.38) percent. In contrast, the mean (median) increase in next-period salary is 3 (2) percent for the lowest-performance decile and 7 (5) percent for the highest-performance decile, a range of only 4 (3) percent. Further analysis shows that almost two-thirds of the CEOs in the lowest-performing decile receive a decrease in bonus.

Effect of Bonus Plans on Incentives

Bonuses, if appropriately structured, can provide the proper incentives to induce the executive to take actions that maximize shareholder value. Further, as noted by Banker et al. (1999, page 2):

> ... performance-based incentives increase an organization's overall productivity by attracting and retaining the more productive employees

Table 5-1:

Percentage Change in Bonus for CEOs with Same Company for Consecutive Years (for Companies Paying Bonus in at Least One of the Years)

Year	Mean Percentage Change In Bonus	Median Percentage Change In Bonus	Average Change in Consumer Price Index CPI-U
1993	1.47	-18.10	2.99%
1994	-3.68	-5.55	2.56%
1995	1.11	3.25	2.83%
1996	7.84	8.71	2.95%
1997	18.45	16.20	2.29%
1998	6.00	6.13	1.56%
1999	10.83	9.09	2.21%
2000	9.98	9.05	3.36%
2001	-7.47	-8.92	2.85%
2002	16.11	14.29	1.58%
2003	18.75	13.04	2.28%
2004	24.31	23.44	2.66%
2005	11.07	8.28	3.39%

Note: Calculations in this table are based upon data contained in the April 2006 version of Standard & Poor's ExecuComp and the Consumer Price Index—All Urban Consumers, as found on the Bureau of Labor Statistics Web site.

(selection effect) and/or by inducing employees to increase or to better allocate their effort (effort effect).

Choice of Performance Measure

If not properly structured however, the bonus plan can lead to dysfunctional behavior. For example, a corporation that has a bonus plan that rewards market share may get increased market share, but at the expense of profitability.[5] Alternatively, depending on the measure or measures used in the bonus plan, executives may be able to manipulate those measures to their advantage. A long line of literature, including Healy (1985) and Balsam (1998), shows managers make accounting choices consistent with increasing their bonus. Bonuses can be based upon stock price performance or returns, which are harder to manipulate. Unfortunately, stock returns are based on factors outside of the control of the corporation's executives, for example, interest rates. Thus, basing the bonus on

Figure 5-1:
Growth in Short-Term Bonus versus Growth in CPI

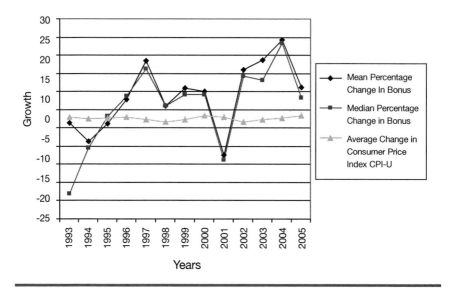

stock returns imposes risk on the executive, and in equilibrium, the executive must be compensated for this risk. Further, executives are already exposed to this risk via the stock-based portion of their compensation package.

Thus, the choice of performance measure or measures is of utmost importance in setting the proper incentives and encouraging desired behaviors. Lambert and Larcker (1987), Ely (1991) and Sloan (1993), among others, argue that accounting-based benchmarks are useful because they shield executives from fluctuations in stock returns that are beyond the manager's control. Consistent with this theory, they show that the greater the corporations' stock price variability, the larger the cash portion of the CEO compensation package. Bushman, Indjejikian and Smith (1996) and Ittner, Larcker and Rajan (1997) argue that subjective or nonfinancial measures are useful for growing, innovative and nontraditional corporations, for whom the traditional accounting model does not work well.[6]

Choice of Parameters

Once the measure or measures[7] of performance to be used is determined, the parameters to be applied must be decided. For example, in his contract with Jefferson Pilot, Dennis Glass does not receive a bonus if earnings growth is less than 5 percent, receives 50 percent of his salary as a bonus if earnings growth equals

Table 5-2:

Percentage Change in Long-term Incentive Payments for CEOs with Same Company for Consecutive Years (for Companies Making Long-Term Incentive Payments in at Least One of the Years)

Year	Mean Percentage Change In Bonus	Median Percentage Change In Bonus	Average Change in Consumer Price Index CPI-U
1993	30.82	100.00	2.99%
1994	-3.69	-2.12	2.56%
1995	10.29	17.63	2.83%
1996	9.66	10.94	2.95%
1997	17.60	20.06	2.29%
1998	5.59	5.84	1.56%
1999	0.59	0.00	2.21%
2000	2.48	1.23	3.36%
2001	-8.59	-9.75	2.85%
2002	3.26	0.00	1.58%
2003	21.30	35.47	2.28%
2004	17.96	27.85	2.66%
2005	20.37	19.57	3.39%

Note: Calculations in this table are based upon data contained in the April 2006 version of Standard & Poor's ExecuComp and the Consumer Price Index—All Urban Consumers, as found on the Bureau of Labor Statistics Web site.

5 percent and can receive 200 percent of his salary as a bonus if earnings growth equals or exceeds 15 percent. In this case, the 5-percent earnings growth would be considered the lower bound, below which no bonus would be paid, while the 15 percent is considered the upper bound, above which additional earnings have no benefit. As will be discussed below, the existence of lower and upper bounds, and the levels set, can affect incentives and thus need to be considered carefully.

Other plans may have a threshold or lower bound, below which no bonus is paid, but no upper bounds. In discussing its Variable Compensation Plan (VCP), which covers approximately 6,400 employees, including executive officers, E. I. DuPont De Nemours (DuPont) notes:

the VCP limits the annual maximum funding to 20% of consolidated net income after deducting 6% of net capital employed.[8]

Figure 5-2:

Growth in Long-Term Bonus versus Growth in CPI

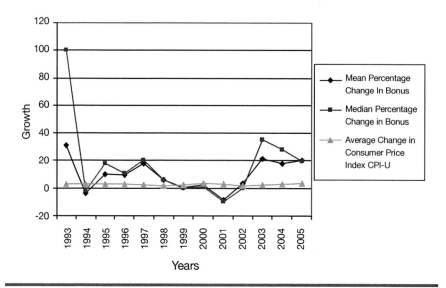

While the funding or, more precisely, the maximum funding is determined by the previous quantitative formula, the payouts themselves are determined separately, and it appears there is much more discretion involved.

In determining VCP payments to participants for 2005, the Committee used a formula, which consisted of equally weighted components of earnings per share (EPS) (excluding significant items) versus the prior year and return on invested capital (ROIC) versus the average of the Peer Group.

Variable compensation differentiation across platforms and business units is based on after-tax operating income (excluding significant items), free cash flow, and revenue versus each unit's financial commitments for the year. In addition, payments may be differentiated by platform and business unit based on a qualitative assessment of performance on the Company's core values: ethics and integrity; workplace environment, treatment and development of people, and strategic staffing (including diversity); and safety, health and environmental stewardship.

In arriving at the level of payments for 2005, the Committee considered that 2005 EPS (excluding significant items) was 98% of 2004, ROIC was 95% of the average of the Peer Group and average platform and business unit performance was 92% of each unit's financial commitments for the year.

Table 5-3:

Relation Between Changes in Performance and Changes in Bonus

Performance Decile	Mean Increase in Bonus	Median Increase in Bonus	Percentage of CEOs with Increase in Bonus	Percentage of CEOs with Decrease in Bonus
Lowest	-31.77	-50.00	30.28	66.73
2	-25.20	-31.82	30.63	66.45
3	-13.89	-14.48	37.70	59.00
4	-2.47	0.00	46.65	49.39
5	13.42	9.09	63.52	32.23
6	18.26	13.62	69.62	26.98
7	22.75	16.67	70.78	24.41
8	27.00	23.78	74.55	22.15
9	36.93	38.73	73.33	23.56
Highest	43.39	50.38	77.66	20.26

Note: Calculations in this table are based upon data contained in the April 2006 version of Standard & Poor's ExecuComp.

The combination of the corporate and business unit performance factors described above resulted in an average payment of 94% of the award target (with individual business unit factors ranging from 19% to 190%). The Committee approved awards for 2005 that totaled 77% of the 2004 grant.

Variable compensation payments for 2005 were 35% of the maximum amount available under the VCP limit. Over the past ten years, the Committee has approved payments on average of 47% of the maximum available.[9]

DuPont's plan differs from the one observed for Jefferson Pilot in that it doesn't have an upper bound—that is, the amount transferred increases linearly with net income. Another difference is that the plan determines the amount transferred to the fund, not the payout from the fund. As discussed above, payments have on average been less than half that available, which may indicate that DuPont has built in a substantial cushion. Further, the amounts not awarded can be carried forward and awarded in future years.[10]

Still other plans contain upper but no lower bounds. For example, Unocal has a plan whereby the amount added to the bonus pool is two percent of Unocal's annual bonus plan. However, while there is no upper bound on the amounts added to the pool, the payout to any individual is capped at 0.25 percent of the company's net cash provided by operating activities, or $2 million, whichever is lower.

Incentive Compensation Plan

The Incentive Compensation Plan (the "ICP") is Unocal's annual bonus plan for senior and middle management. Each award period under the ICP is one year. The annual bonus pool for a calendar year equals 2% of Unocal's "Net Cash Provided by Operating Activities," which is the maximum amount of annual cash bonuses that may be awarded in a calendar year.

Prior to March of each year, the Compensation Committee establishes a percentage of this bonus pool as the maximum target award for the CEO and certain other executive officers. The Compensation Committee also establishes individual target awards for the remaining participants based on salary grade.

For 2004, the Compensation Committee approved a bonus award payout based 25% on Comparative Return to Shareholders, 37.5% on financial performance ("Return on Capital Employed" and "Free Cash Flow") and 37.5% on an evaluation of the calendar year activities that will affect future performance. The Compensation Committee determined that Unocal performed significantly above the established goals with respect to the financial and future performance measures based on a set commodity price determined by the Compensation Committee, while Unocal's TSR relative to the Peer Group resulted in a 0% of target payout with respect to this factor. After a downward adjustment for other factors, the bonus award pool for the entire eligible group for 2004 was set at 85% of the target amount. Awards were subject to further adjustment to reflect business unit and individual performance.[11]

The maximum cash award that may be payable to a participant for a year is 0.25% of the Company's Net Cash Provided by Operating Activities (which was $1.668 billion and $2.125 billion in 2000 and 2001, respectively) or, if less, $2,000,000.[12]

Effect of Lower and Upper Bounds

These parameters themselves can affect incentives. Consider the executive who is approaching or over the upper bound of his/her bonus program, a program based upon accounting income numbers. The incentive exists for the executive to defer income to a future period. If the executive does this through an income-decreasing choice of accounting methods, the cost to the corporation will be minimal. However, if the executive does so by accelerating future expenditures into the current period and/or deferring sales to the future, there may be real costs to the corporation. As noted by Healy (1985), a similar incentive exists for executives sufficiently below the lower bound. That is, they too have the incentive to defer income to a future period. The incentives for the executives below their lower bound and above their upper bound are twofold. First, by pushing income to future periods they increase their bonus in those future periods, while not affecting current-period bonus. Second, to the extent that future-period bounds or targets are based upon current-period performance, lowering current period performance reduces those future targets, also having the effect of increasing future bonuses. This can be illustrated using the contract between Dennis Glass and Jefferson-Pilot contained in Appendix 5-1. Recall Glass' bonus is based on the growth in operating earnings per share. Thus, explicitly, this period's performance becomes the threshold for determining the bonus paid in the next period. So growth in excess of the upper bound, in this case 15 percent, not only does not increase Glass' bonus for the current period, but by increasing the threshold for the next period, reduces his expected bonus for that period.

The following example, where an executive is rewarded on growth in reported income, will further illustrate the effect of bounds on incentives. Net income in the base year was $100 million, unmanipulated income for the current year is $120 million and expected income for the next year is $125 million. Assume that this corporation pays its CEO a bonus equal to 1 percent of the growth in income, up to a maximum of $150,000. If the CEO is unable to manipulate reported income, the bonus in the current year will be $150,000, which is calculated as the lesser of $150,000 or 1 percent of the excess of $120 million over $100 million, and the bonus in the next year will be $50,000, which is calculated as the lesser of $150,000 or 1 percent of the excess of $125 million over $120 million. If, however, the CEO is able to shift income from the current to the next period, so that income in the current period is $115 million, and income in the next period is $130 million, he or she can receive a bonus of $150,000 in each year. In both cases, total income across the two periods is $245 million, yet in the absence of income shifting, the CEO receives a total bonus of $200,000 ($150,000 plus $50,000) over the two years, but with income shifting the CEO receives $300,000 ($150,000 in each year).

Empirically, Healy (1985) finds corporations below the lower bound and above the upper bound are more likely to make income-decreasing accounting choices, whereas Holthausen, Larcker and Sloan (1995) and Gaver, Gaver and Austin (1995) only find that corporations above the upper bound are more likely to make income-decreasing accounting choices. A possible explanation for the latter result is that executives who find themselves below the lower bound may be reluctant to reduce income further for fear of losing their jobs. Weisbach (1988), among others, finds that poor accounting performance is associated with subsequent CEO turnover.

If after considering the effect on incentives, the board of directors decides to include lower and/or upper bounds in its bonus plan, it then has to consider the placement of those bounds. Perverse incentives exist if bounds are set too high or too low. If the bounds are too high, then executives can get discouraged and not even try to achieve those goals, adversely affecting corporation performance and value. If they are set too low, especially the upper bound, then there is little incentive to work hard.

How the bounds are set matters, too. As previously illustrated, if this year's performance becomes the hurdle for next year's bonus, or the base upon which next year's bonus is computed, then the incentive exists to keep this year's performance down. The frequency with which current-year performance is used as a hurdle for next year's evaluation is unclear. However, consistent with current performance being used in future-performance evaluation, a long line of accounting and financial literature notes that income smoothing or income manipulation to meet certain goals/targets is prevalent. For example, Burgstahler and Dichev (1997) show evidence consistent with earnings management to avoid reporting losses and decreases in earnings, while Brown (1999), Degeorge, Patel and Zeckhauser (1999) and Burgstahler and Eames (2006) provide evidence consistent with executives manipulating earnings measures to meet analysts' earnings expectations. Further, consistent with the incentives previously discussed, these papers find corporations are more likely to report earnings that just meet the threshold under examination.

Adherence to Plan

Finally, the incentive effect of the plan will be nullified if the compensation committee does not adhere to the plan. That is, most compensation committees have the ability to override/change plan provisions. For example, the compensation committee may switch performance metrics as Home Depot's did with its CEO's incentive compensation. According to Murray (2006b), "with shareholder returns in the dumps, they changed his incentive pay from a formula based on shareholder returns to one based on earnings per share." Similarly, Silver (2006) reports that Verizon shifted a portion of CEO Ivan Seidenberg's compensation from shareholder returns to attaining strategic objectives, this after a year in which its stock price had dropped by more than 25 percent. Another example is AT&T Wireless, which when it became aware that its targets would not be met, simply reset those targets:

The original performance targets were developed and approved in January 2002 in conjunction with the Company's business plan for 2002. Several factors, including slower than anticipated subscriber and revenue growth for the wireless industry, a challenging economy, the earlier-than-expected completion of a significant acquisition, other changes in the industry, and certain strategic decisions during the first half of 2002 resulted in the original targets no longer providing meaningful incentives. In light of these factors, the Committee reset the performance measures for the second half of the year to represent challenging yet realistic targets.[13]

Alternatively, compensation committees can pay bonuses aside from the plans. Consider the example of Big Lots:

During fiscal 2005, the Company's executives, including the CEO and the other Named Executive Officers, participated in the 2001 Bonus Plan; however, no bonuses were paid under the 2001 Bonus Plan as the performance criteria established by the Committee were not met. As discussed below, one-time bonuses were paid to the CEO and the other Named Executive Officers in fiscal 2005. Mr. Fishman received a bonus in connection with the commencement of his employment in July 2005, and each of the other Named Executive Officers (excluding Mr. Potter) received a bonus in connection with the fulfillment of their obligations under their respective retention packages dated Jan. 6, 2005.[14]

Or the committee could adhere to the terms of the plan and not pay, or pay a reduced bonus, but then increase some other component of the compensation package to make the executive whole. For example, the following is taken from Gap Inc.'s 2006 proxy statement:

For fiscal year 2005, cash incentive bonuses under the Executive MICAP were based on performance compared to goals for earnings (70% weight), economic profit (20% weight) and free cash flow (10% weight) set for the Company and/or each division. Executive officers were eligible to receive a target bonus of between 50% and 125% of their base salary. Based on performance against these goals, payouts could have ranged from 33% of the executive's target bonus at threshold performance to 200% of the executive's target bonus at maximum performance. However, we determined that the Company's performance in fiscal 2005 did not meet the threshold criteria for bonus payments to executive officers set forth at the beginning of the period. Accordingly, executive officers, including the CEO, did not receive any cash awards under Executive MICAP except for Cynthia Harriss, who received a modest bonus based on the portion of fiscal 2005 during which she led the Outlet Division and the performance of that division.[15]

However, while Paul S. Pressler, the president and CEO, did not receive a bonus, he did receive a substantial option grant that year that more than offset the loss of his bonus. Thus, while his bonus went from $1,119,140[16] to zero, the present value of the options he received (excluding replacement options) increased from $5,121,105[17] to $15,244,400.[18]

It should be clarified that on average, corporations do indeed reduce conditional compensation when performance decreases. This was shown in Table 5-3 and has been implied by a long line of academic research (see for example, Lewellen and Huntsman 1972, Antle and Smith 1985, Lambert and Larcker 1987, Balsam 1998). This is also shown by corporations where executives neither get bonuses, nor get an increase elsewhere in their compensation package to make up for it. For example, in 2005 General Motors did not pay a bonus to its top executives, including Chairman and CEO Richard Wagoner. As discussed below, it does not appear the committee increased any other portion of his compensation package. The compensation committee reported:

… we determined Mr. Wagoner's compensation as follows:
   Base Salary—Mr. Wagoner did not receive a salary increase for 2005. His last salary increase was on Jan. 1, 2003.
   Annual Incentives—Given the overall financial performance of the Corporation during 2005, no bonus award was paid to Mr. Wagoner.
   Stock Options—As part of a continuing compensation review process, the Committee considered the number and expected value of the options granted to Mr. Wagoner in comparison with option grants to CEOs of our comparator group and to other executives internally. After consideration of the number of options granted to Mr. Wagoner in prior years and in keeping with our strategy to reduce dilution levels, which has been in place since 2003, the Committee set his 2005 stock option grant at 400,000 shares of Common Stock, a number of shares which is the same

as the 2004 grant. We believe that rather than increase Mr. Wagoner's grant level in light of the decline in the intrinsic value of the shares, a grant at this level is more consistent with our current business conditions and strategy to manage dilution levels.

Other Long-Term Incentives—Mr. Wagoner's Long-Term Incentive Plan target award covering the three-year period 2005-2007 was set at 102,224 share units and is disclosed on page 24. Because the relative, cumulative TSR for the 2003-2005 performance period was below threshold as described above, no such award was paid to Mr. Wagoner.[19]

Effectiveness of Bonus Plans

Bonus plans can and are designed to encourage certain forms of behavior, presumably with a goal of maximizing shareholder wealth. Examining whether they are successful is another story. One approach possible when bonus plans are designed to achieve specific goals is to examine if those goals are met. For example, Larcker (1983) shows that the introduction of long-term incentive plans is associated with subsequent increases in capital expenditures, whereas White (1996) shows basing bonuses on dividend payout increases dividends paid.[20] Mishra et al. (2000a) find that earnings-per-share growth and return on equity exceed industry medians after adoption of long-term accounting-based performance plans, while Leonard (1990) found companies with long-term incentive plans had significantly greater increases in return on equity. However, as noted above, it is possible that an increase in the performance measure is not value increasing, but rather a response to the incentives provided, for example passing up profitable investments to pay dividends. In general, it is hard to measure whether a bonus or other incentive-based compensation arrangement achieves its goal of increasing shareholder value. Empirically, researchers can observe associations, such as the one between compensation and accounting and market performance measures, but have difficulty attributing causality. One approach is the "event study" approach, whereby the market reaction to public disclosure of the plan adoption is used to infer whether or not the plan is value increasing. The event study methodology, which is based upon the assumption that markets are efficient, assumes market participants make unbiased, and on average correct, predictions, about the effect of the plan on shareholder value at the time they first learn about it, that is at public disclosure. Thus if the market reaction is positive, that is, the corporation's share price increases upon announcement—as in Larcker (1983), Brickley et al. (1985), Tehranian and Waegelein (1985), Kumar and Sopariwala (1992)—it is assumed the plan is value increasing.[21] Unfortunately, while such studies find that, on average, adoption of long-term incentive plans are associated with an increase in shareholder value, it is hard (once again) to draw those conclusions for any given corporation and plan. One reason is that the positive reaction to plan adoption may not be associated with the expected effects of the plan on firm performance, but rather to the information released by the plan adoption. That is, management is more likely to propose tying its compensation to firm performance when it expects the firm to perform well in the future. Investors realize this tendency, and thus, react positively when they first learn the plan is being adopted. A second reason is that stock prices are volatile, and the return or price change at any time is affected by many factors, including adoption of the incentive plan. In a large sample study, researchers assume they have randomized away all factors other than those under examination and thus can draw a conclusion, a conclusion that cannot be definitively drawn with a sample size of one.

Political Costs

The selection of bonus plan parameters is important for another reason. If the amounts involved are too low, there may be no motivational effect. However, if the amounts are too large, there may be political costs for the corporation and executive. As with salary, large bonuses can be criticized by politicians, regulators, shareholders and employees. This may explain, in part, the motivation corporations have for putting an upper bound or cap on their bonus payouts. Oracle notes:

> The maximum bonus payment that our Chief Executive Officer may receive under the Bonus Plan for fiscal year 2007 would be $11,269,000. The maximum bonus payment that any other participant may receive under the Bonus Plan for fiscal year 2007 is based on a fixed multiple of a target bonus for such participant and would be less than the maximum bonus payment that our Chief Executive Officer may receive under the Bonus Plan.[22]

While Oracle and many other corporations have limited their bonuses, perhaps to avoid the adverse publicity, some corporations do not appear to. Tables 5-4 and 5-5 list the largest bonuses and long-term incentive payments by year. The largest short-term bonus payment, by far, was the $121,271,000 paid by JDS Uniphase to Gregory Dougherty, executive vice president and chief operating officer (COO) in 2001, whereas the largest long-term incentive payment was the $84,800,000 paid by iSTAR Financial to its chairman and CEO, Jay Sugarman, in 2003.

An interesting, if dated, example of the political costs associated with the payment of large bonuses, and a corporation's response to those costs, involved the securities firm Bear Stearns. After a long history as a privately held partnership, Bear Stearns went public in October 1985. As a partnership, its compensation was private information, but as a publicly held corporation, its compensation was public knowledge and immediately became an issue. In a *Wall Street Journal* article entitled "How Embarrassing! Bear Stearns Officials Wallow in a Windfall—Concern

Table 5-4:
Largest Bonuses

Year	Executive	Position	Company	Bonus
1992	Alan C. Greenberg	Chairman & CEO	Bear Stearns	$11,726,000
1993	Lawrence Coss	Chairman & CEO	Conseco Finance	$13,601,000
1994	Lawrence Coss	Chairman & CEO	Conseco Finance	$28,544,000
1995	Lawrence Coss	Chairman & CEO	Conseco Finance	$65,147,000
1996	Lawrence Coss	Chairman & CEO	Conseco Finance	$102,015,000
1997	Richard Handler	Executive Vice President	Jefferies Group	$17,105,000
1998	Lawrence Lasser	President-Putnam Investments	Marsh & Mclennan	$17,000,000
1999	Lawrence Lasser	President-Putnam Investments	Marsh & Mclennan	$26,000,000
2000	Lawrence Lasser	President-Putnam Investments	Marsh & Mclennan	$33,000,000
2001	Gregory Dougherty	Executive Vice President & Chief Operating Officer	JDS Uniphase	$121,271,000
2002	Milan Panic	Chairman & CEO	Valeant Pharmaceuticals Intl.	$33,550,000
2003	Sanford Weill	Chairman	Citigroup	$29,000,000
2004	Robert Toll	Chairman & CEO	Toll Brothers	$30,402,000
2005	Stanford Kurland	President & Chief Operating Officer	Countrywide Financial	$78,785,000

Table 5-5:
Largest Long-Term Incentive Payments

Year	Executive	Position	Company	Bonus
1992	Constantine Hampers	Executive Vice President	Grace (W.R.) & Co.	$26,468,000
1993	Harry Merlo	Chairman, President & CEO	Louisiana-Pacific	$11,306,000
1994	Maurice Greenberg	Chairman & CEO	American International Group	$8,330,000
1995	Joe Roby	Chief Operating Officer	Credit Suisse First Boston USA	$11,083,000
1996	Joe Roby	President & Chief Operating Officer	Credit Suisse First Boston USA	$23,984,000
1997	Alexander Trotman	Chairman, President & CEO	Ford Motor Co.	$24,137,000
1998	Maurice Greenberg	Chairman & CEO	American International Group	$15,460,000
1999	John Welch Jr.	Chairman & CEO	General Electric	$31,325,000
2000	Maurice Greenberg	Chairman & CEO	American International Group	$23,655,000
2001	Joseph Nacchio	Chairman & CEO	Qwest Communications	$24,374,000
2002	James Mulva	President & CEO	ConocoPhillips	$14,978,000
2003	Jay Sugarman	Chairman & CEO	iSTAR Financial	$84,800,000
2004	C. Wilder	President & CEO	TXU	$36,908,000
2005	John Kilroy Jr.	President & CEO	Kilroy Realty	$38,706,000

Says Its Bonus Plan Has Provided Executives With 'Exorbitant' Sums," it was noted that for the six months ending April 30, 1986, which coincided with Bear Stearns' first six months as a public company, its chairman and CEO, Alan C. Greenberg, made $4 million, more than any other executive at a publicly held securities firm made during the entire previous year.[23] The following year *The Wall Street Journal* published a follow-up article entitled "Bear Stearns Aides, Despite Pay Cuts, Can Grin and Bear It—Six Executives at Concern Outearned All Others At Major Public Firms." The article notes that for their fiscal year ending April 30, 1987, the "six top executives of the securities firm earned more last year than any other executive of a major publicly held Wall Street firm."[24] A review of proxy statements for the period shows that Bear Stearns did indeed modify the parameters of its bonus plan, decreasing the percent of adjusted pretax income allocated to the bonus fund. For example, for the fiscal year ending April 30, 1988, the amounts allocated to the fund were determined as follows:

Percentage of Increment of Adjusted Pretax Income

Amount of Adjusted Pretax Income—FY 1988	Allocated to Bonus Fund
up to $20 million	0%
over $20 million but not exceeding $100 million	24.5%
over $100 million but not exceeding $180 million	26.0%
over $180 million but not exceeding $260 million	28.5%
over $260 million but not exceeding $340 million	31.0%
over $340 million	33.5%

Whereas for the fiscal year ending June 30, 1989, the amounts allocated to the bonus fund were calculated as:

Percentage of Increment of Adjusted Pretax Income

Amount of Adjusted Pretax Income—FY 1989	Allocated to Bonus Fund
up to $15 million	0%
over $15 million but not exceeding $85 million	7.4%
over $85 million but not exceeding $150 million	8.5%
over $150 million but not exceeding $215 million	9.2%
over $215 million but not exceeding $275 million	11.0%
over $275 million	11.9%[25]

Given income before taxes and extraordinary items was $287,383,000 for the year ended June 1989, the change in formula reduced the allocation to the bonus fund by almost two-thirds, from $71,688,730 to $24,758,577.

Another interesting case involved Stephen M. Wolf, chairman, and Rakesh Gangwal, CEO, of US Airways Group. One day after the approval of the US Airways Group Inc. long-term compensation plan by a margin of 63,019,913 to 3,843,023,[26] but after receiving complaints from unions about the size of their compensation (approximately $34 million and $36 million, respectively for 1998)[27], the two decided not to accept annual cash bonuses[28], a fact confirmed by the following year's proxy statement:

both the Chairman and the Chief Executive Officer have declined to accept payments for the performance period ending with fiscal year 1999.[29]

Financial Consequences
Cash Flows
As noted previously, each component of the executive compensation package impacts the corporation's cash flows, directly via the actual payment and indirectly via the corporation's tax returns. If paid in cash, a bonus is a cash outflow, whereas the benefit from the tax deduction is a cash inflow (alternatively it can be viewed as a reduction of another cash outflow, income taxes). Sometimes, however, the corporation may not pay bonuses immediately or may not use cash to pay those bonuses, that is, the bonus may be deferred to a future period or may be paid in the form of stock. For example, Sears Holdings allows executives to defer cash bonuses into restricted shares and even provides a 20-percent premium as an inducement:

> Pursuant to a deferred equity exchange feature available to participants in the Sears Deferred Compensation Plan, Mr. Lacy elected to exchange and defer 20% of his 2004 bonus ($153,746 of the $768,731 reflected in the table) at the closing market price of $33.18 per share of Sears common stock on March 15, 2005. As a result of his election to exchange and defer, Mr. Lacy received a 20% premium ($30,749) on the portion of the bonus he elected to exchange and defer. He received a premium in restricted common share equivalents, which will vest on March 15, 2008.[30]

Tax Deductibility
Sometimes the executive defers part, or all, of the bonus earned. Also, while compensation is normally deductible as an ordinary business expense under section 162 of the Internal Revenue Code, if the executive is subject to the limitations of section 162(m), the corporation may not be able to fully deduct the bonus payment, whether made in cash or stock.

As noted previously, section 162(m) limits deductibility of compensation to $1 million per covered individual, where covered individual is defined as the CEO plus the next four highest-paid executives. The $1-million limitation is not binding if the amounts involved are specified in a contract executed prior to Feb. 17, 1993. Further, amounts meeting the performance-based criteria set forth in section 162(m) are not subject to the limitation. If bonuses are not paid pursuant to a qualified plan, they are subject to the $1 million deductibility cap (which includes all nonqualifying compensation, such as salary). Bonuses, however, may be performance based and hence may meet the criteria set forth in Section 162(m).

As illustrated by Table 5-6, many corporations pay at least one executive more than

$1 million in salary and bonus, and this number has been increasing over time. In fact, in 2005, 177 corporations paid each of their top five executives more than $1 million, yet few claim to be able to deduct the full amount due to a pre-existing contract. When salary is less than $1 million, corporations paying more than $1 million in salary plus bonus have three choices. As with salary, the corporation can elect to forfeit the deductions. Balsam and Yin (2005) report that from 1994 through 1998, almost 40 percent of affected corporations report that they forfeit deductions due to Section 162(m). While that number is almost certainly higher today, corporations have become more reserved in their disclosures over time, so it is hard to identify whether or not a corporation has forfeited deductions, and even harder to estimate the amount forfeited.

Example of a Corporation Forfeiting Deductions

As an example of a corporation forfeiting deductions, consider Tyco International. Tyco, in its proxy statement, provides the following discussion of the tax deductibility of executive compensation:

Table 5-6:
Number of Firms in Which Salary Plus Bonus Exceeds $1 Million, by Executive

Year	CEO	2nd Highest Paid	3rd Highest Paid	4th Highest Paid	5th Highest Paid
1992	84	22	12	3	5
1993	128	38	18	9	7
1994	178	49	24	16	10
1995	226	58	35	23	15
1996	309	76	50	26	22
1997	382	102	63	41	26
1998	426	122	67	39	31
1999	497	169	91	63	38
2000	562	193	120	72	57
2001	559	199	110	74	56
2002	702	245	158	120	86
2003	823	370	228	169	128
2004	1002	477	303	236	164
2005	986	533	346	246	177

Section 162(m) of the Internal Revenue Code imposes a limit of $1 million on the amount of compensation that may be deducted by Tyco with respect to the Chief Executive Officer and any of the other four most highly compensated officers; however, this limitation does not apply to compensation that qualifies as "performance-based" under federal tax law. It is the Committee's policy to have compensation payable to our executive officers qualify as performance-based and deductible for federal income tax purposes unless there are valid compensatory reasons for paying nondeductible amounts, such as the recruitment and retention of key employees. We have endeavored to structure our incentive plans so that annual bonuses, stock options and performance share awards should be fully deductible. Deferred stock units (DSUs) are paid following an executive's termination of employment when the deduction limits of Internal Revenue Code Section 162(m) do not apply. Examples of potentially non-deductible compensation would include nondeferred base salary in excess of $1 million, sign on/relocation bonuses, and time-based restricted stock awards.[31]

Examining potentially nondeductible compensation, we see that the chairman and CEO of Tyco, Edward D. Breen, received a salary of $1,570,617 in 2005, with the $570,617 not being deductible. In addition, Tyco granted time-based restricted stock to each of the top five executives, totaling $11,456,000. Consequently, an estimate of the nondeductible amount is more than $12 million, yielding additional tax payments of $4.2 million at a corporate tax rate of 35 percent.

Examples of Executives Deferring Compensation to Preserve Deductions

Alternatively, the corporation can preserve the tax deduction if the executive defers compensation to a period in which he or she is no longer subject to the provisions of Section 162(m), that is, a period in which he or she is no longer the CEO or one of the next four highest-paid individuals. For example, Edward J. Zander's employment agreement with Motorola specifies:

Payment of the Target Bonus shall be guaranteed for fiscal year 2004 (the "Guaranteed Bonus"). The Executive has agreed to defer receipt of the Guaranteed Bonus pursuant to the terms of the Company's Management Deferred Compensation Plan until after the Executive's Date of

Termination (as defined below). However, notwithstanding the immediately preceding sentence, the Executive shall not be required to defer receipt of the Guaranteed Bonus beyond the first day on which the deductibility of the Guaranteed Bonus by the Company is no longer precluded by the provisions of Section 162(m) of the Internal Revenue Code of 1986, as amended (the "Code"), and in no event shall the Executive be required to defer receipt beyond Jan. 1 of the year following the year in which his Date of Termination (as defined below) occurs.[32]

Other companies reporting that their executives have agreed to defer compensation include Brunswick:

Section 162(m) of the Internal Revenue Code of 1986 (the "Code"), added by The Omnibus Budget Reconciliation Act of 1993, places a $1 million tax deduction limit on compensation paid to any executive employed by Brunswick on Dec. 31 of each year and named in the summary compensation table, with certain exceptions. Currently, Senior Executives must defer receipt of compensation in excess of $1,500,000, under the terms of an automatic deferral plan established for this purpose. Accordingly, Brunswick may not be entitled to deduct up to $500,000 for each named executive under these rules.[33]

Balsam and Yin (2005) report that approximately 12 percent of affected corporations deferred compensation to preserve deductions due to Section 162(m).

Example of a Corporation Qualifying Its Plan to Preserve Deductions

The final option companies have with their bonus plans is to qualify them as performance based, because if the plan is qualified under section 162(m), deductibility of those bonus payments is not limited (as long as the payments are made pursuant to the plan). Note that when a corporation qualifies a bonus or other compensation plan, it does not assure all compensation paid by the corporation is deductible, only the compensation paid pursuant to the plan. The corporation may still pay salary and other nonqualified compensation in excess of $1 million and hence lose deductions. To qualify a bonus plan under Section 162(m), the plan must be designed so that compensation is paid solely on account of the executive's attainment of one or more performance goals determined by objective formulae; those performance goals must be established by a compensation committee of two or more independent directors; and the material terms of the plan must be disclosed to and approved by shareholders.[34] Because negative, but not positive, discretion is allowed under Section 162(m), the incentive exists for corporations to set loose targets. Thus, if the compensation committee desires, it can reduce compensation. An example of a company modifying its bonus plan to meet Section 162(m) requirements is American International Group:

> The EIP was designed so that all awards under the EIP are considered "performance-based compensation" within the meaning of Section 162(m)(4)(C) of the Internal Revenue Code and the regulations thereunder. Section 162(m) limits the deductibility of compensation paid to certain executive officers in excess of $1 million, but excludes "performance-based compensation" from this limit. Awards under the EIP are intended to constitute "performance-based compensation" for these purposes. Likewise, compensation realized by executive officers through the exercise of stock options should be fully deductible to AIG as "performance-based compensation" under Section 162(m).[35]

Financial Reporting

Beyond the cash-flow effects, there is the financial reporting, or accounting costs, involved. Each component of the compensation package has an impact on reported profitability. Bonuses, like salary, are recorded as an expense in the period earned, whether deferred or paid currently, and whether deductible for tax purposes or not. In that respect, salary and bonuses are more expensive for financial accounting purposes than, say, stock options or restricted stock, which are expensed over their vesting periods. These amounts can be significant. For example, the United Parcel Service (UPS) reported it expensed $404 million during 2005 for management incentive awards, including restricted stock units.[36] To illustrate the differential accounting treatments among the various forms of payment, the 2005 expense was actually $334 million lower than it would have been otherwise, as starting in 2005, 50 percent of its incentive payout took the form of restricted stock units with a five-year graded vesting period.[37] Consequently, only one-fifth of the expense related to the restricted stock units was recognized in 2005.

Summary

This chapter reviewed the issues surrounding executive bonuses. Bonuses are traditionally considered to be a variable, or at-risk, form of compensation, although the amount of risk the executive is subject to depends upon the parameters of the plan. In some cases the bonus, or a minimum amount of bonus, is guaranteed, thus there is little risk. The bonus amount can be subjective or based upon objective criteria. It can be based upon financial or nonfinancial measures, or a combination of the two.

If structured properly, bonuses can provide the proper incentives to induce the executive to take actions that maximize shareholder value. However, if not structured properly, the bonus plan itself can lead to dysfunctional behavior. For example, if the performance threshold is unachievable, it provides no motivation. Alternatively, if the bonus is based upon a measure over which the executive has some discretion, the executive may manage that measure to increase his or her bonus at shareholders' expense. Thus, the performance measures, targets and other parameters must be chosen with extreme care.

Bonuses, like the other components of the compensation package, have political, as well as financial, reporting costs. Consequently, bonuses, and/or bonus plans, should be structured to minimize these costs. For example, the tax deductions associated with bonuses can be maximized if the corporation meets the requirements set out in Section 162(m) of the Internal Revenue Code.

Footnotes

[1] Page 39, Coca-Cola proxy statement filed with the Securities and Exchange Commission, March 10, 2006.

[2] Page 26, Citigroup proxy statement filed with the Securities and Exchange Commission, March 17, 2000.

[3] Pages 10 and 11, Exhibit 99.1 of 3M form 8-K filed with the Securities and Exchange Commission, Dec. 9, 2005.

[4] In Table 4-2 the assumption was that an increase (decrease) in salary would occur in the following year, as only after the close of the year would full-year performance be known. In contrast, SEC reporting requirements allow firms to pay bonuses for year T after the close of the year, and still report it in the proxy statement for year T. Consequently, the bonus disclosed for year T is the reward for year-T performance.

[5] Kato (1997) notes that for Japanese companies with financial keiretsu affiliation, CEO compensation is positively related to capital investment. Financial keiretsu are organized around a main bank, which is the principal lender to member firms and also a major shareholder. Thus structuring executive compensation to encourage capital investment may be optimal, even if it comes at the expense of profitability, because the main bank earns interest on the financing. That is, it maximizes shareholder profit.

[6] The traditional accounting model, developed over hundreds of years, better fits manufacturing firms with lots of fixed assets that can be easily measured and valued. In contrast, firms like Microsoft have little in the way of fixed assets, yet are incredibly valuable, yielding astronomical market-to-book ratios. One of the reasons is that the traditional accounting model undervalues companies like Microsoft, in that it undervalues the intangible assets created by the organization, which includes both the value of the people and products created by those people.

[7] Murphy (1998) table 2 shows that the majority of firms use multiple measures.

[8] Page 19, DuPont proxy statement filed with the Securities and Exchange Commission, March 17, 2006.

[9] Page 20, DuPont proxy statement filed with the Securities and Exchange Commission, March 17, 2006.

[10] Page A-2, DuPont proxy statement filed with the Securities and Exchange Commission, March 21, 2002.

[11] Page 27, Unocal proxy statement filed with the Securities and Exchange Commission, April 11, 2005.

[12] Page 28, Unocal proxy statement filed with the Securities and Exchange

Commission, April 8, 2002.

[13] Page 13, AT&T Wireless proxy statement filed with Securities and Exchange Commission, April 14, 2003.

[14] Page 17, Big Lots proxy statement filed with the Securities and Exchange Commission, April 19, 2006.

[15] Page 36, GAP Inc., proxy statement filed with the Securities and Exchange Commission, March 28, 2006.

[16] Page 22, GAP Inc., proxy statement filed with the Securities and Exchange Commission, March 28, 2005.

[17] Page 23, GAP Inc., proxy statement filed with the Securities and Exchange Commission, March 28, 2005.

[18] Page 30, GAP Inc., proxy statement filed with the Securities and Exchange Commission, March 28, 2006.

[19] Pages 19 and 20, General Motors proxy statement, filed with the Securities and Exchange Commission, April 28, 2006.

[20] This is an example of how one component of the compensation can be designed to offset a side or negative effect of another component. As discussed in the next chapter, stock options give managers a disincentive to pay dividends. Thus a provision whereby bonuses are at least partially based upon dividends is useful in that it provides some counterincentive to that provided by the options.

[21] Under the efficient market hypothesis, the stock price immediately after public announcement is an unbiased representation of the firms' value, and any stock price changes after that point would not be attributable to the plan itself, but to other factors.

[22] Page 41, Oracle proxy statement filed with the Securities and Exchange Commission, Aug. 23, 2006.

[23] Swartz (1986).

[24] Swartz (1987).

[25] Page 12, Bear Stearns proxy statement filed with the Securities and Exchange Commission, Aug. 4, 1988.

[26] Page 23, US Airways 10-Q filed with the Securities and Exchange Commission, Aug. 6, 1999.

[27] Pages 9 and 11, US Airways proxy statement filed with the Securities and Exchange Commission, April 1, 1999.

[28] *The Wall Street Journal* (1999).

[29] Page 18, US Airways proxy statement filed with the Securities and Exchange Commission, April 14, 2000.

[30] Page 19, Sears Holding proxy statement filed with the Securities and Exchange Commission, March 16, 2006.

[31] Page 40, Tyco International proxy statement filed with the Securities and Exchange Commission, Jan. 23, 2006.

[32] Page 2 of employment agreement between Motorola and Edward J. Zander, incorporated as exhibit 10.27 to Motorola 10-K filed with Securities and Exchange Commission, March 12, 2004.

[33] Page 18, Brunswick proxy statement filed with Securities and Exchange Commission, March 23, 2006.

[34] Balsam and Ryan (1996) find that approximately 50 percent of their sample firms qualify their bonus plans upon enactment of Section 162(m). In contrast, Rose and Wolfram (2000) found that only 40 percent of the firms in their sample qualified their bonus plans, and 20 percent, their long-term incentive plans. The difference in findings can partially, if not totally, be explained by difference in sample composition. That is, while Balsam and Ryan only included firms paying more than $1 million in cash composition, Rose and Wolfram included firms below that level.

[35] Page 46, American International Group proxy statement filed with Securities and Exchange Commission, April 5, 2006.

[36] Page F-31, United Parcel Service 10-K filed with Securities and Exchange Commission, March 14, 2006.

[37] Page 24, United Parcel Service 10-K filed with Securities and Exchange Commission, March 14, 2006.

Appendix 5-1

Bonus Formula from Contract Between Dennis R. Glass and Jefferson Pilot Corp., dated Dec. 6, 2003[1]

3.3 Annual Bonus Computation. The additional cash compensation payable under Section 3.2 hereof with respect to a Bonus Year shall be in an amount equal to a portion of the Base Salary for such Bonus Year determined as follows:

(a) JP's income from operations (disregarding realized capital gains and losses), as reflected in JP's audited financial statements ("Operating Income"), per share of common stock for the year immediately preceding the Bonus Year (the "Prior Year's Operating EPS") shall be subtracted from JP's Operating Income per share of common stock for the Bonus Year. If the result is negative, no additional compensation shall be payable, and no further computation will be necessary.

(b) The amount determined in clause (a) above shall be divided by the Prior Year's Operating EPS. If the result is less than 0.05 (that is, the growth in Operating Income per share is less than 5%), no additional compensation shall be payable, and no further computation will be necessary.

(c) If the amount determined in clause (b) above is .05 or greater, a percentage of Base Salary shall be obtained by straight line interpolation between applicable points shown in the table under (d) below.

(d) The percentage determined in clause (c) above shall be multiplied by the Base Salary for the Bonus Year (or one-sixth of the Base Salary in the case of the 2007 Bonus Year), and the result obtained shall be the additional compensation paid to Glass with respect to such Bonus Year.

In making the foregoing computation, appropriate adjustments shall be made for any stock splits and dividends, so that the Company's Operating Income per share of common stock for consecutive years is properly comparable. Without limiting the foregoing, the following table illustrates the application of the foregoing provisions:

Percentage Increase in Operating Income Per Share	Percentage of Base Salary Paid as Bonus
less than 5%	0%
5%	50%
10%	100%
15%	200%
more than 15%	200%

Notwithstanding the provisions of this Section 3.3, either Glass or the Compensation Committee of the Board of Directors of the Company may propose adjustments to the annual bonus in light of extraordinary transactions or circumstances that affect materially the Company's income, and any such adjustment agreed to by both Glass and the Compensation Committee of the Company's Board of Directors shall be given effect.

Appendix 5-2

Excerpt from American Express Co. Proxy Statement Report of Compensation and Benefits Committee[2]

Annual Incentive Awards. The Company's annual incentive (i.e., bonus) awards compensate executive officers for annual performance.

For 2005, the Company paid annual incentive awards to each of the executive officers, except for James Cracchiolo and another executive officer who transferred to Ameriprise upon its spin-off from the Company in September 2005. The Committee considered each individual's goal achievement and leadership performance, as well as Company and business unit or staff group performance, in making discretionary awards, giving equal weight to the goal and leadership categories. In addition, the Committee considered current competitive market data.

The Committee considered each individual's goal achievement, including the evaluation by the CEO, in the following three areas:

- Shareholder (50% weight). Includes financial results, such as shareholder return, earnings growth, revenue growth, return on equity, reengineering and cost savings.
- Customer (25% weight). Includes customer survey results, expansion and retention of customer base, development of products and services and improvements in competitive position.
- Employee (25% weight). Includes employee survey results, success in achieving long-term, world-class targets for employee satisfaction, retention of talented employees and diversity.

The Committee also considered each individual's leadership results, including the evaluation by the CEO of a variety of factors, including: developing winning strategies, achieving results, focusing on the customer and client, driving innovation and change, building and leveraging relationships, communicating effectively, building diverse talent and demonstrating personal excellence.

The Committee used similar factors to evaluate the goal and leadership performance of the CEO, Mr. Chenault. The specific factors the Committee used to evaluate Mr. Chenault's goal performance are described on pages 24 and 25. The Committee did not assign weights to the goal achievement categories in evaluating Mr. Chenault's performance. In addition, the Committee evaluated his overall leadership of the senior management team and of the Company.

To recognize the Company's outstanding financial performance in 2005 (see "2005 Financial Performance" on page 24 below), the Committee approved cash annual incentive awards for all executive officers (as reflected in the "Bonus" column of the Summary Compensation Table on page 26), except for Mr. Cracchiolo and a second executive officer who transferred to Ameriprise. In addition, for 2005 performance and as an incentive for future performance, in the first quarter of 2006 the Committee (i) issued restricted stock awards that vest after three years from grant for four of the executive officers named in the Summary Compensation Table, (ii) issued restricted stock awards that vest in equal installments after one and two years from grant for two named executives, as well as another executive officer not named in such Table and (iii) issued a letter of intent entitling one of the named executives to receive shares of the Company's common stock after three years from grant (as reflected in the "Restricted Stock Awards" column of the Summary Compensation Table). The vesting of each of these non-cash awards is subject to continuous employment and the attainment of certain Company financial goals.

Long-Term Incentive Awards. The Company's long-term incentive award (LTIA) program rewards executive officers for Company performance over periods longer than one year. The Committee believes these awards are important components of the Company's compensation philosophy because they help to align the interests of management and shareholders over a longer time horizon than the annual incentive awards described above and to retain executive talent. For 2005, LTIAs included annual stock option and Portfolio Grant (PG) awards, as well as performance-based restricted stock awards and letters of intent.

- Stock Options. Ten-year stock options reward executive officers if the Company's share price increases over the market price at grant. Executives may exercise up to 25% of the 2005 grant after one year, 50% after two years, 75% after three years, and 100% after four years.

- PG Awards. PG awards reward executive officers based on the Company's financial and relative total shareholder return performance over a three-year period. Each PG award has two parts. The first part is the Financial Incentive Component (FIC), which accounts for 60% of the target value of the award. The FIC is based on the Company's average annual earnings per share, revenue and return on equity results over the three-year period. The Financial Incentive Component will earn value if the Company achieves at least a threshold level of performance on any of these financial measures. The second part is the Stock Incentive Component (SIC), which accounts for 40% of the target value of the award. The SIC is based on the total shareholder return (i.e., return due to share price appreciation plus dividends, assuming reinvestment) of the Company's common stock compared to the return of the S&P Financial Index over the three-year period. In determining actual payouts at the end of the three-year period, the Committee may adjust the maximum values produced by these performance measures downward based on its judgment of Company, business unit and individual performance over the performance period. To receive his or her payout under a PG award, an executive officer generally must be employed by the Company through the vesting and payment date of the award, which has historically occurred in the January or February following the completion of the performance period.

- Restricted Stock and Letters of Intent. The Committee may, in its judgment, award to executive officers shares of restricted stock and/or letters of intent, which represent the right to receive shares of the Company's common stock at a future date, as a component of the executive's annual incentive award, PG payout or in other circumstances it deems appropriate, including to recognize an executive's contributions in respect of annual or multi-year performance, as an incentive for future performance or for retention purposes. The vesting period of these awards is determined by the Committee in its discretion and is generally subject to the executive's continuous employment during the vesting period and the Company's attainment of certain financial goals.

In 2005, the Committee approved the grant of long-term incentive awards to executive officers after reviewing factors similar to those identified above for annual incentive awards, as well as the incentive and retention value of existing stock option, PG and restricted stock awards held by each officer, and talent assessments. In addition to the annual stock option grants, the Committee granted annual PG awards (PG-XVI) to the executive officers that cover a 2005-2007 performance period. In the first quarter of 2006, the Committee approved the payouts under PG-XIV awards (granted in 2003), which covered 2003-2005 performance.

The Committee granted restricted stock awards in the first quarter of 2005 to four named executives, including Mr. Chenault, for retention purposes. The grants vest in equal installments on the first, second, third and fourth anniversaries of the grant date, subject to continuous employment and attainment of certain Company financial goals. In addition, as described above under "Annual Incentive Awards" and below under "Chief Executive Officer Compensation," in the first quarter of 2006, the Committee granted restricted stock awards to Mr. Chenault, four other named executives and one other executive officer, and it also issued a letter of intent to Mr. Chenault.

Appendix 5-3

Lucent Technologies Inc. 2003 Long-Term Incentive Program[3]
SECTION 1.1 PURPOSE

The purposes of the Lucent Technologies Inc. 2003 Long Term Incentive Program (the "Plan") are to encourage selected Employees of Lucent Technologies Inc. (the "Company") and its Affiliates to acquire a proprietary and vested interest in the growth and performance of the Company, to generate an increased incentive to contribute to the Company's future success and prosperity, thus enhancing the value of the Company for the benefit of shareowners, and to enhance the ability of the Company and its Affiliates to attract and retain individuals of exceptional talent upon whom, in large measure, the sustained progress, growth and profitability of the Company depend.

SECTION 1.2 ESTABLISHMENT AND TERM OF THE 2003 PLAN

The Company establishes the Plan effective as of February 19, 2003, subject to the Plan having been approved by the Company's shareowners on or prior to that date. The Plan shall remain in effect until the earlier of: (i) the date that no additional Shares are available for issuance under the Plan, (ii) the date that the Plan has been terminated in accordance with Section 13 or (iii) the close of business on February 28, 2008. Upon the Plan becoming effective, no further awards shall be made under the 1996 Plan. Upon the termination or expiration of the Plan as provided in this Section 1.2, no Award shall be granted pursuant to the Plan, but any Award theretofore granted may extend beyond such termination or expiration.

SECTION 2. DEFINITIONS

As used in the Plan, the following terms shall have the meanings set forth below:

(a) "Affiliate" shall mean (i) any Person that directly, or through one or more intermediaries, controls, or is controlled by, or is under common control with, the Company or (ii) any entity in which the Company has a significant equity interest, as determined by the Committee.

(b) "Award" shall mean any Option, Stock Appreciation Right, Restricted Stock Award, Performance Share, Performance Unit, Dividend Equivalent Other Stock Unit Award, or any other right, interest, or option relating to Shares or other securities of the Company granted pursuant to the provisions of the Plan.

(c) "Award Agreement" shall mean any written or electronic agreement, contract, or other instrument or document evidencing any Award granted by the Committee hereunder and signed or otherwise authenticated by both the Company and the Participant.

(d) "Board" shall mean the Board of Directors of the Company.

(e) "Cause" shall mean for termination of employment of an Employee the definition given to it under the applicable Award Agreement or, in the absence of such a definition, (A) the definition given to it under applicable law, (B) for Employees who are subject to legislation which does not explicitly give such a definition, such circumstances which entitle the Company or the Affiliate to terminate the employment of the Employee without severance payments, or (C) for Employees who are subject to an employment agreement or severance policy with the Company or an Affiliate, the definition given to it under such employment agreement or severance policy.

(f) "Change in Control" shall mean the happening of any of the following events:

(i) An acquisition by any individual, entity or group (within the meaning of Section 13(d)(3) or 14(d)(2) of the Exchange Act) (an "Entity") of beneficial ownership (within the meaning of Rule 13d-3 promulgated under the Exchange Act) of 20% or more of either (A) the then outstanding shares of common stock of the Company (the "Outstanding Company Common Stock") or (B) the combined voting power of the then outstanding voting securities of the Company entitled to vote generally in the election of directors (the "Outstanding Company Voting Securities"); excluding, however, the following: (1) any acquisition directly from the Company, other than an acquisition by virtue of the exercise of a conversion privilege unless the security being so converted was itself acquired directly from the Company, (2) any acquisition by the Company, (3) any acquisition by any employee benefit plan (or related trust) sponsored or maintained by the Company or any corporation controlled by the Company, or (4) any acquisition by any corporation pursuant to a transaction which complies with clauses (A), (B) and (C) of subsection (iii) of this Section 2(f); or

(ii) A change in the Composition of the Board during any two year period such that the individuals who, as of the beginning of such two year period, constitute the Board (such Board shall be hereinafter referred to as the "Incumbent Board") cease for any reason to constitute at least a majority of the Board; provided, however, that for purposes of this definition, any individual who becomes a member of the Board subsequent to the beginning of the two year period, whose election, or nomination for election by the Company's shareowners, was approved by a vote of at least a majority of those individuals who are members of the Board and who were also members of the Incumbent Board (or deemed to be such pursuant to this proviso) shall be considered as though such individual were a member of the Incumbent Board; and provided further, however, that any such individual whose initial assumption of office occurs as a result of or in connection with a solicitation subject to Rule 14a-12(c) of Regulation 14A promulgated under the Exchange Act or other actual or threatened solicitation of proxies or consents by or on behalf of an Entity other than the Board shall not be so considered as a member of the Incumbent Board; or

(iii) The approval by the shareowners of the Company of a merger, reorganization or consolidation or sale or other disposition of all or substantially all of the assets of the Company (each, a "Corporate Transaction") or, if consummation of such Corporate Transaction is subject, at the time of such approval by shareowners, to the consent of any government or governmental agency, the obtaining of such consent (either explicitly or implicitly by consummation); excluding however, such a Corporate Transaction pursuant to which (A) all or substantially all of the individuals and entities who are the beneficial owners of the Outstanding Company Common Stock and Outstanding Company Voting Securities immediately prior to such Corporate Transaction will beneficially own, directly or indirectly, more than 60% of the outstanding shares of common stock, and the combined voting power of the then outstanding voting securities entitled to vote generally in the election of directors of the corporation resulting from such Corporate Transaction (including, without limitation, a corporation or other Person which as a result of such transaction owns the Company or all or substantially all of the Company's assets either directly or through one or more subsidiaries (a "Parent Company")) in substantially the same proportions as their ownership, immediately prior to such Corporate Transaction, of the Outstanding Company Common Stock and Outstanding Company Voting Securities, (B) no Entity (other than the Company, any employee benefit plan (or related trust) of the Company, such corporation resulting from such Corporate Transaction or, if reference was made to equity ownership of any Parent Company for purposes of determining whether clause (A) above is satisfied in connection with the applicable Corporate Transaction, such Parent Company) will beneficially own, directly or indirectly, 20% or more of, respectively, the outstanding shares of common stock of the corporation resulting from such Corporate

Transaction or the combined voting power of the outstanding voting securities of such corporation entitled to vote generally in the election of directors unless such ownership resulted solely from ownership of securities of the Company prior to the Corporate Transaction, and (C) individuals who were members of the Incumbent Board will immediately after the consummation of the Corporate Transaction constitute at least a majority of the members of the board of directors of the corporation resulting from such Corporate Transaction (or, if reference was made to equity ownership of any Parent Company for purposes of determining whether clause (A) above is satisfied in connection with the applicable Corporate Transaction, of the Parent Company); or

(iv) The approval by the shareowners of the Company of a complete liquidation or dissolution of the Company.

(g) "Change in Control Price" means the higher of (A) the highest reported sales price, regular way, of a Share in any transaction reported on the New York Stock Exchange Composite Tape or other national exchange on which Shares are listed or on NASDAQ during the 60-day period prior to and including the date of a Change in Control or (B) if the Change in Control is the result of a tender or exchange offer or a Corporate Transaction, the highest price per Share paid in such tender or exchange offer or Corporate Transaction; provided however, that in the case of Incentive Stock Options and Stock Appreciation Rights relating to Incentive Stock Options, the Change in Control Price shall be in all cases the Fair Market Value of a Share on the date such Incentive Stock Option or Stock Appreciation Right is exercised or deemed exercised. To the extent that the consideration paid in any such transaction described above consists all or in part of securities or other noncash consideration, the value of such securities or other noncash consideration shall be determined in the sole discretion of the Board.

(h) "Code" shall mean the Internal Revenue Code of 1986, as amended from time to time, and any successor thereto.

(i) "Committee" shall mean the Corporate Governance and Compensation Committee of the Board (or any successor committee); provided, however, that (i) with respect to Awards to any Employees who are Officers or members of the Board for purposes of Section 16, Committee means all of the members of the Compensation Committee who are "non-employee directors" within the meaning of Rule 16b-3 adopted under the Exchange Act, (ii) with respect to Awards to any Employees who are Officers or members of the Board for purposes of Section 16 and who are intended to satisfy the requirements for "performance based compensation" within the meaning of Section 162(m)(4)(C) of the Code, the regulations promulgated thereunder, and any successors thereto, Committee means all of the members of the Compensation Committee who are "outside directors" within the meaning of Section 162(m) of the Code, and (iii) with respect to all Awards, the Committee shall comprise of "independent" directors as required under the New York Stock Exchange listing requirements.

(j) "Company" shall mean Lucent Technologies Inc., a Delaware corporation.

(k) "Covered Employee" shall mean a "covered employee" within the meaning of Section 162(m)(3) of the Code.

(l) "Dividend Equivalent" shall mean any right granted pursuant to Section 14(h) hereof.

(m) "Employee" shall mean any employee of the Company or of any Affiliate. Unless otherwise determined by the Committee in its sole discretion, for purposes of the Plan, an Employee shall be considered to have terminated employment and to have ceased to be an Employee if his or her employer ceases to be an Affiliate, even if he or she continues to be employed by such employer.

(n) "Exchange Act" shall mean the Securities Exchange Act of 1934, as amended from time to time, and any successor thereto.

(o) "Exercise Period" shall have the meaning set forth in Section 11(b) hereof.

(p) "Good Reason" shall mean "good reason" as such term is defined in the Award Agreement or, in the absence of such a definition, for Employees who are subject to an employment agreement or severance policy with the Company or an Affiliate, the definition given to it under such employment agreement or severance policy.

(q) "Fair Market Value" shall mean, (i) with respect to Shares, the average of the highest and lowest reported sales prices, regular way, of Shares in transactions reported on the New York Stock Exchange on the date of determination of Fair Market Value, or if no sales of Shares are reported on the New York Stock Exchange for that date, the comparable average sales price for the last previous day for which sales were reported on the New York Stock Exchange, and (ii) with respect to any other property, the fair market value of such property determined by such methods or procedures as shall be established from time to time by the Committee.

(r) "Incentive Stock Option" shall mean an Option granted under Section 6 hereof that is intended to meet the requirements of Section 422 of the Code or any successor provision thereto.

(s) "Net Income" shall mean the net income of the Company as determined under generally accepted accounting principles, excluding (a) extraordinary items (net of applicable taxes); (b) cumulative effects of changes in accounting principles; (c) securities gains and losses (net of applicable taxes); and (d) nonrecurring items (net of applicable taxes) including, but not limited to, gains or losses on asset dispositions and sales of divisions, business units or subsidiaries, restructuring charges, gains and losses from qualified benefit plan curtailments and settlements, and income or expenses related to deferred tax assets.

(t) "Nonstatutory Stock Option" shall mean an Option granted under Section 6 hereof that is not intended to be an Incentive Stock Option.

(u) "Officer" shall mean any manager of the Company or any Affiliate holding a position above the executive level (E band) or any future salary grade that is the equivalent thereof.

(v) "Option" shall mean any right granted to a Participant under the 2003 Plan allowing such Participant to purchase Shares at such price or prices and during such period or periods as the Committee shall determine.

(w) "Other Stock Unit Award" shall mean any right granted to a Participant by the Committee pursuant to Section 10 hereof.

(x) "Participant" shall mean an Employee who is selected by the Committee to receive an Award under the Plan.

(y) "Performance Award" shall mean any Award of Performance Shares or Performance Units pursuant to Section 9 hereof.

(z) "Performance Period" shall mean that period, established by the Committee at the time any Performance Award is granted or at any time thereafter, during which any performance goals specified by the Committee with respect to such Award are to be measured.

(aa) "Performance Share" shall mean any grant pursuant to Section 9 hereof of a unit valued by reference to a designated number of Shares, which value may be paid to the Participant by delivery of such property as the Committee shall determine, including, without limitation, cash, Shares, or any combination thereof, upon achievement of such performance goals during the Performance Period as the Committee shall establish at the time of such grant or thereafter.

(bb) "Performance Unit" shall mean any grant pursuant to Section 9 hereof of a unit valued by reference to a designated amount of property other than Shares, which value may be paid to the Participant by delivery of such property as the Committee shall determine, including, without limitation, cash, Shares, or any combination thereof, upon achievement of such performance goals during the Performance Period as the Committee shall establish at the time of such grant or thereafter.

(cc) "Person" shall mean any individual, corporation, partnership, association, joint-stock company, trust, unincorporated organization, limited liability company, other entity or government or political subdivision thereof.

(dd) "Plan" shall mean the Long Term Incentive Program set forth herein known as the "Lucent Technologies Inc. 2003 Long Term Incentive Program", as the same may be amended from time to time.

(ee) "Restricted Stock" shall mean any Share issued with the restriction that the holder may not sell, transfer, pledge, or assign such Share and with such other restrictions as the Committee, in its sole discretion, may impose (including, without limitation, any restriction on the right to vote such Share, and the right to receive any cash dividends), which restrictions may lapse separately or in combination at such time or times, in installments or otherwise, as the Committee may deem appropriate.

(ff) "Restricted Stock Award" shall mean an award of Restricted Stock under Section 8 hereof.

(gg) "Section 16" shall mean Section 16 of the Exchange Act and the rules promulgated thereunder and any successor provision thereto as in effect from time to time.

(hh) "Shares" shall mean the shares of common stock, $.01 par value, of the Company and such other securities of the Company as the Committee may from time to time determine.

(ii) "Stock Appreciation Right" shall mean any right granted to a Participant pursuant to Section 7 hereof to receive, upon exercise by the Participant, the excess of (i) the Fair Market Value of one Share on the date of exercise or, if the Committee shall so determine in the case of any such right other than one related to any Incentive Stock Option, at any time during a specified period before the date of exercise over (ii) the grant price of the right on the date of grant, or if granted in connection with an outstanding Option on the date of grant of the related Option, as specified by the Committee in its sole discretion, which, other than in the case of Substitute Awards, shall not be less than the Fair Market Value of one

Share on such date of grant of the right or the related Option, as the case may be. Any payment by the Company in respect of such right may be made in cash, Shares, other property, or any combination thereof, as the Committee, in its sole discretion, shall determine.

(jj) "Subsidiary" shall mean a "subsidiary corporation" of the Company as defined in Section 424(f) of the Code, an entity in which the Company directly or indirectly owns 50% or more of the voting interests or an entity in which the Company has a significant equity interest, as determined by the Board or the Committee.

(kk) "Substitute Award" shall have the meaning set forth in Section 4(d).

(ll) "1996 Plan" shall mean the Company's 1996 Long-Term Incentive Program.

(mm)"1997 Plan" shall mean the Company's 1997 Long-Term Incentive Plan.

SECTION 3. ADMINISTRATION

(a) AUTHORITY OF COMMITTEE. The Plan shall be administered by the Committee. The Committee shall have full power and authority, subject to such resolutions not inconsistent with the provisions of the Plan as may from time to time be adopted by the Board, to: (i) select the Employees of the Company and its Affiliates to whom Awards may from time to time be granted hereunder; (ii) determine the type or types of Award to be granted to each Participant hereunder; (iii) determine the number of Shares to be covered by each Award granted hereunder; (iv) determine the terms and conditions, not inconsistent with the provisions of the Plan, of any Award granted hereunder; (v) determine whether, to what extent and under what circumstances Awards may be settled in cash, Shares or other property or canceled or suspended; (vi) determine whether, to what extent and under what circumstances cash, Shares and other property and other amounts payable with respect to an Award under this Plan shall be deferred either automatically or at the election of the Participant; (vii) interpret and administer the Plan and any instrument or agreement entered into under the Plan; (viii) establish such rules and regulations and appoint such agents as it shall deem appropriate for the proper administration of the Plan; and (ix) make any other determination and take any other action that the Committee deems necessary or desirable for administration of the Plan. Notwithstanding anything in this Section 3(a) to the contrary, the Committee shall not have the authority to reduce the exercise price for Options and Stock Appreciation Rights other than in connection with adjustments as provided in Section 4(g).

(b) DECISIONS BINDING. Decisions of the Committee shall be final, conclusive and binding upon all Persons, including the Company, any Participant, any shareowner, and any employee of the Company or of any Affiliate.

(c) DELEGATION. Subject to the terms of the Plan and terms and limitations as the Committee shall determine, the Committee may delegate its authority as identified herein to any individual or committee of individuals (who need not be directors of the Board), including without limitation the authority to make Awards to Participants who are not Officers or directors of the Company for purposes of Section 16 or who are otherwise not subject to such Section. To the extent that the Committee delegates its authority to make Awards as provided by this Section 3(c), all references in the Plan to the Committee's authority to make Awards and determinations with respect thereto shall be deemed to include the Committee's delegate. Any such delegate shall serve at the leisure of, and may be removed at any time by, the Committee.

SECTION 4. SHARES SUBJECT TO THE 2003 PLAN

(a) NUMBER OF SHARES AVAILABLE FOR GRANTS. Subject to adjustment as provided in Section 4(g), the aggregate number of Shares that may be issued to Participants pursuant to Awards granted under the Plan shall not exceed the sum of one hundred seventy million (170,000,000) Shares.

(b) LAPSED AWARDS. If any Award is canceled, terminates, expires, or lapses for any reason, any Shares subject to such Award shall not count against the aggregate number of Shares that may be issued under the Plan set forth in Section 4(a) above.

(c) SHARES USED TO PAY OPTION PRICE AND WITHHOLDING TAXES. If a Participant pays the option price for an Option by tendering previously owned Shares in accordance with the provisions of Section 6 herein or satisfies any tax withholding requirement by having the Company withhold Shares in accordance with Section 14 herein, then such Shares surrendered to pay the option price or used to satisfy such tax withholding requirements shall not count against the aggregate number of Shares that may be issued under the Plan set forth in Section 4(a) above.

(d) OTHER ITEMS NOT INCLUDED. The following items shall not count against the aggregate number of Shares that may be issued under the Plan set forth in Section 4(a) above:

(i) the payment in cash of dividends or dividend equivalents under any outstanding Award; (ii) any Award that is settled in cash rather than by issuance of Shares; or (iii) Awards granted through the assumption of, or in substitution for, outstanding awards previously granted to individuals who become Employees as a result of a merger, consolidation, acquisition or other corporate transaction involving the Company or any Subsidiary ("Substitute Award").

(e) AWARD LIMITS. Notwithstanding any provision herein to the contrary, the following provisions shall apply (subject to adjustment as provided in Section 4(g) below):

(i) in no event shall a Participant receive an Award or Awards during any one (1) calendar year covering in the aggregate more than six million (6,000,000) Shares (whether such Award or Awards may be settled in Shares, cash or any combination of Shares and cash) or twenty million Shares (20,000,000) covering the term of the Plan; provided that, during the initial year of employment, the limit shall be increased to ten million (10,000,000) Shares;

(ii) in no event shall there be granted during the term of the Plan Incentive Stock Options covering more than an aggregate of forty million (40,000,000) Shares; and

(iii) in no event shall there be granted during the term of the Plan Shares of Restricted Stock, Performance Units, Performance Shares or Other Stock Based Awards (or any similar plan or program as determined by the Committee) covering more than fifty-one million (51,000,000) Shares.

(f) SOURCE OF SHARES. Shares issued under the Plan may be original issue shares, treasury stock or shares purchased in the open market or otherwise, all as determined by the Chief Financial Officer of the Company (or the Chief Financial Officer's designee) from time to time.

(g) ADJUSTMENTS. In the event of any merger, reorganization, consolidation, recapitalization, stock dividend, stock split, reverse stock split, spin-off or similar transaction or other change in corporate structure affecting the Shares, such adjustments and other substitutions shall be made to the Plan and to Awards as the Committee in its sole discretion deems equitable or appropriate, including without limitation such adjustments in the aggregate number, class and kind of Shares which may be delivered under the Plan, in the aggregate or to any one Participant, in the number, class, kind and option or exercise price of Shares subject to outstanding Options, Stock

Appreciation Rights or other Awards granted under the Plan, and in the number, class and kind of Shares subject to Awards granted under the Plan (including, if the Committee deems appropriate, the substitution of similar options to purchase the shares of, or other awards denominated in the shares of, another company) as the Committee may determine to be appropriate in its sole discretion, provided that the number of Shares or other securities subject to any Award shall always be a whole number.

SECTION 5. ELIGIBILITY

Any Employee (excluding any member of the Committee) shall be eligible to be selected as a Participant.

SECTION 6. STOCK OPTIONS

Options may be granted hereunder to Participants either alone or in addition to other Awards granted under the Plan. Options may be granted for no consideration or for such consideration as the Committee may determine. Any Option granted under the Plan shall be evidenced by an Award Agreement in such form as the Committee may from time to time approve. Any such Option shall be subject to the following terms and conditions and to such additional terms and conditions, not inconsistent with the provisions of the Plan, as the Committee shall deem desirable:

(a) OPTION PRICE. The exercise price per Share under an Option shall be determined by the Committee in its sole discretion; provided that, except in the case of an Option pursuant to a Substitute Award, such purchase price shall not be less than the Fair Market Value of a Share on the date of the grant of the Option.

(b) OPTION PERIOD. The term of each Option shall be fixed by the Committee in its sole discretion; provided that no Option shall be exercisable after the expiration of seven years from the date the Option is granted.

(c) EXERCISABILITY. Options shall be exercisable at such time or times as determined by the Committee at or subsequent to grant.

d) METHOD OF EXERCISE. Subject to the other provisions of the 2003 Plan and any applicable Award Agreement, any Option may be exercised by the Participant in whole or in part at such time or times, and the Participant may make payment of the option price in such form or forms, including, without limitation, payment by delivery of cash, Shares or other consideration (including, where permitted by law and the Committee, Awards) having a Fair Market Value on the exercise date equal to the total option price, or by any combination of cash, Shares and other consideration as the Committee may specify in the applicable Award Agreement.

(e) INCENTIVE STOCK OPTIONS. In accordance with rules and procedures established by the Committee, the aggregate Fair Market Value (determined as of the time of grant) of the Shares with respect to which Incentive Stock Options held by any Participant which are exercisable for the first time by such Participant during any calendar year under the Plan (and under any other benefit plans of the Company or of any parent or Subsidiary of the Company) shall not exceed $100,000 or, if different, the maximum limitation in effect at the time of grant under Section 422 of the Code, or any successor provision, and any regulations promulgated thereunder. The terms of any Incentive Stock Option granted hereunder shall comply in all respects with the provisions of Section 422 of the Code, or any successor provision, and any regulations promulgated thereunder.

(f) FORM OF SETTLEMENT. In its sole discretion, the Committee may provide, at the time of grant, that the shares to be issued upon an Option's exercise shall be in the form of Restricted Stock or other similar securities, or may reserve the right so to provide after the time of grant. Similarly, the Committee may require Shares to be held for a specific period of time.

SECTION 7. STOCK APPRECIATION RIGHTS

Stock Appreciation Rights may be granted hereunder to Participants either alone or in addition to other Awards granted under the Plan and may, but need not, relate to a specific Option granted under Section 6. The provisions of Stock Appreciation Rights need not be the same with respect to each recipient. Any Stock Appreciation Right related to a Nonstatutory Stock Option may be granted at the same time such Option is granted or at any time thereafter before exercise or expiration of such Option. Any Stock Appreciation Right related to an Incentive Stock Option must be granted at the same time such Option is granted. In the case of any Stock Appreciation Right related to any Option, the Stock Appreciation Right or applicable portion thereof shall terminate and no longer be exercisable upon the termination or exercise of the related Option, except that a Stock Appreciation Right granted with respect to less than the full number of Shares covered by a related Option shall not be reduced until the exercise or termination of the related Option exceeds the number of Shares not covered by the Stock Appreciation Right. Any Option related to any Stock Appreciation Right shall no longer be exercisable to the extent the related Stock Appreciation Right has been exercised. The Committee may impose such conditions or restrictions on the exercise of any Stock Appreciation Right as it shall deem appropriate.

SECTION 8. RESTRICTED STOCK AWARDS

Restricted Stock Awards may be issued hereunder to Participants, for no cash consideration or for such minimum consideration as may be required by applicable law, either alone or in addition to other Awards granted under the Plan. The provisions of Restricted Stock Awards need not be the same with respect to each recipient. Any Restricted Stock Award issued hereunder may be evidenced in such manner as the Committee in its sole discretion shall deem appropriate, including, without limitation, book-entry registration or issuance of a stock certificate or certificates. In the event any stock certificate is issued in respect of a Restricted Stock Award, such certificate shall be registered in the name of the Participant, and shall bear an appropriate legend referring to the terms, conditions, and restrictions applicable to such Award. Except as otherwise determined by the Committee and subject to Section 11 hereof, upon termination of employment for any reason during the restriction period, any portion of a Restricted Stock Award still subject to restriction shall be forfeited by the Participant and reacquired by the Company.

SECTION 9. PERFORMANCE AWARDS

Performance Awards in the form of Performance Units or Performance Shares may be issued hereunder to Participants, for no cash consideration or for such minimum consideration as may be required by applicable law, either alone or in addition to other Awards granted under the Plan. The performance criteria to be achieved during any Performance Period and the length of the Performance Period shall be determined by the Committee upon the grant of each Performance Award or at any time thereafter. Except as provided in Section 11, Performance Awards will be distributed only after the end of the relevant Performance Period. Performance Awards may be paid in cash, Shares, other property or any combination thereof, in the sole discretion of the Committee. The performance levels to be achieved for each Performance Period and the amount of the Award to be distributed shall be conclusively determined by the Committee. Performance Awards may be paid in a lump sum or in installments following the close of the Performance Period.

SECTION 10. OTHER STOCK UNIT AWARDS

Other Awards of Shares and other Awards that are valued in whole or in part by reference to, or are otherwise based on, Shares or other property ("Other Stock

Unit Awards") may be granted hereunder to Participants, either alone or in addition to other Awards granted under the Plan. Other Stock Unit Awards may be paid in Shares, other securities of the Company, cash or any other form of property as the Committee shall determine. Shares (including securities convertible into Shares) granted under this Section 10 may be issued for no cash consideration or for such minimum consideration as may be required by applicable law. Shares (including securities convertible into Shares) purchased pursuant to a purchase right awarded under this Section 10 shall be purchased for such consideration as the Committee shall in its sole discretion determine, which shall not be less than the Fair Market Value of such Shares or other securities as of the date such purchase right is awarded. Subject to the provisions of the Plan, the Committee shall have sole and complete authority to determine the Employees of the Company and its Affiliates to whom and the time or times at which such Awards shall be made, the number of Shares to be granted pursuant to such Awards, and all other conditions of the Awards. The provisions of Other Stock Unit Awards need not be the same with respect to each recipient.

SECTION 11. CHANGE IN CONTROL PROVISIONS

(a) IMPACT OF EVENT. Notwithstanding any other provision of the Plan to the contrary, unless the Committee shall determine otherwise at the time of grant with respect to a particular Award, in the event of a Change in Control:

    (i) All outstanding Awards other than Performance Awards shall become fully and immediately exercisable unless such Awards are converted, assumed, or replaced by a successor. If a Participant's employment is subsequently terminated without Cause or for Good Reason within 24 months of the Change in Control, any such Awards (other than Performance Awards) so converted, assumed, or replaced that remain unvested shall become fully and immediately exercisable upon the date of the Participant's termination and all deferral and restriction limitations applicable shall lapse.

    (ii) All Performance Awards earned and outstanding as of the date of the Change in Control is determined to have occurred shall be payable in full in accordance with the payout schedule pursuant to the Award Agreement. Any remaining Performance Awards (including any applicable Performance Period) for which the payout level has not been determined shall be prorated at the target payout level up to and including the date of such Change in Control and shall be payable in full in accordance with the payout schedule pursuant to the Award Agreement. Any existing deferrals or other restrictions shall remain in effect. If the Participant's employment is terminated without Cause following the Change in Control, any Awards remaining to be paid will be paid in accordance with the employment termination provision of the Award Agreement. If the Participant's employment is terminated for Good Reason following the Change in Control, any Awards remaining to be paid will be paid in accordance with the payout schedule pursuant to the Award Agreement.

(b) CHANGE IN CONTROL CASH-OUT. Notwithstanding any other provision of the Plan, during the 60-day period from and after a Change in Control (the "Exercise Period"), if the Committee shall determine at, or at any time after, the time of grant, a Participant holding an Option shall have the right, whether or not the Option is fully exercisable and in lieu of the payment of the purchase price for the Shares being purchased under the Option and by giving notice to the Company, to elect (within the Exercise Period) to surrender all or part of the Option to the Company and to receive cash, within 30 days of such notice, in an amount equal to the amount by which the Change in Control Price per Share on the date of such election shall exceed the purchase price per Share under the Option multiplied by the number of Shares granted under the Option as to which the right granted under this Section 11(b) shall have been exercised.

SECTION 12. CODE SECTION 162(m) PROVISIONS

(a) Notwithstanding any other provision of this Plan, if the Committee determines at the time Restricted Stock, a Performance Award or an Other Stock Unit Award is granted to a Participant that such Participant is, or may be as of the end of the tax year for which the Company would claim a tax deduction in connection with such Award, a Covered Employee, then the Committee may provide that this Section 12 is applicable to such Award under such terms as the Committee shall determine.

(b) If an Award is subject to this Section 12, then the lapsing of restrictions thereon and the distribution of cash, Shares or other property pursuant thereto, as applicable, shall be subject to the Company having a level of Net Income for the fiscal year preceding lapse or distribution set by the Committee within the time prescribed by Section 162(m) of the Code or the regulations thereunder in order for the level to be considered "pre-established". The Committee may, in its discretion, reduce the amount of any Performance Award or Other Stock Unit Award subject to this Section 12 at any time prior to payment based on such criteria as it shall determine, including but not limited to individual merit and the attainment of specified levels of one or any combination of the following: net cash provided by operating activities, earnings per Share from continuing operations, operating income, revenue growth, gross margin, operating return on sales, return on operating assets, return on equity, economic value added, stock price appreciation, total shareowner return (measured in terms of stock price appreciation and dividend growth), or cost control, of the Company or the Affiliate or division of the Company for or within which the Participant is primarily employed.

(c) Notwithstanding any contrary provision of the Plan other than Section 11, the Committee may not adjust upwards the amount payable pursuant to any Award subject to this Section 12, nor may it waive the achievement of the Net Income requirement contained in Section 12(b), except in the case of the death or disability of a Participant.

(d) Prior to the payment of any Award subject to this Section 12, the Committee shall certify in writing that the Net Income requirement applicable to such Award was met.

(e) The Committee shall have the power to impose such other restrictions on Awards subject to this Section 12 as it may deem necessary or appropriate to ensure that such Awards satisfy all requirements for "performance-based compensation" within the meaning of Section 162(m)(4)(C) of the Code, the regulations promulgated thereunder, and any successors thereto.

SECTION 13. AMENDMENTS AND TERMINATION

The Board may amend, alter or discontinue the 2003 Plan, but no amendment, alteration, or discontinuation shall be made that would impair the rights of an optionee or Participant under an Award theretofore granted, without the optionee's or Participant's consent, or that without the approval of the shareowners would:

(a) except as is provided in Section 4 of the Plan, increase the total number of shares reserved for the purpose of the Plan;

(b) change the employees or class of employees eligible to participate in the Plan; or

(c) reduce the exercise price for Options and Stock Appreciation Rights by repricing or replacing such Awards.

The Committee may amend the terms of any Award theretofore granted, prospectively or retroactively, but no such amendment shall impair the rights of any Participant without his consent. Except as provided in Section 4 and Section 14(e), the Committee shall not have the authority to cancel any outstanding Option and issue a new Option in its place with a lower exercise price; provided, however, that this sentence shall not prohibit an exchange offer whereby the Company provides certain Participants with an election to cancel an outstanding Option and receive a grant of a new Option at a future date if such exchange offer only occurs with shareowner approval.

SECTION 14. GENERAL PROVISIONS

(a) Unless the Committee determines otherwise at the time the Award is granted, no Award, and no Shares subject to Awards described in Section 10 which have not been issued or as to which any applicable restriction, performance or deferral period has not lapsed, may be sold, assigned, transferred, pledged or otherwise encumbered, except by will or by the laws of descent and distribution and all Awards shall be exercisable, during the Participant's lifetime, only by the Participant or, if permissible under applicable law, by the Participant's guardian or legal representative; provided that, if so determined by the Committee, a Participant may, in the manner established by the Committee, designate a beneficiary to exercise the rights of the Participant with respect to any Award upon the death of the Participant.

(b) The term of each Award shall be for such period of months or years from the date of its grant as may be determined by the Committee; provided that in no event shall the term of any Option or any Stock Appreciation Right related to any Option exceed a period of seven (7) years from the date of its grant.

(c) No Employee or Participant shall have any claim to be granted any Award under the Plan and there is no obligation for uniformity of treatment of Employees or Participants under the Plan.

(d) The prospective recipient of any Award under the Plan shall not, with respect to such Award, be deemed to have become a Participant, or to have any rights with respect to such Award, until and unless such recipient shall have complied with the then applicable terms and conditions.

(e) Except as provided in Section 12, the Committee shall be authorized to make adjustments in Performance Award criteria or in the terms and conditions of other Awards in recognition of unusual or nonrecurring events affecting the Company or its financial statements, or changes in applicable laws, regulations or accounting principles. The Committee may correct any defect, supply any omission or reconcile any inconsistency in the Plan or any Award in the manner and to the extent it shall deem desirable. In the event the Company shall assume outstanding employee benefit awards or the right or obligation to make future such awards in connection with the acquisition of another corporation or business entity, the Committee may, in its discretion, make such adjustments in the terms of Awards under the Plan as it shall deem appropriate.

(f) Subject to Section 13, the Committee shall have full power and authority to determine whether, to what extent and under what circumstances any Award shall be canceled or suspended. In particular, but without limitation, all outstanding Awards to any Participant shall be canceled if the Participant, without the consent of the Committee, while employed by the Company or after termination of such employment, engages in any activity which is in competition with the Company, as determined by the Committee, one or more Officers of the Company or a committee of Officers of the Company to whom the authority to make such determination is delegated by the Committee. The Committee shall have the discretion with respect to any Award granted under this Plan to establish, upon its grant, conditions under which (i) the Award may be subsequently forfeited, cancelled, rescinded, suspended, withheld or otherwise limited or restricted; or (ii) the gains that are realized by the grantee in connection with an Award or the exercise of an Award may be recovered; provided, however, that such conditions and their consequences are: (a) clearly set forth in the Award Agreement or other grant document; and (b) comply with applicable laws. These conditions may include, without limitation, actions by the Participant which constitute a conflict of interest with the Company, are prejudicial to the Company's interests, or are in violation of any non-compete agreement or obligation, any confidentiality agreement or obligation, the Company's applicable policies, or the Participant's terms and conditions of employment.

(g) All certificates for Shares delivered under the Plan pursuant to any Award shall be subject to such stock-transfer orders and other restrictions as the Committee may deem advisable under the rules, regulations, and other requirements of the Securities and Exchange Commission, any stock exchange upon which the Shares are then listed, and any applicable Federal or state securities law, and the Committee may cause a legend or legends to be put on any such certificates to make appropriate reference to such restrictions.

(h) Subject to the provisions of this Plan and any Award Agreement, the recipient of an Award (including, without limitation, any deferred Award) may, if so determined by the Committee, be entitled to receive, currently or on a deferred basis, interest or dividends, or interest or dividend equivalents, with respect to the number of Shares covered by the Award, as determined by the Committee, in its sole discretion, and the Committee may provide that such amounts (if any) shall be deemed to have been reinvested in additional Shares or otherwise reinvested.

(i) Except as otherwise required in any applicable Award Agreement or by the terms of the Plan, recipients of Awards under the Plan shall not be required to make any payment or provide consideration other than the rendering of services.

(j) [Intentionally omitted]

(k) The Committee is authorized to establish procedures pursuant to which the payment of any Award may be deferred.

(l) The maximum value of the property, including cash, that may be paid or distributed to any Participant pursuant to grants of Performance Units and/or Other Stock Unit Awards or any other Award (paid or payable in cash or other property) that are valued with reference to property other than Shares made in any one calendar year is $10,000,000.

(m) The Company is authorized to withhold from any Award granted or payment due under the Plan the amount of withholding taxes due in respect of an Award or payment hereunder and to take such other action as may be necessary in the opinion of the Company to satisfy all obligations for the payment of such taxes. The Committee shall be authorized to establish procedures for election by Participants to satisfy such withholding taxes by delivery of, or directing the Company to retain, Shares, and will not issue Shares or Awards until such tax obligations have been satisfied.

(n) Nothing contained in this Plan shall prevent the Board of Directors from adopting other or additional compensation arrangements, subject to shareowner approval if such approval is otherwise required; and such arrangements may be either generally applicable or applicable only in specific cases.

(o) The validity, construction, and effect of the Plan and any rules and regulations relating to the Plan shall be determined in accordance with the laws of the State of Delaware and applicable Federal law.

(p) If any provision of this Plan is or becomes or is deemed invalid, illegal or unenforceable in any jurisdiction, or would disqualify the Plan or any Award under any law deemed applicable by the Committee, such provision shall be construed or deemed amended to conform to applicable laws or if it cannot be construed or deemed amended without, in the determination of the Committee, materially altering the intent of the Plan, it shall be stricken and the remainder of the Plan shall remain in full force and effect.

(q) Awards may be granted to Employees who are foreign nationals or employed outside the United States, or both, on such terms and conditions different from those specified in the Plan as may, in the judgment of the Committee, be necessary or desirable in order to recognize differences in local law or tax policy. The Committee also may impose conditions on the exercise or vesting of Awards in order to minimize the Company's obligation with respect to tax equalization for Employees on assignments outside their home country.

IN WITNESS WHEREOF, the Company has caused this Plan, which was approved by the Board of Directors on November 25, 2002, to be executed effective the 19th day of February, 2003.

For Lucent Technologies Inc.

By: /s/ Pamela O. Kimmet

_____

Pamela O. Kimmet, Senior Vice President, Human Resources

Attest: /s/ Richard J. Rawson

_____

Richard J. Rawson, Senior Vice President, General Counsel and Secretary

Footnotes

[1] Pages E-12 and E-13 of Exhibit 10(ii) of Jefferson Pilot form 10-K filed with the Securities and Exchange Commission, March 15, 2004.

[2] Pages 21 and 22, American Express proxy statement, filed with the Securities and Exchange Commission, March 22, 2006.

[3] Exhibit 10.2 to Lucent Technologies Form 8-K filed with the Securities and Exchange Commission, April 11, 2003.

Chapter 6

Stock Grants and Options

Introduction

Stock-based compensation, like bonuses, is a variable, or at-risk, form of compensation, although the risk to which the executive is subject depends upon the type of compensation. Stock-based compensation normally falls into one of two broad categories; stock options/stock appreciation rights, or stock grants. While the ultimate value of either is based upon stock price performance after the date of grant, the payoffs and risks are different. For example, when Ford Motor Co. hired Alan Mulally as president and CEO, it granted him two types of options, as well as restricted stock units, as follows:

Effective Sept. 1, 2006, the Company granted Mr. Mulally (i) 3,000,000 10-year nonqualified options that vest 33% one year after the grant date, 33% two years after the grant date and 34% three years after the grant date and (ii) 1,000,000 five year nonqualified performance-based options that vest based on the regular way trading closing price of Ford common stock on the New York Stock Exchange reaching certain thresholds that are maintained for a period of at least 30 consecutive trading days as follows: 250,000 options vest after Ford common stock closes at least $15 per share for such a period, an additional 250,000 options vest after Ford common stock closes at least $20 per share for such a period, an additional 250,000 options vest after Ford common stock closes at least $25 per share for such a period and an additional 250,000 options vest after Ford common stock closes at least $30 per share for such a period. All of the options granted to Mr. Mulally have an option price equal to the grant date's current fair market value of $8.28/share (based on the average of the high and low trading price on the New York Stock Exchange on the grant date).

In addition, effective Sept. 1, 2006, the Company granted Mr. Mulally 600,000 restricted stock units. The units vest as to 200,000 units one year after the grant date, 200,000 units two years after the grant date and 200,000 units three years after the grant date. Dividend equivalent payments will be made in cash until the restrictions lapse. When the restrictions lapse, the units will be valued based on the closing price of Ford common stock on the New York Stock Exchange on the date of lapse and paid out in cash as soon as practicable thereafter.[1]

Several details are worth discussing. First, Mulally received 4 million nonqualified stock options, which as discussed below, mean that the options do not qualify for preferential tax treatment. Three million of these options vest based upon time, meaning that they vest over the three years following grant regardless of performance. The other 1 million vests based upon Ford's stock price performance, meaning that if Ford's stock price does not hit the thresholds put forth in the contract, the options will be forfeited. All of the options were issued with an exercise price equal to the market price on the date of grant, $8.28, consequently the stock price has to increase beyond this level for Mulally to profit from them.

In contrast, the 600,000 restricted stock units (RSUs), which are not performance based and vest over three years, are valuable to Mulally as long as Ford's stock price is greater than zero. While many companies issue restricted stock, under which an employee owns shares of stock upon vesting, Ford issued restricted stock units, under which Mulally will receive the value of the underlying shares in cash as soon as the restricted stock units vest. In addition, for a public company, the RSUs are accounted for as deferred compensation representing an underfunded promise to pay.

Another difference between the options and the restricted stock units is that while an option can be outstanding for up to 10 years (five years with regard to the performance-based options), the restricted stock units effectively have a life, and thus an incentive/retentive value for only one, two or three years. That is, while Mulally may hold on to his options for as long as 10 years before exercising, the restricted stock units are cashed in as soon as they vest. In addition, for a public company, the RSUs are accounted for as deferred compensation representing an underfunded promise to pay.

Appendix 6-1 provides an example of an incentive stock option agreement, that of Amerigroup Corp., including the form completed by the company when granting the option/SAR and the form the employee is required to complete when exercising. It is obvious the agreement is a legal document. The agreement, when complete, provides the number of options granted; the option term; the conditions under which the employee can exercise; the method(s) of payment allowable; and the effect of termination, including change in control. This agreement is for a "tax-qualified option," which will be discussed below, so paragraph 24 outlines some of the conditions the employee must meet to retain the tax-preferential treatment.

Types of Equity Compensation

As illustrated previously with respect to Mulally, equity compensation can take many forms. That is, while the two main categories are stock options and restricted stock, even within those categories there are many variations from which to choose. Thus, while a number of variations will be discussed below, given the nearly limitless permutations, not all can be discussed.

Stock Options/Stock Appreciation Rights

Stock options allow their holder to purchase one or more shares of stock at a fixed "exercise" price over a fixed period of time. That period, however, does not necessarily start on the date the options are granted to the executive. While some options vest immediately, most of the time the executive does not have the right to exercise some or all of the options until a specified time period has passed or performance goal has been met. At Motorola, for example, options vest 25 percent per year over a four-year period:

> On May 3, 2005, the Committee granted 37.7 million stock options to approximately 24,000 employees as part of the Company's annual award of stock options. These options vest and become exercisable in four equal annual installments, with the first installment vesting on May 3, 2006.[2]

In contrast, at Coca-Cola Enterprises Inc., certain senior-management options vest with the achievement of performance goals. The following extract pertains to options granted to John Brock, president and CEO.

> Filer has been awarded an initial grant of 900,000 stock options, which will become exercisable only upon the satisfaction of both a graduated, three-year service condition and performance conditions. Specifically, one-half of the options will become exercisable only if the trading price of the Company's stock increases by 25% and the other one-half of the options will become exercisable only if the trading price of the Company's stock increases by 50%.[3]

The options, once vested, can then be exercised until they expire. Most options expire over periods no longer than 10 years from the date of grant, as illustrated by the following extract from Merck's proxy statement:[4]

Table 6-1:

Option/SAR Grants In Last Fiscal Year

Name	Date of Grant	Expiration Date
Richard T. Clark	2/25/05	2/24/15
	5/05/05	5/04/15
Raymond V. Gilmartin	2/25/05	2/24/15
Judy C. Lewent	2/25/05	2/24/15
Peter S. Kim	2/25/05	2/24/15
Per Wold-Olsen	2/25/05	2/24/15
Kenneth C. Frazier	2/25/05	2/24/15

When the stock price increases between the time of grant and the time of vesting (a.k.a., the vesting period), the effect is to tie the employee to the corporation, as the employee would forfeit the increase in value if he or she leaves before the option has vested. Of course, there is never any assurance an employee will not leave before the option vests. The raise offered by the new employer may be more than sufficient to make up for value of the unvested options. Alternatively, as noted in Chapter 3, if the new employer wants the executive badly enough, it can reimburse the executive for the value of the unvested options. The example presented in Chapter 3 was that of the hiring of James McNerney by Boeing. Another example is that of Alan Mulally being hired away from Boeing by the Ford Motor Co.

> As part of the hiring arrangement, the Company also agreed to pay Mr. Mulally, no later than Sept. 15, 2006, $7,500,000 as a hiring bonus and $11,000,000 as an offset for forfeited performance and stock option awards at his former employer.[5]

At any time prior to exercise, the value of an option is comprised of its intrinsic and time values (see Appendix 6-3). The intrinsic value of the option is the excess of the current market price of the shares over the exercise price at any point in time. The time value of the option is the value attached to the potential increase in the stock price over the remaining life of the option. While all options have a positive value at the date of grant (because of the time value), ultimately they will only prove profitable to the executive if the corporation's share price is greater than the exercise price at the exercise date. Otherwise they will expire unexercised. Because the exercise price is normally set at the share price on the date of grant,[6] the ultimate value of the option depends upon the performance of a corporation's share price subsequent to the date of grant. That is, options can be extremely valuable when the share price rises dramatically, but can also expire worthless if the share price declines.[7] In some cases, though, the corporation can guarantee a payoff. When Joseph Galli took the position of president at Amazon.com, Amazon effectively guaranteed him a minimum profit of $20 million over the subsequent 10 years by promising to make up the difference via a special bonus payment.[8]

Table 6-2 shows that the percentage of CEOs that hold options on their employer's common stock has increased over time, from a low of 72 percent in 1992 to a high of 95 percent at the end of 2002/2003, dropping slightly to 93 percent in 2005. In contrast, restricted shares are only held by 47 percent of CEOs in 2005, but that is a major increase from the 33 percent who held restricted shares only two years earlier. To some extent these numbers parallel those in Table 2-2, which show the yearly flow and growth in usage over time of options and restricted shares. The table also shows some of the risk associated with options. That is, for some CEOs, even though they have options, all of their options have exercise prices in excess

Table 6-2:
Status of Equity Compensation Held by CEOs

Year	Percentage of CEOs with Options	Percentage of CEOs with In-the-Money Options	Percentage of CEOs Holding Restricted Shares
1992	72.28	68.13	32.12
1993	84.71	79.42	33.94
1994	86.18	75.79	29.98
1995	86.98	79.84	28.32
1996	89.22	80.92	30.1
1997	90.36	82.99	29.68
1998	90.72	79.76	29.06
1999	91.16	78.22	27.03
2000	91.52	77.85	26.12
2001	93.72	84.06	28.38
2002	94.74	77.18	29.21
2003	95.02	88.33	32.94
2004	93.97	90.01	39.72
2005	93.34	87.49	46.63

Note: Calculations in this table are based upon data contained in the April 2006 version of Standard & Poor's ExecuComp.

of the current market price and hence are referred to as "out of the money." This percentage ranges from 4 percent in 2004 to 19 percent in 2002. Of course, while these options currently have no intrinsic value (cannot be exercised profitably), the possibility exists that at some point prior to their expiration they will be valuable.

Stock appreciation rights are similar to options in their payoff structure, that is, they are only valuable if the stock price increases beyond the exercise price. The difference between stock options and stock appreciation rights relates to the form of the payoff. With stock options, the executive exercises the options by paying cash and, in exchange, receives shares of stock. He or she may then turn around and sell those shares at the current market price, the profit being the difference between the price paid (the exercise price) and the current market price. Alternatively, recognizing that raising cash to pay the exercise price may be a constraint for executives, some corporations grant stock appreciation rights. When the executive elects to exercise the stock appreciation right, the corporation simply pays the executive, in cash and/or shares, the difference between the current market price and the exercise price for the number of stock appreciation rights held. In most cases, stock appreciations rights are granted in tandem with stock options, so that the executive may exercise one or the other depending upon whether he or she wants to receive shares or cash.[9]

Alternative ways around the executive's cash constraint include cashless exercise and payment with previously owned shares. In a cashless exercise, the executive simply calls the program administrator, which would normally be a brokerage firm like Merrill Lynch, and states he or she would like to exercise the options and sell the shares. The administrator would then handle the transaction and deposit the profits, less any transaction costs, in the executive's brokerage account or send a check to the executive. An example of a corporation that allows both cashless exercise (except for Section 16 officers) and payment with shares of stock is DuPont:

> Payment of the option price must be made in cash, through the sale of option shares issued pursuant to the exercise (except for Section 16 officers), or in DuPont common stock, valued at the fair market value (the average of the high and low prices on the NYSE-Composite Transactions Tape) on the date of exercise, or a combination thereof as determined by the Compensation Committee. When payment is made in shares, the optionee must have owned such shares for at least six months.[10]

Stock Grants

Stock grants differ from stock options in that they have no exercise price. Whereas a stock option only has value if the corporation's share price is above the exercise price, a stock grant has value as long as the share price is above zero. Stock grants can be unrestricted or restricted. An example of a restriction imposed upon a stock grant might be that the employee cannot sell the shares until he or she has worked for the corporation for a period of time. For example, General Electric discusses its use of restricted stock units (RSUs), which convert into shares of GE stock with the passage of time:

> RSUs will convert into shares of GE stock only if the individual continues to be employed by GE when the restrictions lapse. During the restricted period, each RSU entitles the recipient to receive quarterly payments from the company equal to the quarterly dividends on one share of GE stock. Restrictions on half of the RSUs granted annually in combination with stock options lapse after three years, and on the other half after five years.[11]

Other restrictions might be based upon performance. For example, PerkinElmer, as described below, conditions the earning of its restricted stock on earnings per share in the three years subsequent to the grant—if the targets are not met, the shares are forfeited:

> Performance-contingent restricted stock: In 2005, all of the executive officers named in the Summary Compensation Table in this proxy statement received awards of performance-contingent restricted stock. For the three-year performance period beginning in 2005, the vesting of these restricted shares is linked to three annual EPS targets. The shares vest upon achievement of the EPS goals (one-third of the shares vest upon achievement of each of the three increasing EPS goals) over a performance period that began on Jan. 1, 2005, and ends Dec. 31, 2007. If performance conditions are not met on or before Dec. 31, 2007, unvested shares are forfeited.[12]

The risk of forfeiture is real. Recall the example from Chapter 2 of John T. Cahill, chairman and CEO of the Pepsi Bottling Group, who forfeited restricted shares worth $3,626,182.

Effect on Executive Retention

As with other forms of compensation, stock options and grants can be used to attract and retain employees (see Balsam and Miharjo 2007), an attraction that works well when stock prices are increasing, but not as well when they are decreasing. When stock prices are rising, executives are reluctant to leave, as if by departing they leave some valuable but unexercisable options (options that have not yet vested) or restricted shares behind. Viewed as a way to retain key people, the vesting period then becomes an important factor. As long as the options/shares are unvested, those individuals would suffer a monetary loss when leaving the corporation.[13] Of course if vesting is too far in the future, executives may leave for a quicker payoff elsewhere. Thus the vesting period is a key factor that must be chosen with care. Further, if those options are "under water," that is the exercise price is greater than the current market price, there is little monetary bond, and thus employees are more willing to leave the corporation.

> ... like so many e-tailers, Skymall has seen its stock plunge since the end of last year, leaving Mr. Goldman with options priced at $16 and the stock trading at under $10. So he did what an increasing number of others in his shoes are doing: He quit ...[14]

Use of Stock Options and Grants in the Compensation Package

As shown in Chapter 2, stock options and grants are a major component of the CEO compensation package, although as shown in Table 2-2, stock options are used much more frequently, even with the recent shift to increased usage of restricted stock. Table 2-2 shows that both stock options and stock grants are awarded with increasing frequency, as the proportion of firms awarding stock options increased from 58 percent in 1992 to 77 percent in 2001 before dropping to 69 percent in 2005, while the percentage of firms making stock grants increased from 20 percent in 1992 to 45 percent in 2005, with most of that increase occurring since 2002. Table 2-5 shows the proportion of compensation comprised of stock options and stock grants also has increased, with the percentage of compensation consisting of stock options increasing from a mean (median) of 21 (18) percent in 1992 to 42 (43) percent in 2001 before declining to 28(24) percent in 2005, and that of stock grants increasing from a mean of 5 percent in 1992 to 14 percent in 2005, with most of that increase coming since 2002.[15] If we combine the percentages, we see that equity compensation increased from a mean of 26 percent in 1992 to 42 percent in 2005. Table 2-8 shows the amounts involved. For example, the value of stock options granted increased from a mean (median) of $703,729 ($304,110) in 1992 to $1,870,255 ($685,749) in 2005. The mean value of stock grants is much lower, 1,054,171, in 2005, but has increased dramatically from a mean value of $215,168 in 1992.[16] Stock options and grants have thus been increasing in frequency (Table 2-2), as a proportion of the compensation package (Table 2-5) and in amount (Table 2-8).

Table 6-3 shows the percentage change in the value of stock options and grants awarded to CEOs that have been with the same corporation (and in the same position) for at least two years. Table 6-3 and Figure 6-1 (see page 184) show that from 1996 to 2001, the value of stock option grants grew at a healthy rate, whereas since 2001 they have generally become smaller. In contrast, Table 6-4 on page 185 and Figure 6-2 on page 186 show that beginning in 2002 and accelerating in 2003, the value of restricted stock grants grew at a rapid clip. Consequently, Tables 6-3 and 6-4 confirm the previous evidence that starting in 2002, executive compensation began to shift from options to restricted shares.

Incentives

More than other forms of compensation, stock compensation provides employees

Table 6-3:
Percentage Change in Value of Stock Option Grants for CEOs with Same Company for Consecutive Years
(for Companies Making Stock Option Grants in at Least One of the Years)

Year	Mean Percentage Change Value of Stock Option Grants	Median Percentage Change Value of Stock Option Grants	Average Change in Consumer Price Index CPI-U
1993	-13.61	-53.74	2.99%
1994	-1.45	1.59	2.56%
1995	-3.88	-13.92	2.83%
1996	23.31	37.59	2.95%
1997	18.61	21.17	2.29%
1998	22.74	30.92	1.56%
1999	26.21	42.26	2.21%
2000	16.63	15.32	3.36%
2001	16.18	19.54	2.85%
2002	3.29	-1.65	1.58%
2003	-7.28	-14.73	2.28%
2004	7.00	7.08	2.66%
2005	0.43	-4.23	3.39%

Calculations in this table are based upon data contained in the April 2006 version of Standard & Poor's ExecuComp and the Consumer Price Index—All Urban Consumers, as found on the Bureau of Labor Statistics Web site.

Figure 6-1:

Growth in Value of Stock Option Granted Versus Growth in CPI

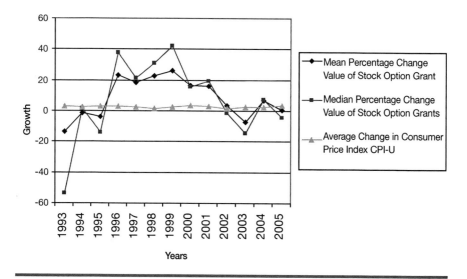

with incentives to increase shareholder value. This is because when executives own shares or options on shares, executive wealth increases/decreases with shareholder wealth. Thus, stock compensation (and ownership) aligns the interests of employees with shareholders (see for example Jensen and Meckling 1976, Murphy 1985, Abowd 1990, Jensen and Murphy 1990a and b, and Murphy 1998). A potential downside of options is that while they provide the incentive to increase stock price, executives may have the incentive to manipulate stock price for short-term gain (for example, they delay disclosing good news until after grant, or disclosing bad news until after exercise). Academics have investigated this possibility. Examining the timing of option grants, Yermack (1997) finds "CEOs receive stock option awards shortly before favorable corporate news," while Chauvin and Shenoy (2001) find an abnormal decrease in stock prices during the 10 days prior to option grants. Examining the timing of option exercise, Huddart and Lang (2000) find the level of option exercise inversely related to future stock returns, whereas Carpenter and Remmers (2001) find little evidence of option exercise prior to adverse stock price performance, only finding "negative stock price performance only after exercise by top managers at small firms." Evidence has also shown that executives with an equity stake, e.g., stock options, manage accounting numbers to shore up stock prices (see, for example, Bartov and Mohanram 2004, Bergstresser and Philippon 2006, Burns and Kedia 2006, Cheng and Warfield

Table 6-4:

Percentage Change in Value of Restricted Stock Grants for CEOs with Same Company for Consecutive Years

(For Companies making Restricted Stock Grants in at Least One of the Years)

Year	Mean Percentage Change Value of Restricted Stock Grants	Median Percentage Change Value of Restricted Stock Grants	Average Change in Consumer Price Index CPI-U
1993	-28.64	-100.00	2.99%
1994	-32.99	-100.00	2.56%
1995	-19.22	-51.97	2.83%
1996	6.90	15.32	2.95%
1997	6.91	14.04	2.29%
1998	4.76	7.89	1.56%
1999	-3.17	-2.99	2.21%
2000	-3.16	-11.69	3.36%
2001	5.32	13.08	2.85%
2002	13.88	18.02	1.58%
2003	26.57	57.36	2.28%
2004	31.30	58.98	2.66%
2005	27.72	32.26	3.39%

Note: Calculations in this table are based upon data contained in the April 2006 version of Standard & Poor's ExecuComp and the Consumer Price Index—All Urban Consumers, as found on the Bureau of Labor Statistics Web site.

2005). Most recently Lie (2005) and Heron and Lie (2006a & b) provide evidence consistent with companies retroactively selecting the grant dates of their options, i.e., backdating, to minimize the exercise prices of their options.

Given the riskiness of stock-based compensation, the amount of stock-based compensation included in the compensation package will affect the type of executives attracted to the corporation. In particular, a corporation with a large proportion of stock in its compensation package is more likely to attract executives with low-risk aversion.

Effect on Incentives to Take Risk

Agrawal and Mandelker (1987) find that variance-increasing investments are more likely to be made by managers with larger holdings of common stock and options. However, including stock in the compensation package may not provide increased

Figure 6-2:

Growth in Value of Stock Grants Versus Growth in CPI

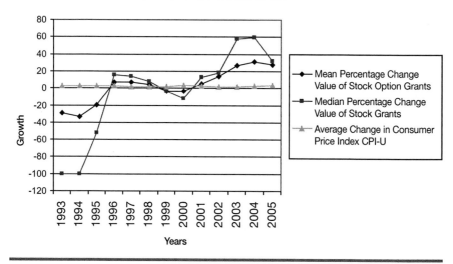

incentive to take risk (also see following discussion with respect to in-the-money options). Rather, stock options, because their ex-ante value increases with risk, provides managers with incentives to take risk. This can be illustrated with the following simple example. The expected share price of corporation A one year from now follows the following probability distribution:

Probability	Share Price
50 percent	$100
50 percent	$50

The corporation has the option to make a risky investment that will alter the above distribution as follows:

Probability	Share Price
50 percent	$180
50 percent	$20

Without the investment, the expected value of a share is $75 (50 percent of $50 plus 50 percent of $100); with the investment, the expected value increases to $100 (50 percent of $20 plus 50 percent of $180). A risk-averse executive, fearing the repercussions of a bad outcome, that is getting fired, might be unwilling to take the investment. However, if the executive were awarded options with an exercise price of $75, his or her incentive would change. Without the investment, the expected value of the options would be $12.50 (50 percent of $25, the value of the option if the share price is $100; the option is worthless if share price is $50). With the investment, the expected value of the options would increase to $52.50 (50 percent of $105, the value of the option if the share price is $180; the option is worthless if share price is $20). The effect of the options is to provide executives with the incentive to take risks.

While it is generally assumed that options provide incentives for managers to take risks (DeFusco et al. 1990), this may not be true in all situations (Wiseman and Gomez-Mejia 1998). While true for options out-of-the-money (exercise price greater than current market price) and at-the-money (exercise price equal to current market price), it is not necessarily true for options in the money. If an option is in the money, the executive may become risk averse, in that he or she has something to lose if the stock price decreases. This is also true with stock grants, as the underdiversified manager will not want to take as much risk as diversified shareholders would like. Thus, the best way to counter managers' risk aversion is to make sure the bulk of their equity incentives comes from holding at-the-money or out-of-the-money options, a situation that can be controlled with reload options, which will be discussed later in this chapter.

Effect of Stock Compensation on Ownership

Incentive effects differ across types of stock compensation. First, consider options, the various choices that have to be made and the effects of those choices on incentives. The corporation can grant, for tax purposes, qualified or nonqualified options. With qualified options, the executive does not pay taxes upon exercise of the option (with a nonqualified option the executive does), but rather pays taxes upon sale of the shares acquired upon exercise. Further, assuming he or she held the shares for one year (or more), the gain is taxed at capital gains rather than ordinary income rates. Deferral of taxability with a tax-qualified option provides incentive, similar to the "lock-in effect," to retain shares. In contrast, with a nonqualified option, there is no tax incentive to retain shares, and thus for liquidity and diversification purposes, the executive may sell shares immediately upon exercise. Empirical and anecdotal evidence suggests that employees generally sell shares upon exercise, although no research has looked at whether this is affected by the tax status of the option. Huddart (1994) and Gilles (1999) report that more than 90 percent of shares received from exercising options are sold immediately. As noted above, some corporations even facilitate this turnover by setting up "cashless exercise" programs with investment bankers. Yet these corporations often state that encouraging employee ownership is one of the goals of their option programs. And more companies are requiring executives to hold shares after exercise. Two examples are Wells Fargo and Walt Disney. Wells Fargo requires:

each executive officer is expected to retain shares of the Company's common stock equal to at least 50% of the after-tax profit shares (assuming a 50% tax rate) acquired through option exercises. The number of shares expected to be owned under these guidelines continues to increase each time an executive officer exercises a stock option. The Chief Executive Officer and each other executive officer named in the Summary Compensation Table have either satisfied or exceeded these ownership guidelines.[17]

While Disney states:

for all stock option grants made beginning in 2005, the executives are required, as long as they remain employed by the Company, to retain ownership of shares representing at least 75% of the after-tax gain realized (100% in the case of the Chief Executive Officer) upon exercise of such options for a minimum of 12 months.[18]

Reload options are options with terms that specify that if they are exercised prior to their stated date of expiration, it will result in the grant of replacement options. Reload options may be used to encourage ownership by employees. Alternatively, reload options allow firms to combat the risk aversion that can result from executives having too many in-the-money options. That is, by removing one of the disincentives an executive has for exercising the option, the loss of the remaining time-value component, the reload provision encourages early exercise. If the underdiversified executive exercises the option, sells the shares and gets new at-the-money options, the options no longer provide a disincentive to take risk. However, if ownership has increased, the shares held may provide a disincentive to take risk. Consider the following from the Tribune Co. (which refers to them as replacement options):

To encourage stock ownership by executives and other key employees, replacement stock options ("replacement options") may be granted simultaneously with the exercise of existing stock options. Replacement options are intended to encourage executives and other key employees to exercise a stock option earlier than might otherwise occur, thus resulting in increased share ownership. Replacement options may be granted when an executive or other key employee exercises an option by surrendering currently owned shares to purchase the shares subject to the option as well as to satisfy related tax withholding obligations. Replacement options will only be granted if at the time of exercise the closing price of Tribune stock exceeds the option exercise price by a predetermined amount. Replacement options are subject to the same terms and conditions as the original options, including the expiration date, except that the option price of a replacement option is the fair market value on the date of its grant rather than the option price of the original option and replacement options do not become exercisable until one year after grant. The grant of replacement options does not result in an increase in the total combined number of shares and options held by an employee. As shown in the table on page 25, Mr. FitzSimons received replacement options during 2004.[19]

While the above passage explicitly states, perhaps for political purposes, that the reload provision exists to encourage share ownership, nothing is mentioned about a requirement that the executive hold onto the shares obtained upon exercise. Without such a requirement, the exercise of the option may not lead to increased share ownership, as noted by Ofek and Yermack (2000). To illustrate, in 2004, Dennis J. FitzSimons, chairman, CEO and president of Tribune, exercised a total of 294,989 options, realizing a profit of $3,381,463,[20] and a total of 255,637 replacement options.[21] As noted below, the number of shares received by FitzSimons was substantially lower:

Represents aggregate number of shares underlying options exercised. The number of shares of Tribune common stock acquired upon the exercise of options in 2004 for each of the above officers was offset by the number of existing or newly acquired shares of Tribune common stock the officer used to pay the exercise price and/or the applicable withholding tax. The net number of shares of Tribune common stock actually acquired by each of the above officers as a result of option exercises in 2004 was as follows: Mr. FitzSimons, 39,352 shares; ...[22]

This is to be expected, however, as 294,989 (number of options exercised/shares received) less 255,637 (replacement options issued for shares used to pay exercise price) is 39,352. Yet, a comparison of shares held as of March 1, 2004, which was 483,054,[23] and March 15, 2005, which was 484,930,[24] shows that FitzSimons did not hold on to most of those 39,352 shares. Thus the reload option did not appear to increase ownership in this case.

Choices the Corporation Must Make in Granting Stock Compensation

Other choices the corporation makes are the vesting period, the exercise price, the number of options or shares and, of course, whether the grant should take the form of options or shares. Each affects the incentives of the executive to remain with the corporation, expend effort and/or take risks.

Vesting Period

As discussed above, the choice of, or rather, the use of, a vesting period provides executives with incentive to remain with the corporation until the options and/or shares are vested. That is, Balsam et al. (2007) shows that voluntary turnover increases after options vest, while Balsam and Miharjo (2007) show the magnitude of unvested options and shares is inversely associated with voluntary executive turnover. Consequently, increasing the vesting period might reduce executive turnover. While the typical vesting period for options is four years or 25 percent per year over a four-year period (see Kole 1997), some companies have begun using extended vesting periods. For example, as discussed below, at Comcast no options vest until two years have passed, and some options remain unvested until 9.5 years have passed.

> Options granted in 2005 become exercisable at the rate of 30% of the shares covered thereby on the second anniversary of the date of grant, another 15% on each of the third, fourth and fifth anniversaries of the date of grant, another 5% on each of the sixth through ninth anniversaries of the date of grant and 5% six months prior to the tenth anniversary of the date of grant.[25]

At Boston Scientific, as explained below, executives have to wait two years before they may exercise any options and have to wait six years from the date of grant until all options are exercisable.

> On July 1, 2005, we granted options to purchase shares of common stock to certain of our key employees, including the Named Officers listed above. These options were granted at the fair market value on the date of grant and vest over five years in equal annual installments beginning on July 1, 2007, the second anniversary of the date of grant.[26]

Cisco requires its president and CEO, John Chambers, to work seven years before his most recent grant can be vested.

> The option granted to Mr. Chambers has a term of nine years measured from the grant date and, if vested, will remain exercisable for the full term

even after his cessation of service except in limited circumstances. The option will vest and become exercisable upon Mr. Chambers' completion of seven years of service from the grant date.[27]

Exercise Price

The choice of exercise price affects the employee's incentives, including risk preferences. If it is set too low relative to the current market price, and hence is in the money, the underdiversified employee becomes risk averse, unwilling to take risks. If set too high, again relative to the current market price, the probability of profiting from the option decreases, as does the employee's incentive to work hard to increase the stock price. Also as noted above, if the options are out of the money, they have no retentive effect. For these and other financial reasons detailed below, the vast majority of options have traditionally been granted with the exercise price equal to the current market price, which Hall and Murphy (2000) show provide maximum pay for performance incentives. However, it is possible that market movements, rather than a standout performance by the company, could result in substantial and unmerited rewards for executives that actually underperform the market. Consider the following example:

On Jan. 1, 2010, and each year thereafter, the CEO of XYZ Corp. is granted options, exercisable over 10 years, to purchase 1 million shares at the current market price on the date of grant. The exercise price of the grants fluctuates with the market price, which was $35 on Jan. 1, 2010, $20 on Jan. 1, 2011, $30 on Jan. 1, 2012, and $40 on Jan. 1, 2013. As of Jan. 1, 2013, the CEO has options to purchase 4 million shares with an intrinsic value of $35 million. In contrast, the shareholder who owned the shares on Jan. 1, 2010, earned appreciation of more than 14 percent on those shares, less than he or she could have earned with U.S. Treasury Securities.

While this is a fictional example, truth can sometimes be stranger than fiction. In its proxy statement filed with the Securities and Exchange Commission on March 12, 2001, Apple Computer reported that it had granted its CEO, Steven Jobs, 20 million options in January of the previous year, and that if its share price rose at a rate of 5 percent per year, at the end of the options term, those options would be worth $548,317,503. Of course, if its share price increased by 5 percent per year, Apple stockholders might have preferred purchasing 30-year U.S. Treasury Bonds that offered a 6.34-percent yield risk-free at that point in time.

The use of Jobs as an example is purely for illustrative purposes and not meant as a comment on either his performance or pay. Over the approximately six-and-two-thirds years (at the time of writing) since the above grant, Apple Computer's share price has increased from a split adjusted $21.80 (closing price Jan. 10, 2000) to $89.07 (closing price Feb. 23, 2007), a total return of 309 percent, or about 17 percent per year on an annual basis. For comparison purposes, over the same time period the NASDAQ composite index dropped from 4,049.67 to 2,515.10. So Apple and Jobs have turned in an outstanding performance over that time period. Had he held onto the 20 million options, which would now be 40 million options post split, they would be worth almost $2.7 billion.

However, the story does not end there. In March 2003, Jobs voluntarily cancelled all of his options and the board gave him 5 million shares of restricted stock. During March 2003, the share price ranged from $14.14 to $15.01, far below the exercise price of the shares. So Jobs availed himself of an opportunity to cancel his underwater stock options and in return receive restricted shares (three-year vesting period) with a grant date value of $74,750,000. Those shares are worth significantly more today, about $900 million taking into account the subsequent split and current share price of $89.07, but substantially less than the $2.7 billion he would have had, had he held on to his options.

From a design/public policy standpoint, this case yields two issues. One, by setting the exercise price equal to the market price on the date of grant, which was a mega-grant by any stretch of the imagination, the executive had the potential for a substantial payout even if the stock price performance was mediocre. The second was allowing the executive the ability to convert those options into restricted shares when it looked like they would not be profitable at all.

There are two possible solutions to these issues—set the exercise price higher than the market price at the date of grant or adjust the exercise price with movements in an underlying market index. An example of the former is Micrel, which on March 20, 2006, granted options to its president and CEO, Raymond Zinn, with an exercise price of $16.21,[28] a more than 20-percent premium to its closing stock price of $13.18. An example of the latter is Level 3 Communications, which as described below, requires its share price to outperform the S&P 500 index before the executive can profitably exercise his or her option.

> Level 3's long-term incentive program has historically consisted of awards of Outperform Stock Options (OSOs), which are an innovative stock-indexed equity-based long term compensation vehicle. OSOs are designed to provide executives with an incentive to maximize stockholder value and to reward executives only when the price of the company's common stock outperforms the S&P 500 Index between the date of grant and the date that the OSO is exercised.[29]

While the former, i.e., issuing options at a premium to the market does mitigate the ability of the executive to profit from mediocre performance, it does not avoid the second issue, where the firm decides to either reprice or exchange its options for restricted shares because of a down market. The latter, indexing the options to a market index, takes care of both, i.e., ensures that the executive has to outperform the market to get a payout and protects the executive from downward movements in market indices.

Grant Size

The number of options granted can also affect the employee's incentives. If the grant is large enough, that is, a "mega-grant," even if the stock price increases very little, the executive can become very rich. Thus the executive, while wanting to increase the stock price, does not necessarily want to take the risks necessary to maximize shareholder wealth.

Options Versus Shares

The biggest choice, perhaps, is between stock options and stock grants. Grants can be considered options with a zero exercise price, with the restriction period being analogous to the vesting period. Both provide incentive for the executive to remain with the corporation, but as noted previously have vastly different effects on the executive's incentive to take risk (see, for example, Guay 1999), in that while options may make the executive more willing to take risk, stock grants will make the executive less willing to take risks.

Stock grants have been increasing in frequency and amount, in part due to the expectation of and promulgation of Statement of Financial Accounting Standards 123(revised), which required that options be expensed, but probably more so due to the market downturn observed starting in March 2000. Grants can be restricted or unrestricted. If restricted, the restrictions either expire with the passage of time or the achievement of performance goals. While both types of restrictions encourage the executive to remain with the corporation, each provides different incentives. If the restrictions expire with the passage of time, the executive need only concern himself or herself with remaining employed until those restrictions expire.[30] In contrast, if the restrictions only expire with the achievement of performance goals, the executive needs to work toward achievement of those goals. Unrestricted stock grants seemingly do not provide any incentives, however perhaps they (and restricted stock grants) work toward the goal of increasing employee ownership.

In addition to affecting risk preferences, stock options and share grants differentially affect the executives' willingness to pay dividends. Consider the following illustration. An executive holds an option to purchase a share of stock at $75 per share at a time when the shares are trading at $100. The executive is deciding whether to pay a dividend of $10 per share. If the executive decides to pay the dividend, the ex-dividend value of the share will drop to $90 (ignoring taxes and other market imperfections), and the value of the option will drop accordingly. In general, options provide the incentive for the executive not to pay dividends, which is confirmed by academic research showing that corporations where executives hold large numbers of options are likely to pay lower dividends (Lambert et al. 1989, Fenn and Liang 1999). In contrast, if the executive owned shares rather than options, and once again ignoring taxes and other market imperfections, the executive would be indifferent to paying the dividend, as the decrease in value of the share would be offset by an increase in his or her cash holdings. This is true as while most corporations pay dividends on restricted shares, see for example American Express,[31] none are paid on stock options— nor is the exercise price adjusted to recognize the decrease in share value as a result of the payout.

Costs
Dilution
Among the commonalities of stock options and stock grants are that they increase the potential number of outstanding shares, and hence potentially dilute the proportionate ownership of existing shareholders. This so called "dilution" is a major, if not the major, cost of stock option and stock grant programs. The term potential is used as not all options are exercised, nor are all stock grants earned. Some have gone as far to assert, "Option plans are redistributing corporate ownership." (Leonhardt 2000)

Dilution has also received significant attention from the popular press. A 2000 BusinessWeek article included the following passage pertaining to the enormous amount of options granted to Linda Wachner, the then-president, CEO and chairman of the board of Warnaco:

> All told, Wachner has received stock options over the last nine years that could give her ownership of a phenomenal 21% of outstanding shares.[32]

As illustrated by Table 6-5, this potential dilution, that is, the number of options granted, has increased over time, ranging from a mean (median) of

3,565,191 (1,561,849) in 1992 to a high of 38,336,771 (6,190,150) in 2000 before dropping to 17,046,184 (5,345,413) in 2005.[33] This decrease in recent years has in part or in whole been offset by an increase in the number of restricted shares granted. However, as explained in note 33, the number of restricted shares granted is not available in machine-readable form for further analysis. This pattern of first increased and then decreased dilution is echoed when examining the number of options granted as a percentage of the number of shares outstanding, which ranges from a mean (median) of 2 (1) percent of shares outstanding in the years 1992-1995, to 4 (2) percent of shares outstanding in the years 1998-2001, and back down to 2 (1) percent of shares outstanding in 2005. To put these numbers in perspective, at a rate of 2 percent per year, the number of shares outstanding would double, and hence the proportional holdings of existing shareholders be halved, in 35 years.

This peaking is also consistent with that found by consultants Pearl Meyer & Partners (2004):

Table 6-5:

Options Granted During Current Year, Both as an Absolute Amount and as a Percentage of Outstanding Shares

Year	Mean Number of Options Granted	Median Number of Options Granted	As a Percentage of Shares Outstanding at Year-End (Mean)	As a Percentage of Shares Outstanding at Year-End (Median)
1992	3,565,191	1,561,849	2.08	1.14
1993	4,464,272	1,813,611	2.21	1.27
1994	5,104,378	2,077,764	2.24	1.35
1995	5,980,626	2,493,766	2.43	1.43
1996	7,237,064	2,920,141	2.78	1.59
1997	10,300,763	3,437,115	3.17	1.84
1998	13,247,785	4,167,845	3.54	2.05
1999	17,671,392	5,272,938	3.75	2.24
2000	38,336,771	6,190,150	3.71	2.46
2001	31,143,337	6,616,026	3.93	2.44
2002	33,026,636	6,328,002	3.24	2.15
2003	20,809,362	5,715,267	2.77	1.88
2004	21,378,429	5,388,260	2.28	1.61
2005	17,046,184	5,345,413	2.01	1.35

Note: Calculations in this table are based upon data contained in the April 2006 version of Standard & Poor's ExecuComp.

... the proportion of shares allocated for management and employee equity incentives declined for the first time since this annual report was first issued 15 years ago. Average allocations dipped from a peak level of 17.32% of outstanding shares in the 2003 report to 16.36% this year. In a corresponding development, average annual grant rates among the Top 200 dropped sharply for a third straight year, to 2.02% of the outstanding—roughly the same level of stock use seen in 1998.

However, even though declining, it should be reiterated that the 2.02 percent average annual grant rate is significantly greater than the 1.2 percent observed by Pearl Meyer in 1994, and the 16.36-percent allocation is still greater than the 13.7 percent they observed in 1999 (Leonhardt 2000).[34] This allocation, or overhang, is the ratio of stock options granted but not yet exercised to the number of outstanding shares. Consequently these large corporations, which are not considered to be the most intense issuers of options, have made promises that can increase their number of shares outstanding by more than 16 percent. Table 6-6 (see page 197) shows for a select group of companies the number of options and shares currently outstanding, and the ratio of the two, the overhang. The ratio varies dramatically. Five of the 10 companies—Cisco, Ford, Intel, IBM and Yahoo—have potential dilution in excess of 12 percent, whereas General Electric has potential dilution of 2.77 percent and for Wal-Mart, outstanding options represent less than 1 percent of outstanding shares.

Stock option plans are normally put to a shareholder vote. This is required by the New York Stock Exchange and NASDAQ for all listed corporations, and by the Securities and Exchange Commission if the issuer wishes the transaction to be exempt from section 16(b).[35, 36, 37] Increasing dilution, among other factors, has led to increased opposition to stock option plans (Lublin and Scism 1999) and to a number of corporate proposals regarding stock option plans being voted down by shareholders. For example, the board of directors of Ben & Jerry's, the ice cream maker, proposed to increase the number of shares authorized for its stock option plan from 900,000 to 1.3 million, a proposal that was rejected by shareholders by a vote of 4,800,368 for; 6,551,058 against; 64,692 abstaining; and 1,307,805 broker nonvotes.[38]

Cash Outflow

To counter the issue of dilution, many companies have made it a policy to fund their option and grant programs with shares they repurchase in the market. To illustrate the magnitude of these repurchases, consider the following from Microsoft and Cisco.

Table 6-6:

Ratio of Options to Shares Outstanding for Select Companies

	Fiscal Year End	Number of Options and Restricted Shares Outstanding at Year End	Number of Shares Outstanding at Year End	Ratio
Amazon.com [1]	Dec. 31, 2005	22,000,000	416,000,000	5.29%
Cisco [2]	July 29, 2006	971,000,000	7,138,000,000	13.60%
eBay [3]	Dec. 31, 2005	129,109,000	1,404,184,000	9.19%
Ford Motor [4]	Dec. 31, 2005	245,400,000	1,837,000,000	13.36%
General Electric [5]	Dec. 31, 2000	290,859,000	10,484,268,000	2.77%
Intel [6]	Dec. 30, 2005	899,900,000	5,919,000,000	15.20%
IBM [7]	Dec. 31, 2005	236,070,040	1,573,979,761	15.00%
Microsoft [8]	June 30, 2006	884,700,000	10,062,000,000	8.79%
Wal-Mart [9]	Jan. 31, 2006	38,348,000	4,165,000,000	0.92%
Yahoo [10]	Dec. 31, 2005	182,694,000	1,430,162,000	12.77%

Note: Calculations in this table are based upon data contained in the April 2006 version of Standard & Poor's ExecuComp and the Consumer Price Index—All Urban Consumers, as found on the Bureau of Labor Statistics Web site.

[1] Pages 73 of Amazon.com form 10-K filed with the Securities and Exchange Commission, Feb. 17, 2006.
[2] Pages 67 & 68 of Exhibit 13-1 filed as part of Cisco Systems form 10-K filed with the Securities and Exchange Commission, Sept. 18, 2006.
[3] Pages 112 & 113, eBay form 10-K filed with the Securities and Exchange Commission, Feb. 24, 2006.
[4] Pages FS-3 & FS-31, Ford Motor form 10-K filed with the Securities and Exchange Commission, March 1, 2006.
[5] Page 94, Exhibit 13, General Electric form 10-K filed with the Securities and Exchange Commission, March 3, 2006.
[6] Pages 50 & 68, Intel form 10-K filed with the Securities and Exchange Commission, Feb. 27, 2006.
[7] Pages 75 & 84, Exhibit 13, International Business Machines form 10-K filed with the Securities and Exchange Commission, Feb. 28, 2006.
[8] Pages 59,63 & 64, Microsoft form 10-K filed with the Securities and Exchange Commission, Aug. 25, 2006.
[9] Pages 31 & 42, Exhibit 13, Wal-Mart form 10-K filed with the Securities and Exchange Commission, March 29, 2006.
[10] Pages 63 & 88, Yahoo form 10-K filed with the Securities and Exchange Commission, March 3, 2006.

Microsoft

On July 20, 2004, our Board of Directors approved a plan to buy back up to $30 billion of Microsoft common stock over the succeeding four years. ... Our Board of Directors had previously approved a program to repurchase shares of our common stock to reduce the dilutive effect of our stock option and stock purchase plans.[39]

Cisco

During the fiscal year, we repurchased $10.2 billion or 540 million shares of our common stock at an average price of $18.95. At the end of fiscal 2005, our cumulative purchases since the inception of the share repurchase program in September 2001 were approximately $27.2 billion, or 1.5 billion shares, at an average price of $18.15.[40]

Despite the large amounts spent, in some years repurchases fail to keep up with share issuances under stock plans, thus dilution resulted. For example, in 2005 Microsoft spent $8 billion to repurchase 312 million shares of common stock, while only issuing 160 million. However in 2003 and 2004 they issued more shares than they repurchased. Thus at the end of a three-year period in which they spent $17.3 billion to repurchase common shares, the net number of shares repurchased was only 8 million.

Table 6-7 documents on a yearly basis the amount corporations included in the S&P 500, S&P MidCap and S&P SmallCap indices spent repurchasing their own shares. On a per-corporation basis, the mean (median) amount increased from about $21 ($0) million in 1992 to about $267 ($8) million in 2005. Similarly, the percent of corporations repurchasing their own shares rose from 25 percent in 1992 to 55 percent in 2005. In aggregate, the corporations under examination spent more than $339 billion in 2005 repurchasing their shares. Table 6-8 on page 200 documents the materiality of those repurchases. Cash spent to repurchase shares ranged from a mean (median) of 8 (0) percent to 25 (6) percent of operating cash flow, and between 11 (0) percent and 33 (10) percent of net income. Finally, Table 6-9 on page 201 shows the percentage increase in shares outstanding on a yearly basis for these corporations. The mean (median) increase, which ranges from 2 (1) to 10 (1) percent per year, indicates that all the resources spent on repurchasing shares is not enough to stem the dilution.[41]

Incentive vs. Dilutive Effect

In theory, the increase in shareholder value from the incentive effects should outweigh the dilutive effect of stock-based compensation, that is, existing shareholders should benefit from the increase in shareholder value despite giving up some of their proportional ownership. However, this may not always be true. For example, Carlin et al. (2005) find that return on assets and return on equity are inversely related to dilution. Further, the assertion that the incentive effects should outweigh the dilutive effect assumes that the individuals who award compensation are acting

Table 6-7:

Amounts Spent to Repurchase Shares

Year	Mean Firm	Median Firm	Percentage of Firms Repurchasing Shares	In Aggregate
1992	$20,776,790	$0	25.35	$32,453,346,000
1993	$21,669,963	$0	27.05	$41,844,699,000
1994	$23,899,756	$0	28.75	$48,397,005,000
1995	$37,064,203	$0	29.95	$78,131,339,000
1996	$48,716,124	$0	35.40	$100,014,203,000
1997	$72,756,111	$34,000	40.32	$144,275,369,000
1998	$95,099,716	$2,583,000	48.30	$185,539,545,000
1999	$104,314,702	$2,852,000	49.95	$196,007,325,000
2000	$106,485,515	$3,116,000	50.98	$189,757,188,000
2001	$92,837,027	$207,000	41.23	$155,316,347,000
2002	$90,086,161	$107,000	41.75	$150,173,630,000
2003	$96,146,467	$81,000	41.39	$156,238,009,000
2004	$154,820,333	$313,000	44.81	$246,319,150,000
2005	$266,620,093	$7,929,500	54.77	$339,140,758,000

Note: Calculations in this table are based upon data contained in the July 2006 version of Standard & Poor's Compustat.

in the best interests of shareholders, and not, for example, in their own self-interest.

Others argue that because options are only valuable if and when the share price increases, that there is no downside to shareholders, that is, employees only benefit if shareholders do. Of course, this presumes the options are granted at or above the market price at time of grant, and does not hold if shares, rather than options, are granted to employees. It also ignores the opportunity costs faced by shareholders.

Effectiveness of Stock-Based Compensation

As noted in Chapter 5, it is not always easy to measure the effectiveness of various types of compensation. As noted above, more so than other forms of compensation, stock compensation provides employees with incentives to exert the effort and take the risks necessary to increase shareholder value. Unfortunately, because neither can be measured directly, researchers have had to rely on indirect accounting and stock return measures. That is, researchers measure accounting returns subsequent to plan adoption and stock price reaction at time of public

Table 6-8:

Amount Spent to Repurchase Shares as a Percentage of Operating Cash Flow and Net Income

Year	Amount Spent to Repurchase Shares as a Percentage of Operating Cash Flow (Mean)	Amount Spent to Repurchase Shares as a Percentage of Operating Cash Flow (Median)	Amount Spent to Repurchase Shares as a Percentage of Net Income (Mean)	Amount Spent to Repurchase Shares as a Percentage of Net Income (Median)
1992	7.54	0.00	10.72	0.00
1993	8.65	0.00	11.96	0.00
1994	9.50	0.00	13.02	0.00
1995	9.39	0.00	12.97	0.00
1996	12.14	0.00	17.16	0.00
1997	15.57	0.09	21.27	0.13
1998	21.34	3.52	28.36	5.87
1999	21.80	4.00	29.27	6.48
2000	19.96	3.69	27.05	6.60
2001	12.86	0.26	19.62	0.41
2002	14.17	0.13	21.42	0.17
2003	14.57	0.08	20.50	0.14
2004	18.54	0.21	25.09	0.34
2005	25.45	6.41	32.98	10.15

Note: Calculations in this table are based upon data contained in the July 2006 version of Standard & Poor's Compustat and use the absolute value of operating cash flow (net income) in those cases where operating cash flow (net income) is negative.

announcement. For example, Mehran (1995) finds that return on assets (an accounting performance measure defined as net income divided by the book value of the corporation's assets) is positively associated with the percentage of compensation that is equity-based, and Hanlon et al. (2003) conclude that future operating performance is positively associated with the value of stock option grants. However, Kimbrough and Louis (2004) show that the "firm's future operating performance is negatively associated with the proportion of total executive compensation granted in the form of options." Table 6-10 on page 202 provides some descriptive information on the effect of stock option grants on firm performance. It divides the firms into deciles by percentage of options granted in the prior year, showing shareholder returns and return on assets in the subsequent year. In general, there does not seem to be an association between grant size and subsequent shareholders returns, as the highest mean and median return are observed in the sixth decile. There does, however, appear

Table 6-9:

Change in Shares Outstanding

Year	Mean Change in Shares Outstanding from Prior Year	Median Change in Shares Outstanding from Prior Year
1993	9.62	1.15
1994	5.45	0.62
1995	8.29	0.86
1996	9.02	0.99
1997	7.58	1.01
1998	6.43	0.60
1999	5.92	0.51
2000	4.52	0.55
2001	4.63	0.99
2002	3.74	0.77
2003	3.41	0.82
2004	3.60	1.10
2005	2.22	0.71

Note: Calculations in this table are based upon data contained in the July 2006 version of Standard & Poor's Compustat.

to be some association between grant size and subsequent return on assets, as mean return on assets is actually negative for firms with the largest option grants.

Using accounting returns is problematic in measuring the effect of stock option plans. For example, the result in Table 6-10 could be a function of firms with large growth opportunities using larger amounts of stock options. And firms in the growth stage may generate losses because of high depreciation and research and development expenses. Additionally, prior to 2006,[42] firms were not required to record an expense for stock option grants if the grants were fixed in nature and the exercise price was equal to or greater than the market price on the date of grant. Thus, if options were substituted for other forms of compensation for which expense is recognized, there would be an upward bias in accounting performance measures unrelated to improvements in performance. Further, some, including Alan Greenspan, former Federal Reserve chairman, asserted that the "spread of shareholding and options among business managers perversely created incentives to artificially inflate reported earnings in order to keep stock prices high and rising."[43]

Similarly, while Billett et al. (2006), among others, find a positive stock price

Table 6-10:

Size of Option Grant (Relative to Shares Outstanding) versus Shareholder Returns in Subsequent Year

Size of Grant	Mean Shareholder Return in Subsequent Year	Median Shareholder Return in Subsequent Year	Mean Return on Assets in Subsequent Year	Median Return on Assets in Subsequent Year
Lowest Decile	13.08	11.25	4.19	3.67
2	11.75	10.03	4.78	4.15
3	12.79	10.81	4.64	4.28
4	13.66	11.10	4.36	4.46
5	14.14	11.28	3.92	4.28
6	16.33	12.56	4.41	4.53
7	14.38	11.83	3.07	4.53
8	15.99	12.12	2.85	4.43
9	13.31	11.53	-0.04	3.74
Highest Decile	14.99	10.79	-3.72	2.56

Note: Calculations in this table are based upon data contained in the April 2006 version of Standard & Poor's ExecuComp.

reaction to first-time equity grants to CEOs, as noted in Chapter 5, looking at stock price performance at time of public announcement may be misleading, as the market reaction to plan adoption may not be associated with the expected effects of the plan on firm performance, but rather to the information released by the plan adoption. That is, management is more likely to propose tying its compensation to share price performance when it expects the share price to perform well in the future. Investors realize this tendency and, thus, react positively when they first learn the plan is being adopted.

What is clear is that stock-based compensation can affect risk preferences. Researchers, including Cohen et al. (2000), Rajgopal and Shevlin (2002), Rajgopal et al. (2004) and Sanders and Hambrick (2004), have found that stock option compensation has a positive effect on future risk taking.

Macro/Market Effects

It has been said that a rising tide lifts all boats. That is, in a rising market, stock prices go up even if the corporation underperforms the market. And executives benefit. Consider the case of Ralston Purina. In 1986, the corporation granted restricted stock that would vest if within the next 10 years the stock price closed above $100 for 10 consecutive days. Based upon the then-current stock price of $63.375, the price had only to rise at a rate of 4.67 percent per year for the next 10 years for the shares to vest. In fact, $100 was reached within five years. However, within its industry, Ralston Purina was somewhat of a laggard. Campbell and Wasley (1999) note that while executives collected their payoffs, shareholders suffered an industry-adjusted loss of $2.1 billion.[44]

While this situation has to some extent been repeated throughout time, it is true that not all corporations have benefited from the run up in stock prices. It is also true that with the mega-grants that have become prevalent, even a small increase in stock price can lead to large payoff. Arbitrarily defining mega-grant as when the present value of the sum of grants to a senior executive in a year exceeds $10 million, Table 6-11 on page 204 shows the increase in the number of mega-grants over time. In 1992, seven executives received grants valued by ExecuComp at more than $10 million. In contrast, in 2000, 353 executives received stock option grants valued by ExecuComp at more than $10 million. However, by 2005, this number had decreased to 59. So, consistent with our other observations about the use of stock options, the use of mega-grants peaked in 2000 and dropped thereafter. In contrast, the number of mega stock grants has increased linearly from 1 in 1992 to 40 in 2005, consistent with the increase in emphasis on restricted stock over time. Table 6-12 on page 205 lists the largest option grant by year, as valued by ExecuComp. These maximums, which ranged in size from $30,285,000 to $52,096,000 between 1992 and 1995, jumped dramatically in 1996 when Michael Eisner, Disney Co. chairman and CEO, received a grant valued at $193,532,000, and then in 2000, when Steven Jobs, Apple Computer CEO, received a grant valued by Standard & Poor's Execucomp at more than $600 million. It should, however, be noted that even these enormous grants do not guarantee a payoff. As shown in Table 6-12, Amazon.com gave Joseph Galli Jr. stock options valued at $201,356,000 to join the company in 1999. Its stock price dropped dramatically after that point, so in 2000 when Galli resigned to become CEO of VerticalNet, he left Amazon without making a penny off those options.[45] Table 6-13 on page 206 lists the largest stock grants by year. One number is a clear outlier, and that is the grant to Charles Wang of CA, which will be discussed later in the chapter.

What happens if the market stops rising and drops? This could be the market for one particular firm's stock, or the overall market. Since the market peak in March 2000, this has become a major issue with companies. Microsoft, for example, gave out new options to employees after a dramatic fall in stock price that made many of its previously granted options worthless.[46] As noted above, once options are worthless or out-of-the-money, incentives change dramatically. For example, out-

Table 6-11:

Number of Executives Receiving Stock Option or Stock Grants Valued at More Than $10 Million in a Given Year

Year	Number of Stock Option Grants Valued at More Than $10 Million	Number of Stock Grants Valued at More Than $10 Million
1992	7	1
1993	10	3
1994	27	2
1995	26	1
1996	63	4
1997	119	14
1998	108	17
1999	212	26
2000	353	30
2001	293	20
2002	150	26
2003	72	30
2004	75	33
2005	59	40

Note: Calculations in this table are based upon data contained in the April 2006 version of Standard & Poor's ExecuComp.

of-the-money options no longer tie the employee to the corporation.

What should the corporation do? One response is to grant additional options at the current price, as Microsoft did. Another response is to reprice existing options, essentially lower the exercise price of the options the executive already holds. The following passage explains the multiple option repricings Apple Computer engaged in during 1996 and 1997:

> In December 1997, the Board of Directors approved an option exchange program which allowed employees to exchange all (but not less than all) of their existing options (vested and unvested) with an exercise price greater than $13.6875, on a one-for-one basis for new options with an exercise price of $13.6875, the fair market value of the Company's common stock on Dec. 19, 1997, and a new four-year vesting schedule beginning in December 1997. A total of 4.7 million options with a weighted-average exercise price of $19.90 per share were exchanged for new options as a result of this program.
>
> In July 1997, the Board of Directors approved an option exchange program which allowed employees to exchange all (but not less than all)

of their existing options (vested and unvested) to purchase Apple common stock (other than options granted and assumed from NeXT) for options having an exercise price of $13.25 and a new three year vesting period beginning in July of 1997. Approximately 7.9 million options were repriced under this program.

On May 14, 1996, the Board of Directors adopted a resolution allowing employees up to and including the level of Vice President to exchange 1.25 options at their existing option price for 1.0 new options having an exercise price of $26.375 per share, the fair market value of the Company's common stock at May 29, 1996. Options received under this program are subject to one year of additional vesting such that the new vesting date for each vesting portion will be the later of May 29, 1997, or the original vesting date plus one year. Approximately 2.9 million options were exchanged and repriced under this program.[47]

Repricing was extremely controversial, as while it protects executives from declines in share prices, it does nothing for shareholders. Some have gone so far

Table 6-12:
Executives Receiving the Highest-Valued Stock Option Grants, by Year

Year	Executive	Position	Company	Amount
1992	Sanford Weill	Chairman & CEO	Citigroup	$36,032,000
1993	Charles Harper	Chairman & CEO	Nabisco Group Holdings	$30,285,000
1994	Stephen Hilbert	Chairman, President & CEO	Conseco	$52,096,000
1995	James Donald	Chairman, President & CEO	DSC Communications	$47,472,000
1996	Michael Eisner	Chairman & CEO	Disney (Walt)	$193,532,000
1997	Henry Silverman	President & CEO	Cendant	$255,630,000
1998	Sanford Weill	Chairman & Co-CEO	Citigroup	$137,045,000
1999	Joseph Galli Jr.	President & COO	Amazon.com	$201,356,000
2000	Steven Jobs	CEO	Apple Computer	$600,347,000
2001	Gregory Reyes	Chairman & CEO	Brocade Communications	$369,312,000
2002	Steven Jobs	CEO	Apple Computer	$89,445,000
2003	Michael Jeffries	Chairman & CEO	Abercrombie & Fitch	$36,501,000
2004	Terry Semel	Chairman & CEO	Yahoo	$119,459,000
2005	Eugene Isenberg	Chairman & CEO	Nabors Industries	$55,825,000

Note: Calculations in this table are based upon data contained in the April 2006 version of Standard & Poor's ExecuComp and are valued using the Black-Scholes value of the option on the grant date.

Table 6-13:

Executives Receiving the Highest-Valued Stock Grants, by Year

Year	Executive	Position	Company	Amount
1992	Eugene Grisanti	Chairman & President	International Flavors & Fragrances	$10,625,000
1993	Millard Drexler	President & COO	GAP	$40,250,000
1994	Roy Wilkens	President-Williams Telecommunications Group	Williams Cos.	$15,237,000
1995	John Welch Jr.	Chairman & CEO	General Electric	$11,425,000
1996	Daniel Akerson	Chairman & CEO	Nextel Communications	$15,375,000
1997	Lawrence Lasser	President-Putnam Investments	Marsh & Mclennan	$22,153,000
1998	John Welch Jr.	Chairman & CEO	General Electric	$27,019,000
1999	Charles Wang	Chairman & CEO	CA	$650,812,000
2000	John Welch Jr.	Chairman & CEO	General Electric	$48,716,000
2001	Douglas Daft	Chairman & CEO	Coca-Cola	$47,880,000
2002	L. Kozlowski	Chairman & CEO	Tyco International	$66,991,000
2003	Steven Jobs	CEO	Apple Computer	$74,750,000
2004	E. O'Neal	Chairman & CEO	Merrill Lynch	$31,300,000
2005	Lee Raymond	Chairman & CEO	Exxon Mobil	$32,087,000

Note: Calculations in this table are based upon data contained in the April 2006 version of Standard & Poor's ExecuComp and are valued using the stock price on the date of the grant.

as to assert that repricing destroys the incentive value of options, because employees assume that repricing will occur, or that they will get additional options if the share price falls (Schroeder and Simon 2001). While repricings were used fairly frequently during the 1990s, they virtually ceased following changes in financial accounting rules, in particular, Financial Accounting Standards Board Interpretation (FIN) No. 44—Accounting for Certain Transactions Involving Stock Compensation—which required that companies recognize expense for options that have been repriced (for example, see Carter and Lynch 2003).

FIN No. 44 required an expense be recognized for options canceled and reissued within six months. Apple (as did other companies) took advantage of this loophole in 2003 (see "Stock Option Exchange Program"), essentially repricing its options but avoiding recognizing an expense under financial accounting rules by waiting six months plus one day to issue the new options. Interestingly enough, while it gave its other employees new options, it gave Steve Jobs, as discussed previously, restricted shares instead.

Stock Option Exchange Program

Due to the downturn in the economy, particularly in the technology industry, the share price of the Company's Common Stock declined significantly over the last couple of years leaving many employees with stock options that were "underwater," that is, options with exercise prices that are significantly higher than the current market price of the Company's stock. The Committee believed that many of those options had little value, were unlikely to be exercised in the foreseeable future and no longer provided an effective incentive to motivate and retain employees. In addition, because of the drop in the stock price over the past couple of years, the number of unexercised options had grown to an undesirable level. Sensitive to shareholder concerns regarding the dilutive effect of stock options, rather than granting additional options to compensate for the underwater options, the Committee determined that a reduction in such potential dilution was more in line with building shareholder value. Accordingly, in March 2003, the Board authorized a stock option exchange program whereby eligible employees, other than executive officers and members of the Board of Directors, have an opportunity to exchange outstanding options with exercise prices at or above $25.00 per share for a predetermined smaller number of new stock options that will be granted at the fair market value on the day of the new grant, which will be at least six-months-plus-one-day after the exchanged options are cancelled.

In March 2003, Mr. Jobs voluntarily cancelled all of his outstanding options, excluding those granted to him in his capacity as a director. Mr. Jobs felt strongly that this would more effectively build shareholder value by reducing the Company's overhang and by providing additional shares that could later be granted to employees whose contributions are critical to the long-term success of the Company. In keeping with its philosophy to relate compensation to corporate performance, in exchange for his cancelled options, the Board approved a new retention and incentive program in the form of long-term equity compensation consisting of five million restricted shares of the Company's Common Stock which generally vest in full on the third anniversary of the grant date.[48]

If the firm wants to continue issuing options and is worried about out-of-the money options, it may consider issuing more frequent option grants, which make it more likely that some options are in the money, and extending the life of the options, which make it more likely the share price will recover so that the options are in-the-money. Other choices in a declining market include replacing options with other forms of compensation, such as cash and stock grants. At its 2000 annual meeting, Genesis Health Ventures and its shareholders approved the following plan to deal with underwater options.

> ... a stock option redemption program under which Genesis' employees and directors may elect to surrender Genesis' stock options for unrestricted shares of Common Stock.[49]

Overall, there does seem to be an increase in stock grants, with the grants getting more frequent and larger in amount. Table 2-2 showed the proportion of CEOs getting stock grants increasing from 20 percent in 1992 to 45 percent in 2005, whereas Table 2-8 showed the average CEO received stock worth $1,054,171 in 2005, up from $215,168 in 1992.

Alternative Forms of Options

While historically companies have granted fixed options (i.e., options granted with an exercise price equal to the market price on the date of grant), theoretically they can choose from a variety of different options. These alternatives include, but are not limited to, discount options, premium options, performance-vested options, repriceable options, purchased options, reload options and indexed options. And now that the accounting bias toward fixed options has been removed, companies are more likely to use these alternatives in the future.

Whereas a standard option is issued with an exercise price equal to the grant date market price, discount options are granted with an exercise price less than the grant date market price, and premium options are issued with an exercise price exceeding the grant date market price. Performance-vested options are options whose exercisability depends upon future performance. Repriceable options can have their exercise price lowered if the corporation's stock price falls, whereas with a purchased option, the executive pays a portion of the exercise price at the time of grant. Reload options allow the executive to pay the exercise price with previously owned shares and then receive new options to replace those used to pay the exercise price. Indexed options are options whose exercise price is adjusted for market and/or industrywide movements. When compared to standard options, each of these alternatives has differing effects on the incentive to increase share value and risk and reduce dividend yields.

Discount Options

Discount options are a cross between an option issued at current market price and a share of restricted stock, which is equivalent to an option with an exercise price of zero. While neither accounting nor tax regulations prohibit the issuance of discount options, because of the bias toward fixed options, in the past, few companies issued discount options, or perhaps more correctly, few companies admitted to issuing discount options (more on this below). From an accounting standpoint, while companies were able to avoid recognition of any expense (in the past) for fixed stock options, they had to recognize an expense equal to the intrinsic value, that is the difference between the exercise price and the higher market price on the date of grant, for discount options. From a tax standpoint, discount options were less favorable as employees were taxed on the intrinsic value at the date of grant, and employers could not claim the options met the performance-based exception under Section 162(m) of the Internal Revenue Code. Perhaps the largest disincentive to granting discount options was the necessity of getting shareholder approval, that is, while shareholders routinely approve stock option plans, companies generally state that options would not be granted at less than market price at the date of grant—to do otherwise would admit the options are not totally performance based.[50] Analysis of grants in the Execucomp database indicates that while discount options are granted, they are not granted very frequently, as out of 128,586 grants recorded in the database, only 1,744 were issued at a discount to market price. And most of these have some sort of justification. For example, in 2003 Dell granted some options at 20 percent below the market price. However, as discussed below, these options were granted in lieu of their bonus and, effectively, the executives involved purchased the 20-percent discount with that bonus:

> These options were granted as a part of the Executive Stock Ownership Incentive Program, under which the executives can elect to receive options in lieu of their annual bonus. The exercise price of the options was 80% of the fair market value of the common stock on the date of grant, and the number of shares awarded was calculated by dividing the designated bonus amount by 20% of the fair market value of the common stock on the date of grant.[51]

An example of a company issuing unconditional discount options is the GAP, which issued discount options to several executives including President and CEO Paul Pressler in September 2002.

In September 2002, upon hire, Mr. Pressler was granted options to purchase 5,000,000 shares. Unlike most options which are granted at market value, Mr. Pressler received a combination of discounted, market and "premium priced" options. The number and exercise price of the shares are as follows: 2,000,000 at $5.92, a price which was 50% of the market value at the date of grant, 1,500,000 at $11.83, the market value at the date of grant, 500,000 at $14.79, a price which was 125% of the market value at the date of grant, 500,000 at $17.75, a price which was 150% of the market value at the date of grant, and 500,000 at $20.70, a price which was 175% of the market value at the date of grant. The "premium price" options are intended to reward Mr. Pressler only after shareholders have been delivered significant growth in the stock price which is consistent with the Committee's philosophies of increasing shareholder value and including at-risk compensation as a significant part of an executive's overall compensation.[52]

However, recent changes in the tax rules governing deferred compensation, that is section 409A of the Internal Revenue Code, may have put the breaks on the issuance of discount stock options even as the unfavorable financial accounting treatment has been removed. Under Section 409A, added as part of the American Jobs Creation Act of 2004, a stock option granted with a per share exercise price that is less than the fair market value per-share of a company's underlying stock on the date of grant is treated as deferred compensation. This will result in tax at vesting as opposed to exercise, as well as an additional 20-percent tax on the optionee under certain conditions. As a result, I am only aware of one company that issued new discount options since the end of 2004—Baldor Electric.

Backdated Options

Early in 2006, the media picked up on research by Professor Erik Lie of the University of Iowa (Lie 2005, Heron and Lie 2006a) showing that the timing of option grants seemed to defy chance. That is, companies were granting options at prices that were the low point for the year, quarter, etc., and doing so time after time. What the media, regulators, prosecutors and plaintiffs bar soon began to suspect was that the firms involved were backdating their option grants, which is retroactively granting options at an earlier, lower price. The effect was to grant discount options, which in and of itself was not illegal. The illegality set in when companies, rather than state they were issuing options currently at a discount, presented the grant to the public as being made at the earlier date and acted accordingly with respect to their financial reports and tax returns. Thus they were overstating income on their financial statements[53] and potentially understating it on their and their executive's tax returns.

The facts across the companies involved varied dramatically. Some of the back-dating appeared relatively innocuous, for example granting options to new hires at the lowest price in the 30 days after they joined the firm. The reason ostensibly was to keep motivation up if the stock price fell and create some equity among employees whose employment start dates were close together. This was especially important with the high-tech Silicon Valley companies that competed for employees with stock options. Microsoft was one such company, which ended the practice and voluntarily took a charge for it in 1999.

> Historically, exercise prices of grants of ESOs were struck at the lowest price in the 30 days following July 1 for annual grants and the 30 days after the start date for new employees. In connection with this practice, which is no longer employed, a charge of $217 million was recorded in the fourth quarter for fiscal 1999 compensation expense.[54]

In another version of backdating, allegedly practiced by Brocade Communications Systems, employees were entered into payroll on a part-time status before their true hire date so that, in a rising market, they would get options at the earlier, lower grant price.

> The Company has determined it incorrectly accounted for, and will record historical stock-based compensation charges relating to, (i) grants that were made to new hires on their offer acceptance date, rather than the date of their commencement of employment, during the period May 1999 to July 2000, and (ii) grants that were made to persons engaged on a part-time basis prior to their new hire full-time employment during the period August 2000 to October 2002.[55]

The impact on Brocade's financial statements was significant.

> These charges will affect the previously filed financial statements for fiscal years 2002 and 2003. The Company also expects to make stock based compensation and associated income tax adjustments to previously reported fiscal year 2004 financial results. These adjustments relate solely to matters pertaining to stock options granted prior to August 2003. For years prior to 2002, the Company will reduce previously reported net

income by approximately $304 million (consisting of a reduction to net income in years 1999 and 2000 of $15 million and $1,019 million, respectively, and an increase to net income in 2001 of $730 million) relating solely to stock based compensation and associated income tax adjustments.[56]

Brocade's executives did not escape unscathed. On July 20, 2006, Gregory Reyes, the former chief executive, and Stephanie Jensen, former HR director, were charged with criminal securities fraud, which carries a maximum penalty of 20 years in prison. They, along with former CFO Antonio Canova, also face civil charges from the SEC of securities fraud and filing false documents (Forelle et al 2006).

Other cases appeared more troubling, for example at United Health, CEO William McGuire was reportedly allowed to pick the date on which his options were granted (The Wall Street Journal 2006). Eventually the fallout from the scandal forced him to resign, even though the company's stock price growth had been astronomical (8,500 percent) during his tenure (Dash and Freudenheim 2006). Somewhat surprisingly, he was allowed to keep his options. While the exercise prices on those options were to be adjusted to the yearly highs, those options were still valued in excess of $1 billion at the time of resignation (Forelle and Maremont 2006).

The fallout from the scandal is widespread and continuing. On Sept. 6, 2006, the U. S. Senate Committee on Banking, Housing and Urban Affairs and the Committee on Finance held hearings on the topic, which included testimony from representatives of the Attorney General's Office, Internal Revenue Service, Public Company Oversight Board, and Securities and Exchange Commission. More than 100 companies are under investigation by either regulators or prosecutors. Executives at McAfee and Vitesse Semiconductor have reportedly lost their jobs because of their involvement in backdating (Hechinger 2006, The Wall Street Journal 2006). Forelle (2006) reports that "the number of dismissals, suspensions and resignations of corporate officials amid probes of stock-option practices" is at least 28. In its 2005 10-K filed March 6, 2006, Micrel disclosed that it had sued its former auditor Deloitte & Touche in April 2003 over conflicting advice provided on this very issue:

Specifically, beginning in 1996, the Company began to follow a practice of granting employee stock options on the date with the lowest closing price within the thirty-day period subsequent to the employee's date of hire (the "Thirty-Day Method"). The Company began this practice after receiving advice from Deloitte that options granted using the Thirty-Day Method would not be compensatory under APB No 25. The Company subsequently determined that options granted using the Thirty-Day Method were compensatory under APB No 25, and discontinued use of the Thirty-Day Method thereafter.[57]

Overall, Heron and Lie (2006b) report that almost 30 percent of option grants during the 1996-2005 period were backdated or otherwise manipulated, indicating the problems were widespread. In addition to firms that backdated their options, their research and that of others suggests firms time their option grants before the increase in stock prices associated with the release of good news, sometimes referred to as springloading.

One response used by corporations to clear the air surrounding option grants is to establish a fixed schedule of grants in advance. For example, Cognos Inc. now states:

> All Option awards are made quarterly three (3) trading days after the Corporation's quarterly earnings release in order to avoid opportunistic grant timing and to ensure that all Options are priced at a time when the marketplace has current financial information.[58]

United Health states:

> While recognizing that the company's exceptional long-term perform-ance has driven unanticipated compensation levels, today the Board:
> - Established the Annual Shareholder Meeting as the grant date for stock options for existing employees (Option grants for new hires will coincide with date of service and promotion grants will coin-cide with regularly scheduled Compensation Committee meetings.)[59]

Premium Options

Premium options differ from standard options in that their exercise price is set to be greater than market price at date of grant. Thus the executive does not profit from the first dollar increase in stock price. While more common than discount options, premium options are used relatively infrequently. Analysis of grants in the Execucomp database shows that out of 128,586 grants recorded in the database, only 2,276 were issued at a premium to market price. Even more interesting, the frequency with which companies are using premium options is actually decreasing over time—with no premium grants recorded in 2005.

Adjusted Options

If options were adjusted for marketwide and/or industrywide movements, then managers would neither be penalized in a market downturn, nor rewarded in a bull market; rather, they would only be rewarded for above-average stock price growth relative to the benchmark. In other words, they would be paid based upon their performance. While reasonable in theory, and research (for example, Gibbons and Murphy 1990) does show that relative performance evaluation is used, market-adjusted options have not caught on in practice. Some (for example, Johnson 1999) explain this unwillingness by pointing to the differential accounting treatments, a motivation which no longer exists. Fixed stock options historically did not result in a charge to earnings. In contrast, market-adjusted options were treated as variable options and, consequently, would result in an expense being recognized on the income statement. For example, RCN in June 2000 adopted its Outperform Stock Option Plan. The following passage from its 2000 annual report (note 12) explains the accounting consequences:

> The Company granted 3,000,000 OSOs to employees during the year ended Dec. 31, 2000, with a fair value under SFAS No. 123 of $42,776. The Company recognized $17,910 of compensation expense during the year 2000 for options granted in 2000. As of Dec. 31, 2000, the Company had not reflected $24,866 of unamortized compensation expense in its financial statements for options granted in 2000.60.[61]

Another explanation for the infrequent use of adjusted options is that executives have to date been profiting from the bull market and want to keep doing so. If the market were to decline substantially, they would then simply reprice or replace the options, effectively making the option market adjusted on the downside, but not the upside.

For these reasons, few publicly held companies issue indexed options. One exception is Level 3 Communications.

> Level 3's long-term incentive program has historically consisted of awards of Outperform Stock Options (OSOs), which are an innovative stock-indexed equity-based long term compensation vehicle. OSOs are designed to provide executives with an incentive to maximize stockholder value and to reward executives only when the price of the company's common stock outperforms the S&P 500 Index between the date of grant and the date that the OSO is exercised.[62]
>
> OSOs have an initial exercise price that is equal to the closing market

price of our common stock on the trading day immediately prior to the date of grant. This exercise price is referred to as the Initial Price. When an employee elects to exercise an OSO, the Initial Price is adjusted upward or downward—as of the date of that exercise—by a percentage that is equal to the aggregate percentage increase or decrease in the S&P 500 Index over the period beginning on the date of grant and ending on the trading day immediately preceding the date of exercise of the OSOs.[63]

Financial Consequences
Cash Flow
As noted previously, each component of the executive compensation package impacts the corporation's cash flows. In the case of stock-based compensation, most of the time there is no direct cash outflow, as the corporation provides stock or options rather than cash as payment.[64] There is an opportunity cost, however. Shares and options that are not given to employees could be sold to outside investors. The opportunity cost is the price these investors would pay for the shares and options.

In most cases, the first-order effect of stock-based compensation is to increase corporate cash flows. First, stock compensation generates tax savings, as stock grants and certain stock options result in deductions on the corporate return. For example, in its fiscal year ending June 30, 2000, Microsoft reported a tax benefit (that is, savings) associated with employee stock plans exceeding $5.5 billion.[65] Second, cash inflows may result from option exercise (whereby the executive pays the exercise price to the corporation in exchange for the promised shares). Indirectly, stock-based compensation may increase corporate cash flow as it reduces the amount of cash compensation that needs to be paid. Core and Guay (2001) provide evidence "consistent with cash constrained" corporations using stock options in lieu of cash compensation. However, as discussed above, to counter the dilution associated with stock compensation programs, many corporations repurchase their own stock in the market, a cash outflow. For example, Microsoft spent $19 billion repurchasing its own shares during its 2006 fiscal year,[66] while both Cisco[67] and Intel[68] spent more than $10 billion during their 2005 fiscal year. While these amounts are larger than most, as shown in Table 6-7, corporations spend substantial sums repurchasing their own shares.

Taxes
Due to the volume of option exercises and stock grants, companies save substantial amounts on their taxes. While the $5.5 billion Microsoft saved in 2000 is the largest

I am aware of, other companies saving significant amounts in taxes during their 2005 fiscal year include Yahoo, $760 million,[69] Intel, $351 million,[70] and eBay, $267 million.[71] Generally, the corporation gets a deduction for the dollar value of the stock granted, or if options, the profit on exercise.

If the stock grant is unrestricted, the corporation gets an immediate deduction equal to the current value of the shares granted. If the grant is restricted, the executive recognizes income and the corporation takes as a deduction the fair value of the shares when the restrictions expire, although an 83(b) election allows the executive to recognize the income (and the corporation the deduction) earlier.

With a stock option, or in particular a nonqualified stock option, as long as the exercise price of the option is equal to or greater than the share price at the date of grant, the employee recognizes no income, nor does the corporation recognize a deduction at that time.[72] Rather, at the time of exercise, the employee recognizes ordinary income, and the employer deducts the difference between the fair value of stock purchased and the exercise price paid. A special type of option, referred to as a qualified or Section 422 (Internal Revenue Code Section 422 which is reproduced in Appendix 6-2 sets the rules options must meet to be considered qualified) option, allows the executive to defer taxation at the time of exercise and, ultimately, recognize income as a capital gain, if certain conditions are met. However, if these conditions are met the employer does not receive a tax deduction. The Internal Revenue Code limits the use of qualified stock options to $100,000 of face value (number of options times exercise price) vesting in any particular year.[73] Thus, qualified stock options are of little relevance to top executives at large corporations who routinely receive options with face values that can run into the millions.

Internal Revenue Code Section 162(m), the million-dollar cap, also applies to stock-based compensation. Consequently, the corporation needs to qualify its plans to deduct any compensation over $1 million. Stock options, as long as they are granted at or above the current market price, are easy to qualify as performance based.[74] That is, because they only have value if the share price increases, they are assumed by Section 162(m) to be performance based. In contrast, stock grants are harder to qualify, because they have value as long as the share price is greater than zero. Thus, the shares would have to be earned based on a performance measure for stock grants to be deductible.

Financial Reporting

Warren Buffett has made the point succinctly: if a company has a choice between paying its employees with a currency that counts against its earnings and another currency that does not, there is not a lot of mystery about which one it will pick.[75]

Historically, most companies did not record any expense for stock options granted to employees for financial accounting purposes. In fact, many critics (see, for example, Welles 1998) have argued that because companies did not record expense, they overused options. In contrast to other forms of compensation, such as salary, bonuses, stock grants and pensions, which are expensed when earned regardless of when they are paid, under Accounting Principles Board Opinion No. 25, stock options do not result in any expense recognition as long as they are fixed in nature, and the exercise price is greater than the market price at the date of grant. An option is considered fixed if the exercise price and number of shares obtainable are known at the date of grant. In contrast, if the options have to be earned, that is, the executive's ability to exercise the option is dependent upon performance after the date of grant, then the options are considered variable for accounting purposes. Under Financial Accounting Standards Board Interpretation No. 28, companies had to recognize an expense for variable options. It has been asserted that companies preferred fixed to variable options for this reason.[76]

Beginning with fiscal years starting after June 15, 2005, companies were required by Statement of Financial Accounting Standards (SFAS) 123(revised) to expense all options granted to employees using the fair value of the option. That fair value could be determined from an option pricing model (see Appendix 6-3) or using the market value of the option (see Appendix 6-4). Consistent with the expectation that expensing would lead to a reduction in the use of stock options, we have seen some reduction in stock option grants over the past few years, in part because of the anticipation of the new rules, but also because the market peaked in March 2000 and has, at best, been flat since then. In a survey conducted by the Controllers' Leadership Roundtable in June of 2006 (Balsam et al. 2006), we found that almost 40 percent of companies responded that they reduced stock option grants in response to the new rules. Perhaps consistent with a leveling of the accounting field between options and grants, we also saw that about 50 percent of the companies that had not previously issued restricted share grants were now doing so.

What we have not observed yet, and may not, is a change in the parameters of the existing options. As noted above, prior to SFAS 123(revised), financial accounting rules discouraged the use of performance/variable options as they were expensed, whereas fixed options were not. Under SFAS 123(revised), fixed and variable options must be expensed, thereby leveling the playing field between the two types of options. Further, given that expense need only be recognized for options that "vest," a plan that adds performance conditions to previously fixed options reduces the likelihood those options will vest, and hence the expense associated with those options.

Observation on Differences Between Tax and Financial Accounting

Potentially there is an enormous difference between the amounts calculated by the valuation models at the date of grant and the actual profits to employees/deductions to the employer at the date of exercise. For example, Microsoft in 2000 disclosed a pro forma reduction in net income of $1.2 billion due to its stock option grants. As noted previously, Microsoft disclosed that it saved $5.5 billion in taxes due to stock option exercises that same year. Utilizing the top federal tax bracket of 35 percent, Microsoft would have had to deduct $15.7 billion on its tax return to save $5.5 billion in taxes. So while it disclosed a cost of $1.2 billion in its financial accounting footnotes, it deducted $15.7 billion on its tax return. The Financial Accounting Standards Board is aware of this discrepancy requiring, in SFAS 123 (revised) that the "excess tax benefit" rather than reduce reported tax expense, be credited to shareholders equity, and that it appear as a financing inflow on the statement of cash flows. A more interesting question might be: Where does the difference come from in the first place? One reason for the difference is that the accounting cost determined at the date of grant is the "present value" of a future amount. Ignoring other factors, given a discount rate of 12 percent and time to exercise of six years, the accounting cost (present value) would be 50 percent of the tax deduction (future amount). A second reason for the difference lies in the types of corporations that elect to issue stock options. The executives and directors of these corporations have insight and inside information on the future performance of their corporation. Consequently, they are more likely to issue options when they expect above-average growth in share price, a fact not reflected in the accounting cost, but if correct, reflected in the future tax deduction.

Political Costs

As with other forms of compensation, stock-based compensation is politically sensitive. While critics, including politicians, complain about compensation being unresponsive to corporate performance, and have encouraged corporations to use more performance-based compensation like stock options, they object when those packages lead to big payouts. Sometimes these criticisms take place when the compensation plan is passed, or the compensation package is put together, whereas in other cases, the criticism only occurs when the enormity of the payouts is realized. For example, CALPERs, the very large and active California Public Employees Retirement System, a major shareholder in many public corporations, objects publicly to compensation packages it deems excessive.

Possibly the most controversial plan involved Computer Associates. Shareholders approved the plan, 1995 Key Employee Stock Ownership Plan, by a vote of 98,427,761 for versus 26,944,563 against, with 1,221,062 abstentions.[77] The criticism, and in this case the lawsuits, began after the corporation awarded its top three executives shares worth more than $1 billion in 1998. As noted in its proxy:

> ... reflects long-term incentive compensation earned in fiscal year 1999 based on the achievement of stock price targets established in connection with the 1995 Plan. Under that plan, previously described in the 1995 Proxy and approved by the stockholders at the 1995 Annual Meeting, Messrs. Wang, Kumar and Artzt, were awarded in the aggregate 20.25 million shares. Such share awards, which vested in their entirety on May 21, 1998, were in the amounts of $645,412,050, $322,706,025, and $107,568,675, for Messrs. Wang, Kumar, and Artzt, respectively.[78]

The award led to lawsuits. The justification for the lawsuits was that the board awarded 20.25 million shares, while the plan only allowed 6 million. The difference between the 6 million approved and the 20.25 million awarded was caused by three stock splits in August 1995, June 1996 and November 1997. However, the plan did not specify that either the number of shares allowed would be increased or that the stock price targets would be reduced in the event of a split. To resolve the case a settlement was arrived at whereby Wang, Kumar and Artzt returned 4.5 million of the 20.25 million shares previously award to the corporation:

> Pursuant to a court approved settlement, Mr. Wang will return to the Company 2,700,000 shares of Common Stock previously issued under the 1995 Plan. Pursuant to a court approved settlement, Mr. Kumar and Mr. Artzt will return to the Company 1,350,000 and 450,000 shares, respectively, of Common Stock previously issued under the 1995 Plan.[79]

While Computer Associates is an extreme, first in amount and second in the fact that executives actually returned shares to the company, large profitable exercises are very visible and lead to criticism even if they result from an increasing stock price. Further, as noted above, mega-grants assure large profits even if the stock price appreciates very little. These profits are required to be reported in corporate proxy statements and are then reported in the annual surveys conducted by the business press, that is, *The Wall Street Journal, BusinessWeek,*

Forbes, etc. Consider the following amounts reported in the *Forbes* compensation survey. The highest compensation recorded to date was that of Lawrence Ellison of Oracle at more than $706 million in 2001. Following close behind was Charles Wang of Computer Associates at more than $650 million in 1999, and Michael Eisner of Disney at more than $589 million in 1998. In most cases, the bulk of these amounts were in the form of stock compensation.

Summary

The focus of this chapter was stock compensation. As noted in earlier chapters, the primary form of stock compensation, in terms of usage and value, is stock options, although stock grants are used by a growing number of corporations. Stock-based compensation is a variable, or an at-risk, form of compensation, although the risk the executive is subject to depends upon the type of compensation. For example, whereas a stock option is only valuable when the share price exceeds the exercise price, a stock grant is valuable as long as the share price is positive.

More than any other form of compensation, stock compensation provides executives with the incentive to increase shareholder value, because as shareholders and as potential shareholders (option holders), they benefit directly from that increase in shareholder value. However, at some point, stock compensation may make the executive more risk averse than optimal, as the underdiversified executive becomes fearful of losing what he or she has already gained. Thus, the terms of grants, for example, vesting period, exercise price, whether the grants have reload provisions, etc., must be chosen carefully.

While stock compensation can have financial reporting and political costs, the major cost associated with stock compensation is dilution. Dilution arises because stock compensation programs have the potential to increase the number of outstanding shares, and hence, dilute the proportionate ownership of existing shareholders. To limit this dilution corporations have spent billions of dollars repurchasing their own shares.

Footnotes

1 Page 2, Ford Motor Co. 8-K filed with the Securities and Exchange Commission, Sept. 8, 2006.

2 Page 14 Motorola proxy statement filed with the Securities and Exchange Commission, March 10, 2006.

3 John Brock Form 4, filed with the Securities and Exchange Commission, April 27, 2006.

4 Page 27, Merck proxy statement filed with the Securities and Exchange Commission, March 9, 2006.

5 Page 2, Ford Motor Co. 8-K filed with the Securities and Exchange Commission, Sept. 8, 2006.

6 Matsunaga (1995, note 6) and Murphy (1998) find about 95 percent of corporations granting options with an exercise price equal to grant-date fair market value.

7 As will be discussed later in this chapter, when share prices fall after the date of grant, resulting in the exercise price of the option being greater than the share price, companies sometimes grant additional options at the lower price and/or reduce the exercise price on the existing option.

8 Page 12, Amazon.com proxy statement filed with the Securities and Exchange Commission, March 29, 2000.

9 See Matsunaga (1995) or Balsam and Paek (2001).

10 Page 4, Exhibit 10.6, E I Du Pont De Nemours 10-Q filed with the Securities and Exchange Commission, May 5, 2005.

11 Page 23, General Electric proxy statement filed with the Securities and Exchange Commission, March 3, 2006.

12 Page 15, PerkinElmer proxy statement filed with the Securities and Exchange Commission, March 17, 2006.

13 For simplification the discussion in the text ignores the fact that if leaving the corporation causes the executive to exercise his or her options earlier than anticipated, he or she forfeits the remaining time value of the option.

14 Carlton (2000).

15 The dollar value for the stock option grants is determined by Standard & Poor's ExecuComp using the Black-Scholes options pricing model, whereas the dollar value for the stock grants is determined (and reported) by the granting corporations using the market price of the shares on the date of grant.

[16] The median stock grant is zero, because as observed in Table 2.1, only 22 percent of corporations grant stock to their CEOs in 2000.

[17] Page 28, Wells Fargo proxy statement filed with the Securities and Exchange Commission, March 17, 2006.

[18] Page 13, Walt Disney proxy statement filed with the Securities and Exchange Commission, Jan. 11, 2006.

[19] Page 22, Tribune proxy statement filed with the Securities and Exchange Commission, April 8, 2005.

[20] Page 26, Tribune proxy statement filed with the Securities and Exchange Commission, April 8, 2005.

[21] Page 25, Tribune proxy statement filed with the Securities and Exchange Commission, April 8, 2005.

[22] Page 26, Tribune proxy statement filed with the Securities and Exchange Commission, April 8, 2005.

[23] Page 4, Tribune proxy statement filed with the Securities and Exchange Commission, April 2, 2004.

[24] Page 4, Tribune proxy statement filed with the Securities and Exchange Commission, April 8, 2005.

[25] Page 35, Comcast proxy statement filed with the Securities and Exchange Commission, March 24, 2006.

[26] Page 28, Boston Scientific proxy statement filed with the Securities and Exchange Commission, April 10, 2006.

[27] Page 33, Cisco Systems proxy statement filed with the Securities and Exchange Commission, Sept. 26, 2005.

[28] Raymond Zinn, form 4 filed with the Securities and Exchange Commission, March 21, 2006.

[29] Page 11, Level 3 Communications proxy statement filed with the Securities and Exchange Commission, April 10, 2006.

[30] More precisely, as will be discussed in more detail in Chapter 8, in most cases the executive only need concern him/herself with being dismissed for cause. That is, in many cases when an executive is dismissed without cause, both restricted shares and options vest immediately.

[31] Page 29, American Express proxy statement filed with the Securities and Exchange Commission, March 22, 2006.

[32] Brady (2000).

33 While corporations have been required to disclose the value of restricted shares granted, but not the number granted, in their proxy statements, this information is not readily available in machine-readable form. Consequently, this analysis ignores restricted share grants, which we know are becoming increasingly important.

34 The 1.2 percent and 13.7 percent are from Leonhardt (2000).

35 New York Stock Exchange Manual Section 312.03.

36 NASDAQ Manual 4350-5.

37 17CFR 240.16b-3.

38 Page 18, Ben & Jerry's 10-Q filed with the Securities and Exchange Commission, Aug. 10, 1999.

39 Page 57 of Microsoft form 10-K filed with Securities and Exchange Commission, Aug. 26, 2005.

40 Page 19 of Cisco annual report, filed as attachment 13.1 of Cisco's form 10-K filed with the Securities and Exchange Commission, Sept. 9, 2005.

41 This increase may not be entirely attributable to stock options and grants, as corporations may also issue additional shares to the general public to raise equity funds.

42 Actually fiscal years beginning after June 15, 2005 (SFAS 123R).

43 Report to Congress, July 16, 2002.

44 The singling out of Ralston-Purina flows from its use in Campbell and Wasley (1999). By setting a hurdle, albeit a low one, Ralston-Purina at least linked executives and shareholder wealth. Even today, most corporations grant restricted stock whose only requirement is the executive remain with the company for a certain period of time.

45 Shortly after arriving at VerticalNet, Galli departed to become president and CEO of Newell Rubbermaid.

46 Buckman (2000).

47 Page 55, Apple Computer 10-K filed with the Securities and Exchange Commission, Dec. 23, 1998.

48 Page 10, Apple Computer proxy statement filed with the Securities and Exchange Commission, March 24, 2003.

49 Page 15 Genesis Health Ventures proxy statement filed with the Securities and Exchange Commission, Jan. 28, 2000.

50 Interestingly, companies have no problem asking shareholders to approve plans allowing for restricted stock grants—which as noted above have a zero exercise price.

[51] Page 21, Dell proxy statement filed with the Securities and Exchange Commission, May 30, 2003.

[52] Page 25, Gap proxy statement filed with the Securities and Exchange Commission, April 1, 2003.

[53] While no expense was required for fixed at-the-money options, if accounted for properly, these were discount options, and the expense needed to be recognized in the amount of the discount.

[54] Page 25, Microsoft annual report included in form 10-K filed with Securities and Exchange Commission, Sept. 28, 1999.

[55] Exhibit 99.1 of Brocade Communications Systems form 8-K filed with Securities and Exchange Commission, Jan. 6, 2005.

[56] Exhibit 99.1 of Brocade Communications Systems form 8-K filed with Securities and Exchange Commission, Jan. 24, 2005.

[57] Page 63, Micrel form 10-K filed with Securities and Exchange Commission, March 6, 2006.

[58] Page 111 Cognos form 10-K filed with Securities and Exchange Commission, Aug. 1, 2006.

[59] Exhibit 1, United Health form 8-K filed with Securities and Exchange Commission, May 1, 2006.

[60] Page 78, RCN form 10-K filed with Securities and Exchange Commission, April 2, 2001.

[61] As discussed elsewhere, there was no expense recognized for fixed stock options under APB Opinion No. 25, whereas FASB Statement No. 123 requires an expense be recognized for both fixed and variable options. Coincidentally, during 2000, RCN also adopted the recognition provisions of SFAS No. 123.

[62] Page 11, Level 3 Communications proxy statement filed with Securities and Exchange Commission, April 10, 2006.

[63] Page 18, Level 3 Communications proxy statement filed with Securities and Exchange Commission, April 10, 2006

[64] An exception would be if the corporation agreed to pay the taxes on the exercise profits, which sometimes happens.

[65] Page 3, Exhibit 13.4 to Microsoft form 10-K filed with the Securities and Exchange Commission, Sept. 28, 2000.

[66] Page 45, Microsoft form 10-K filed with the Securities and Exchange Commission, Aug. 25, 2006.

[67] Page 42 of exhibit 13.1 to Cisco Systems form 10-K filed with the Securities and Exchange Commission, Sept. 19, 2005.

[68] Page 51, Intel form 10-K filed with the Securities and Exchange Commission, Feb. 27, 2006.

[69] Page 60, Yahoo form 10-K filed with the Securities and Exchange Commission, March 3, 2006.

[70] Page 51, Intel form 10-K filed with the Securities and Exchange Commission, Feb. 27, 2006.

[71] Page 82, eBay form 10-K filed with the Securities and Exchange Commission, Feb. 24, 2006.

[72] If however, the exercise price is less than the market price on the date of grant, the employee must recognize ordinary income, and the corporation takes a deduction at that point in time for the excess of the market price over the exercise price.

[73] Section 422 options, while having preferential tax treatment for executives, must satisfy a number of requirements in addition to those mentioned in the text. For example, the exercise price may not be less than the fair market price at the date of grant, nor may the option be exercisable more than 10 years after the date of grant.

[74] In addition to granting the options with an exercise price at or above the market price on the date of grant, the options must be granted pursuant to a plan approved by shareholders, which specifies the number of options that may be granted, overall and to any one individual. While my expectation is that the percentage of corporations qualifying their stock option plans will be close to 100 percent, Rose and Wolfram (2000) only find 76 percent of their sample qualify their stock option plans. An explanation for the relatively low percentage of qualifiers is that Rose and Wolfram include corporations not subject to section 162(m) in their sample, which biases the percentage of qualifiers downward.

[75] Leonhardt (2000).

[76] Gilles (1999).

[77] Item 4, Computer Associates 10-Q filed with Securities and Exchange Commission, Nov. 2, 1995.

[78] Computer Associates proxy statement filed with Securities and Exchange Commission, July 12, 1999.

[79] Computer Associates proxy statement filed with Securities and Exchange Commission, July 14, 2000.

Appendix 6-1

AMERIGROUP Corp.[1]

2005 Equity Incentive Plan, Incentive Stock Option Agreement

This Incentive Stock Option Agreement (the "Option Agreement") is made and entered into as of ___, 200___ (the "Date of Grant"), by and between AMERI-GROUP Corporation, a Delaware corporation (the "Company"), and ___ (the "Optionee"). Capitalized terms not defined herein shall have the meaning ascribed to them in the Company's 2005 Equity Incentive Plan (the "Plan").

1. **Number of Shares.** The Company hereby grants to Optionee an option (this "Option") to purchase ___ Shares (the "Option Shares") at an Exercise Price per Share of $ ___ , subject to all of the terms and conditions of this Option Agreement and the Plan. The Option is intended to be treated as an Incentive Stock Option.

2. **Option Term.** The term of the Option (the "Option Term") shall commence on the Date of Grant set forth above and, unless the Option is previously terminated pursuant to Section 5 below, shall terminate on the [___] anniversary thereof (the "Expiration Date"). As of the Expiration Date, all rights of Optionee hereunder shall terminate.

3. **Conditions of Exercise.**

   [If granted pursuant to AMERIGROUP's Bonus Plan]

   (a) Subject to Section 5 below, the Option shall become vested on the Date of Grant as to ___ percent (___ %) of the Option Shares, as to an additional ___ percent (___ %) of the Option Shares on April 1, 200___ and as to an additional ___ percent (___ %) of the Option Shares quarterly thereafter, such that the Option shall become fully (100%) vested on ___, 200___.

   [If granted other than under AMERIGROUP's Bonus Plan]

   (a) Subject to Section 5 below, the Option shall become vested as to ___ of the Option Shares on the first anniversary of the Date of Grant, and as to an additional ___ of the Option Shares quarterly thereafter, such that the Option shall become fully (100%) vested on ___.

   (b) Prior to the Expiration Date, this Option may, subject to Section 5 below, be exercised in whole or in part at any time, but only as to Option Shares that have vested. Without limiting Section 5, if Optionee's employment with the Company and all Subsidiaries and Affiliates terminates, then from and after such Termination Date (as defined in Section 5 below), this Option may be exercised only with respect to Option Shares that have vested as of the Termination Date and only as expressly permitted pursuant to Section 5.

(c) This Option may not be exercised for a fraction of a share.

4. Method of Exercise of Option.

(a) The Option may be exercised by delivering to the Company an executed stock option exercise agreement in the form attached hereto as Exhibit A, or in such other form as may be approved by the Administrator from time to time (the "Exercise Agreement"), which shall set forth, inter alia, (i) Optionee's election to exercise the Option and (ii) the number of vested Option Shares being purchased, and payment in full of the aggregate Exercise Price of such Option Shares. If someone other than Optionee exercises the Option, then such person must submit documentation reasonably acceptable to the Company verifying that such person has the legal right to exercise the Option.

(b) The Option may not be exercised unless such exercise is in compliance with all applicable federal and state securities law, as they are in effect on the date of exercise.

(c) Payment of the aggregate Exercise Price for Option Shares being purchased and any applicable withholding taxes may be made (i) in cash or by check, (ii) to the extent permitted by applicable law, by means of a cashless exercise procedure through a broker acceptable to the Administrator, or (iii) through delivery of unrestricted Shares already owned by Optionee for more than six months on the date of surrender, to the extent the shares have an aggregate Fair Market Value on the date of surrender equal to the aggregate Exercise Price of the Shares as to which such Option shall be exercised.

5. Effect of Termination of Employment, Change in Control and Disabling Conduct.

(a) Termination of Employment Generally.

(i) Upon the termination of Optionee's employment with the Company and all Subsidiaries and Affiliates, the Option shall immediately terminate as to any Option Shares that have not previously vested as of the date of such termination (the "Termination Date").

(ii) Any portion of the Option that has vested as of the Termination Date shall be exercisable in whole or in part for a period of 90 days following the Termination Date (the "Post-Termination Exercise Period") unless Optionee has been terminated for Cause or engaged in Disabling Conduct (defined below); provided, in no event may the Option be exercised after the Expiration Date.

(iii) In the event of termination by reason of Optionee's death or Disability, the Post-Termination Exercise Period shall extend until the date that is twelve months from the Termination Date; provided, in no event may the Option be exercised after the Expiration Date.

(iv) Upon the expiration of the Post-Termination Exercise Period any unexercised portion of the Option shall terminate in full (whether or not then exercisable).

(b) Termination for Cause; Disabling Conduct.

(i) The Option shall terminate in full (whether or not then exercisable) immediately upon the termination of Optionee's employment with the Company or any Subsidiary or Affiliate for Cause.

(ii) The Option also shall terminate in full (whether or not then exercisable) immediately if Optionee engages in Disabling Conduct.

[At the discretion of the Administrator, either]

(c) Change in Control. For purposes of Section 5(a) above, any portion of the Option that has not previously vested shall be deemed fully vested if Optionee's employment or service with the Company or any Subsidiary or Affiliate is terminated by the Company or any Subsidiary or Affiliate or any successor entity for any reason (other than for Cause or as a result of Disabling Conduct) within two years following a Change in Control or if Optionee terminates employment or service with the Company or any Subsidiary or Affiliate within two years following the Change in Control and after there is a material adverse change in the nature or status of Optionee's duties or responsibilities from those in effect immediately prior to the Change in Control. [or]

(c) Change in Control. Any portion of the Option that has not previously vested shall become fully vested upon a Change in Control.

(d) Definition of Disabling Conduct. As used herein, "Disabling Conduct" shall mean conduct involving a breach of the covenants made in Section 6 below.

6. Covenant Not to Compete.

(a) In consideration for the grant of the Option, and as a material condition to the grant, Optionee hereby expressly agrees as follows:

(i) Optionee will act in the best interests of the Company and its Subsidiaries and Affiliates (each, an "AMERIGROUP Company" and collectively, the "AMERIGROUP Companies") throughout the period of Optionee's employment with any of the AMERIGROUP Companies; and

(ii) at all times while employed by any AMERIGROUP Company and at all times during the Covered Post-Employment Period (defined below), Optionee will not (A) compete with any AMERIGROUP Company by serving a Competitor (defined below) in any managerial capacity, or in any capacity that influences business strategy, with respect to a Covered Product or Service (defined below) that the Competitor is offering in a Covered Area (defined below) or developing to offer in a Covered Area, or (B) solicit for employment, interfere with the employment relationship of or endeavor to entice away any employee of any AMERIGROUP Company.

(b) As used herein,

(i) The "Covered Post-Employment Period" means the twelve (12) month period beginning on the first day on which Optionee is no longer employed by any AMERIGROUP Company as a result of Optionee's resignation or termination for Cause and ending on the first anniversary of such date. (In the event the Company terminates Optionee without Cause, there shall not be a Covered Post-Employment Period.)

(ii) "Competitor" means any entity or person that provides or is planning to provide a Covered Product or Service in competition with a Covered Product or Service that an AMERIGROUP Company is actively developing, marketing, providing or selling.

(iii) "Confidential Information" means an AMERIGROUP Company's material non-public information concerning its business and affairs, including, without limitation, trade secrets, strategies, business plans, marketing and advertising plans, member and provider information, employee and personnel information, contracts, training manuals, financial projections, budgets and non-public financial data (including, without limitation, statements with premium revenue and/or provider compensation terms, reports of actuaries, medical loss reports, balance sheets and income statements).

(iv) A "Covered Product or Service" shall mean a managed health care product or service offered or provided to any beneficiary of and/or participant in any Medicaid, Medicaid-related, or SSI program, any government-funded children's health insurance program or any federal and/or state sponsored health care program that is substantially similar to any of such programs.

(v) The "Covered Area" shall consist of each city, county and other similar governmental territory in which an AMERIGROUP Company provides or has made material efforts to develop and provide a Covered Product or Service to its members, if in the course of Optionee's employment with an AMERIGROUP Company he or she (A) has provided services to an AMERIGROUP Company with respect to the Covered Products or Services in such city, county or governmental territory, or (B) reviewed or discussed Confidential Information of an AMERIGROUP Company with respect to the Covered Product or Service in such city, county or governmental territory.

(c)   Optionee agrees that any breach by Optionee of the covenants made in Section 6(a) above may cause irreparable damage to one or more of the AMERIGROUP Companies and that in the event of such breach each AMERIGROUP Company shall have, in addition to any and all remedies of law, the right to an injunction, specific performance or other equitable relief to prevent the violation of Optionee's obligations hereunder. Optionee agrees that any such AMERIGROUP Company may seek and obtain injunctive relief without posting an injunction bond. Optionee hereby acknowledges and agrees that Optionee will have access to confidential and proprietary information and trade secrets concerning the AMERIGROUP Companies during Optionee's employment and that the covenants in Section 6(a) are reasonable in scope and necessary to protect the legitimate business interests of the AMERIGROUP Companies. Optionee hereby further expressly acknowledges and agrees that each AMERIGROUP Company is an express third party beneficiary of the terms of this Agreement. (For the avoidance of doubt, Optionee acknowledges and agrees that the experience and/or knowledge that Optionee acquires in the course of his or her employment with an AMERIGROUP Company may relate not only to the Covered Products and Services of the AMERIGROUP Company with which he or she is employed, but also those of other AMERIGROUP Companies.)

7.   Adjustments. In the event of any Change in Capitalization, the Administrator shall take such actions pursuant to Section 5 of the Plan (including the provisions thereof relating to the cancellation of Awards in exchange for a payment in cash or other property) as it deems appropriate.

8.   Certain Changes. The Administrator may accelerate the date on which the Option becomes exercisable, waive or amend the operation of the provisions of this Agreement respecting exercise after termination of

employment or otherwise adjust any of the terms of the Option; provided that no action under this Section 8 shall adversely affect Optionee's rights hereunder or cause the Option to be treated as other than an Incentive Stock Option without the consent of Optionee.

9. Nontransferability of Option. Except under the laws of descent and distribution, Optionee shall not be permitted to sell, transfer, pledge or assign the Option or this Option Agreement, and the Option shall be exercisable, during Optionee's lifetime, only by Optionee. Without limiting the generality of the foregoing, except as otherwise provided herein, the Option may not be assigned, transferred, pledged or hypothecated in any way, shall not be assignable by operation of law, and shall not be subject to execution, attachment or similar process. Any attempted assignment, transfer, pledge, hypothecation or other disposition of the Option contrary to the provisions hereof, and the levy of any execution, attachment or similar process upon the Option shall be null and void and without effect.

10. Notices. All notices and other communications under this Agreement shall be in writing and shall be given by facsimile or first class mail, certified or registered with return receipt requested, and shall be deemed to have been duly given three days after mailing or 24 hours after transmission by facsimile to the respective parties named below:

If to the Company: AMERIGROUP Corporation
4425 Corporation Lane
Virginia Beach, VA 23462
Facsimile: (757) 557-6743
Attn: Stanley F. Baldwin

If to Optionee:
Facsimile:

Either party hereto may change such party's address for notices by notice duly given pursuant hereto.

11. Tax Consequences. The tax laws and regulations applicable to the exercise of the Option and the disposition of the Option Shares are complex and subject to change. Optionee should consult a tax adviser before exercising the Option or disposing of the Shares.

12. Securities Laws Requirements. The Option shall not be exercisable to any extent, and the Company shall not be obligated to transfer any Option Shares to Optionee upon exercise of such Option, if such exercise, in the opinion of counsel for the Company, would violate the

Securities Act of 1933 (the "Securities Act") or any other Federal or state statutes having similar requirements as may be in effect at that time.

13. No Obligation to Register Option Shares. The Company shall be under no obligation to register the Option Shares pursuant to the Securities Act or any other Federal or state securities laws.

14. Investment Representation. Optionee hereby represents and warrants to the Company that Optionee, by reason of Optionee's business or financial experience (or the business or financial experience of Optionee's professional advisors who are unaffiliated with and who are not compensated by the Company or any affiliate or selling agent of the Company, directly or indirectly), has the capacity to protect Optionee's own interests in connection with the transactions contemplated under this Option Agreement.

15. Market Stand-Off. In connection with any underwritten public offering by the Company of its equity securities pursuant to an effective registration statement filed under the Securities Act for such period as the Company or its underwriters may request (such period not to exceed 180 days following the date of the applicable offering), Optionee shall not, directly or indirectly, sell, make any short sale of, loan, hypothecate, pledge, offer, grant or sell any option or other contract for the purchase of, purchase any option or other contract for the sale of, or otherwise dispose of or transfer, or agree to engage in any of the foregoing transactions with respect to, any Option Shares acquired under this Option Agreement without the prior written consent of the Company or its underwriters.

16. Protections Against Violations of Agreement. No purported sale, assignment, mortgage, hypothecation, transfer, pledge, encumbrance, gift, transfer in trust (voting or other) or other disposition of, or creation of a security interest in or lien on, any of the Option Shares by any holder thereof in violation of the provisions of this Agreement or the Certificate of Incorporation or the Bylaws of the Company, will be valid, and the Company will not transfer any of said Option Shares on its books nor will any of said Option Shares be entitled to vote, nor will any dividends be paid thereon, unless and until there has been full compliance with said provisions to the satisfaction of the Company. The foregoing restrictions are in addition to and not in lieu of any other remedies, legal or equitable, available to enforce said provisions.

17. Failure to Enforce Not a Waiver. The failure of the Company to enforce at any time any provision of this Option Agreement shall in no way be construed to be a waiver of such provision or of any other provision hereof.

18. Governing Law. With the exception of Section 6 above, this Option Agreement shall be governed by and construed according to the laws of the State of Delaware without regard to its principles of conflict of laws. The provisions of Section 6 above shall be governed by and construed according to the laws of the Commonwealth of Virginia without regard to its principles of conflict of laws.

19. Incorporation of Plan. The Plan is hereby incorporated by reference and made a part hereof, and the Option and this Option Agreement shall be subject to all terms and conditions of the Plan.

20. Amendments; Construction. The Administrator may amend the terms of this Option Agreement prospectively or retroactively at any time, but no such amendment shall impair the rights of Optionee hereunder (or cause the Option to be treated as other than an Incentive Stock Option) without his or her consent. To the extent the terms of Section 6 above conflict with any prior agreement between the parties related to such subject matter, the terms of Section 6 shall supersede such conflicting terms and control. Headings to Sections of this Option Agreement are intended for convenience of reference only, are not part of this Option Agreement and shall have no affect on the interpretation hereof.

21. Rights as a Stockholder. Neither Optionee nor any of Optionee's successors in interest shall have any rights as a stockholder of the Company with respect to any shares of Common Stock subject to the Option until the date of issuance of a stock certificate for such shares of Common Stock.

22. Agreement Not a Contract for Services. Neither the Plan, the granting of the Option, this Option Agreement nor any other action taken pursuant to the Plan shall constitute or be evidence of any agreement or understanding, express or implied, that Optionee has a right to continue to provide services as an officer, director, employee, consultant or advisor of the Company or any Subsidiary or Affiliate for any period of time or at any specific rate of compensation.

23. Authority of the Administrator. The Administrator shall have full authority to interpret and construe the terms of the Plan and this Option Agreement. The determination of the Administrator as to any such matter of interpretation or construction shall be final, binding and conclusive.

24. Certain Tax Matters. If Optionee fails to comply with the requirements of Section 422(a) of the Code (as from time to time redesignated or amended), subsection (a)(1) of which currently requires that any Option Shares not be disposed of within two (2) years of the date of grant and one (1) year from the date on which such shares are acquired, Optionee understands that the

tax treatment otherwise applicable to the Option shall not be available. Optionee agrees to notify the Company in writing immediately after Optionee makes a disqualifying disposition (within the meaning of Sections 421 and 422 of the Code) of any Option Shares. The Company's obligations under this Option Agreement shall be subject to all applicable tax and other withholding requirements, and the Company shall, to the extent permitted by law, have the right to deduct any withholding amounts from any payment or transfer of any kind otherwise due to Optionee. The Company may, in its discretion, require that Optionee pay to the Company at or after (as determined by the Administrator) the time of exercise of any portion of the Option any such additional amount as the Company deems necessary to satisfy its liability to withhold federal, state or local income tax or any other taxes incurred by reason of the exercise or the transfer of Option Shares.

25. Survival of Terms. This Option Agreement shall apply to and bind Optionee and the Company and their respective permitted assignees and transferees, heirs, legatees, executors, administrators and legal successors. The terms of Section 6 shall expressly survive the termination of the Option and this Agreement.

26. Acceptance. Optionee hereby acknowledges receipt of a copy of the Plan and this Option Agreement. Optionee has read and understand the terms and provision thereof, and accepts the Option subject to all the terms and conditions of the Plan and this Agreement.

27. Severability. Should any provision of this Option Agreement be held by a court of competent jurisdiction to be unenforceable, or enforceable only if modified, such holding shall not affect the validity of the remainder of this Option Agreement, the balance of which shall continue to be binding upon the parties hereto with any such modification (if any) to become a part hereof and treated as though contained in this original Option Agreement. Moreover, if one or more of the provisions contained in this Option Agreement shall for any reason be held to be excessively broad as to scope, activity, subject or otherwise so as to be unenforceable, in lieu of severing such unenforceable provision, such provision or provisions shall be construed by the appropriate judicial body by limiting or reducing it or them, so as to be enforceable to the maximum extent compatible with the applicable law as it shall then appear, and such determination by such judicial body shall not affect the enforceability of such provisions or provisions in any other jurisdiction.

IN WITNESS WHEREOF, the parties hereto have executed and delivered this

Option Agreement on the day and year first above written.

AMERIGROUP Corporation

By

Stanley F. Baldwin

Executive Vice President, General Counsel

and Secretary

Address:

Social Security Number:

EXHIBIT A
AMERIGROUP CORPORATION
2005 EQUITY INCENTIVE PLAN
STOCK OPTION AGREEMENT
NOTICE OF EXERCISE

_____, ____

AMERIGROUP Corporation

[Address]

Attn:

On___, I was granted an option (an "Option") by AMERIGROUP Corporation (the "Company") under the Company's 2000 Equity Incentive Plan (the "Plan") and a stock option agreement, between me and the Company (the "Agreement"). This letter is to notify you that I wish to purchase Option Shares under the Agreement as set forth below.

Exercise of Option

1. I wish to purchase___Option Shares at the current exercise price of $___per share for a total cost of $___.
2. I am paying for these Option Shares as follows:

    ___By enclosing cash and/or a certified or cashier's check payable to the Company in the amount of $___.

    ___By means of a cashless exercise procedure through the following broker: .

    ___By delivery of unrestricted shares of Company stock already owned by me for more than six months on the date of surrender, and which have an aggregate fair market value on the date of surrender equal to the aggregate exercise price of the Option Shares as to which the Option is being exercised, with any fractional share amounts to be settled by cash and/or a certified or cashier's check.

3. I am paying the local, state and federal withholding taxes and/or all other taxes that the Company has advised me are due as follows:

___By enclosing cash and/or a certified or cashier's check payable to the Company in the amount of $___.

___By authorizing the Company to withhold from the number of Option Shares I would otherwise receive that number of whole Shares having a fair market value equal to the minimum tax withholding due, with any fractional share amounts to be settled by cash and/or a certified or cashier's check.

___By delivery of unrestricted shares of Company stock already owned by me for more than six months on the date of surrender, and which have an aggregate fair market value on the date of surrender equal to the minimum tax withholding due, with any fractional share amounts to be settled by cash and/or a certified or cashier's check.

4. In exercising my Option I hereby warrant and represent to the Company that I have not engaged in Disabling Conduct and acknowledge that the Company has no obligation to issue a certificate evidencing any Option Shares purchasable by me until the purchase price of such Option Shares is fully paid as set forth in the Option Agreement.

Very truly yours,

Optionee

Name and Address (please print)

Telephone Number (   )

Social Security Number

Appendix 6-2
§ 422 Incentive Stock Options

(a) In general.

Section 421(a) shall apply with respect to the transfer of a share of stock to an individual pursuant to his exercise of an incentive stock option if—

    (1) no disposition of such share is made by him within 2 years from the date of the granting of the option nor within 1 year after the transfer of such share to him, and

    (2) at all times during the period beginning on the date of the granting of the option and ending on the day 3 months before the date of

such exercise, such individual was an employee of either the corporation granting such option, a parent or subsidiary corporation of such corporation, or a corporation or a parent or subsidiary corporation of such corporation issuing or assuming a stock option in a transaction to which section 424(a) applies.

(b) Incentive stock option.

For purposes of this part, the term "incentive stock option" means an option granted to an individual for any reason connected with his employment by a corporation, if granted by the employer corporation or its parent or subsidiary corporation, to purchase stock of any of such corporations, but only if—

(1) the option is granted pursuant to a plan which includes the aggregate number of shares which may be issued under options and the employees (or class of employees) eligible to receive options, and which is approved by the stockholders of the granting corporation within 12 months before or after the date such plan is adopted;

(2) such option is granted within 10 years from the date such plan is adopted, or the date such plan is approved by the stockholders, whichever is earlier;

(3) such option by its terms is not exercisable after the expiration of 10 years from the date such option is granted;

(4) the option price is not less than the fair market value of the stock at the time such option is granted;

(5) such option by its terms is not transferable by such individual otherwise than by will or the laws of descent and distribution, and is exercisable, during his lifetime, only by him; and

(6) such individual, at the time the option is granted, does not own stock possessing more than 10 percent of the total combined voting power of all classes of stock of the employer corporation or of its parent or subsidiary corporation.

Such term shall not include any option if (as of the time the option is granted) the terms of such option provide that it will not be treated as an incentive stock option.

(c) Special rules.

(1) Good faith efforts to value stock.

If a share of stock is transferred pursuant to the exercise by an individual of an option which would fail to qualify as an incentive stock option under subsection (b) because there was a failure in an attempt, made in good faith, to meet the requirement of subsection (b)(4), the requirement of subsection (b)(4) shall be considered to have been met. To the extent provided in regulations by the Secretary, a similar rule shall apply for purposes of subsection (d).

(2) Certain disqualifying dispositions where amount realized is less than value at exercise.

If—

(A) an individual who has acquired a share of stock by the exercise of an incentive stock option makes a disposition of such share within either of the periods described in subsection (a)(1), and

(B) such disposition is a sale or exchange with respect to which a loss (if sustained) would be recognized to such individual, then the amount which is includible in the gross income of such individual, and the amount which is deductible from the income of his employer corporation, as compensation attributable to the exercise of such option shall not exceed the excess (if any) of the amount realized on such sale or exchange over the adjusted basis of such share.

(3) Certain transfers by insolvent individuals.

If an insolvent individual holds a share of stock acquired pursuant to his exercise of an incentive stock option, and if such share is transferred to a trustee, receiver, or other similar fiduciary in any proceeding under title 11 or any other similar insolvency proceeding, neither such transfer, nor any other transfer of such share for the benefit of his creditors in such proceeding, shall constitute a disposition of such share for purposes of subsection (a)(1).

(4) Permissible provisions.

An option which meets the requirements of subsection (b) shall be treated as an incentive stock option even if—

(A) the employee may pay for the stock with stock of the corporation granting the option,

(B) the employee has a right to receive property at the time of exercise of the option, or

(C) the option is subject to any condition not inconsistent with the provisions of subsection (b).

Subparagraph (B) shall apply to a transfer of property (other than cash) only if section 83 applies to the property so transferred.

(5) 10-percent shareholder rule.

Subsection (b)(6) shall not apply if at the time such option is granted the option price is at least 110 percent of the fair market value of the stock subject to the option and such option by its terms is not exercisable after the expiration of 5 years from the date such option is granted.

(6) Special rule when disabled.

For purposes of subsection (a)(2), in the case of an employee who is disabled (within the meaning of section 22(e)(3)), the 3-month period of subsection (a)(2) shall be 1 year.

(7) Fair market value.

For purposes of this section, the fair market value of stock shall be determined without regard to any restriction other than a restriction which, by its terms, will never lapse.

(d) $100,000 per year limitation.

(1) In general.

To the extent that the aggregate fair market value of stock with respect to which incentive stock options (determined without regard to this subsection) are exercisable for the 1st time by any individual during any calendar year (under all plans of the individual's employer corporation and its parent and subsidiary corporations) exceeds $100,000, such options shall be treated as options which are not incentive stock options.

(2) Ordering rule.

Paragraph (1) shall be applied by taking options into account in the order in which they were granted.

(3) Determination of fair market value.

For purposes of paragraph (1), the fair market value of any stock shall be determined as of the time the option with respect to such stock is granted.

Appendix 6-3

An Introduction to Option-Pricing Models

A stock option is a right to buy a share of stock at a precontracted price over a predetermined period of time. For example, a stock option might allow its holder the right to buy a share of stock for $10 at any time during the next ten years. The issue faced by academics and nonacademics alike, is how to value that right. The right is valuable because, if the share price increases beyond $10 before the right expires, the holder can exercise that right to buy the share at a price less than its worth in the marketplace. As a precursor to explaining option-pricing models, the two components of an option's value,2 the intrinsic and time value, need to be defined. The intrinsic value of an option is equal to the excess of the current market price of a share of stock over the exercise price of the option at any point in time. Continuing with the above example, if the current market price is $12 per share, and the holder of the option can purchase the share for $10, the intrinsic value of the option is $2. The time value of an option is the value attached to the potential increase in the share price over the life of the option. While the intrinsic value is easily determinable, the time value is not, and requires the use of an option-pricing model. Examples of option-valuation models include the Black-Scholes-Merton and a Binomial model. In paragraph A15 of Statement 123(revised), the Financial Accounting Standards Board discusses some of the differences between those two models:

> The Black-Scholes-Merton formula assumes that option exercises occur at the end of an option's contractual term, and that expected volatility, expected dividends, and risk-free interest rates are constant over the option's term. If used to estimate the fair value of instruments in the scope of this Statement, the Black-Scholes-Merton formula must be adjusted to take account of certain characteristics of employee share options and similar instruments that are not consistent with the model's assumptions (for example, the ability to exercise before the end of the option's contractual term). Because of the nature of the formula, those adjustments take the form of weighted average assumptions about those characteristics. In contrast, a lattice model can be designed to accommodate dynamic assumptions of expected volatility and dividends over the option's contractual term, and estimates of expected option exercise patterns during the option's contractual term, including the effect of **blackout periods.** Therefore, the design of a lattice model more fully reflects the substantive characteristics of a particular employee share option or similar instrument.

To illustrate the complexity of option-pricing models, consider the formula used by Foster et al. (1991) to calculate the value of options under the Black-Scholes-Merton model:[3]

$$V = [e^{-\ln(1+k)t}S\_(Z) - e^{-\ln(1+r)t}X\_(Z-\_\sqrt{t})],$$

where V = the value of the option,
  S = the current stock price,
  X = the exercise price,
  r = the risk-free rate,
  $\_^2$ = the variance of return on the optioned stock,
  t = the time until the option matures,
  k = the continuous-dividend yield as a constant proportion of the underlying share price,

$_(.) = $ the cumulative normal density function, and

$Z \quad = \quad [\ln(S/X)+(\ln(1+r)-\ln(1+k)+\_^2/2)t]/\_\sqrt{t}$

As can be seen from the formula, the option-pricing model estimates the option's value by considering the current stock price, the exercise price, the time until the option matures, the continuous dividends, the risk-free rate and the variance of return on the optioned stock. It can be shown that the value of the option increases with increases in the current stock price, the variance of return on the optioned stock and the time until the option matures, and that it decreases with increases in the exercise price, the risk-free rate and the continuous dividend yield. To illustrate, continuing with the above example so that the current price is $12 and the exercise price is $10, assume that the variance of return on the optioned stock is 0.5 or 50 percent per year, the time to maturity is six years, the risk free rate is 5 percent and the stock does not pay dividends. The Black-Scholes-Merton value of the option would be slightly more than $7. Given the intrinsic value of $2, that would mean that the time value of the option was $5.

Although few are familiar with the formula itself, readily available computer software can perform the actual calculation. However, effort must be expended to get the inputs for the model, and some of the models require significant amounts of data. For example, the binomial model requires historical knowledge of employee exercise patterns. Perhaps for that reason most firms use the Black-Scholes-Merton model for financial accounting purposes.[4]

It has been asserted by many (see discussion in Balsam 1994) that these models tend to overvalue employee stock options because they assume tradeability, the ability to sell short, and ignore the effect of the continued employment requirement, all of which reduce the value of the option to the employee. This has motivated some, for example Zions Bancorporation, to look for alternatives to option-pricing models to minimize the expense on the income statement. Their alternative is discussed in Appendix 6-4.

Appendix 6-4

A number of companies are attempting to apply the market value alternative to option-pricing models allowed by paragraph 22 of SFAS 123R. In January of 2007, Zions Bancorporation was the first to receive Securities and Exchange Commission (SEC) approval for its Employee Stock Option Appreciation Rights Securities (ESOARS), which are derivative securities designed to provide a market basis for estimating the fair value of stock options granted to employees. Zions not only plans to use these securities itself, but is also marketing these securities and its expertise in designing these securities to other corporations.

What Are ESOARS?

Put simply, ESOARS represents a derivative security whose value depends not only on the price of the underlying share of stock, but also the vesting and exercise patterns of the underlying stock options (hereafter reference options) that it is tied to. Page seven of Zion's Sept. 22, 2006, submission to the SEC describes:

> The net realized value is calculated as the difference between the trading price per share of Zions' common stock at the time employees exercise their ESOs and the exercise price of the reference options, multiplied by the number of shares of common stock obtained by ESO holders on exercise. Payments to ESOARS holders will be made quarterly.

But it is not so simple. Unlike an option that has one exercise date, the payout to the ESOARS will be quarterly and will be based upon the percentage of reference options exercised during that quarter.[5] Consider the following example:

- The number of ESOARS sold equals 100,000, which is 10 percent of the number of reference options, which were 1 million.
- The exercise price of those options is $20.
- The average market price during the fourth quarter of 2007 is $25.
- 5% of reference options are exercised during the fourth quarter.

Under these circumstances, the payout to all ESOARS holders would equal 100,000 units x 5% exercised x ($25 market – $20 exercise price), or a total of $25,000. The ESOARS would remain outstanding, with the holders continuing to receive payments in future quarters when/if the remaining 95 percent of reference options are exercised.

The Benefit to Corporations

The benefit to the corporation ostensibly is a better measure of the cost of the options. In practice this may mean a lower measure of the cost. Based upon the results of its initial auction, Zions Bancorporation estimates the value of the options granted at $8.57 per option (see page 16 of Sept. 22, 2006, submission), whereas the Black-Scholes-Merton model yields a per-option value of $12.65 (see page 17 of its submission). In other words, the accounting expense could be substantially reduced using the market-based approach. While they expect auction prices to increase over time as more investors enter the market and become familiar with the securities, they expect "given the well-publicized criticisms of the

Black-Scholes-Merton model, … the market value to be somewhat lower than the modeled price …" (see page 18 of their submission). "ESOARS seek to solve the problem of Black-Scholes overstating the options value," said Evan Hill, a vice president of Zions who helped develop the security. "If Black-Scholes is not over-stating the value, then ESOARS does not solve anyone's problem." (Norris 2007)

Costs to the Corporation

ESOARS are SEC-registered traded securities. Issuing a security involves substantial transaction costs. In addition to paying Zions for its "assistance," the company will need to engage law firms and accountants in the preparation of an offering prospectus, advertise to attract potential investors (page 9 of Zions' submission indicated it spent "in excess of $100,000 on this") and screen those investors to ensure a sufficient level of expertise, set up an auction and set up a record-keeping system for these securities that is tied to the record-keeping system for existing options (recall the value of these options is tied to the vesting and exercise behavior of the underlying options). While not breaking down the costs, Zions' prospectus supplement, filed with the SEC on July 3, 2006, notes that while there were 21 winning bidders who paid a total of $702,075, proceeds were $340,075, indicating that expenses of the offering absorbed more than half of the gross proceeds. As the underlying options are exercised, they then will have to make payments to the holders of the ESOARS, which will involve additional transaction costs.

Another cost is whether the corporation can, or even wants to, get fair value for the securities. For example, will the sales price be less than the present value of the expected future cash flows, and if so, by how much? Kowsmann (2006) quotes Cindy Ma, who was a member of the FASB group set up to create option valuation guidelines, as questioning Zions' strategy, saying that "the intimidating complexity of the Zions derivative will deter investors from offering full value." She also quotes Joel D. Hornstein, chief executive of Structural Wealth Management LLC, a poten-tial bidder who points out "the normal incentives in a stock offering are turned upside-down in the Zions case … Companies, after all, have reason to seek a higher price for their securities, while Zions' purpose is to establish a value for stock options that is below the value produced by current accounting methods."

Will sophisticated investors be interested? There are costs involved to determine how much the securities are worth, and the size of the auctions may not provide sufficient opportunity for these investors to recover those costs, forcing the securities to trade at a large discount. On page 15 of Zions' filing with the SEC, it notes that it set the maximum bid amount at $350,000 per bidder, with a lower level of $10,000 for employees, and as noted earlier, there were 21 winning bidders who paid a total of $702,075. Consequently, the amount involved averaged less than $35,000 per successful bidder.

Other Issues

The SEC in its letter to Zions recommends:

> ... each ESOARS auction be analyzed to determine whether it results in an appropriate market pricing mechanism. Specifically, the analysis should determine if the auction clearing price is representative of the fair valuation of the underlying employee share-based payments. Factors that should be considered in determining whether an auction was an appropriate market pricing mechanism include, but are not limited to, the following:
>
> - The size of the ESOARS offering relative to market demand
> - The number of bidders (e.g., Did a sufficient number of bidders participate in the auction? Were they independent?)
> - Technology issues, including delays
> - Bidder perception concerning costs of holding, hedging, or trading the instrument

Adequate consideration of these factors is important to ensure that the auction process results in the sale of ESOARS at what can truly be deemed market prices. The letter implies that not all ESOARS will qualify. Who will make this determination, the independent auditor? There is some anecdotal evidence (see Balsam, et al. 2007) that auditors discouraged the use of the binomial model as they were concerned with their ability to audit the output. Will they take the same position with ESOARS?

Footnotes

[1] Exhibit 10.1 to Amerigroup Corporation form 8-K filed with the Securities and Exchange Commission, May 13, 2005.

[2] The value of the option is equal to the sum of its intrinsic and time values.

[3] While more commonly known as the Black-Scholes model, the model normally used is the Merton modification.

[4] According to a 2007 study by Aon and Radford Surveys + Consulting, as of Jan. 10, 2007, 356 publicly traded companies used the Binomial model, including 80 of the S&P 500.

[5] While the payout to the initial ESOARS will be in cash, Zions' indicates that in the future, settlements will involve the payment of company stock (Page 21 of Sept. 22, 2006, submission).

Chapter 7

Deferred Compensation

As New York Stock Exchange chairman, Richard Grasso had a well-paying high-profile position. And, by most accounts, he performed well. However, his performance became irrelevant in September 2003 as the magnitude of his deferred compensation, $140 million, held in a supplemental executive retirement plan, became known. Segments of the public were appalled, the New York attorney general sued and members of the board asked for his resignation. Some claimed they were unaware of the amounts involved. At the time this was written, the judge in the case ruled that Grasso must return at least $95 million. Grasso plans to appeal (Luchetti and Lublin 2006). While the ultimate outcome is unresolved, many lessons are to be learned. The first lesson is executives will usually pay far more attention to their compensation than the board of directors awarding that compensation. As reported by Lucchetti and Craig (2005), the chairman of the NYSE's compensation committee signed Grasso's final contract "without fully understanding or reading all of it." A second lesson is executives will use this asymmetry to their advantage. And a third lesson is the information will eventually become public.

Introduction

In the past few years, the attention paid to deferred compensation in the form of pensions has exploded. In addition to the Grasso case discussed above, there were large and widely criticized payments to Lee Raymond, former Exxon Mobil CEO, who received a lump-sum payment of $98 million[1], and Henry McKinnell, former Pfizer CEO, whose lump-sum retirement benefit was valued at $83 million[2]. What made McKinnell's pension even more controversial was Pfizer's stock price dropped by 37 percent during his time as CEO (Hensley 2006). Even prospective payments to current executives have been highlighted on the AFL-CIO's Executive Paywatch Web site. This is despite the fact that disclosure for pension lags that of other components of the compensation package. Bebchuk and Fried (2004b) refer to pensions as "stealth compensation," which may explain how the New York Stock Exchange's boards and other boards have allowed them to get so large. In this regard, there are two possible explanations. First, the board didn't realize how large the promised payments were. Second, the board did realize the amount but felt the amounts were justified. To address the issue, the Securities and Exchange Commission recently passed rules increasing and clarifying disclosures with respect to deferred compensation and pensions.

Types of Deferred Compensation

When an employee performs services in one period and receives payment in a subsequent period, the compensation is said to be deferred. The future payment can be in cash—for example, a pension or annuity, stock or benefits—such as the employer continues to pay the employee's health-insurance premiums after the employee retires. On some level, stock-based compensation granted in the current period can be considered deferred as, while the options and/or shares are granted in the current period, the executive does not have full rights to them until they vest in a future period. Further, with options, if the exercise price is greater than or equal to the market price at the date of grant, executives will not be taxed at least until the options are exercised.[3] Compensation may be deferred to a future period for a number of reasons including, but not limited to, incentives and taxation.

Pensions

The most common form of deferred compensation for most employees is their pension, whereby they earn benefits while working and receive payments after they retire. Pension plans fall into two categories—defined benefit and defined contribution.

Defined Benefit Plans

Defined benefit plans provide employees with guaranteed payments based upon predetermined benefits formulas, formulas that may take into account retirement age, length of service and preretirement earnings. Formulas include those based on terminal earnings, career earnings, dollar amount and cash account. Terminal-earnings formulas base benefits on average earnings during a specified number of years at the end of a worker's career. In contrast, career-earnings formulas base benefits on average career earnings. Dollar-amount formulas calculate benefits based on a dollar amount for each year of service, whereas cash-account formulas are based on employer contributions plus interest earned on those contributions.

The benefits payment can be fixed in amount at the time of retirement or, in certain cases, can vary, for example, with increases in the consumer price index. An example of the latter is our Social Security system, in which payments increase with the rate of inflation.

Appendix 7-1, which provides a description of the General Motors defined benefit retirement plan for its executives, also illustrates the magnitude and materiality of these plans. The plans encompass a tax-qualified plan subject to the requirements of the Internal Revenue Code (IRC) or Employee Retirement Income Security Act (ERISA) and a nonqualified supplemental plan. The latter provides significant flexibility to GM as well as to its employees. For example, while GM normally requires a minimum of 10 years of service, it only requires five years of service for Devine and Lutz. Beyond that, while the plan payouts are based upon either salary (Appendix 7-1, Pension Plan Table I on page 264) or salary plus bonus (Appendix 7-1, Pension Plan Table II on page 265), and years of service, the company has the ability to credit extra years of service to an executive. Finally the pension will be calculated using the regular (Table I) and alternative (Table II) SERP formulas, and if certain conditions are met, the executive may chose the larger of the two. Consequently, it appears Wagoner would receive a pension of approximately $2 million per year based upon the alternative formulation.

Defined Contribution Plans

In contrast, with a defined contribution plan, the plan defines the employers' contribution. The employee may add to those contributions. He or she then directs those contributions into employer-provided investment vehicles, which may include company stock, professionally managed mutual funds, fixed-interest securities, etc. The employee's benefit is then based upon the investment choices made by the employee, and how well those investments perform.

A corporation may have multiple pension plans. In fact, most large corporations do. They can have defined benefit and defined contribution plans. They can have different plans for different bargaining units. They can have different plans for the different countries in which they operate. The following excerpt from IBM's

2005 10-K discusses, in very generic terms, its defined contribution plans, which include a 401(k) plan, open to all employees, and an executive deferred compensation plan:

Defined Contribution Plans

IBM Savings Plan

U.S. regular, full-time and part-time employees are eligible to participate in the IBM Savings Plan, which is a tax-qualified defined contribution plan under section 401(k) of the Internal Revenue Code. For employees hired prior to Jan. 1, 2005, the company matches 50 percent of the employee's contribution up to the first 6 percent of the employee's eligible compensation. For employees hired or rehired after Dec. 31, 2004, who have also completed one year of service, the company matches 100 percent of the employee's contribution up to the first 6 percent of eligible compensation. All contributions, including the company match, are made in cash, in accordance with the participants' investment elections. There are no minimum amounts that must be invested in company stock, and there are no restrictions on transferring amounts out of the company's stock to another investment choice. The number of employees receiving distributions under this plan were 2,786 and 2,659 as of Dec. 31, 2005, and 2004, respectively.[4]

In January 2006, the company announced its intention to amend the plan effective Jan. 1, 2008. The announced change will consist of two components including an automatic contribution for all eligible U.S. employees and an increase in the amount of company matching contribution for all eligible U.S. employees hired on or before Dec. 31, 2004.

IBM Executive Deferred Compensation Plan

The company also maintains an unfunded, nonqualified defined contribution plan, the IBM Executive Deferred Compensation Plan (EDCP), which allows eligible executives to defer compensation and to receive company-matching contributions under the applicable IBM Savings Plan formula (depending on the date of hire as described above), with respect to amounts in excess of IRS limits for tax-qualified plans. Amounts contributed to the plan as a result of deferred compensation, as well as company-matching contributions, are recorded as liabilities. Deferred compensation amounts may be directed by participants into an account that replicates the return that would be received had the amounts been invested in similar IBM

Savings Plan investment options. Company-matching contributions, which are provided in the "Plan Financial Information" section, are directed to participant accounts and appreciate or depreciate each reporting period based on changes in the company's stock price. The total participants receiving benefits payments under this plan were 384 and 356 as of Dec. 31, 2005, and 2004, respectively.

Supplemental Executive Retirement Plans

As demonstrated by the General Motors and IBM examples, employees can participate in more than one plan—their employers' defined benefit and defined contribution plans. Executives also usually participate in supplemental executive retirement plans (SERPs). The reasons are partly institutional. Pension plans are governed by ERISA, which includes the IRC, and both groups set limits on contributions and payouts. To provide their executives' retirement payouts beyond those allowed under ERISA and the IRC, most corporations have set up supplemental executive retirement plans.[5] The following excerpt, from IBM's 2006 proxy statement, discusses its supplemental plan and how it is coordinated with the primary tax-qualified defined benefit plan. In fact, the benefit offset mentioned in the second sentence implies the supplemental plan exists primarily because of ERISA and IRC limitations on qualified plans.

> Retirement benefits are provided to the executive officers of the Company, including the named executive officers, under an unfunded, nonqualified defined benefit pension plan known as the Supplemental Executive Retention Plan ("SERP"). Benefits under the SERP are offset by benefits under the Company's defined benefit pension plan known as the IBM Personal Pension Plan, which provides funded, tax-qualified benefits up to IRS limits and unfunded, non-qualified benefits in excess of IRS limits. The SERP and the IBM Personal Pension Plan are referred to collectively as the "Plans."[6]

The following sentence illustrates one of the benefits of a supplemental plan. Unlike the qualified primary plan, for which benefits formulas must be computed in a nondiscriminatory fashion in accordance with ERISA and IRC regulations, a supplemental plan allows the corporation flexibility to deviate from its formulae and negotiate separately with each executive. Thus IBM, rather than setting former CEO Louis Gertner's pension based upon the formula, set it by contract.

Mr. Gerstner's annual pension from the Company under his employment agreement has been set at approximately $1,140,000 at age 60.[7]

The following from Disney illustrates the relative importance of supplemental versus qualified pension plans. For example, an executive with 35 years of experience and an average annual base compensation (five highest consecutive years) of $2 million (the amount CEO Robert Iger receives) would receive $170,000 from the primary qualified pension plan and $1,181,362 from the supplemental plan, yielding a grand total of $1,351,362.

Retirement Plans

The Company maintains a tax-qualified, noncontributory retirement plan, called the Disney Salaried Retirement Plan, for salaried employees who have completed one year of service. Benefits are based primarily on participants' credited years of service and average base compensation (excluding other compensation such as bonuses) for the highest five consecutive years of compensation during the ten-year period prior to termination or retirement, whichever is earlier. In addition, a portion of each participant's retirement benefit is comprised of a flat-dollar amount based solely on years and hours of credited service. Retirement benefits are nonforfeitable after five years of vesting service, and actuarially reduced benefits are available for participants who retire on or after age 55 after five years of vesting service.

In calendar year 2005, the maximum compensation limit under a tax-qualified plan was $210,000, and the maximum annual benefit that may be accrued under a tax-qualified defined benefit plan was $170,000. To provide additional retirement benefits for key salaried employees, the Company maintains a supplemental nonqualified, unfunded plan, the Amended and Restated Key Plan, which provides retirement benefits in excess of the compensation limitations and maximum benefit accruals for tax-qualified plans. This plan recognizes deferred amounts of base salary for purposes of determining applicable retirement benefits. Benefits under this plan are provided by the Company on a noncontributory basis.

The proceeding table illustrates the total combined estimated annual benefits payable under these retirement plans to eligible salaried employees for various years of service assuming normal retirement at age 65 and assuming all years of service are after 1984 (benefits are less for service in or before 1984). The table illustrates estimated benefits payable determined on a straight-life annuity basis. There is no offset in benefits under either plan for Social Security benefits.

Average Annual Base Compensation Highest Five Consecutive Years	Years of Credited Service				
	15	20	25	30	35
$250,000	$74,319	$99,121	$124,031	$148,800	$172,300
500,000	146,507	195,371	244,344	293,175	340,73
750,000	218,694	291,621	364,656	437,550	509,175
1,000,000	290,882	387,871	484,969	581,925	677,613
1,250,000	363,069	484,121	605,281	726,300	846,050
1,500,000	435,257	580,371	725,594	870,675	1,014,488
1,750,000	507,444	676,621	845,906	1,015,050	1,182,925
2,000,000	579,632	772,871	966,219	1,159,425	1,351,362
2,250,000	651,819	869,121	1,086,531	1,303,800	1,519,800

As of December 1, 2005, annual payments under the Disney Salaried Retirement Plan and the Amended and Restated Key Plan would be based upon an average annual compensation of $1,809,616 for Mr. Iger, $840,981 for Mr. Staggs, $832,135 for Mr. Murphy, $756,164 for Mr. Braverman and $372,654 for Ms. McCarthy. Mr. Iger has six years, Mr. Staggs has 16 years, Mr. Murphy has 17 years, Mr. Braverman has three years and Ms. McCarthy has six years of credited service.[8]

One thing worth noting is that the computations vary by company, with major differences in the formulas, including amounts considered in determining the pension. For example, while Disney's plan only considers base compensation (i.e., salary) in computing pension payments, other plans, for example Pepsico's, consider salary and bonus in determining pension payments:

The pay covered by the Pension Plans noted below is based on the salary and annual bonus included in the Summary Compensation Table in this Proxy Statement for each of our five most highly compensated executive officers.[9]

Deferred Compensation Plans

In addition to pension plans, many corporations have plans that allow, encourage and/or mandate their executives defer portions of their salary and/or bonuses.[10] The passage below provides more information about IBM's deferred compensation, which was introduced previously under the section of defined contribution plans. What is particularly interesting, and well illustrated by this example, is the effect the tax code has on the plans. First, given the limitation on contributions, which was $154,500 in 2007, IBM has set up the Executive Deferred Compensation Plan. Second, to avoid taxation, the Executive Deferred Compensation Plan has to be unfunded, with the participants becoming general creditors of the corporation.

The IBM Savings Plan allows all eligible employees to defer up to 80% of their salary and performance bonus on a tax-favored basis into a tax exempt trust pursuant to Internal Revenue Service guidelines. IBM matches these deferrals at the rate of 50 percent for the first 6 percent of compensation deferred. Effective Jan. 1, 2005, for newly hired and rehired employees, IBM matches these deferrals at the rate of 100% for the first 6% of compensation. The employee accounts are invested by the plan trustee in a selection of investment funds, including an IBM Stock Fund, as directed by the employees. Corporate officers participate in the IBM Savings Plan on the same basis as all other employees. For 2005, Internal Revenue Service limits on the IBM Savings Plan precluded an annual deferral of more than $14,000 ($18,000 for participants who were at least age 50 during such year) or an eligible compensation base of more than $210,000 for any one employee.

IBM established the IBM Executive Deferred Compensation Plan (the "EDCP") in 1995. The EDCP allows any U.S. executive, including officers, to defer additional income and receive a Company match on the same basis as the IBM Savings Plan except that the Company match for the EDCP is credited only in units of IBM common stock which are not transferable to other investment alternatives during employment. In addition, participants can defer all or a portion of their annual incentive until termination of employment under the EDCP. In the event that the salary of a Company officer who is subject to the limits of section 162(m) of the Code exceeds $1,000,000, such officer may defer up to 100 percent of his or her salary. The EDCP is not funded and participants are general creditors of the Company. All amounts deferred in the EDCP increase or decrease based on the investment results of the executive's selected investment alternatives, but plan distributions after employment ends are paid out of Company funds rather than from a dedicated investment portfolio.

The Company also provided executives with the opportunity to defer certain restricted stock unit awards under the LTIP on terms similar to the

EDCP. These amounts are not funded (participants are general creditors of the Company) and there is no Company match on these amounts. The restricted stock unit award deferrals are recorded as deferred units of Company stock and are not transferable to any other investment alternatives until paid out.[11]

Another example of a company offering a nonqualified deferred compensation plan to its employees is Dell Computer.

Deferred Compensation Plan—Dell also maintains a nonqualified deferred compensation plan that is available to executives. Under the terms of this plan, Dell matches 100% of each participant's voluntary deferrals up to 3% of the participant's compensation. A participant vests ratably in the matching contributions over the first five years of employment (20% per year). A participant's funds are distributed upon the participant's death or retirement or, under certain circumstances, at the request of the participant during the participant's employment.[12]

There are a variety of instruments into which compensation can be deferred.[13] For example, the deferral can be into an account that is credited with interest according to some interest rate, such as the rate on six-month treasury bills; an account that is tied to some stock market index, for example, the S&P 500; or into an account whose payout is dependent on the firm's stock price performance. Sometimes, to encourage executives to take advantage of these plans, corporations provide additional monetary rewards. For example, Dell matches "100 percent of each participant's voluntary deferrals up to 3 percent of the participant's compensation," while IBM "matches these deferrals at the rate of 50 percent for the first 6 percent of compensation deferred."[14] Clark Consulting (2005) found that 47 percent of its survey respondents matched at least some of the executive deferrals. Beyond matching some or all of the contribution, to induce deferral, the corporation can offer a rate in excess of that available in the marketplace. An illustration of a premium rate occurs when the rate of return promised equals some market rate, for example return on long-term treasury bonds, plus a bonus, such as 2 percent per year. These amounts can be significant. Take, for instance, General Electric. It reported that during 2005, Vice Chairman Robert C. Wright earned $463,825 from above-market interest rates paid on his deferred compensation.[15] Both employer matching and the existence of a premium rate increase the monetary reward and, hence, the desirability of deferring compensation from the viewpoint of the executive.

Funding Limitations

While qualified pension plans are required to be ERISA funded, nonqualified supplemental pension plans and deferred compensation arrangements are not required to be funded. Further, to avoid current taxation, the executive has to avoid constructive receipt of the amounts involved in the supplemental retirement plan and nonqualified deferred compensation plan. Thus, formally, the corporation does not fund[16] an "account" at the time of deferral, rather the corporation promises to pay the amount in the "account" at the end of the deferral period. Many corporations informally fund and secure those benefits via techniques like rabbi trusts.[17] A rabbi trust sets aside assets to be used to satisfy the employer's obligations to the executive. Similar to an escrow account, it is an irrevocable trust established for the benefit of the participant by an employer. However, the employer cannot touch those assets but the creditors of the employer can. It is this last provision, the ability of creditors of the employer to attach those assets if necessary, that allows the executive to avoid constructive receipt and current taxation.

Incentives

Deferral of compensation can affect the executives' incentives, with the effect on incentives depending on the structure of the deferral. For example, different incentives will arise if the deferral is into an interest-bearing account, or into a stock-type account, where the payout is based upon firm performance. Consider first the effect of vesting on the pension benefit.

Vesting

The pension benefit, while nominally fixed, or at least independent of performance, does provide certain incentives. Most pension plans are structured so that the benefits do not vest immediately. This provides the executive with the incentive to remain with the firm at least until the pension vests. That is, there is a monetary cost to leaving the firm before then, as the unvested pension would be forfeited. ERISA mandates that vesting occur over no longer than five years, however, ERISA does not apply to supplemental plans. Thus, the corporation is free to set its vesting requirements for its supplemental plans. And, given that supplemental plans—see previous Disney example —provide the bulk of retirement income to executives, the supplemental plan is usually the more important plan in providing incentives to executives.

Pension Backloading

Beyond vesting, there are other techniques the corporation can use to encourage executives to remain with the firm (or retire early). For example, the pension plan can be structured so the benefit increases with the individual's tenure with the firm, something referred to as "pension backloading." Kotlikoff and Wise (1989) write:

> Pension backloading refers to pension plans that provide very little pension accrual up to a specific age and substantial pension accrual after a specific age. This feature of pension plans typically means that pension benefits are much smaller for employees who change jobs than for those who don't.

Pension backloading may be achieved by basing the pension on final compensation or average compensation over the last three to five years, using a terminal earnings formula. Alternatively, the pension can be a percentage of final compensation, and that percentage can increase with the number of years employed. In such a case, assuming compensation increases over time, the executive has a double monetary incentive to stay. The pension is an increasing percentage of an increasing amount.

Consider the following example. For employees with more than 20 but less than 40 years of service, the promised annual pension payout is equal to the number of years employed times 1.5 percent of the executive's final compensation. For employees with 40 or more years of service, the promised annual pension payout is equal to the number of years employed times 2 percent of the executive's final compensation. Suppose an executive with 39 years of service is deciding on whether to return for his or her 40th year. If he or she returns and works the duration of that 40th year, total compensation other than pension will be $150,000, which is $5,000 more than he or she earned in the previous year. Thus, the promised future pension would be 80 percent of $150,000, or $120,000, rather than 58.5 percent of $145,000 or $84,825. The executive's real earnings on returning for year 40 would thus be the $150,000 minus the pension he or she would have received that year, $84,825, plus the present value of the increase in the annual pension payment of $35,175 ($120,000 - $84,825). If by working the additional year, the executive increases the present value of his or her pension annuity, the pension plan provides incentive for the executive to continue working. Given reasonable assumptions as to the length of time the executive will collect the pension, and the discount rates to be applied to that pension, it is likely the present value of an annuity of $35,175 will exceed $84,825; thus, the pension accrual is positive and the pension plan provides a significant incentive for the executive to continue working.[18]

Alternatively, some corporations may decide to structure their plans to avoid giving executives an incentive to stay too long.[19] They could design their plan so that the maximum benefit is reached when the executive reaches a certain age or a certain number of years of service.

Consider the following modification to the above example. Assume the corporation caps the payout at 80 percent of final salary. The executive is now deciding whether to return for his or her 41st year. If he or she returns, total compensation other than pension will be $155,000, which is $5,000 more than he or she earned in the previous year. Thus, the promised future pension would be 80 percent of $155,000, or $124,000, rather than $120,000. The executive's real earnings on returning for year 41 would thus be $155,000, minus the pension he or she would have received in year 41, $120,000, plus the present value of the increase in the annual pension payment of $4,000. Given that it is unlikely the present value of an annuity of $4,000 is anywhere near $120,000,[20] the pension accrual in this case is actually negative. That, is the corporation is saving more by not paying a pension this year than the incremental increase in pension amount it will have to pay out in the future. Hence, the pension plan provides a significant disincentive for the executive to continue working.

Effect on Risk Preferences

Pensions and/or deferred compensation can also affect the executive's risk preferences. As noted above, ostensibly the promised payments are not related to firm or individual performance. However, if the deferred amounts are invested in company stock, then the ultimate payout will depend on corporate performance.[21] Alternatively, if the deferral is not funded, the corporation's ability to make those payments are not guaranteed and become dependent upon future performance. At the extreme, if the firm goes out of business, the executive would lose all deferred compensation not funded. And note that much of an executive's retirement package comes from supplemental plans, which are not funded and hence are at risk.[22] Thus, an executive with large amounts of unfunded deferred compensation has the incentive to reduce firm risks, which could involve foregoing otherwise profitable projects.[23] Sundaram and Yermack (2006) explain that pensions and other forms of deferred compensation make the executive a debt holder in the firm, showing that consistent with their incentives, "CEOs with high debt-based incentives manage their firms conservatively to reduce default risk."

Bond on Performance

Deferred compensation, if the corporation can refuse to pay it later, can also work as a bond on performance. For example, if the executive is later found to have embezzled funds or misrepresented results while employed with the company, or violated a noncompete agreement after leaving the company, the company could refuse to pay the amounts deferred. Take, for example, Thomas Coughlin, former Wal-Mart vice chairman. After being accused of embezzlement and being forced to resign, the company "rescinded Mr. Coughlin's retirement agreement, which included about $14 million in forfeited restricted stock and salary" (Zimmerman and Hudson 2005). An example of the latter condition—the explicit statement that the benefit spelled out in the agreement may be stopped if the executive takes a position with a competitor—was found in the proxy statement of SCBT Financial Corp.

These executives will forfeit their retirement benefits if they compete with the Company.[24]

Resolving Horizon Problem

Depending upon how it is structured, deferred compensation may also help resolve the horizon problem that arises when an executive's decisions affect performance after his or her retirement. If the executive is paid based upon current performance, he or she has no incentive to care about firm performance after he or she retires, and thus, at a minimum, has no incentive to invest in projects where the payback begins after retirement. Consistent with this theory, Dechow and Sloan (1991) find investment in research and development (R&D) decreases as the CEO nears retirement. While in theory, stock compensation and stock ownership are forward-looking forms of compensation, that is, the value of a share is the present value of expected future cash flows, in the presence of asymmetric information, that may not always be the case. To control for this, Bizjak et al. (1993) suggest the executive be paid based on stock-price performance after retirement. This would be achieved if the executive defers compensation into stock units. Stock units qualify as deferred compensation because shares are not issued at the time of grant, rather an unfunded promise is made by the firm to issue a number of shares in the future.

Political Costs

Deferred compensation is not as political an issue as other components of the compensation package. Consequently, the Richard Grasso case and the controversy surrounding the payments to Lee Raymond and Henry McKinnell are the exception rather than the rule. This is primarily because the payments have not been reported in proxy statements, as they normally occur after retirement when they are no longer required to be disclosed. While that will not change in the near future, the recently adopted changes in proxy statement disclosure rules will make it easier for interested parties to determine what those promised future payments are as they are being earned.

Financial Consequences

Cash Flows

Deferred compensation, like the other components of the executive compensation package, impacts the corporation's cash flows. Although depending on the type of compensation, cash flow may be affected in either the current or some future period(s). The cash-flow consequences of deferred compensation depend upon whether the deferred compensation is funded or unfunded, and whether it is considered "qualified" for tax purposes or not. If the plan is funded, the corporation will have a cash outflow equal to the amount funded in the current period. If the plan is funded and tax qualified, it will be able to deduct the amount contributed to the plan and thus offset some of the cash outflow from the funding with the tax savings. If the plan is informally funded, for example, the Rabbi Trust discussed previously, the corporation will have a current cash outflow for the funding but will receive the deduction and tax savings in the future when the recipient recognizes the taxable income. Finally, if the plan is unfunded, the cash outflow and tax savings will occur in the future when the payments are made.

Taxes

The U.S. tax system provides incentives for employees to defer compensation. At its most basic form, Miller and Scholes (1982) show that if the employee's tax rate is higher than the corporation's tax rate, it makes tax sense to have the employee defer, and have the corporation invest those funds. Deferral also makes tax sense if the executive can postpone the recognition of income to a period in which he or she has a lower tax rate and/or a period in which the corporation has a higher tax rate.[25]

Specific provisions of the tax code encourage deferred compensation. For example, if a pension plan is qualified, the corporation is required to fund the plan while the employee is working and gets to deduct the amount it pays into the pension fund at the time it makes those payments. Those amounts then compound on a tax-deferred basis, with the employee only taxed at the future date when he or she receives payments from the pension fund. The ability of the corporation to take an immediate tax deduction, as well as for the amounts invested to grow on a tax-deferred basis, provide incentive for the corporation to provide qualified pensions. In contrast, there are no tax incentives associated with nonqualified pension plans or other nonqualified deferred compensation arrangements. For nonqualified plans, funding will trigger a tax liability on the part of the employee, hence those plans are not usually formally funded.[26]

Another section of the Internal Revenue Code that encourages deferral of compensation by executives is Section 162(m), the million-dollar cap. It encourages deferral of compensation, as amounts that would not be deductible if paid currently can be fully deductible if payment is deferred until the executive is no longer subject to its limitations, such as once the executive is retired. To preserve tax deductions, some companies require the deferral of any amounts that would not be currently deductible because of Section 162(m). The effect of such a policy is to push the cash outflow to a future period, but more importantly, preserve a deduction which otherwise would be lost. An example of a company requiring deferral is Temple Inland, which states:

> The Committee has adopted a policy requiring the deferral of any compensation that exceeds the permissible deduction under Section 162(m) of the Internal Revenue Code (Section 162(m)) until such time as the maximum deduction under Section 162(m) may be taken.[27]

Section 409A of the IRC sets out a series of requirements that must be met for nonqualified deferred compensation to avoid the income being taxable in the period earned. For example, it generally requires the deferral election be made in the period prior to the income being earned and sets strict rules on when the deferred compensation can be distributed. Failure to comply with the requirements of Section 409A will cause income to be recognized immediately, interest charged as if the tax should have been paid in the year deferred, and both the tax and interest increased by an additional 20-percent penalty.

Financial Reporting Consequences

For financial accounting purposes, amounts deferred are expensed when earned, regardless of when paid. At the same time as the amounts are expensed, the related income tax accounting consequences are recognized. That is, for its financial accounting records, the company records the expense and income tax deduction when the amounts are earned, rather than when they are paid or actually deducted on the corporate tax return.

If the amounts are recorded at the present value of the future payment, as with pension and other postretirement benefits, or if the corporation pays interest on the amounts deferred, then that increase in the present value of the liability[28], or interest on the deferred amount, is also recognized as an expense with the passage of time. These amounts are offset by interest or returns earned on prefunded amounts, if any. For example, as discussed above, qualified pension plans are funded when the employee is employed. The amount contributed by the company to the pension fund is less than the future promised payment because it is expected that the pension fund will invest that money profitably.

Summary

The focus of this chapter was deferred compensation, which occurs when an employee performs services in one period and receives payment in a subsequent period. The most common form of deferred compensation, at least to most employees, is their pension, where the payment is not received until after the employee retires. Pensions can be either defined benefit or defined contribution, with many executives having both types of plans. In addition to their primary tax-qualified plans, which are limited in amount, most upper-level executives have supplemental unfunded plans. As illustrated in the chapter, these supplemental plans, which are not subject to Internal Revenue Code or ERISA regulations, usually provide the preponderance of an upper-level executive's retirement benefits. In addition to pension plans, many corporations have plans that allow, encourage, and/or mandate their executives defer portions of their salary and/or bonuses.

Deferred compensation can be structured to provide incentives. For example, vesting and the formula used to determine retirement benefits can provide incentive for the executive to remain with the corporation. Deferred compensation can also affect risk preferences. In particular, unfunded deferred compensation decreases the executive's willingness to take risk. However, deferred compensation, especially if the payout is tied to the corporation's stock price, can help mitigate the horizon problem.

Footnotes

1 Page 25, Exxon Mobil proxy statement filed with the Securities and Exchange Commission, April 12, 2006.

2 Page 65, Pfizer proxy statement filed with the Securities and Exchange Commission, March 16, 2006.

3 As noted in Chapter 6, if the options are tax qualified (under Internal Revenue Code Section 422), the executive will not realize taxable income until he or she sells the shares acquired upon exercise of the option.

4 Page 86, International Business Machines form 10-K filed with Securities and Exchange Commission, Feb. 28, 2006.

5 Clark Consulting (2005) found that 69 percent of corporations in its survey of the *Fortune* 1,000 have supplemental plans.

6 Page 20, International Business Machines proxy statement filed with the Securities and Exchange Commission, March 9, 2006.

7 Page 18, International Business Machines proxy statement filed with Securities and Exchange Commission, March 13, 2000.

8 Pages 21 and 22, Walt Disney proxy statement filed with the Securities and Exchange Commission, Jan. 11, 2006.

9 Page 22, Pepsico Proxy Statement filed with Securities and Exchange Commission, March 24, 2006.

10 Clark Consulting (2005) found that 91 percent of corporations in its survey of the *Fortune* 1,000 have nonqualified deferred compensation plans.

11 Page 22, International Business Machines proxy statement filed with the Securities and Exchange Commission, March 9, 2006.

12 Page 29, Dell Computer proxy statement filed with Securities and Exchange Commission, June 5, 2006.

13 Actually, because the deferral is unfunded, no investment is made. Rather the value of the deferral increases with the increases in the value of the investment chosen.

14 As noted in the passage above, the match increases to 100 percent of 6 percent for employees hired or rehired after Jan. 1, 2005.

15 Page 35, General Electric proxy statement filed with the Securities and Exchange Commission, March 3, 2006.

16 Clark Consulting (2005) reports that 73 percent of firms in its survey of the *Fortune* 1,000 informally fund their nonqualified deferred compensation arrangements, and

54 percent informally fund their supplemental executive retirement plans.

[17] The term "Rabbi Trust" arose because the Internal Revenue Service Private Letter Ruling No. 8,113,107, which approved the technique, pertained to a trust set up by a temple to benefit its rabbi.

[18] It is worth noting that the average individual retiring at age 65 can expect to live an additional 20 years.

[19] The issue arises of why a corporation would even have to consider this situation. That is, it could always fire an executive who refuses to retire. However, it would be politically untenable, inside and outside the corporation, to fire a previously valued employee in the twilight of his or her career. Given the United States' legal environment, the corporation might even face an age-discrimination lawsuit.

[20] The employee would have to collect the increase of $4,000 in his or her pension for 30 years before the nominal amount equaled $120,000. At a discount rate of 2 percent per year, it would take almost 50 years.

[21] Kadlec (2001) discusses how many 401(K) plans include a disproportionate amount of employer stock.

[22] While it could be funded with a Rabbi Trust, recall that Rabbi Trusts may be attached by creditors of the firm.

[23] Hence the need for other forms of compensation whose value increases with risk.

[24] Page 10, SCBT Financial Corp. proxy statement filed with the Securities and Exchange Commission, March 17, 2006.

[25] The executive and the corporation want to minimize the taxes paid on this transaction. For the executive, to whom this is taxable income, that means recognizing income when his or her tax rate is low. For the corporation, to whom this is a tax deduction, that means recognizing the deduction when its tax rate is high.

[26] Funding the plan results in constructive receipt (and hence taxability to the executive) under the Internal Revenue Code. In effect, the executive must be a general creditor of the firm to avoid taxation. As discussed above, funding deferred compensation via a Rabbi Trust provides some security to the executive while avoiding constructive receipt.

[27] Page 12, Temple Inland proxy statement filed with the Securities and Exchange Commission, March 22, 2006.

[28] As the payment date gets closer, the present value of a liability increases, and at the payment date, equals the face value of the liability.

Appendix 7-1

Executive Pension Benefits

from General Motors Proxy Statement filed April 28, 2006 (pages 25 & 26)

Retirement Programs Applicable to Executive Officers

General Motors executives in the United States may receive benefits in retirement from both a tax-qualified plan that is subject to the requirements of ERISA and from a non-qualified plan that provides supplemental benefits under one of two formulas described below. Together, these plans are referred to here as the "GM Salaried Program." Retired executives' tax-qualified benefits are pre-funded and paid out of the assets of the General Motors Retirement Program for Salaried Employees; however, non-qualified benefits are not pre-funded and are paid out of the Corporation's general assets.

Two formulas are used to calculate the total of both the tax-qualified and non-qualified retirement benefits available to eligible U.S. executives, both of which require a minimum of ten years of eligible service (however, in the case of Mr. Devine and Mr. Lutz, the Executive Compensation Committee has permitted them to be eligible for the SERP after a minimum of five years of eligible service). One formula, the Regular SERP Formula, offers benefits that are calculated based upon the average of the highest five years of base salary during the ten years preceding retirement, and also takes into account the executive's eligible contributory or non-contributory service at GM. These benefits are subject to an offset of a portion of the maximum Social Security benefit available to an individual in the year of retirement, regardless of actual receipt. The Board of Directors has delegated to the Executive Compensation Committee discretionary authority to grant additional eligible years of credited service to selected key executives under such terms and conditions as the Executive Compensation Committee determines for purposes of computing the regular and alternative forms of SERP for such executives.

The Alternative SERP Formula determines benefits based upon average annual total direct compensation, calculated as the sum of (i) the average of the highest five years of base salary during the ten years preceding retirement, plus (ii) the average of the highest five years of bonus received in the ten years preceding retirement — each average calculated independently. The Alternative SERP Formula also takes into account the executive's eligible contributory (or non-contributory) service subject to a maximum of 35 years and provides for an offset of 100 percent of the maximum Social Security benefit available to an individual in the year of retirement, regardless of actual receipt. Only those executives who satisfy certain criteria, including not working for a competitor or otherwise acting in any manner that is not in the best interests of the Corporation, are eligible to receive benefits calculated under the Alternative SERP Formula in lieu of benefits calculated under the Regular SERP Formula. If the executive is eligible for the alternative formula, total tax-qualified and non-qualified retirement benefits payable under both SERP formulas are compared, and the executive receives whichever retirement benefit is greater. Both the regular and alternative forms of the SERP benefit are provided under a program that is non-qualified for tax purposes and not pre-funded. Non-qualified benefits under either the regular or alternative formulas can be reduced or eliminated for both retirees and active employees by the Executive Compensation Committee and/or the Board of Directors.

Pension Plan Table I shows the estimated total of both the tax-qualified and non-qualified retirement benefits, as calculated under the Regular SERP Formula (based upon an Average Annual Base Salary as of December 31, 2005), that would be paid in monthly installments as a single life annuity to GM executives retiring as early as age 62 in 2005.

Pension Plan Table II shows the estimated total of both the tax-qualified and non-qualified retirement benefits as calculated under the Alternative SERP Formula (based upon Average Annual Total Direct Compensation as of December 31, 2005) that would be paid in monthly installments as a single life annuity to GM executives retiring as early as age 62 in 2005.

If an eligible executive elects to receive the retirement benefits shown in Pension Plan Tables I or II in the form of a 65 percent joint and survivor annuity, the single life annuity amounts shown in each of the tables generally are reduced by 5 percent to 12 percent, depending upon the age differential between spouses. In addition, certain executives grandfathered under the American Jobs Creation Act of 2004 may elect to receive a portion of the non-qualified SERP benefit paid in a lump sum, calculated using mortality tables and a 7 percent discount rate.

On February 7, 2006, the Corporation announced that these pension plans would be capped effective December 31, 2006. All actively employed U.S. executives will be eligible to receive a frozen accrued benefit based on the current formulas, current credited service, and current compensation history. Effective January 1, 2007, new pension arrangements for U.S. executives will be implemented.

PENSION PLAN TABLE I

Projected Total Annual Retirement Benefits from All Components of the GM Salaried Program
Assuming Executive's Benefits Are Calculated Under the Regular SERP Formula (a)

Average Annual Base Salary	Years of Credited Service				
	10	15	25	35	45
$	$	$	$	$	$
500,000	95,350	143,020	238,370	333,710	429,060
1,000,000	195,350	293,020	488,370	683,710	879,060
1,500,000	295,350	443,020	738,370	1,033,710	1,329,060
2,000,000	395,350	593,020	988,370	1,383,710	1,779,060
2,500,000	495,350	743,020	1,238,370	1,733,710	2,229,060

(a) The Average Annual Base Salary and the Eligible Years of Credited Service as of December 31, 2005, for each of the Named Executive Officers were as follows: Mr. Wagoner, $2,120,000 (28 years); Mr. Devine $1,510,000 (5 years); Mr. Gottschalk $927,500 (23 years); and Mr. Cowger $761,250 (39 years). Mr. Lutz completed 52 months of service with the Corporation as of December 31, 2005, and his Average Annual Base Salary for such 52-month period was $1,519,231 per annum. The Annual Base Salaries for the most recent years considered in the calculations reported here will be found in the Summary Compensation Table on page 20 in the column headed "Salary." For retirement benefit calculation purposes, the original salaries for 2006 for Messrs. Wagoner, Devine, Lutz, and Gottschalk will be used.

PENSION PLAN TABLE II

Projected Total Annual Retirement Benefits from All Components of the GM Salaried Program Assuming Executive's Benefits Are Calculated Under the Alternative SERP Formula (a)

Average Annual Total Direct Compensation	Eligible Years of Credited Service				
	10	14	21	28	35
$	$	$	$	$	$
1,125,000	145,480	212,980	331,110	449,230	567,360
2,200,000	306,730	438,730	669,730	900,730	1,131,730
3,275,000	467,980	664,480	1,008,360	1,352,230	1,696,110
4,350,000	629,230	890,230	1,346,980	1,803,730	2,260,480
5,425,000	790,480	1,115,980	1,685,610	2,255,230	2,824,860
6,500,000	951,730	1,341,730	2,024,230	2,706,730	3,389,230
7,575,000	1,112,980	1,567,480	2,362,860	3,158,230	3,953,610

(a) The Average Annual Total Direct Compensation and the Eligible Years of Credited Service (capped at 35 years) which may be considered in the Alternative SERP calculation as of December 31, 2005, for each of the Named Executive Officers were as follows: Mr. Wagoner, $4,767,400 (28 years); Mr. Devine $2,911,200 (5 years); Mr. Gottschalk $1,831,700 (23 years); and Mr. Cowger $1,460,050 (35 years). Mr. Lutz completed 52 months of service with the Corporation as of December 31, 2005, and his Average Annual Total Direct Compensation for such 52-month period was $2,905,231 per annum. The Annual Total Average Direct Compensation for the most recent years considered in the calculations reported here will be found in the Summary Compensation Table on page 20 in the columns headed "Salary" and "Bonus." For 2002 an amount equal to the hypothetical cash value of a payout under the Annual Incentive Plan was used to calculate the average of the highest five years of bonus received in the ten years before retirement for purposes of calculating Alternative SERP Formula. For retirement benefit calculation purposes, the original salaries for 2006 for Messrs. Wagoner, Devine, Lutz, and Gottschalk will be used.

Chapter 8

Severance Packages and Change-in-Control Agreements

Heads I win, tails you lose. Sometimes it seems that's the way with executive compensation. If the corporation does well, the executive makes millions, sometimes hundreds of millions. And if the corporation does poorly, the executive gets fired and makes millions, sometime hundreds of millions.

Introduction

Severance and change-in-control payments are fairly common and have become very controversial. Severance payments occur when an executive leaves the company or is fired without cause, while a change-in-control payment occurs when the company is acquired by another company. So when an executive receives a large severance payment, shareholders are incensed that he or she is receiving a payment, in essence, for failure. One example of a controversial severance payment was when Michael Ovitz was paid $140 million after Walt Disney Co. fired him, a payment that led to shareholder-initiated litigation that dragged on for several years. In addition to the amount involved, the payment was controversial because Ovitz had been on the job barely a year before being fired. Similarly, shareholders and others are incensed when an executive receives a large change-in-control payment, sometimes retaining a position at the newly merged company, while the merger often results in the loss of jobs. An example of a controversial change-in-control payment was the reported $185 million paid to James Kiltz when Gillette was acquired by Procter & Gamble (Forelle and Maremont 2005). Procter & Gamble forecasted that 6,000 jobs would be cut in the combined company (Maremont 2005).

Justification for Severance/Change-in-Control Payments
Severance

The justification for severance packages is that they protect the executive and induce him/her to take risk (Almazan and Suarez, 2004). In the case of an outsider joining the company, the severance package serves to reduce the executive's financial risk if things don't work out as planned. This is necessary because if the executive perceives the move as too risky, he or she may elect not to join the company. While a large severance payment cannot reduce this risk, it can cushion the blow. And as illustrated by the Ovitz case, this risk is real and the amounts involved, substantial. Ovitz sold his business Creative Artists Agency (CAA), a business that earned him a reported $20 million a year (Stewart 2006, p. 213), to take the position at Disney. To induce him to leave his position, and take the position at Disney, which involved some risk, Disney promised him severance if things did not go as planned. Consider one last item about Ovitz. Prior to his stint at Disney, he was known as the most powerful man in Hollywood. Since his fall from grace at Disney, he has failed to re-emerge in a comparable public position. Consequently, it appears, based upon publicly available data at least, that Ovitz's reputation and earning power was reduced dramatically by his Disney stint.

And while the Ovitz case is an aberration in many ways, the risk to an executive of being fired is real, with CEO turnover increasing and CEO tenure decreasing dramatically in recent years. Lucier et al. (2006) find that CEO turnover has increased from 9 percent annually in 1995 to 15.3 percent in 2005. This risk exists for executives recruited from the outside and executives that have been with the company for a number of years—and there are significant costs involved. According to an analysis of a group of almost 500 executives from the ExecuComp database that Balsam and Miharjo (2007) deemed to have been forced from their positions, only 6 percent subsequently take positions with other companies in the database.

In the absence of a severance provision, executives will be less likely to take longer-term, value-increasing yet risky investments on the firm's behalf. However, executives who have been with the company for a number of years, for example, their entire careers, are less likely to have formal employment and/or severance agreements. While they may be covered by a companywide agreement/policy that covers all executives, they may not be covered by any explicit severance agreement/policy. Yet Yermack (2006) finds:

> Dismissed CEOs also obtain the large majority of their separation pay— 76%—from discretionary awards rather than existing employment contracts.

Why is this prevalent? One potential explanation for severance in the absence of a contractual requirement is that it is a gift from the company, or more appropriately, from the board, to the dismissed executive, perhaps in part to assuage guilt for dismissing him or her. Alternatively, the implicit promise of severance provides the executive with the safety net necessary for him or her to take risks on the company's behalf or, in the case of an outsider, to take the risk to join the company. As Yermack (2006) suggests, severance, even in the absence of a contractual requirement, is a method of damage control, enabling the board to "protect corporate secrets and head off litigation or adverse publicity." Consequently, for an executive to receive his or her severance, whether contractually promised or not, he or she usually must execute an agreement releasing the firm from legal liability and which may include "a variety of noncompetition, nondisclosure, nonhire, and consulting positions" (Yermack 2006).

Change-in-Control Payments

The justification for change-in-control payments is slightly different. Mergers and acquisitions are fairly common in the United States and are becoming more common internationally. While shareholders of the acquired firm normally make out well in these transactions, receiving premiums averaging as much as 50 percent of the share price prior to the acquisition (Gaspar et al. 2005), executives frequently lose their positions, e.g., the merged corporation does not usually need two CEOs. Hartzell et al. (2004) find that about half of acquired-firm CEOs accept a position in the acquiring company, indicating that the other half leave the company at the merger's conclusion. Of those who stay, they find that approximately one-third leave in the first year. Finally, they note that "the vast majority of target CEOs who exit the firm do not obtain further employment." Given the likelihood of the loss of a high-paying and prestigious position (see also, Walsh 1988, Walsh 1989), in the absence of monetary incentives, executives are likely to oppose mergers that are beneficial to their shareholders (Walkling and Long 1984, Cotter and Zenner 1994). Change-in-control provisions, also known as golden parachutes, were originally intended to counter the incentives of executives to fight takeovers. However, as the amounts of these payments have grown large, the question has been raised (Morgenson 2005) whether some executives are motivated to seek out an acquirer to receive these payments.

Typical Agreement

A typical severance or change-in-control agreement includes the explicit compensation paid by the company upon the signing of a separation agreement or the consummation of the change in control, plus the vesting of pre-existing compensation. The former normally includes a payment equal to a multiple of promised or target salary plus bonus and perhaps long-term incentive payments, while the latter includes the immediate vesting of options and restricted shares. While many consider the explicit compensation paid by the corporation to be the severance payment, critics and litigants focus on the value of the explicit compensation paid, plus the benefits vested, which in many cases can dwarf the value of the explicit compensation paid. Disney reported paying Ovitz a severance of $38,869,000, significantly less than the $140 million reported in the press. Additionally, corporations often promise items such as continued medical benefits and outplacement assistance, however, these benefits pale in magnitude to those already discussed.

In exchange for these payments, corporations generally require the executive to release the corporation from all claims, that is promise not to sue for more, and not to compete with the corporation for a period of time, which could encompass a provision that he or she not share privileged information about the company or attempt to hire executives away from the corporation. To deter these behaviors, sometimes the corporation will make the payout over a period of time, or tie the payout to a postemployment consulting agreement.

The Ovitz/Disney Fiasco

In probably the most celebrated case involving a severance payment, that of Michael Ovitz, critics have focused on a severance package worth a reported $140 million for less than 14 months' work. What critics have not acknowledged is that in taking the Disney position, Ovitz sold CAA. To persuade him to leave his prior position to work for Disney, which always involved some risk, Disney, as most corporations do, included the following severance provision in his contract if things did not go as planned.

11. Termination

(c) If a Non-Fault Termination of Executive's employment with Company shall occur, Executive or his estate shall be entitled to receive a lump sum payment equal to the sum of (x) the present value (based on Company's then current cost of borrowing for the remainder of the scheduled Term) of 100% of Executive's base salary for the balance of the term of this Agreement (the percentage of Executive's salary to be paid in such lump sum after such present value calculation being referred to herein as the "PRESENT VALUE PERCENTAGE") and (y) of an amount equal to

$7,500,000 multiplied by the product of (A) the Present Value Percentage (expressed as a decimal) and (B) the number of fiscal years of Company in the Term not yet completed at the time of termination. The sum of clauses (x) and (y) above is hereinafter referred to as the "NON-FAULT PAYMENT".[1]

After 15 months as president, Ovitz was fired by Disney's chairman and CEO, Michael Eisner. According to Disney, Ovitz was paid $38,869,000 in severance.[2] How then do critics figure the value of the package at $140 million? The difference is primarily driven by the 3 million nonqualified stock options that vested upon his termination as explained by the following provision in his employment contract.

5. Stock Options

(c)   In the event that Executive's employment shall be terminated and such termination shall constitute a Non-Fault Termination (as defined in subparagraph (d) below), then the vesting schedule of Option A shall be accelerated and Option A shall become immediately exercisable in its entirety upon such termination.[3]

As noted, the severance was rather controversial, and consequently led to the filing of several shareholder lawsuits that have continued for almost a decade. The following excerpt from Disney's most recent 10-K describes this litigation.

In re The Walt Disney Company Derivative Litigation. William and Geraldine Brehm and thirteen other individuals filed an amended and consolidated complaint on May 28, 1997, in the Delaware Court of Chancery seeking, among other things, a declaratory judgment against each of the Company's directors as of December 1996 that the Company's 1995 employment agreement with its former president Michael S. Ovitz, was void, or alternatively that Mr. Ovitz's termination should be deemed a termination "for cause" and any severance payments to him forfeited. On Oct. 8, 1998, the Delaware Court of Chancery dismissed all counts of the amended complaint. Plaintiffs appealed, and on Feb. 9, 2000, the Supreme Court of Delaware affirmed the dismissal but ruled also that plaintiffs should be permitted to file an amended complaint in accordance with the Court's opinion. The plaintiffs filed their amended complaint on Jan. 3, 2002. On Feb. 6, 2003, the Company's directors' motion to dismiss the amended complaint was converted by the Court to a motion for summary judgment and the plaintiffs were permitted to take discovery. The Company and its directors answered the amended complaint on April 1, 2003. On May 28, 2003, the Court (treating as a motion to dismiss the motion for summary judgment into which it had converted the original motion on February 6, 2003) denied the directors' motion to dismiss the amended complaint. Trial commenced on Oct. 20, 2004, and on Aug. 9, 2005, the Delaware Court of Chancery issued an order entering judgment against the plaintiffs and in favor of all defendants on all counts. Plaintiffs have appealed from the order.

Similar or identical claims have also been filed by the same plaintiffs (other than William and Geraldine Brehm) in the Superior Court of the State of California, Los Angeles County, beginning with a claim filed by Richard and David Kaplan on Jan. 3, 1997. On May 18, 1998, an additional claim was filed in the same California court by Dorothy L. Greenfield. All of the California claims were consolidated and stayed pending final resolution of the Delaware proceedings. The Claim filed by Dorothy L. Greenfield was voluntarily dismissed with prejudice on Oct. 24, 2005.[4]

Given the importance of the case, some analysis is needed. The basic questions are whether a lesser amount could have been paid when Ovitz was terminated, or if he could have been terminated for cause. Ovitz's employment agreement contained the following passage regarding dismissal for cause:

Termination by Company of Executive's employment for "good cause" as used in this Agreement shall be limited to gross negligence or malfeasance by Executive in the performance of his duties under this Agreement.[5]

As discussed below, gross negligence and malfeasance are hard to prove, and therefore, the board did not try to dismiss him for cause. While the plaintiffs tried to make the case that he should have been dismissed for cause, the court did not feel the evidence was sufficient to overrule the board's decision. The next question was whether the amount paid could have been less. The provisions cited above promised Ovitz payment of the present value of his base salary, which the agreement set at $1 million plus $7.5 million annually for the remainder of his contractual term. Because Ovitz was fired after 15 months of a five-year contract, the minimum he was due was an amount equal to the present value of $1 million for 3.75 years, $7.5

million paid annually for four years (number of not-yet-completed fiscal years) and a $10 million contract termination payment as specified below.

10. CONTRACT TERMINATION PAYMENT

In the event that Company shall not have made a Qualifying Offer (as hereinafter defined) to Executive by July 1, 2000, and no other agreement between Executive and Company relating to the extension of Executive's employment shall have been entered into by Sept. 30, 2000, Executive shall be entitled to receive, after Executive's:

(a) having given Company written notice of its failure to deliver a Qualifying Offer; and

(b) not having received such Qualifying Offer from Company within five business days from the delivery of such notice to Company,

a contract termination payment of $10,000,000 (the "TERMINATION PAYMENT") from Company. Such Termination Payment shall be due by the earlier of 30 days after the date that such payment shall not be subject to Section 162(m) of the Code or four months after the end of the last fiscal year of the Company during which Executive was employed by Company, but in no event shall such Termination Payment be due earlier than October 1, 2000, except as provided in Section 11(c) hereof.[6]

Given a nominal value of the payments of $43,750,000, it appears quite reasonable the present value could be $38,869,000. As noted above, the other major component of his severance package was the immediate vesting of 3 million options of Disney shares, which they were contractually required to provide. Critics do not mention that there were options of 2 million shares that he was granted under his employment agreement, but were forfeited because of his early termination.

Other Well-Compensated Disappointments

Feeding the fury is the perception that executives make enormous amounts whether they perform well or not. Besides Ovitz, there have been other well-publicized instances where top executives who were forced to leave their companies received multimillion-dollar severance packages.

A case working its way through the courts is that involving the severance package paid by Hewlett-Packard to Carly Fiorina. She left Hewlett-Packard at the beginning of 2005 and received a severance package valued at as much as $42 million (Darlin 2006). Fiorina had been CEO of HP since July 1999, having been recruited from Lucent Technologies. The explicit terms of her severance agreement, as filed with the SEC, are reproduced below:[7]

- Severance Agreement: We will honor all the terms of the HP severance policy.
- Severance Payment: A severance payment equal to 2.5 times your base pay and bonus at target less such tax as the company is obliged to deduct. This amount will be paid six months from the termination date in one lump sum with interest based on the January 2005 annual short term Applicable Federal Rate (AFR) of 2.78%:
- $14,000,000 [2.5 x ($1,400,000 + $4,200,000)] – on August 9, 2005 (or as soon as practical)
- Release and Waiver of Claims: As a condition to receiving these payments, you must sign a general waiver and release agreement in the attached form.
- Equity:
- Stock Options: Upon termination, all your non-qualified options (6,065,852 shares) will be fully vested. You will have the lesser of the expiration date or up to one year from your termination date to exercise the options.
- Long Term Performance Cash: You will receive a payout of the first year's Long Term Performance Cash at Target and the subsequent year's Long Term Performance Cash will be pro-rated at Target less applicable tax withholding based on the number of whole months of active service during the performance period. These amounts will be paid in one lump sum on February 18, 2005 or as soon as administratively practical.
- 2003 LTPC at Target = $5,880,000
- 2004 LTPC pro-rated = 9/36 of $6,010,800 = $1,502,700
- Benefits: You will receive a payout of any accrued retirement benefits that are applicable, this includes: tax and US Pension Benefits. Please note that you may be able to rollover some of the retirement pay outs into a qualified account to preserve favorable tax treatment. In addition, you will receive a cash payment of the balance of your unused vacation time.
- Health: You are eligible to participate in HP's continued Group Medical through COBRA for up to 18 months.

- Computer/Technical Support: You may retain all your home computer equipment. Your HP email and phone number will remain active for three months following termination. Technical support will be available two days per week during this three month period. HP will provide continued support for transition phone services for three months.
- Administrative Support: HP will provide access to administrative support for six months after termination.
- Financial/Legal/Career Fees: A lump sum payment of $50,000 for any financial counseling, legal fees and career counseling will be paid on February 18, 2005 or as soon as administratively practical.
- Security: HP will pay reasonable costs for your home security through Feb. 8, 2006.
- Transportation: The Company provided automobile must be returned upon termination. The use of the Corporate Aircraft will also cease upon termination.

As with Ovitz, Fiorina's severance was contested in court, by the pension funds of the Indiana Electrical Workers and the Service Employees International unions (Darlin 2006), as violating the limit shareholders approved in 2003 that restricted such compensation to 2.99 times an executive's base pay plus bonus. The payment also seems to be generous when compared with the term's of Fiorina's initial employment agreement (see below).[8] For example, while the employment contract specifies a payment of two times her target pay, HP paid her 2.5 times base pay plus bonus at target. Similarly, while the original agreement specified vesting of 50 percent of options, HP fully vested all her nonqualified options.

4. Termination of Employment.

...

(c) Voluntary Termination for Good Reason; Involuntary Termination Other Than for Cause.

...

(iv) a severance amount equal to two (2) times Executive's then Target Pay, payable in substantially equal installments over 24 months in accordance with the Company's standard payroll practice; provided, however, that (i) if Executive competes with the Company or materially violates Sections 7(c) or (d) hereof, any severance payments due thereafter shall cease and be forfeited as of the commencement of such competition, (ii) in the event of a Change of Control after such termination, the unpaid portion of such severance amount, if any, shall be paid to Executive in full in a single lump sum cash payment within fifteen (15) business days following such Change of Control, and

(iii) if such termination occurs in contemplation of, at the time of, or within two (2) years after a Change of Control, Executive shall instead be entitled to a lump sum cash payment within fifteen (15) business days after delivery of the aforesaid release equal to three (3) times the sum of (A) Executive's then Base Salary and (B) the higher of (x) Executive's then current Target Pay and (y) the highest variable pay and annual incentive bonus received by Executive for the two (2) fiscal years last ending prior to such termination. For purposes of this Section 4(c)(iv), "competition" shall mean engaging in any business that materially competes with the Company.

(vii) any forfeiture provision of any Restricted Stock or Restricted Unit shall lapse and Executive shall be fully vested in such Restricted Stock and Restricted Unit;

(viii) full vesting of 50% of Executive's unvested Stock Option and each traunche of each other grant of stock options or other equity awards, provided that if such termination takes place in contemplation of, at the time of, or within two (2) years after a Change of Control, Executive shall be entitled to full vesting of the Stock Option and all other stock options and equity awards, except that if such Change of Control occurs within one (1) year after the Employment Commencement Date, (A) the foregoing proviso shall not apply and (B) the additional vesting beyond that occurring upon the Change of Control shall not occur if the termination is at the time of or within three (3) months after the Change of Control.[9]

The cost of the severance award becomes magnified when the executive has a relatively short tenure. For example, in March 2005, Stephen Crawford became co-president of Morgan Stanley. About 100 days later, he quit, leaving with a severance package which included two years' salary and bonus valued at $32 million. Crowley (2005) notes that based upon his time in office, Crawford earned $54,000 an hour.

Dismissal for Cause

The question becomes why are we rewarding these people for doing a bad job—why do we have to give them severance at all? Why can't we dismiss them for cause, where the cause is poor performance? In the Ovitz case, plaintiffs asserted that the board should have dismissed him for cause, which would have negated the need to pay him severance. Employment/severance agreements are legal documents, which in most cases define dismissal for cause, which as noted above with respect to Ovitz is limited to gross negligence or malfeasance.

Unfortunately, short of a criminal conviction, it is hard to prove either gross negligence or malfeasance. The case of Robert J. O'Connell, former Massachusetts Mutual Life Insurance Co. CEO, proves instructive in this regard. Bandler (2005) detailed the allegations against O'Connell, who the board fired for "willful gross misconduct":

> Mr. O'Connell improperly added about $30 million to a special retirement account in his name; he purchased a company-owned condominium for an amount substantially below market price; and he interfered with the investigation and reprimand of two family members who were company employees.

O'Connell appealed, and Creswell (2006) reports that a three-arbitrator panel concluded that while:

> Mr. O'Connell did, in fact, have affairs with two female employees; made millions in profit in a deferred compensation account by trading using closing prices from the day before, and perhaps even stepped over the line in use of the company aircraft, none of these acts constituted "willful gross misconduct" on his part or resulted in "material harm" to the company.

Consequently, the company must pay him benefits worth as much as $50 million (Creswell 2006). Cases such as these make one question why corporations enter into contracts that make it so hard to fire someone for "cause." Why can't "cause" be poor performance?

Two potential explanations are (1) the corporation is better, in an economic sense, at bearing risk than the executive, or (2) we have a negotiation between a very interested party, the executive, and a board that, for better or worse, is playing with other people's money, so they agree to terms they might not otherwise. Among other things, while the amounts involved are large in dollar amounts, they are not necessarily large relative to company assets or market value. In the case of an outsider, where the sought-after individual must be induced to leave a job at which he/she has presumably been successful (or else why would another corporation want to hire him/her in the first place), the new employer needs to reduce his/her risk to induce the move. Thus, executive search firms advise their candidates to negotiate severance up front, and pre-existing severance agreements are more likely to be observed when the executive has been recruited from outside the corporation.

Summary

The focus of this chapter has been on severance and change-in-control agreements. Both agreements are utilized to reduce the risk of the executive, although change-in-control agreements are also utilized to mitigate the incentive the executive has to resist takeovers that otherwise might be in the best interests of shareholders. Unfortunately, as discussed in this chapter, both types of payments can be controversial. For example, severance payments usually occur when an executive is dismissed when the firm performed poorly, consequently many refer to it as pay for failure. And change-in-control payments, while not necessarily pay for failure, are associated with takeovers that in many cases lead to layoffs of rank-and-file workers.

Footnotes

1 Page 12, Exhibit 10(e), Walt Disney form 10-K filed with the Securities and Exchange Commission, Dec. 19, 1995.

2 Page 14, Walt Disney proxy statement filed with the Securities and Exchange Commission, Jan. 9, 1997.

3 Page 3, Exhibit 10(e), Walt Disney form 10-K filed with the Securities and Exchange Commission, Dec. 19, 1995.

4 Page 27, Walt Disney form 10-K filed with the Securities and Exchange Commission, Dec. 7, 2005.

5 Page 11, Exhibit 10(e), Walt Disney form 10-K filed with the Securities and Exchange Commission, Dec. 19, 1995.

6 Page 9, Exhibit 10(e), Walt Disney form 10-K filed with the Securities and Exchange Commission, Dec. 19, 1995.

7 Exhibit 99.1 Hewlett-Packard form 8-K filed with the Securities and Exchange Commission, Feb. 22, 2005.

8 Unlike Ovitz's employment contract that had a five-year term, Fiorina's contract stated: Executive and the Company understand and acknowledge that Executive's employment with the Company constitutes "at-will" employment. Subject to the Company's obligation to provide severance benefits as specified herein, Executive and the Company acknowledge that this employment relationship may be terminated at any time ... (Page 2, Exhibit QQ, Hewlett-Packard form 10-Q filed with the Securities and Exchange Commission, Sept. 20, 1999.)

9 Pages 15 & 16, Exhibit QQ, Hewlett-Packard form 10-Q filed with the Securities and Exchange Commission, Sept. 20, 1999.

Appendix 8-1[1]

Exhibit 10(gg)

Hewlett-Packard Co.

Employment Agreement

This Agreement is made as of the 17th day of July, 1999 by and between Hewlett-Packard Company (the "Company"), and Carleton S. Fiorina (the "Executive").

1. Duties and Scope of Employment.

    (a) Positions; Duties. During the Employment Term (as defined in Section 2), the Company shall employ Executive as the President and Chief Executive Officer of the Company. Executive shall report solely and directly to the Board of Directors of the Company (the "Board"). All other employees of the Company shall report to Executive or her designee and not directly to the Board. During the Employment Term, Executive shall have such responsibilities, duties and authorities as commensurate with chief executive officers of public entities of similar size and, in particular, shall be, in addition to being responsible for the operations of the Company, the chief external representative of the Company. The role and responsibilities of the Chairman of the Company shall be limited to chairing the Board and mentoring and counseling the Chief Executive Officer when and as requested by her and such other matters as the Chairman and Executive may agree, and within thirty (30) days after the Employment Commencement Date, the By-laws of the Company shall be amended accordingly. The Board shall, in good faith, consider Executive's advice and recommendations, if any, in connection with any appointments or nominations to the Board. For so long as Executive remains President and Chief Executive Officer of the Company, the Board will nominate Executive to the Board and, if elected, Executive shall serve in such capacity without additional consideration.

    (b) Obligations. During the Employment Term, Executive shall devote substantially all of her business efforts and time to the Company. Executive agrees, during the Employment Term, not to actively engage in any other employment, occupation or consulting activity for any direct or indirect remuneration without the prior approval of the Board; provided, however, that Executive may (i) serve in any capacity with any professional, community, industry, civic, educational or charitable organization, (ii) serve as a member of corporate boards of directors on which Executive currently serves and, with the consent of the Board (which consent shall not be unreasonably withheld or delayed), other corporate boards of directors and (iii) manage her and her family's personal investments and legal affairs so long as such activities do not materially interfere with the discharge of Executive's duties.

2. Employment Term. The Company hereby agrees to employ Executive and Executive hereby accepts employment, in accordance with the terms and conditions set forth herein, commencing on July 17, 1999 (the "Employment Commencement Date"). The period of Executive's employment hereunder is referred to herein as the "Employment Term." Executive and the Company understand and acknowledge that Executive's employment with the Company constitutes "at-will" employment. Subject to the Company's obligation to provide severance benefits as specified herein, Executive and the Company acknowledge that this employment relationship may be terminated at any time, upon written notice to the other party, with or without Cause or Good Reason and for any or no cause or reason, at the option of either the Company or Executive.

3. Compensation/Benefits. During the Employment Term, the Company shall pay and provide Executive the following:

   (a) Cash Compensation. As compensation for her services to the Company, Executive shall receive a base salary ("Base Salary") and shall be eligible to receive additional variable compensation. As of the Employment Commencement Date, Executive's annualized Base Salary shall be $1,000,000, and her annual variable compensation amount shall be targeted at no less than $1,250,000 (the "Target Bonus" which, together with the Base Salary, shall be referred to herein as "Target Pay"), with an opportunity to earn up to at least $3,750,000 in annual variable compensation. Except as provided herein, during the Employment Term, Executive's Base Salary and variable compensation for the fiscal year of the Company shall be determined in accordance with the Company's 1999 Variable Pay Plan as in effect as of the Employment Commencement Date, as amended, or any successor plan (the "Variable Pay Plan"). During the Employment Term, the Compensation Committee of the Board (the "Compensation Committee") shall review Executive's Base Salary and variable compensation then in effect at least annually and shall increase such amounts as the Compensation Committee may approve. Such Base Salary and variable compensation shall be payable in accordance with the Company's normal payroll practices and, in the case of variable compensation, in accordance with the terms of the Variable Pay Plan, except as otherwise provided herein. No increase in Base Salary shall be used to offset or otherwise reduce any obligations of the Company to Executive hereunder or otherwise.

(b) Joining Bonus. Within fifteen (15) business days after the Employment Commencement Date, the Company shall pay Executive a one-time lump sum cash payment in the amount of $3,000,000, reduced by any annual cash bonus Executive receives from her prior employer for the fiscal year ending September 30, 1999. If such annual cash bonus is paid after Executive receives the aforesaid payment, Executive shall refund to the Company an amount equal to the amount of such annual cash bonus received by her.

(c) Fiscal Years 1999 and 2000 Bonuses.

    (i) Pro-Rated Fiscal Year 1999 Bonus. Executive shall receive a cash bonus on account of, and subject to, her employment with the Company through the end of the Company's 1999 fiscal year equal to $1,250,000 multiplied by a fraction, determined by dividing the number of days from the Employment Commencement Date through the Company's 1999 fiscal year-end, by 365, payable as a single lump sum cash payment in accordance with the normal payment practices under the Variable Pay Plan (the "Guaranteed 1999 Bonus").

    (ii) Fiscal Year 2000 Bonus. For the Company's 2000 fiscal year, subject, except as otherwise provided herein, to her continued employment with the Company through the end of the 2000 fiscal year, Executive shall be guaranteed a minimum bonus of $1,250,000, payable as a single lump sum cash payment in accordance with the normal payment practices under the Variable Pay Plan (the "Guaranteed 2000 Bonus").

(d) Equity Compensation.

    (i) Stock Options. The Compensation Committee of the Board, which administers the Company's 1995 Incentive Stock Plan (the "1995 Plan"), has awarded Executive, as of the Employment Commencement Date, a non-qualified stock option (the "Stock

Option") under the Company's 1995 Plan to purchase a total of 600,000 shares of Company common stock, $1 par value (the "Common Stock"), with a per share exercise price equal to 100% of the fair market value of the Company's Common Stock as of the Employment Commencement Date as determined under the 1995 Plan. The Stock Option is for a term of 10 years (subject to earlier termination as provided in the 1995 Plan. In the case of termination by the Company without Cause, voluntary termination by Executive for Good Reason, death or a Disability Termination, the Stock Option and any other Company stock option then held by Executive shall remain exercisable (to the extent vested on the date of termination) until the earlier of one year from the employment termination date or the expiration of the option. Subject to accelerated vesting as set forth in this Agreement, the Stock Option shall vest and become exercisable as to 25% of the shares originally subject to the Stock Option on each anniversary of the Employment Commencement Date, so as to be 100% vested on the four year anniversary thereof, conditioned upon Executive's continued employment with the Company as of each vesting date. Executive may, but need not, exercise the Stock Option or any other stock option granted to Executive with a loan from the Company in accordance with Section IX of the 1995 Plan. The Stock Option shall in all respects be subject to the terms, definitions and provisions of the 1995 Plan and the standard form of stock option agreement, a copy of which has been given to Executive, as modified by the terms of this Agreement.

(ii) Restricted Stock. The Compensation Committee of the Board has awarded Executive as of the Employment Commencement Date, 290,000 shares of the Company's Common Stock under the 1995 Plan (the "Restricted Stock"). Subject to accelerated vesting as set forth in this Agreement, the Restricted Stock shall vest (i.e., the forfeiture of the Restricted Stock upon Executive's termination of employment shall lapse) as to one-third (1/3) of the Restricted Stock shares on each anniversary of the Employment Commencement Date, so as to be 100% vested on the three year anniversary thereof, conditioned upon Executive's continued employment with the Company as of each vesting date. Executive shall be entitled to all cash dividends paid on the Restricted Stock. If there is (i) any stock dividend, stock split or other change in the Restricted Stock, or (ii) any merger or sale of all or substantially all of the assets or other acquisition of the Company, any and all new, substituted or additional securities attributable to the Restricted Stock shall be included thereafter as "Restricted Stock" for purposes of this Agreement. The Restricted Stock shall in all respects be subject to the terms, definitions and provisions of the 1995 Plan and the standard form of restricted stock agreement, a copy of which has been given to Executive, as modified by the terms of this Agreement.

(iii) Restricted Share Units.

(A) As of the Employment Commencement Date, the Company shall credit Executive's account on the books of the Company with 290,000 "restricted share units" (the "Restricted Units"). The Restricted Units may not be sold, assigned, exchanged, pledged or otherwise transferred and are subject to the Forfeiture Restrictions (as hereinafter defined). In the event of a termination of employment prior to the lapse of the Forfeiture Restrictions, Executive shall, for no consideration, forfeit to the Company all Restricted Units to the extent then subject to the Forfeiture Restrictions. The forfeiture of Restricted Units upon such a termination of employment is herein referred to as "Forfeiture Restrictions." Except as otherwise provided herein, the Forfeiture Restrictions shall lapse as to one-third (1/3) of the Restricted Units on each anniversary of the Employment Commencement Date, so as to be 100% vested on the three year anniversary thereof, conditioned upon Executive's continued employment with the Company as of each vesting date.

(B) If on any date the Company shall pay any dividend on the Common Stock (other than a dividend payable in Common Stock), the number of Restricted Units credited to Executive shall as of such date be increased by an amount equal to: (x) the product of the number of Restricted Units credited to Executive as of the record date for such dividend multiplied by the per share amount of any dividend (or, in the case of any dividend payable in property other than cash, the per share value of such dividend, as determined in good faith by the Board), divided by (y) the fair market value of a share of Common Stock on the payment date of such dividend as determined under the 1995 Plan.

In the case of any dividend declared on Common Stock which is payable in Common Stock, the number of Restricted Units credited to Executive shall be increased by a number equal to the product of (x) the aggregate number of Restricted Units that have been credited to Executive through the related dividend record date multiplied by (y) the number of shares Common Stock (including any fraction thereof) payable as a dividend on a share of Common Stock. In the event of any change in the number or kind of outstanding shares of Common Stock by reason of any recapitalization, reorganization, merger, consolidation, stock split or any similar change affecting the Common Stock (other than a dividend payable in Common Stock) the Company shall make an appropriate adjustment in the number and terms of the Restricted Units credited to Executive so that, after such adjustment, the Restricted Units shall represent a right to receive the same consideration (or if such consideration is not available, other consideration of the same value) that Executive would have received in connection with such recapitalization, reorganization, merger, consolidation, stock split or any similar change if she had owned on the applicable record date a number of shares of Common Stock equal to the number of Restricted Units credited to Executive's account prior to such adjustment.

    (C) On the first to occur of the fifth (5th) anniversary of the Employment Commencement Date, the date of any termination of employment, or the first date on which occurs a Change of Control, the Company shall pay to Executive a number of shares of Common Stock equal to the aggregate number of vested Restricted Units credited to Executive as of such date.

    (iv) When Executive incurs tax liability in connection with the exercise of the Stock Option or options, Restricted Stock or Restricted Units, Executive may elect to satisfy her resulting withholding tax obligation by having the Company retain shares of Common Stock having a fair market value equal to the Company's minimum withholding tax obligation.

    (v) Ongoing Awards. Executive shall fully participate in annual restricted stock and stock option grants and any other long-term incentive program at levels commensurate with her position.

    (vi) Registration. At all times, the Company shall maintain registrations on Form S-8 or another applicable form so that the Restricted Stock, Common Stock issued in connection with Restricted Units or upon exercise of the Stock Option or other options or other equity awards are immediately saleable by Executive on the public market (subject to the non-registration limitations of applicable laws).

  (e) Employee Benefits. Executive shall, to the extent eligible, be entitled to participate at a level commensurate with her position in all employee benefit welfare and retirement plans and programs, as well as equity plans, provided by the Company to its senior executives in accordance with the terms thereof as in effect from time to time. Such plans and programs currently include, without limitation, the 1995 Plan, the Variable Pay Plan, the Employee Stock Purchase Plan, the Tax Saving Capital Accumulation Plan, the Retirement Plan, the Deferred Profit-Sharing Plan, the Excess Benefit Retirement Plan, the Executive Deferred Compensation Plan, financial counseling program, automobile program, group term life insurance plan, comprehensive health, major medical, dental insurance plans and short-term and long-term disability plans.

(f) Perquisites. The Company shall provide to Executive, at the Company's cost, all perquisites to which other senior executives of the Company are entitled to receive and such other perquisites which are suitable to the character of Executive's position with the Company and adequate for the performance of her duties hereunder but not less than the level being provided on the date hereof to her predecessor as Chief Executive Officer except as otherwise required because of changes in law. To the extent consistent with the Company's past practice, the Company shall not treat such amounts as income to Executive.

(g) Business and Entertainment Expenses. Upon submission of appropriate documentation in accordance with its policies in effect from time to time, the Company shall pay or reimburse Executive for all business expenses which Executive incurs in performing her duties under this Agreement, including, but not limited to, travel, entertainment, professional dues and subscriptions, and all dues, fees, and expenses associated with membership in various professional, business, and civic associations and societies in which Executive participates in accordance with the Company's policies in effect from time to time.

(h) Flexible Time Off. Executive shall be entitled to paid time off in accordance with the standard written policies of the Company with regard to senior executives, but in no event less than twenty-five (25) days, per calendar year.

(i) Relocation. Executive shall be entitled to relocation benefits pursuant to the Company's relocation benefit program, as supplemented by the provisions of the side letter entered into by the Company and Executive.

4. Termination of Employment.

(a) Death or Disability. The Company may terminate Executive's employment for disability in the event Executive has been unable to perform her material duties hereunder for six (6) consecutive months because of physical or mental incapacity by giving Executive notice of such termination while such continuing incapacity continues (a "Disability Termination"). Executive's employment shall automatically terminate on Executive's death. In the event Executive's employment with the Company terminates during the Employment Term by reason of Executive's death or a Disability Termination, then upon the date of such termination (i) any forfeiture provision of any Restricted Stock or Restricted Units shall lapse and Executive shall be fully vested in such Restricted Stock and Restricted Units, (ii) the Stock Option and all other stock option or equity grants to Executive shall vest in full so as to become fully exercisable, (iii) the Company shall promptly pay and provide Executive (or in the event of Executive's death, Executive's estate) (A) any unpaid Base Salary through the date of termination and any accrued vacation, (B) any unpaid bonus accrued with respect to the fiscal year ending on or preceding the date of termination, (C) reimbursement for any unreimbursed expenses incurred through the date of termination and (D) all other payments, benefits or fringe benefits to which Executive may be entitled subject to and in accordance with, the terms of any applicable compensation arrangement or benefit, equity or fringe benefit plan or program or grant and amounts which may become due under Sections 6, 9 and 10 hereof (collectively, items under (iii) are referred to as "Accrued Benefits"), (iv) the Company shall pay the Guaranteed 1999 Bonus and the Guaranteed 2000 Bonus to the extent not previously paid or paid under (v) below and (v) the Company shall pay to Executive at the time other senior executives are paid under any Variable Pay Plan or cash bonus or long term incentive plan, a pro-rata bonus equal to the amount Executive would have received if employment continued (without any discretionary cutback) multiplied a fraction where the numerator is the number of days in each respective bonus period prior to Executive's termination and the denominator is the number of days in the bonus period (the "Prorated Bonus").

(b) Termination for Cause. The Company may terminate Executive's employment for Cause. In the event that Executive's employment with the Company is terminated during the Employment Term by the

Company for Cause, Executive shall not be entitled to any additional payments or benefits hereunder, other than Accrued Benefits (including, but not limited to, any then vested Stock Option, Restricted Stock, Restricted Units or other stock options or equity grants). For the purposes of this Agreement, "Cause" shall mean (i) the willful failure by Executive to attempt to substantially perform her duties with the Company (other than any such failure resulting from her incapacity due to physical or mental impairment), unless any such failure is corrected within thirty (30) days following written notice by the Board that specifically identifies the manner in which the Board believes Executive has substantially not attempted to materially perform her duties or (ii) the willful gross misconduct by Executive with regard to the Company that is materially injurious to the Company. No act, or failure to act, by Executive shall be "willful" unless committed without good faith and without a reasonable belief that the act or omission was in the best interest of the Company. No event shall be deemed the basis for Cause unless Executive is terminated therefore within sixty (60) days after such event is known to the Chairman of the Company, or, if Executive is Chairman, known to the Chairman of any committee of the Board. Notwithstanding the foregoing, Executive shall not be deemed to have been terminated for Cause without (i) advance written notice provided to Executive not less than fourteen (14) days prior to the date of termination setting forth the Company's intention to consider terminating Executive and including a statement of the proposed date of termination and the specific detailed basis for such consideration of termination for Cause, (ii) an opportunity of Executive, together with her counsel, to be heard before the Board at least ten (10) days after the giving of such notice and prior to the proposed date of termination, (iii) a duly adopted resolution of the Board stating that in accordance with the provisions of the next to the last sentence of this paragraph (b), that the actions of Executive constituted Cause and the basis thereof, and (iv) a written determination provided by the Board setting forth the acts and omissions that form the basis of such termination of employment. Any determination by the Board hereunder shall be made by the affirmative vote of at least a two-thirds (2/3) majority of all of the members of the Board (other than Executive). Any purported termination of employment of Executive by the Company which does not meet each and every substantive and procedural requirement of this paragraph (b) shall be treated for all purposes under this Agreement as a termination of employment without Cause.

(c) Voluntary Termination for Good Reason; Involuntary Termination Other Than for Cause. Executive may terminate her employment for Good Reason at any time within one hundred eighty (180) days after the occurrence of the Good Reason event by written notice to the Company. If Executive's employment with the Company is voluntarily terminated by Executive for "Good Reason" or is involuntarily terminated by the Company other than for "Cause," then, subject to Executive executing and not revoking the Release Agreement attached hereto as Exhibit A (other than with respect to subsections 4(c)(i) and (vii) below), the Company shall pay or provide Executive with the following:

(i) any Accrued Benefits;

(ii) the Prorated Bonus;

(iii) the Guaranteed 1999 Bonus and the Guaranteed 2000 Bonus to the extent not previously paid or paid under (i) or (ii) above;

(iv) a severance amount equal to two (2) times Executive's then Target Pay, payable in substantially equal installments over 24 months in accordance with the Company's standard payroll practice; provided, however, that (i) if Executive competes with the Company or materially violates Sections 7(c) or (d) hereof, any severance payments due thereafter shall cease and be forfeited as of the commencement of such competition, (ii) in the event of a Change of Control after such termination, the unpaid portion of such severance amount, if any, shall be paid to Executive in full in a single lump sum cash payment within fifteen (15) business days following such Change of Control, and (iii) if such termination occurs in contemplation of, at the time of, or within two (2) years after a Change of Control, Executive shall instead be entitled to a lump sum cash payment within fifteen (15) business days after delivery of the aforesaid release equal to three (3) times the sum of (A) Executive's then Base Salary and (B) the higher of (x) Executive's then current Target Pay and (y) the highest variable pay and annual incentive bonus received by Executive for the two (2) fiscal years last ending prior to such termination. For purposes of this Section 4(c)(iv), "competition" shall mean engaging in any business that materially competes with the Company.

(v) to the extent eligible on the date of termination, continued participation, at no additional after tax cost to Executive than Executive would have as an employee, in all welfare plans until two (2) years after the date of termination; provided, however, that if such termination occurs within two (2) years after a Change of Control, Executive shall be entitled to continued participation in all welfare plans for three (3) years rather than two (2) years. In the event Executive obtains other employment that offers substantially similar or improved benefits, as to any particular welfare plan, such continuation of coverage by the Company for such benefits under such plan shall immediately cease. To the extent such coverage cannot be provided under the Company's welfare benefit plans without jeopardizing the tax status of such plans, for underwriting reasons or because of the tax impact on Executive, the Company shall pay Executive an amount such that Executive can purchase such benefits separately at no greater after tax cost to Executive than Executive would have had if the benefits were provided to Executive as an employee;

(vi) in the event such termination occurs in contemplation of, at the time of, or within two (2) years after a Change of Control, three (3) additional years of service and compensation credit (at Executive's then compensation level) for benefit purposes under any defined benefit type retirement plan, including but not limited to any tax-qualified retirement plan and any excess benefit retirement plan if then in effect, and, if Executive is not eligible to receive benefits under any such plan on the date of termination, two (2) additional years of age for determining eligibility to receive such benefits, provided that benefits under any such plan will not commence until Executive actually attains the required distribution age under the plan or Executive's spouse qualifies for death benefits under such plan and further provided that, with regard to any plan qualified under Section 401(a) of the Internal Revenue Code of 1986, as amended (the "Code"), the additional amounts may be provided on a nonqualified plan basis.

(vii) any forfeiture provision of any Restricted Stock or Restricted Unit shall lapse and Executive shall be fully vested in such Restricted Stock and Restricted Unit;

(viii) full vesting of 50% of Executive's unvested Stock Option and each traunche of each other grant of stock options or other equity awards, provided that if such termination takes place in contemplation of, at the time of, or within two (2) years after a Change of Control, Executive shall be entitled to full vesting of the Stock Option and all other stock options and equity awards, except that if such Change of Control occurs within one (1) year after the Employment Commencement Date, (A) the foregoing proviso shall not apply and (B) the additional vesting beyond that occurring upon the Change of Control shall not occur if the termination is at the time of or within three (3) months after the Change of Control; and

(ix) outplacement services at a level commensurate with Executive's position, including use of an executive office and secretary, for a period of one (1) year commencing on Executive's date of termination but in no event extending beyond the date on which Executive commences other full time employment.

For the purposes of this Agreement "Good Reason" means, without the express written consent of Executive, the occurrence of any of the following events: (i) any reduction or diminution (except temporarily during any period of disability) in Executive's titles or positions, any material diminution in Executive's authority, duties or responsibilities with the Company (it being acknowledged that, in the event any entity becomes the owner (directly or indirectly) of more than 35% of the Common Stock, it shall be Good Reason if Executive is not the Chief Executive Officer of such entity); (ii) a breach by the Company of any material provision of this Agreement, including, but not limited to, a breach of the Company's obligation under Section 1(a), any reduction, (other than a reduction (not to exceed ten percent (10%)) that applies, in equal percentages, to all U.S. officers (within the meaning of Section 16 of the Securities Exchange Act of 1934, as amended) of the Company), in Executive's Base Salary or any material failure to timely pay any part of Executive's compensation (including, without limitation, Base Salary, annualized Target Pay and bonus) or to materially provide in the aggregate the level of benefits contemplated herein; (iii) the failure of the Company to obtain and deliver to Executive a satisfactory written agreement from any successor to the Company to assume and agree to perform this Agreement in accordance with Section 8 hereof; or (iv) the failure to appoint or elect Executive to the Board within thirty (30) days of the Employment Commencement Date or at any time thereafter or the removal of Executive therefrom.

(d) Without Good Reason. Executive may terminate her employment at any time without Good Reason by written notice to the Company. In the event that Executive's employment with the Company is terminated during the Employment Term by Executive without Good Reason, Executive shall not be entitled to any additional payments or benefits hereunder, other than Accrued Benefits (including, but not limited to, any then vested Stock Option, Restricted Stock, Restricted Units or other stock options or equity grants).

(e) No Mitigation/No Offset. Executive shall not be required to seek other employment or otherwise mitigate the value of any severance benefits contemplated by this Agreement, nor shall any such benefits be reduced by any earnings or benefits that Executive may receive from any other source. The amounts payable hereunder shall not be subject to setoff, counterclaim, recoupment, defense or other right which the Company may have against Executive or others.

5. Change of Control Vesting Acceleration. In the event of a "Change of Control" (as defined below), on the date of such Change of Control (a) any forfeiture provision of any Restricted Stock or Restricted Unit shall lapse and Executive shall be fully vested in such Restricted Stock and Restricted Unit and (b) 50% of any remaining unvested shares subject to the Stock Option and of each tranche of each other stock option or equity award shall be immediately vested. Following such partial acceleration of the Stock Option or each tranche of each other stock option or equity award, the remaining unvested shares of such Stock Option or tranche shall continue to vest as otherwise provided in the grant.

For the purposes of this Agreement, "Change of Control" is defined as:

(a) Any "person" (as such term is used in Sections 13(d) and 14(d) of the Securities Exchange Act of 1934, as amended) becomes the "beneficial owner" (as defined in Rule 13d-3 under said Act), directly or indirectly, of securities of the Company representing 35% or more of the total voting power represented by the Company's then outstanding voting securities; or

(b) A change in the composition of the Board occurring within a two-year period, as a result of which fewer than a majority of the directors are Incumbent Directors. "Incumbent Directors" shall mean directors who either (i) are directors of the Company as of the date hereof or (ii) are elected, or nominated for election, to the Board with the affirmative votes of at least a majority of the Incumbent Directors at the time of such election or nomination (but shall not include an individual whose election or nomination is in connection with an actual or threatened proxy contest relating to the election of directors to the Company); or

(c) The consummation of a merger or consolidation of the Company with any other corporation, other than a merger or consolidation which would result in the voting securities of the Company outstanding immediately prior thereto continuing to represent (either by remaining outstanding or by being converted into voting securities of the surviving entity) at least 50% of the total voting power represented by the voting securities of the Company or such surviving entity outstanding immediately after such merger or consolidation; or

(d) The consummation of the sale or disposition by the Company of all or substantially all of the Company's assets; or

(e) The approval by the stockholders of the Company of a plan of complete liquidation of the Company.

Notwithstanding the foregoing, a Change of Control shall not be deemed to occur by reason of the divestiture of the Company's test and measurement and related businesses in connection with the contemplated spin-off of such business or any events directly attributable thereto.

6. Golden Parachute Excise Tax Gross-Up.

(a) In the event that Executive shall become entitled to payments and/or benefits provided by this Agreement or any other amounts in the "nature of compensation" (whether pursuant to the terms of this Agreement or any other plan, arrangement or agreement with the Company, any person whose actions result in a change of ownership or effective control covered by Section 280G(b)(2) of the Code or any person affiliated with the Company or such person) as a result of such change in ownership or effective control (collectively the "Company Payments"), and such Company Payments will be subject to the tax (the "Excise Tax") imposed by Section 4999 of the Code (and any similar tax that may hereafter be imposed by any taxing authority) the Company shall pay to Executive at the time specified in paragraph (d) below an additional amount (the "Gross-up Payment") such that the net amount retained by Executive, after deduction of any Excise Tax on the Company Payments and any U.S. federal, state, and local income or payroll tax upon the Gross-up Payment provided for by this paragraph

(a) but before deduction for any U.S. federal, state, and local income or payroll tax on the Company Payments, shall be equal to the Company Payments.

(b) For purposes of determining whether any of the Company Payments and Gross-up Payments (collectively the "Total Payments") will be subject to the Excise Tax and the amount of such Excise Tax, (i) the Total Payments shall be treated as "parachute payments" within the meaning of Section 280G(b)(2) of the Code, and all "parachute payments" in excess of the "base amount" (as defined under Section 280G(b)(3) of the Code) shall be treated as subject to the Excise Tax, unless and except to the extent that, in the opinion of the Company's independent certified public accountants appointed prior to any change in ownership (as defined under Section 280G(b)(2) of the Code) or tax counsel selected by such accountants (the "Accountants") such Total Payments (in whole or in part) either do not constitute "parachute payments," represent reasonable compensation for services actually rendered within the meaning of Section 280G(b)(4) of the Code in excess of the "base amount" or are otherwise not subject to the Excise Tax, and (ii) the value of any non-cash benefits or any deferred payment or benefit shall be determined by the Accountants in accordance with the principles of Section 280G of the Code.

(c) For purposes of determining the amount of the Gross-up Payment, Executive shall be deemed to pay U.S. federal income taxes at the highest marginal rate of U.S. federal income taxation in the calendar year in which the Gross-up Payment is to be made and state and local income taxes at the highest marginal rate of taxation in the state and locality of Executive's residence for the calendar year in which the Company Payment is to be made, net of the maximum reduction in U.S. federal income taxes which could be obtained from deduction of such state and local taxes if paid in such year. In the event that the Excise Tax is subsequently determined by the Accountants to be less than the amount taken into account hereunder at the time the Gross-up Payment is made, Executive shall repay to the Company, at the time that the amount of such reduction in Excise Tax is finally determined, the portion of the prior Gross-up Payment attributable to such reduction (plus the portion of the Gross-up Payment attributable to the Excise Tax and U.S. federal, state and local income tax imposed on the portion of the Gross-up Payment being repaid by Executive if such repayment results in a reduction in Excise Tax or a U.S. federal, state and local income tax deduction), plus interest on the amount of such repayment at the rate provided in Section 1274(b)(2)(B) of the Code. Notwithstanding the foregoing, in the event any portion of the Gross-up Payment to be refunded to the Company has been paid to any U.S. federal, state and local tax authority, repayment thereof (and related amounts) shall not be required until actual refund or credit of such portion has been made to Executive, and interest payable to the Company shall not exceed the interest received or credited to Executive by such tax authority for the period it held such portion. Executive and the Company shall mutually agree upon the course of action to be pursued (and the method of allocating the expense thereof) if Executive's claim for refund or credit is denied. In the event that the Excise Tax is later determined by the Accountant or the Internal Revenue Service to exceed the amount taken into account hereunder at the time the Gross-up Payment is made (including by reason of any payment the existence or amount of which cannot be determined at the time of the Gross-up Payment), the Company shall make an additional Gross-up Payment in respect of such excess (plus any interest or penalties payable with respect to such excess) at the time that the amount of such excess is finally determined.

(d) The Gross-up Payment or portion thereof provided for in paragraph

(c) above shall be paid not later than the thirtieth (30th) day following an event occurring which subjects Executive to the Excise Tax; provided, however, that if the amount of such Gross-up Payment or portion thereof cannot be finally determined on or before such day, the Company shall pay to Executive on such day an estimate, as determined in good faith by the Accountant, of the minimum amount of such payments and shall pay the remainder of such payments (together with interest at the rate provided in Section 1274(b)(2)(B) of the Code), subject to further payments pursuant to paragraph (c) hereof, as soon as the amount thereof can reasonably be determined, but in no event later than the ninetieth (90th) day after the occurrence of the event subjecting Executive to the Excise Tax. In the event that the amount of the estimated payments exceeds the amount subsequently determined to have been due, such excess shall constitute a loan by the Company to Executive, payable on the fifth (5th) day after demand by the Company (together with interest at the rate provided in Section 1274(b)(2)(B) of the Code).

(e) In the event of any controversy with the Internal Revenue Service (or other taxing authority) with regard to the Excise Tax, Executive shall permit the Company to control issues related to the Excise Tax (at its expense), provided that such issues do not potentially materially adversely affect Executive, but Executive shall control any other issues. In the event the issues are interrelated, Executive and the Company shall in good faith cooperate so as not to jeopardize resolution of either issue, but if the parties cannot agree Executive shall make the final determination with regard to the issues. In the event of any conference with any taxing authority as to the Excise Tax or associated income taxes, Executive shall permit the representative of the Company to accompany Executive, and Executive and Executive's representative shall cooperate with the Company and its representative.

(f) The Company shall be responsible for all charges of the Accountant.

(g) The Company and Executive shall promptly deliver to each other copies of any written communications, and summaries of any verbal communications, with any taxing authority regarding the Excise Tax covered by this Section 6.

7. Non-Compete; Non-Solicit.

(a) The parties hereto recognize that Executive's services are special and unique and that the level of compensation and the provisions herein for compensation under Section 3 are partly in consideration of and conditioned upon Executive's not competing with the Company, and that Executive's covenant not to compete or solicit as set forth in this Section 7 during and after employment is essential to protect the business and good will of the Company.

(b) Executive agrees that during the term of employment with the Company and for a period of twenty-four (24) months thereafter (the "Covenant Period"), Executive shall not render services for any of the three (3) organizations designated by the Board in a writing delivered to Executive within thirty (30) days after the Employment Commencement Date (the "Prohibited List"). The Prohibited List may be changed by the Board from time to time (but there may never be more than three (3) entities listed) by written notice to Executive, such notice to be effective only if Executive's commencement of rendering services for such entity is ninety (90) or more days after the giving of such notice. The scope of the non-competition clause under any equity plan, benefit plan or other plan, agreement or arrangement of the Company shall not be deemed to prohibit Executive's actions or, except as provided in Section 4(c) of this Agreement or pursuant to a provision in a Company plan or grant agreement that precludes future vesting or exercisability at the time competition is entered into, serve as a basis for any reduction or forfeiture of benefits or payments thereunder unless such actions violate this Section 7(b) of this Agreement.

(c) During the Covenant Period, Executive shall not, directly or indirectly, disrupt, damage or interfere with the operation or business of the Company by soliciting or recruiting its employees for Executive or others, but the foregoing shall not prevent Executive from giving reference.

(d) During the Covenant Period, Executive shall not, without prior written authorization from the Company, violate the agreement entered into pursuant to Section 13 hereof.

(e) Executive agrees that the Company would suffer an irreparable injury if Executive was to breach the covenants contained in Sections 7(b), (c) or (d) and that the Company would by reason of such breach or threatened breach be entitled to injunctive relief in a court of appropriate jurisdiction and Executive hereby stipulates to the entering of such injunctive relief prohibiting Executive from engaging in such breach.

(f) If any of the restrictions contained in this Section 7 shall be deemed to be unenforceable by reason of the extent, duration or geographical scope or other provisions thereof, then the parties hereto contemplate that the court shall reduce such extent, duration, geographical scope or other provision hereof and enforce this Section 7 in its reduced form for all purposes in the manner contemplated hereby.

8. Assignment. This Agreement shall be binding upon and inure to the benefit of (a) the heirs, beneficiaries, executors and legal representatives of Executive upon Executive's death and (b) any successor of the Company, provided that any successor shall within ten (10) days of such assumption deliver to Executive a written assumption in a form reasonably acceptable to Executive. Any such successor of the Company shall be deemed substituted for the Company under the terms of this Agreement for all purposes. As used herein, "successor" shall mean any person, firm, corporation or other business entity which at any time, whether by purchase, merger or otherwise, directly or indirectly acquires all or substantially all of the assets or business of the Company. Notwithstanding such assignment, the

Company shall remain, with such successor, jointly and severally liable for all of its obligations hereunder. This Agreement may not otherwise be assigned by the Company.

None of the rights of Executive to receive any form of compensation payable pursuant to this Agreement shall be assignable or transferable except through a testamentary disposition or by the laws of descent and distribution upon the death of Executive or as provided in Section 18 hereof. Any attempted assignment, transfer, conveyance or other disposition (other than as aforesaid) of any interest in the rights of Executive to receive any form of compensation hereunder shall be null and void; provided, however, that notwithstanding the foregoing, Executive shall be allowed to transfer vested shares subject to the Stock Option or other stock options or equity awards and vested Restricted Stock consistent with the rules for transfers to "family members" as defined in Securities Act Form S-8.

9. Liability Insurance.

    (a) The Company shall cover Executive under directors and officers liability insurance both during and, while potential liability exists, after the Employment Term in the same amount and to the same extent, if any, as the Company covers its other officers and directors.

    (b) The Company shall during and after the Employment Term indemnify and hold harmless Executive to the fullest extent permitted by applicable law with regard to actions or inactions taken by Executive in the performance of her duties as an officer, director and employee of the Company and its affiliates or as a fiduciary of any benefit plan of the Company and its affiliates.

10. Payment of Legal Fees. The Company shall pay Executive's reasonable legal and financial consulting fees and costs associated with entering into this Agreement.

11. Notices. All notices, requests, demands and other communications called for hereunder shall be in writing and shall be deemed given if (a) delivered personally or by facsimile, (b) one (1) day after being sent by Federal Express or a similar commercial overnight service, or (c) three (3) days after being mailed by registered or certified mail, return receipt requested, prepaid and addressed to the parties or their successors in interest at the following addresses, or at such other addresses as the parties may designate by written notice in the manner aforesaid:

If to the Company: Hewlett-Packard Company 3000 Hanover Street Palo Alto, CA 94304 Attn: General Counsel

If to Executive: at the last residential address known by the Company.

12. Severability. In the event that any provision hereof becomes or is declared by a court of competent jurisdiction to be illegal, unenforceable or void, this Agreement shall continue in full force and effect without said provision.

13. Proprietary Information. Concurrently with the execution of this Agreement, Executive shall enter into a confidentiality and proprietary information agreement with the Company in the form mutually agreed on by the parties (the "Confidentiality Agreement"), provided, however, that the foregoing shall not preclude Executive from complying with due legal process or from removing Company property from the Company's premises in furtherance of her duties and obligations as provided herein.

14. Entire Agreement. This Agreement represents the entire agreement and understanding between the Company and Executive concerning Executive's employment relationship with the Company, and supersedes and replaces any and all prior agreements and understandings concerning Executive's employment relationship with the Company entered into prior to the date hereof but not any written agreements entered into simultaneous with this Agreement or thereafter.

15. Arbitration.

    (a) Agreement. The Company and Executive agree that any dispute or controversy arising out of, relating to, or in connection with this Agreement, or the interpretation, validity, construction, performance, breach, or termination thereof shall be settled by binding arbitration to be held in Santa Clara, California or such other location agreed by the parties hereto, in accordance with the National Rules for the Resolution of Employment Disputes then in effect of the American Arbitration Association. The arbitrator may grant injunctions or other relief in such dispute or controversy. The decision of the arbitrator shall be final, conclusive and binding on the parties to the arbitration. Judgment may be entered on the arbitrator's decision in any court having jurisdiction.

    (b) Governing Law. The arbitrators shall apply California law to the merits of dispute or claim, without reference to rules of conflicts of law. Executive and the Company hereby expressly consent to the personal jurisdiction of the state and federal courts located in California for any action or proceeding arising from or relating to this Agreement or relating to any arbitration in which the parties are participants.

(c) Costs and Fees of Arbitration. Executive shall pay the initial arbitration filing (not to exceed $200), and the Company shall pay the remaining costs and expenses of such arbitration (unless Executive requests that each party pay one-half of the costs and expenses of such arbitration or unless otherwise required by law). Unless otherwise required by law or pursuant to an award by the arbitrator, the Company and Executive shall each pay separately its counsel fees and expenses. Notwithstanding the foregoing, the arbitrator may, but need not, award the prevailing party in any dispute its or her legal fees and expenses.

16. No Oral Modification, Cancellation or Discharge. This Agreement may only be amended, canceled or discharged in writing signed by Executive and the Company's General Counsel, the Chairman of the Company (provided Executive is not Chairman) or a member of the Compensation Committee.

17. Survivorship. The respective rights and obligations of Company and Executive hereunder shall survive any termination of Executive upon her employment to the extent necessary to the intended preservation of such rights and obligations.

18. Beneficiaries. Executive shall be entitled, to the extent permitted under any applicable law, to select and change the beneficiary or beneficiaries to receive any compensation or benefit payable hereunder upon her death by giving the Company written notice thereof. If Executive dies, severance then due or other amounts due hereunder shall be paid to her designated beneficiary or beneficiaries or, if none are designated or none survive Executive, her estate.

19. Withholding. The Company shall be entitled to withhold, or cause to be withheld, any amount of federal, state, city or other withholding taxes required by law with respect to payments made to Executive in connection with her employment hereunder.

20. Governing Law. This Agreement shall be governed by the laws of the State of California, without reference to rules of conflicts of law.

IN WITNESS WHEREOF, the undersigned have executed this Agreement:

HEWLETT-PACKARD COMPANY

/s/Lewis E. Platt

_____

Lewis E. Platt

EXECUTIVE

/s/Carleton S. Fiorina

_____

Carleton S. Fiorina

Address: _____

_____

EXHIBIT 10 (ii)

Hewlett-Packard Co. Incentive Stock Plan Stock Option Agreement (Non-Qualified)

THIS AGREEMENT, dated July 17, 1999 ("Grant Date") by and between HEWLETT- PACKARD COMPANY, a Delaware corporation ("Company"), and 00547500 Carleton S. Fiorina ("Employee"), is entered into as follows:

WITNESSETH:

WHEREAS, the Company has established the Hewlett-Packard Company 1995 Incentive Stock Plan ("Plan"), a copy of which can be found on the Stock Options Web Site at: http://hpweb.corp.hp.com/publish/hwp/stock/stok_opt.htm or by written or telephonic request to the Company Secretary, and which Plan made a part hereof; and

WHEREAS, the Compensation Committee of the Board of Directors of the Company ("Committee") determined that the Employee be granted an option under the Plan as reflected in the terms and conditions contained in the Employment Agreement by and between the Employee and the Company made as of July 17, 1999 (the "Employment Agreement") and as hereinafter set forth;

NOW THEREFORE, the parties hereby agree that in consideration of services to be rendered, the Company grants the Employee an option ("Option") to purchase 600,000 shares of its $1.00 par value voting common stock of the Company ("Stock") upon the terms and conditions set forth herein.

1. This Option is granted under and pursuant to the Plan and is subject to each and all of the provisions thereof.

2. The Option price shall be $113.03 per share of Stock.

3. Except as may be provided in this Paragraph 3, this Option is not transfer-able by the Employee otherwise than by will or the laws of descent and distribution, and is exercisable only by the Employee during her lifetime. Except as may be provided in this Paragraph 3, this Option may not be transferred, assigned, pledged or hypothecated by the Employee during her lifetime, whether by operation of law or otherwise, and is not subject to execution, attachment or similar process. The Employee may transfer this

Option (to the extent vested) consistent with the rules for transfers to "family members" as defined in Form S-8 of the Securities Act of 1933, as amended; provided, however, that any such transfer shall comply with all procedural rules reasonably established by the Committee.

4. This Option shall become exercisable as to 25% of the Stock subject to such Option on the first anniversary date of the Grant Date, and as to an additional 25% on each succeeding anniversary date, so as to be 100% vested on the fourth anniversary thereof, conditioned upon the Employee's continued employment with the Company as of each vesting date. Notwithstanding the foregoing, this Option shall become exercisable as to:

(a) 100% of the then unvested Stock subject to this Option upon the termination of the Employee's employment due to a "Disability Termination" (as defined in the Employment Agreement), death or retirement due to age or permanent and total disability;

(b) 50% of the then unvested Stock subject to this Option upon the Employee's voluntary termination of employment for "Good Reason" (as defined in the Employment Agreement) or involuntary termination by the Company other than for "Cause" (as defined in the Employment Agreement); provided, however, that if such termination takes place in contemplation of, at the time of, or within two (2) years after a Change of Control (as defined in the Employment Agreement), this Option shall become exercisable in full, except that if such Change of Control occurs within one (1) year after the Grant Date (i) such full vesting shall not occur, and (ii) the additional vesting beyond that occurring upon the Change of Control under sub-paragraph (c) below shall not occur if the termination is at the time or within three (3) months after the Change of Control; or

(c) 50% of each vesting tranche of the then unvested Stock subject to this Option in the event of a Change of Control. Following such partial acceleration of this Option as provided in Paragraphs 4(b) or (c), the remaining unvested Stock subject to this Option shall continue to vest as otherwise provided in this Agreement.

5. This Option will expire ten (10) years from the date hereof, unless sooner terminated or canceled in accordance with the provisions of the Plan and this Agreement. This means that the Option must be exercised, if at all, on or before July 16, 2009.

6. This Option may be exercised by delivering to the Secretary of the Company

at its head office a written notice stating the number of shares of Stock as to which the Option is exercised; provided, however, that no such exercise shall be with respect to fewer than twenty-five (25) shares or the remaining shares covered by the Option if less than twenty-five. The written notice must be accompanied by the payment of the full Option price of such shares. Payment may be by:

(a) Cash;

(b) Shares of Stock owned for at least six (6) months;

(c) Delivery of the Employee's promissory note ("Note") in the form attached hereto as Exhibit A bearing interest at the "applicable federal --------- rate" prescribed under the Internal Revenue Code of 1986, as amended and its regulations at time of purchase and secured by a pledge of the Stock purchased by the Note pursuant to the Security Agreement attached hereto as Exhibit B; or --------- (f)d Consideration received by the Company under a cashless exercise program implemented by the Company in connection with the Plan; or

(e) A combination thereof; provided, however, that any payment in Stock or by delivery of a Note shall be in strict compliance with all procedural rules established by the Committee.

7. All rights of the Employee in this Option, to the extent that it has not been exercised, shall terminate upon the death of the Employee (except as hereinafter provided) or termination of her employment for any reason other than retirement due to age or permanent and total disability, a Disability Termination, termination by the Company without Cause, or voluntary termination by the Employee for Good Reason, except as provided in Paragraph 4(b) with regard to the contemplation of a Change of Control. In the event of the Employee's retirement due to age or permanent and total disability, the Employee may exercise the Option within three (3) years after such retirement. In the event of the Employee's termination of employment due to a Disability Termination (other than due to a permanent and total disability), termination by the Company without Cause, or voluntary termination by the Employee for Good Reason, the Employee may exercise the Option within one (1) year after such termination. In the event of the Employee's death, her legal representative or designated beneficiary shall have the right to exercise all or a portion of the Employee's right under this Option. The representative or designee must exercise the

Option within one (1) year after the death of the Employee, and shall be bound by the provisions of the Plan. In all cases, however, the Option will expire no later than the expiration date set forth in Paragraph 5.

8. The Employee shall remit to the Company payment for all applicable with-holding taxes and required social security contributions at the time the Employee exercises any portion of this Option. The Employee may elect to satisfy such withholding tax obligation by having the Company retain Stock having a fair market value equal to the Company's minimum withholding obligation.

9. Neither the Plan nor this Agreement nor any provision under either shall be construed so as to grant the Employee any right to remain in the employ of the Company, and it is expressly agreed and understood that employment is terminable at the will of either party subject to the provisions of the Employment Agreement.

HEWLETT-PACKARD COMPANY
By /s/ Susan P. Orr

_____

Susan P. Orr Chairman of the Compensation Committee
By /s/ Ann Baskins

_____

Ann Baskins Associate General Counsel

Exhibit A --------- NOTE

FOR VALUE RECEIVED, _____ promises to pay to HEWLETT-PACKARD COMPANY, a Delaware corporation (the "Company"), or order, the principal sum of _____ ($_____), together with interest on the unpaid principal hereof from the date hereof at the rate of _____ percent (____%) per annum, compounded semiannually.

Principal and interest shall be due and payable on _____,
_____. Payment of principal and interest shall be made in lawful money of the United States of America.

The undersigned may at any time prepay all or any portion of the principal or interest owing hereunder.

This Note is subject to the terms of the Company's 1995 Incentive Stock Plan, the Incentive Stock Plan Stock Option Agreement (Non-Qualified) between the Company and the undersigned, dated as of July 17, 1999 and the Employment Agreement between the Employee and the Company made as of July 17, 1999. This Note is secured in part by a pledge of the Company's $1.00 par value voting common stock ("Stock") under the terms of a Security Agreement of even date herewith and is subject to all the provisions thereof.

The holder of this Note shall have full recourse against the undersigned, and shall not be required to proceed against the collateral securing this Note in the event of default.

In the event the undersigned shall cease to be an employee of the Company for any reason, this Note shall, at the option of the Company, be accelerated, and the whole unpaid balance on this Note of principal and accrued interest shall be immediately due and payable.
Should any action be instituted for the collection of this Note, the reasonable costs and attorneys' fees therein of the holder shall be paid by the undersigned.

Dated:_____

Signature _____

Print Name_____

EXHIBIT B --------- SECURITY AGREEMENT

This Security Agreement is made as of _____, _____ between HEWLETT-PACKARD COMPANY, a Delaware corporation ("Pledgee"), and _____ ("A Pledgor").

Recitals --------

WHEREAS, pursuant to Pledgor's election to purchase shares of $1.00 par value voting common stock of the Company ("Stock") under the Option Agreement dated July 17, 1999 (the "Option Agreement"), between Pledgor and Pledgee under Pledgee's 1995 Incentive Stock Plan, and Pledgor's election under the terms of the Option Agreement to pay for such Stock with her promissory note (the "Note"), Pledgor has purchased _____ shares of Pledgee's Stock at a price of $_____ per share, for a total purchase price of $_____. The Note and the obligations thereunder are as set forth in Exhibit A to the Option Agreement.

NOW, THEREFORE, it is agreed as follows:

1. Creation and Description of Security Interest. In consideration of the pursuant to the Delaware Commercial Code, hereby pledges all of such Stock (herein sometimes referred to as the "Collateral") represented by certificate number _____, duly endorsed in blank or with executed stock powers, and herewith delivers said certificate to the Secretary of Pledgee ("Pledgeholder"), who shall hold said certificate subject to the terms and conditions of this Security Agreement.The pledged Stock (together with an executed blank stock assignment for use in transferring all or a portion of the Stock to Pledgee if, as and when required pursuant to this Security Agreement) shall be held by the Pledgeholder as security for the repayment of the Note, and any extensions or renewals thereof, to be executed by Pledgor pursuant to the terms of the Option, and the Pledgeholder shall not encumber or dispose of such Stock except in accordance with the provisions of this Security Agreement.

2. Pledgor's Representations and Covenants. To induce Pledgee to enter into this Security Agreement, Pledgor represents and covenants to Pledgee, its successors and assigns, as follows:

    (a) Payment of Indebtedness. Pledgor will pay the principal sum of the Note secured hereby, together with interest thereon, at the time and in the manner provided in the Note.

    (b) Encumbrances. The Stock is free of all other encumbrances, defenses and liens, and Pledgor will not further encumber the Stock without the prior written consent of Pledgee.

    (c) Margin Regulations. In the event that Pledgee's Stock is now or later becomes margin-listed by the Federal Reserve Board and Pledgee is classified as a "lender" within the meaning of the regulations under Part 207 of Title 12 of the Code of Federal Regulations ("Regulation G"), Pledgor agrees to cooperate with Pledgee in making any amendments to the Note or providing any additional collateral as may be necessary to comply with such regulations.

3. Voting Rights. During the term of this pledge and so long as all payments of principal and interest are made as they become due under the terms of the Note, Pledgor shall have the right to vote all of the shares of Stock pledged hereunder.

4. Stock Adjustments. In the event that during the term of the pledge any stock dividend, reclassification, readjustment or other changes are declared or made in the capital structure of Pledgee, all new, substituted and additional shares or other securities issued by reason of any such change shall be delivered to and held by the Pledgee under the terms of this Security Agreement in the same manner as the Stock originally pledged hereunder. In the event of substitution of such securities, Pledgor, Pledgee and Pledgeholder shall cooperate and execute such documents as are reasonable so as to provide for the substitution of such Collateral and, upon such substitution, references to "Stock" in this Security Agreement shall include the substituted shares of capital stock of Pledgor as a result thereof.

5. Options and Rights. In the event that, during the term of this pledge, subscription options or other rights or options shall be issued in connection with the pledged Stock, such subscription options or other rights or options shall be the property of Pledgor and, if exercised by Pledgor, all new stock or other securities so acquired by Pledgor as it relates to the pledged Stock then held by Pledgeholder shall be immediately delivered to Pledgeholder, to be held under the terms of this Security Agreement in the same manner as the Stock pledged.

6. Default. Pledgor shall be deemed to be in default of the Note and of this Security Agreement in the event:

    (a) Payment of principal or interest on the Note shall be delinquent for a period of 10 days or more; or

    (b) Pledgor fails to perform any of the covenants set forth in the Option or contained in this Security Agreement for a period of 10 days after written notice thereof from Pledgee. In the case of an event of default, as set forth above, Pledgee shall have the right to accelerate payment of the Note upon notice to Pledgor, and Pledgee shall thereafter be entitled to pursue its remedies under the Delaware Commercial Code.

7. Release of Collateral. Subject to any applicable contrary rules under Regulation G, there shall be released from this pledge a portion of the pledged Stock held by Pledgeholder hereunder upon payments of the principal of the Note. The number of the pledged shares of Stock which shall be released shall be that number of full shares which bears the same proportion to the initial number of shares pledged hereunder as the payment of principal bears to the initial full principal amount of the Note.

8. Withdrawal or Substitution of Collateral. Pledgor shall not sell, withdraw, pledge, substitute or otherwise dispose of all or any part of the Collateral without the prior written consent of Pledgee.

9. Term. The within pledge of Stock shall continue until the payment of all indebtedness secured hereby, at which time the remaining pledged Stock shall be promptly delivered to Pledgor, subject to the provisions for prior release of a portion of the Collateral as provided in paragraph 7 above.

10. Insolvency. Pledgor agrees that if a bankruptcy or insolvency proceeding is instituted by or against it, or if a receiver is appointed for the property of Pledgor, or if Pledgor makes an assignment for the benefit of creditors, the entire amount unpaid on the Note shall become immediately due and payable, and Pledgee may proceed as provided in the case of default.

11. Pledgeholder Liability. In the absence of willful or gross negligence, Pledgeholder shall not be liable to any party for any of his or her acts, or omissions to act, as Pledgeholder.

12. Invalidity of Particular Provisions. Pledgor and Pledgee agree that the enforceability or invalidity of any provision or provisions of this Security Agreement shall not render any other provision or provisions herein contained unenforceable or invalid.

13. Successors or Assigns. Pledgor and Pledgee agree that all of the terms of this Security Agreement shall be binding on their respective successors and assigns, and that the term "Pledgor" and the term "Pledgee" as used herein shall be deemed to include, for all purposes, the respective designees, successors, assigns, heirs, executors and administrators.

14. Governing Law. This Security Agreement shall be interpreted and governed under the internal substantive laws, but not the choice of law rules, of California.

IN WITNESS WHEREOF, the parties hereto have executed this Agreement as of the day and year first above written.

"PLEDGOR" _____ Signature

_____ Print Name

"PLEDGEE" HEWLETT-PACKARD COMPANY a Delaware corporation

_____ Signature
_____ Print Name
_____ Title:

"PLEDGEHOLDER" _____

Signature

_____ Print Name
_____ Title: Secretary of

HEWLETT-PACKARD COMPANY

EXHIBIT 10(jj)
Hewlett-Packard Co. Restricted Stock Agreement

THIS AGREEMENT, dated as of July 17, 1999 ("Grant Date") by and between Hewlett-Packard Company, a Delaware Corporation ("Company"), and 00547500 Carleton S. Fiorina ("Employee"), is entered into as follows:

WHEREAS, the Company has established the Hewlett-Packard Company 1995 Incentive Stock Plan ("Plan"), a copy of which can be found on the Stock Options Web Site at: http://hpweb.corp.hp.com/publish/hwp/stock/stok-opt.htm or by written or telephonic request to the Company Secretary, and which Plan made a part hereof; and

WHEREAS, the Compensation Committee of the Board of Directors of the Company ("Committee") determined that the Employee be granted shares of the Company's $1.00 par value Common Stock ("Stock") subject to the restrictions stated below, as reflected in the terms and conditions contained in the Employment Agreement by and between the Employee and the Company made as of July 17, 1999 (the "Employment Agreement") and as hereinafter set forth;

NOW, THEREFORE, the parties hereby agree as follows:
1. Grant of Stock. Subject to the terms and conditions of this Agreement and of the Plan, the Company hereby grants to the Employee 290,000 shares of Stock.
2. Vesting Schedule.
    The interest of the Employee in the Stock shall vest as to one-third of such Stock on the first anniversary of the Grant Date, and as to an additional one-third on each succeeding anniversary date, so as to be 100% vested on the third anniversary thereof, conditioned upon the Employee's continued employment with the Company as of each vesting date. Notwithstanding the foregoing, the interest of the Employee in the Stock shall vest as to:
    (a) 100% of the then unvested Stock upon the Employee's termination of employment due to death, a "Disability Termination" (as defined in the Employment Agreement), involuntary termination by the Company other than for "Cause" (as defined in the Employment Agreement) or voluntary termination by the Employee for "Good Reason" (as defined

in the Employment Agreement); or

(b) 100% of the then unvested Stock upon a "Change of Control" (as defined in the Employment Agreement).

3. Restrictions.

   (a) The Stock or rights granted hereunder may not be sold, pledged or otherwise transferred until the Stock becomes vested in accordance with Section 2. The period of time between the date hereof and the date Stock becomes vested is referred to herein as the "Restriction Period."

   (b) If the Employee's employment with the Company is terminated by the Company for Cause or voluntarily by the Employee (other than for Good Reason), the balance of the Stock subject to the provisions of this Agreement which have not vested at the time of the Employee's termination of employment shall be forfeited by the Employee, and ownership transferred back to the Company.

4. Legend.

   All certificates representing any shares of Stock of the Company subject to the provisions of this Agreement shall have endorsed thereon the following legend: "The shares represented by this certificate are subject to an agreement between the Corporation and the registered holder, a copy of which is on file at the principal office of this Corporation."

5. Escrow.

   The certificate or certificates evidencing the Stock subject hereto shall be delivered to and deposited with the Secretary of the Company as Escrow Agent in this transaction. The Stock may also be held in a restricted book entry account in the name of the Employee. Such certificates or such book entry shares are to be held by the Escrow Agent until termination of the Restriction Period, when they shall be released by said Escrow Agent to the Employee.

6. Employee Shareholder Rights.

   During the Restriction Period, the Employee shall have all the rights of a shareholder with respect to the Stock except for the right to transfer the Stock, as set forth in Section 3 and except as set forth in Section 7. Accordingly, the Employee shall have the right to vote the Stock and to receive any cash dividends paid to or made with respect to the Stock.

7. Changes in Stock.

   In the event that as a result of (a) any stock dividend, stock split or other change in the Stock, or (b) any merger or sale of all or substantially all of the assets of other acquisition of the Company, and by virtue of any such change the Employee shall in her capacity as owner of unvested shares of Stock which have been awarded to her (the "Prior Stock") be entitled to new or additional or different shares or securities, such new or additional or different shares or securities shall thereupon be considered to be unvested Stock and shall be subject to all of the conditions and restrictions which were applicable to the Prior Stock pursuant to this Agreement.

8. Disability Termination or permanent and total disability of Employee.
   In the event of a Disability Termination or permanent and total disability of the Employee, any unpaid but vested Stock shall be paid to the Employee if legally competent or to a legally designated guardian or representative if the Employee is legally incompetent.

9. Death of Employee.
   In the event of the Employee's death after the vesting date but prior to the payment of Stock, said Stock shall be paid to the Employee's estate or designated beneficiary.

10. Taxes.
    The Employee shall be liable for any and all taxes, including withholding taxes, arising out of this grant or the vesting of Stock hereunder. The Employee may elect to satisfy such withholding tax obligation by having the Company retain Stock having a fair market value equal to the Company's minimum withholding obligation.

11. Miscellaneous.
    (a) The Company shall not be required (i) to transfer on its books any shares of Stock of the Company which shall have been sold or transferred in violation of any of the provisions set forth in this Agreement, or (ii) to treat as owner of such shares or to accord the right to vote as such owner or to pay dividends to any transferee to whom such shares shall have been so transferred.

    (b) The parties agree to execute such further instruments and to take such action as may reasonably be necessary to carry out the intent of this Agreement.

    (c) Any notice required or permitted hereunder shall be given in writing and shall be deemed effectively given upon delivery to the Employee at her address then on file with the Company.

    (d) Neither the Plan nor this Agreement nor any provisions under either shall be construed so as to grant the Employee any right to remain in the employ of the Company.

(e) This Agreement and the Employment Agreement constitute the entire agreement of the parties with respect to the subject matter hereof.

HEWLETT-PACKARD COMPANY

By /s/ Susan P.Orr

Susan P.Orr Chairman of the Compensation Committee

By /s/ Ann Baskins

Ann Baskins Associate General Counsel

EXHIBIT 10(kk)
Hewlett-Packard Co. Restricted Stock Unit Agreement

THIS AGREEMENT, dated as of July 17, 1999 ("Grant Date") by and between Hewlett-Packard Company, a Delaware Corporation ("Company"), and 00547500 Carleton S. Fiorina ("Employee"), is entered into as follows:

WHEREAS, the Company has established the Hewlett-Packard Company 1995 Incentive Stock Plan ("Plan"), a copy of which can be found on the Stock Options Web Site at:
http://hpweb.corp.hp.com/publish/hwp/stock/stok_opt.htm or by written or telephonic request to the Company Secretary, and which Plan made a part hereof; and

WHEREAS, the Compensation Committee of the Board of Directors of the Company ("Committee") determined that the Employee be granted stock units subject to the restrictions stated below, as reflected in the terms and conditions contained in the Employment Agreement by and between the Employee and the Company made as of July 17, 1999 (the "Employment Agreement") and as hereinafter set forth;

NOW, THEREFORE, the parties hereby agree as follows:

1. Grant of Units.

   Subject to the terms and conditions of this Agreement and of the Plan, the Company hereby credits to a separate account maintained on the books of the Company ("Account") 290,000 units ("Units"). On any date, the value of each Unit shall equal the fair market value of a share of the Company's $1.00 par value Common Stock ("Stock"). For purposes of this Agreement, "fair market value" shall be deemed to be the mean of the highest and lowest quoted selling prices for a share of Stock on that date as reported on The New York Stock Exchange Composite Tape.

2. Vesting Schedule.

   The interest of the Employee in the Units shall vest as to one-third of such Units on the first anniversary of the Grant Date, and as to an additional one-third on each succeeding anniversary date, so as to be 100% vested on the third anniversary thereof, conditioned upon the Employee's continued employment with the Company as of each vesting date. Notwithstanding the foregoing, the interest of the Employee in the Units shall vest as to:

(a) 100% of the then unvested Units upon the Employee's termination of employment due to death, a "Disability Termination" (as defined in the Employment Agreement), involuntary termination by the Company other than for "Cause" (as defined in the Employment Agreement) or voluntary termination by the Employee for "Good Reason" (as defined in the Employment Agreement); or

(b) 100% of the then unvested Units upon a "Change of Control" (as defined in the Employment Agreement).

3. Restrictions.

(a) The Units granted hereunder may not be sold, pledged or otherwise transferred and may not be subject to lien, garnishment, attachment or other legal process. The period of time between the date hereof and the date the Units become vested is referred to herein as the "Restriction Period."

(b) If the Employee's employment with the Company is terminated by the Company for Cause or voluntarily by the Employee (other than for Good Reason), the balance of the Units subject to the provisions of this Agreement which have not vested at the time of the Employee's termination of employment shall be forfeited by the Employee.

4. Dividends.

If on any date the Company shall pay any dividend on the Stock (other than a dividend payable in Stock), the number of Units credited to the Employee's Account shall as of such date be increased by an amount equal to: (a) the product of the number of Units credited to the Employee's Account as of the record date for such dividend, multiplied by the per share amount of any dividend (or, in the case of any dividend payable in property other than cash, the per share value of such dividend, as determined in good faith by the Board of Directors of the Company), divided by (b) the fair market value of a share of Stock on the payment date of such dividend. In the case of any dividend declared on Stock which is payable in Stock, the number of Units credited to the Employee shall be increased by a number equal to the product of (x) the aggregate number of Units that have been credited to the Employee's Account through the related dividend record date, multiplied by (y) the number of shares of Stock (including any fraction thereof) payable as a dividend on a share of Stock.

5. Changes in Stock.

In the event of any change in the number and kind of outstanding shares of Stock by reason of any recapitalization, reorganization, merger, consolidation, stock split or any similar change affecting the Stock (other than a dividend payable in Stock) the Company shall make an appropriate adjustment in the number and terms of the Units credited to the Employee's Account so that, after such adjustment, the Units shall represent a right to receive the same consideration (or if such consideration is not available, other consideration of the same value) that the Employee would have received in connection with such recapitalization, reorganization, merger, consolidation, stock split or any similar change if she had owned on the applicable record date a number of shares of Stock equal to the number of Units credited to the Employee's Account prior to such adjustment.

6. Form and Timing of Payment.

   On the first to occur of the following, the Company shall pay to the Employee a number of shares of Stock equal to the aggregate number of vested Units credited to the Employee as of such date:

   (a) The fifth anniversary of the Grant Date;

   (b) The first date on which occurs a Change of Control; or

   (c) The date of the Employee's termination of employment for any reason.

7. Disability Termination of Employee.

   In the event of a Disability Termination of the Employee, any unpaid but vested Units shall be paid to the Employee if legally competent or to a legally designated guardian or representative if the Employee is legally incompetent.

8. Death of Employee.

   In the event of the Employee's death after the vesting date but prior to the payment of the Units, said Units shall be paid to the Employee's estate or designated beneficiary.

9. Taxes.

   The Employee shall be liable for any and all taxes, including withholding taxes, arising out of this grant or the vesting of Units hereunder. The Employee may elect to satisfy such withholding tax obligation by having the Company retain Stock having a fair market value equal to the Company's minimum withholding obligation.

10. Miscellaneous.

    (a) All amounts credited to the Employee's Account under this Agreement shall continue for all purposes to be a part of the general assets of the Company. The Employee's interest in the Account shall make her only a general, unsecured creditor of the Company.

(b) The parties agree to execute such further instruments and to take such action as may reasonably be necessary to carry out the intent of this Agreement.

(c) Any notice required or permitted hereunder shall be given in writing and shall be deemed effectively given upon delivery to the Employee at her address then on file with the Company.

(d) Neither the Plan nor this Agreement nor any provisions under either shall be construed so as to grant the Employee any right to remain in the employ of the Company.

(e) This Agreement and the Employment Agreement constitute the entire agreement of the parties with respect to the subject matter hereof.

HEWLETT-PACKARD COMPANY

By /s/ Susan P. Orr

_____

Susan P. Orr Chairman of the Compensation Committee

By /s/ Ann Baskins

_____

Ann Baskins Associate General Counsel

Footnote

1 Hewlett-Packard form 10-Q filed with the Securities and Exchange Commission, Sept. 20, 1999.

Part III
Related Issues

Chapter 9

Ownership of the Corporation

As the ownership of corporate wealth has become more widely dispersed, ownership of that wealth and control over it have come to lie less and less in the same hands. Under the corporate system, control over industrial wealth can be and is being exercised with a minimum of ownership interest. Conceivably, it can be exercised without any such interest. (Berle and Means 1932)

Introduction

It has long been believed that many of the problems associated with the modern corporation arise from the separation of the ownership from the control of the corporation.[1] This separation, and the conflicting incentives of owners (value maximization) and managers (utility maximization), has been termed the agency problem, with the resulting costs called agency costs. Consequently, many (for example, Jensen and Meckling 1976) have argued that increasing managerial ownership will reduce agency costs by aligning the interests of management and shareholders.

Consider the following example. The CEO of a major corporation is considering the purchase of a corporate jet for $10 million. While the corporation does not need the jet, the CEO wants it for the status it conveys. If the CEO owns 1 percent of the corporation, his or her wealth will decrease by $100,000 as a result of the purchase. Consequently, as long as the value placed on the jet by the CEO exceeds $100,000, he or she will have the corporation purchase the jet. However, if the CEO owns 10 percent of the corporation, his or her wealth would decrease by $1 million as a result of the purchase. Obviously, it is less likely he or she will value the jet at $1 million, and hence the corporation is less likely to purchase the jet. In generic terms, as CEO ownership increases, he or she bears more of the costs of his or her nonvalue maximizing actions, such as overconsumption of perquisites, and as a result, is more likely to act in a manner that will maximize firm value.

Many of those making the argument that increasing managerial ownership will reduce agency costs assert that current levels of ownership are too low (see, for example, Jensen and Murphy 1990a). Although it has not been empirically established that higher managerial ownership leads to better firm performance (Loderer and Martin 1997; Himmelberg et al. 1999), to increase executive ownership, many corporations have instituted stock option and grant programs, and have set minimum levels for executive ownership. For example, Wells Fargo sets ownership goals for executives, part of which require the executive to retain some of the shares acquired upon exercise of a stock option:

> Under stock ownership guidelines established by the Committee, each executive officer is expected to retain shares of the Company's common stock equal to at least 50% of the after-tax profit shares (assuming a 50% tax rate) acquired through option exercises. The number of shares expected to be owned under these guidelines continues to increase each time an executive officer exercises a stock option. The Chief Executive Officer and each other executive officer named in the Summary Compensation Table have either satisfied or exceeded these ownership guidelines.[2]

Wells Fargo also sets ownership goals for directors, as well as a time line for achieving those goals:

> Within five years after joining the Board, directors are expected to own Company common stock (including shares credited to a director's account under the Directors Plan deferral program discussed below) having a value equal to five times the cash portion of the annual retainer. Each director has met, or for any director who has served fewer than five years is on track to meet, these ownership requirements.[3]

Conyon and Murphy (2000) find that in 1997, the average CEO owned 3.1 (median 0.29) percent of the shares in his or her corporation. However, once they aggregate ownership, options and long-term incentives, they arrive at an effective ownership percentage of 4.18 (median 1.48). Incorporating options and other long-term components of the compensation package provides a better measure of the CEO's incentives to increase shareholder value than looking at ownership alone. It shows the percentage of the increase in shareholder wealth that would flow to the CEO. Consequently, Tables 9-1 through 9-4 show CEO stock ownership, and stock ownership including stock options, for large U.S. corporations (firms in the S&P 500, MidCap and SmallCap indexes). Table 9-1 shows ownership as a

Table 9-1:

Ownership, as a Percentage of Shares Outstanding, by Year

Year	Mean			Median		
	Shares	Options	Shares+ Options	Shares	Options	Shares+ Options
1992	2.27	0.40	2.67	0.12	0.17	0.40
1993	2.80	0.72	3.52	0.28	0.33	0.92
1994	3.32	0.96	4.29	0.43	0.48	1.50
1995	3.17	0.99	4.16	0.41	0.56	1.50
1996	3.01	1.09	4.09	0.40	0.63	1.61
1997	3.19	1.23	4.41	0.37	0.71	1.72
1998	3.25	1.25	4.50	0.39	0.78	1.77
1999	3.36	1.40	4.77	0.46	0.90	1.94
2000	3.12	1.47	4.59	0.42	1.00	2.06
2001	2.73	1.54	4.27	0.36	1.07	2.01
2002	2.55	1.58	4.13	0.34	1.11	1.93
2003	2.32	1.58	3.90	0.32	1.11	1.90
2004	2.21	1.44	3.65	0.32	0.99	1.74
2005	2.01	1.29	3.30	0.31	0.84	1.52

Note: Calculations in this table are based upon data contained in the April 2006 version of Standard & Poor's ExecuComp.

percentage of outstanding shares. Mean (median) ownership is comparable to that found by Conyon and Murphy, ranging from a low of 2.01 (0.31) percent in 2005 to a high of 3.36 (0.46) in 1999. After including options (exercisable and unexercisable), this percentage increases to 3.30 (1.52) percent in 2005 and 4.77 (1.94) percent in 1999. In both cases, it is interesting to note the decline in ownership from 1999 to 2005, which may be coincidental, or may be associated with the overall market decline since 2000.[4] Table 9-2 on page 326 shows mean and median share, and option-ownership percentage is generally inversely related to size, with ownership dropping from 5.55 (median 3.24) percent for the smallest to 1.70 (0.46) percent for the largest corporations. The latter finding makes sense given an executives' wealth constraint. That is, it costs more to buy a given percentage of a larger corporation than it does to purchase the same percentage of a smaller corporation. Overall, the ownership percentages are rather low, indicating the potential for agency problems. To be more precise, ownership percentages are low relative to 100 percent, where the owner-manager bears the full cost/receives the full benefit of his or her actions. As illustrated in the introduction to this chapter,

Table 9-2:

Ownership, as a Percentage of Shares Outstanding, by Company Size (for 2005)

	Size Decile	Mean Shares	Mean Options	Mean Shares+ Options	Median Shares	Median Options	Median Shares+ Options
Smallest	1	3.26	2.29	5.55	0.64	1.95	3.24
	2	3.14	2.00	5.14	0.56	1.44	2.64
	3	2.37	1.74	4.11	0.37	1.38	2.01
	4	2.17	1.30	3.47	0.36	1.01	1.65
	5	1.82	1.16	2.98	0.48	0.86	1.62
	6	1.78	1.26	3.03	0.37	0.93	1.61
	7	1.98	1.05	3.03	0.28	0.75	1.50
	8	1.23	0.92	2.15	0.24	0.66	1.11
	9	1.14	0.70	1.84	0.15	0.54	0.82
Largest	10	1.25	0.45	1.70	0.08	0.30	0.46

Note: Calculations in this table are based upon data contained in the April 2006 version of Standard & Poor's ExecuComp.

Table 9-3:

Dollar Value of Ownership, by Year

Year	Mean Shares	Mean Options	Mean Shares+ Options	Median Shares	Median Options	Median Shares+ Options
1992	$83,176,006	$3,783,649	$86,959,655	$5,003,840	$1,147,073	$7,857,228
1993	$57,070,826	$3,746,328	$60,817,154	$4,757,692	$953,137	$7,105,778
1994	$46,237,042	$3,032,020	$49,269,062	$4,380,225	$635,079	$7,059,999
1995	$55,935,967	$5,475,565	$61,411,532	$5,114,440	$1,131,250	$8,484,713
1996	$68,312,856	$7,371,655	$75,684,511	$5,572,380	$1,720,400	$9,729,335
1997	$100,061,683	$10,815,344	$110,877,027	$6,979,684	$2,673,869	$14,074,097
1998	$129,186,581	$13,886,524	$143,073,104	$6,622,042	$2,173,693	$13,851,991
1999	$163,407,044	$22,008,319	$185,415,363	$7,304,494	$1,892,657	$14,373,819
2000	$149,410,339	$24,589,099	$173,999,437	$6,634,371	$2,523,126	$14,685,690
2001	$116,507,365	$24,070,133	$140,577,498	$5,848,749	$2,660,353	$12,490,670
2002	$98,599,557	$8,549,178	$107,148,735	$4,867,444	$1,481,145	$9,613,435
2003	$105,193,900	$12,919,184	$118,113,084	$6,209,848	$3,663,645	$13,663,555
2004	$109,182,112	$16,209,729	$125,391,841	$7,068,137	$4,929,815	$17,398,232
2005	$127,988,652	$17,340,177	$145,328,829	$7,880,157	$4,841,751	$17,915,551

Note: Calculations in this table are based upon data contained in the April 2006 version of Standard & Poor's ExecuComp.

as the ownership percentage increases, the owner becomes less likely to take costly actions (for example, purchase a corporate jet) that reduce shareholder value because he or she bears a greater percentage of that cost.

Tables 9-3 and 9-4 provide the dollar value of CEO ownership as of the end of the year. It is calculated by multiplying the number of shares owned by the year-end share price and adding to that amount the intrinsic value of in-the-money options (the intrinsic value of the options is the profit that would be realized if the options were exercised at that point in time). As shown in Table 9-3, the amounts are quite large, with the value of share and option ownership increasing from a mean (median) of $86,959,655 ($7,857,228) in 1992 to $185,415,363 ($14,373,819) in 1999 before dropping to $145,328,829 ($17,915,551) in 2005. Thus, CEOs have substantial investments in their firms, even if, as a percentage of total shares outstanding, their ownership is low.

Table 9-4 shows that the dollar amounts increase with firm size, with the value of share and option ownership ranging from a mean (median) of $8,363,596 ($1,865,224) for the smallest firms to $867,035,259 ($63,693,078) for the largest firms. This holds despite the inverse relationship between firm size and ownership percentage documented in Table 9-2, indicating that while the dollar value of ownership increases with firm size, it does not increase as much as market value.

Table 9-4:
Dollar Value of Ownership, by Company Size (for 2005)

	Size Decile	Mean			Median		
		Shares	Options	Shares+ Options	Shares	Options	Shares+ Options
Smallest	1	$7,365,995	$997,601	$8,363,596	$1,141,206	$289,714	$1,865,224
	2	$16,615,964	$2,758,147	$19,374,111	$3,117,799	$1,204,139	$5,529,867
	3	$20,634,241	$5,092,985	$25,727,225	$3,212,030	$2,277,384	$7,947,918
	4	$29,215,352	$5,449,179	$34,664,531	$4,510,452	$3,278,564	$10,599,765
	5	$31,582,994	$7,838,160	$39,421,155	$8,626,415	$4,338,075	$18,448,214
	6	$47,282,317	$11,518,604	$58,800,921	$9,573,889	$7,267,245	$21,982,804
	7	$77,727,881	$14,156,665	$91,884,546	$10,947,380	$7,529,510	$25,520,054
	8	$83,883,675	$27,370,083	$111,253,758	$16,318,627	$12,283,520	$36,017,562
	9	$161,393,550	$31,387,164	$192,780,714	$17,732,782	$19,176,420	$43,057,213
Largest	10	$800,422,302	$66,612,957	$867,035,259	$35,135,985	$22,499,130	$63,693,078

Note: Calculations in this table are based upon data contained in the April 2006 version of Standard & Poor's ExecuComp.

Effect of Executive Ownership on Incentives

Table 9-5 shows CEO ownership for a sample of well-known U.S. corporations. Firms like Berkshire Hathaway and Amazon.com, which are at the top of the list, can pay less attention to their compensation packages simply because their ownership structure provides their CEO with the proper incentives. As discussed in Chapter 3, both compensate their chief executives solely with salary.[5] And yet each has done a good job of increasing shareholder wealth. Their large ownership provides the incentive to exert effort and take actions to increase firm value. Thus, ownership can take the place of stock options and grants in providing executives with the proper set of incentives.[6] In fact, a growing body of research shows (Jensen and Murphy 1990a, Hall and Liebman 1998 and Murphy 1998) that CEO ownership (including options) accounts for the bulk of the sensitivity of CEO wealth to firm performance.

Table 9-5:

Examples of CEO Ownership

Corporation	Executive	Position	Percentage Ownership
Berkshire Hathaway	Warren Buffett	Chairman and Chief Executive Officer	32.30[1]
Amazon.com	Jeffrey Bezos	Chairman and Chief Executive Officer	24.30[2]
Nike	Philip Knight	Chairman	23.90[3]
Dell Computer	Michael Dell	Chairman	9.88[4]
Microsoft	William Gates	Chairman	9.73[5]
Cisco	John T. Chambers	President and Chief Executive Officer	0.48[6]
Xerox	Anne M. Mulcahy	Chairman and Chief Executive Officer	0.43[7]
Eastman Kodak	Antonio M. Perez	Chairman and Chief Executive Officer	0.25[8]
Starbucks	James Donald	President and Chief Executive Officer	0.18[9]
General Electric	Jeffrey R. Immelt	Chairman and Chief Executive Officer	0.04[10]

[1]Page 8, Berkshire Hathaway proxy statement filed with Securities and Exchange Commission, March 13, 2006.
[2]Page 6, Amazon.com proxy statement filed with Securities and Exchange Commission, April 20, 2006.
[3]Page 10, Nike proxy statement filed with Securities and Exchange Commission, Aug. 9, 2006.
[4]Page 31, Dell Computer proxy statement filed with Securities and Exchange Commission, June 5, 2006.
[5]Page 8, Microsoft proxy statement filed with Securities and Exchange Commission, Oct. 4, 2006.
[6]Page 19, Cisco proxy statement filed with Securities and Exchange Commission, Sept. 25, 2006.
[7]Page 15, Xerox proxy statement filed with Securities and Exchange Commission, April 10, 2006.
[8]Page 23, Eastman Kodak proxy statement filed with Securities and Exchange Commission, March 24, 2006.
[9]Page 13, Starbucks proxy statement filed with Securities and Exchange Commission, Dec. 16, 2005.
[10]Page 18, General Electric proxy statement filed with Securities and Exchange Commission, March 3, 2006.

It should be noted, though that CEO ownership does not have to be high for the shareholders to do well. Analyzing the ExecuComp database, the corporation with the highest return to shareholders, almost 300 percent, during the 2001-2005 period was Joy Global. John Nils Hanson, who has been the corporation's chairman and CEO during that period, has beneficial ownership of less than 1 percent of the company.[7] However, Hanson receives many incentives via his compensation package. In contrast to Warren Buffett and Jeff Bezos, CEOs of Berkshire Hathaway and Amazon.com only receive salary, and minimal amounts, at that. Hanson received, in 2005, $782,400 in salary, $1,351,840 in bonus, payout from a long term incentive plan of $4,070,250, a restricted stock grant valued at $429,908 and 163,125 in stock options.[8]

Effect of Executive Ownership on Risk Preferences

The issue, however, is much more complex. While ownership provides incentive to increase firm value, as any increase in stock price increases the executive's wealth, it also affects risk preferences. An executive with much of his or her wealth tied up in the firm may be more risk averse than optimal, passing up value-increasing investments that also increase firm risk and reducing the firm's use of leverage. For example, Capozza and Sequin (2003) find "firms with greater insider holdings tend to invest in assets with lower systematic risk," and they, along with Friend and Lang (1988) and Jensen et al. (1992), find these firms have "less debt in their capital structure." To mitigate that risk, Bettis et al. (2001) find some executives engage in hedging transactions that reduce the risk associated with their share ownership, and that not surprisingly, firm risk, as measured by the volatility of stock returns, increases after the executive hedges are implemented. We also observe executives and major shareholders, for example, Michael Dell and Bill Gates, selling shares in their companies from time to time.[9] Consistent with this diversification argument, Murphy (1998, page 37) finds evidence suggesting that "executives with large option holdings rationally reduce their unrestricted stock holdings."

Effect of Executive Ownership on Corporate Performance

Academic research is inconclusive as to whether increased executive ownership leads to improved performance, however. Himmelberg et al. (1999) note "we cannot conclude (econometrically) that changes in managerial ownership affect firm performance." Yet Core and Larcker (2002), who examine a sample of firms that institute ownership requirements, conclude "for this sample of firms, required increases in the level of managerial equity ownership are associated with improvements in firm performance." And earlier, Mehran (1995) concluded "firm performance is positively related to the percentage of equity held by managers."

One possible explanation for these conflicting results is that while insider ownership does affect performance, the relationship is not a linear one. At low levels, increases in ownership improve firm performance, but once ownership increases beyond a certain level, management becomes entrenched (Morck et al. 1988). Once their ownership exceeds a certain level, management is unlikely to be fired and, hence, a major incentive to perform well is removed.

Executive Ownership Requirements

Despite the inconclusive academic evidence, there has been a trend toward requiring executives to own stock. Equilar (2006) reports, "In 2005, 63.8 percent of *Fortune* 500 companies disclosed ownership guidelines for executive officers…" In general, these guidelines require an executive to hold shares equal in value to a multiple of his or her salary or compensation, where the multiple often increases with the rank of the executive. One example of a company utilizing ownership guidelines is American Express, which requires ownership for approximately 135 of its most senior executives, as illustrated by the following passage:

> *Share Ownership.* The Company's share ownership policy requires approximately 135 senior executives, including executive officers, to have an ongoing ownership stake in the Company, linking their interests to those of the shareholders. The policy has these key features:
> - Participants are expected to own Company shares with a target value of a multiple of their base salary, ranging from one times base salary for certain participants to 10 times for Mr. Chenault. Only the value of shares held in identified brokerage accounts, in registered form or in accounts under Company benefit programs are counted under the policy.
> - If a participant has not yet reached the target ownership requirement, he or she must retain 75% of the net after-tax shares acquired from any stock option exercise or restricted stock award vesting.
> - In addition, after achieving their stock ownership targets, executive officers and selected other senior executives must retain for at least one year shares with a value of 50% of the net after-tax gain from any stock option exercise or restricted stock award vesting.[10]

American Express also expects its directors to own shares:

> The Company believes that each Director should have a substantial personal investment in the Company. A personal holding of 20,000 shares of the Company is recommended for each Director. Directors are expected to acquire and maintain this share ownership threshold within five years of joining the Board.[11]

As shown in the passage above, the 135 executives are required to own shares equal to a multiple of their base salary, and that multiple ranges from a low of one to 10 for Kenneth I. Chenault, its chairman and CEO. If the executive is below his or her assigned multiple, he or she must retain at least 75 percent of the net after-tax shares acquired from a stock option exercise or restricted stock vesting. And even after achieving his or her stock ownership target, the executive must retain at least 50 percent of the net after-tax shares acquired from a stock option exercise or restricted stock vesting.

If the executive ownership on performance is inconclusive, the question arises as to why firms are so concerned with managerial ownership. The answer is simple. Instituting mandatory or voluntary guidelines is good politics; it looks good for the shareholders and politicians.

Effect of Executive Ownership on Executive Compensation

Some CEOs who are major shareholders take relatively modest compensation; for example, Warren Buffett, owner of approximately 32 percent[12] of Berkshire Hathaway, receives an annual salary of $100,000[13], and Jeff Bezos, owner of approximately 24 percent[14] of Amazon.com, receives an annual salary of $81,840[15].

Effect of Executive Ownership on the Level of Compensation

CEO ownership provides two sets of incentives with respect to compensation, as illustrated by these divergent examples. This arises from the owner-manager conflict and the ability of the CEO to control the transfer of wealth from shareholders to managers and vice versa. On the one hand, because the pay of subordinates is usually related to that of the CEO, a CEO with large shareholdings has the incentive to reduce his or her pay. Doing so will decrease that of subordinates and increase shareholder wealth. However, a CEO with large shareholdings has the ability to control the corporation, and with it, his or her own compensation. If the CEO owns 50 percent of the corporation, each $1 increase in his or her own compensation decreases the value of his or her shares by only 50 cents.[16] Thus, the CEO has some incentive to increase his or her compensation at the expense of the other shareholders. In this very simple example, the CEO will increase his or her compensation as long as he or she is able to keep the total increase in compensation to lower-level employees to $1 or less.[17] Given that few CEOs own anywhere near 50 percent of their corporation, the latter effect, that is, enriching himself or herself at the expense of shareholders, may predominate. Empirical research on this issue is mixed, with Dyl (1988) and Mallette et al. (1995) finding increases in CEO ownership lead to increases in CEO compensation, and Allen (1981) and Core et al. (1999) finding that increases in CEO ownership lead to lower CEO compensation.

Effect of Executive Ownership on the Composition of the Compensation Package

CEO ownership also influences the composition of the compensation package. As noted above, Buffett and Bezos' compensation packages are solely comprised of cash. There is no need for any form of incentive compensation as their ownership provides all the necessary incentives. At lower levels of ownership, however, incentive compensation is needed. Toyne et al. (2000) find at low levels of ownership, the proportion of stock-based compensation in the compensation package is positively related to board (including the CEO) ownership. As ownership increases, however, the association between the proportion of stock-based compensation and board ownership decreases, consistent with the marginal incentive effect of additional stock-based compensation being outweighed by the risk to the CEO caused by underdiversification, which reduces the valuation placed on that stock-based compensation by the CEO.

Effect of Director's Ownership on Executive Compensation

As will be discussed more fully in the next chapter, to some extent, the agency problem that exists between shareholders and managers also exists between shareholders and directors. In the absence of a substantial equity investment on the part of directors, their interests may lie with those of management, whom they are supposed to supervise, rather than shareholders, to whom they owe a fiduciary responsibility. Bhagat et al. (1998) argue:

> Without the direct economic incentive of substantial stock ownership, directors, given a natural loyalty to their appointing party and the substantial reputation enhancement and monetary compensation board service came to entail, had little incentive other than their legal fiduciary duties to engage in active managerial oversight.

Bhagat et al. (1998) and Core et al. (1999) find the average director owns a relatively small proportion of corporation stock. Bhagat et al. (1998) find mean (median) ownership of 0.57 (0.02) percent, while Core et al. find mean (median) ownership of 0.136 (0.005) percent. Core et al. (1999) find CEO compensation inversely related to percentage stock ownership per director, while Conyon and He (2004) find the existence of a 5-percent shareholder on the compensation committee reduces CEO compensation and is associated with greater CEO equity incentives. Tables 9-6 and 9-7 provide some descriptive information about outside director ownership for the years 2001 through 2005. Table 9-6 shows the mean (median) ownership of an individual director, which ranges from $11,071,229 ($247,686) per director in 2001 to $37,090,969 ($212,660) in 2002, or in percentage terms from 0.26 (0.01) percent in 2005 to 0.36 (0.01) in 2002. Table 9-7 shows the mean (median) ownership of the outside directors as a group, which

Table 9-6:
Average Ownership of Outside Director, by Year

	Dollar Value of Director Ownership		Percentage Director Ownership	
Year	Mean	Median	Mean	Median
2001	$11,071,299	$247,686	0.35	0.01
2002	$37,090,969	$212,660	0.36	0.01
2003	$28,370,743	$229,551	0.33	0.01
2004	$31,305,144	$245,632	0.35	0.01
2005	$14,319,735	$266,806	0.26	0.01

Note: Calculations in this table are based upon data obtained from The Corporate Library in March 2006.

Table 9-7:
Average Ownership of All Outside Directors in the Corporation, by Year

	Dollar Value of Board Ownership		Percentage Board Ownership	
Year	Mean	Median	Mean	Median
2001	$72,852,110	$3,534,060	2.33	0.20
2002	$286,799,948	$5,837,591	2.75	0.39
2003	$212,321,635	$5,387,948	2.45	0.26
2004	$236,292,416	$5,774,105	2.61	0.24
2005	$111,666,493	$6,056,862	1.99	0.22

Note: Calculations in this table are based upon data obtained from The Corporate Library in March 2006.

per corporation ranges from $72,852,110 ($3,534,060) in 2001 to $286,799,948 ($5,837,591) in 2002, or in percentage terms from 1.99 (0.22) percent in 2005 to 2.75 (0.39) percent in 2002. Whether viewed individually, or as a group, outside directors do own a relatively small proportion of the corporation.

Effect of Large Shareholders and Institutional Ownership on Executive Compensation

Executives in general, and CEOs in particular, may be able to enrich themselves at the expense of shareholders who, for the most part, lack the resources and/or incentive to resist. The existence of large shareholders, and the trend toward institutional ownership (e.g., Balsam et al. (2002) found that approximately 50 percent of shares are held by institutions) may mitigate this problem because those shares have the incentives and ability to monitor and resist management, and coalesce to oppose management if necessary. Large shareholders have this incentive because, if they can affect a policy change that increases firm value, they will garner a larger portion of that increase than small shareholders. Further, large shareholders, because they cannot readily sell their shares without causing a stock price decline, may have no choice but to be active in monitoring management. They have the ability to impact management in general, and executive compensation in particular, through their ability to vote for and elect board members willing to act in their interests.

In fact, the mere existence of a large shareholder, or ownership by an activist institutional shareholder such as CALPERS (California Public Employees Retirement System), may be enough to persuade executives to moderate their compensation demands. These shareholders may persuade executives to mitigate their compensation demands privately or via a shareholder proposal, which is allowed under Securities and Exchange Commission Rule 14a-8 (§240.14a-8).[18] In addition, if a proposal on executive compensation is made, large shareholders are more likely to pay for and receive advice from voting advisory services, such as Institutional Shareholder Services (www.isstf.com/).

Effect of Large and Institutional Shareholders on the Level of Compensation

Allen (1981) found CEOs of corporations where no shareholder owned 5 percent or more of the firm received higher compensation. Lambert et al. (1993) and Core et al. (1999) found the existence of an insider other than the CEO owning 5 percent of the firm decreased the CEO's compensation, as did the existence of an outside blockholder owning 5 percent or more of the firm. Hartzell and Starks (2003) found a significantly negative relation between the level of compensation and the concentration of institutional ownership. David et al. (1998) found that large noninstitutional shareholders and pressure-resistant institutional shareholders reduce the level of CEO compensation.

Effect of Large and Institutional Shareholders on the Composition of the Compensation Package

Looking at the relationship between pay and performance, Gomez-Mejia et al. (1987) found compensation most tightly linked to performance in firms defined as owner controlled, which they defined as firms that had a 5-percent shareholder. Similarly, Hartzell and Starks (2003) find "institutional ownership concentration positively related to the pay-for-performance sensitivity of executive compensation."

Looking at the composition of the compensation package, David et al. (1998) found the proportion of long-term incentives to total compensation increasing with the ownership of pressure-resistant institutional shareholders. In contrast, they found the proportion of long-term incentives to total compensation decreasing with the existence of a large noninstitutional shareholder. They attribute this latter finding to the ability of such shareholders to monitor management directly; there is less need for incentive mechanisms in the compensation package. Mehran (1995) found a similar result, that is, "firms in which a higher percentage of shares are held by insiders or outside blockholders use less equity-based compensation."

Effect of Shareholder Proposals on Executive Pay

Johnson et al. (1997) find that firms targeted by CALPERS reduce the level of executive compensation, and the sensitivity of that compensation to performance. While the two findings are seemingly inconsistent, and the latter finding surely is not what CALPERS intended, the findings are consistent with economic theory. That is, in equilibrium, the only way to reduce compensation is to reduce the risk associated with that compensation. Thomas and Martin (1999) find that "target companies do not increase average total CEO compensation levels as rapidly in the year after receiving a shareholder proposal (on average 2-percent increases) as firms not receiving such proposals (on average 22.3 percent increases)." Further, they find that the higher the level of voting support for a proposal, the smaller the subsequent increases in CEO compensation.

Another interesting result is found by Williams et al. (2000). They examine the effects of shareholder proposals sponsored by public pension funds and labor unions on executive compensation, finding that while there is an increase in option-based compensation, that increase does not appear to enhance the sensitivity of pay to performance. An explanation for their finding is that, while options are assumed to be performance based because their value is a function of future share-price performance, at the time of grant, the grant date value of the options need not be related to contemporaneous performance. Looking at the effect of anti-takeover legislation on executive pay, Bertrand and Mullainathan (2000) found that subsequent to the passage of anti-takeover legislation, "firms with a large shareholder increased pay for performance, while firms without a large shareholder increased mean pay." Recall from Chapter 1 that the market for corporate control and the compensation package are two ways to provide executives with incentives to increase shareholder value. Passage of the anti-takeover legislation reduced the effectiveness of the market for corporate control in providing those incentives. In response, corporations with large shareholders increased the incentives provided via the compensation package. In contrast, executives in corporations without large shareholders responded by increasing their pay.

Summary

This chapter examined ownership and its effect on the executive compensation package. In percentage terms, CEO ownership is rather small, with mean ownership approximating 2 percent to 3 percent over time, and median ownership well below 1 percent. Including options to arrive at an effective ownership percentage raises these numbers somewhat, but the percentages are still rather low, always less than 5 percent. These amounts are rather low in that they indicate that the CEO bears less than 5 percent of the cost of his or her actions, and analogously, receives less than 5 percent of the benefits. However, while low in percentage terms, in dollar amounts, ownership is extremely significant, with the value of shares and options held by the CEO averaging over $145 million (median $17,915,551) in 2005.

As pointed out in Chapter 1, the goals of executives and shareholders can be aligned through executive share ownership. This chapter discusses the steps certain corporations have taken to increase executive share ownership, providing examples along the way. Yet as noted, there is no conclusive evidence that increasing share ownership improves corporate performance. One possible explanation for the lack of association is that, in addition to affecting incentives to increase shareholder value, executive ownership affects executive risk preferences, as well. An executive who has both his or her human capital, as well as a good portion of his or her financial wealth, tied to the firm is not optimally diversified. That makes him or her less willing to take on risky new projects, even when the expected value of those projects is positive.

Executive ownership and the executive compensation package are ways to provide the incentives to increase shareholder value. Thus, the higher the level of executive ownership, the less the need for conditional compensation in the compensation package to motivate executives to increase shareholder value. Similarly, monitoring by the board of directors and/or large shareholders is a way to provide executives with incentives to increase shareholder value independent of the executive compensation package. While the evidence of the effect of CEO ownership on the level of CEO compensation is mixed, there is some evidence that the level of CEO compensation decreases as the ownership of outside directors increases. Similarly, there is some evidence that the level of compensation is lower when there are large shareholders. Looking at the composition of the compensation package, there is also some evidence that the portion of stock in the compensation package decreases with increases in insider, board and large shareholder ownership.

Footnotes

[1] The modern literature on this topic can be traced back to Berle and Means (1932).

[2] Page 28, Wells Fargo proxy statement filed with the Securities and Exchange Commission, March 17, 2006.

[3] Page 23, Wells Fargo proxy statement filed with the Securities and Exchange Commission, March 17, 2006.

[4] Note that none of the major indexes had reached its previous highs by the end of 2005.

[5] This is an oversimplification, as each also receives pension and other benefits. They do not, however, receive any compensation conditioned on performance.

[6] Researchers have looked at whether ownership does take the place of stock options and grants, finding conflicting results. Mehran (1995) finds an inverse relation between ownership and stock-based compensation, whereas Lewellen, et al., (1987) and Yermack (1995) do not.

[7] Page 2, Joy Global proxy statement filed with Securities and Exchange Commission, Jan. 23, 2006.

[8] Page 10, Joy Global proxy statement filed with Securities and Exchange Commission, Jan. 23, 2006.

[9] For example, on Nov. 20, 2006, Bill Gates filed a form 4 indicating that he had sold or otherwise disposed of 1 million shares of Microsoft common stock on Nov. 16, 2006.

[10] Page 23, American Express proxy statement filed with the Securities and Exchange Commission, March 22, 2006.

[11] Page 6, American Express proxy statement filed with the Securities and Exchange Commission, March 22, 2006.

[12] Page 8, Berkshire Hathaway proxy statement filed with the Securities and Exchange Commission, March 13, 2006.

[13] Page 5, Berkshire Hathaway proxy statement filed with the Securities and Exchange Commission, March 13, 2006.

[14] Page 6, Amazon.com proxy statement filed with the Securities and Exchange Commission, April 20, 2006.

[15] Page 8, Amazon.com proxy statement filed with the Securities and Exchange Commission, April 20, 2006.

16 Ignoring taxes and/or transaction costs which may make the actual cost higher or lower.

17 To elaborate, if the CEO who owns 50 percent of the corporation increases his or her own compensation by $1 and that of subordinates by $1, then the increase in the CEO's compensation will be exactly offset by the decrease in value of the CEO's shareholdings.

18 To be eligible to submit a proposal, rule 14a-8 requires that a shareholder continuously hold at least $2,000 in market value, or 1 percent of the corporation's voting securities, for at least one year and continue to hold those securities through the date of the meeting. Consequently both small and large shareholders have the ability to submit shareholder proposals. However, large shareholders can make more of an impact because of the larger number of shares they vote in support of their proposal, and their ability, to communicate with other shareholders.

Chapter 10

Corporate Governance

In a decision that underscores the increased scrutiny corporate boards face over executive compensation, a New York judge has ruled a shareholder lawsuit against Viacom Inc. can proceed.

The case was brought by two small shareholders last year against Viacom, its directors and top executives. It contends that the media company's directors breached their fiduciary duty in approving nearly $160 million in compensation to three top executives in 2004, a year when the company reported an $18-billion loss.[1]

Introduction

As the introduction to this chapter alludes, executive compensation and corporate governance are intertwined. Boards and directors can be sued for paying excessive compensation, and although no cases have been lost to this point and no payments have been made, this might not always be true. Consequently, directors, especially those on the compensation committee, must pay close attention to executive compensation and be able to justify the amounts awarded.

Statutory Regulations

In the United States, corporate charters are issued by the individual states. Delaware, the home to more than half a million business entities "including more than 50 percent of all U.S. publicly traded companies and 60 percent of the *Fortune* 500,"[2] requires "The business and affairs of every corporation organized under this chapter shall be managed by or under the direction of a board of directors ..."[3] The major tasks of these directors include the hiring, firing and compensating of top executives.

When the corporation goes public or has an initial public offering, it also becomes subject to the rules promulgated by the Securities and Exchange Commission and the exchange upon which it is listing.

The New York Stock Exchange requires that listed companies have a majority of independent directors.[4] Listed companies must also have audit[5], compensation[6] and nominating/corporate governance[7] committees composed entirely of independent directors. The NASDAQ has similar requirements, that is, it requires a majority of independent directors and an audit committee comprised solely of independent directors, while it only requires that the compensation and nominating committees have a majority of independent directors.[8]

The Internal Revenue Code imposes additional requirements for those companies wishing to deduct compensation in excess of $1 million per executive. To meet Section 162(m) requirements, the performance goals under which compensation is paid must be established by a compensation committee comprised solely of two or more independent or outside directors. Treasury Regulation §1.162-27 defines an outside director as a director who (A) is not a current employee of the publicly held corporation; (B) is not a former employee of the publicly held corporation who receives compensation for prior services (other than benefits under a tax-qualified retirement plan) during the taxable year; (C) has not been an officer of the publicly held corporation; and (D) does not receive remuneration from the publicly held corporation, either directly or indirectly, in any capacity other than as a director. For this purpose, remuneration includes any payment in exchange for goods or services.

Responsibilities/Loyalties of Directors

The shareholders of the corporation elect the directors. Legally, the directors of a corporation are responsible to those shareholders, that is, they have a fiduciary duty to put the interests of shareholders first. There are many, see for example Mace (1971) and Crystal (1991), who believe this does not occur in practice, as the directors themselves are agents, with little or no equity investment in the corporation, and consequently, their interests are not necessarily aligned with those of shareholders. Or, as Baker et al. (1988) suggest, outside directors lack the economic incentives to curb executives' rent-seeking behavior. Further, Hermalin and Weisbach (1998) and Shivdasani and Yermack (1999) suggest outside board members serve at the CEO's discretion. Pfeffer (1972, p. 220) writes:

> ... in most cases board members are handpicked by management. In many practical respects, then, management is, therefore, in control of the board.

Or as Bhagat et al. (1998) note:

> Through control of the proxy process, incumbent management nominated its own candidates for board membership. The board of directors, theoretically composed of the representatives of various shareholding groups,

instead was comprised of individuals selected by management. The directors' connection with the enterprise generally resulted from a prior relationship with management, not the stockholding owners, and they often had little or no shareholding stake in the company.

Categories of Directors

Few directors are completely independent of the CEO. The board is comprised of two broad groups, inside directors whose full-time employment is with the corporation, and outside directors. In many cases, an insider, the CEO, is also the chairman of the board,[9] which adversely affects the board's ability to independently monitor and discipline the CEO (see Jensen 1993, Fama and Jensen 1983). For example, Goyal and Park (2000) conclude "that the sensitivity of CEO turnover to firm performance is significantly lower when the CEO and chairman titles are vested in the same individual." Perhaps, because of this, Yermack (1996) provides evidence consistent with corporations being more highly valued when the positions are separated.

The other inside directors are executive-level subordinates whose compensation may be linked to that of the CEO. Some (Main et al. 1995) believe the CEO actually controls the wage-setting process of subordinates. At a minimum, the CEO influences the compensation of his or her subordinates.

Outside directors are those for whom the corporation is not their primary employer. They can include former employees of the corporation relatives of the CEO, individuals with business relationships with the corporation and individuals who sit on other boards with the corporation's CEO or on whose board the CEO sits, with the latter being known as an interlocking directorate.[10,11] Sometimes these individuals are referred to as "gray directors" because, while they are not full-time employees of the corporation, they are not independent of the corporation either (Shivdasani and Yermack 1999). More formally, "gray directors," while not directly employed by the company, have business ties or affiliations to the company and/or its executives that may compromise their independence.

Acknowledging this lack of independence, NASDAQ and the New York Stock Exchange have tightened their definitions of independent directors. Under NASDAQ rule 4200, if any of the following occur, the director would not be considered independent.

(A) a director who is, or at any time during the past three years was, employed by the company or by any parent or subsidiary of the company;

(B) a director who accepted or who has a Family Member who accepted any payments from the company or any parent or subsidiary of the company in excess of $60,000 during any period of twelve consecutive months within the three years preceding the determination of independence, other than the following:

(i) compensation for board or board committee service;

(ii) payments arising solely from investments in the company's securities;

(iii) compensation paid to a Family Member who is a non-executive employee of the company or a parent or subsidiary of the company;

(iv) benefits under a tax-qualified retirement plan, or non-discretionary compensation;

(v) loans from a financial institution provided that the loans (1) were made in the ordinary course of business, (2) were made on substantially the same terms, including interest rates and collateral, as those prevailing at the time for comparable transactions with the general public, (3) did not involve more than a normal degree of risk or other unfavorable factors, and (4) were not otherwise subject to the specific disclosure requirements of SEC Regulation S-K, Item 404;

(vi) payments from a financial institution in connection with the deposit of funds or the financial institution acting in an agency capacity, provided such payments were (1) made in the ordinary course of business; (2) made on substantially the same terms as those prevailing at the time for comparable transactions with the general public; and (3) not otherwise subject to the disclosure requirements of SEC Regulation S-K, Item 404; or

(vii) loans permitted under Section 13(k) of the Act. Provided, however, that in addition to the requirements contained in this paragraph (B), audit committee members are also subject to additional, more stringent requirements under Rule 4350(d).

(C) a director who is a Family Member of an individual who is, or at any time during the past three years was, employed by the company or by any parent or subsidiary of the company as an executive officer;

(D) a director who is, or has a Family Member who is, a partner in, or a controlling shareholder or an executive officer of, any organization to which the company made, or from which the company received, payments for property or services in the current or any of the past three fiscal years that exceed 5% of the recipient's consolidated gross revenues for that year, or $200,000, whichever is more, other than the following:

(i) payments arising solely from investments in the company's securities; or

(ii) payments under non-discretionary charitable contribution matching programs.

(E) a director of the listed company who is, or has a Family Member who is, employed as an executive officer of another entity where at any time during the past three years any of the executive officers of the listed company serve on the compensation committee of such other entity; or

(F) a director who is, or has a Family Member who is, a current partner of the company's outside auditor, or was a partner or employee of the company's outside auditor who worked on the company's audit at any time during any of the past three years.

(G) in the case of an investment company, in lieu of paragraphs (A)–(F), a director who is an "interested person" of the company as defined in Section 2(a)(19) of the Investment Company Act of 1940, other than in his or her capacity as a member of the board of directors or any board committee.[12]

While tightening the rule considerably, that is, clearly defining scenarios related to the firm that would compromise the director's independence, the rules ignore personal relationships, other than family. For example, a director who was a personal friend of the CEO but did no business with the corporation would be considered independent. For example, Reveta F. Bowers, who was a director of Disney from 1993 to 2003, was "administrator and the Head of School for the Center for Early Education, an independent school for pre-school through sixth grade located in Los Angeles,"[13] a school attended by Michael Eisner's children. Backer (2005) notes that the plaintiffs in the Ovitz litigation attempted to have her declared nonindependent because of this relationship and "because Bowers' salary as a teacher is low compared to her director's fees and stock options, 'only the most rigidly formalistic or myopic analysis' would view Bowers as not beholden to Eisner." Similarly, Backer (2005) reported the plaintiffs sought to have Irwin Russell, a Disney director from 1987 to 2001, declared nonindependent because he was Eisner's personal attorney (interestingly, he negotiated Eisner's employment agreement with Disney). While the court did not ultimately rule on these issues, it is clear that at least in appearance, the independence of these two directors could be questioned.

Westphal and Zajac (1994, 386) caution that "increasing the number and/or proportion of outsiders on the board of directors as recommended by some activists interested in governance reform, could be a more symbolic than substantive action, given that CEOs may simply recruit sympathetic outsiders to the board."

Director Compensation

Director compensation can be significant in amount and can include cash retainers (a fixed amount, analogous to salary), board meeting fees, fees for chairing committees, stock options, stock grants and pensions. The following example is from General Motors:

Director Compensation

Only non-employee directors receive payment for serving on the Board. Since Mr. Wagoner is an employee of the Corporation, he is not compensated as a director. Non-employee directors are not eligible to participate in the executive incentive program, GM S-SPP, or any of the retirement programs for General Motors employees. Other than as described in this section, there are no separate benefit plans for directors. Compensation paid to non-employee directors in 2005 was as follows:

2005 Nonemployee Director Compensation Table Director

Director	Annual Retainer	Audit Committee Retainer	Chair Retainer	Other Compensation	Total Compensation
	$ (a)	$	$	$ (b)	$
Percy N. Barnevik (c)	200,000		10,000	23,488	233,488
Erskine B. Bowles (d)	116,667			9,077	125,744
John H. Bryan	200,000		10,000	17,513	227,513
Armando M. Codina	200,000			19,694	219,694
George M.C. Fisher	200,000		10,000	14,904	224,904
Karen Katen	200,000			19,766	219,766
Kent Kresa	200,000	20,000		15,529	235,529
Ellen J. Kullman (e)	200,000	11,667		19,766	231,433
Philip A. Laskawy	200,000	20,000	10,000	17,223	247,223
E. Stanley O'Neal (f)	200,000		10,000	19,766	229,766
Eckhard Pfeiffer	200,000	20,000		23,488	243,488

(a) Under the General Motors Corporation Compensation Plan for Non-Employee Directors (the "Compensation Plan for Non-Employee Directors"), non-employee directors were required to defer $140,000 of the annual retainer noted above in restricted units denominated in shares of Common Stock. In addition, under this plan directors could also elect to defer all or a portion of the remaining compensation in cash or restricted units denominated in shares of Common Stock.

(b) "Other Compensation" includes imputed income and reimbursement of associated taxes for the use of company vehicles, as well as personal accident and liability insurance elected by non-employee directors.

(c) Since Mr. Barnevik is headquartered outside the U.S., non-cash items in "Other Compensation" may not be comparable.

(d) Mr. Bowles was elected to the Board on June 7, 2005.

(e) Ms. Kullman joined the Audit Committee effective June 7, 2005.

(f) Mr. O'Neal resigned from the Board effective Feb. 6, 2006.

Under the Compensation Plan for Non-Employee Directors, RSUs are credited with dividend equivalents in the form of additional stock units. Amounts deferred under this plan are not available until after the director retires from the Board or otherwise terminates service. After the director leaves the Board, payment under this plan is made in cash based on the number of stock units valued at the average quarterly mean market price prior to payment.

Directors are reimbursed for travel expenses incurred in connection with their duties as directors. Directors, like all active GM employees in the U.S., are eligible to participate in a matching contributions program to accredited four-year colleges, universities, and community colleges, and all eligible contributions are matched on a dollar-for-dollar basis up to $5,000 annually.

To support GM's on-going turnaround plan to reduce costs and business risks and to further enhance financial flexibility, the Board of Directors voluntarily reduced its annual $200,000 retainer by 50 percent effective March 1, 2006. This reduction eliminates the $60,000 cash portion of director compensation and $40,000 of the mandatory deferred stock portion.[14]

General Motors was paid an annual retainer of $200,000 in 2005, of which $140,000 had to be deferred into restricted stock units, effectively making the majority of compensation performance based and at risk. Further, as noted at the bottom of the passage, in 2006 General Motors directors voluntarily reduced their retainer by 50 percent, and are now taking the entire reduced amount in the form of restricted stock units. General Motors also paid extra compensation to directors who were committee chairmen, or for serving on the audit committee, recognizing the extra effort, and perhaps risk, involved.

In theory, having directors defer some or all of their compensation into restricted stock units aligns their interests with those of shareholders. In practice, adding risk and reducing the cash portion of the compensation package (to zero in the case of General Motors) may serve to limit the pool of qualified individuals willing to serve as directors of public corporations.

In General Motors' case, while the amount ultimately payable is at risk, as long as its share price is positive, directors will receive some remuneration for serving on the board. In contrast, Coca-Cola just revised its director compensation plan so that director compensation is fully based upon firm performance.

> The Compensation Plan grants directors equity share units each year equal to a flat fee of $175,000 payable only upon the attainment of predefined performance targets. When the performance target is met at the end of the performance period, the share units will be payable in cash. Should the performance target not be met, all share units and hypothetical dividends would be forfeited in their entirety.
>
> For 2006, the Board of Directors set an initial three-year performance target of 8 percent compounded annual growth in earnings per share.[15]

If the company fails to meet the target, the directors get nothing for their service. As Meyer (2006) points out, not all qualified directors "can afford the risk of no compensation for their time and services if business performance goals are not met." Consequently, plans such as this limit the pool of qualified individuals willing to serve as directors. As such, it should be pointed out that General Motors and Coca-Cola are the exceptions, as most corporations still pay fixed-cash retainers, as will be discussed below.

Trends in Director Compensation

Director compensation has increased dramatically over time. Please note that when Coca-Cola instituted the plan discussed above, it also increased the nominal amount of director compensation from $125,000 to $175,000.[16] As an illustration of the steady increase over time and across a broad group of corporations, consider that while Yermack (1996) reports that director compensation over the 1984-1991 period averaged just under $30,000 (in 1991 dollars), Table 10-1 shows total director compensation increasing steadily from a mean (median) of $33,002

(30,000) in 1992 to a mean (median) of $131,528 ($107,158) in 2005.

Table 10-1 provides some detail on director pay. As with executives, the bulk of the increase from 1992 to 2005 is in the form of equity-based compensation. For example, while the mean (median) retainer (base remuneration) approximately doubled from $16,582 ($16,500) in 1992 to $33,688 ($30,000) in 2005, the mean (median) value of stock grants increased from $1,895 (0) to $32,108 (0), slightly less than 1,600 (0) percent, and the mean (median) value of stock option grants increased from $7,032 (0) to $58,083 ($26,656), more than 700 percent.

Table 10-1:

Directors Compensation, by Year

(means on top, medians below)

	Retainer	Per-Meeting Fee	Value of Stock Grants	Value of Option Grants	Total Compensation
1992	$16,582	$883	$1,895	$7,032	$33,002
	$16,500	$1,000	$0	$0	$30,000
1993	$16,432	$910	$2,139	$11,522	$37,181
	$16,000	$1,000	$0	$0	$30,060
1994	$17,158	$950	$2,530	$16,017	$42,860
	$17,500	$1,000	$0	$0	$34,984
1995	$17,654	$982	$3,627	$16,849	$45,794
	$18,000	$1,000	$0	$0	$36,047
1996	$16,981	$989	$4,655	$25,513	$54,401
	$16,000	$1,000	$0	$5,118	$40,000
1997	$17,064	$989	$7,140	$29,388	$61,222
	$16,000	$1,000	$0	$8,538	$45,027
1998	$17,410	$1,003	$7,129	$31,949	$63,598
	$17,000	$1,000	$0	$10,025	$48,427
1999	$17,862	$1,017	$7,333	$38,741	$71,619
	$18,000	$1,000	$0	$13,091	$50,933
2000	$18,774	$1,030	$9,391	$62,615	$99,101
	$19,500	$1,000	$0	$15,358	$56,560
2001	$19,848	$1,072	$9,958	$61,517	$99,006
	$20,000	$1,000	$0	$19,778	$64,682
2002	$21,640	$1,093	$9,238	$53,112	$92,453
	$20,000	$1,000	$0	$23,240	$69,249
2003	$27,250	$1,177	$16,531	$51,103	$101,805
	$24,000	$1,000	$0	$21,439	$76,149
2004	$29,303	$1,229	$23,291	$63,886	$124,332
	$26,634	$1,200	$0	$27,008	$98,823
2005	$33,688	$1,276	$32,108	$58,083	$131,528
	$30,000	$1,500	$0	$25,656	$107,158

Note: Calculations in this table are based upon data contained in the April 2006 version of Standard & Poor's ExecuComp, and total assumes directors attended all meetings of the full board.

This increase in director pay and the increase in the portion of director pay that is stock based is consistent with two factors. The first is the increase in director responsibilities over time, especially in the period following the passage of the Sarbanes-Oxley Act (SOX) of 2002. Kooker (2005) reports that due to rising responsibilities, the number of hours spent by directors has, in the case of one director, doubled in recent years, in part due to an increase in board meetings. Consistent with this, Kooker (2005) also reports that directors are serving on fewer boards. Linck et al. (2006) report that as a result of the Sarbanes-Oxley Act of 2002, not only has board workload and risk increased, but the composition of the board has changed.

SOX also had a dramatic effect on the makeup of the corporate director pool: more post-SOX directors are lawyers/consultants, financial experts and retired executives, and fewer are current executives.

The second is the pressure by pension funds and governance watchdogs to compensate directors with incentive/stock-based compensation (National Association of Corporate Directors 2000, Teachers Insurance and Annuity Association—College Retirement Equities Fund 2000, Lublin 1996, California Public Employees Retirement System 1998).

As observed with CEO compensation, director compensation also increases with the size of the corporation. Table 10-2 shows that in 2005, mean (median) total director compensation was $67,480 ($49,972) for the smallest decile of corporations, increasing to $193,586 ($171,875) for the largest corporations. In terms of composition, directors in large corporations seem to be getting less of their compensation in the form of retainers and more in the form of stock. As with CEOs, this finding is driven by the magnitude of stock in the compensation package, not by a reduction in the value of the retainer, as directors of large corporations also get larger retainers (mean $51,985, median $50,000) than their smaller corporation counterparts (mean $21,948, median $20,000).

Determinants of Director Incentives

If the directors are agents with little equity investment, and whose interests are not necessarily aligned with those of shareholders, a possibility raised previously, then the director compensation package may be the only way to align their interests with those of shareholders.[17] Only recently have researchers begun looking at the determinants of director compensation. One of the first studies on the topic is Bryan et al. (2000). As noted in Chapter 2, and will be discussed further in Chapter 14, prior research has found executive compensation related to the growth oppor-

Table 10-2:

Directors Compensation, by firm size (for 2005)

(means on top, medians below)

	Size Decile	Retainer	Meeting Fees	Value of Stock Grants	Value of Options Grants	Total Compensation
Smallest	1	$21,498	$1,214	$12,842	$30,322	$67,480
		$20,000	$1,200	$0	$15,038	$49,972
	2	$23,944	$1,243	$10,484	$46,020	$86,864
		$23,250	$1,000	$0	$34,391	$74,600
	3	$26,685	$1,247	$14,289	$53,383	$101,442
		$26,000	$1,000	$0	$36,233	$89,739
	4	$26,964	$1,340	$24,607	$62,466	$120,675
		$25,000	$1,500	$0	$39,220	$112,570
	5	$30,134	$1,368	$17,685	$57,402	$112,145
		$30,000	$1,500	$0	$30,476	$91,419
	6	$32,388	$1,307	$38,946	$65,448	$140,784
		$30,000	$1,250	$19,236	$25,188	$111,793
	7	$35,969	$1,611	$40,044	$58,022	$141,945
		$35,000	$1,500	$14,594	$21,331	$111,413
	8	$39,284	$1,384	$34,351	$66,316	$149,428
		$40,000	$1,500	$13,386	$29,203	$135,131
	9	$45,727	$1,031	$61,668	$59,273	$171,281
		$45,000	$1,000	$47,175	$13,908	$140,708
Largest	10	$51,985	$1,002	$63,131	$72,591	$193,586
		$50,000	$1,000	$54,356	$15,897	$171,875

Note: Calculations in this table are based upon data contained in the April 2006 version of Standard & Poor's ExecuComp.

tunities of the firm. Similarly, Bryan et al. (2000) find the level of outside director stock option awards positively related to the corporation's growth opportunities, whereas the level of director stock grants is negatively associated with the corporation's growth opportunities. As discussed in Chapter 9, institutional shareholdings are also associated with executive compensation. Similarly, Bryan et al. (2000) find the level of outside director stock option awards positively related to the level of institutional shareholdings in the corporation. In general, Bryan et al. (2000) find that firm characteristics that explain executive compensation also explain director compensation, a finding consistent with directors being treated as agents of the shareholders who need economic incentives to increase shareholder value. While Bryan et al. (2000) limited their analysis to director compensation, Yermack (2004) incorporated the incentives arising from director ownership, as well as those arising from the gain (loss) of other directorships if the firm performs well (poorly). He estimates that a one-standard deviation increase in market performance increases director wealth by $285,000.

Effect of Director Compensation on Director Independence

In contrast to Bryan et al. (2000), who looked at multiple determinants of director compensation, Moskowitz (1998) focuses on one item and finds that the level of director pay is positively related to CEO overcompensation. The latter leads to a very interesting, and controversial, hypothesis: a corporate version of you scratch my back and I'll scratch yours. Board memberships can be quite lucrative, and that may impair the director's objectivity. Further, as with executives, this compensation can serve as a bond to be forfeited if their performance is not satisfactory. However, outside directors do not have any operational duties upon which to be judged. Rather, because outside directors are appointed by, and serve with the approval of, the CEO[18, 19], their performance may be judged on how well they get along (or go along) with the CEO. For example, Tejada (1997) reports that when Jesse L. Upchurch resigned as Tandy director, he claimed he was being penalized for criticizing the CEO's performance. Similarly, Tharp (2003) reports that Andrea Van de Kamp was forced from the Disney board for taking stands against Eisner. Thus, for financial and social reasons, board members may be more loyal to the CEO who has appointed them than to the shareholders they legally represent. Further, the greater the pay, the greater the loyalty.

Effect of the Board of Directors on CEO Compensation

The lack of an arms-length relationship between the CEO and the board creates opportunity for self-dealing when determining compensation. However, even with an arms-length relationship, the CEO has strong incentives to increase his or her compensation, while the board, normally not consisting of large shareholders, has little or no incentive to resist. To provide some incentive, rule changes implemented in 1993 by the Securities and Exchange Commission required the compensation committee to provide a report in the proxy statement detailing how it set executive compensation. And the rule changes which went into effect Dec. 15, 2006, require a new Compensation Discussion and Analysis that requires even greater disclosure and clarity in discussing how the board set executive compensation.

Appendix 10-1 contains, as an example of this report, the compensation committee report incorporated into the Dow Jones proxy statement filed with the Securities and Exchange Commission March 17, 2006.

The first section of the report, The Compensation Committee and the Compensation Program, describes the compensation committee—five independent directors and the general charge of the committee—as administering the compensation program to enhance stockholder value. The next section, Elements of Compensation Program Considered by the Committee, discusses the focus of the committee—senior management—and the elements of compensation considered. The report then goes on to discuss how committee members establish and administer the program. In Establishing and Administering a Competitive Program, they discuss the use of outside compensation consultants, performance studies and peer companies. They then go on to explain that the amount of compensation that will be awarded to the CEO in the forthcoming year will be substantially based upon the achievement of predetermined financial objectives, which they describe, for example, as earnings-per-share growth, without disclosing the actual quantitative goal. The last part of the section discusses the effect of Section 162(m) on the deductibility of compensation, noting that the deductibility of certain compensation paid to four of the executives was affected, but not disclosing how much compensation was affected or the amount of additional taxes paid as a result. The last section, Committee Reporting, discusses the actual compensation paid and the reasons for awarding the compensation, for example, individual contribution and performance, value of jobs in the marketplace, and company performance measured against predetermined financial and nonfinancial criteria.

Note that to justify compensation, the committee refers to vaguely worded financial, strategic and individual performance goals, without giving details on those goals. Furthermore, in the course of the report, the committee refers to the "unnamed" compensation consultants multiple times. This is not uncommon. Clarke et al. (1998) find the use of external advisers and pay surveys are prevalent among large companies (see also Crystal 1991, Thomas and Martin 1999). By surveying the competition, compensation consultants help a corporation determine and justify the compensation paid. Unfortunately, the process is susceptible to biases. For example, if the goal is to justify an increase in compensation, the survey might focus on high-paying corporations. Alternatively, if the survey shows that the CEO earns less salary but a larger bonus than his or her peers, the compensation consultants/committee might focus on the relatively low salary to justify a raise, totally ignoring the relatively high bonus. A more general problem with surveys is they can lead to an endless spiraling upward of compensation. Many corporations state that it is their objective to set compensation so that it is above the median, sometimes explicitly stating that it should be in the 50th to 75th percentile relative to their competition. Of course, all corporations cannot be above the median. However, in striving to be above the median, corporations can justify continual increases in compensation.

Corporations must justify the compensation they pay their executives, so the question is whether corporate governance, or more precisely, the composition of the board of directors and the compensation committee, affects compensation. While the assumption is that outside directors, because they are independent, will better represent the interests of shareholders, that need not always be the case. As discussed above, while their primary employer may not be the corporation, they may have relationships with the corporation and/or the CEO that impair their independence. Further, even if they are independent, their low level of shareholdings in the corporation may not provide them with the proper incentives.

Core et al. (1999) conduct a comprehensive study of the effect of corporate governance on CEO compensation. In general, they find that compensation for CEOs was higher at corporations with ineffective governance structures. Mallette et al. (1995), Sridharan (1996), Core et al. (1999) and Conyon and Murphy (2000) all find compensation higher when the same person is CEO and board chairman. While this could be the result of the influence the individual holds over the compensation committee, it could also be remuneration for the additional duties the individual holds. Core et al. (1999) also find compensation increases with board size, that is, number of directors on board. Sridharan (1996) finds that compensation increases with increases in the percent of insiders on the board of directors. While consistent with the finding of Mayer et al. (1997) that mutual insurance companies with more outside directors spend less on salaries and wages, it is inconsistent with the findings of Lambert et al. (1993) and Core et al. (1999). They find compensation *decreases* with the percentage of insiders on the board.[20] However, Core et. al. (1999) find that compensation increases when the CEO has influence over the outside directors, as measured by the percentage of outside directors appointed by the CEO, the percentage of "gray" outside directors, the percentage of outside directors older than age 69, and the percentage of busy outside directors. Hallock (1997) found the existence of an interlock increases CEO compensation by as much as 52 percent. In contrast, Daily et al. (1998) find no evidence that "captured" directors pay higher levels of CEO compensation. Wade et al. (1990) found the greater the percentage of outside board members appointed after the CEO, the more likely the CEO will have a golden parachute. More recent research by Larcker et al. (2005) and Barnea and Guedj (2006) find that even subtle relationships between directors and executives, e.g., "backdoor links," increase executive compensation.

Focusing on the compensation committee, Mallette et al. (1995), as did O'Reilly et al. (1988), find "the value of compensation received by members of the compensation committee with their primary employer is a significant predictor of CEO cash compensation." The more highly paid the members of the compensation committee, the higher the compensation they will award the CEO. Among the theoretical explanations for this finding is that compensation committee members use their own pay as a benchmark or reference point in setting CEO pay. Additionally, Conyon and He (2004) find that the more highly paid compensation committee members believe the longer their board service, the greater the CEO compensation. Main et al. (1995) found that CEO compensation was higher when the CEO's tenure was greater than that of the compensation committee chairman. One potential explanation for this finding is that the compensation committee chairman was only appointed with the approval of the CEO, with whom he or she may have some relationship. In contrast, the presence of a significant shareholder (5 percent) on the compensation committee reduces CEO compensation (Conyon and He 2004).

Turning to the relationship between pay and performance, Conyon and Peck (1998) find it was stronger for corporations with boards that have larger proportions of outside directors. Meanwhile, Conyon and He (2004) find it stronger when a 5-percent shareholder is represented on the compensation committee. Similarly, Mehran (1995) and Ryan and Wiggins (2004) find that equity-based compensation, which is performance based by definition, is used more extensively in corporations with more outside directors. Yermack (1996) finds evidence showing that as board size increases, the association between pay and performance decreases, consistent with CEOs receiving "stronger compensation incentives in companies with smaller boards."

As noted in the introduction to this chapter, Section 162(m) of the Internal Revenue Code requires that a corporation have a compensation committee consisting of two or more independent directors if the corporation wishes to deduct compensation in excess of $1 million per executive. This is not an issue with all corporations, as not every corporation has executives receiving compensation in excess of $1 million. Further, as noted by Balsam and Yin (2005), a growing number of corporations have elected to forfeit deductions. As such, corporations willing to forfeit deductions can have insiders on their compensation committees. In a finding similar to what they found for the entire board, Conyon and Peck (1998) find the link between pay and performance stronger for corporations with fewer insiders on the compensation committee. Newman and Mozes (1999) find that insider participation on the compensation committee weakens the relation between CEO compensation and corporate performance in poorly performing corporations. In contrast, Lavelle (2000) finds "independent committees are now more likely to dole out raises when the stock tanks than committees stacked with insiders."

Effect of the Board of Directors on CEO Turnover

As noted above, the board's role is to hire, fire and monitor the CEO. Historically, boards have traditionally been reluctant to fire CEOs, although that has changed somewhat in recent years. Cross-sectionally, Coughlan and Schmidt (1985), Warner et al. (1988) and Weisbach (1988) all find evidence consistent with the theory that outside directors are more willing than inside directors to dismiss CEOs following poor performance. Yermack (1996) shows that the probability of CEO dismissal as the result of poor performance decreases as board size increases, consistent with smaller boards being more effective monitors of management.[21] Goyal and Park (2000), as noted above, find the sensitivity of CEO turnover to corporate performance is weaker when the CEO is also the chairman of the board.

What Makes a Good Board?

As noted above, a board can have an effect on executive compensation, and for the most part, executive compensation is more restrained at firms with good governance. More importantly, good governance can improve the performance of the firm. But how is good governance or a good board defined?

It has been a maintained assumption that a good board is made up of a majority of independent directors, which as discussed in Chapter 10, the New York Stock Exchange and NASDAQ now require. In addition, a number of experts have advocated the separation of the CEO and chairman of the board positions. While not all agree, an increasing number of corporations are separating the positions, 29 percent in a recent survey (Deutsch 2006).

Several noted authorities have called for increased equity ownership on the part of directors as a way to align their incentives with those of shareholders (for example, Hambrick and Jackson 2000). As noted in Chapter 9, many corporations are imposing ownership requirements on executives and directors.

The number of boards on which a director serves can be viewed as a measure of the capabilities of that director. For example, Ferris et al. (2003) find support for the argument that director quality is positively associated with the number of boards on which they serve. However, the more boards on which a director serves, the less time he or she can devote to any one board. Consequently, some (Core et al. 1999) find that, at some point, director quality declines with the number of boards on which a director serves. This trend has become exacerbated over the past few years.

There is also the question of how long an individual should serve as a director. On the one hand, over time the director builds up knowledge of the firm. On the other hand, over time, the director becomes linked with the firm and its executives, possibly compromising his or her independence. Vafeas (2003) examines this issue, finding evidence consistent with the latter, that is, independence being compromised for long-serving directors, and suggests term limits for directors.

Movement Toward More Corporate Democracy

It cannot be pointed out enough that the current board controls the proxy machinery. That is, the board of directors, or its nominating subcommittee, nominates directors, who are then rubber-stamped by absentee owners with little choice, as there is usually only one nominee per position. Only in the presence of a proxy contest generated by a large shareholder or outsider attempting to gain control of the corporation does the investor have a choice. In response to this environment, Peter H. Arkison submitted the following proposal, which was incorporated in Walt Disney's 2000 proxy statement, asking that shareholders be given at least two qualified individuals to choose from for each board position.[22]

RESOLVED that the Board of Directors should submit the names of at least two qualified individuals to the shareholders for each position on the board of directors to be voted upon by the shareholders. Each nominee should be submitted in such a manner as to make it impossible for the shareholders to know which is the one preferred by the Board, except that a simple statement may be included indicating that person's time of service on the board. Proxies submitted on behalf of management should be prepared in such a way that each candidate will receive approximately the same number of votes if the shareholders do not make a choice in favor of particular candidates.

STATEMENT IN SUPPORT OF RESOLUTION

It is the legal right and duty of the shareholders to elect the Board of Directors. At the present time, the Board of Directors nominates one candidate for each position to be filled on the Board. Under the proxy system, the shareholders do not have a meaningful way of saying that they do not like a particular candidate.

It is possible for a shareholder to withhold authority for voting for a particular director; however, since there is not a meaningful alternative choice presented, the chosen candidate wins.

The shareholders have the right to make a choice of whom they want to run their company; this Resolution takes a step toward allowing them to exercise that right. With the vast number of shareholders, only those whose names appear on the proxy ballot submitted with the Notice of the Annual Meeting have a chance at being elected to the board. This Resolution attempts to address this problem by seeking to have the Board submit two equally qualified candidates for each position.

Discretion is left with the Board to determine how information about the candidates is presented; the only requirement is that they be presented in a similar manner.

The proxy ballots are to be designed and distributed in a manner that would result in all candidates receiving approximately the same number of votes. That means that those shareholders who actually take the time and effort to vote for specific candidates will be the ones who choose the new members of the Board. Every vote then becomes very important.

The Resolution seeks to change the way that the company is governed. It seeks return of the control of the corporation to the shareholders. It seeks to terminate the Board of Directors becoming a self perpetuating body by giving shareholders the opportunity to remove the present directors by voting for the alternative choices. The Board then would become more accountable to the shareholders for its actions.

A YES vote is needed for effective shareholder governance.

While a seemingly reasonable proposal, it was opposed by management and turned down by shareholders by a vote of 74,914,596 for and 1,229,835,340 against.23 Yet slowly, many corporations are moving toward more corporate democracy. As an illustration, the general rule is that the individuals who receive the highest number of affirmative votes are elected directors. There was no requirement that the director receive a majority of either shares outstanding or shares voted. Recently, however, in response to public pressure, a number of corporations—more than 140 according to Chan (2006)—are voluntarily requiring that directors win a majority of votes. For example, Wal-Mart's board recently passed the following amendment, which, while it requires a director who has not received a majority vote to submit his or her resignation, doesn't assure the board will actually accept it:

On Sept. 21, 2006, the Board of Directors (the "Board") of Wal-Mart Stores, Inc. (the "Company") adopted amendments to Articles II and III of the Company's Amended and Restated Bylaws (the "Bylaws") to provide for a majority vote standard for the election of directors. In future uncontested elections of directors, each director of the Company will be elected by a majority of the votes cast by the shares present in person or represented by proxy at the meeting and entitled to vote on the election of directors. Under previous Bylaw provisions, directors were elected by a plurality of the votes of the shares present in person or represented by proxy at the meeting and entitled to vote on the election of directors. In contested elections, directors will continue to be elected by the vote of a plurality of the shares present in person or by proxy at the meeting and entitled to vote on the election of directors. For purposes of the Bylaws as amended, a "contested election" is an election in which the number of nominees for director is greater than the number of directors to be elected.

Under the Bylaws as amended, following any uncontested election, an incumbent director who does not receive the required majority vote must promptly tender his or her resignation. The Board committee responsible for recommending nominees for appointment or election to the Board, which is currently the Compensation, Nominating and Governance Committee, will consider the resignation and make a recommendation to the Board as to whether the resignation should be accepted.[24]

Summary

This chapter describes the corporate governance system in the United States. In the United States, corporate charters are issued by the states, which are the primary regulators of those corporations. In general, states require that corporations have boards of directors. The shareholders of the corporation elect those directors to oversee the operations of the corporation. When the corporation decides to go public, it then becomes subject to the regulations of the exchange upon which it is listed, and of the Securities and Exchange Commission. These entities impose additional requirements on the corporation, for example, requiring that the corporation have an audit committee to oversee the financial reporting process, and specifying the composition of that committee.

Among the board's responsibilities is the setting of executive compensation. The possibility exists that the board, which is supposed to oversee and set compensation for the CEO, may not be independent of the CEO. And note that, even if the board is totally independent, while the CEO has strong incentives to increase his or her compensation, the board has little or no incentive to resist.

Few directors are completely independent of the CEO. That is, while their fiduciary duty lies with the shareholders who elected them, their true loyalties may lie with the CEO who nominated them in the first place. The board is comprised of inside directors whose full-time employment is with the corporation, and outside directors who are not currently employed by the corporation. In many cases, an insider, the CEO, is also the board chairman, which adversely affects the board's ability to independently monitor and discipline the CEO. Outside directors, while not currently employed by the corporation, may be retired employees, or have other business ties or affiliations to the corporation and/or its executives.

Director's compensation can be significant, averaging $131,528 (median $107,158) in 2005. Like the executive compensation package, it includes multiple components such as cash retainers, board meeting fees, fees for chairing committees, stock options and stock grants. These amounts, while necessary to attract high-quality directors, also may compromise directors' independence. That is, when the amounts get large, directors may be afraid to challenge the CEO if by doing so, they risk losing their position and compensation.

Academic evidence generally shows that executive compensation is higher at firms with ineffective governance structures, for example, when outside directors have ties to the company, or when they hold multiple outside directorships. However, given the extensive networks and backdoor links between executives and directors, it is hard to imagine a way to avoid these relationships. CEO compensation is also higher when the same person is CEO and board chairman, although this finding could be remuneration for the additional duties the individual holds.

Footnotes

1 Karnitschnig (2006).

2 http://www.state.de.us/corp/.

3 Delaware General Corporation Law § 141.

4 New York Stock Exchange Manual Section 303A.01.

5 New York Stock Exchange Manual Section 303A.07.

6 New York Stock Exchange Manual Section 303A.05.

7 New York Stock Exchange Manual Section 303A.04.

8 NASDAQ Manual Section 4350(c).

9 Shivdasani and Yermack (1999) find this duality for 84 percent of the firms in the *Fortune* 500.

10 Fich and White (2005) find that "about one company in seven was part of a relationship whereby the CEO of one company sat on a second company's board and the second company's CEO sat on the first company's board."

11 An extreme case is the interlocking compensation committee where the CEO of ABC is a director of XYZ and serves on its compensation committee, while the CEO of XYZ is a director of ABC and serves on its compensation committee. Fierman (1990) provides some examples.

12 NASDAQ manual, rule 4200.

13 Page 5, Walt Disney proxy statement filed with the Securities and Exchange Commission, Jan. 4, 2002.

14 Pages 8 and 9, General Motors proxy statement filed with the Securities and Exchange Commission, April 28, 2006.

15 Page 2, Coca-Cola form 8-K filed with the Securities and Exchange Commission, April 5, 2006.

16 Page 2, Coca-Cola form 8-K filed with the Securities and Exchange Commission, April 5, 2006.

17 An interesting question is who would have the incentives and ability to design such a package, given the divergence in interests between management and shareholders, and the dispersion of shareholders in most companies.

18 See, for example, Mace (1971) and Lorsch and MacIver (1989).

19 "Directors appointed during the tenure of an incumbent CEO have been termed 'interdependent' directors." Daily et al. (1998).

[20] Hebner and Kato (1997) develop an interesting theory to explain why executive compensation would increase with the number of insiders on the board of directors. In equilibrium, executive compensation consists of explicit compensation plus the implicit profits to be made from trading on inside information. As the number of insiders increases, the ability to profit from inside information decreases, and thus the explicit component of the compensation package must increase. In the absence of direct data on insider profits, they indirectly test their theory using explicit executive compensation, finding that executive compensation does in fact increase with the number of officers.

[21] This may be a function of smaller groups being able to arrive at consensus more easily.

[22] Pages 22 and 23 of Walt Disney Co. proxy statement filed with Securities and Exchange Commission, Jan. 5, 2000.

[23] Page 2 of Walt Disney Co. 10-Q filed with Securities and Exchange Commission, May 15, 2000.

[24] Page 2, Wal-Mart form 8-K, filed with the Securities and Exchange Commission, Sept. 25, 2006.

Appendix 10-1

Dow Jones Comp. Committee Report on Executive Compensation[1]

The Compensation Committee and the Compensation Program

The Compensation Committee consists of five independent directors. The principal role of the Committee is to: review and approve corporate goals and objectives relevant to Chief Executive Officer compensation, evaluate the Chief Executive Officer's performance in light of those goals and objectives and determine and approve (along with the other independent directors) the Chief Executive Officer's compensation level based on this evaluation; and make recommendations to the Board with respect to the Chairman's compensation, senior executive officer compensation, and incentive compensation and equity-based plans. The Committee's objective is to establish and administer a "total compensation program" that fairly and competitively rewards Company executives for current and long-term performance and that enhances stockholder value. To this end, the Committee reviews and exercises judgment on all elements of the executive compensation program, including salary increases and annual incentive compensation, and the Company's long-term incentive program.

The purpose of this report is to explain the Company's executive compensation program and the operation of the Compensation Committee.

Elements of Compensation Program Considered by the Committee

The Committee reviews and approves corporate goals and objectives relevant to the Chief Executive Officer's compensation and evaluates his performance in light of those goals and objectives. In addition, the Committee recommends to the Board financial, strategic and individual performance measures for the other top executive officers at the Company and evaluates the individual performance of each in light of these measures.

We consider four elements of compensation: (i) base salary; (ii) annual incentive compensation; (iii) long-term incentive compensation; and (iv) retirement and other compensation.

Establishing and Administering a Competitive Program

The Committee retains outside compensation consultants and reviews competitive compensation and performance studies in developing and administering the total compensation program. We give continuing attention to changes in compensation practices, business trends and changes in applicable law and regulations in order to establish and administer a sound competitive compensation program. The competitive universe that we primarily consider includes the five largest newspaper publishers in the Dow Jones U.S. Publishing Index (the "Company's peer group") (see page 27), and we also review data on general industry trends and on certain other public companies which compete with one or more of the Company's business segments.

With regard to annual and long-term incentive compensation for 2005, the Committee, in working with management and the Committee's outside compensation consultants, determined that a substantial portion of executives' awards would be based on the achievement of certain pre-established financial objectives. For Mr. Kann, a substantial portion of his annual incentive compensation for 2005 was based on the achievement of these pre-established financial objectives (60% based on earnings per share and 10% based on return on investment) and the balance was based on the achievement of specified strategic goals. For most of the remaining executive officers, a substantial portion of their annual incentive compensation was based on the achievement of pre-established financial objectives and the balance was based on the achievement of strategic goals and on individual performance.

Federal tax legislation in effect since 1994 eliminates the deductibility of compensation in excess of $1,000,000 paid to the Chief Executive Officer and the other four executive officers whose compensation is disclosed in the proxy statement. The law exempts compensation paid under plans that objectively tie compensation to performance.

Although the Company's incentive compensation plans are designed to relate compensation to performance, certain elements of the plans used during 2005 did not meet the tax law's requirements because they allow the Committee to exercise discretion in setting compensation. The Committee retained some measure of discretion with respect to the annual incentive plan and certain long-term incentive compensation; and therefore, for 2005, the deductibility of certain compensation paid to Messrs. Kann, Zannino and Crovitz and Ms. House was affected by this limitation.

Initial awards of contingent stock rights were granted under the 2001 Long-Term Incentive Plan (as amended) for the 2006-2008 performance period. In order for final awards to qualify as "performance-based compensation" under federal tax law, the Committee is not permitted, and currently does not intend, to exercise upward discretion in connection with the determination of final awards for the 2006-2008 performance period.

Starting in 2006, assuming approval by the Company's stockholders, the annual incentive compensation of the Chief Executive Officer and the four most highly compensated executive officers of the Company (the "Named Executive Officers") will be based on certain objective performance criteria in order for annual incentives to qualify as "performance-based compensation" under federal tax law. As the initial step, the Company would create a bonus pool, the funding of which would be based on Company performance with respect to the pre-established objective criteria, for the executives who have a reasonable chance of being one of the Named Executive Officers. The Compensation Committee would retain downward discretion with respect to the final payouts from the pool.

Committee Reporting

The Committee makes recommendations to the other independent directors regarding the total compensation of the Chief Executive Officer, and together with the other independent directors determines and approves the total compensation of the Chief Executive Officer. It also makes recommendations to the Board regarding the total compensation of the other members of senior management. More specifically, the Committee recommends to the Board (or in the case of the Chief Executive Officer, to the other independent directors) the Final Awards under the Company's incentive plans for the Company's top executives for each performance period. The Committee also recommends to the Board (or in the case of the Chief Executive Officer, to the other independent directors) stock-based awards for the Company's executives.

Mr. Kann's salary for 2005 was set at $995,000 during 2005. Normally, salaries for members of senior management are set after evaluating their individual contributions and performance, increased responsibilities in certain cases and the value of their jobs in the marketplace based on a review of the competitive compensation guidelines that were developed with advice from the Committee's outside compensation consultants.

The annual incentive compensation for 2005 for the Named Executive Officers listed in the table on page 16 reflects the Company's performance measured against financial and qualitative criteria established in the beginning of the year by the Committee. Financial criteria included earnings per share, return on investment and, where applicable, direct operating income at the executive's business unit. It is the Committee's view that the executive officers performed well on the qualitative measures in a difficult business environment by, among other things, controlling costs, continuing to invest in and enhance the quality of the Company's products, improving operational efficiency and executing on the Company's long-range strategic initiatives.

In January 2006, we determined contingent stock right payouts to Mr. Kann and other members of senior management under the Company's 2001 Long-Term Incentive Plan (as amended). The Final Awards covered performance for the period 2002-2005 and were made after reviewing the Company's performance on total stockholder return relative to other newspaper, media and financial services companies. We also considered progress toward achieving other Company objectives (quality of Dow Jones' publications and services, level of customer satisfaction and commitment to innovative products and services), and individual performance. In the case of the 2002-2005 performance period, satisfactory performance (as judged by the Compensation Committee in its discretion at the time of the payouts) would be deemed rewarded at target levels when the Final Award approximated two-thirds of the number of shares in the Initial Award. Exceptional performance would have supported a Final Award in excess of two-thirds of the Initial Award.

Final Awards were made in January 2006 to Messrs. Kann, Zannino, Crovitz and Steiger and to Ms. House in amounts equal to 53.2% to 54.2% of their Initial Awards for the 2002-2005 period. The Named Executive Officers received their Final Awards in the form of Common Stock.

Mr. Kann's Final Award for the 2002-2005 period was 17,888 shares of Common Stock. That represented a decrease of 687 shares from his Final Award for the 2001-2004 period. The fair market value of Mr. Kann's Final Award for the 2002-2005 period was $681,712 (based on the closing stock price of $38.11 on the date Final Awards were determined), an amount approximately 11% lower in value than the Final Award for the 2001-2004 period of $764,176 (based on the closing stock price of $41.14 on the date Final Awards were determined).

In early 2006, we granted members of senior management (i) stock options and (ii) contingent stock rights for the 2006-2008 performance period. These grants tie a significant portion of each senior executive's potential compensation to the Company's long-term objectives and to the market value of the Company's stock. The Committee will determine the actual number of shares of stock payable to an executive under the contingent stock rights following the end of the three-year performance period. It is expected that the final awards to all those receiving these grants will be based solely on the Company's performance with respect to total shareholder return relative to an established group of newspaper and media companies.

The Committee believes that the number of contingent stock rights and stock options granted to individual executives should be set annually by the Committee after consultation with its consultants concerning competitive compensation levels and after consideration of each individual executive's performance and potential future contributions to the Company.

The view of the Committee is that salaries for the senior executives of the Company generally should not deviate substantially from the median, and bonus and other incentive compensation opportunities should be somewhat above the median, of the competitive guidelines developed with the advice of the Committee's consultants. The Committee believes that the compensation levels for the Chairman and the Chief Executive Officer and other senior executives reflect these criteria and are appropriate given performance during the periods covered.

Irvine O. Hockaday, Jr., Chairman
Christopher Bancroft
Harvey Golub
M. Peter McPherson
Frank N. Newman

Footnote

1 Pages 21-23, Dow Jones proxy statement filed with the Securities and Exchange Commission, March 17, 2006.

Part IV

Is Executive Compensation Really that High?

Chapter 11

The Relation Between Pay and Performance

*A recent survey found 82 percent of respondents thought CEO pay was excessive.
(Philadelphia Business Journal 2006) In another survey 90 percent of institutional
investors said top executives were "dramatically overpaid." (Hymowitz 2006)*

Introduction

Implicit in the above statistic is the argument that American CEOs are overpaid.
Perhaps more shocking:

> Nearly 40 percent of directors feel CEO pay is "too high in most cases."
> (Corporate Board Survey 2006)

While similar sentiments have been expressed annually, CEO pay continues to
increase.

> Last year, total direct compensation for chiefs—which includes salary,
> bonus and the value of restricted stock when it was granted—jumped nearly
> 16 percent to a median of $6.05 million, according to an analysis of 350
> major companies by Mercer for The Wall Street Journal. (Hymowitz 2006).

And CEO pay is expected to continue increasing:

> Sixty-four percent of directors expect to see continued increases in CEO cash
> compensation. Fifty-eight percent expect an increase in stock-based compen-
> sation. (Corporate Board Survey 2006)

In reality, whether CEOs are overpaid depends on how the issue is framed. When
framed as a multiple of blue-collar worker pay, it does appear CEOs are overpaid.
The amounts involved are high by most people's standards. However, when viewed
relative to corporate profits, dividends or increases in shareholder wealth, the
numbers seem less excessive.

Compensation Relative to Performance

CEO Compensation Relative to Corporate Profits

One way to gauge if compensation is excessive is to compare it to corporate profits. Given the widespread belief that pay should be related to performance, it is widely accepted, and expected, that pay will be greater the better the measure or measures of performance. In fact, one of the criticisms of Richard Grasso's compensation at the NYSE was that his pay was excessive when compared with reported income. In fact, Lahart (2004) writes, "The $130 million in compensation and benefits the NYSE expensed for Mr. Grasso for the years 2000 to 2002 was equal to 98% of the NYSE's reported income of $133 million."

Tables 11-1 through 11-3 show CEO pay as a percentage of net income.[1] Table 11-1 shows how CEO pay as a percentage of net income varies over time, while Table 11-2 shows how it varies with the size of the corporation. As can be seen from Table 11-1, as a percentage of net income, mean (median) annual CEO compensation ranges from a low of 2.74 (0.90) percent of profit in 1992 to a high of 9.65 (3.51) percent in 2001. As found by previous research going back to Taussig

Table 11-1:

CEO Compensation as a Percentage of Net Income, By Year

Year	Mean	Median
1992	2.74	0.90
1993	5.44	1.72
1994	6.34	2.41
1995	6.21	2.36
1996	6.71	2.54
1997	7.35	2.64
1998	7.66	2.84
1999	8.74	2.99
2000	8.30	3.08
2001	9.65	3.51
2002	8.33	2.92
2003	7.23	2.77
2004	7.82	2.92
2005	6.79	2.59

Note: Calculations in this table are based upon data contained in the April 2006 version of Standard & Poor's ExecuComp and use the absolute value of net income in those cases where net income is negative.

Table 11-2:

CEO Compensation as a Percentage of Corporate Profits, By Firm Size (for 2005)

	Size Decile	Mean	Median
Smallest	1	19.52	7.47
	2	11.81	5.67
	3	11.09	5.06
	4	6.18	3.30
	5	5.00	2.94
	6	4.18	2.62
	7	3.36	1.96
	8	3.61	1.60
	9	2.62	1.11
Largest	10	0.77	0.55

Note: Calculations in this table are based upon data contained in the April 2006 version of Standard & Poor's ExecuComp and uses the absolute value of net income in those cases where net income is negative.

and Barker (1925), Table 11-2 shows that CEO compensation as a percentage of profit is inversely related to the size of the corporation, dropping from 19.52 (median 7.47) percent of profits for the smallest corporations to 0.77 (median 0.55) percent of profits for the largest corporations. This latter finding, when combined with the earlier observation that compensation increases with the size of the corporation (see Table 2-10), indicates that while compensation increases with size of the corporation, the increase is not proportional.

CEO Compensation Relative to Dividends Paid

Tables 11-3 and 11-4 on page 374 show CEO compensation as a percentage of dividends paid to common shareholders. Typically, dividends are less than profits because corporations normally retain some profits to internally fund projects. A number of well-known profitable corporations, such as Cisco, don't pay any dividends. Consistent with dividends being lower than net income, the percentages in Tables 11-3 and 11-4 are higher than those in Tables 11-1 and 11-2. Table 11-3 shows mean (median) annual CEO compensation ranges from a low of 11.26 (3.46) percent of dividends in 1994 to a high of 21.43 (8.78) percent in 2003. Table 11-4 shows CEO compensation as a percentage of dividends is inversely related to the size of the corporation, dropping from 24.34 (median 20.56) percent of dividends for the smallest corporations, to 7.57 (median 2.52) percent of dividends for the largest corporations.

Table 11-3:

CEO Compensation as a Percentage of Common Dividends, By Year

Year	Mean	Median
1992	17.02	3.77
1993	12.51	2.47
1994	11.26	3.46
1995	14.55	5.60
1996	17.40	6.07
1997	19.90	7.46
1998	16.74	6.01
1999	18.39	7.09
2000	20.96	7.52
2001	20.42	8.28
2002	18.76	7.05
2003	21.43	8.78
2004	20.76	9.08
2005	17.60	7.53

Note: Calculations in this table are based upon data contained in the April 2006 version of Standard & Poor's ExecuComp.

Table 11-4:

CEO Compensation as a Percentage of Common Dividends, By Firm Size (for 2005)

	Size Decile	Mean	Median
Smallest	1	24.34	20.56
	2	24.25	18.65
	3	25.61	14.94
	4	20.89	10.72
	5	20.72	10.92
	6	23.89	8.74
	7	14.47	7.57
	8	18.24	6.72
	9	11.54	3.30
Largest	10	7.57	2.52

Note: Calculations in this table are based upon data contained in the April 2006 version of Standard & Poor's ExecuComp.

CEO Compensation Relative to Increase in Shareholder Wealth

Perhaps the most relevant measure of executive performance is increase in shareholder wealth, as at least in theory, the executives are agents of the shareholders. Consequently, when the executive makes millions while the share price is decreasing, shareholders complain and the media tends to pick up on it. One CEO on the hot spot is Robert Nardelli of Home Depot. Terhune (2006) writes,

> Mr. Nardelli has come under intense criticism because Home Depot shares have slid 11% since he took the helm in 2000, while shares of archrival Lowe's Cos. have nearly tripled. Over that same period, Mr. Nardelli has pocketed more than $100 million in compensation, including nearly $32 million last year.

Tables 11-5 and 11-6 show CEO compensation as a percentage of the increase in common shareholder wealth, where increase in common shareholder wealth is

Table 11-5:
CEO Compensation as a Percentage of Increase in Shareholder Wealth (Price Appreciation Plus Dividends Paid), By Year

Year	Mean	Median
1992	6.08	0.56
1993	3.39	0.40
1994	3.37	0.71
1995	2.50	0.53
1996	3.30	0.72
1997	2.60	0.59
1998	2.84	0.63
1999	3.10	0.59
2000	2.65	0.56
2001	3.81	0.83
2002	3.89	0.95
2003	2.76	0.65
2004	2.89	0.76
2005	3.42	0.91

Note: Calculations in this table are based upon data contained in the April 2006 version of Standard & Poor's ExecuComp and uses the absolute value of increase in shareholder wealth in those cases where shareholder wealth decreases during the year.

Table 11-6:

CEO Compensation as a Percentage of Increase in Shareholder Wealth (Price Appreciation Plus Dividends Paid), By Size (for 2005)

	Size Decile	Mean	Median
Smallest	1	4.17	1.97
	2	4.89	1.25
	3	4.63	1.53
	4	5.06	1.34
	5	3.21	1.08
	6	2.88	1.02
	7	2.63	0.76
	8	3.49	0.62
	9	2.77	0.41
Largest	10	0.55	0.27

Note: Calculations in this table are based upon data contained in the April 2006 version of Standard & Poor's ExecuComp and use the absolute value of increase in shareholder wealth in those cases where shareholder wealth decreases during the year.

defined as the dividends paid to common shareholders plus the increase in the value of their shares. Table 11-5 shows that mean (median) annual CEO compensation ranges from a low of 2.60 (0.59) percent of the increase in shareholder wealth in 1997, to a high of 6.08 (0.56) percent in 1992. Table 11-6 shows that CEO compensation as a percentage of the increase in shareholder wealth is inversely related to the size of the corporation, dropping from 4.17 (median 1.97) percent of the increase in shareholder wealth for the smallest corporations to 0.55 (median 0.27) percent of the increase in shareholder wealth for the largest corporations.

Summarizing Tables 11-1 through 11-6, it appears that CEO compensation is a material component of corporate profits and dividends, but a less significant proportion of the increase in shareholder wealth. Which is the appropriate percentage to use in determining reasonability? Some would argue that because the CEO is an agent of the shareholders that the increase in shareholder wealth should be the appropriate benchmark. If you subscribe to this view, then compensation seems reasonable, especially for the largest corporations, where the mean and median percentages are less than 1 percent. Others would argue that because stock prices are influenced by factors outside the CEO's control, that net income is a more appropriate benchmark. If you subscribe to this view, then the means and medians, for example, 9.65 percent and 3.51 percent respectively, for 2001, seem less reasonable. And note this is compensation for one individual. The mean (median) firm in 2001 employed more than 19,000 (5,000) individuals.

CEO Worth

While the above numbers provide some descriptive statistics on the relative magnitudes of CEO compensation, they do not address the issue of whether the CEOs are worth those amounts. Hayes and Schaefer (1999) provide some academic evidence on whether executives are worth their pay by examining the effect of executive departures on stock market returns. They reason that if an executive is overpaid relative to his or her marginal product or value to the corporation, the market will react positively to his or her departure. Conversely, if the executive is underpaid relative to his or her marginal product, the market will react unfavorably to his or her departure. They find that when executives depart for other corporations, the market reacts unfavorably, indicating that those executives were underpaid, relative to their contributions to the corporation (which may explain why they were desired by another employer). In contrast, when executives die unexpectedly, the market reacts positively, indicating that those executives were overpaid.[2] Of course, it must be pointed out that the market reaction also takes into account the expected pay and performance of the executive's successor. If an overpaid executive, where overpaid is defined relative to his or her marginal product, is expected to be replaced by another executive who is even more overpaid, then the market will react negatively to the departure. Unfortunately, a direct examination of marginal product is not possible. Thus, whether or not executive pay is excessive depends upon your perspective. Consider the following proposal made by the International Brotherhood of Dupont Workers:

Stockholder's Statement

Mr. Holliday has served as CEO since 1998 and during that time his total compensation has been made up of three elements—salary, cash bonus and stock.

While his salary and bonus for 2004 was 3.6 million, a 50% increase over what he received during 2003, that amount is dwarfed by what he has received in stock. As of October 2005, Mr. Holliday has been provided with over 460,000 shares of stock, over 3.5 million stock options and over 130,000 restricted stock units. Also, Mr. Holliday can look forward to a pension, were he to retire right now, of close to $2 million per year.

In contrast with the white glove treatment that Mr. Holliday has received, the stockholders and employees have been subject to very different treatment. For stockholders, since 1998 when Mr. Holliday took over as CEO, DuPont stock is down over 30% (with DuPont stock at $40) while the S&P

is up 30%. Dow Chemical, a competitor, is up over 40% for that same period.

For employees, they have received a yearly wage increase that has averaged significantly less than 3%, and in just the last four years, their contribution toward health care costs have gone up almost four fold. For DuPont pensioners, the picture is even worse, with retirees often paying more in health care costs than they receive from their pension!

It is said that success comes with its price and that price can be expensive. In the case of DuPont and its treatment of Mr. Holliday, it can also be said that failure comes with its price—and that price is also expensive.

While DuPont has many formulas for calculating executive compensation, all detailed within the proxy statement, you have to wonder what all these formulas really mean since Mr. Holliday has been accumulating enormous wealth while the shareholders, employees and pensioners have been suffering. It is past time for DuPont to rethink the criteria used for compensating its senior executives.[3]

Or the following proposal, made in the same proxy statement by The United Brotherhood of Carpenters and Joiners of America, which made it clear that executives should not get bonuses unless DuPont outperforms a disclosed group of peer companies.

1. The annual incentive component of the Company's Plan should utilize financial performance criteria that can be benchmarked against peer group performance, and provide that no annual bonus be awarded based on financial performance criteria unless the Company exceeds the median or mean performance of a disclosed group of peer companies on the selected financial criteria;

2. The long-term equity compensation component of the Company's Plan should utilize financial and/or stock price performance criteria that can be benchmarked against peer group performance, and any options, restricted shares, or other equity compensation used should be structured so that compensation is received only when Company performance exceeds the median or mean performance of the peer group companies on the selected financial and stock price performance criteria;[4]

While seemingly reasonable, DuPont's board recommended shareholders vote against the proposals, and neither resolution came close to getting majority approval.[5]

Statistical Relationship Between Executive Compensation and Firm Performance

Executive salaries are subject to few and infrequent changes. What movement appears in the individual cases is almost entirely upward. In part, this upward movement is accounted for by the circumstance that prices and money incomes in general advanced during the period in question. But no doubt it is chiefly accounted for by the fact that while salaries are raised in the course of time, even though not promptly, for an efficient and money-making staff in the reverse case, they are not likely to be reduced. Poor management leads to a change in personnel, not a decrease in salary.

The above quotation, which implies that compensation is not related to performance, at least poor performance, is from Taussig and Barker (1925). Since then, a long line of literature has argued that compensation should be related to performance.[6] The reasons for the linkage are normative and positive. In a normative sense, compensation is considered fair if it has been "earned" through superior performance. In a positive sense, agency theorists argue that linking compensation to firm performance measures provides incentive to increase firm value.

More recent research has also shown that CEO compensation is related to firm performance measures. For example, Masson (1971) shows that CEO compensation is significantly associated with stock market performance. Lewellen and Huntsman (1972) show compensation is significantly related to profits and market value. Murphy (1985) shows compensation is related to stock returns and sales growth, whereas Coughlan and Schmidt (1985) show compensation is related to cumulative abnormal returns.[7] Looking at relative performance, Antle and Smith (1986) show compensation related to systematic (industry-related) and unsystematic components of stock market returns and accounting return on assets, while Gibbons and Murphy (1990) show compensation is related to stock market returns after industry, and market returns are filtered out. Yet some researchers, for example, Tosi et al. (2000), have found that, while performance has some explanatory power for compensation, firm size explains more of the variation in compensation. The difference in findings between the more recent research and the early findings of Taussig and Barker (1925) may have to do with changes in the compensation package over time. Taussig and Barker examined compensation in the early 20th century, before the widespread use of conditional compensation such as bonuses and stock options. Even today, decreases in salary are infrequent. An analysis of year-to-year changes in salary for the corporations available on the Standard & Poor's ExecuComp database found about 95 percent of the changes to be increases, and only 5 percent to be decreases.

Some researchers argue that the size of the relationship between compensation and firm performance is too small. For example, Jensen and Murphy (1990b) find that CEO wealth increases by $3.25 for every $1,000 change in shareholder wealth. Hall and Liebman (1998), however, re-examine this relationship, finding "the level of CEO compensation and the sensitivity of compensation to performance have risen dramatically ... largely because of increases in stock option grants." They note:

> Our main empirical finding is that CEO wealth often changes by millions of dollars for typical changes in firm value. For example, the median total compensation for CEOs is about $1 million if their firm's stock has a thirtieth percentile annual return (-7.0 percent) and is $5 million if the firm's stock has a seventieth percentile annual return (20.5 percent). Thus, there is a difference of about $4 million dollars in compensation for achieving a moderately above average performance relative to a moderately below average performance. The difference in compensation between a tenth percentile firm performance and a ninetieth percentile performance is more than $9 million.

It should be noted that both Jensen and Murphy (1990b) and Hall and Liebman (1998) look not at responsiveness of compensation to corporate performance, but of the association of CEO wealth, which includes compensation but also includes stock and option holdings with corporate performance. Hall and Liebman (1998) conclude "that stock and stock option revaluations increase median CEO wealth by about $1.25 million in response to a 10-percent increase in firm value. This is 53 times larger than our estimated $23,400 increase in salary and bonus emanating from the same change in firm value ..."

While much of the above literature looks at the contemporaneous association between pay and performance, Boschen and Smith (1995), focusing on salary and bonus, show that CEO compensation responds to firm performance with a lag, that is over a period of four to five years, with the "cumulative response of pay to performance ... roughly 10 times that of the contemporaneous response." Additionally, Hayes and Schaefer (2000) note that, if compensation contracts incorporate measures unobservable to outsiders, measures that are correlated with future performance, then current compensation will be correlated with future performance. Consistent with their theory, they show that current compensation is associated with future performance. Consequently, both papers demonstrate that by examining the contemporaneous relationship between pay and performance, the prior research has underestimated the strength of the relationship.

One additional caveat should be made. Most of the above studies, in particular Jensen and Murphy (1990b), focus on stock price as a measure of performance. Yet, it is well known that stock price movements are caused by many factors, some of which are outside of the control of management and thus not reflective of management performance. Maximizing shareholder value in the principal-agent model requires a trade-off between incentive alignment and risk sharing, whereby the principal must compensate the agent for risk imposed upon the agent. Tying managerial pay to a variable out of the control of management imposes additional risk upon the agent, and thus may be an inefficient (and costly) way to align incentives. Consequently, the observed linkage between pay and performance, while low, may be optimal. Consistent with this logic, Aggarwal and Samwick (1999) demonstrate "the pay-performance sensitivity for executives at firms with the least volatile stock prices is an order of magnitude greater than the pay-performance sensitivity for executives at firms with the most volatile stock prices."

To summarize the above research, there is a link between pay and performance, although some researchers do not believe it is strong enough. Further, the research is based upon analysis across large groups of companies. That does not preclude executives, perhaps in firms with weak governance, from being paid for poor performance, or being paid despite missing their bonus targets.

Further, recent changes in compensation plans, in particular the substitution of restricted stock for options, have taken the incentive out of "incentive compensation." That is, while an option has no value if the share price does not appreciate, a share of restricted stock does. Consequently, the link between pay and performance may be weaker going forward.

The Politics of Executive Compensation

In the United States, executive compensation has been a political issue for some time. Scores of bills and resolutions have been introduced in Congress (see appendices 11.1 and 11.2 for examples) to directly limit compensation, and although none have passed, as discussed in earlier chapters, Congress did pass section 162(m) of the Internal Revenue Code in 1993, which limited deductibility of executive compensation in general, and Section 280(g) of the Internal Revenue Code in 1984, which limited deductibility of, and imposed excise taxes on, "golden parachutes" (see Appendix 11-3).[8] Another bill that did pass, the *Comprehensive Thrift and Bank Fraud Prosecution and Taxpayer Recovery Act of 1990* (public law no. 101-647), added section 18(k)(1) to the *Federal Deposit Insurance Act* which permitted the Federal Deposit Insurance Corp., to prohibit golden parachutes, which it did on Feb. 15, 1996.[9]

While most of the bills did not pass, many of them achieved their intended goals indirectly. For example, the goal of the *Corporate Pay Responsibility* Act (Bill No. S. 1198) was:

> To provide that the compensation paid to certain corporate officers shall be treated as a proper subject for action by security holders, to require certain disclosures regarding such compensation, and for other purposes.

Similarly, the goal of Protection Against Executive Compensation Abuse Act (Bill No. H.R. 4291) was to amend Securities Exchange Act of 1934 to require additional disclosure to shareholders of executive compensation.

While neither bill passed, both were closely followed by the Securities and Exchange Commission promulgated rules achieving the same goals. Companies must now include increased disclosure in their proxy statements, and include a report from the compensation committee (or equivalent) explaining how executive compensation was determined. (See Chapter 1 for a discussion of the rules governing this disclosure and Chapter 10 for a discussion and example of this report.) Further, shareholders may now raise issues pertaining to executive compensation at the annual meeting.

Similarly, the goal of the Corporate Executives' Stock Option Accountability Act (Bill Nos. S.259 and H.R. 2878) was to require that the stock option compensation paid to corporate executives be recorded as a compensation expense in corporate financial statements.

Once again, while the bill did not pass (actually, neither of the bills made it to the floor of their respective chambers), at approximately the same time, the Financial Accounting Standards Board made a similar proposal,[10] and beginning in 1997, required disclosure of the costs of stock option grants in the footnotes to the financial statements.[11]

Effect of the Political Process

While executive compensation is an extremely political issue, and actions have been taken by politicians and regulators, the effect of those actions is unclear. Take, for example, the increased/improved disclosure of executive compensation in proxy statements beginning in 1993. As shown in Table 2-8, executive compensation has increased dramatically since 1993, thus it does not appear the increased disclosures had the effect of reducing compensation. Of course, one never knows what compensation would have been in the absence of those disclosures, but there are those who believe that increased disclosure leads to increased compensation as executives find out what other executives are receiving and push for parity. Interestingly, while there was no evidence that the footnote disclosures of the cost of employee stock option grants has decreased the number of options granted, there appears to be some evidence that the expensing of options, or the anticipation of the expensing of options, has led to a decrease in the number of options granted. That is, examining Table 6-5, we see an upward trend peaking at either 2000 (mean) or 2001 (median) and declining since then. This is not to say the expensing of options has led to a decrease in compensation, merely a decrease in the number of options granted. As we have observed in recent years, there has been an upswing in other non-option forms of compensation. Carter et al. (2007), examining a group of firms that voluntarily began expensing options in 2002 and 2003, "find that these firms reduce their option use and increase their restricted stock use after starting to expense options but exhibit no decrease in total compensation."

Moving on to actual legislation, there are some who believe the tax code changes involving executive compensation have had perverse effects. For example, Harris and Livingstone (2002) argue that section 162 (m) has had the effect of raising compensation of CEOs earning less than $1 million, by setting that number as a benchmark. Rose and Wolfram (2000) conclude that the "limit on the deductibility of executive pay has led firms near the $1 million cap to restrain their salary increases, and perhaps to increase the performance components of their pay packages." Other researchers, Johnson, et. al (1997) and Perry and Zenner (2001), examined CEOs earning more than $1 million and found contradictory results as to whether section 162 (m) made compensation more responsive to firm performance. Using a more refined hypothesis and method, Balsam and Ryan (2007) find that section 162(m) did increase the sensitivity of pay to performance, but that increase was greatest for CEOs appointed after section 162(m) went into effect.

Research also suggests that the limit on the deductibility of golden parachutes, which is set at 2.99 times average pay, and the associated 20-percent excise tax on excess payments has not had the intended effect of reducing those payments. Rather, many corporations are willing to not only forgo deductions for excess parachute payments as defined under Section 280(g), but are also grossing up the executive's compensation to pay for the excise taxes levied on the executive. For example, when North Fork Bancorp was acquired by Capital One Financial, its chairman and CEO, John Kanas, received about $185 million, including tax gross-ups estimated at $111 million (Drucker and Bandler 2006). According to Morgenson (2004), this is the norm, as "contracts almost always require the companies to pay" the taxes associated with merger-related compensation payments.

Summary

The focus on executive pay in public corporations is good and bad. As a major expense and a tool for providing executives with proper incentives, executive compensation should be scrutinized carefully by shareholders and their representatives. On the other hand, too much scrutiny, artificial caps and slander may drive talented executives to other lines of work, where their compensation will be shielded from public view. For example, James Kiltz, formerly of Gillette, and Stephen Crawford, formerly of Morgan Stanley, are now with Centerview Partners, an investment banking firm. Among other commonalities is that their final compensation packages at Gillette and Morgan Stanley, respectively, were savaged as excessive by the press. Whether this is the motivation for their not taking jobs at public corporations, and Sorkin (2006) reports Kiltz had opportunities, is uncertain. However, it is a possible explanation.

The bottom line is that few object to high compensation when it is earned. The problem is that sometimes executives get huge sums of money regardless of performance. In that case, the losers are all of us, not just the shareholders, as our capital markets, which are a large part of our economy, become less efficient. Consequently, the public policy question is not whether it is appropriate to limit the amount of compensation that a company is able to deduct, but rather how can we utilize the tools available to us, be it the Internal Revenue Code or the Securities and Exchange Commission, to ensure that corporations are managed for the benefit of their shareholders.

Footnotes

1 The denominators used to calculate the percentages in Tables 11-1 through 11-6 are net income, common dividends and increase in shareholder wealth. The possibility of a small or negative value for each of these variables exists, with the potential to disproportionately influence the calculation of the mean. Consequently, medians, which are not disproportionately influenced by outliers, are more representative of the true patterns.

2 An alternative explanation is the sudden departure makes the firm more likely to be acquired at a premium to the current stock price.

3 Pages 31 and 32, DuPont proxy statement filed with the Securities and Exchange Commission, March 17, 2006.

4 Page 35, DuPont proxy statement filed with the Securities and Exchange Commission, March 17, 2006.

5 Page 38, DuPont 10-Q filed with the Securities and Exchange Commission, May 4, 2006.

6 While this is true, most of the theories introduced in Chapter 1, for example, tournament theory, do not posit a linkage between compensation and performance.

7 Abnormal returns are returns in excess of those explained by market movements.

8 Golden parachutes are payments to executives if they lose their jobs as part of a change in control of the corporation.

9 61 Federal Register 5927.

10 Financial Accounting Standards Board. 1993. Proposed Statement of Financial Accounting Standards: Accounting for Stock-based Compensation. Norwalk, Conn: FASB.

11 Statement of Financial Accounting Standards No. 123: Accounting for Stock-Based Compensation is required for all fiscal years beginning after Dec. 15, 1995.

Appendix 11-1

Selection of Bills Introduced, But Not passed, with the Potential to Affect Amounts, Deductibility or Disclosure of Compensation

Bill Number	Date Introduced	Goals
S. 2556 H.R. 5113	April 6, 2006 April 14, 2006	To amend title 11, United States Code, with respect to reform of executive compensation in corporate bankruptcies.
H.R. 4291	Nov. 10, 2005	To amend the Securities Exchange Act of 1934 to require additional disclosure to shareholders of executive compensation.
H.R. 3269	July 12, 2005	To amend the Internal Revenue Code of 1986 to deny employers a deduction for payments of excessive compensation.
H.R. 3031	June 22, 2005	To require the advance disclosure to shareholders of certain executive pension plans.
S. 991 (similar bill introduced on same date in House, H.R. 2233)	May 10, 2005	To amend title I of the Employee Retirement Income Security Act of 1974 to limit the availability of benefits under an employer's nonqualified deferred compensation plans in the event that any of the employer's defined benefit pension plans are subjected to a distress or PBGC termination in connection with bankruptcy reorganization or a conversion to a cash balance plan; to provide appropriate funding restrictions in connection with the maintenance of nonqualified deferred compensation plans; and to provide for appropriate disclosure with respect to nonqualified deferred compensation plans.
H.R. 913	Feb. 17, 2005	To direct the Securities and Exchange Commission to require enhanced disclosures of employee stock options; to require a study on the economic impact of broad-based employee stock option plans; and for other purposes.

H.R. 4208	April 22, 2004	To discourage the abuse of stock options by executives of public companies by preventing unjust enrichment through the recapture of profits when shareholders suffer losses.
H.R. 5432	Sept. 24, 2002	To amend the Internal Revenue Code of 1986 to require the same holding period for company stock acquired upon exercise of options as is applicable to company stock in its 401(k) plan; to require disclosure to shareholders of the amount of corporate perks provided to retired executives; and to provide parity for secured retirement benefits between the rank and file and executives.
S. 2901	Sept. 3, 2002	To provide that bonuses and other extraordinary or excessive compensation of corporate insiders and wrongdoers may be included in the bankruptcy estate.
S. 2877	Aug. 1, 2002	To amend the Internal Revenue Code of 1986 to ensure that stock options of public companies are granted to rank-and-file employees as well as to officers and directors, and for other purposes.
S. 2822	July 30, 2002	To prevent publicly traded corporations from issuing stock options to top management in a manner that is detrimental to the long-term interests of shareholders.
S. 2722	July 11, 2002	To amend the Internal Revenue Code of 1986 to ensure the proper tax treatment of executive compensation, and for other purposes.
S. 1940 H.R. 4075	Feb. 13, 2002 March 20, 2002	To amend the Internal Revenue Code of 1986 to provide that corporate tax benefits from stock option compensation expenses are allowed only to the extent such expenses are included in a corporation's financial statements.

H.R. 2691	July 31, 2001	To limit the amount of total compensation for top executives of air carriers that receive certain Federal relief.
H.R. 740	Feb. 11, 1999	To amend the Internal Revenue Code of 1986 to deny employers a deduction for payments of excessive compensation.
H.R. 3562	March 26, 1998	To amend the Internal Revenue Code of 1986 to allow a credit against income tax to C corporations which have substantial employee ownership; to encourage stock ownership by employees by excluding from gross income stock paid as compensation for services; and for other purposes.
H.R. 2788	Oct. 31, 1997	To amend the Internal Revenue Code of 1986 to promote the grant of incentive stock options to nonhighly compensated employees.
S. 576	April 15, 1997	To amend the Internal Revenue Code of 1986 to provide that corporate tax benefits from stock option compensation expenses are allowed only to the extent such expenses are included in corporate accounts.
H.R. 687	Feb. 11, 1997	To amend the Internal Revenue Code of 1986 to deny employers a deduction for payments of excessive compensation.
H.R. 620	Jan. 20, 1995	To increase minimum wage and to deny employers a deduction for payments of excessive compensation.
H.R. 3278	Oct. 13, 1993	To increase the minimum wage and to deny employers a deduction for payments of excessive compensation.

H.R. 1725	April 20, 1993	To limit excessive compensation and bonuses paid by the Resolution Trust Corp. and for other purposes.
S. 565	March 11, 1993	To amend the Internal Revenue Code of 1986 to improve disclosure requirements for tax-exempt organizations.
S. 259 H.R. 2878	Jan. 28, 1993 Aug. 5, 1993	To require that stock option compensation paid to corporate executives be recorded as a compensation expense in corporate financial statements.
H.R. 3331	Sept. 12, 1991	To amend the Internal Revenue Code of 1986 to simplify the definitions of highly compensated employees and compensation for pension plan purposes, and for other purposes.
H.R. 3056	July 25, 1991	To amend the Internal Revenue Code of 1986 to deny employers a deduction for payments of excessive compensation.
S. 1198/ H.R. 2522	June 4, 1991 June 4, 1991	To provide that the compensation paid to certain corporate officers shall be treated as a proper subject for action by security holders, to require certain disclosures regarding such compensation, and for other purposes.

Appendix 11-2
Resolutions Introduced to Limit Executive Compensation

Resolution	Date	Resolution
H. Con. Res. 118	July 1, 1993	Expressing the sense of the Congress that any limitation under federal tax law on the deductibility of compensation exceeding $1 million paid to executives individually should be expanded to apply to compensation paid to entertainers and athletes.

Appendix 11-3

Laws that Restrict Executive Compensation

Resolution Law Number	Date Enacted Into Law	Restrictions Placed Upon Executive Compensation
98-369	July 18, 1984	Limits tax deductibility of payments made contingent on a change in the ownership or control of the corporation, a.k.a. golden parachutes. No deduction is allowed for "excess" parachute payments (Internal Revenue Code Section 280G), and a 20-percent excise tax is imposed upon such payment (Internal Revenue Code Section 4999).
101-647	Nov. 29, 1990	Authorizes the Federal Deposit Insurance Corp. to prohibit or limit golden parachute or indemnification payments.
103-66	Aug. 10, 1993	Disallowance of deduction for certain employee remuneration in excess of $1 million (Internal Revenue Code Section 162(m)).
108-357	Oct. 22, 2004	Increased rules and regulations pertaining to the payment of deferred compensation (Internal Revenue Code Section 409A). Effect is to tighten the rules under which executive can avoid recognizing constructive receipt.
109-8	April 20, 2005	Modifies bankruptcy code to limit retention bonuses, severance pay and other payments to executives.

Chapter 12

International Comparisons

The once-yawning gap between U.S. CEOs and their counterparts abroad is fast closing. The stock options mania has spread globally. In an era when big business seeks talent wherever it can find it, companies no longer restrict their search to their own nationals. With this internationalizing of the executive talent market, companies everywhere must pay international scales.[1]

Introduction

Rules governing executive compensation vary across the globe. For example, while stock options are, and have been, a major part of the executive compensation package in the United States, it was illegal for companies in Germany and Finland to use stock options to compensate executives until 1998 (Ratnesar 2000). Even today, "executive stock options, outright stock ownership, and stock appreciation rights are missing ingredients in most CEO reward systems" for Chinese companies (Firth et. al. 2006), although this may change now that state-owned enterprises have been allowed to grant options (Fairclough 2007). Similarly, while (nonqualified) stock options result in a tax deduction for the granting corporation in the United States, in several countries, Britain for example, no tax deduction is allowed (Conyon and Murphy 2000).

A recent study by the consulting firm Towers Perrin (2006) estimates pay as of April 1, 2005, in industrial companies with approximately $500 million in sales. It estimates that CEOs for U.S. companies of that size earn $2,164,952, whereas Japanese CEOs earn $543,564, German CEOs $1,181,292, French CEOs $1,202,145, British CEOs $1,184,936, Indian CEOs $290,854 and Chinese (Shanghai) CEOs $211,255. A U.S. CEO makes 10 times that of his or her counterpart in Shanghai. Some, but not all, of these difference are driven by stock and other variable forms of compensation. For example, while a U.S. CEO receives 27 percent (in the Towers Perrin study) of his or her compensation in the form of base salary and 62 percent in the form of variable pay (the remaining 11 percent consists of benefits and perquisites), for CEOs in the United Kingdom, the comparable percentages are 43 percent and 35 percent. But note that given the larger total amounts earned by U.S. CEOs, even with the lower percentage, they still earn higher base salaries than most of their counterparts in other countries.

A separate study by Mercer Human Resource Consulting (2006) examined salaries and cash compensation for finance, marketing and human resources directors, finding, for all three positions, U.S. executives earned the most, and executives in India the least, among the 14 countries examined. And some of the differences were substantial. For example, a finance director receives an average of $324,600 in the United States, $262,700 in Canada (which is second highest) and $63,800 in India. The findings of both of these surveys is consistent with the general notion that executive compensation in the United States exceeds that of the rest of the world, although recent years have seen other countries adopting more of the "American" approach.

The International Politics of Executive Compensation
Similar to the United States, executive compensation in other countries has become very politicized, causing action on the part of regulators. For example, after an uproar over executive compensation in Britain, Kenneth Clarke, Exchequer chancellor, "decreed that henceforth share options would not be subject to capital gains tax but income tax" (Blackhurst 1995). A comparable example occurred when Spain, in response to the political uproar associated with the $17 million in stock option gains of Juan Villalonga of Telefónica, and his unwillingness to renounce that profit, doubled the tax on share-option gains (Ratnesar 2000). In France, the so-called Jaffré affair, which occurred when the CEO of Elf-Aquitaine, Philippe Jaffré, received a stock option package worth $35 million when his company was acquired by TotalFina, derailed government plans to lower the tax rate on stock option earnings from 40 percent to 26 percent and led to an unsuccessful campaign to increase the rate to 50 percent (Ratnesar 2000).

Perhaps most disturbing was the attempt by German authorities to criminalize the payment of bonuses by Mannesmann AG in connection with its takeover by the British firm Vodafone PLC in 2000. In this case, former officials were "accused of committing or abetting breaches of fiduciary trust" for making the bonus payments (The Economist 2004). While acquitted in their first trial, four officials, only one of whom actually received the disputed bonus, paid amounts ranging from 60,000 to 3.2 million euros out of their own pockets to avoid a second trial (Landler 2006).

Discussion of Compensation in Other Countries

While the Securities and Exchange Commission requires U.S. companies to disclose compensation paid to their top five executives, not all countries are as open in their disclosures (Orr and Holloway 1999). For example, in some countries compensation is disclosed for the board or management as a group, and thus the amount earned by any one executive is not easily determined. Therefore, evidence on the level and performance sensitivities of executives in other countries is not as easy to obtain. Consequently, the following discussion is based upon a much more limited data set than that available for United States companies.

Britain

Conyon and Murphy (2000) note that in 1997, Disney's Eisner single-handedly outearned "the aggregate paycheques of the top 500 CEOs in the U.K." While Eisner is clearly an outlier, they find "CEOs in the U.S. earn 45% higher cash compensation and 190% higher total compensation ...," although they also note that the pay-performance elasticity of cash compensation for U.S. CEOs is "more than double the elasticity for U.K. CEOs," and that U.S. CEOs have much larger ownership. They attribute many of the differences in pay packages to the greater use of stock options in the United States, that is, the "median option grant in the U.S. ... is nearly *twenty times* the median grant for U.K. CEOs ..."[2]

More recently, Ossinger (2006) notes the phenomenon continues to exist, with the average CEO in the United States earning $2.2 million versus $1.2 million for his (or her) British counterpart. Conyon et al. (2006) find that this difference has narrowed over the years because of "substantial increases in U.K. pay and incentives and flat U.S. pay and incentives," and that the difference in pay can be explained by "risk premiums related to their relatively greater equity incentives."

This explanation, that the differences are explained by the additional risk imposed upon U.S. CEOs, does makes some sense, as in theory, there is substitutability between CEOs in the United States, United Kingdom, Canada, etc., that share a common language and customs. However, it does not explain why the differences in risk exist in the first place. That is, what cultural, institutional or legal/regulatory differences exist? As noted above, stock options are treated differently in the United Kingdom than in the United States. The United Kingdom stock (or share) options do not result in a tax deduction for the issuing corporation and are taxed as ordinary income to the executive. In theory, this difference, which raises the after-tax cost of stock options, should lead to less use of options in the United Kingdom. Additionally, Ossinger (2006) notes that there is a greater concentration of shareholdings in the United Kingdom, as members of the Association of British Insurers and the National Association of Pension Funds together own about one-third of listed shares. As discussed in Chapter 9, concentrated ownership may result in increased monitoring and hence alleviate the need for the compensation package to provide incentives. Thus, in theory, greater concentration of ownership leads to less use of not just stock options, but variable compensation in general.

While not causing the observed differences in compensation which preceded it by many years, the regulation passed in 2002 that requires that U.K. companies have an advisory shareholder vote on the "Directors' Report on Remuneration" has the ability to widen the gap. There is some belief that even this advisory vote will have a dampening effect on executive pay in the United Kingdom (Gordon 2006), and some evidence that it has so already. One good example is when the shareholders of GlaxoSmithKline were asked to approve a proposed golden parachute for CEO J.P. Garnier, and they immediately rejected it (Naik 2003). This caused the board to submit a plan with reduced benefits for shareholder approval (Flynn and Naik 2003).

Canada

The Towers Perrin (2006) survey previously cited found that Canadian CEOs earned approximately half of U.S. counterparts, $1,068,964 versus $2,164,952. This is despite Canada and the United States sharing a common language and having similar customs (not to mention a long border). They do have differing tax and regulatory systems, however. For example, the Canadian system is more progressive, with higher tax rates for executives. Further, with respect to stock options, Mawani (2003) notes that in contrast to U.S. companies, Canadian companies do not receive a tax deduction at any time for stock options granted to employees. Still, Klassen (2002) finds that all of the top 100 companies on the Toronto Stock Exchange grant options. Zhou (1999) finds, when comparing corporations in Canada with those in the United States, that "Canadian CEOs were paid substantially lower than their U.S. counterparts." He also found that when comparing Canadian to U.S. corporations, salary made up a higher proportion, and bonuses and options a lower proportion, of the compensation package for Canadian corporations. Overall, he concludes that the relationship of pay to performance is weaker in Canada than it is in the United States.

Germany

The Towers Perrin (2006) survey previously cited, found that German CEOs earned slightly more than half of their U.S. counterparts, $1,181,292 versus $2,164,952. As with the United Kingdom and Canada, a large part of the gap is caused by the lower use of stock options. As noted above, until 1998 it was illegal for German corporations to use stock options. However, they quickly began issuing options once allowed to. More than 80 percent of the DAX 30 companies now have stock option programs (Preen and Glaeser 2005). "The main reason is globalization. When Daimler Benz took over Chrysler Corp. last year, CEO Jurgen E. Schrempp had to confront the fact that Chrysler CEO Robert Eaton, who earned over $11 million in 1997, including exercised options, appears to have made more than the rest of Daimler's management board members put together. Worse, Daimler had to pay out $395 million, primarily in stock, to Chrysler's top 30 executives to cash out their options. Since cutting the pay of Chrysler managers wasn't possible, Daimler was forced to boost pay for its own execs" (Ewing et al. 1999). Some cynics may wonder if this was indeed the motivation for the merger.

Japan

"For years the pay package of Japanese chief executives ... have lagged badly behind those in the U.S." (Bremner 1999). Nakazato et al. (2006) are more direct: "Japanese executives earn far less than U.S. executives—holding firm size constant, about one-third the pay of their U.S. peers." Further, until recently, Japanese companies did not make much use of stock options. It was not until a 1997 amendment to the Japanese Commercial Code that companies could grant options on as many as 10 percent of their outstanding shares for up to 10 years. Although much more restricted than in the United States, for example, the law requires that corporations at the date of grant own enough shares to cover the options granted; formerly, Japanese companies were only allowed to hold a maximum of 3 percent of their own shares, and for no more than six months at a time (*The Economist* 1997). Subsequently, from 1997 through 2001 Kato et. al. (2005) found 644 firms adopted stock option plans, in general, offering modest amounts of grants. That is, in contrast to the United States where corporations on average have options outstanding equal to 16.36 percent of outstanding shares (see Pearl Meyer & Partners 2004), Kato et. al. (2005) found the Japanese firms in their sample offered options equal to approximately 0.6 percent of their outstanding shares. Overall, the Japanese seem to lag in the use of performance pay, as Nakazato et. al. (2006) note "executive pay in Japan depends on firm size, ... but not on accounting profitability or stock returns."

Why Do These Differences Exist?

Part of the reason for these differences is cultural, part regulatory and part tax. It is simply unacceptable in many countries to earn the amounts American executives make. This culture is reinforced by, or perhaps results in, a system that restrains and taxes such compensation. For example, as noted above, until rather recently, few Japanese and German corporations were able to issue options, and few Chinese companies do today. As alluded to above, in Japan, a corporation had to purchase and hold in its own treasury sufficient shares to fund its stock option program. However, the amount it could hold, and the period it could hold it for, was extremely limited. Even now, it is limited to owning 10 percent of its stock, a large amount, but much less than many U.S. companies (Carpenter and Yermack 1999 note the typical large U.S. corporation reserves more than 10 percent of its equity for stock plans). Other countries have their own quirks that make options less valuable. For example, in Germany, shares have to beat an index before the holder can profit from his or her options. In Singapore, options are limited to five years (Yeo et. al. 1999), and in Holland, options are taxed upon vesting.

Can These Differences Continue to Exist?

Corporations, or at least, large corporations, are increasingly becoming more multinational. Not only do they sell their products and services in all corners of the globe, many of them maintain securities listings in multiple countries and boast shareholders and board members of many nationalities. Assuming these trends continue, the differences in executive compensation will, by necessity, shrink. Lipschultz (2002) reports that CEOs from nearly 100 foreign countries run American corporations, and American corporations will increasingly search worldwide for executives. This will have two effects. First, increasing the potential supply of executives should decrease the wages paid. Second, to compete, foreign corporations will have to raise their compensation levels to retain their executives.

While not as common (Lipschultz 2002), foreign corporations occasionally hire American executives to run some or all of their operations, which requires paying U.S. levels of compensation. Browne (2004) reports:

> After quitting his job running Microsoft China, Tang Jun, a naturalized U.S. citizen, joined Chinese online gaming company Shanda Interactive Entertainment and picked up 2.6 million stock options now valued at more than $90 million.

While Solomon (2005) reports:

> In one recent case, an Indian company offered an American executive a base salary of $350,000 plus a potential bonus of $2 million over two years to join its U.S. operations, according to an executive with knowledge of the deal. The executive's salary at his U.S. company was $300,000 annually plus stock options equal to around $1.2 million over four years.

China and India have been particularly persistent in attracting U.S. executives. In some cases, the U.S. executives recruited are Chinese or Indian born (for an example, see Kaufman 2003) who came to the United States earlier to study.

Additionally, as foreign corporations enter the U.S. market, they will have to increase their levels of compensation to attract American executives to staff their U.S. subsidiaries. They will then have to increase compensation in their home country to avoid having the executives in their U.S. subsidiary making more than their corporate superiors. If they are traded on U.S. exchanges, shareholders may pressure them to use more performance-based pay. Fackler and Barboza (2006) note that:

> Companies with large overseas presences, like Sony or Honda, are more likely to have adopted American-style stock options and performance-linked bonuses. That is because they have large numbers of foreign shareholders, who have raised the pressure in recent years to increase pay based on performance.

However, this means the differences should decrease over time, although not entirely. Executives from different countries are not perfect substitutes, with language and culture creating impediments to cross-country hiring of executives. Similarly, culture and regulatory environment, which differ across countries, govern the compensation of executives within a country. For example, Bryan et. al. (2002 & 2006) find that the use of equity compensation varies predictably across countries, and is heaviest in those countries with "equity-oriented capital markets" and where "shareholder rights are strong." Tax rates differ across countries, as does the taxation of various items of compensation. Thus, while we should see a convergence between compensation paid to executives of U.S. and non-U.S. companies, the degree of convergence will depend on language, culture and regulatory environment.

Summary

This chapter has examined compensation across the globe, noting that compensation for U.S. executives exceeds, sometimes by a factor as great as 10, compensation of executives in other countries. Some explanations are offered for these differences, such as differences in culture that will not permit the levels of compensation paid in the United States, differences in tax and regulatory systems that discourage certain forms of compensation used in the United States such as stock options, and differences in share ownership that leads to more concentrated ownership for non-U.S. corporations. While the market for executive services is a global market, executives are not a commodity. Thus, while they may be substitutes, they are not perfect substitutes because of differences in language and culture. Consequently, while we do observe movement of CEOs both to and from the United States, and that movement will drive compensation outside the United States closer to U.S. levels, differences may always exist.

Footnotes

1 Kroll (1998).

2 It is worth noting that Conyon and Schwalbach (1999) find in their study of European countries that the use of long-term incentives is the most prevalent in the United Kingdom.

Chapter 13

Comparison to Other Occupations

According to Institutional Investor's Alpha *magazine, hedge fund manager James Simons earned an estimated $1.5 billion in 2005, while the average pay for the top 26 managers in their survey was $363 million. (Taub 2006)*

Introduction

By most standards (certainly this author's), executives of publicly traded corporations make a lot of money. The question, as posed earlier in this book, is do they make too much? As a way of shedding light on this question, Chapter 11 examined the relation between pay and firm performance, whereas Chapter 12 examined compensation internationally. This chapter sheds additional light on this issue by making comparisons to highly paid individuals other than executives of publicly traded corporations.

Managers of Privately Held Companies

Privately held companies compete with publicly held companies for managerial talent. Further, given that concentrated ownership leads to more monitoring and control by owners, it is less likely a manager would be able to extract excessive pay from these firms. In the past, privately held companies have been smaller than publicly held corporations. However, with advances in private equity markets, the largest privately held companies rival all but the largest publicly held companies. According to Reifman and Wong (2006), there were 396 privately held companies with at least $1 billion of revenue in 2005, with the largest (by revenue) being Koch Industries, with an estimated revenue of $90 billion and 85,000 employees. By comparison, the mean corporation in the ExcecuComp database had revenue of $6.4 billion and 19,000 employees in 2005. And less than 1 percent of the companies had more than $90 billion in revenue, and just 5 percent of the companies had more than 85,000 employees.

Thus, privately held companies provide a good benchmark for comparison. Unfortunately, pay on data of privately held companies is hard to come by, but extremely relevant, as these companies compete with Corporate America for managerial talent. Yet anecdotal and survey evidence suggest that the amounts they pay equal and/or exceed that of public corporations, perhaps because they are not encumbered by public disclosures.

One example, provided by Kranhold and Lublin (2006), discusses how privately held Dutch media firm VNU NV lured General Electric Vice Chairman David Calhoun to be its chairman and chief of its executive board. Reportedly courted by companies such as Boeing and 3M, Calhoun was lured by a package speculated to be at least $100 million, which included $50 million to replace compensation he left behind at GE. A survey by Watson Wyatt Worldwide (2004) found the CEO of a private company with at least 10,000 employees received mean (median) salary of $735,500 ($656,300), which compares favorably to salary for CEOs of publicly held companies, where the mean (median) from Table 2-8 was $685,181 ($635,114) in 2003. However, the mean bonus of $411,500 received by privately held company CEOs was significantly lower than that observed in Table 2-8, $872,487. While the latter is consistent with CEOs of privately held companies requiring less variable compensation because of a higher level of monitoring by the concentrated ownership, it also means that cash compensation is lower for private versus public CEOs. Also, CEOs of privately held companies are less likely to have stock-based incentive plans. And yet, a number of large, publicly held companies have been taken public over the years by their managers, for example, RJR Nabisco. Why would managers do so if their compensation goes down? The answer is when the company goes private or when the executive accepts a position at a privately held company, the executive gets a significant equity share.

Investment Managers

A 2006 *Wall Street Journal* article (Grant and Buckman 2006) alluded to a problem that exists with respect to pay of public institutions, not just corporations. That is, pay is de facto capped to avoid controversy. The article discussed how the manager of Stanford University's endowment, Michael McCaffery, was leaving to join Makena Capital Management LLC, an investment fund. The reporters noted that "the most successful managers can make hundreds of millions of dollars a year. Managers of college endowments rarely make more than $2 million in salary and bonus." A year earlier, Harvard University had lost its endowment chief, Jack Meyer, who resigned to start his own investment firm. While making less at Harvard than many investment fund managers, the multimillion-dollar pay he received and paid his top managers caused controversy among Harvard alumni, employees and students (Bulkeley 2004, Zimmerman 2006). The controversy was not necessarily unreasonable, given the then-president of Harvard, Lawrence Summers, only received $637,824 in total compensation in 2004.[1] Consequently, the question is, are they worth it, or conversely, how much does the firm/university lose or gain by not having access to these individuals? With endowments in the $15-billion (Stanford) to $25-billion (Harvard) range, a one percentage point increase in return is worth $150 million or $250 million, a significant sum. According to Stein (2005), Harvard's endowment during the previous 10 years "earned an average return of 16.1 percent a year.[2] That compares to a median return of 9.4 (percent) for institutional investors and 12.5 percent for the 25 largest endowments." And according to Grant and Buckman (2006), Stanford's endowment had a "70-percent cumulative investment gain during" McCaffery's tenure, "compared with a 15-percent decline in the Standard & Poor's 500-stock index during the same period."

Lawyers

Average profits per partner at the top-earning 100 law firms exceeded $1 million in 2005 (Frankel 2006), with Wachtell Lipton Rosen & Katz leading the list at $3.8 million per partner (Willing 2006). Examples also exist of class-action lawyers winning paydays exceeding that of all but a few of the most highly paid CEOs. For example, it has been estimated (Cohen 2000) that Dickie Scruggs will receive "about a third of the $1.2 billion being paid to his firm" as a result of the tobacco settlement. Similarly, Lenzner and Maiello (2006), in discussing the Redux litigation note that if the plaintiffs attorneys "took the typical 33-percent fee, then they raked off $333 million in legal fees."

Sports and Entertainment

In 1930, Babe Ruth was asked to justify his new annual salary, $80,000, for which he was paid to hit baseballs a long way, in light of the fact that the president of the United States was making a mere 75 grand. "I had a better year than he did," Ruth replied.[3]

One of the interesting things about this quote is that in 1930, it was newsworthy that Babe Ruth, by any definition one of the greatest athletes of his time, was being questioned for earning $5,000 more than the U.S. president. In 2005, the average NBA salary was $4.9 million, average major league baseball salary $2.6 million and average NFL salary $1.4 million (Weinbach 2005), all in excess of the U.S. president, who earns $390,000.[4] However, this is no longer news, because in the world of sports and entertainment, individuals barely out of, or still in, their teens can make millions.[5]

For example, in 2003, before he was even drafted for the NBA, LeBron James, 18 at the time, signed a $90-million, seven-year endorsement deal with Nike (Tkacik 2003). Similarly, just after turning pro, 16-year-old golfing sensation Michelle Wie signed multiyear deals with Nike and Sony Electronics that pay her an estimated $10 million per year (Goodison 2005). *Advertising Age* (Thomaselli 2005) estimates that 18-year-old Maria Sharapova earned $20 million in endorsements after winning Wimbledon in 2004. Led by Tiger Woods, the top 10 athletes all earned in excess of $25 million in 2005 (Hoffer 2006). Most recently, soccer star David Beckham signed a deal that would pay him $250 million over five years (Zinser and Lyall 2007).

Movie stars such as Julia Roberts can make $20 million or more for a single movie (Rickey 2001). Lippman (2001) estimates that actor Tom Hanks made more than $40 million from his performance in the movie *Cast Away*. Topping this, Marr (2006a) reports, "The studio's forecast anticipates Mr. (Tom) Cruise and his production company earning as much as $80 million" from *Mission: Impossible III*.

The July 3, 2006, issue of *Forbes* magazine reports the following earnings for the following athletes/entertainers for 2005:[6]

Steven Spielberg, Director/Producer	$332 million
Howard Stern, Talking Head	$302 million
Jerry Seinfeld, Comedian	$100 million
Tiger Woods, Athlete	$90 million
Dan Brown, Author	$88 million
Tom Cruise, Actor	$67 million

Difference Between Executives and Other Highly Paid Individuals

There are two major differences between executive pay and pay for the individuals discussed above. In many of the cases above, we can see the difference an individual makes, for example, the number of books sold by an author, or tournaments won by a golfer. It is harder to see what an executive does, and what impact he or she has on the organization.

A second major difference between executive pay and the examples above is that unlike the executive, the above individuals have little control over the parties that pay them. That is, they do not set their own pay, or exercise influence over those that do set their pay. For example, when Paramount Pictures paid Cruise as much as $80 million for *Mission: Impossible III*, it was an arms-length transaction between two independent parties—one that could and was ended when the studio felt that Cruise no longer warranted that level of compensation and Cruise was unwilling to take the amount offered (Marr 2006b).

On the other hand, when the board of directors of a major corporation awards compensation to its chairman of the board and CEO, the parties are not independent. They are not independent for many reasons. First of all, as noted in Chapter 9, directors may be employees of the corporation and hence answer to the CEO. Alternatively, while the director may be an outside or "independent" director, he or she may still not be independent of the CEO. For example, the director may be an executive of another corporation, upon whose board this CEO serves. This is known as an interlocking directorate. In some extreme cases, the CEOs will sit on each other's compensation committees (Fierman 1990). Alternatively, the outside director may have some other business relationship, such as being a partner in the corporation's outside law firm. In both of these situations, the outside director is not totally independent of the corporation whose board he or she serves, and hence has been termed a "gray" outside director by many (see, for example, Core et al. 1999). Even when the relationship is not overt, as in an interlocking directorate or documented business relationship, Larcker et al. (2005) demonstrate that "backdoor" links or relationships between directors can influence, i.e., increase, executive compensation.

As Leonhardt (2006) states:

> It's difficult, in fact, to come up with a single example of a company and its chief executive splitting up over pay. Chief executives retire and are fired. But as long as they remain on the job, they evidently don't end up disagreeing with their boards about how valuable they are. The negotiation over a chief executive's pay is one that never seems to fail, which, of course, means that it isn't much of a negotiation at all. It's more like a friendly conversation.

Summary

If you compare executives to others at the top of their professions, their compensation does not seem as outrageous as when you compare them to the average worker. A major difference between executive compensation and that of others discussed in this section is that executives, especially CEOs who are also the chairmen of the board, have more influence over their own compensation than many of those discussed above. Thus, when the university president agrees to pay his endowment manager more than he makes himself, he is doing it voluntarily, presumably in the best interest of the university. In contrast, that presumption may not always hold with respect to executive compensation. Christopher Cox, Securities and Exchange Commission chairman, summed it up well when he said:

The difference with executive compensation, ... "is that boards of directors of public companies don't always negotiate at arms' length with their executives. And as a result, the executives are often able to influence the level of their own compensation." Scannell (2006).

Footnotes

1 Form 990 filed with the Internal Revenue Service for fiscal year ending June 30, 2004.

2 In the year after he left, Harvard's endowment achieved an investment return of 16.7 percent (Levitz and Hechinger 2006).

3 Sullivan (2000/2001).

4 H.R. 5658, Treasury and General Government Appropriations Act of 2001, raised the compensation of the president from the $200,000 earned by William Jefferson Clinton.

5 Interestingly enough, high-powered individuals are willing take enormous pay cuts for high-profile government jobs. For example, Henry Paulson left a position as head of Goldman Sachs that paid him more than $38 million in 2005 to become secretary of the treasury, a position that paid $183,500. Others taking substantial pay cuts for high-profile government positions include Vice President Richard Cheney, formerly CEO of Halliburton, and New Jersey Gov. Jon Corzine, formerly CEO of Goldman Sachs.

6 The Celebrity 100: Top Earners by Category.

Part V
Considerations in Designing the Executive Compensation Package

Chapter 14

The Effect of Corporate and Executive Characteristics on Designing an Optimal Compensation Contract

Introduction

A good compensation package is customized to take into account the characteristics of the corporation and executive. Trade-offs need to be made based upon those characteristics. In particular, the optimal contract involves a trade-off between incentive alignment and risk sharing. That is, while the corporation wants to provide the executive with incentives to increase firm value (incentive alignment), it does not want to put too much risk on the executive, as (1) it may affect executive decision-making in a suboptimal way,[1] and (2) in equilibrium, the corporation must increase remuneration to compensate the executive for bearing that risk. Yet, to provide incentive alignment, a portion of the compensation package should be linked to firm performance. Consequently, to minimize executive risk, the corporation may want to use multiple measures of firm performance. Further, the measures and weights used should take into account the informativeness of those measures, as well as their noisiness[2] in evaluating executive performance. Research shows (for example, Lambert and Larcker 1987, Sloan 1993, Aggarwal and Samwick 1999) that the weights placed on performance measures in contracts are consistent with the trade-off between noise and informativeness.

Consider the following example. An oil-exploration company is designing a CEO compensation package. To simplify things, we assume that future firm profitability is a function of only two factors, the company's success in finding oil and the price of oil. While the CEO has some impact on the former, for example, by deciding where to drill, he or she has little impact on the latter. However, the traditional performance measures, accounting earnings and stock prices, while being affected by the success in finding oil, are also greatly impacted by oil prices. Thus, accounting earnings and stock prices, while providing some information about CEO performance, are noisy measures. Further, they reflect oil discoveries at different points. Assuming market efficiency, stock prices increase at the time the oil is discovered. In contrast, accounting earnings only reflect the discovery when the oil is produced, which may not begin for some time after the oil is discovered. Further production would occur over a period of years, including after the CEO retires.

Despite the weaknesses of these measures, oil companies continue to use them to measure performance and reward executives. For example, Exxon-Mobil uses accounting measures such as net income in determining short-term bonus awards.[3] While not explicitly using stock price as a performance measure, it makes grants of restricted stock to its executives, effectively tying compensation to stock price performance. Exxon-Mobil is not alone among the large, integrated oil companies in its use of accounting and stock price performance measures. Chevron uses "earnings, return on capital employed (ROCE), cash flow, operating expense and other key operating measures."[4] Only Hess in its compensation committee report even mentions an "increase in year-end proven reserves and extension of the company's reserve life,"[5] which is a more direct and, hence, better measure of the company's exploration success, and one unaffected by oil prices, accounting regulations or broad stock market trends.

Why do companies persist in using accounting earnings and stock prices, which are known to be noisy measures? One reason is that any indirect measure of performance is imperfect, and direct observation of performance is impractical and perhaps impossible. Previously, we assumed that there were only two factors that influence performance—success in finding oil and and the price of oil. Yet only one of the corporations previously mentioned even alluded to oil reserves in its discussion of compensation. A potential explanation is that oil exploration is risky, and directly tying compensation to success in finding oil imposes too much risk on the CEO. For example, because of the boom or bust nature of oil exploration, major oil discoveries do not occur every year. Thus, tying compensation to oil discoveries would result in an extreme variation in compensation from one year to the next. Thus, the fact that few corporations use a measure indicates that they feel the noise in the measure, or the risk imposed upon the executive by using the measure, outweighs the benefit from using the measure to provide incentives to the executive.

As noted above, to minimize risk and maximize incentive effects, corporations may use a combination of measures, subjective and objective, to evaluate performance. As an example, consider the following overview of compensation philosophy included as part of General Electric's compensation committee report:

Overview of Compensation Philosophy and Program

We believe that the quality, skills and dedication of our senior executive officers are critical factors affecting the long-term value of our company. Our key compensation goals are to attract world-class executive talent; retain our key leaders; reward past performance; incent future performance; and align our executives' long-term interests with those of our investors. We use a variety of compensation elements to achieve these goals, including base salary, annual bonuses, contingent long-term performance awards, stock options, restricted stock units, performance share units, deferred salary plans and a supplementary pension plan, all of which we discuss in detail below.

Our decisions on senior executive officer compensation are based primarily upon our assessment of each executive's leadership and operational performance and potential to enhance long-term shareowner value. We rely upon our judgment about each individual—and not on rigid formulas or short-term changes in business performance—in determining the amount and mix of compensation elements and whether each particular payment or award provides an appropriate incentive and reward for performance that sustains and enhances long-term shareowner value. Key factors affecting our judgment include: performance compared to the financial, operational and strategic goals established for the executive at the beginning of the year; nature, scope and level of responsibilities; contribution to the company's financial results, particularly with respect to key metrics such as cash flow, revenue, earnings and return on total capital; effectiveness in leading our initiatives to increase customer value and productivity; contribution to the company's commitment to corporate responsibility, including success in creating a culture of unyielding integrity and compliance with applicable laws and our ethics policies; and commitment to community leadership and diversity.[6]

General Electric uses a variety of compensation elements and a multitude of performance measures, including financial and nonfinancial, to measure performance. That is, General Electric's incentive program includes salary, bonus, contingent long-term performance awards, stock options, restricted stock units, performance share units, deferred salary plans and a supplementary pension plan. To reduce the riskiness of any one performance measure, General Electric, like most companies, uses multiple market, accounting and nonfinancial measures. It also uses objective measures like performance compared to the financial, operational and strategic goals established for the executive at the beginning of the year;

nature, scope and level of responsibilities; contribution to the company's financial results, particularly with respect to key metrics such as cash flow, revenue, earnings and return on total capital; and subjective measures like creating a culture of unyielding integrity; compliance with applicable laws and ethics policies; and commitment to community leadership and diversity. Baker et al. (1994) show that the use of objective and subjective performance measures can reduce risk, as the "firm can subjectively evaluate the incentive distortions caused by the imperfect objective performance measure."

The remainder of this chapter addresses the impact of corporate goals, and corporate and executive characteristics, on the optimal contract. In particular, the focus is on determining how much and how to pay. How much is important, because setting pay too high imposes unnecessary costs upon the corporation, while setting it too low increases the probability of executives being lured away by competitors.[7] How is equally important because the compensation package is used to provide the proper incentives to executives. How is also important because the form of compensation affects accounting earnings, cash flow and the after-tax cost to shareholders.

Goals

A precursor to designing the executive compensation package is to determine the package's goals, that is, what forms of behavior the board of directors want to encourage. While a maintained assumption is that all boards want to encourage the maximization of shareholder value, they may have different approaches, depending on the characteristics of the corporation and the market(s) in which it operates. For example, if the corporation operates in a mature industry, the board may seek increased efficiencies, growth in market share in existing markets or expansion into new markets. It may also want to encourage (or minimize) risk-taking on the part of management. Once these goals are set, the board then tries to achieve them at a minimum cost to shareholders, which involves minimizing cash outflows and/or maximizing tax deductions. An important item to be recognized in designing the package is that the different components of the package must be coordinated with each other and with the goals of the corporation.

Effect of Corporate Characteristics on the Optimal Contract

Most corporations use multiple forms of compensation and multiple performance measures, but which corporate characteristics influence the level of pay, the components of the compensation package, the performance measures to be used and the extent to which they are to be used?

Size

The firm's size influences the compensation package in several ways, some of them subtle. First, in general, the larger the corporation, the greater the set of skills necessary to manage it effectively. Second, the larger the corporation, the greater the effect of the manager in dollar terms. That is, a managerial decision that increases shareholder value by 10 percent translates into a greater dollar increase in value for a billion-dollar corporation than for a million-dollar corporation. Both of these factors should increase the level of compensation. In fact, Table 2-10 shows that in 2005, mean (median) total CEO compensation increases from $1,331,332 ($926,136) for corporations in the smallest decile to $14,938,239 ($12,488,782) for the largest corporations. On a more subtle level, as the size of the corporation increases, percentage of managerial ownership drops due to wealth constraints. Referring to Table 9-4, the mean (median) value of shares and options held in 2005 by CEOs in the smallest corporations was $8,363,596 ($1,865,224), while the mean (median) value of shares and options held by CEOs in the largest firms was $867,035,259 ($63,693,078). In contrast, Table 9-2 shows that the mean (median) percentage ownership of shares and options of CEOs in the smallest corporations was 5.55 (3.24) percent, while the mean (median) percentage ownership of shares and options of CEOs in the largest firms was 1.70 (0.46) percent. Thus the composition of the compensation package must be adjusted to provide incentives to increase equity value.[8] This, of course, can be accomplished by adding or increasing the amount proportion of stock-based compensation in the compensation package. In fact, Table 2-7 shows that for the smallest corporations, the mean (median) proportion of the value of the 2005 CEO compensation package comprised of stock options was 19 (11) percent, whereas for the largest corporations it was 33 (32) percent. Similarly, large corporations were more intensive users of restricted stock, as the mean (median) proportion of the value of the 2005 CEO compensation package comprised of restricted stock grants was 9 (0) percent for the smallest corporations and 18 (13) percent for the largest.

Political Costs

Political costs are related to the corporation's size. Everything about large publicly traded corporations is visible, including its executive compensation, which is publicly available via proxy statements filed with the Securities and Exchange Commission and widely disseminated via surveys published in business publications such as *Forbes, BusinessWeek* and *The Wall Street Journal*. When compensation is high, political costs may be imposed upon the corporation and executive. Political costs include the taxes the corporation and the executive pay, and regulations that either require or prohibit the corporation from taking certain actions. Section 162(m) of the tax code is an example of a cost imposed upon corporations and their executives because of executive compensation. It limits deductions for executive compensation and, consequently, increases the corporation's tax bill. To minimize political costs, boards, in designing or adding components to existing packages, must "justify" that compensation to stakeholders (Zajac and Westphal 1995). They do so in one of two ways: the first is to justify the package in terms of the need to attract and retain qualified executives; the second is to justify the components by making reference to how the components will align the interests of management and shareholders. Microsoft, in proposing its 2001 Stock Plan to shareholders, incorporated both. Microsoft states that the plan will "allow the Company to continue to attract and retain the best available employees and provide an incentive for employees to use their best efforts on the Company's behalf."[9]

Westphal and Zajac (1994) suggest some corporations may add incentive-based compensation plans for symbolism rather than substance. They adopt long-term incentive plans to "symbolically" control agency costs.

Political costs have the potential to reduce executive compensation. Depending upon the market for executive services, executives may be made to bear all, some or none of the political costs in the form of lower compensation and/or higher risk. For example, if the market for an executive's services is perfectly inelastic, the executive bears none of the cost and the corporation takes on the entire cost. This would arise when there is a competitive market for his or her services, for example from entities not subject to similar political constraints, such as privately held corporations, consulting firms, investment banks or law firms, none of whom must publicly disclose compensation. In this environment, to get an executive to accept lower compensation, the corporation would have to reduce the risk of the compensation package. Thus, one side effect of the political pressure to reduce executive compensation is to make the compensation package less responsive to performance, that is, reduce incentives to increase shareholder value. Alternatively, the executive might be willing to accept less explicit compensation if combined with more perquisites, for example, a bigger office. However, if the executive values a dollar spent on perquisites less than a dollar in compensation, the increase in the amount the corporation spends on perquisites will exceed the decrease in compensation, reducing shareholder value.

In contrast, if the market for an executive's services is perfectly elastic, the executive will bear all the costs. In reality, the market for an executive's services is neither perfectly elastic nor perfectly inelastic. Thus, the executive and corporation will bear some of the costs and, hence, have the incentive to work together to reduce those costs.

Risk

The riskier the corporation, the greater the amount of risk imposed upon an underdiversified executive via performance-based compensation and stock ownership. Consequently, risk-averse executives will demand greater levels of compensation to compensate themselves for bearing that risk. Risk can take many forms. For example, there is the risk of bankruptcy, whereby the most likely outcome is that the executive loses his or her job, and most, if not all, of his or her investment in the corporation. More generally, there is the riskiness of the corporation's share price, which impacts executives via their stock ownership and stock-based compensation. This risk can be decomposed into systematic and unsystematic components, where the former is market related and the latter a function of the corporation's unique characteristics.

The systematic risk of the corporation, also known in finance circles as Beta, is the movement of the corporation's share price in response to overall market movements. For example, the share price of a corporation with a Beta of 1, which is by definition average, will increase by 20 percent in response to an overall increase in the market of 20 percent. In contrast, the share price of a corporation with a Beta of 2 will increase by 40 percent for that same market increase of 20 percent. As noted elsewhere, stock price movements are a noisy measure of a corporation's/executive's performance. The higher the systematic risk, the noisier a measure it is. Consequently, the higher the Beta, the lesser the extent compensation should be based upon share price performance, and the less the stock-based component of the compensation package should be (Lewellen et al. 1987).

In contrast, the effect of unsystematic risk on the compensation package is a bit more ambiguous. While unsystematic risk reduces the desirability of stock ownership and stock-based compensation to the executive, unsystematic movements in a corporation's share price reflect the performance of the corporation and, hence, are less noisy than systematic movements that mirror those of the overall market. Consistent with this, Lewellen et al. (1987) find that while the proportion of stock in the compensation package decreases with Beta, they find it increases with the variance of stock returns.

From the above discussion, it is clear that structuring stock-based compensation to filter out the systematic risk would be optimal. As discussed in Chapter 6, such market-adjusted options have not been observed in practice, perhaps because of their unfavorable accounting treatment, or because corporations can always informally adjust for downside risk via repricings.

Share price fluctuation is not the only risk a corporation should be concerned with when designing the executive compensation contract. It needs to be aware of the riskiness of all measures used in performance evaluation and bonus allocation. For example, if conditional compensation is based upon accounting income, and certain drivers of accounting income are beyond an executive's control, then accounting income becomes a noisy measure of performance.

Growth and Liquidity

Empirical research shows that the level of compensation, and the use of conditional compensation, varies with the investment opportunity set of the corporation. Finkelstein and Boyd (1998) note in corporations where managers have a large amount of discretion, their potential impact on the organization is greater, as will be their marginal product and compensation. Smith and Watts (1992) and Gaver and Gaver (1993 and 1995) show that corporations with more growth options have higher executive compensation. Smith and Watts (1992) also show that corporations with more growth options have a greater use of bonus and stock option plans, while Gaver and Gaver (1995) show that corporations with more growth options pay a larger portion of their total compensation in the form of long-term incentives. Baber et al. (1996) find stronger associations between pay and performance, and more use of market, rather than accounting-based, performance indicators for high-growth corporations.

Unfortunately, stock-based compensation is most risky for these same growth corporations. As an illustration, Pulliam and Thurm (2000) note that in 2000, the "25 worst-performing Internet stocks … are down a staggering 95.7%." Because of this risk, one might expect growth corporations to use less market-based compensation. While some might argue that this market risk implies the need for more accounting-based compensation, for many growth companies the traditional accounting model does not work well.

Consider the following example. A newly established company invests significant amounts in product development and marketing, with the goal of establishing a brand name for itself and its products. If the investments are successful, the corporation will acquire a large market share, and be able to charge a premium price in the future. Generally accepted accounting principles, while allowing the current capitalization (and future expensing) of expenditures on fixed assets, requires the immediate expensing of most research and development and marketing expenses. Thus, while a $100,000 expenditure on a new warehouse will only reduce current income by the current depreciation expense, which could be $2,500 if the company depreciated the warehouse over 40 years, a $100,000 expenditure on marketing would reduce current income by $100,000. Basing compensation, or a large portion of compensation, on accounting-based measures would provide disincentive to invest in product development and marketing. This problem is greatest for growth firms, or alternatively, firms with the most investment opportunities.

If there are problems and risks associated with using market and accounting-based compensation, it would imply growth corporations should include more fixed cash compensation in their compensation packages. But from the empirical research cited above and anecdotal evidence, this does not appear to be the case. One potential explanation revolves around another corporate characteristic—liquidity.

Fast-growing corporations, with many investment opportunities, are often cash constrained. Thus, many have argued that because of liquidity constraints, they can only pay minimal cash compensation, and instead must give large stock and option grants to attract employees.[10] This added risk may in part, or in whole, explain the above findings of Smith and Watts (1992) and Gaver and Gaver (1993 and 1995) that growth corporations pay higher levels of compensation. Mitigating this risk may also be an explanation for the stock option repricings and additional grants of options, often observed after the share price drops. For example, Horn (2000) reported that Sprint allowed "employees to cancel stock options granted to them in 2000 in exchange for an equal number of new options in the future" and that "Microsoft doubled its annual stock-option grants to 3,400 full-time employees in a bid to keep workers after its stock price tumbled on a variety of bad news."

Labor Intensity

Growth corporations are not the only corporations for which the accounting model does not work well. Consider labor-intensive firms, whose investments in training (also known in academic jargon as "human capital") are expensed immediately rather than capitalized and expensed over time. Using accounting measures in setting compensation provides a disincentive to invest in human capital.

Ownership and Board Composition

As noted in earlier sections of this book, concentrated ownership, and monitoring by the board of directors, can act to provide incentives to maximize shareholder value, independent of the compensation package.[11] Thus, the existence of large, nonmanagement shareholders and/or an active board of directors may mitigate the need for the compensation package to provide those incentives. Large shareholders, because they internalize more of the gains from monitoring, are more likely to expend resources on monitoring management. Consistent with the reduced need for the compensation package to provide executives with incentives, Beatty and Zajac (1994) find the existence of a large shareholder is associated with a lower percentage of the compensation package being performance based. Kraft and Niederprum (1999) find when a large shareholder dominates a corporation, the corporation pays less, and has a lower pay-performance sensitivity. Kato (1997) points out that the ownership and control structure of financial keiretsu, which are groups of firms organized around their major lender and having extensive cross-shareholdings, is an effective constraint on executives and executive pay. As evidence, Kato then shows that pay is lower for executives in these firms than those in Japanese firms not affiliated with any financial keiretsu.

Concentrated shareholdings may, in fact, substitute for other forms of monitoring. Hebner and Kato (1997) note that the average corporate board in Japan includes less than one (0.7 to be exact) outside director, perhaps because of the extensive cross-shareholdings of financial keiretsu. Kaplan (1999) suggests that, in Japan, where capital markets are relatively illiquid and hence market-oriented control mechanisms are less useful, corporate and bank ownership in Japan plays the major monitoring and disciplinary role.

The ability and incentive of the board to monitor executives affects the need to use the compensation package to align the interests of executives and shareholders. An example of where monitoring may be weak, and thus the compensation package especially important in providing the proper incentives, occurs when the CEO also holds the position of board chairman. Research summarized in Chapter 10 has found that, whether it is because of the additional responsibilities they shoulder or the influence they have over the remainder of the board, CEOs, who are also board chairmen, earn higher compensation than their counterparts who are not also board chairmen. Other research cited in Chapter 10 shows that the sensitivity of CEO turnover to corporate performance was lower when the same person holds both jobs. Considering the evidence, and incentives, when the CEO is also the board chairman, his or her compensation package should consist mainly of performance-based compensation. Beatty and Zajac (1994) find empirical evidence consistent with this hypothesis.

The composition of the remainder of the board of directors influences the ability of that board to monitor executives, and hence, the importance of the compensation package in providing incentives. An independent board is one in which independent directors are defined as directors whose primary employment is not with the corporation and who do not conduct business with the corporation. It has the ability to monitor executives. However, the directors may lack the incentives to do so. Perhaps the relevant factor in terms of incentives is the amount of shares they own. If one or more directors own a significant amount of stock, they have the incentive to monitor executives, to look after their investment. Alternatively, if board ownership is low, and most, if not all, of the directors have been appointed by the current CEO, then they lack the incentive to monitor the CEO, and the importance of the compensation package in providing incentives is paramount. Beatty and Zajac (1994) find the percentage of incentive compensation increases with the percentage of inside, that is, nonindependent, directors.

Regulated Industries

As noted in Chapter 1, the need for incentive alignment via the executive compensation package arises from the fact that monitoring by definition is imperfect. The board cannot review every decision, and even if it could, it may lack the expertise and/or firm-specific knowledge necessary to evaluate those decisions. Still, variation does exist in the ability of boards and shareholders to monitor executive behavior across corporations. This variation may arise from variation in the ability/incentives of the board and/or from the variation in the investment opportunity set of the corporation. The better the boards and shareholders are able to monitor management, the less the need for incentive alignment via executive compensation packages. Consider, for example, regulated or government-owned firms. Managers of these firms may find their decision-making ability limited by an inability to lay off workers, increase prices or shift production overseas. In some cases, if they do too well, regulators may even force them to reduce future rates and/or return excess profits to ratepayers.

Consider the following example of a rate-regulated utility, which also faces a ceiling on the amount of profit it can report, a profit that is a function of its rate base (normally capital investment). Basing compensation on reported profit may not be optimal, as there are political and regulatory constraints upon how much profit the utility can make. However, because the amount of allowed profit increases with the rate base, the plan needs to provide incentive for capital investment. Yet the plan should only encourage relatively low-risk investments, as the payoff function to the firm is asymmetric. Regulators limit the upside payoff to investments but may not necessarily limit the downside losses.[12] Thus for two reasons, stock options—also with an asymmetric payoff function but tied to the upside potential of the corporation—are a suboptimal compensation strategy. The first reason is that the payoff structure of at-the-money or out-of-the-money stock options encourages risk taking. The second reason is the limited upside potential for the share price of a regulated utility. The optimal package, from the view of shareholders, needs to encourage managers to minimize the variances of cash flows and earnings. Such a package is likely to include more fixed components, that is, salary, than that of the average unregulated corporation.

Consistent with this, evidence has shown that regulated corporations use less incentive compensation. Abdel-Khalik (1988), in examining executive compensation in regulated utilities, notes that few firms in his sample use stock options. He also finds that compensation is positively associated with overcapacity, consistent with the incentive noted above to increase the rate base. Similarly, an analysis of 2005 compensation for public utilities (SIC code 4900-4999) shows that the portion of the compensation made up of salary (mean 31, median 26 percent) is at the high end, and that of stock options (mean 12 percent, median zero) is at the low end when compared to the industry groupings shown in Table 2.6.[13] It should be noted that these percentages have changed dramatically to reflect the deregulation that has taken place during the 1990s. In 1992, the corresponding mean (median) percentages were 58 (62) percent for salary, and 9 (0) percent for stock options.

This finding is consistent with the academic research showing changes in the compensation package when regulations are lifted. For example, Cragg and Dyck (2000), who examine British firms that were privatized from 1982 to 1984, find that prior to privatization, when managers were relatively constrained in their decision-making, there was no pay for performance. In contrast, after privatization, when many of the political constraints on their decision-making were lifted, the level of compensation and intensity of their pay for performance measure increased. Bryan et al. (1999) find similar results for electric utilities, and Ezzell and Miles (1995) for banks, in the United States.

Financial Distress

Corporations in financial distress, that is, in bankruptcy or close to it, have many problems, one of which is the retention of key employees. As an example, McCracken and Lublin (2006) recently reported on retention issues at Ford Motor Co. One issue is "top managers at Ford can get 40% to 100% of their salary in bonuses—if the auto maker does well." However, when the firm does not do well and does not pay bonuses, top managers lose a large chunk of their income.[14] Similarly, when the firm is not doing well, any options the manager holds are likely to be worth less. The corporation can increase fixed compensation to retain key employees or pay retention bonuses. However, if the corporation seems to favor executives while trying to negotiate concessions with other employees and/or suppliers, it may run into political problems. For example, McCracken (2006) reports that disclosure that Delphi would provide "$60 million in additional compensation to its salaried employees and managers" would likely "complicate Delphi's efforts to extract concessions from the United Auto Workers union." Norris (2006) reports that the justice department, unions and creditors have joined to oppose a proposed pay system for top executives of Dana Corp., currently in bankruptcy protection. The basis for the opposition is a provision of the Bankruptcy Abuse Prevention and Consumer Protection Act of 2005, which "bars retention bonuses for corporate insiders unless the company can show that the executives in question have a bona fide job offer that would pay at least as much as they were already receiving."

From a compensation/employment viewpoint there are two major issues. The first is that financial distress imposes more than the normal amount of risk on employees, in terms of both job loss and the loss of any amounts directly (stock, options) or indirectly (pensions) invested in the corporation. The second is that they may have little cash with which to pay those employees. Further, for the corporation to maximize its chances of survival, it needs to retain key employees. While the above applies to all employees in the corporation, executive departures are particularly painful because they may cause a ripple effect. That is, a well-publicized executive departure can send negative signals[15] about the corporation's chances of survival and lead to lower-level employees departing.

How should the corporation in financial distress structure the compensation package? The first and second issues provide conflicting directions. That is, because of the risk involved, the employee would place an extremely high discount rate on the value of any equity-based compensation. In other words, the employee would require much more in the way of uncertain stock-based compensation than he or she would in the form of certain cash compensation. Unfortunately, because of its financial circumstances, as well as the political and regulatory environment, the corporation normally would need to conserve cash.

The situation is somewhat similar with startup corporations, that is, the risk of failure is great and the amount of cash is normally low. Thus, the compensation package at these corporations will normally have a large equity component. However, there are several differences between a startup and a corporation in financial distress. The first is the optimism surrounding a startup, which contrasts with the pessimism surrounding a corporation in financial distress. That is, while employees are optimistic about the chances of success for a startup and, hence, a large payoff when the corporation makes it big, for example, when the corporation goes public. Employees are less likely to envision a big payoff for a corporation already in financial distress. Another difference is that a startup, by virtue of its ability to start with a clean slate, is able to attract employees who are less risk averse (more willing to endure risk) than an existing corporation with employees who may have been attracted to it because of its stability.

Because of its risk, the corporation in financial distress must include a risk premium in its compensation package, that is, additional remuneration to compensate for the risk involved. Depending upon its cash situation, it may have to pay much of it in the form of equity, promising a large portion of the firm to employees if the corporation succeeds.

Effect of Executive Characteristics
on the Optimal Compensation Contract

This section builds on the earlier discussion by more fully incorporating executive characteristics into the design of the compensation package. Factors to be considered include the executive's opportunity cost, risk aversion, horizon and share ownership.

While executive characteristics are important, it should be noted that incorporating individual characteristics into the package is more difficult than incorporating the corporation's characteristics. While the corporation can tailor its package(s) to its circumstances, or the characteristics of its executives as a group, tailoring the package to specific individuals becomes expensive from a design and political point of view. From a design point of view, the board or the consultants it hires has to analyze each executive's characteristics and then design a plan for that particular individual. From a political viewpoint, designing individual plans can be costly if it breeds the perception of favoritism, or inequity, across the executive ranks.

Still, incorporating executive characteristics, including tailoring the contract to the specific characteristics of an individual, can be beneficial. A prudent approach would be to tailor the plan to the general characteristics of the group, making modifications where appropriate and justifiable.

Opportunity Cost

In the context of attracting a new CEO, Chapter 3 briefly discussed the need for the value of the compensation package offered to exceed the executive's next best opportunity, which is his or her "opportunity cost." When an individual's opportunity cost is "established," the contract can, but does not have to, be customized to the individual executive. Consider the following example. The vice president of marketing, highly regarded inside and outside the corporation, is offered a comparable position at a competitor, but at a 20-percent raise. His or her opportunity cost has been established, and given the corporation wants to retain the executive, it matches the offer. Previously, all vice presidents (marketing, finance, manufacturing) were making comparable compensation. The corporation has justification for paying this vice president more than the others because he or she has attracted an outside offer, and the corporation needs to act to retain him or her. Unfortunately, as discussed in an earlier chapter of this book, paying one executive more than his or her colleagues on the same level breeds resentment and the perception of inequity. In the extreme, the executive is viewed as being rewarded for being disloyal, that is, seeking out alternative employment. The other vice presidents may then look for competing offers, diverting their attention from their corporate responsibilities. If they are successful in attracting new offers, the corporation then must decide whether to match them or lose the executive. If they do not attract new offers, they may become discouraged, which may adversely affect their job performance. Thus, when increasing the compensation of one executive, the corporation may find it wise to increase the pay of all executives at that level, to maintain internal equity. One factor that should influence the decision to increase the compensation of executives on the same level is the number of executives on that level. It is more costly to the corporation if there are 100 executives at the same level than it is if there are three executives at the same level.[16] Another factor that should influence the decision is whether the corporation determines that its current pay is too low.

But how does a corporation make the determination that pay is too low? In some cases, where the corporation is trying to attract a new executive who is employed elsewhere, or is trying to retain an executive who is being offered a position outside the company, that individual's opportunity cost is usually easy to determine.[17]

Consider that, when attempting to hire an executive from outside the corporation, one measure of the executive's opportunity cost is his or her current compensation. The example, given in Chapter 3, of Robert Rubin and Citigroup illustrates this is not always the case. Rubin was previously employed as the U.S. Secretary of the Treasury, earning $151,800 per year. Yet, for 2000 alone, Citigroup promised him a $1-million salary, $14-million bonus and 1.5 million stock options. In this case, Rubin's opportunity cost was best measured by what he could have earned elsewhere, rather than what he was earning as treasury secretary.[18] However, this case is the exception; usually current compensation is the opportunity cost.

In most other circumstances, that is executives without competing offers, determining the opportunity cost is not as simple. But it is important. Paying the executive too much reduces shareholder value. Paying too little makes it more likely the executive leaves, or gets a more costly offer the corporation elects to match. Corporations can, and do, use a variety of means to determine an executive's opportunity costs. Regularly (Clarke et al. 1998), corporations, or more likely the consultants they hire (Ezzamel and Watson 1998), conduct surveys of what comparable firms (based on size and industry) pay their executives, using that information to set compensation accordingly. In addition, the media publicly reports on executive compensation (for example, *Forbes*, *BusinessWeek*, *The Wall Street Journal*). Surveys in trade journals often report compensation for lower-level executives.

Risk Aversion

The effect of risk aversion on the compensation package is complex and originates with the effect of risk aversion on executive incentives. Risk aversion, in the absence of any incentives (monetary or otherwise) to take risk, will cause executives to pass up projects that increase their risk, even those that increase shareholder value. The solution is to provide compensation in which value increases with the risk of the corporation, such as stock options. However, Beatty and Zajac (1994) note, "linking a manager's compensation too closely to firm performance might lead to risk-avoiding behavior on the part of the manager." They suggest "the ability of firms to use executive compensation contracts to address managerial incentive problems is hampered by risk-bearing concerns that stem from the risk aversion of top managers."

The primary effect of executive risk aversion is on the composition of the compensation package, that is, the compensation package will contain less conditional or risky compensation than it would if the executive was risk neutral. This occurs because a risk-averse individual will demand a higher expected payout if the compensation package is risky than he or she would if the package was risk free. This expected payout will increase with the risk of the payout and the executive's risk aversion. In equilibrium, corporations will use risky compensation only up to the level where the marginal benefits equals their marginal cost, which is the higher level of expected compensation. Similarly, in equilibrium, executives will self-select into positions appropriate for the level of risk they are willing to bear.

The corporation must be extremely careful in designing a package to control for risk aversion. Conventional wisdom is that stock options, because their value increases with the risk of the firm, provide incentives to take risk. However, consider the case where an executive holds in-the-money stock options, that is, options in which the exercise price is less than the current market price. The executive then has something to lose if the share price goes down, which may make him or her reluctant to take risks. For this reason, at-the-money or out-of-the money options provide the appropriate incentive for the executive to take the risks necessary to increase firm value. One mechanism to ensure that an executive's option portfolio does not provide disincentive to take risk is to grant reload options. As discussed earlier, reload options enable the holder to exercise in-the-money options and receive new at-the-money options, that is, new options exercisable at the current market price.

Horizon/Age

An executive's horizon is the amount of time he or she expects to spend in a particular job. It has been noted (for example, Dechow and Sloan 1991, Murphy and Zimmerman 1993, Pourciao 1993) that executives approaching retirement have differing incentives. In particular, they have less incentive to invest in a project with a payback that comes after their retirement. For example, Dechow and Sloan (1991) find evidence that CEOs spend less on research and development in their final years in office. While theoretically, in an efficient market, the present value of those payoffs should be reflected in the stock price at the time of investment, the market may not be efficient, or the decision maker may not believe it is. In addition to passing up potentially profitable projects, executives have the incentive to manipulate accounting income to pull future income into current periods. This would increase their bonuses, and potentially, if they can fool the market, inflate the corporation's stock price. Of course, pulling income from the future into the current period reduces future income and potentially the future stock price. One way to mitigate these incentives is to tie the executive's payoffs to income and/or stock price after retirement. For example, the executive may be given options and/or restricted stock that do not vest until after retirement, at which time any manipulation will presumably be revealed. Consistent with firms acting to mitigate these problems, Lewellen et al. (1987) find that the percentage of current compensation in the compensation package decreases with executive age, and Cheng (2004) finds a positive association between changes in option compensation and research and development expenditures as the CEO approaches retirement.

An additional consideration increasing the importance of the compensation package is the decreased incentives provided by the managerial labor market as the executive gets older. In general, while the managerial labor market provides some discipline/incentives in the form of attracting outside offers, the older the executive, the less relevant those incentives are (Beatty and Zajac 1994, Lewellen et al. 1987). This can be because an older executive is less likely to attract an offer, or even if he or she does receive an offer, he or she would have fewer years to earn the new higher level of compensation associated with that offer, thus making it less valuable than it would have been to a younger executive.

Ownership

Executive ownership theoretically provides the incentive to increase shareholder value. In the extreme, it provides all the incentives necessary. Thus, firms like Berkshire Hathaway and Amazon.com, because their CEOs own such large stakes in the firm, do not need to use their compensation package to align the interest of those CEOs with shareholders. As noted earlier, Warren Buffett of Berkshire Hathaway and Jeff Bezos of Amazon.com receive relatively small salaries and no conditional compensation at all. However, there is still the need to provide incentives to lower-level executives who will not have such a large stake in the firm. For example, in 2005, Amazon.com made restricted stock grants to its next two highest-ranking executives, Richard L. Dalzell and Diego Piacentini.[19] Still, when the CEO has such a large stake in the firm, he or she has the incentive, and presumably the ability, to monitor lower-level executives. Thus, there is less need for incentive compensation in the compensation package of these lower-level executives, and less need for other shareholders to monitor executives.

Dollar and percentage executive ownership play a role in determining executive incentives, and the need to augment those incentives through the compensation package. When executive ownership is large in dollar terms, it is likely that the executive has a large portion of his or her wealth tied to the firm. In that case, the executive, while having the incentive to maximize shareholder value, will also be more risk averse than a diversified shareholder would like. As noted by Beatty and Zajac (1994), "the magnitude of the existing equity positions held by top managers may influence their willingness to accept further risk bearing." To provide the executive with the appropriate incentives, two divergent approaches might be tried. The first is the standard approach of giving the executive more options, as out-of-the-money, or at-the-money, options encourage risk taking. This may only have a marginal effect on an executive with an already large investment in the firm. An alternative, which is consistent with the empirical evidence in Lewellen et al. (1987), Beatty and Zajac (1994) and Toyne et al. (2000), would be to reduce the equity portion and increase the cash-based portion of the executive's compensation to reduce his or her risk.

When executive ownership is large in percentage terms, it is likely that the executive's incentives are aligned with those of shareholders, as he or she shares in wealth gains and losses to that extent. Once again, there is less need for incentive compensation. There is one caveat, however. Research has shown (for example, Denis et al. 1997) that as executive ownership increases, executives are less likely to be replaced.[20] Thus, the incentive to work hard to avoid being fired is lessened.

In contrast, when executive ownership is low, ownership provides little incentive to increase firm value. Thus, the compensation package must provide those incentives via stock options and stock grants.

Effect of Joint Characteristics on the Optimal Contract

This next section discusses how the firm's tax characteristics and its executives interact to influence the executive compensation contract.

Tax Status

The effect of taxes on the compensation package is discussed separately from the firm and executive characteristics above because the tax status of the corporation and the executive jointly influence the compensation package. Taxes matter, because if the compensation package can be structured to minimize the taxes paid by the corporation and the executive, which is referred to as the joint tax burden, those tax savings can be shared by the two parties, making both better off. However, the corporation and executive must be careful and not ignore the incentives provided by the compensation package. That is, while tax savings are important, they should not be pursued without taking incentive effects into consideration.

Tax-Qualified Options

We begin with a discussion of tax-qualified options. Tax-qualified options provide certain benefits to employees, that is, if the employee need not pay taxes on the exercise profit until the shares are sold, and if the shares are held for more than a year, the gain is taxed at capital gains rates. However, the employer does not receive a deduction if the option is tax qualified. The use of tax-qualified options thus increases the corporate tax burden. However, if the corporation is in a low tax bracket, or more appropriately, anticipates being in a low tax bracket at the time of exercise,[21] tax-qualified options minimize the joint tax burden. In many cases, especially when the corporation is in the top tax bracket, the increase in corporate taxes may exceed the savings to the executive from the option. Yet, tax-qualified options have certain incentive effects that may still make them worthwhile. The ability to defer taxation as long as the executive owns the shares creates what is known as the lock-in effect, a disincentive to sell those shares, and consequently may also increase the possibility the executive remains with the firm. As Balsam et al. (1997) show, in some cases the benefits from incentive alignment and executive retention outweigh the tax costs, and cause firms to grant what appears to be tax disadvantageous compensation.

Deferred Compensation

In minimizing the joint tax burden, the current and future tax rates of the executive and the corporation must be taken into consideration. An interesting situation surrounded the adoption of the Tax Reform Act of 1986. The act, which was phased in from 1986 to 1988, dramatically reduced the top marginal tax rate for corporations and individuals. An individual in the top bracket saw his or her rate drop from 50 percent in 1986 to 28 percent in 1988, whereas a corporation in the top bracket saw its rate drop from 46 percent to 34 percent. Because of the lower tax rates on income for an individual in the top bracket, deferring income from 1986 to 1988 saves $22,000 in taxes for every $100,000 deferred. However, from the corporation's perspective, because of the lower tax rates, deductions are less valuable. That is, while a $100,000 deduction in 1986 saves $46,000 in taxes, one in 1988 only saves $34,000 in taxes, a difference of $12,000. From a joint-tax perspective, the savings for every $100,000 deferred from 1986 to 1988 is $10,000, the difference between the $22,000 the executive saves and the $12,000 additional the corporation has to pay.

A more common situation arises when an executive defers income until retirement, under the assumption that he or she will be in a lower bracket at that time. In this situation, the assumption is that the corporation's tax status does not change, thus the deduction is equally valuable, but the executive's tax rate drops, resulting in less tax paid.

Fringe Benefits

The use of nontaxable fringe benefits, for example health and life insurance, almost by definition reduces the joint-tax burden. The reason is that while the payments are deductible to the corporation, they are not taxable to the employee. Holding total compensation constant, taxes paid by the corporation are unchanged, while those paid by the executive are lower, because some of his or her compensation is in the form of a nontaxable fringe benefit. However, as noted by Scholes and Wolfson (1992), while tax beneficial, the contracting costs of these plans may outweigh the tax benefits. First are the compliance costs. These are the costs of drawing up plans and ensuring that they meet Internal Revenue Code requirements. A major cost is the requirement that to qualify for favorable tax treatment, that is exclusion from income by the executive, the benefits have to be offered on a nondiscriminatory basis to essentially all employees. The corporation is willing to incur these costs because, in equilibrium, the executive will accept less explicit compensation. To be more precise, the corporation is only willing to incur these costs if they are less than the reduction in explicit compensation the executive(s) are willing to accept. However, while the benefits have to be offered across the board, the valuation of the benefits, and hence the reduction in compensation the employee is willing to accept, differs by employee. For example, while health insurance might be valued highly by an executive with a nonworking spouse and two dependent children, a single employee would place a lower valuation on those benefits, and an employee covered by a spouse's plan would place an even lower valuation.

Corporate Tax Status

Consider now the corporation's tax status. Because of the structure of our federal tax system, the marginal tax rate for most profitable corporations is 35 percent. But some corporations pay no federal taxes; for example, newly established corporations that have yet to achieve profitability, or established companies that are in financial distress. Those corporations cannot currently use the tax deductions associated with executive compensation.[22] Their preference would be for forms of compensation that generate future, rather than current, deductions. These forms could include stock options and restricted stock, or more simply, the deferral of salary and bonus. That is, nonqualified stock options generate tax deductions in the future when they are exercised, restricted stock generates tax deductions when the restrictions expire and deferred compensation generates deductions when payment is actually made.

Summary

The focus of this chapter was on how corporate goals, and corporate and executive characteristics, influence the level and composition of executive pay. Corporate characteristics that influence executive pay include size, political costs, risk, growth, liquidity, tax status, ownership, board composition, regulation and degree of labor intensity. Executive characteristics include opportunity cost, risk aversion, horizon and ownership.

In general, larger corporations should and do pay a higher level of compensation. In addition, because the wealth constraint limits the percentage ownership in the corporation, larger corporations should and do make a higher proportion of the compensation package equity based. Fast-growing corporations, perhaps because of the risk involved, pay a higher level of compensation, with a larger component of that compensation being equity based. To mitigate some of the risk involved, these corporations often resort to additional option grants and/or option repricing after share price decreases. When ownership is concentrated, or the board of directors takes an active role in monitoring, there is less need to provide incentives via the executive compensation package. Labor-intensive corporations, and corporations with large investments in marketing or research and development, should minimize their use of accounting numbers in performance evaluation and reward, or alternatively adjust, those numbers before using them. Regulated corporations, given the constraints on their operations, have less need for conditional compensation. Further, performance measures have to be carefully tailored to what the regulatory environment allows. Corporations in financial distress, because of cash constraints, must include a large equity component in their compensation package, despite the risks involved.

Additionally, the executive compensation contract should consider the characteristics of executives individually and as a group. While it is costly to tailor contracts to individual executives, in some circumstances it may be worthwhile. In those circumstances, the corporation should take into account the executive's opportunity cost in setting the level of compensation. The corporation should also consider the executive's risk aversion, horizon and ownership in determining the composition of the compensation package.

It is important to recognize in designing the package that the different components of the package should be coordinated, so that the incentives they provide do not conflict with one another, or with the corporation's goals. For example, a corporation trying to encourage long-term growth, which requires major investments in research and development, should utilize long-term performance measures. It should not utilize short-term measures of accounting performance, due to the accounting requirement that research and development be expensed immediately, the effect of which would be to discourage such investment if the executive were compensated based upon accounting income. Alternatively, if accounting measures are to be used, adjustments should be made for research and development. For example, rather than using reported accounting income, the corporation could use income before research and development.

Decisions have to be made as to participation in plans. For example, is the bonus plan limited to the CEO, the top five executives or all executives earning above a certain amount? A related decision is how much, either in dollars or shares, does the corporation want to spend on the plan? The decisions are related in that, all else equal, the greater the number of participants, the greater the cost to the corporation. And how are amounts allocated from the plans? Do all participants get equal allocations, or are the allocations based upon rank, salary, performance, etc.? In many corporations, bonus targets are set based upon the participant's salary. For example, Brocade Communications Systems recently amended its compensation plan "to increase the annual incentive target for Michael Klayko, chief executive officer, from 75% to 100% of his base salary, effective beginning Oct. 29, 2006."[23] Related to the allocation, what, if any, performance criteria should be used in determining the size of the plan, and allocating amounts to participants? For example, a corporation can set aside a specific proportion of profits for its bonus plan. It may then allocate the bonus to participants based upon rank, individual performance evaluations, etc.

Footnotes

[1] Mishra et al. (2000b) find that when too much risk is placed on the CEO, firm performance suffers.

[2] For example, stock returns are a "noisy" measure of executive performance as they are influenced by economywide and industry factors, as well as executive decisions.

[3] Page 16, Exxon Mobil proxy statement filed with the Securities and Exchange Commission, April 12, 2000.

[4] Page 18, Chevron proxy statement filed with the Securities and Exchange Commission, March 20, 2006.

[5] Page 18, Hess proxy statement filed with the Securities and Exchange Commission, March 27, 2006.

[6] Page 21, General Electric proxy statement filed with the Securities and Exchange Commission, March 3, 2006.

[7] With the ensuing cost of either matching the offer, or recruiting and training a replacement.

[8] Dollar and percentage ownership are important in terms of incentives. The differing incentives and effects of each are discussed later in the chapter.

[9] Microsoft proxy statement filed with the Securities and Exchange Commission, Sept. 28, 2000.

[10] As noted earlier, Core and Guay (2001) find that firms that are cash constrained are more likely to use stock options to compensate their employees.

[11] This section will discuss ownership by individuals not employed by the firm, whereas the next will discuss the effect of executive ownership on incentives.

[12] Examples abound in the 1980s of regulated power utilities, for example the Long Island Lighting Company and the Public Service Co. of New Hampshire, investing billions in nuclear power generating facilities that were never opened. Because these facilities were never opened they were never included in the rate base (or only partially included in the rate base), which pushed the companies into bankruptcy and caused major losses to shareholders.

[13] SIC codes 4900-4999 are included in the broader industry grouping 4000-4999 in Table 2-6.

[14] McCracken and Lublin (2006) report that Ford has only paid a bonus in two of the previous five years.

15 The higher the level of the executive, the more information that executive is perceived to have (by other employees, investors, lenders and suppliers) about the firm and its chances for survival.

16 This same factor, the number of contemporaries of the executive in question, should influence whether or not the corporation matches the offer. As the number of contemporaries increases so does the cost of matching the offer, either in terms of disgruntled contemporaries who are paid less, or in terms of the cost of increasing the pay of those contemporaries.

17 Where the executive is employed at another company, his or her opportunity cost is his or her existing compensation. When a current executive is offered a position outside the company, his or her opportunity cost is the new offer.

18 Individuals often take high-level jobs in the government that pay substantially less than they could make in the private sector. Another example is Richard Cheney, who resigned as Halliburton chairman and CEO to run for U.S. vice president. In his final full year at Halliburton, Cheney received a salary of $1,283,000, other compensation of $640,914 and options for 300,000 shares, with a potential realizable value of between $7,452,401 and $18,885,848 (pages 20 and 21 of Halliburton proxy statement filed with the Securities and Exchange Commission, April 3, 2000). Now, as vice president, he earns a salary of $171,500 per year.

19 Page 8, Amazon.com proxy statement filed with the Securities and Exchange Commission, April 20, 2006.

20 As executive ownership increases, the executive is said to be more "entrenched."

21 Recall that with nonqualified employee stock options the corporation takes a tax deduction at the time of exercise. Thus, in deciding which type of option minimizes the joint tax burden, the corporation must estimate the time of exercise and tax rate at that time. Given the difficulties involved in such estimation, the corporation could always grant qualified options and, later, if nonqualified options appear to be more advantageous, induce employees to disqualify those options, which would allow those options to be treated as nonqualified for tax purposes. Matsunaga et al. (1992) document such activity after the Tax Reform Act of 1986, which reduced the relative tax advantages of qualified stock options.

22 While the tax code allows losses (the excess of deductions over taxable income) to be carried forward for 20 years, the present value of a future deduction is less than one, and if the company never becomes profitable, those deductions will never be used.

23 Form 8-K, Brocade Communications Systems filed with Securities and Exchange Commission, Nov. 24, 2006.

Chapter 15

Designing a Compensation Contract

The key to a company achieving its strategic goals often lies in its ability to attract and retain experienced senior executives—and this, in turn often depends on the quality of its compensation and benefits programs.[1]

Introduction

This chapter will extend, and be a more detailed discussion, of the factors that enter into the design of the executive compensation contract. As discussed in Chapter 3, the executive compensation contract has four major objectives. It must be (1) attractive enough to employ the executive initially, (2) provide the proper incentives, (3) tie the executive to the corporation and (4) minimize the costs to the corporation. In designing the compensation contract, these four objectives must then be integrated with the corporation's goals, and the corporate and executive characteristics discussed in Chapter 14.

Salary

As noted in Chapter 2 (see Table 2-2), the overwhelming majority of compensation contracts include a salary component. The issue is then how much or what portion of the compensation package should be in the form of salary. Many factors, executive and corporation specific, are incorporated into the decision. An underlying constraint in determining salary is that an individual's salary is not determined in isolation. That is, other executives' salaries and reactions must be taken into consideration.

Impact of Executive Characteristics
Opportunity Cost

Let's start by considering the impact of executive characteristics on salary. Whether the individual is a current employee, or one the corporation wishes to recruit, the individual's opportunity cost must be taken into consideration. Generally, an individual will not accept a lower salary than is offered elsewhere, although if the other components of the package are more attractive, the individual may accept the lower salary. However, the onus is on the corporation to make those other components more attractive, as many times those other components are tied to salary. As an example, consider the following passage linking bonus, or as they refer to it, annual award opportunity, to base salary, which appeared in the proxy statement of R.H. Donnelley.

> The target annual award opportunity for the Named Executive Officers range from 60% (45% in cash and 15% in deferred shares) to 100% (70% in cash and 30% in deferred shares) of base salary for the CEO. Accordingly, approximately 25% to 33% of each annual incentive award to all executive officers will be paid in deferred shares vesting over the following two years so that each officer is properly motivated to remain with the Company and to continue to create stockholder value over the next several years. As discussed above, we take into account the executive officer's target annual incentive award as part of the targeted total compensation for the executive.[2]

Risk Aversion

An executive's risk aversion must be considered in determining salary. A risk-averse individual always prefers a certain to an uncertain amount. Thus, holding the value of the compensation package constant, he or she would prefer that the salary, which is the certain component, be as large as possible. In equilibrium, he or she would even be willing to accept a lower amount in exchange for reducing the uncertainty/risk of the package. This desire on the part of the executive must be weighed against the corporation's goals. If risky investments are needed to provide incentives to the executive to achieve the corporations' goals, then the compensation package must include some risky compensation. On the other hand, if the executive already has a substantial investment in the corporation, then the necessary incentives may already be present. In that situation, including a risky component in the compensation package may be counterproductive, because it would increase the executive's risk beyond the optimal level.

Executive Ownership

As alluded to in the immediately preceding paragraph, executive ownership affects the need for incentives to be provided via the compensation package. In particular, the greater an executive's ownership, the less the need for conditional compensation. Thus, the amount and proportion of salary in the compensation package should increase with executive ownership.

Horizon

The executive's horizon also must be considered in determining salary. If the executive is approaching the traditional retirement age, he or she may be reluctant to make long-term investments that pay off after his or her retirement. To provide incentive for the executive to make such investments, the corporation should consider reducing the amount of current salary, replacing it with deferred compensation conditional upon the performance of the corporation after the executive retires.

Impact of Corporate Characteristics
Size

In general, it has been observed that the dollar amount of salary increases with the size of the corporation (Table 2-10), while salary as a percentage of the total compensation package decreases with the size of the corporation (Table 2-7). As noted in Chapter 14, the latter may be due to the fact that the percentage of the corporation owned by executives decreases with increases in the size of the corporation, and thus, the compensation package has to increasingly provide those equity-related incentives. The finding that salary (and total compensation) increases with size is attributable to the greater set of skills required to run a more complex organization, and the greater demand and willingness to pay for people who can run those organizations.

Growth

The growth of the corporation must be taken into consideration. As noted in Chapter 14, growth corporations, while in general paying a higher level of compensation, make more of that compensation conditional on performance. Providing incentives to maximize shareholder value in the compensation package is more important for growing corporations because, as the amount of discretion an executive has increases, it becomes harder for shareholders and directors to effectively monitor the executive. Thus, salary becomes a smaller part of the compensation package.

Financial Considerations

The financial circumstances of the corporation also affect the composition of the compensation package. Salary, if currently paid, reduces the corporation's cash availability, financial accounting income and taxable income. If the corporation is cash constrained, it may substitute noncash items such as stock grants and options for cash salary (Core and Guay 2001). Similarly, if the corporation wishes to increase financial accounting income, it can substitute stock compensation, which is expensed over a period of time rather than immediately. While corporations rarely seek to increase taxable income, if the corporation has little taxable income, it may seek to replace salary, which yields current tax deductions, with components that yield tax deductions in the future, when the corporation can utilize them. Finally, if the executive is subject to Internal Revenue Code Section 162(m) limitations, the corporation may want to either defer salary until the executive is not subject to those limitations, and/or substitute other forms of compensation that meet the performance-based criteria specified in Section 162(m) (Rose and Wolfram 2000).

Ownership/Board Composition

Monitoring from large shareholders and/or an active board of directors may lessen the role of the compensation package in motivating executives. In the absence of active monitoring, a large portion of the compensation package should be performance based to provide executives with incentive to increase shareholder value. However, when performance-based compensation is used, executive risk aversion requires an increase in the expected value of the compensation package. Active monitoring allows corporations to reduce the amount of performance-based compensation in the compensation package, and hence, the expected value of the package. Thus, salary should be higher and a larger component of a smaller compensation package when there are large shareholders and/or an active board of directors.

Bonus

Approximately 80 percent of corporations pay their CEOs bonuses in a given year. (See Table 2-2.) While some of the remaining companies may not have bonus plans, others may have them and not pay bonuses because performance standards were not met. Take, for example, the following passage from Ohio Casualty. It explains that a bonus was not paid because the performance target was not met.

> Under the 2003 Annual Incentive Program (the "2003 Program"), the CEO and the CFO did not meet the target levels established for the before-tax corporate operating income or the accident year combined ratio. Consequently, they did not receive a bonus in 2004.[3]

Because of situations like this, the percentage of corporations that paid their CEOs bonuses understates the number of corporations that have bonus plans.

The standard procedure is to set a target bonus as a percentage of salary, with the percentage of salary usually increasing as the executive moves up through the executive ranks. For example, with R.H. Donnelley (see page 440) the percentage for named executive officers ranged from 60 percent to 100 percent for CEO. Thus, consistent with economic theory, as the executive moves up the ranks, more of his or her pay is at risk. For a CEO, the target bonus might be 100 percent of salary, if the target is met. If the target is exceeded by a certain amount, the executive might get more, for example, 120 percent of salary, whereas if the target is missed the executive might get less, perhaps 80 percent of bonus. Generally speaking, these plans are nonlinear, that is, to achieve a higher bonus, the executive/corporation must achieve a series of thresholds. Additionally, plans may have upper bounds beyond which increased performance does not increase the bonus, and/or lower bounds below which no bonus is paid. The following passage describing the contract between Mae Numata and Fisher Communications illustrates the linkage between salary and bonus. Bonus is expressed as a percentage of salary and the use of an upper bound.

> She will also be eligible for participation in the Fisher Communications, Inc. Short-Term Incentive Plan, with a payout target equal to 45 percent of her base salary and a maximum payout equal to 200 percent of the payout target.[4]

This lack of linearity causes problems, as it provides executives with incentives to manipulate performance measures to maximize the present value of bonus payments, even if the current period's bonus cannot be affected. For example, assume the bonus is based on accounting earnings, and the corporation is either above the upper bound or below the lower bound. The executive has the incentive to reduce current-period income so that he or she may shift that income to future periods, increasing the bonus paid in those future periods.[5] An extreme example of this has been referred to as the "big bath" (Kinney and Trezevant 1996). A big bath occurs when a corporation having a loss year takes a series of accounting charges to increase the magnitude of the loss. The benefit of the big bath is that because those charges do not have to be taken in the future (and in some cases may be reversed), income and bonuses in future periods will be higher.

The compensation committee, assuming it decides to pay bonuses/have a bonus plan, must make the following determinations. First, should the bonus be implicit or explicit? If the bonus is implicit, no formal plan exists, and the committee determines the bonus after the end of the period in question based upon whatever criteria, objective and/or subjective, it decides to use. If the bonus is explicit, a formal plan must be drawn, normally prior to the start of the period in question. While an implicit plan has advantages in terms of flexibility, explicit plans have advantages in terms of clarity, that is, the executive knows his or her goals, and the payoff if he or she achieves those goals.[6] The plan, if explicit, must address the targeted bonus payout; the performance period (i.e., will performance be judged quarterly, annually or over a longer period?); the performance measure or measures to be used; the target or thresholds for those performance measures and the means of payment. As will be illustrated below, characteristics of the executive and corporation should be taken into consideration in making these determinations.

Targeted Bonus Amount

For those corporations that have a bonus plan, the corporation must decide how much, and what proportion of the compensation package, the targeted bonus amount should be. As noted above, most explicit bonus plans state that the bonus will be a percentage of salary if a certain level of performance is achieved. Casual observation notes that for CEOs, the target bonus is normally 100 percent of salary.

The target bonus should depend on a number of factors. Consider first, two generic factors. If salary is relatively low, to raise total compensation to the level required to attract and retain executives, bonuses must be higher. The following example, which ignores executive risk aversion and assumes that the targeted bonus is the expected bonus, illustrates the need to consider salary when setting the targeted bonus amount. Corporation A pays its CEO $1 million in salary and will pay a bonus of 100 percent of salary if the performance targets are met, leading to expected salary plus bonus of $2 million. Corporation B pays its CEO $500,000 in salary. To be competitive with Corporation A, Corporation B needs its expected bonus to be $1.5 million. Thus, it should pay a bonus of 300 percent of salary if the performance targets are met. A second factor to be considered is the performance goals themselves. The targeted bonus amount should take into account the ease with which the goals can be achieved. If the goals are easy to achieve because there is little risk involved, the bonus becomes akin to salary. Alternatively, if the goals are difficult to achieve, then the actual payment is uncertain, and a risk premium should be built into the targeted bonus amount.

Effect of Executive Characteristics on Targeted Bonus Amount

Executive characteristics influence the targeted bonus amount. The executive's risk aversion may influence the breakdown of compensation between certain salary and uncertain bonus, with the amount of bonus decreasing with risk aversion. Similarly, an executive's opportunity cost may influence the targeted bonus amount, as the greater the executive's opportunity cost, the greater total compensation. If an executive has significant share and/or option ownership, the current compensation package should reflect that, and mitigate some of the market-based risk, via more bonus and less stock-based compensation. In contrast, if an executive is nearing retirement, the corporation may want to increase the percentage of compensation that is forward looking, that is, stock based, consequently decreasing the targeted bonus amount.

Effect of Corporate Characteristics on Targeted Bonus Amount

As with salary, the magnitude of the bonus will increase with the size of the corporation. Similarly, the amount of bonus will be affected by liquidity and tax considerations. A corporation with liquidity constraints may be more likely to pay a smaller cash bonus and devote a larger portion of the compensation package to stock-based compensation.[7] Analogously, a corporation wishing to report higher financial-accounting income will pay less bonus, which is recorded as an expense in the current period, and grant more stock compensation, for which the expense can be spread over several periods. Similarly, if the corporation has little taxable income, even if it is not cash constrained, it may seek to replace the bonus, which yields current tax deductions, with components like stock options that yield tax deductions in the future when the corporation can utilize them.[8] If the executive is subject to Internal Revenue Code Section 162(m) limitations, the corporation should either structure its bonus plan to qualify for the performance-based exceptions under Section 162(m), defer the bonus until the executive is not subject to those limitations and/or substitute into other forms of compensation, such as stock options, that meet the performance-based criteria specified in Section 162(m). Finally, the noise and informativeness of performance measures, in particular share prices, affect the decision to use bonuses versus stock-based compensation. That is, if share prices are very noisy and/or do not provide much information on the performance of an executive, then the conditional compensation component of the compensation package should primarily be composed of bonuses (and share price should not be the performance measure).

Performance Period

In general, the longer the performance period or time frame the bonus is calculated over, the greater the retentive effect (Kole 1997). That is, the greater the window, the greater the monetary amount forfeited if the executive leaves. Consider the following illustration of the effect of a one-year versus three-year plan. An executive has a bonus plan that pays him (or her) 1 percent of net income. Income in the first year is $250 million, in the second year, the corporation incurs a loss of $75 million, and in the third year, the corporation has a profit of $150 million. If the plan is based on yearly income, the executive receives $2.5 million in the first year, 0 in the second and $1.5 million in the third. If the plan is for three years, the executive receives a bonus of $3.25 million at the end of three years. Under the three-year plan, the executive gets a smaller bonus, but also somewhat surprisingly, at times has a greater incentive to remain with the corporation. If the plan is annual, it provides no monetary incentive for the executive to remain with the corporation during year two. In contrast, if the plan is based upon three years of performance, and hence no payout is made at the end of year one, if the executive leaves during year two, he or she forfeits the accumulated bonus at that point in time, which despite the loss, is still $1.75 million at the end of year two. Of course sometimes the incentives work in reverse. For example, if the corporation loses money in the first year of the three-year term, the executive has incentive to leave. To earn a bonus, not only does the corporation have to earn money in years two and three, that amount must exceed the losses in year one. The executive, if he or she has the choice, may simply prefer to go elsewhere and start with a clean slate.

A longer period also minimizes the opportunity for shifting income across periods. Consider the example above, where net income is $250 million in the first year, a loss of $75 million in the second year and $150 million in the third year. If the executive receives bonuses based on yearly income, he or she has the incentive to shift expenses (revenues) from year three (two) to year two (three), thereby increasing the loss in year two (big bath), but more importantly increasing income and bonus in year three. In contrast, there are fewer monetary incentives to shift income if the bonus is based on income for the three-year period. That is, while there are no incentives to shift income across the three years, there are still incentives to shift income from earlier and later periods.

Effect of Executive Characteristics on Choice of Performance Period

What factors should influence the performance period to be used? Risk aversion would probably cause the executive to prefer a shorter period for the simple reason that the amount of the bonus, or even the existence of the bonus, is uncertain until completion of the performance period. In addition, the executive would prefer more frequent payments to smooth his or her income. That is, if the performance period is three years, the executive will not receive a payment in two of the three years, creating fluctuations in income. Then, of course, there is the issue of present value. A dollar received today is worth more than a dollar received in the future. Assuming that the nominal value of the bonus is the same regardless of the performance period,[9] the present value of the bonus is greater if paid yearly, rather than if paid at the end of three years. If the executive has other opportunities, he or she may elect the one with the shortest payout period. While it is difficult, first, to measure those other opportunities, and second, to tailor the contract to one executive, the corporation can proxy for those opportunities by examining the terms used by its competitors. These competing corporations, because of executives' industry-specific expertise, are the most likely alternative employers for a corporation's current executives.

An approach used by many corporations that mitigates the problems discussed above, that is, uncertainty about and fluctuations in executive income, is the use of overlapping periods. A corporation may measure performance over three years, but have three performance periods accumulating at the same time. For example, one period may consist of years one through three, a second period consist of years two through four and a third period consist of years three through five. Thus, assuming performance is satisfactory, the executive could expect to receive a bonus every year. In terms of executive income, this may create a smoother income stream than basing the bonus on income for a single year, as the longer time period can filter out fluctuations in the performance measure.

Effect of Corporate Characteristics on Choice of Performance Period

The corporation's investment opportunities influence the choice of performance period. The greater the corporation's investment opportunities, the more important it is to the corporation to retain existing executives. So, the length of the performance period should be positively associated with growth. In addition, the choice of performance period should be positively associated with the corporation's operating cycle. Consider two companies, one that constructs housing and the other that sells clothing. The time from initiation of a housing development until its completion could be years. In contrast, the operating cycle for a clothing retailer or the design of a new line of clothing is less usually than a year. If direct observation of an executive's actions is impossible or impractical, to properly evaluate the performance of an executive requires the completion of an operating or production cycle.

Performance Measure(s)

The choice of performance measure or measures must be made with extreme care, as the compensation committee does not want to provide the wrong set of incentives or impose unnecessary risk on the executive. For example, rewarding managers based upon market share or sales growth alone may yield unprofitable sales that decrease shareholder value. Nor does a corporation want to use accounting earnings as a measure if it provides incentives to avoid certain investments, or if the accounting model does not accurately represent the corporation's true performance. In general, the goal is to maximize the informativeness and minimize the noise/riskiness in the performance measures chosen. Assuming that the measures chosen are not perfectly correlated with each other, and are positively correlated with true, yet unobservable, performance, using multiple measures can be more informative than using a single measure. Basing compensation on these measures can also reduce executive risk and, consequently, the level of compensation the corporation is required to pay.

Effect of Executive Characteristics on the Choice of Performance Measures

Executive characteristics play a role in determining the measures used. If an executive has significant share and option holdings, the corporation should not use share price as a performance measure, as doing so would increase the executive's risk.[10] Conversely, for an executive nearing retirement, share price would be a good measure, as, if markets are efficient, share price reflects the long-run consequences of an executive's actions.

Effect of Corporate Characteristics on Choice of Performance Measures

A growing corporation might want to use revenues, rather than net income or cash flows, because the investments required to sustain growth decrease those measures of performance. Similarly, as noted in Chapter 14, a corporation with profits that are capped by regulators would not want to use net income as a performance measure. Generally, corporations want to use measures that are informative and under the executives' control. That is, not only should the measure be informative about corporate performance, but it should also reflect the efforts of the executive. For example, airline profits are highly influenced by factors, such as fuel prices, outside of the CEO's control. Should a CEO be punished if an increase in fuel prices leads to a decrease in net income? As noted above, using multiple measures can be beneficial in measuring performance and in reducing executive risk. These measures can include financial and nonfinancial metrics. Consider again the airline. Customer service provides another measure of performance, one more controllable, or at least responsive to the CEO's actions, than fuel prices. In general, a corporation dealing with the ultimate consumer, like an airline, might want to include one or more measures of customer service, whereas a manufacturer might want to include one or more measures of product quality.

Performance Targets

Targets or thresholds can be absolute, or they can be relative to either prior performance or the performance of competitors. An example of an absolute target: No bonus is paid unless return on equity equals or exceeds 12 percent. An example of a relative target: No bonus is paid unless the growth in earnings per share relative to the prior year equals or exceeds 6 percent. Absolute and relative targets can be combined. For example: No bonus will be paid unless return on equity equals or exceeds 12 percent and equals or exceeds the median return on equity for the benchmark group of corporations.

Effect of Corporate Characteristics on Choice of Performance Target

Corporate characteristics will influence whether the target is absolute or relative. If the corporation is growing, then the target can be expressed in terms of growth—the level of performance relative to prior years. In contrast, if the corporation is mature, absolute performance would be a better measure. If the corporation is not expected to grow, and thus, the change in the level of performance is expected to be zero, then using the change in net income to measure performance provides no incentives. Analogously, if the corporation has many close competitors, it should measure performance relative to those competitors to control for industry-specific risks that may be outside of the executive's control. In contrast, the lack of similar corporations, where similarity is defined as size, industry, product line, etc., suggests the use of absolute measures.

The magnitude of the target, whether the goal is 10-percent growth in EPS or a 15-percent return on shareholders' equity, should be dependent on the historical growth rate of the corporation and industry in which it operates. Certain corporations and industries have higher rates of return than others. For example, pharmaceutical companies traditionally have high return on equity relative to industrial corporations. Taking these differences into account is important, as a threshold that is too low and is thus easily achieved provides no motivation. Neither does a threshold that is too high, and thus, unachievable.

Method of Payment

Corporate and executive characteristics will influence the method of payment. If the corporation is cash constrained then it would be more likely to, (A) defer the bonus, (B) pay the bonus in stock or (C) both. Independent of whether the corporation faces cash constraints, deferring bonuses can help with retention and the horizon problem. Deferring the bonus helps with retention. If the executive does not remain with the corporation for the period required, he or she loses the amount deferred. Making the bonus dependent on the future share price may help mitigate the incentive problems associated with a looming retirement. The ultimate value of the bonus is dependent on the stock price after the executive retires. Deferring the bonus also provides a bond if the executive is found to have misstated current-period results and/or later decides to breach his or her contract by, for example, going to work for a competitor. Peoples Bancorp, as illustrated by the following passage, requires executives to defer 25 percent of their incentive compensation for three years:

> Executive officers are required to defer 25% of their incentive compensation for a period of three years and have the option to defer any remaining incentive compensation until they reach retirement age.[11]

Stock Compensation

The corporation must decide whether to grant any stock-based compensation. If it decides to, should that compensation be in the form of options, grants or both? It also must decide on how much, and consequently, what proportion of the compensation package, should be stock based. As shown in Table 2-2, most companies (69 percent in 2005) award stock options to their CEOs, and roughly half (45 percent in 2005) issue share grants.

Amount of Stock Compensation

There are two separate issues when granting stock compensation. The first is how much, and what portion of the compensation package should be stock based. The second, which, perhaps, should precede the first, is how to value that stock compensation. Consider the following example. A corporation decides that the compensation package should be composed of one-third salary, one-third bonus and one-third stock options. It sets salary at $1 million and targeted bonus at $1 million, and wishes to grant $1 million worth of options, with an exercise price equal to the current share price of $25. Theoretically, the most appropriate way to value the option is with an option-pricing model. Assuming the value of the option is $10 per share, the corporation would then grant 100,000 options.

However, while theoretically a correct measure of the cost to the corporation, in that these options could have been sold to investors for this value, research, such as Lambert et al. (1991), demonstrates that under reasonable assumptions about individual risk aversion and diversification, undiversified executives, who cannot sell the options, place a much lower value on the options than that generated by an option-pricing model. This occurs because option-pricing models "assume tradeability, the ability to sell short, and ignore the effect of the continued employment requirement, all of which reduce the value of the option to the employee" (Balsam 1994). Hence, the option's cost to the corporation is greater than the value placed upon the option by the executive. The employer will always have to pay more in stock-based compensation than it would have in fixed cash compensation. Put another way, the employee values stock-based compensation at less than the cost to the corporation. Meulbroek (2001) estimates that "undiversified managers at rapidly growing, entrepreneurially based firms, such as Internet-based firms, value their option-based compensation at only 53% of their cost to the firm ..." More recent evidence in Bettis et al. (2005) confirms early exercise behavior on the part of executives and finds that the "subjective value of the options are uniformly lower than the corresponding objective values and that the difference is increasing in stock price volatility." However, in contrast to conventional wisdom and most of academic research, Hodge et al. (2006) "find that managers, on average, systematically overvalue stock options relative to both the Black-Scholes (B-S) value and fair value equivalent restricted stock grants." Still, the preponderance of research suggests that options are worth less to employees than to risk-neutral investors. Hall (2003) sums it up well:

> Most stock options are worth considerably less to the executives they are meant to motivate than to the shareholders of the companies that grant them. This "wedge" in value represents a significant cost to the firm's shareholders-one that could tilt the balance toward the use of restricted stock or cash-based compensation instead.

In a recent development, Google Inc. has developed a *Transferrable Stock Option* in an attempt to increase the value of the option to its nonexecutive-management employees.[12] Under the program, employees would be allowed to sell their vested options to participating financial institutions. By allowing the employee to capture some, if not all, of the time value of his or her option, it would increase the value of the option to the employee.[13] Consider two situations. In the first, the option is out of the money, yet has a positive time value. At any time after vesting and prior to expiration, the employee may sell the option for its time value. In the second, the employee has decided to exercise the option prior to expiration. Rather than exercising the option early and entirely giving up the time value of the option, the employee could sell the option to a purchaser who would value not only the intrinsic, but also the remaining, time value.

Another approach would be to value the options at their nominal value, that is, their exercise price. In that situation, given the exercise price of $25, the corporation would grant 40,000 options. Yet a third approach would be to value the option based upon the expected gain upon exercise, that is, as some corporations choose to do in their proxy statements. Assuming a 10-year exercise period and appreciation of 5 percent per year, the expected profit from each option would be just under $16 per option, thus the corporation would need to issue about 64,000 options. But is 5 percent the correct rate of appreciation? At a rate of 10 percent, the expected profit per option jumps to almost $40, thus the corporation would only need to grant about 25,000 options. The last couple of sentences illustrate that not only is the valuation of the option subject to the method chosen—that is, grant date option model valuation, versus nominal value, versus expected gain upon exercise—it is also highly influenced by the inputs into those models. Valuation is also an issue with restricted stock grants. While unrestricted stock grants should be valued at the current market price on the date of grant, restricted stock grants, because of the restrictions imposed, are less valuable to executives.

Effect of Executive Characteristics on Amount of Stock Compensation

Assuming the corporation can resolve the valuation issue, it can then return to the issue of how much and what portion of the compensation package is comprised of stock-based compensation. If an executive owns few shares, it would be optimal to make a large portion of the compensation package stock based. However, as noted above, politically it is difficult to tailor a specific package to each executive. Thus, the relevant benchmark would be shares owned by executives as a group. If their ownership was low (high), the corporation should make a larger (smaller) portion of the compensation package stock based.

The risk aversion of the executive group will also influence the portion of the compensation package that is made up of stock-based compensation. The difference in the value placed upon stock-based compensation by the executive and the cost to the corporation arise in part, from executive risk aversion. That is, because of risk aversion, the corporation will have to replace $1 of fixed compensation with stock compensation costing more than $1. The corporation will do this as long as the marginal benefits from the improved incentives exceed the marginal cost. However, the greater the risk aversion, the greater the amount of stock the executive will demand to substitute for $1 of fixed compensation. Alternatively, as executive risk aversion increases, the lower the amount of fixed compensation the executive will accept in lieu of a given amount of stock compensation. Either way, using stock-based compensation becomes more costly to the corporation as executive risk aversion increases. Consequently, the portion of stock-based compensation should decline with executive risk aversion.

The horizon of the executive(s) will influence the composition of the compensation package. As noted above, an executive has little incentive to make investments that pay off after his or her retirement. This problem becomes greater as the executive approaches retirement age. Stock-based compensation may mitigate this problem because stock prices, in an efficient market, reflect the expected benefits and the costs of investments at the time the investment is made. Thus, as an executive approaches retirement age, the amount and portion of stock-based compensation in the compensation package should increase.

Also relevant is opportunity cost. As noted above, in many cases, the most likely employers of a corporation's executives are the corporation's industry competitors. Thus, to retain executives, not only should the corporation's level of compensation be comparable with those of its competitors, but the composition of the package should also be comparable. So, the portion of the compensation package comprised of stock-based compensation should be influenced by industry norms.

Effect of Corporate Characteristics on Amount of Stock Compensation

Growing corporations should grant a large amount of stock-based compensation, due to the value implications of managerial decisions (Kole 1997). However, consider a corporation in a nongrowth industry that basically pays out all of its earnings as dividends. There is little or no expectation for stock price appreciation. Thus, standard stock options provide no incentives. The corporation needs to grant restricted stock or a special dividend-protected option. While this type of option would provide the proper incentives and counteract the incentive to reduce dividends (Lambert et al. 1989), it has not been observed in practice due to the accounting, tax and implementation issues. For example, for accounting purposes these options would be defined as variable options under Financial Accounting Standards Board Interpretation No. 28, and thus, prior to 2006, an expense would have to be recognized, whereas no expense was recognized for most traditional options under Accounting Principles Board Opinion No. 25. For tax purposes, the executive would recognize income each time the option's exercise price was reduced, if that price were below the current market value. And implementation would have to be done carefully. Recall the confusion and ensuing lawsuits when Computer Associates (see Chapter 6) adjusted the number of shares given to its top executives for stock splits, an adjustment which was not stipulated in the original plan submitted to shareholders (Johnston 1999).

As noted above with respect to bonuses, the use of a performance measure depends in part on the noise relative to the informativeness of that measure with respect to executive performance. The performance measure implicit in all stock-based compensation is share price. As discussed in Chapter 14, the greater the association between share prices and overall market movements, referred to as Beta, the more noisy share prices are as a measure of executive performance. Thus as Beta increases, the percentage of stock compensation in the compensation package should decrease.

A corporation's financial circumstances can also affect its preferences for stock-based compensation. As neither options nor restricted stock require a cash outflow, the use of stock-based compensation can conserve cash. In fact, stock compensation can be a source of cash in that executives must pay to exercise their options,[14] and shares and options lead to tax savings (recall that Microsoft was able to reduce its tax bill by $5.5 billion in 2000 due to tax deductions associated with its stock plans). For financial accounting purposes, the cost of stock compensation is spread over several periods. Thus, if the corporation desires to increase current cash flow and/or financial reporting income, it could substitute stock-based compensation for salary and bonus. Similarly, a corporation with little need for current tax deductions should increase the amount of stock, either options or restricted stock grants, in the compensation package, as it allows the corporation to push those deductions into the future, when it may better be able to utilize those deductions. In the extreme case where the corporation does not anticipate being able to utilize those deductions in the future, it should consider granting tax-qualified stock options, which give the executive tax benefits in lieu of tax deductions for the corporation.

The amount of monitoring of executives should influence the amount of stock in the compensation package. As noted earlier in this book, monitoring in the form of active board members and/or owners can provide incentives for executives to increase shareholder value. In the absence of this monitoring, the compensation package must provide the incentives for executives to increase shareholder value. Thus, corporations with limited monitoring from owners/directors should issue a large amount of stock-based compensation.

Share Versus Option Grants[15]

Once the corporation decides on the amount of stock-based compensation to include in the executive compensation package, it needs to decide whether the stock component should be shares, options or some combination of the two. While both are valuable to employees, each possesses attributes that make it more or less valuable than the other. First, a share is implicitly an option with a zero exercise price. Thus, it is more valuable than an option. Holding the value of stock-based compensation constant, the employee would receive a larger number of options than shares. Further, as noted in Chapter 6, a share has value as long as the share price exceeds zero, whereas an option is only valuable when the share price exceeds the option's exercise price. Consequently, while a share grant imposes less risk on the executive, it also has less of an impact on the executives' willingness to take risks.

Impact of Executive Characteristics on Choice Between Option and Share Grants

There is less risk with shares because, as long as the market price is positive, the employee is guaranteed the shares will have value. In contrast, options can, and do, expire out of the money, effectively making them worthless to the executive. Thus, as executive risk aversion increases, so does the executive's preference for shares over options.

To some extent, the decision to grant options or restricted shares will be influenced by the executive's opportunity cost, as proxied for by industry norms. For example, if one potential employer grants shares and the other grants options, the executive will choose the form of compensation he or she perceives to be more valuable. As noted in Table 2-3, there is substantial variation in the use of share grants across industries.

Impact of Corporate Characteristics on Choice Between Option and Share Grants

Options and shares, because of their different payoff structures, have different effects on executive incentives and decision-making. Shares can actually decrease an executive's incentive to take risks, as the executive can suffer monetary losses as a result of the investment. In contrast, options, as long as they are not in the money, provide incentives to take risks, as the executive profits from increases in the corporation's share price, but does not suffer any monetary loss from a decrease in share price. Thus corporations with a lot of investment opportunities should primarily grant options, to provide incentive to take risks.

As alluded to previously, for a corporation with a relatively fixed share price, that is, little upward potential or growth, options have no incentive effect. In those situations, the corporation should grant shares. Yet as shown in Table 2-2, most corporations grant options to their CEOs annually. Perhaps these corporations grant shares in addition to, rather than in place of, options.[16]

The corporation's financial circumstances can also influence the choice between share and option grants. First, share and option grants have differing cash and financial reporting consequences. While options may result in a cash inflow when the executive exercises his or her options, if the corporation pays dividends, share grants may lead to cash outflows. Thus, a corporation with little cash will prefer options to grants. Tax considerations are subtler, as options and shares, assuming they are restricted, result in deductions in the future. Because future taxable income is uncertain, there is a chance the corporation will not be able to utilize those deductions. If that is a possibility, options may be more efficient in terms of minimizing the joint taxes paid by the corporation and executive. Consider first share grants. Assuming the Section 83(b) election is not taken, income will be recognized by the executive and a deduction taken by the corporation at the time the restrictions expire for the fair value of those shares at that time. While the executive will always pay tax on that income, the possibility exists the corporation will not be able to utilize the deduction. Consider now stock options. Assuming they are granted with an exercise price equal to the then-market price, options are only valuable if the market price rises. This will generally occur only if the corporation is profitable, which will generally coincide with the corporation having taxable income. Thus, in scenarios where the corporation would be unable to benefit from additional tax deductions, the option would be out of the money and hence the executive would not have any taxable income.[17] A second approach would be to grant tax-qualified options. Thus, while the corporation would not receive any deductions from those options, the executive would receive preferential tax treatment. If, in the future, the corporation needs tax deductions, it could provide monetary incentives to the executive to disqualify the options for tax purposes. If the executive agrees and disqualifies those options, they are then treated as nonqualified and he or she recognizes ordinary income upon exercise, while the corporation gets a deduction for that same amount.

Restrictions/Vesting

Shares and options may be granted with restrictions, some of which may expire with the passage of time (also known as the vesting period), and some of which require the executive and/or corporation to meet certain performance hurdles. Consider first share grants. These grants are commonly referred to as restricted stock because the executive does not have full rights to the shares until the restrictions expire. For example, while the executive may have voting and dividend rights immediately, he or she will not be able to sell the shares until the restrictions expire. These restrictions may expire with the passage of time, achievement of performance objectives or some combination of the two. Consider next options. Options can have two levels of restrictions, the first imposed on the executive's ability to exercise the option, and the second, on the executive's ability to sell the shares obtained upon exercise.

These restrictions affect the incentive and retentive effects. That is, assuming the shares and/or options are valuable, the longer the restriction period, the longer the executive is tied to the corporation. Of course, as mentioned in Chapter 6, if vesting is too far in the future, the executive may leave for a quicker payoff elsewhere. Further, as the restrictions on the executive's ability to sell the shares and diversify his or her risk increase, a risk-averse executive will decrease the value he or she places on the stock-based compensation. Additionally, forcing an executive to hold shares and options that are in the money can make the undiversified executive less likely to take on new, risky projects. Thus, as the restriction period increases, the corporation would have to provide additional incentives to make the executive willing to take on new risks.

Effect of Executive Characteristics on Restrictions

Restrictions on the ability to sell the shares, whether restricted shares and/or shares acquired upon exercise of options, will be important if the corporation feels it necessary to increase executive share ownership for incentive or political purposes. Thus, when executive ownership is low, the corporation should grant more stock-based compensation and impose restrictions on the ability of executives to sell those shares.

These restrictions will also be important as the executive nears retirement, to guard against policies that lead to short-term gains in the corporation's stock price at the expense of long-term profitability. Thus, restrictions on the ability of the executive to dispose of the shares should extend beyond normal retirement age. The time frame for which the restrictions remain in effect depends on a number of factors, including the gestation period for an investment.

As noted above, imposing restrictions on the ability to exercise options and/or sell shares increases the risk of the executive. Consequently, the executive will place a lower value on those options/shares than if there were fewer restrictions. Similarly, the increased risk may cause the executive to be less willing to take on risky projects. These issues become more important as executive risk aversion increases.

Finally, the executive's opportunity costs must be taken into consideration when determining these restrictions. All else equal, the executive will select the alternative with the fewest constraints. Thus, if a competitor offers the same compensation package with fewer constraints, the executive will elect to work for the competitor. Given that the most likely employers of an executive are the corporation's industry competitors, industry norms should be taken into consideration in setting restrictions.

Effect of Corporate Characteristics on Restrictions

The investment opportunities of the corporation should also affect the restriction decisions. The greater the growth opportunities and, in particular, the longer the gestation period of the corporation's projects, the more important it is to retain executives. Consequently, the longer the restriction period should be.

The corporation's financial circumstances affect the restrictions. Consider restricted stock. In the absence of a Section 83(b) election, the executive will recognize income, and the corporation will receive a deduction, when the restrictions expire. Similarly, with nonqualified options, the executive will recognize income, and the corporation will receive a deduction, when the shares are exercised. A corporation that does not foresee a need for these deductions in the near future will try to push these deductions as far as possible into the future by extending the restriction/vesting period. In contrast, a corporation in need of cash may want to make the vesting period for its options as short as possible, and require payment of the exercise price in cash to improve its liquidity.

The accounting treatment also influences the restriction period for options and share grants. The cost of stock options and restricted shares is recognized as an expense over the restriction period. Hence, the longer the restriction period, the less expense is recognized in each period. So, if the corporation desires to increase its accounting income, it will increase the length of the restrictions.

Grant Frequency

Shares and options should be granted as frequently as practical. More frequent grants work like the investment technique referred to as "dollar-cost averaging." That is, the executive receives options with a variety of exercise prices. This portfolio of options makes it likely that at least some are in the money at any point in time. Consequently, it reduces the risk due to market fluctuations, and minimizes the need to engage in costly repricings.

The frequency of grants will also be related to the restrictions referred to in the previous section. Given that shares and options provide incentives to increase shareholder value, the corporation wants to make sure executives always have some stock-based incentives. Thus, a corporation that grants shares and/or options every other year, but only imposes a one-year restriction/vesting period, would have a problem if executives exercised their options and sold their shares as soon as they were eligible to. The problem would arise as the executives would have no incentives to increase shareholder value in the second year of the cycle.

Related to grant frequency is the use of reload options. Recall from Chapter 6 that as the stock price increases beyond the exercise price, executives become more risk averse, in that they now have something to lose if the share price drops. To prepare for this possibility, corporations should use reload options, which allow executives to exercise their existing options and get replacement options with an exercise price equal to the current share price.

Exercise Price

The vast majority of options are granted whereby the exercise price is fixed and equal to the current market price on the date of grant.[18] They need not be. As discussed earlier, it is possible to adjust the exercise price to some market or industry index to filter out marketwide or industrywide movements that have nothing to do with performance of the corporation or its executives. Alternatively, options can be granted at a fixed price, but at a price that is at a premium to the then-existing market price. This premium could be set so that the executive does not benefit unless shareholders do well. As noted in Chapter 6, both are infrequently observed in practice. And yet, both have strong theoretical justifications and would play well in the political arena.[19] Consider the following proposal by the AFL-CIO contained in the Chubb Corp. proxy statement filed with the Securities and Exchange Commission March 24, 1999.

> That the shareholders of The Chubb Corporation (the "Company") urge the board of directors to adopt an executive compensation policy that all future stock option grants to senior executives shall be performance-based. For the purposes of this resolution, a stock-option is performance-based if its exercise price is either 1) linked to an industry index, such as Standard and Poor's Property-Casualty Insurance Index; or 2) significantly above the current market price of the stock at the grant date."

While the proposal was not approved, it did receive almost 39 million votes, approximately one-third of the total cast,[20] indicating the proposal had appeal beyond the AFL-CIO, which owned only 26,900 shares.[21]

Adjusted options, that is, options with exercise prices that are adjusted for movements in a selected index after the grant date, reduce an executive's risk by removing items that are out of the executive's control. To some extent, executives have been able to control their downside risk, for example via repricings in the 1990s and later with additional grants, while at the same time benefiting from upward marketwide movements, which may be why adjusted options have not been observed more frequently.[22] Further, adjusted options have implementation issues. For example, if the exercise price is to be adjusted, what index should be used? Should adjustments to the exercise price be based on market or industry returns? Should those returns be calculated based upon the relative market values of the companies in the index or an equal weighting of all the corporations in the index? Should the returns be adjusted for risk, etc.?

Premium options, or options granted with an exercise price greater than the share price on the date of grant, have fewer implementation problems. The corporation could simply select a hurdle below which the executive should not benefit, and then price the option accordingly. While executives would obviously prefer options at a lower price, the corporation could make the executive whole by increasing the number of options granted. Further, premium options would provide more incentive to take risks. However, if it appears the options will expire out of the money, which is more likely with a premium option, they have no retention effects.

Consider the following example, which illustrates the intuitive benefit of premium options. At the time the options are granted, the current market price is $100 a share, and the rate of return on 10-year U.S. Treasury bonds is 7.2 percent. If the options are granted with an exercise price of $100, executives will profit from any appreciation in share price. Shareholders will not, however, because there is an opportunity cost for their money. They could invest in another corporation or in treasury bonds, to name just two possibilities. If they invest in 10-year treasury bonds, at the end of 10 years they would have $200. So at any price below $200, they would have been better off investing in risk-free Treasury bonds, whereas executives benefit whenever the price exceeds $100.[23] There is a range, when the share price is between $100 and $200, where executives benefit, while investors suffer opportunity losses.[24] Thus, setting the exercise price at a premium, $200, aligns the payouts of executives and shareholders.

Options can also be issued at a discount to the current market price. Effectively a cross between a stock grant, which has a zero exercise price, and a market or premium-priced option, discount options have both incentive problems, in that they discourage executive risk taking, and are costly from a tax viewpoint. Perhaps most importantly, they are politically incorrect, that is in contrast to at-the-money or out-of-the-money options, which send a bullish signal that stock prices are going to increase, discount options send the wrong signal. That is, discount options convey management's uncertainty about future stock price increases and ensure stock prices don't have to increase for managers to make money.

Deferred Compensation[25]

Corporations have tax and incentive motivations to offer pensions and other forms of deferred compensation. As discussed in Chapter 7, tax benefits can arise from the executive's deferral of taxation from the current to a future period. For example, if the executive expects his or her tax rate to drop in the future, he or she will prefer to receive that income in that future period. While the tax benefits accrue to the executive whose tax bill is being deferred, implicitly, the corporation will benefit by paying a lower level of compensation than it would have otherwise. In contrast, when the tax benefits accrue to the corporation, for example, where the deferral is motivated by Internal Revenue Code Section 162(m), the corporation may have to provide a monetary incentive for the executive to engage in the deferral, perhaps matching a portion of the deferral or paying a premium rate on the amounts deferred. In either case, the corporation has to be careful that the cost of obtaining those tax benefits, that is, the cost to the corporation of complying with Internal Revenue Code (for example, making the plan nondiscriminatory) and Employee Retirement Income Security Act requirements, does not exceed the value of those benefits.

In addition to being used to minimize the joint tax burden, deferred compensation can be structured, for example via vesting requirements, to provide monetary incentives to executives to remain with the corporation. Focusing on pensions for the moment, recall from Chapter 7 that for highly paid executives, the majority of their pension comes from supplemental plans not subject to ERISA regulations. Thus, the corporation is free to design the plan to improve incentives and retain employees.

Amount Deferred

When an executive defers compensation, the ultimate payout is determined by the amount deferred and the returns on that amount. In some cases, the corporation mandates the deferral, for example, to comply with Section 162(m). Most of the time, however, it is the executive who determines the amount deferred, although the corporation can encourage deferral via matching and premium interest rates.

From the viewpoint of the executive, deferral is beneficial for tax purposes if he or she expects a lower tax rate in the future. From the viewpoint of the corporation, deferral may be beneficial for tax purposes by preserving deductions under Section 162(m), helping provide the proper incentives. For example, as discussed earlier, to counteract the horizon problem, the corporation should provide compensation that is paid after retirement, with the ultimate payout tied to corporate performance after the executive retires.

Length of Deferral

For tax purposes, the maximum benefit may be achieved if the executive defers compensation until retirement, when he or she will possibly be in a lower tax bracket and will no longer be subject to Section 162(m) requirements. However, taxes are not the only consideration. To the executive, the deferral is also a way of providing retirement income. Thus, he or she may prefer that the payout be in the form of a lifetime annuity that begins after retirement. For incentive purposes, the corporation may want the deferral to continue for a period after retirement, so that its value might more fully reflect the actions the executive took prior to retirement.

Deferral Vehicle

The returns can be based upon a fixed interest rate agreed to in advance; an interest rate that varies with some published rate (for example, the rate on U.S. Treasury Bills); the rate of return on a stock index (for example, the S&P 500); or the rate of return on the corporation's own shares. As executives are risk averse, all else equal, they would generally prefer the more certain payout of the fixed interest rate or the rate of return on treasury bills to the more uncertain payouts associated with the rates of return on the stock index or corporations shares. However, all else is not equal, as the expected return on the market, that is, the stock index, is generally higher than the expected return on treasury bills. Further, the corporation can offer premiums to encourage executives to defer their compensation into corporate shares. If executive ownership is low, making the payout dependent upon the corporation's share price provides incentives for the executive to increase shareholder value. Thus, the corporation may want to provide incentives to defer compensation into corporate stock, for example, by offering that stock at a discount. Of course, if executive ownership is high, then tying the payout to the corporation's share price imposes unnecessary risk on the executive, possibly causing him or her to take suboptimal actions to reduce risk. Similarly, if the executive is nearing retirement, and hence, his or her horizon is affecting his or her incentives to invest in projects that pay off subsequent to retirement, the corporation wants to encourage deferral into corporate stock.

If the executive is risk averse, he or she is also concerned that the corporation have the wherewithal to make the promised payments in the future. While as noted earlier, funding the deferral results in adverse tax consequences, the corporation can use a Rabbi Trust to provide some security for the deferred compensation, although even a Rabbi Trust does not guarantee payment.[26]

Restrictions

As noted above, the bulk of deferred compensation is not governed by ERISA. Consequently the corporation is free to impose any restrictions it chooses, subject to the caveat that those restrictions will reduce the value of the deferred compensation to the executive. Consider the following example, which illustrates how restrictions can be used to encourage retention. The corporation has a lot of investment opportunities and, consequently, wants to structure the deferral to encourage the executive to remain with the corporation until retirement. Thus, it makes payment conditional upon the executive remaining with the corporation until age 65. The executive, while valuing those benefits, places a lower value on those benefits than he or she would have in the absence of restrictions. In particular, the executive will discount for the possibility that he or she does not remain with the corporation until retirement, and hence does not receive the benefit.

Benefits and Perquisites

Corporations normally provide benefits including, but not limited to, health and life insurance to their executives. One reason is that these benefits have become so common that they are expected, not only by executives, but by lower-level employees as well. Given that individuals can buy these "benefits" directly, why have they so often become associated with employment? One reason is the Internal Revenue Code encourages them. Consider the following example. An executive in the 40-percent tax bracket wishes to purchase a health insurance policy that costs $6,000. To obtain the funds to pay for the policy, the individual has to earn $10,000. Of the $10,000, $4,000 will go to taxes, while the remaining $6,000 will then go toward the purchase of the insurance policy. Alternatively, the employer can purchase the insurance policy directly and pay $4,000 to the employee. The tax code encourages the latter. The reason is, from the employer point of view, whether it directly pays the executive $10,000, or pays the executive $4,000 and buys them an insurance policy costing $6,000, the corporation has a tax-deductible expense of $10,000. In contrast, in the first situation the executive has taxable income of $10,000, whereas in the second, if the corporation meets certain requirements (to be discussed below), the executive only has taxable income of $4,000. After the payment of $1,600 in taxes, the executive has $2,400 left under the second alternative, whereas under the first alternative, nothing remained.[27] So, the executive is $2,400 better off. In theory, the tax savings that arise from minimizing their joint tax burden will be shared between the executive and the corporation, thus while the corporation will buy the policy, it may not pay the executive the full remaining $4,000.

It would be remiss not to, at least in general terms, discuss the requirements necessary for most benefits to qualify for this preferential tax treatment. A primary requirement is that the plan is nondiscriminatory, that is the plan does not discriminate in favor of highly paid executives. Effectively, for the executive benefit to qualify for favorable tax treatment, benefits must be offered to all employees. If not, then the premiums paid by the corporation will be taxable to the executive. Thus, if they do not have a qualified plan, corporations should weigh the benefits, tax savings to employees—some of which the corporation may be able to capture—against the costs to the corporation of implementing a qualified plan. If the corporation is not able to capture any of the benefits, then obviously the costs outweigh the benefits.

As noted in Chapter 14, a problem arises if the benefits must be offered to all employees on a nondiscriminatory basis, when employees value those benefits differentially. In equilibrium, the largest amount by which the corporation can reduce explicit compensation by is the valuation placed upon the benefits by the employee. In some cases, the valuation placed upon the benefits by the employee is less than the cost to the corporation, hence there are no benefits to capture. Scholes and Wolfson (1992) and Jones (2001) note that the use of "cafeteria plans" may mitigate this problem by giving the employee the choice between a menu of taxable and nontaxable benefits, and taxable salary. Thus, at a minimum, the corporation can reduce its explicit salary by the amount it provides employees via the cafeteria plan.

While benefits such as health and life insurance are offered to executives as well as lower-level employees, certain perquisites, such as access to the company plane, chauffeur service and country club memberships, are limited to top executives.

While these perquisites have a business purpose if they allow executives to work more efficiently and securely, they have also been viewed as evidence of corporate waste and executive greed. Perhaps for this reason and in light of the revised/increased SEC disclosure requirements, White and Lublin (2007) found a number of companies cutting back on perquisites.

Summary

The focus of this chapter was on designing a compensation contract. The various components of the compensation package, that is, salary, bonus, stock compensation, deferred compensation and benefits, were reviewed, with an eye toward how the executive and corporate characteristics identified in Chapter 14 influence the inclusion of the component in the compensation package, as well as the amount of the component.

The overwhelming majority of compensation contracts include a salary component, thus the issue is not whether to pay salary, but rather, how much to pay. Salary, the primary fixed component of the compensation package, is important not just because it is a major component of the compensation package, but because other components are sometimes linked to it, for example, when the target bonus is a percentage of salary. In general, salary should increase with increases in an executive's opportunity cost, risk aversion and ownership. As a proportion of the compensation package, salary should increase with the executive's risk aversion and ownership, and decrease as the executive approaches retirement age. Salary should also increase with the size of the corporation and the degree of monitoring, and be lower for firms that are cash constrained.

While most corporations pay bonuses to their executives, in most cases the amount is neither fixed in advance, nor guaranteed. Thus, bonuses are conditional compensation. The payments are made conditional upon implicit or explicit performance measures to provide the executive with the proper incentive to exert effort to increase shareholder value. Unfortunately, in some cases, the existence of an explicit performance measure provides executives with dysfunctional incentives, for example, to manipulate results to increase the performance measure. Thus, the performance measure should be chosen with care, and consideration should be given to using multiple financial, as well as nonfinancial, measures. Also to be chosen with care are the targeted bonus amount, performance period, performance target and method of payment.

Executive characteristics, as do corporate characteristics, influence these choices. For example, the targeted bonus amount, or the bonus as a portion of the compensation package, will decrease with risk aversion and increase with the executive's opportunity cost. Similarly, a corporation with liquidity constraints is more likely to pay a smaller cash bonus and devote a larger portion of the compensation package to stock-based compensation.

In designing its executive compensation package, a corporation must decide not only whether it will award stock compensation, but also, if it does, if that compensation should take the form of stock options or grants. It must also decide on the amount of compensation, which will involve valuation issues, and the terms of the compensation. For example, if the stock compensation takes the form of stock options, the corporation needs to decide if the options should be tax qualified or nonqualified, what the exercise price should be, and the length, if any, of the vesting period. The corporation will also have to decide on the frequency with which it makes grants. Given that stock-based compensation provides a direct incentive for the executive to increase shareholder value, the choices made are essential in providing the proper incentives. As with salary and bonus, executive and corporate characteristics influence these choices. In general, if executive ownership is low, it would be optimal to make a large portion of the compensation package stock based. However, other factors need to be considered, such as executive risk aversion, the systematic risk of the corporation's shares and the corporation's financial circumstances. For example, as executive risk aversion increases, so does the executive's preference for shares over options.

Deferred compensation, while not as sexy or politically visible as the other components of the compensation package, can be material in amount—note the $1 million-plus retirement packages discussed in Chapter 7—and valuable in providing executives with the proper incentives. For example, the choice of vesting period, as well as the benefit formula, can be chosen to provide executives with monetary incentive to remain with the corporation. Other choices that need to be made are the amount to be deferred, the length of the deferral, the deferral vehicle and whether the corporation will match part or all of the deferral or provide a premium rate on the deferral. If used effectively, deferred compensation is also a way to maximize corporate tax deductions and minimize taxes paid by the executive.

Footnotes

1 Compensation Resources Group (2000).

2 Page 35, R.H. Donnelley proxy statement filed with the Securities and Exchange Commission, April 25, 2006.

3 Page 20, Ohio Casualty proxy statement filed with the Securities and Exchange Commission, March 12, 2004.

4 Page 4, Fisher Communications form 8-K filed with the Securities and Exchange Commission, Oct. 27, 2006.

5 Healy (1985) discusses these incentives in more detail.

6 Further, to qualify for exemption from the $1 million deductibility limit under Internal Revenue Code Section 162(m), bonuses must be paid based upon an explicit performance-based plan approved by shareholders. If the bonuses are not deductible, the after-tax cost to the corporation is increased.

7 Alternatively, the corporation facing liquidity constraints can require the bonus be deferred to a future period.

8 Alternatively, rather than replace the bonus, the corporation could require, or provide incentives for the executive, to defer the bonus until a future period in which it expects to have taxable income.

9 This may not always be true. Recall in the example above, because of the loss in year two, the total bonus paid over three years was $4 million if a one-year performance period was used, and $3.25 million if a three-year period was used.

10 It would also serve no purpose, as the share and options holdings already provide the incentive to maximize share price.

11 Peoples Bancorp proxy statement filed with the Securities and Exchange Commission, March 14, 2006.

12 Google form 8-K filed with the Securities and Exchange Commission, Dec. 13, 2006.

13 Upon transfer, the remaining life of the option would be reduced to a maximum of two years.

14 Some corporations allow the executive to pay the exercise price with shares already held, in which cash payment of the exercise price would not be a cash inflow to the corporation.

15 Other forms of stock compensation exist but are omitted for brevity and to focus on the most important and commonly used forms. For example, a

third possibility is stock or share appreciation rights. Stock appreciation rights, which are sometimes offered in tandem with stock options, can be structured to provide the same incentives and payoffs as options. The major difference is that with a stock appreciation right, the corporation pays, in either cash or stock, to the executive the difference between market and exercise price at the time of exercise, whereas with an option the executive has to pay cash and then may either retain the shares or sell them in the market. Thus, while payment of the exercise price with a stock option is a source of cash to the corporation, a stock appreciation right may result in a cash outflow. A second difference is that the financial reporting differs for stock appreciation rights, as rather than the cost being determined at the grant date, the cost is estimated as the intrinsic value at the grant date and then adjusted for changes in intrinsic value until the exercise date–thus the final charge is uncertain and can vary greatly from period to period.

[16] Alternatively, perhaps corporations are unwilling to admit/accept a stagnant share price and thus grant options regardless.

[17] Recall, however, that in equilibrium, the executive will receive a larger amount of options than share grants to make up for both this risk and the fact that he or she needs to pay an exercise price with options.

[18] For example, Matsunaga (1995, note 6) finds only 5 percent of his sample corporations issued options with an exercise price below the fair market value at the grant date. Similarly, Hall and Murphy (2000) find that "94 percent of options grants to S&P 500 CEOs in 1998 were at-the-money grants."

[19] While there are strong theoretical justifications for granting premium and/or indexed options, Hall and Murphy (2000) argue that setting the exercise price at the grant date exercise price is optimal. They assert that risk-averse executives discount the value of the option based upon the probability of payout, "and setting exercise prices at (or near) the grant-date market price maximizes incentives by ensuring a relatively high probability of ultimate payout."

[20] Page 20, Chubb form 10-Q filed with Securities and Exchange Commission, Aug. 13, 1999.

[21] Page 22, Chubb proxy statement filed with Securities and Exchange Commission, March 24, 1999.

[22] One interesting transaction involved UnitedHealth Group. In 1999, with its stock price depressed, the company issued additional options to replace those whose exercise price far exceeded the then-current market price. The original options were to be suspended, but not cancelled in an attempt to avoid the financial accounting consequences that would have been associ-

ated with a repricing. Later on, when the stock price increased, the suspended options were reactivated, meaning that employees got to exercise both the original and replacement options (Forelle and Bandler 2006).

23 The example assumes the corporation does not pay any dividends.

24 In advocating its above proposal, the AFL-CIO noted that Chubb stock price had lagged behind the S&P 500 and other relevant indexes over the previous five years, and that "Chairman and CEO Dean O'Hare stands to gain nearly $3.8 million from last year's grant of 99,250 stock options by achieving a mere 5% annual shareholder return over the term of the grant."

25 The primary focus of this section is on nonqualified deferred compensation, for example, supplemental executive retirement plans, which make up the vast majority of deferred compensation for top executives of major corporations.

26 Recall that the only reason the executive is able to avoid taxation when the corporation funds the Rabbi Trust is because the funds are available to the general creditors of the corporation in case of bankruptcy.

27 While in theory medical expenses, including insurance premiums, are deductions by individuals, in practice few are able to benefit from that deduction as the amount must exceed 7.5 percent of adjusted gross income before any benefit.

Part VI
Conclusion

Chapter 16

Recent Trends and Their Implication for the Future of Executive Compensation

Executive compensation, while always high, continues to increase. As illustrated in Table 2-8, mean (median) compensation increased 139 (93) percent during the period from 1992 to 2005, a period over which the Consumer Price Index increased by 39 percent. These increases continued despite the long standing outcry over excessive compensation, an outcry which led to increased Securities and Exchange Commission disclosure requirements in 1993 and 2007, Internal Revenue Code restrictions on the deductibility of executive compensation and Financial Accounting Standards Board modifications in the accounting treatment for employee stock options. Table 2-8 also shows that while each component of the compensation package increased over the period, the increase in compensation was primarily driven by the performance-based components of compensation. That is, while mean total CEO compensation increased from \$2,333,037 in 1992 to \$5,578,289 in 2005, for an increase of 139 percent, the mean value of bonus increased from \$492,553 to \$1,200,417, an increase of 144 percent, the mean value of stock option grants increased from \$703,729 in 1992 to \$1,870,255, an increase of 166 percent, and the mean value of stock grants increased from \$215,168 to \$1,054,171, an increase of 390 percent. In contrast, mean salary increased from \$634,985 to \$745,962, an increase of only 17 percent, less than the increase in the Consumer Price Index of 39 percent.

Before continuing, however, three points should be made. First, when the press refers to average CEO compensation, it uses means (as given above), which are driven by outliers. In contrast, median compensation is "more reasonable." For example, median total CEO compensation for 2005 was \$3,346,766, 40 percent less than the mean of \$5,578,289. Second, is that this is CEO compensation for the approximately 1,500 largest corporations, whereas there are more than 10,000 publicly traded companies in the United States. Given the relationship between CEO compensation and firm size, average total compensation for CEOs of all publicly traded corporations is probably significantly lower than either the $5,578,289 or $3,346,766. Finally, when discussing excessive "executive compensation," most observers cite CEO compensation; as shown in Table 2-13, lower-level executives make significantly less. For example, the fifth highest-ranking executive received mean (median) total compensation of $1,604,787 ($956,075) in 2005, less than 30 percent of what the CEO received.

Attempts to Explain Past Increases in Compensation

To predict the future, one needs to interpret the past. At many points over the last 75 years (see *New York Times* 1930, Baker 1977 and 1978, Kraus 1980, Unger 1984, Patton 1985 and Crystal 1991), critics have asserted that executive compensation was excessive and out of control. Yet it continues to grow. More so, it continues to grow at rates far in excess of the rates of inflation, the growth of the economy and the average worker. For example, Murphy and Zabojnik (2004) note CEO cash compensation has increased from 25 times that of the average production worker in 1970 to 90 times in 2000. And this was without even considering stock compensation. Why has this happened? Bebchuk et al. (2002) argue that entrenched CEOs use their power over the board to extract high compensation. However, while their theory might explain the level of CEO compensation, it does not necessarily explain the increases. That is, if the CEO compensation reflects rent extraction, why is it greater today than it was 30 years ago? Murphy and Zabojnik (2004) argue that it is the competition for CEOs that has driven the increase in pay levels, providing as evidence consistent with their hypothesis the fact that more CEOs have been appointed from outside the corporation in recent years, CEOs who would not be able to extract rents from captive boards, but who would presumably receive market levels of compensation.

Can this trend of increased compensation continue in the future? Frydman and Saks (2005), who examined executive compensation from 1936 to 2003, find that it has not always increased. During World War II, there was a sharp decline in total compensation, followed by a modest increase from the mid-1940s to the 1970s. Perhaps more importantly, "executive compensation declined steadily relative to both market value and sales from the 1940s to the 1960s." Frydman and Saks find that tax policy has an effect on executive compensation; in particular, passage of the 1950 Revenue Act led to the use of stock options. Further high personal tax rates tend to have a moderating effect on compensation overall and on the form of compensation, that is, at higher tax rates, preferences for options are greater.

Use of Compensation Surveys

Another explanation suggested (for example, see Williams 1985) for the increase in executive compensation has been the use of pay surveys and the information in them to "impart an upward bias on compensation" (Ezzamel and Watson 1998). Most corporations aim to pay between the 50th and 75th percentile, and almost none aim to pay below average compensation. Given that no one expects consulting firms to stop conducting these surveys, or for corporations and their executives to stop using them as justification for compensation packages, theoretically there is no end in sight, short of a restructuring of the corporation and its control processes.[1] That is, short of ending the separation between the ownership and control of the corporation, executive compensation will continue to climb.[2]

Along these lines, Thomas and Martin (1999) suggest that, and Park et al. (2001) find evidence consistent with, the increased disclosure and dissemination of information about executive compensation increases compensation, as knowledge about what others are receiving fuels pay demands by executives. It will be interesting to examine whether the recent increase in executive compensation disclosure mandated by the SEC will lead to even higher compensation.

Performance

Another potential explanation for the vast increase in compensation is firm performance. Hence, the increase in compensation represents pay for performance. For example, at the end of 1992, the Dow Jones Industrial Average was 3,301, the Standard & Poor's 500 Index was 433 and the NASDAQ Index 677. By the end of 2005, the Dow Jones Industrial Average had increased to 10,718, the Standard & Poor's 500 Index to 1,248 and the NASDAQ to 2,205. Thus, while mean CEO compensation increased by 139 percent during the 13-year period, the Dow increased by 225 percent, the Standard & Poor's 500 by 189 percent and the NASDAQ by 226 percent during that same period.

The period under examination included a bull market (1992-1999), accounting for nearly all of the increases in the indices reported above. However for the six years through the end of 2005, each of these indices was, at best, flat. Perhaps not coincidentally, mean total CEO compensation reached a maximum of $6,798,501 in 2000, declining for four consecutive years afterward.

Increased Demand on Executives

Tosi et al. (2000), in conducting a "meta-analytic review of the empirical literature on the determinants of CEO pay," find that "firm size accounts for more than 40% of the variance in total CEO pay." In contrast, they find that "firm performance accounts for less than 5% of the variance" in CEO pay. Murray (2001) points out that growth in size increases the demands on the CEO. Gabaix and Landier (2006) develop a model that predicts the level of CEO compensation should increase with the size of the firm. Consequently, they argue that the "six-fold increase of CEO pay between 1980 and 2003 can be fully attributed to the six-fold increase in market capitalization of large US companies." More than increasing the demand on the CEO, firm size or scale also increases the marginal product or value of the CEO to shareholders. For example, Wal-Mart has gotten so large that the decisions of its executives not only influence its results, they also affect rivals and the economy as a whole (Whitehouse 2006). More important, from a shareholder perspective, the decisions made by the CEO of Wal-Mart, for example to cut prices or scale back expansion, have the potential to generate enormous changes in market value. In fact, a decision by Wal-Mart to cut capital spending increased its share price by more than 5 percent (Hudson 2006). With a market value of about $200 billion, that decision increased shareholder value by more than $10 billion.

Increased Demand for Executives

> Where there is a powerful need for a scarce resource, there will be equivalent payment made for it. And few resources in business are as scarce as good CEOs. This is a supply-side problem, not a demand-side one, and demand-side interventions that seek to cap compensation will simply drive compensation packages into gray- and black-market status, not effectively cap them.[3]

An alternative economic explanation for the growth in executive compensation requires executives to be viewed as products in limited supply (see for example, Kay 1998). That is, few people are qualified to be CEO of a large public corporation. And as demand increases for a product in limited supply, the price will rise. Empirically, Himmelberg and Hubbard (2000) find:

> The compensation packages for the CEOs of larger, more complex firms, however, require highly skilled CEOs. Empirically, the compensation packages for the CEOs of these firms are more sensitive to aggregate shocks,

which we interpret as evidence that the supply of highly skilled CEOs is relatively inelastic.

Similarly, Chen (2003) finds CEO compensation is positively related to the rate of entry in a specific industry, concluding "this appears to explain a portion of the dramatic increase in CEO compensation during the time period examined."

Consistent with this hypothesis explaining some, or all of the increase in executive compensation, the number of publicly traded corporations listed on Compustat, a database maintained by Standard & Poor's of large, publicly traded U.S. companies, was 7,488 at the end of 1992 and 10,194 at the end of 2005. While this trend may or may not continue, a trend that is sure to continue for some time is the increasing globalization of capital markets, which will increase the demand for professional managers to run companies outside the United States. For example, as of Dec. 31, 1992, there were 9,240 companies included in Global Vantage, a database maintained by Standard & Poor's of large, publicly traded corporations around the world. By Dec. 31, 2005, Global Vantage included 17,642 corporations.

Increased Use of Stock Compensation

A big factor in the increase in compensation is the increase in the amount and proportion of stock-based compensation. The increase in stock-based compensation has been driven by a number of factors. For example, until recently, academics, politicians and shareholders, among others, have argued for the increased alignment of shareholder and management interests. That is, granting stock-based compensation will make executives act like shareholders, thereby remedying the problems associated with low executive ownership. In addition, stock compensation satisfies the call for "pay for performance," as the ultimate value of stock-based compensation is theoretically based on firm performance. Beyond this, the almost uninterrupted bull market that ran from the early 1980s until the beginning of 2000 caused executives to think of stock compensation as riskless, the lack of accounting recognition (prior to 2006) caused corporations to think of stock options as costless and their tax deductibility caused corporations to view stock compensation as a source of cash. However, the first two of these factors, the extended bull market and the favorable accounting treatment, have now changed. Perhaps because of the end of the bull market, and the anticipation of the less favorable accounting treatment for stock options, corporations in recent years have begun shifting equity compensation to restricted stock from options.

Increased Risk

Risk has increased over time. Compensation risk has increased as the package has shifted toward conditional and stock-based compensation. In particular, it has been argued by many that because of risk aversion, underdiversification, nontransferability and the consequent early exercise, the value placed upon employee stock options by executives is substantially less than the cost to the firm (for example, see Hall and Murphy 2000). Consequently, the value placed on the compensation package by the executive is less than that which is reported in the proxy statement and popular press. Additionally, as corporations increasingly demand that executives own larger amounts of stock, the incentives derived from ownership exceed those associated with the compensation.[4] However, that share ownership also increases the risk of the underdiversified executive. Finally, the risk of being replaced has increased (Lucier et al. 2006), as shareholders have become more involved and boards more proactive (Lear 2000).[5] As discussed in Chapter 8, being replaced is costly to the executive, as only 6 percent of executives find comparable jobs. In equilibrium, CEOs have to be compensated for all these increased risks via increased monetary rewards.

The Future of Executive Compensation, or Can These Trends Continue?

Can these trends continue? As noted above, consultants will continue to produce, and corporations continue to use (or misuse) compensation surveys, driving pay higher. In addition, the increased globalization of business and demand for professional managers should continue to increase, at least for the near future. Both of these factors will continue to drive executive compensation higher. The increase in executive turnover, and the riskiness of executive compensation, that is pay for performance, also seems to be a permanent fixture, although as discussed below, corporations may take steps to reduce that riskiness. If they do so, that could reduce the level of compensation. Similarly, the risk of turnover, while it may not increase, seems to be permanent, as greater expectations are being placed on the board of directors by shareholders.

One major unknown is the effect of the new standard on accounting for share-based payments, in the United States and internationally, which should, in theory at least, eliminate some of the bias toward fixed-price share options. Rather, compensation committees may focus on using equity compensation to create value rather than on minimizing accounting expense. The consequences are many. First, we will probably see fewer fixed stock options as compensation committees are forced to recognize that options are not costless. Second, compensation committees are likely to increase the use of other forms of equity compensation, including restricted stock and variable/performance-based stock options. Depending on which way they decide to go, we could either see less or more pay for performance. Time-based restricted stock, while increasing in value with share price performance, has less of a tie to performance than fixed stock options which only have value if the share price increases. Alternatively, we may see more variable or performance-based options, where the exercise price may adjust according to some market index, or the options may only become exercisable if some performance condition is met.

The major uncertainty is future performance, in particular, future stock price performance. Consider two scenarios, the first being that the market, which has been flat since 2000, resumes its upward climb, the latter being that the market remains stagnant or even declines.

Bull Market Resumes

The 2000 market decline and the lack of new highs by the major indices through the end of 2005 should have convinced most executives that stock compensation is not riskless. Still, if the market should resume its climb, executives will demand increasing amounts of stock compensation. Rising dilution, however (see discussion in Chapter 6), as well as the increased proxy statement disclosure requirements and developments in accounting for stock-based compensation, have convinced many, if not most, shareholders that stock-based compensation is costly. In addition, academics and politicians have come to realize that stock compensation is not the panacea they once imagined it to be. For example, Reingold and Grover (1999) report on a study that found returns to shareholders in companies with the highest overhang, which is potential dilution associated with stock options, was lower than that of firms with medium or low overhang. Thus, there will be resistance, in many quarters, to increases in the level of stock compensation, and in fact, there may be resistance to stock compensation continuing at the same level. However, a share-the-wealth mentality makes it more likely that the level of stock and overall compensation can be maintained, or even increased, in a bull market than is likely in a down or stagnant market.

Market Remains Stagnant or Declines

"When the market is up, executives all want equity," said James A. Hatch, an executive vice president at Compensation Resource Group, a pay adviser. "When the market is down, they all say 'The market has nothing to do with the performance of this company.'"[6]

The extended bull market ended in the early part of 2000. During 2000, all major stock indexes showed losses. The NASDAQ composite index dropped 39.3 percent, the Standard & Poor's 500 Index 10.1 percent and the Dow Jones Industrial Index 6.2 percent (Ip 2001). Former highfliers Priceline.com and eToys dropped 97 percent and 99 percent, respectively. Since that time, the broad market indices have recovered, but the six-year period from the beginning of 2000 to the end of 2005 was, at best, flat.

This is important because, as noted throughout this book, stock compensation makes up a large portion of the executive compensation package. For example, Table 2-5 shows that in 2005, a mean (median) of 28 (24) percent of the value of the compensation package consists of stock-option grants, with an additional 14 (0) percent coming from stock grants. What should a corporation do after a steep fall in its share price that results in options being out of the money? Should those corporations stop granting stock-based compensation? Should they shift from stock options to stock grants? Microsoft was one of the corporations affected by this decline and, while retaining equity compensation, it took a number of approaches. First, in April of 2000, it gave about 70 million new stock options to its employees at a lower exercise price to make up for the stock's decline since the company's previous option grant in July 1999 (Sloan 2000). Then, as discussed in Chapter 1, as its price stagnated, in 2003, Microsoft shifted its equity compensation from stock options to restricted stock.

One could say the compensation package as designed is optimal and continue to include stock in the package. To maintain the incentives intended to result from the grant of options, which are now far out of the money, and hence, have little incentive and retentive effect for executives, the corporation would have to grant new options and/or reprice existing options at the new lower price. Repricing options, while a commonly used technique in the 1990s, fell out of favor as discussed below, and is no longer a viable option for companies. First of all, it is politically unpopular with shareholders, whose shares are not repriced, and consequently who have lost money.[7] For example, the State of Wisconsin Investment Board introduced the following resolution, which would require shareholder approval of any future repricings, at the General Datacomm Industries 1999 annual meeting:

"WHEREAS, the General DataComm Industries, Inc. (GDC) board has supported the adoption of numerous incentive compensation plans over the years, regardless of company or stock performance; and

WHEREAS, during the previous several years, the company has granted options for millions of GDC shares leading to an unacceptable level of potential dilution; and

WHEREAS, notwithstanding high dilution and poor company performance over the past 3 years, GDC continues to retain a policy that outstanding
options can be repriced to a lower exercise price at such time as the board
shall determine;

NOW THEREFORE, BE IT RESOLVED:
PURSUANT TO THE AUTHORITY OF SHAREHOLDERS TO CHANGE
BYLAWS, THE FOLLOWING BYLAW SHALL BE ADDED TO THE
BYLAWS OF GENERAL DATACOMM INDUSTRIES, INC.: OPTION
REPRICING. THE COMPANY SHALL NOT REPRICE ANY STOCK
OPTIONS ALREADY ISSUED AND OUTSTANDING TO A LOWER
STRIKE PRICE AT ANY TIME DURING THE TERM OF SUCH OPTION,
WITHOUT THE PRIOR APPROVAL OF SHAREHOLDERS.

SUPPORTING STATEMENT
Stock option plans have been used for many years by corporate manage-
ment as incentives for attracting and retaining qualified employees.
Shareholders generally support the use of reasonable levels of incentive
compensation to provide a competitive employment environment.
However, excessive reliance on such plans is unfair to existing shareholders.

Certain companies have continued to expand the use of such plans to
the point where existing shareholders face serious potential dilution. As
of July 31, 1998, GDC had options granted or available for grant to
employees of over 4,936,688 shares, representing potential dilution of
over 22%. This level of potential dilution and the trend toward even higher
grants should not be supported.

GDC has a history of repricing "underwater-options". In May, June and July,
1997, the Company repriced 863,400 options with exercise prices as high as
$15.50 down to a low of $6.75. GDC again repriced another 93,900 options in
June, July and August, 1998 from as high as $15.88 to a low of $3.94 per share.
GDC feels it can restart the clock on any number of options at anytime without
regard for shareholder concerns. We are concerned about further repricings if
GDC stock price continues to drop and have asked that the Company disclose
any additional repricings it may engage in prior to the meeting. We urge
management to raise the stock price, not lower the exercise price.

We believe GDC has been irresponsible in its use of incentive compensation, since options are authorized, issued and can be repriced without regard to performance. While we support the concept of incentive compensation, the above program is unjustified and inequitable to existing shareholders. Notwithstanding repeated requests, the company has refused to adopt a policy against repricing of "underwater-options". The above resolution will help ensure a measure of fairness to the use of incentive compensation at GDC."[8]

The proposal passed by a vote of 5,755,519 for, versus 4,947,119 against, with 195,563 abstained.[9] Second, taking advantage of the broad opposition to repricings, the Financial Accounting Standards Board (FASB) imposed the requirement that companies recognize an expense for options repriced. Under FASB Interpretation No. 44: Accounting for Certain Transactions Involving Stock Compensation, any time a company cancels options and reissues new ones within six months, the transaction would be considered a repricing and would result in earnings charges over the remaining life of the option. Carter and Lynch (2003) show that repricings nearly dried up as a result of the new rule. However, if the company cancels options and waits at least six months to issue new ones, there is no charge. Leonhardt (2001) reports companies such as Sprint, Ariba, Lante, RealNetworks and Pumatech have all taken advantage of this loophole to avoid the earnings charge. While avoiding the spirit of the FASB ruling, this maneuver is perfectly legal. More troubling, however, is the effect of the transaction on incentives. Consider the following paragraph from the 8-K filed by Sprint with the Securities and Exchange Commission on Oct. 17, 2000.

On October 17, 2000, Sprint Corporation announced that its Board of Directors had approved a proposal to offer employees a choice to cancel certain stock options granted to them in 2000 in exchange for new options to purchase an equal number of the same class of shares. The new options will be granted six months and one day from the date the old options are cancelled. The exercise price of the new options will be the market price on the grant date.

Given the exercise price will be the market price on the grant date, which is six months and one day later, executives do not have the incentive to increase the share price between the date of cancellation and the future date of grant (Brown 2001). More to the point, they have the incentive to make the price as low as possible on the future grant date so that their options will be worth more. The lower the grant date market price, the lower the exercise price, and the greater the value of the option. Executives can do this in part by delaying the release of good news and accelerating the release of bad news. Yermack (1997), Aboody and Kasznik (2000) and Callaghan et al. (2004) find that the timing of stock option awards and stock option repricings is consistent with such behavior. For the record, Sprint's share price on Oct. 17, 2000, was $23.19, and its price on May 18, 2001, was $20.90.

Taking the political and incentive aspects into consideration, unless the corporation is constrained in terms of its ability to grant new options, it should grant new options rather than reprice existing ones. Further, the corporation should consider granting a larger than average number of options, as it is likely that a large part of the executive's option portfolio will be out of the money.[10] In addition, corporations should resort to more frequent grants to minimize risk and maintain compensation now that the market is no longer increasing.[11] However, the corporation must be careful because, as noted in Chapter 6, executives can benefit from fluctuations in corporations' shares even if the long-term trend is flat. In those situations, the executive, but not the shareholders, will benefit. To control for this possibility, the corporation should consider issuing indexed options. In a declining market, executives may be more willing to accept indexed options, as rather than depend on an uncertain repricing, the downward adjustment in stock price is automatic, if the index to which it is tied decreases.

An alternative view is that the optimal compensation package should contain more cash and/or stock grants to compensate for the loss in value of existing stock options and decrease in desirability of future stock options. While this may be optimal, there are some who take a more cynical view:

> A look back at history would suggest that even in a slow or bear market, executives always manage to get theirs. When the market doesn't cooperate, the rules simply change. In the 1970s, for example, a prolonged bear market made options worthless. So companies switched over to bonus plans based on the achievement of cash-based internal goals and restricted stock; although those shares can't immediately be sold, unlike options they retain their value even if they fall below their grant price.[12]

Osterland (2001) reports that following the market downturn in 2000, "consultants confirm that renegotiated employment contracts and pay packages being offered to new hires involve a large cash element." Among the companies taking this approach are Amazon.com, which, in 2000, increased the magnitude of the signing bonuses it paid to its new executives and paid, for the first time, cash bonuses other than signing bonuses to four of its top executives (all but CEO Jeff Bezos).[13] Similarly, Condon (2001) reported that Globix gave Marc Bell, its CEO, $6 million of restricted stock, the first time it had granted restricted stock, after its stock price dropped by 95 percent.

While executives will always look for ways to increase their compensation or maintain it at the current level, shareholders and their representatives on the board of directors may not be willing to acquiesce, especially in a declining market. In a declining market, large absolute amounts of CEO compensation cannot be justified even as a small percentage of the increase in shareholder wealth. In fact, while in an up market, compensation amounts to a sharing of the gains, in a declining market, compensation, especially stock grants, can be viewed as a transfer of ownership from shareholders to executives. Further, in a declining market, the marginal product of an executive will be perceived to be lower.

Overall, the expectation is that in a declining market, compensation should decrease, and we should see a change in the composition of the executive compensation package away from stock and toward cash. The shift toward cash can be explained by at least two reasons. First, in a declining market, the perceived riskiness of stock compensation increases, so executives require a larger amount of stock to substitute for a given level of cash compensation. Thus, from the corporate point of view, the relative costliness of stock to cash compensation increases, and in equilibrium, the corporation itself will elect to replace stock with cash. Second, as noted above, in a declining market, the amount shareholders and directors are willing to pay decreases. In equilibrium, the only way executives would be willing to accept a lower level of compensation is to reduce the risk of that compensation.

Summary

Predicting the future level and composition of the executive compensation package is wrought with uncertainty. An uncertainty caused by an unpredictable stock market, political environment and tax system. Still, some educated guesses can be made. The market gyrations of recent years have convinced many, if not most, executives that stock-based compensation is risky. Similarly, the events of the past decade—increasing dilution, revamped disclosure requirements and revised accounting treatment—have convinced most executives, as well as investors, politicians and regulators, that stock-based compensation is costly. Combined with the fact that executives perceive the value of stock-based compensation at amounts lower than that publicized in proxy statements and the popular press, we should see a shift from stock to cash compensation. This shift, because it reduces the risk of the executive, may reduce the overall level of compensation. That is, it may reduce the cost to the firm/amount disclosed to shareholders, although it may actually increase the value of the compensation package to the executive.

Footnotes

[1] Some argue that the recent trend of the compensation committee hiring its own compensation consultants may put a brake on the increase in executive compensation.

[2] Interestingly, the increase in stock compensation and the associated dilution could achieve this goal by transferring the ownership of the corporation from the shareholders to the executives, if the executives were then required to hold on to those shares.

[3] Formaini (2006).

[4] See for example Conyon (2006), who finds the magnitude of incentives provided by ownership nine times the magnitude of incentives provided by the compensation package.

[5] Leonard (2000), as well as Bianco and Lavelle (2000), Lear (2000), Martin (2000) and Lyons (1999), document that CEO turnover has gotten higher and CEO tenure shorter in recent years.

[6] Leonhardt (2000).

[7] While shareholders are not insulated from losses, sometimes employees are. Simon and Bryan-Low (2001) and Schroeder and Weil (2001) report that some companies, whose prices had declined, were "wiping out" prior stock option transactions that had occurred at higher prices. To be more precise, these companies were, following a decline in their share prices, allowing employees to reverse previous option exercises.

[8] Page 13, General Datacomm Industries Proxy Statement filed with the Securities and Exchange Commission, Jan. 15, 1999.

[9] Page 23, General Datacomm Industries Form 10-Q filed with the Securities and Exchange Commission, May 17, 1999.

[10] Some companies have already taken this step. Osterland (2001) reports, "after its stock had plunged by 40 percent, Microsoft doubled its option grants to 34,000 full-time employees to make up for the underwater options issued in 1999."

[11] Osterland (2001) reports that Cisco Systems is "considering stepping up the frequency of its grants to a quarterly or monthly basis."

[12] Reingold and Grover (1999).

[13] Page 11 Amazon.com proxy statement filed with the Securities and Exchange Commission, April 13, 2001.

Glossary

Academic research: the hypothesizing, gathering, analyzing and interpretation of information that is done by educators.

Agency costs: the costs that arise because of the separation of the ownership from the management of the corporation.

Agent: an individual who performs services for compensation on behalf of one or more other individuals, collectively known as the "principal."

Annuity: a series of payments of equal amount, usually made at fixed intervals.

Assets: economic resources owned by a company.

Arms-length transaction: a transaction occurring between unrelated parties who are looking out for their own interests.

At-the-money option: when the exercise price of an option is equal to the current market price.

Audit committee: a group within a company's board of directors, established to oversee and provide a check on the company's financial controls. Its duties include the hiring and supervision of the CPA firm engaged to conduct an audit.

Backdating of stock options: pretending an option was granted at an earlier date, when the stock price was lower.

Beta: a measure of the extent to which the returns on a given stock move in tandem with the stock market. Also known as *systematic risk*.

Big bath: when a company is having a "bad" financial year and takes additional accounting charges to increase the company's loss in that year.

Bonus: a form of compensation conditioned upon individual, group or firm performance.

Black-Scholes option-pricing model: a model developed by Fisher Black and Myron Scholes to value stock options.

Blockholder: a large shareholder.

Board of Directors: a group of individuals elected by shareholders to represent their interests.

Bond: a long-term promissory note issued by a business or governmental unit.

Cafeteria plan: a compensation plan under which employees may choose among a menu of taxable and nontaxable fringe benefits and taxable salary.

Capital markets: financial markets for stocks and long-term debt (can be either public or private).

Capital expenditures: costs incurred to acquire a long-lived asset.

Capital gain: the gain realized on the sale of a capital asset (as defined by the Internal Revenue Code). For individuals, capital gains, if held for more than one year, are taxed at favorable (that is, lower) rates.

Capital stock: transferable units of ownership in a company.

Cash flow: the corporation's change in cash, based on its operating, investing and financing activities.

CEO: chief executive officer.

Chairman of the Board: a director selected by his or her peers to lead the board.

Change-in-control payment: the payment an executive receives due to a change in control of the employer.

Class hegemony theory: the theory which argues that executives share a common bond, and that through boards composed primarily of CEOs, executives are able to pursue their own goals and interests.

Common stock: a basic type of capital stock that possesses the rights of ownership, including the right to elect the corporation's directors.

Compensation: all forms of financial payments and/or tangible services and benefits employees receive as part of an employment relationship.

Compensation committee: a subcommittee of the board of directors responsible for setting executive compensation.

Compensation package: the different forms of remuneration that are included in an employee's compensation.

Compliance costs: costs associated with drawing up benefits plans to meet regulations, for example, the requirements of the Internal Revenue Code.

Conditional compensation: compensation dependent on individual, group or corporate performance.

Consumer price index: measure of the average change over time in the prices paid by consumers for a market basket of goods and services.

Compensation contract: an agreement that provides specific details of the executive's employment with the corporation.

Corporate governance: laws, regulations and customs affecting the control of the corporation, including, but not limited to, the hiring, firing and compensating of executives.

Deduction: a subtraction in the calculation of taxable income.

Deferred compensation: compensation earned in the current period that an employee agrees to receive, and the employer agrees to pay, in a future period.

Deferred compensation plan: a plan that allows, encourages and/or mandates that executives defer portions of their salary and/or bonuses.

Defined benefit plan: a pension plan that provides employees with promised payments after retirement based upon predetermined benefits formulas.

Defined contribution plan: a pension plan under which the employer makes contributions to an employees's retirement account without specifying payments the employee receives in retirement.

Depreciation: the allocation of the cost of a tangible asset to expense in the periods in which benefits are received from the asset.

Dilution: the reduction in percentage ownership of existing shareholders associated with the increase in the number of shares outstanding over time. Dilution is a major cost of stock option and stock grant programs.

Diversification: the reduction in risk achieved by the distribution of investments.

Dividends: a distribution of resources made by a corporation to its stockholders.

Dollar-amount formula: a defined benefit pension formula where the benefits are based on a dollar amount for each year of service.

Earning per share: net income divided by the weighted-average number of common shares outstanding during the year.

Efficiency wage theory: a theory which suggests that employees are paid a premium to provide them with the incentive to exert effort to avoid being fired, hence to increase productivity and reduce employee turnover.

Efficient market: a market in which prices rapidly reflect all information concerning the security.

Employee: an individual who performs services for compensation under the direction and control of the employer.

Employee Retirement Income Security Act (ERISA): a federal law that sets the provisions and standards for defined benefit and defined contribution pension plans.

Employee Stock Option Appreciation Rights Securities (ESOARS): derivative securities designed to provide a market basis for estimating the fair value of stock options granted to employees.

Equity-based compensation: compensation whose value varies with the company's share price.

Event study: a research method that uses market reaction to a public disclosure of an action or event to infer the effect of the action on firm value.

Executives: the top managers of a corporation.

Exercise price: the price at which an option allows the holder to purchase shares of stock.

Expenses: decreases in the company's assets associated with its profit-directed activities.

Explicit contract: a formal, written contract between two parties.

External equity: the comparison of one's compensation to that of peers outside the corporation. That is, a comparison of compensation with peers in similar jobs, but in different organizations.

Fiduciary: a person entrusted to oversee the investment of another, with the responsibility to make decisions in accordance with those individuals' interests.

Figurehead theory: a theory that suggests the CEO should not be paid based upon operating results, but rather for his or her role as leader or political figurehead.

Financial Accounting Standards Board (FASB): a private-sector organization that is in charge of determining generally accepted accounting principles in the United States.

Financial keiretsu: groups of firms, common in Japan, organized around their major lender and holding a large amount of cross-shareholdings.

Firm: the generic name for business organization. Firms include sole proprietorships, partnerships and corporations.

Fixed compensation: compensation that does not vary with firm performance.

Fixed costs: costs that do not vary with output.

Fringe benefit: usually a noncash item received by an employee as additional compensation.

Generally Accepted Accounting Principles (GAAP): the set of accounting methods required by the Securities and Exchange Commission (SEC) and the Financial Accounting Standards Board (FASB) for financial reporting.

Golden handcuffs: a monetary incentive that the executive will receive only if he/she remains with the corporation for a specified period of time.

Golden parachute: large payment made to a departing executive of a company, usually made after the corporation is acquired.

Gray directors: directors who are not employed by the corporation but have a relationship with it or its executives.

Hedging: the strategy of taking offsetting positions to minimize risks.

Horizon: the amount of time a person expects to spend in a particular job.

Horizontal equity: the equity within a level of the organization.

Human capital: the value of an individual's skills and abilities.

Human capital theory: the theory which posits that the value of the executive, and hence, his or her compensation, is based upon his or her accumulated knowledge and skills.

Implicit contract: promises and shared understandings that are not expressed in a formal written contract between two parties.

Inelastic: the demand for the product or service is constant regardless of price.

In-the-money option: an option where the exercise price is less than the current market price (an option that has a positive intrinsic value).

Income statement: an activity statement that subtracts from the corporation's revenue those expenses that have generated the revenues; the result is a net income or a net loss.

Independent directors: individuals (directors) whose primary employment is not with the corporation. Also known as *outside directors*.

Indexed options: options whose exercise price is adjusted for market and/or industrywide movements. Also known as market-adjusted options.

Inside directors: those individuals (directors) who are employed full time with that corporation.

Interlocking directorate: when a director is an executive of another corporation upon whose board this CEO serves.

Internal equity: equity within the organization, both vertical and horizontal.

Internal Revenue Code (IRC): the foundation of all U.S. federal tax law, containing all the tax laws enacted by Congress. Contains provisions addressing income taxes, estate and gift taxes, employment taxes, alcohol and tobacco taxes and other excise taxes.

Intrinsic value of an option: the excess of the current market price of a share of stock over the exercise price of the option at a point in time.

Liabilities: debts or obligations, which will require the future expenditure of assets.

Liquidity: a company's ability to meet its continuing obligations.

Managerialism theory: the theory which suggests that the separation of ownership and control gives executives the power to increase the level, and reduce the risk, of their compensation.

Marginal benefit: the incremental benefit associated with an action.

Marginal cost: the additional cost associated with an action.

Marginal product: the additional output associated with the employment of one additional resource unit, with other factors held constant.

Marginal productivity theory: the theory which suggests that, in equilibrium, the executive should receive, as compensation, his or her value to the corporation.

Market-adjusted option: an option whose exercise price is adjusted for market and/or industrywide movements. Also known as an indexed option.

Market share: a company's percentage of total sales within its industry.

Megagrants: large grants of options or shares.

Merger: the combination of two or more business entities to form a single entity.

Net income: the excess of revenue earned over expenses in a given period.

Noncompete agreement: a contract that prohibits an employee from working for other potential employers.

Nonqualified deferred compensation plan: a deferred compensation plan that does not meet Internal Revenue Code requirements for favorable tax treatment.

Nonqualified option: options that do not meet Internal Revenue Code requirements for favorable tax treatment.

Operating cycle: the period of time it takes a company to convert its inventory into cash.

Opportunity cost: the value of a resource in its next best alternative use.

Option-pricing model: calculates the value of a stock option, normally incorporating the price of the underlying share, exercise price, share-price volatility, risk-free interest rate, dividend yield and time to expiration.

Ordinary income: any income that is not a capital gain (or loss).

Out-of-the-money option: options with an exercise price that exceeds the current market price (an option that has no intrinsic value). Also known as an *underwater option*.

Outside directors: those individuals (directors) where the corporation is not their primary employer. Also known as *independent directors*.

Pension: deferred compensation that provides income to an employee after retirement from the corporation.

Pension back loading: a way of structuring a pension plan so that benefits paid from it increase with the individual's tenure with the firm.

Performance-based compensation: compensation paid based on performance of the individual, group or corporation.

Performance-vested options: options whose exercisability depends upon future performance.

Political costs: costs imposed by the government's ability to tax and regulate.

Premium options: options issued with an exercise price exceeding the current market price at the time of grant.

Present value: the amount that an investor would pay today for the right to receive a future cash flow.

Principal: one who employs another to act on his or her behalf subject to his or her general control and authority.

Prospect theory: the theory of executive compensation that focuses on the executive's loss aversion, and the need to overcome that aversion.

Proxy: a document giving one person the authority to act for another person (usually the power to vote shares of common stock).

Proxy statement: a statement given to stockholders prior to a stockholders meeting.

Qualified options: options that meet Internal Revenue Code requirements for favorable tax treatment. As a result, the employee will be able to defer taxation upon exercise and, if certain holding requirements are met, will pay taxes at the lower capital gains rate. Also see *Tax-qualified options*.

Qualified deferred compensation plan: a deferred compensation plan that meets Internal Revenue Code requirements for favorable tax treatment. As a result, the employer will be able to claim a tax deduction when the plan is funded, while the employee will be able to defer taxation until receipt of the compensation.

Rabbi trust: a trust established for the benefit of the participant by an employer, which the employer cannot touch, but creditors of the employer can. Allows a corporation to fund deferred compensation without the deferred compensation becoming taxable to the employee.

Reload options/replacement options: options that allow the executive to pay the exercise price with previously owned shares and then receive new options to replace those used to pay the exercise price.

Repurchase program: a program whereby a corporation buys back its own shares, sometimes to mitigate the dilutive impact of employee compensation programs.

Repricing options: either decreasing or increasing the exercise price of options that the executive already holds.

Restricted stock: stock that has certain limitations.

Return on assets: net income expressed as a percentage of average total assets.

Return on equity: net income expressed as a percentage of average total stock-holders equity.

Revenue: the dollar amount of goods and services charged to customers for these goods and services delivered by a company.

Risk: the uncertainty regarding an outcome.

Risk averse: the assumed preference of an individual for less risk.

Risk premium: the difference between the return generated on a given risky item and a riskless one.

Salary: a fixed contractual amount of compensation that does not explicitly vary with performance.

Securities and Exchange Commission (SEC): a governmental organization that has the legal authority to set accounting principles and financial reporting requirements for publicly held corporations in the United States. Also regulates U.S. securities markets.

Severance package: the payment the executive receives when leaving a company.

Shareholder: owner of capital stock in a corporation.

Share price: the amount someone would pay to purchase one share of capital stock in a corporation.

Social comparison theory: the theory by which board members use their own pay as a reference point when setting pay of executives.

Spring-loading: awarding options just before the release of good news.

Stock appreciation rights: a form of compensation whereby the corporation pays the executive, in cash and/or shares, the difference between the current market price and the exercise price of the stock appreciation rights.

Stock-based compensation: stock options and stock grants given to employees of the corporation.

Stock grants: the transfer of shares from the corporation to the individual, normally an employee, in exchange for services rendered.

Stock options: allows their holder to purchase one or more shares of stock at a fixed "exercise" price over a fixed period of time.

Stock units: a compensation plan whose ultimate value is limited to the corporation's stock price.

Supplemental executive retirement plans: additional pension plans and/or agreements designed for executive officers.

Systematic risk: a measure of the extent to which the returns on a given stock move in tandem with the stock market. Also known as *Beta*.

Tax-qualified options: options that meet IRS requirements for preferential tax treatment. As a result, the employee will be able to defer taxation upon exercise and if certain holding requirements are met, will pay taxes at the lower capital gains rate. Also see *qualified options*.

Terminal earnings formulas: a pension whereby benefits are based on average earnings during a specified number of years, at the end of a worker's career.

Time value of an option: the value attached to the potential increase in the stock price over the life of the option.

Tournament theory: a theory that suggests that executive compensation is set to provide incentives not to the executives themselves, but rather to their subordinates, so that those subordinates will strive for promotion to the executive ranks.

Treasury bond: a U.S. government security with a maturity of more than 10 years that pays interest periodically.

Unsystematic risk: the movement of a company's stock price that is not caused by market movements.

Underwater options: when the exercise price of an option is greater than the current market price. Also known as an *out-of-the-money option*.

Vertical equity: refers to equity in compensation across levels of the organization.

Vesting period: the amount of time which must pass before the employee has the unconditional right to pension, to exercise his or her options or to sell restricted shares of stock.

References

Abdel-Khalik, A. Rashad. 1988. "Incentives for Accruing Costs and Efficiency in Regulated Monopolies Subject to ROE Constraint." *Journal of Accounting Research*, 26 (Supplement): 144-174.

Aboody, David and Ron Kasznik. 2000. "CEO Stock Option Awards and the Timing of Corporate Voluntary Disclosures." *Journal of Accounting & Economics*, 29(1): 73-100.

Abowd, John M. 1990. "Does Performance-Based Managerial Compensation Affect Corporate Performance?" *Industrial and Labor Relations Review*, 43(3): 52-73.

Adams, Marilyn and Dan Reed. 2003. "Analysts Fret Over Turnaround as Delta CEO Plans Resignation." *USA Today*, Nov. 25: B1.

Agarwal, Naresh C. 1981. "Determinants of Executive Compensation." *Industrial Relations*, 20 (Winter): 36-46.

Agrawal, Anup and Gershon Mandelker. 1987. "Managerial Incentives and Corporate Investment and Financing Decisions." *Journal of Finance*, 42 (September): 823-837.

Aggarwal, Rajesh and Andrew A. Samwick. 1999. "The Other Side of the Tradeoff: The Impact of Risk on Executive Compensation." *Journal of Political Economy*, 107(1): 65-105.

Allen, Michael P. 1981. "Power and Privilege in the Large Corporation: Corporate Control and Managerial Compensation." *American Journal of Sociology*, 86: 1,112-1,123.

Almazan, Andres and Javier Suarez. 2004. "Entrenchment and Severance Pay in Optimal Governance Structures." *Journal of Finance*, 58, 519-547.

Antle, Rick and Abbie Smith. 1985. "Measuring Executive Compensation: Methods and an Application." *Journal of Accounting Research*, 23: 296-325.

Antle, Rick and Abbie Smith. 1986. "An Empirical Investigation of the Relative Performance Evaluation of Corporate Executives." *Journal of Accounting Research*, 24: 1-39.

Baber, William R., Surya N. Janakiraman and Sok-Hyon Kang. 1996. "Investment Opportunities and the Structure of Executive Compensation." *Journal of Accounting and Economics*, 21(3): 297-318.

Backer, Larry Cata. 2005. "Director Independence and the Duty of Loyalty: Race, Gender, Class, and the Disney-Ovitz Litigation." *St. Johns Law Review*, 79: 1,011-1,103.

Baker, George, Robert Gibbons and Kevin J. Murphy. 1994. "Subjective Performance Measures in Optimal Incentive Contracts." *The Quarterly Journal of Economics*, 109(4): 1,125-1,156.

Baker, George P., Michael C. Jensen and Kevin J. Murphy. 1988. "Compensation and Incentives: Practice vs. Theory." *Journal of Finance*, 43 (3): 593-616.

Baker, John C. 1977. "Are Corporate Executives Overpaid?" *Harvard Business Review*, 55(4): 51-56.

Baker, John C. 1978. "Are Executives Overpaid? Readers Respond." *Harvard Business Review*, 56(4): 54-66.

Balsam, Steven. 1998. "Discretionary Accounting Choices and CEO Compensation." *Contemporary Accounting Research.*

Balsam, Steven. 1994. "Extending the Method of Accounting for Stock Appreciation Rights to Employee Stock Options." *Accounting Horizons.*

Balsam, Steven. 1995. "The Effect of the Tax Reform Act of 1986 on the Composition of the Executive Compensation Package." *Advances in Taxation.*

Balsam, Steven. 1993. "Treatment of Executive Compensation." *Pennsylvania CPA Journal.*

Balsam, Steven, Eli Bartov and Carol Marquardt. 2002. "Accruals Management, Investor Sophistication and Equity Valuation: Evidence from 10-Q Filings." *Journal of Accounting Research*, 40 (4): 987-1,012.

Balsam, Steven, Richard H. Gifford and Sungsoo Kim. 2007. "The Effect of Stock Option Grants on Voluntary Employee Turnover." *Review of Accounting and Finance*, forthcoming at press time.

Balsam, Steven and Setiyono Miharjo. 2007. "The Effect of Equity Compensation on Voluntary Executive Turnover." *Journal of Accounting and Economics*, 43: 95-119.

Balsam, Steven, Haim Mozes and Harry A. Newman. 2000b. "Reporting of Stock Option Grant Information Under FASB 123." Working paper, Temple and Fordham universities.

Balsam, Steven, Robert Halperin and Haim A. Mozes. 1997. "Tax Costs and

Nontax Benefits: The Case of Incentive Stock Options." *Journal of the American Taxation Association.*

Balsam, Steven, Sebastian O'Keefe and Mark M. Wiedemer. 2006. "From the Frontlines, Initial Firm Reaction to SFAS 123R: Share-Based Payments." *Journal of Accountancy*, forthcoming at press time.

Balsam, Steven and Wonsun Paek. 2001. "Insider Holding Requirements, Stock Options and Stock Appreciation Rights." *Journal of Accounting, Auditing and Finance*, 16 (Summer): 227-248.

Balsam, Steven and David Ryan. 1996. "Response to Tax Law Changes Involving the Deductibility of Executive Compensation: A Model Explaining Behavior." *Journal of the American Taxation Association*, 18: 1-12.

Balsam, Steven and David Ryan. 2007. "Limiting Executive Compensation: The Case of CEOs Hired after the Imposition of 162(m)." *Journal of Accounting, Auditing and Finance.*

Balsam, Steven and Qin Jennifer Yin. 2005. "Explaining Firm Willingness to Forfeit Tax Deductions Under Internal Revenue Code Section 162(m): The Million-Dollar Cap." *Journal of Accounting and Public Policy*, 24: 300-324.

Bandler, James. 2005. "MassMutual Fires O'Connell, Citing Misconduct." *The Wall Street Journal*, June 24.

Bank, David. 1999. "Microsoft to Increase Pay, Stock Options As Demand for Skilled Workers Grows." *The Wall Street Journal*, May 10.

Banker, Rajiv D., Seok-Young Lee, Gordon Potter and Dhinu Srinivasan. 1999. "An Empirical Analysis of Continuing Improvements Following the Implementation of a Performance-Based Compensation Plan." Working paper, University of Pittsburgh.

Barnea, Amir and Ilan Guedj. 2006. "But, Mom, All the Other Kids Have One! CEO Compensation and Director Networks." Working paper, University of Texas at Austin.

Bartov, Eli and Partha Mohanram. 2004. "Private Information, Earnings Manipulations and Executive Stock Option Exercises." *The Accounting Review*, 79(4): 889-920.

Beatty, Randolph P. and Edward J. Zajac. 1994. "Managerial Incentives, Monitoring and Risk Bearing: A Study of Executive Compensation, Ownership and Board Structure in Initial Public Offerings." *Administrative Science Quarterly*, 39: 313-335.

Bebchuk, Lucien and Jesse Fried. 2004a. "Pay Without Performance: The Unfulfilled Promise of Executive Compensation." Harvard University Press.

Bebchuk, Lucien and Jesse Fried. 2004b. "Stealth Compensation Via Retirement Benefits." *Berkeley Business Law Journal*, Vol. 1, No. 2, Fall 2004, 291-326.

Bebchuk, Lucien, Jesse Fried and David Walker. 2002. "Managerial Power and Rent Extraction in the Design of Executive Compensation." *University of Chicago Law Review*, 69(3): 751-761.

Berle, Adolf Augustus and Gardiner Coit Means. 1932. *The Modern Corporation and Private Property*. New York: Commerce Clearing House.

Bergstresser, Daniel and Thomas Philippon. 2006. "CEO Incentives and Earnings Management: Evidence from the 1990s." *Journal of Financial Economics*, 80(3): 511-529.

Bertrand, Marianne and Sendhil Mullainathan. 2000. "Agents With and Without Principals." *The American Economic Review*, 90 (2): 203-208.

Bettis, J. Carr, John M. Bizjak and Michael L. Lemmon. 2005. "Exercise Behavior, Valuation and the Incentive Effects of Employee Stock Options." *Journal of Financial Economics*, 76: 445-470.

Bettis, J. Carr, John M. Bizjak and Michael L. Lemmon. 2001. "Managerial Ownership, Incentive Contracting, and the Use of Zero-Cost Collars and Equity Swaps by Corporate Insiders." *Journal of Financial and Quantitative Analysis*, 36(3): 345-370.

Bhagat, Sanjai, Dennis C. Carey and Charles M. Elson. 1998. "Director Ownership, Corporate Performance and Management Turnover." Working paper.

Bianco, Anthony and Louis Lavelle. 2000. "The CEO Trap." *BusinessWeek*, Dec. 11: 86-92.

Billett, Matthew T., David C. Mauer and Yilei Zhang. 2006. "Stockholder and Bondholder Wealth Effects of CEO Incentive Grants." Working paper, University of Iowa and Southern Methodist University.

Bizjak, John M., James A. Brickley and Jeffrey L. Coles. 1993. "Stock-Based Incentive Compensation and Investment Behavior." *Journal of Accounting and Economics*, 16: 349-372.

Blackhurst, Chris. 1995. "The Sorry Saga of Share Options." *Management Today*, November: 66-69.

Boschen, John F. and Kimberly J. Smith. 1995. "You Can Pay Me Now and You Can Pay Me Later: The Dynamic Response of Executive Compensation to Firm Performance." *Journal of Business*, 68(4): 577-608.

Brady, Diane. 2000. "Who Does Linda Wachner Answer To?" *BusinessWeek*, August 7: 37.

Bremner, Brian. 1999. "The Stock-Option Option Comes to Japan." *BusinessWeek*, April 19: 39.

Brickley, James A., Sanjai Bhagat and Ronald C. Lease. 1985. "The Impact of Long-Range Managerial Compensation Plans on Shareholder Wealth." *Journal of Accounting and Economics*, 7(1-3): 115-130.

Brickley, James A., James S. Linck and Jeffrey L. Coles. 1999. "What Happens to CEOs After They Retire? New Evidence on Career Concerns, Horizon Problems, and CEO Incentives." *Journal of Financial Economics*, 52: 341-377.

Brown, Larry. 1999. "Managerial Behavior and the Bias in Analysts' Earnings Forecasts." Working paper, Georgia State University.

Brown, Ken. 2001. "Now, Some Hope for Their Stock to Tank." *The Wall Street Journal*, June 4: C1.

Browne, Andrew. 2004. "Chinese Recruit Top Executives Trained Abroad." *The Wall Street Journal*, November 30: B1.

Brubaker, Harold. 2000. "Genesis Offers Stock for Worthless Options." *Philadelphia Inquirer*, March 12, P E1.

Bryan, Stephen, Lee-Seok Hwang, April Klein and Steven Lilien. 2000. "Compensation of Outside Directors: An Empirical Analysis of Economic Determinants." Working paper, Wake Forest University, Baruch College and New York University.

Bryan, Stephen, Lee-Seok Hwang and Steven Lilien. 1999. "The Change in Operating and Regulatory Environment and the CEO Compensation-Performance Sensitivity: An Empirical Analysis of Electric Utilities." Working paper, Baruch College.

Bryan, Stephen and April Klein. 2004. "Non-Management Director Options, Board Characteristics, and Future Firm Investments and Performance." Working paper, Wake Forest and New York Universities.

Bryan, Stephen H., Robert C. Nash and Ajay Patel. 2002. "The Equity Mix in Executive Compensation: An Investigation of Cross-Country Differences." Working paper, Wake Forest University.

Bryan, Stephen H., Robert C. Nash and Ajay Patel. 2006. "The Structure of Executive Compensation: International Evidence from 1996-2004." Working paper, Wake Forest University.

Buckman, Rebecca. 2000. "Microsoft Uses Stock Options to Lift Morale." *The Wall Street Journal*, April 26: A3.

Bulkeley, William M. 2004. "Harvard Key Asset Managers Receive Pay Cut—to $25 Million." *The Wall Street Journal*, Nov. 23: C3.

Burgstahler, David and Ilia Dichev. 1997. "Earnings Management to Avoid Earnings Decreases and Losses." *Journal of Accounting and Economics*, 24: 99-126.

Burgstahler, David and Michael Eames. 2006. "Management of Earnings and Analysts' Forecasts to Achieve Zero and Small Positive Earnings Surprises." *Journal of Business Finance and Accounting*, 33(5&6): 633-652.

Burns, Natasha and Simi Kedia. 2006. "The Impact of Performance-Based Compensation on Misreporting." *Journal of Financial Economics*, 79: 35-67.

Bushman, Robert M., Raffi J. Indjejikian and Abbie Smith (1996). "CEO Compensation: The Role of Individual Performance Evaluation." *Journal of Accounting and Economics*, 21(2): 161-193.

Byrne, John A. 1996. "And You Thought CEOs Were Overpaid." *BusinessWeek*, Aug. 26: 34.

California Public Employees Retirement System. 1998. *Corporate Governance Core Principles & Guidelines: The United States*, April 13. Sacramento, Calif. California Public Employees Retirement System.

Callaghan, Sandra Renfro, P. Jane Saly and Chandra Subramaniam. 2004. "The Timing of Option Repricing." *The Journal of Finance*, 59: 1,651-1,676.

Campbell, Cynthia J. and Charles E. Wasley. 1999. "Stock-Based Incentive Contracts and Managerial Performance: The Case of Ralston Purina Company." *Journal of Financial Economics*, 51: 195-217.

Capozza, Dennis R. and Paul J. Seguin. 2003. "Inside Ownership, Risk Sharing and Tobin's Q-Ratios: Evidence from REITs." *Real Estate Economics*, 31(3): 367-404.

Carlin, Tyrone M., G. William Ford and Ruiyan W. Huang. 2005. "Executive Option Plans and Firm Performance—Bigger Isn't Better." Working paper, Macquarie University.

Carlton, Jim. 2000. "Dot-Com Executives Depart for Pre-IPO Start-Ups." *Wall Street Journal*, April 27, P. B6.

Carpenter, Jennifer N. and Barbara Remmers. 2001. "Executive Stock Option Exercises and Inside Information." *Journal of Business*, 74(4): 513-534.

Carpenter, Jennifer N. and David Yermack. 1999. "Introduction: Executive Compensation and Shareholder Value." *Executive Compensation and Shareholder Value: Theory and Evidence*, Jennifer Carpenter and David Yermack, editors.

Carter, Mary Ellen and Luann J. Lynch. 2003. "The Consequences of the FASB's 1998 Proposal on Accounting for Stock Option Repricing." *Journal of Accounting and Economics*, 35(1): 51-72.

Carter, Mary Ellen, Luann J. Lynch and Irem Tuna. 2007. "The Role of Accounting in the Design of CEO Equity Compensation." *The Accounting Review*, March.

Chan, Gilbert. 2006. "New State Law Empowers Voting by Shareholders." *The Sacramento Bee*, Oct. 4: D1.

Chauvin, Kevin W. and Catherine Shenoy. 2001. "Stock Price Decreases Prior to Executive Stock Option Grants." *Journal of Corporate Finance*. 7: 53-76.

Chen, Jie. 2003. "The Demand Shift for CEOs and CEO Compensation in the 1990s." Working paper, Washington University.

Cheng, Qiang and Terry Warfield. 2005. "Equity Incentives and Earnings Management." *The Accounting Review*, 80 (2): 441-476.

Cheng, Shijun. 2004. "R&D Expenditures and CEO Compensation." *The Accounting Review*, 79 (2): 305-328.

Clark Consulting. 2005. "Executive Benefits—A Survey of Current Trends." 2005 results.

Clarke, Robert N., Martin J. Conyon and Simon I. Peck. 1998. "Corporate Governance and Directors' Remuneration: Views from the Top." *Business Strategy Review*, 9(4): 21-30.

Cohen, Adam. 2000. "Are Lawyers Running America?" *Time*: July 17, 22-25.

Cohen, Randolph B., Brian J. Hall and Luis M. Viceira. 2000. "Do Executive Stock Options Encourage Risk-Taking?" Working paper, Harvard Business School.

Compensation Resources Group. 2000. "Executive Benefits: A Survey of Current Trends."

Condon, Bernard. 2001. "Share Scare." *Forbes*, May 14: 146-148.

Conyon, Martin J. 2006. "Executive Compensation and Incentives." *Academy of Management Perspectives*, February: 25-44.

Conyon, Martin J., John E. Core and Wayne Guay. 2006. "How High Is U.S. CEO Pay?

A Comparison with U.K. CEO Pay." Working paper, University of Pennsylvania.

Conyon, Martin J. and L. He. 2004. "Compensation Committees and CEO Compensation Incentives in U.S. Entrepreneurial Firms." *Journal of Management Accounting Research*, 16: 35-56.

Conyon, Martin J. and Kevin J. Murphy. 2000. "The Prince and the Pauper? CEO Pay in the U.S. and U.K.," *The Economic Journal*, 110: F640-F671.

Conyon, Martin J. and Simon I. Peck. 1998. "Board Control, Remuneration Committees, and Top Management Compensation." *Academy of Management Journal*, 41(2): 146-157.

Conyon, Martin J. and Joachim Schwalbach. 1999. "Corporate Governance, Executive Pay and Performance in Europe." *Executive Compensation and Shareholder Value: Theory and Evidence*, Jennifer Carpenter and David Yermack, editors.

Conwell, Alan. 2001. "Overseas, Salaries are Kept Hush-Hush." *New York Times*, April 1.

Core, John E. and Wayne Guay. 2001. "Stock Option Plans for Non-Executive Employees." *Journal of Financial Economics*, 61(2): 253-287.

Core, John E. and David F. Larcker. 2002. "Performance Consequences of Mandatory Increases in Executive Stock Ownership." *Journal of Financial Economics*, 64: 317-340.

Core, John E, Robert W. Holthausen and David F. Larcker, 1999. "Corporate Governance, Chief Executive Officer Compensation and Firm Performance." *Journal of Financial Economics*, 51:371-406.

Corporate Board Survey: Study Highlights. 2006. Center for Effective Organizations, Marshall School of Business, University of Southern California; Heidrick & Struggles.

Cotter, James F. and Marc Zenner. 1994. "How Managerial Wealth Affects the Tender Offer Process." *Journal of Financial Economics*, 35: 63-97.

Coughlan, Anne T. and Ronald M. Schmidt. 1985. "Executive Compensation, Management Turnover and Firm Performance: An Empirical Investigation." *Journal of Accounting and Economics*, 7, 44-66.

Cowherd, Douglas M. and David I. Levine. 1992. "Product Quality and Pay Equity Between Lower-Level Employees and Top Management: An Investigation of Distributive Justice Theory." *Administrative Science Quarterly*, 37: 302-320.

Cragg, Michael I. and I. J. Dyck. 2000. "Executive Pay and U.K. Privatization: The Demise of 'One Country, Two Systems.'" *Journal of Business Research*, 47: 3-18.

Creswell, Julie. 2006. "Firing Chief Was Wrong, Panel Says." *The New York Times*, Oct. 21: C1.

Cross, P. 1977. "Not Can But Will College Teaching Be Improved." *New Directions for Higher Education*, 17: 1-15.

Crowley, Michael. 2005. "That's Outrageous." *Readers Digest*, October: 39.

Crystal, Graef. 1991. In Search of Excess: *The Overcompensation of the American Executive*. New York: W.W. Norton & Co.

Daily, Catherine M., Jonathan L. Johnson, Alan E. Ellstrand and Dan R. Dalton. 1998. "Compensation Committee Composition as a Determinant of CEO Compensation." *Academy of Management Journal*, 41: 209-220.

Darlin, Damon. 2006. "Pay Deal At Hewlett Is Contested." *The New York Times*, March 6: C1.

Dash, Eric and Milt Freudenheim. 2006. "Chief Executive at Health Insurer is Forced Out in Options Inquiry." *The New York Times*, Oct. 16: A1.

David, Parthiban, Rahul Kochbar and Edward Levitas. 1998. "The Effect of Institutional Investors on the Level and Mix of CEO Compensation." *Academy of Management Journal*, 41: 200-208.

DeAngelo, Harry and Linda DeAngelo. 1991. "Union Negotiations and Corporate Policy: A Study of Labor Concessions in the Domestic Steel Industry During the 1980s." *Journal of Financial Economics*, 30(1), 3-44.

Dechow, Patricia M. and Richard G. Sloan. 1991. "Executive Incentives and the Horizon Problem: An Empirical Investigation." *Journal of Accounting and Economics*, 14(1): 51-90.

Defusco, Richard A., Robert R. Johnson and Thomas S. Zorn. 1990. "The Effect of Executive Stock Option Plans on Stockholders and Bondholders." *Journal of Finance*, 45(2): 617-627.

Degeorge, Francois, Jayendu Patel and Richard Zeckhauser. 1999. "Earnings Management to Exceed Thresholds." *Journal of Business*, 72(1): 1-33.

Delaney, Kevin J. 2005. "Judge Grants Microsoft's Request." *The Wall Street Journal*, July 29.

Denis, David J., Diane K. Denis and Atulya Sarin. 1997. "Ownership Structure and Top Executive Turnover." *Journal of Financial Economics*, 45: 193-221.

Deutsch, Claudia. 2006. "Fewer Chiefs Also Serving as Chairmen." *The New York Times*, March 16.

Drucker, Jesse and James Bandler. 2006. "North Fork Executives to Receive $288 Million for Capital One Deal." *The Wall Street Journal*, March 14: A1.

Dyl, Edward A. 1988. "Corporate Control and Management Compensation." *Managerial and Decision Economics*, 9: 21-25.

Ely, Kirsten. 1991. "Interindustry Differences in the Relation Between Executive Compensation and Firm Performance Variables." *Journal of Accounting Research*, 29, 37-58.

Equilar Inc. 2006. *Executive Compensation Trends*, October.

Ewing, Jack, Stephen Baker, William Echikson and Kerry Capell. 1999. "Eager Europeans Press their Noses to the Glass." *BusinessWeek*, April 19: 40.

Ezzamel, Mahmoud and Robert Watson. 1998. "Market Comparison Earnings and the Bidding-up of Executive Cash Compensation: Evidence from the United Kingdom." *Academy of Management Journal*, 41(2): 221-231.

Ezzell, John R. and James A. Miles. 1995. "Bank CEO Pay-Performance Relations and the Effects of Deregulation." *Journal of Business*, 68 (2): 231-256.

Fackler, Martin and David Barboza. 2006. "In Asia, Executives Earn Much Less." *The New York Times*, June 16.

Fama, Eugene F. 1980. "Agency Problems and the Theory of the Firm." *Journal of Political Economy*, 88: 288-307.

Fama, Eugene F. and Michael C. Jensen. 1983. "Separation of Ownership and Control." *Journal of Law and Economics*, 26 (2): 301-325.

Fairclough, Gordon. 2007. "Heard in Asia: China's Option Play, State-Run Firms Embrace Plans." *The Wall Street Journal*, Jan. 5: C5.

Fairclough, Gordon 2000. "Philip Morris to Pay Special Bonuses to Executives, Citing an 'Unusual Year.'" *The Wall Street Journal*, March 14: A22.

Favole, Jared A. 2007. "More Pressure on Executive Pay." *The Wall Street Journal*, Jan. 24: B9A.

Fenn, George W. and Nellie Liang. 1999. "Corporate Payout Policy and Managerial Stock Incentives." Working paper, Federal Reserve.

Ferris, Stephen, Murali Jagannathan and A. C. Pritchard. 2003. "Too Busy to Mind the Business? Monitoring by Directors with Multiple Board Appointments." *The Journal of Finance*, 58: 1,087-1,112.

Fich, Eliezer M. and Lawrence J. White. 2005. "Why Do CEOs Reciprocally Sit on Each Other's Boards?" *Journal of Corporate Finance*, 11: 175-195.

Fierman, Jaclyn. 1990. "The People Who Set The CEO's Pay." *Fortune*, March 12: 58-61.

Finkelstein, Sydney and Brian K. Boyd. 1998. "How Much Does the CEO Matter? The Role of Managerial Discretion in the Setting of CEO Compensation." *Academy of Management Journal*, 41(2): 170-199.

Firth, Michael, Peter M. Y. Fung and Oliver M. Rui. 2006. "Corporate Performance and CEO Compensation in China." *Journal of Corporate Finance*. 12(4): 693-714.

Flynn, Julia and Gautam Naik. 2003. "Glaxo Sets Plan to Better Link Pay to Performance." *The Wall Street Journal*, Dec. 16: D5.

Forbes. 2006. "The Celebrity 100: Top Earners by Category." July 3: 128.

Forelle, Charles. 2005. "Gillette CEO Defends P&G Pact as Well as His Big Pay Package." *The Wall Street Journal*, Sept. 9: B4.

Forelle, Charles. 2006. "BCGI, Sanmina Employees Leave Over Backdating." *The Wall Street Journal*, Oct. 13: A3.

Forelle, Charles and James Bandler. 2006. "How Did UnitedHealth's McGuire Get Same Options Twice?" *The Wall Street Journal*, Oct. 20: B1.

Forelle, Charles, James Bandler and Steve Stecklow. 2006. "Brocade Ex-CEO, 2 Others Charged In Options Probe." *The Wall Street Journal*, July 21: A1.

Forelle, Charles and Mark Maremont. 2005. "Gillette CEO Payday May Be Richer; Massachusetts Opens Probe Of P&G Deal Amid News, Kilts May Get $185 Million." *The Wall Street Journal*, Feb. 3: B2.

Forelle, Charles and Mark Maremont. 2006. "UnitedHealth's McGuire Could Leave With $1.1 Billion." *The Wall Street Journal*, Oct. 17: B1.

Formaini, Robert. 2006. "Regulating Executive Pay Is a Futile Exercise." *The Wall Street Journal*, Oct. 23: A15.

Foster, Taylor W., Paul R. Koogler and Don Vickrey. 1991. "Valuation of Executive Stock Options and the FASB Proposal." *The Accounting Review* (July): 595-610.

Frankel, Alison. 2006. "Growing Pains; While Am Law 100 Firms Keep Adding More Lawyers, Converting Those Bodies into Revenue Can Pose a Challenge. It Turns Out, Big Isn't Always Better." *American Lawyer*, May 1 (vol 28 issue 5).

Freedman, Michael. 2001. "Judgment Day." *Forbes*, May 14: 132.

Friend, Irwin and Larry H. P. Lang. 1988. "An Empirical Test of the Impact of Managerial Self-Interest on Corporate Capital Structure." *Journal of Finance*, 43(2): 271-281.

Frydman, Carola and Raven E. Saks. 2005. "Historical Trends in Executive Compensation 1936-2003." Working paper, Harvard University and Federal Reserve Board of Governors.

Gabaix, Xavier and Augustin Landier. 2006. "Why Has CEO Pay Increased So Much?" Working paper, Massachusetts Institute of Technology, National Bureau of Economic Research and New York University.

Gaspar, José-Miguel, Massimo Massa and Pedro P. Matos. 2005. "Shareholder Investment Horizons and the Market for Corporate Control." *Journal of Financial Economics*, 76(1): 135-165.

Gaver, Jennifer J. and Kenneth M. Gaver. 1993. "Additional Evidence on the Association Between the Investment Opportunity Set and Corporate Financing, Dividend and Compensation Policies." *Journal of Accounting and Economics*, 16 (1-3): 125-160.

Gaver, Jennifer J. and Kenneth M. Gaver. 1995. "Compensation Policy and the Investment Opportunity Set." *Financial Management*, 24(1): 19-32.

Gaver, Jennifer J., Kenneth M. Gaver and Jeffrey Austin. 1995. "Additional Evidence on Bonus Plans and Income Management." *Journal of Accounting and Economics*, 19(1): 3-28.

Gaver, Jennifer J., Kenneth M. Gaver and George P. Battistel. 1992. "The Stock Market Reaction to Performance Plan Adoptions." *The Accounting Review*, 67(1): 172-182.

Gibbons, Robert and Kevin J. Murphy. 1990. "Relative Performance Evaluation for Chief Executive Officers." *Industrial and Labor Relations Review*, 43(3): 30-51.

Gibbons, Robert and Kevin J. Murphy. 1992. "Optimal Incentive Contracts in the Presence of Career Concerns: Theory and Evidence." *Journal of Political Economy*, 100(3): 468-505.

Gilles, Paul L. 1999. "Alternatives for Stock Options." *HR Magazine*, January: 40-48.

Gomez-Mejia, Luis R. 1994. "Executive Compensation: A Reassessment and a Future Research Agenda." *Research in Personnel and Human Resources Management*, 12: 161-222.

Gomez-Mejia, Luis. R., Henry Tosi and Timothy Hinkin. 1987. "Managerial Control, Performance and Executive Compensation." *Academy of Management Journal*, 30 (1): 51-70.

Goodison, Donna. 2005. "Wie Reaches Green." *The Boston Herald*, Oct. 10: 27.

Gordon, Jeffrey N. 2006. "Executive Compensation: If There's a Problem, What's the Remedy? The Case for 'Compensation Discussion and Analysis.'" *The Journal of Corporation Law*, 31 (Summer): 102-130.

Goyal, Vidhan K. and Chul W. Park. 2000. "Board Leadership Structure and CEO Turnover." Working paper, Hong Kong University of Science and Technology.

Grant, Peter and Rebecca Buckman. 2006. "Fatter Pay Lures University Endowment Chiefs." *The Wall Street Journal*, June 27: C1.

Guay, Wayne R. 1999. "The Sensitivity of CEO Wealth to Equity Risk: An Analysis of the Magnitude and Determinants." *Journal of Financial Economics*, 53(1): 43-71.

Guth, Robert A. and Joann S. Lublin. 2003. "Microsoft Ushers Out Golden Era of Options: Software Giant Exchanges Symbol of Bull Market for Restricted Stock." *The Wall Street Journal*, July 9: A1.

Hall, Brian J. 2003. "Six Challenges in Designing Equity-Based Pay." *Journal of Applied Corporate Finance*, 15(3): 21-33.

Hall, Brian J. and Jeffrey B. Liebman. 1998. "Are CEOs Really Paid Like Bureaucrats?" *The Quarterly Journal of Economics*, 113: 653-691.

Hall, Brian J. and Kevin J. Murphy. 2000. "Optimal Exercise Prices for Executive Stock Options." *American Economic Review*, 90(2): 209-214.

Hallinan, Joseph T. 2000. "Wendt Gave Up $20 Million to Take Conseco's CEO Post." *Wall Street Journal*, July 12, C16.

Hallinan, Joseph T. 2000b. "Conseco Removes Two Directors Who Failed To Pay Back Loans." *Wall Street Journal*, Dec. 13: B10.

Hallock, Kevin F. 1998. "Layoffs, Top Executive Pay and Firm Performance." *The American Economic Review*, 88(4): 711-723.

Hallock, Kevin F. 1997. "Reciprocally Interlocking Boards of Directors and Executive Compensation." *Journal of Financial and Quantitative Analysis*, 32: 331-344.

Hambly, Bob. 2000. *Time*, April 24: 25.

Hambrick, Donald C. and Eric Abrahamson. 1995. "Assessing Managerial Discretion Across Industries: A Multimethod Approach." *Academy of Management Journal*, 38 (5): 1427-1441.

Hambrick, Donald C. and Eric M. Jackson. 2000. "Outside Directors with a Stake: The Linchpin in Corporate Governance." *California Management Review*, 42 (4): 108-127.

Hanlon, Michelle, Shivaram Rajgopal and Terry Shevlin. 2003. "Are Executive Stock Options Associated with Future Earnings?" *Journal of Accounting and Economics*, 36: 3-43.

Harris, David and Jane Livingstone. 2002. "Federal Tax Legislation as a Political Cost Benchmark." *The Accounting Review*, 77 (October): 997-1,018.

Hartzell, Jay C., Eli Ofek and David Yermack. 2004. "What's In It For Me? CEOs Whose Firms are Acquired." *The Review of Financial Studies*, 17(1): 37-61.

Hartzell, Jay C. and Laura T. Starks. 2003. "Institutional Investors and Executive Compensation." *Journal of Finance*, 58 (6): 2,351-2,374.

Hayes, Rachel M. and Scott Schaefer. 1999. "How Much are Differences in Managerial Ability Worth?" *Journal of Accounting and Economics*, 27 (2): 125-148.

Hayes, Rachel M. and Scott Schaefer. 2000. "Implicit Contracts and the Explanatory Power of Top Executive Compensation for Future Performance." *Rand Journal of Economics*, 31 (2): 273-293.

Healy, Paul. 1985. "The Effect of Bonus Schemes on Accounting Decisions." *Journal of Accounting and Economics*, 7: 85-107.

Hebner, Kevin J. and Takao Kato. 1997. "Insider Trading and Executive Compensation: Evidence from the U.S. and Japan." *International Review of Economics and Finance*, 6(3): 223-237.

Hechinger, John. 2006. "McAfee Fires Top Lawyer Amid Stock-Option Probe." *The Wall Street Journal*, May 31: A3.

Hensley, Scott. 2006. "Pfizer's New CEO Gets a Big Checkup." *The Wall Street Journal*, Oct. 14: A2.

Hermalin, B. and M. Weisbach. 1998. "Endogenously Chosen Boards of Directors and Their Monitoring of the CEO." *American Economic Review*, 88: 96-118.

Heron, Randall A. and Erik Lie. 2006a. "Does Backdating Explain the Stock Price Pattern Around Executive Stock Option Grants?" *Forthcoming Journal of Financial Economics*.

Heron, Randall A. and Erik Lie. 2006b. "What Fraction of Stock Option Grants to Top Executives Have Been Backdated or Manipulated?" Working paper, Indiana University and University of Iowa.

Himmelberg, Charles P. and Glenn R. Hubbard. 2000. "Incentive Pay and the Market for CEOs: An Analysis of Pay-for-Performance Sensitivity." Working paper, Columbia University.

Himmelberg, Charles P; Glenn R. Hubbard and Darius Palia. 1999. Understanding the Determinants of Managerial Ownership and the Link Between Ownership and Performance. *Journal of Financial Economics*, September, 53(3): 353-384.

Hodge, Frank, Shiva Rajgopal and Terry Shevlin. 2006. "How Do Managers Value Stock Options and Restricted Stock?" Working paper, University of Washington.

Hoffer, Richard. 2006. "It's Great to be Average." *Sports Illustrated*. 105 (4): July 31.

Holmes, Stanley. 1999. "Boeing Gives Lots of Extras to Make Sure Mulally Stays—His Deal Stands Out Among Execs." *The Seattle Times*, March 19, A1.

Holthausen, Robert, David Larcker and Richard Sloan. 1995. "Annual Bonus Schemes and the Manipulation of Earnings." *Journal of Accounting and Economics*, 19(1): 29-74.

Horn, Patricia. 2000. "Loose Change." *The Philadelphia Inquirer*, Oct. 22: A1, A6.

Huddart, Steven. 1994. "Employee Stock Options." *Journal of Accounting & Economics*.

Huddart, Steven and Mark Lang. 2000. "Information Distribution Within Firms: Evidence from Stock Option Exercises." Working paper, Pennsylvania State University.

Hudson, Kris. 2006. "Wal-Mart Scales Back Expansion Spending as Sales Growth Slows." *The Wall Street Journal*, Oct. 24: A1.

Hymowitz, Carol. 2006. "Sky-High Payouts To Top Executives Prove Hard to Curb." *The Wall Street Journal*, June 26: B1.

Ip, Greg. 2001. "Year of Living Dangerously." *The Wall Street Journal*, Jan. 2: R1, R6.

Ittner, Christopher D., David F. Larcker and Madhav V. Rajan. 1997. "The Choice of Performance Measures in Annual Bonus Contracts." *The Accounting Review*, 72, 231-255.

Jensen, Gerald R., Donald P. Solberg and Thomas S. Zorn. 1992. "Simultaneous Determination of Insider Ownership, Debt and Dividend Policies." *Journal of Financial and Quantitative Analysis*, 27(2): 247-263.

Jensen, Michael J. 1993. "Presidential Address: The Modern Industrial Revolution, Exit and the Failure of Internal Control Systems." *Journal of Finance*, 48: 831-880.

Jensen, Michael J. and William H. Meckling. 1976. "Theory of the Firm: Managerial Behavior, Agency Costs and Ownership Structure." *Journal of Financial Economics*, 3, 305-360.

Jensen, Michael J. and Kevin J. Murphy. 1990a. "Performance Pay and Top-Management Incentives." *Journal of Political Economy*, 98 (2): 225-64.

Jensen, Michael and Kevin J. Murphy. 1990b. "CEO Incentives: It's Not How Much, but How." *Harvard Business Review*, May/June.

Johnson, Alan. 1999. "Should Options Reward Absolute or Relative Shareholder Returns." *Compensation and Benefits Review*, 31(1): 38-43.

Johnson, Marilyn F., Susan Porter and Margaret B. Shackell. 1997. "Stakeholder Pressure and the Structure of Executive Compensation." Working paper, University of Michigan and University of Texas at Austin.

Johnson, Shane A. and Yisong S. Tian. 2000. "The Value and Incentive Effects of Nontraditional Executive Stock Option Plans." *Journal of Financial Economics*, 57 (1): 3-34.

Johnston, David Cay. 1999. "Computer Associates to Appeal Ruling on 3 Executives' Stock." *The New York Times*, Nov. 11: C8.

Jones, Sally M. 2001. *Principles of Taxation for Business and Investment Planning*. Boston: McGraw-Hill Higher Education.

Kadlec, Daniel. 2001. "Time Bomb: 401(k)s Stuffed With Employer Stock are a National Calamity. Here's How to Fix It." *Time*, March 5: 84.

Kaplan, Steven N. 1999. "Top Executive Incentives in Germany, Japan and the USA: A Comparison." *Executive Compensation and Shareholder Value: Theory and Evidence*. Jennifer Carpenter and David Yermack, editors.

Kaplan, Steven N. 1994. "Top Executive Rewards and Firm Performance: A Comparison of Japan and the United States." *Journal of Political Economy*, 102(3): 510-546.

Karnitschnig, Matthew. 2006. "Viacom Lawsuit On Executive Pay Can Go Forward." *The Wall Street Journal*, June 30: B2.

Kato, Hideaki Kiyoshi, Michael Lemmon, Mi Luo and James Schallheim. 2005. "An Empirical Examination of the Costs and Benefits of Executive Stock Options: Evidence from Japan." *Journal of Financial Economics*, 78(2): 435-461.

Kato, Takao. 1997. "Chief Executive Compensation and Corporate Groups in Japan: New Evidence from Micro Data." *International Journal of Industrial Organization*, 15: 455-467.

Kaufman, Jonathan. 2003. "China Reforms Bring Back Executives Schooled in U.S." *The Wall Street Journal*, March 6: 1.

Kay, Ira T. 1998. *CEO Pay and Shareholder Value: Helping the U.S. Win the Global Economic War*. Boca Raton, Fla.; London: St. Lucie Press.

Kimbrough, Michael D. and Henock Louis. 2004. "Financial Reporting Incentives, Managerial Influence and the Trade-Off Among Alternative Forms of Executive Compensation." Unpublished working paper, Harvard and Penn State universities.

Kinney, Michael and Robert Trezevant. 1996. "Smoothing, Big Baths and Special Items." Working paper, Texas A&M and University of Southern California.

Klassen, Kenneth J. 2002. "Options for Compensation." *CA Magazine*, 135(6): 41-44.

Kole, Stacey R. 1997. "The Complexity of Compensation Contracts." *Journal of Financial Economics*, 43: 79-104.

Kooker, Naomi R. 2005. "Reality Check for Boards." *Boston Business Journal*, July 29.

Kotlikoff, Laurence J. and David A. Wise. 1989. "The Wage Carrot and the Pension Stick." W.E. Upjohn Institute for Employment Research, Kalamazoo, Mich.

Kowsmann, Patricia. 2006. "Zions Seeks Bidders In Bid To Change Options Accounting." *Dow Jones Newswires*, June 27.

Kranhold, Kathryn and Joann S. Lublin. 2006. "$100 Million Helps Lure Away General Electric Veteran." *The Wall Street Journal*, Aug. 24: B1.

Kraft, Kornelius and Antonia Niederprum. 1999. "Determinants of Managerial Compensation With Risk-Averse Agents and Dispersed Ownership of the Firm." *Journal of Economic Behavior & Organization*, 40: 17-27.

Kraus, David. 1980. "Executive Pay: Ripe for Reform?" *Harvard Business Review*, 58(5): 36-48.

Kroll, Luisa. 1998. "Warning: Capitalism is Contagious." *Forbes*, May 18: 220-221.

Kumar, Raman and Parvez R. Sopariwala. 1992. "The Effect of Long-Term Performance Plans on Stock Prices and Accounting Numbers, *Journal of Financial and Quantitative Analysis*, 27 (4): 561-573.

Lahart, Justin. 2004. "Street Sleuth: Grasso's Pay Topped Most Peers, Drained Profit." *The Wall Street Journal*, June 2: C3.

Lambert, Richard A., William N. Lanen and David F. Larcker. 1989. "Executive Stock Option Plans and Corporate Dividend Policy." *Journal of Financial and Quantitative Analysis*, 24: 409-425.

Lambert, Richard A. and David F. Larcker. 1987. "An Analysis of the Use of Accounting and Market Measures of Performance in Executive Compensation Contracts." *Journal of Accounting Research*, 25, Supplement, 85-121.

Lambert, Richard A., David F. Larcker and Robert E. Verrecchia. 1991. "Portfolio Considerations in Valuing Executive Compensation." *Journal of Accounting Research*, 29 (Spring): 129-149.

Lambert, Richard A., David F. Larcker and Keith Weigelt. 1993. "The Structure of Organizational Incentives." *Administrative Science Quarterly*, 38: 438-461.

Landler, Mark. 2006. "6 in Germany Settle Landmark Case on Bonuses." *The New York Times*, Nov. 25.

Larcker, David F. 1983. "The Association Between Performance Plan Adoption and Corporate Capital Investment." *Journal of Accounting and Economics*, 5: 3-30.

Larcker, David F., Scott A. Richardson, Andrew J. Seary and Irem Tuna. 2005. "Back Door Links Between Directors and Executive Compensation." Working paper, University of Pennsylvania and Simon Frasier University.

Latour, Almar and Kevin J. Delaney. 2002. "Foreign Business Scofflaws Aren't Hurting Much at All." *The Wall Street Journal*, Aug. 16: A1.

Lavelle, Louis. 2000. "CEO Pay: The More Things Change ..." *BusinessWeek*, Oct. 16: 106,108.

Lazear, Edward P. and Sherwin Rosen. 1981. "Rank-Order Tournaments As Optimum Labor Contracts." *Journal of Political Economy*, 89(5): 841-864.

Lear, Robert W. 2000. "Fire the CEO!" *Chief Executive*, 153: 12.

Leggett, Karby. 2000. "Small Investors Rail Against China." *The Wall Street Journal*, Dec. 28: p. C1, C10.

Lenzner, Robert and Michael Maiello. 2006. "The $22 Billion Gold Rush." *Forbes*, April 10: 86-82.

Leonard, Bill. 2000. "CEO's Length of Tenure is Becoming Quite Short-Lived." *HR Magazine*, 45(5): 20.

Leonard, Jonathan S. 1990. "Executive Pay and Firm Performance." *Industrial and Labor Relations Review*, 43(3): 13-30.

Leonhardt, David. 2000. "Report on Executive Pay: Will Today's Huge Rewards Devour Tomorrow's Earnings?" *New York Times*, April 2.

Leonhardt, David. 2001. "The Letter, If Not the Spirit, on Options Pricing." *New York Times*, April 1.

Leonhardt, David. 2006. "Why CEOs Aren't Sitting in the Dugout." *New York Times*, Oct. 4: C1.

Levitz, Jennifer and John Hechinger. 2006. "Harvard's Endowment Surpasses $29 Billion." *The Wall Street Journal*, Sept. 20: C3.

Lewellen, Wilbur G. and B. Huntsman. 1972. "Managerial Pay and Corporate Performance." *American Economic Review*, 60: 710-720.

Lewellen, Wilbur G. Claudio Loderer and Kenneth Martin. 1987. "Executive Compensation and Executive Incentive Problems; An Empirical Analysis." *Journal of Accounting and Economics*, 9, 287-310.

Lie, Erik. 2005. "On the Timing of CEO Stock Option Awards." *Management Science*, 51(5): 802-812.

Linck, James S., Jeffry M. Netter and Tina Yang. 2006. "Effects and Unintended Consequences of the Sarbanes-Oxley Act on Corporate Boards." Working paper, University of Georgia and Clemson University.

Lippman, John. 2001. "Creative Differences: Battle Over Residuals Could Set the Stage for a Hollywood Strike." *The Wall Street Journal*, March 28: A1.

Lipschultz, David. 2002. "Bosses from Abroad." *Chief Executive*, Jan. 1.

Loderer, Claudio and Kenneth Martin. 1997. "Executive Stock Ownership and Performance: Tracking Faint Traces." *Journal of Financial Economics*, August: 223-255.

Lorsch, Jay L. and Elizabeth M. MacIver. 1989. *Pawns or Potentates? The Reality of America's Corporate Boards*. Boston: Harvard Business School Press.

Lublin, Joann S. 1996. "Sunbeam's Chief Picks Holder Activist and Close Friend as Outside Director." *The Wall Street Journal*, Sept. 26: B9.

Lublin, Joann. S. and L. Scism. 1999. "Stock Options at Firms Irk Some Investors." *The Wall Street Journal*, Jan. 12: C1-4.

Lublin, Joann S., Matt Murray and Rick Brooks. 2000. "Home Depot Nabs GE's Nardelli as CEO." *The Wall Street Journal*, Dec. 6: A3.

Lucchetti, Aaron and Joann S. Lublin. 2006. "Grasso is Ordered to Repay Millions in Compensation." *The Wall Street Journal*, Oct. 20: A1.

Lucchetti, Aaron and Susanne Craig. 2005. "NYSE Report Shows Excesses Under Grasso." *The Wall Street Journal*, Feb. 3: C1.

Lucier, Chuck, Paul Kocourek and Rolf Habbel. 2006. "CEO Succession 2005: The Crest of the Wave." *Strategy + Business*, Summer.

Lyons, Dennis B. K. 1999. "CEO Casualties: A Battlefield Report." *Directors and Boards*, 23(4): 43-45.

Mace, Myles L. 1971. Directors: *Myth and Reality*. Harvard Business School Press.

Main, Brian. 1999. "The Rise and Fall of Executive Share Options in Britain." *Executive Compensation and Shareholder Value: Theory and Evidence*, Jennifer Carpenter and David Yermack, editors.

Main, Brian, Charles A. O'Reilly and James Wade. 1995. "The CEO, the Board of Directors and Executive Compensation: Economic and Psychological Perspectives." *Industrial and Corporate Change*. 4: 293-332.

Mallette, Paul, R. Dennis Middlemist and Willie E. Hopkins. 1995. "Social, Political and Economic Determinants of Chief Executive Compensation." *Journal of Managerial Issues*, 7(3): 253-276.

Maremont, Mark. 2005. "No Razor Here: Gillette Chief to Get a Giant Payday; About $153 Million Awaits Kilts After P&G Deal, His Second Merger Score." *The Wall Street Journal*, Jan. 31: A1.

Maremont, Mark and Laurie P. Cohen. 2002. "Tyco Spent Millions for Benefit of Kozlowski, Its Former CEO: Company Secretly Forgave Loans, Financed Extravagant Lifestyle." *The Wall Street Journal*, Aug. 7: A1.

Marr, Merissa. 2006a. "In Hollywood, the Picture Blurs for Studio Profits." *The Wall Street Journal*, Sept. 2: A1.

Marr, Merissa. 2006b. "Summer Redstone Gives Tom Cruise His Walking Papers." *The Wall Street Journal*, Aug. 23: A1.

Martin, Justin. 2000. "CEOs in Danger." *Chief Executive*, 160: 22-28.

Masson, Robert T. 1971. "Executive Motivations, Earnings and Consequent Equity Performance." *Journal of Political Economy*, 79: 1,278-1,292.

Matsunaga, Steven R. 1995. "The Effects of Financial Reporting Costs on the Use of Employee Stock Options." *The Accounting Review*, 70(1): 1-26.

Matsunaga, Steve, Terry Shevlin and D. Shores. 1992. "Disqualifying Dispositions of Incentive Stock Options: Tax Benefits Versus Financial Reporting Costs." *Journal of Accounting Research*, 30 (Supplement): 37-68.

Mawani, Amin. 2003. "Cancellation of Executive Stock Options: Tax and Accounting Income Considerations." *Contemporary Accounting Research*, 20(3): 495-517.

Mayers, David, Anil Shivdasani and Clifford W. Smith Jr. 1997. "Board Composition and Corporate Control: Evidence from the Insurance Industry." *Journal of Business*, 70 (1): 33-62.

McBride, Sarah. 2006. "Stern, Agent to Get Early Payout of $219.8 Million in Sirius Stock." *The Wall Street Journal*, Jan. 6: A3.

McCracken, Jeffrey. 2006. "Delphi Plans Salaried Payouts As Hourly Union Wages Are Cut." *The Wall Street Journal*, May 11: A15.

McCracken, Jeffrey and Joann S. Lublin. 2006. "Managers See Leaving Ford as a Better Idea." *The Wall Street Journal*, Aug. 28: B1.

Mehran, Hamid. 1995. "Executive Compensation Structure, Ownership and Firm Performance." *Journal of Financial Economics*, 38, 163-184.

Menn, Joseph. 2000. "Apple's Reward to Jobs in Options May Be Most Ever." *Philadelphia Inquirer*, Jan. 23, E3.

Mercer Human Resource Consulting. 2006. *2006 Global Pay Summary*.

Meulbroek, Lisa K. 2001. "The Efficiency of Equity-Linked Compensation: Understanding the Full Cost of Awarding Executive Stock Options." *Financial Management*, Summer: 5-30.

Meyer, Harvey. 2000. "Boards Take on the Heavy Lifting." *Journal of Business Strategy*, July/August: 18-23.

Meyer, Pearl. 2006. "Aligning the Interests of Directors and Shareholders." *Workspan*, September: 12-13.

Miller, Merton H. and Myron S. Scholes. 1982. *Executive Compensation, Taxes, and Incentives: Financial Economics: Essays in Honor of Paul Cootner*. Prentice-Hall, Englewood Cliffs, N.J., 179-201.

Mishra, Chandra S., David H. Gobeli and Don O. May. 2000a. "The Effectiveness of Long-Term Accounting-Based Incentive Plans." *Journal of Managerial Issues*, 12(1): 48-60.

Mishra, Chandra S., Daniel L. McConaughy and David H. Gobeli. 2000b. "Effectiveness of CEO Pay-For-Performance." *Review of Financial Economics*, 9: 1-13.

Morck, Randall, Andre Shleifer and Robert Vishney. 1988. "Management Ownership and Market Valuation: An Empirical Analysis." *Journal of Financial Economics*, 20: 293-315.

Morgan, Angela G. and Annette B. Poulsen. 2000. "Linking Pay to Performance—Compensation Proposals in the S&P 500." Working paper, Clemson University and the University of Georgia.

Morgenson, Gretchen. 1998. "Stock Options are Not a Free Lunch." *Forbes*, 10: 212-217.

Morgenson, Gretchen. 2004. "No Wonder CEOs Love Those Mergers." *The New York Times*, July 18.

Morgenson, Gretchen. 2005. "What are Mergers Good For?" *The New York Times*, June 5.

Moskowitz, Gary. 1998. "Incentive Alignment or Cooptation? Outside Director Compensation at Large Publicly Traded U.S. Firms." Working Paper.

Murphy, Kevin J. 1985. "Corporate Performance and Management Remuneration: An Empirical Analysis." *Journal of Accounting and Economics*, 7: 11-42.

Murphy, Kevin J. 1999. *Executive Compensation, Handbook of Labor Economics 3*. Orley Ashenfelter and David Card (Editors), North Holland, 2,485-2,525.

Murphy, Kevin J. 1998. "Executive Compensation." Working paper, University of Southern California.

Murphy, Kevin J. 1995. "Politics, Economics and Executive Compensation." *University of Cincinnati Law Review*, 63: 713-746.

Murphy, Kevin J. 1996. "Reporting Choice and the 1992 Proxy Disclosure Rules." *Journal of Accounting, Auditing & Finance*, 11: 497-515.

Murphy, Kevin J., Andrei Shleifer and Robert W. Vishny. 1991. "The Allocation of Talent." *Quarterly Journal of Economics*, 106(2): 503-530.

Murphy, Kevin J. and Jan Zabojnik. 2004. "CEO Pay and Appointments: A Market-Based Explanation for Recent Trends." *AEA Papers and Proceedings* (May): 192-196.

Murphy, Kevin J. and Jerold L. Zimmerman. 1993. "Financial Performance Surrounding CEO Turnover." *Journal of Accounting and Economics*, 16: 273-317.

Murray, Alan. 2006. "In Setting CEO Pay, 'Stern Factor' Isn't a Good Role Model." *The Wall Street Journal*, Jan. 11: A2.

Murray, Alan. 2006b. "A Tale of Two CEOs: How Public Perception Shapes Reputations." *The Wall Street Journal*, July 12: A2.

Murray, Matt. 2001. "Critical Mass: As Huge Companies Keep Growing, CEOs Struggle to Keep Pace." *The Wall Street Journal*, Feb. 8: A1.

Naik, Gautam. 2003. "Glaxo Holders Reject CEO's Compensation Package." *The Wall Street Journal*, May 20: D8.

Nakazato, Minoru, J. Mark Ramseyer and Eric Bennett Rasmusen. 2006. "Executive Compensation in Japan: Estimating Levels and Determinants From Tax Records." Working paper, University of Tokyo, Harvard Law School and Indiana University.

National Association of Corporate Directors. 2000. *1999-2000 Director Compensation Survey*. Washington, D.C.: National Association of Corporate Directors.

New York Times. 1930. "Grace's Large Pay Stirs Bonus Debate." July 27:33.

Newman, Harry A. and Haim A. Mozes. 1999. "Does the Composition of the Compensation Committee Influence CEO Compensation Practices?" *Financial Management*, 28: 3, Autumn, pp. 41-53.

Norris, Floyd. 2007. "SEC Approves New Method for Companies to Value Stock Options." *The New York Times*, C7.

Norris, Floyd. 2006. "U.S. Opposes Bankruptcy Bonus Plan." *The New York Times*, Sept. 5: C1.

Ofek, Eli and David Yermack. 2000. "Taking Stock: Equity-Based Compensation and the Evolution of Managerial Ownership." *The Journal of Finance*, June: pp. 1,367-1,384.

O'Reilly, Charles A., Brian G. Main and Graef S. Crystal. 1988. "CEO Compensation as Tournament and Social Comparison: A Tale of Two Theories." *Administrative Science Quarterly*, 33: 257-274.

O'Reilly, Charles A., James Wade and Tim Pollock. 1996. "Overpaid CEOs and Underpaid Managers: Equity and Executive Compensation." Working paper, Stanford University.

Orr, Deborah and Nigel Holloway. 1999. "Earning More and Hiding It." *Forbes*, May 17: 206-207.

Ossinger, Joanna L. 2006. "CEO Compensation Survey (A Special Report)— Poorer Relations: When It Comes to CEO Pay, Why are the British So Different?" *The Wall Street Journal*, April 10: R6.

Osterland, Andrew. 2001. "Keeping Options Afloat." *CFO*, March: 37-40.

Palia, Darius. 2000. "The Impact of Regulation on CEO Labor Markets." *RAND Journal of Economics*, 31(1) Spring: 165-179.

Park, Yun W., Toni Nelson and Mark R. Huson. 2001. "Executive Pay and the Disclosure Environment: Canadian Evidence." *Journal of Financial Research*, 24 (3): 347-365.

Patton, Arch. 1985. "Those Million-Dollar-a-Year Executives." *Harvard Business Review,* 63(1): 56-62.

Pearl Meyer & Partners. 2004. "Study of Management Equity Participation in The Top 200 Corporations."

Perry, Todd and Marc Zenner. 2001. "Pay for Performance? Government Regulation and the Structure of Compensation Contracts." *Journal of Financial Economics,* 62(3): 453-488.

Perez, Evan. 2003. "Delta's Top Executives Won't Receive Bonuses—Carrier's New CEO Says Other Managers Will Defer Retention-Program Awards." *The Wall Street Journal*, Dec. 24: A3.

Philadelphia Business Journal. 2006. "Readers Say Top Execs' Pay is Just Too High." June 26.

Pfeffer, Jeffrey and Nancy Langton. 1993. "The Effect of Wage Dispersion on Satisfaction, Productivity and Working Collaboratively: Evidence from College and University Faculty." *Administrative Science Quarterly*, 38: 382-407.

Pfeffer, Jeffrey and Alison Davis-Blake. 1992. "Salary Dispersion, Location in the Salary Distribution and Turnover Among College Administrators." *Industrial and Labor Relations Review*, 45(4): 753-763.

Pfeffer, Jeffrey. 1972. "Size and Composition of Corporate Boards of Directors." *Administrative Science Quarterly*, 17: 218-228.

Pourciau, Susan. 1993. "Earnings Management and Nonroutine Executive Changes." *Journal of Accounting and Economics*, 16: 317-336.

Preen, Alexander von and Marc Glaeser. 2005. "Developments in Top-Level Compensation in Germany" in *Top Pay and Performance: International and Strategic Approach* edited by Shaun Tyson and Frank Bournois.

Prendergast, Canice.1999. "The Provision of Incentives in Firms." *Journal of Economic Literature*, 37: 7-63.

Pulliam, Susan. 2000. "New Dot-Com Mantra: 'Just Pay Me in Cash, Please.'" *The Wall Street Journal*, Nov. 28: C1.

Pulliam, Susan and Scott Thurm. 2000. "What Goes Up: For Some Executives the Internet Dream has a Deep Downside." *The Wall Street Journal*, Oct. 20: A1, A6.

Puri, Shaifali. 1997. "The GM-VW Battle: Blood Feud." *Fortune*, April 14: 90-102.

Rajan, Raghuram G. and Julie Wulf. 2006. "Are Perks Purely Managerial Excess?" *Journal of Financial Economics*, 79:1-33.

Rajgopal, Shivaram and Terry Shevlin. 2002. "Empirical Evidence on the Relation Between Stock Option Compensation and Risk Taking." *Journal of Accounting and Economics*, 2 (33), 145–171.

Rajgopal, Shivaram, Michelle Hanlon and Terry Shevlin. 2004. "Large Sample Evidence on the Relation Between Stock Option Compensation and Risk Taking." Working paper, University of Washington and University of Michigan.

Rappaport, Alfred. 1999. "New Thinking on How to Link Executive Pay with Performance." *Harvard Business Review*, 77(2): 91-101.

Ratnesar, Romesh. 2000. "Get Rich Quick! Europe's Executives are Finally Following the Lead of Their U.S. Counterparts and Making a Bundle on Stock-Option Bonuses." *Time*, May 8: B7-8.

Reifman, Shlomo and Samantha N. Wong. 2006. "The Largest Private Companies." *Forbes*, Nov. 9.

Reingold, Jennifer. 2000. "An Options Plan Your CEO Hates." *BusinessWeek*, Feb. 28: 82-87.

Reingold, Jennifer and Ronald Grover. 1999. "Executive Pay: The Numbers are Staggering, but So is the Performance of American Business. So How Closely are They Linked?" *BusinessWeek*, April 19: 72-74.

Reingold, Jennifer and Fred Jespersen. 2000. "Executive Pay: It Continues to Explode—and Options Alone are Creating Paper Billionaires." *BusinessWeek*, April 17: 100-112.

Rickey, Carrie. 2001. "Why We Love Julia: Film's $20 Million Woman, Poised to Pocket an Oscar Tonight, Has it All—Plus Vulnerability and Spunk. We Love Vulnerability and Spunk." *The Philadelphia Inquirer*, March 25: H1.

Rose, Nancy L. and Catherine Wolfram. 2000. "Has the 'Million-Dollar Cap' Affected CEO Pay?" *The American Economic Review*, 90(2): 197-202.

Rosen, Sherwin. 1986. "Prizes and Incentives in Elimination Tournaments." *The American Economic Review*, 76(4): 701-715.

Ryan, Harley E. and Roy A. Wiggins. 2004. "Who is in Whose Pocket? Director Compensation, Board Independence and Barriers to Effective Monitoring." *Journal of Financial Economics*, 73: 497-524.

Sanders, William Gerard and Donald C. Hambrick. 2004. "The Effects of CEO Incentive Compensation on Subsequent Firm Investments and Performance." Working paper, Brigham Young and Penn State universities.

Scannell, Kara. 2006. "SEC May Scrap 'Couric' Rule on Pay Disclosure." *The Wall Street Journal*, July 20: C1.

Scholes, Myron S. and Mark A. Wolfson. 1992. *Taxes and Business Strategy: A Planning Approach*, Prentice Hall.

Schroeder, Michael and Ruth Simon. 2001. "Tech Firms Object, as SEC Gets Tougher on Their Practice of Repricing Options." *The Wall Street Journal*, Feb. 7: C1.

Schroeder, Michael and Jonathan Weil. 2001. "Firms Must Disclose Effect of Accords Rescinding Stock Purchases, SEC Says." *The Wall Street Journal*, Feb. 2: C15.

Seigel, Phyllis A. and Donald C. Hambrick. 2005. "Pay Disparities Within Top Management Groups: Evidence of Harmful Effects on Performance of High-Technology Firms." *Organization Science*, 16(3): 259-274.

Sessa, Danielle and Laura Saunders Egodigwe. 1999. "Incentive Plans Can Fuel Insider Buying." *The Wall Street Journal*, Jan. 13: C1.

Shaw, Jason D., Nina Gupta and John E. Delery. 2002. "Pay Dispersion and Workforce Performance: Moderating Effects of Incentives and Interdependence." *Strategic Management Journal*, 23: 491-512.

Shivdasani, Anil and David Yermack. 1999. "CEO Involvement in the Selection of New Board Members: An Empirical Analysis." *Journal of Finance*, 54(5): 1,829-1,853.

Silver, Sara. 2006. "Verizon Ties CEO Pay to Project Success Instead of Company Stock Performance." *The Wall Street Journal*, Oct. 18: C1.

Silverman, Rachel Emma. 2000. "The Jungle/ What's News in Recruitment and Pay." *The Wall Street Journal*, Aug. 1: B12.

Silverman, Rachel Emma. 2000b. "The Jungle/What's News in Recruitment and Pay," *The Wall Street Journal*, Oct. 31: B18.

Simon, Ruth and Cassell Bryan-Low. 2001. "Unlike Most Investors, Some Insiders Can Cancel Unprofitable Stock Purchases." *The Wall Street Journal*, Feb. 15: C1.

Sloan, Allan. 2000. "The Geeks Microsoft Cares About." *Newsweek*, May 15.

Sloan, Richard. 1993. "Accounting Earnings and Top Executive Compensation." *Journal of Accounting and Economics*, 16, 55-100.

Smith, Clifford W. and Ross L. Watts. 1992. "The Investment Opportunity Set and Corporate Financing, Dividend and Compensation Policies." *Journal of Financial Economics*, 32(3): 263-292.

Smith, Randall. 2000. "Citigroup Chief Weill's Pay Package Rose 37% to $14.1 Million Last Year." *The Wall Street Journal*, March 8: A4.

Solomon, Jay. 2005. "India Poaches U.S. Executives for Tech Jobs." *The Wall Street Journal*, Feb. 22: B1.

Sorkin, Andrew Ross. 2006. "Ex-Head of Gillette to Lead Private Equity Fund." *The New York Times*, Sept. 20: C3.

Sridharan, Uma V. 1996. "CEO Influence and Executive Compensation." *The Financial Review*, 31(1): 51-66.

Stein, Charles. 2005. "As Exec Exits, Harvard Endowment Grows More Than 19 Percent." *The Boston Globe*, Oct. 1.

Stewart, James B. 2006. *Disney War*. Simon & Schuster.

Stodghill, Ron, Christina Del Valle, Greg Sandler and Lois Therrien. 1992. "United They Stand," *BusinessWeek*, Oct. 19: 40-41.

Sullivan, Robert. 2000/2001. "Big Bucks and Baseball: The Idea of Overpaying for an Athlete's Services Didn't Start with A-Rod, and It Won't End With Him." *Time*, Dec. 25/Jan. 1:144.

Sundaram, Rangarajan and David Yermack. 2006. "Pay May Later: Inside Debt and Its Role in Managerial Compensation." *Journal of Finance*. Forthcoming.

Swartz, Steve. 1986. "How Embarrassing! Bear Stearns Officials Wallow in a Windfall—Concern Says Its Bonus Plan Has Provided Executives With 'Exorbitant' Sums." *The Wall Street Journal*, Aug. 26.

Swartz, Steve. 1987. "Bear Stearns Aides, Despite Pay Cuts, Can Grin and Bear It—Six Executives at Concern Outearned All Others at Major Public Firms." *Wall Street Journal*, Aug. 18.

Taub, Stephen. 2006. "Really Big Bucks." *Alpha*, May.

Taussig, Frank W. and W.S. Barker. 1925. "American Corporations and Their Executives: A Statistical Inquiry." *The Quarterly Journal of Economics*, November: 1-51.

Teachers Insurance and Annuity Association—College Retirement Equities Fund. 2000. *Corporate Governance: TIAA-CREF's Policy Statement on Corporate Governance.* New York. Teachers Insurance and Annuity Association—College Retirement Equities Fund.

Tehranian, Hassan and James F. Waegelein. 1985. "Market Reaction to Short-Term Executive Compensation Plan Adoption." *Journal of Accounting and Economics* 7(1-3): 131-144.

Tejada, Carlos. 1997. "Longtime Tandy Director Quits Board, Says He was Punished for Faulting CEO." *The Wall Street Journal*, Jan. 16: B9.

Terhune, Chad. 2006. "Showdown Looms at Home Depot." *The Wall Street Journal*, May 20: A2.

Tharp, Paul. 2003. "Disney Board Critic Silenced." *New York Post*, Feb. 1: 20.

The Economist. 1997. "Exercised." Aug. 2: 59-60.

The Economist. 2004. "Bankers! Glum Prosecutors Lose Their Grip." Jan. 31.

The Wall Street Journal. 2006. "Backdate Backlash." May 27: A6.

The Wall Street Journal. 1999. "Chairman and CEO of US Air Decline Their Cash Bonuses." May 20.

The Wall Street Journal. 2000a. "JCPenney Co. CEO's Salary is Raised 73%, But Bonus is Cut by 93%." April 17: B13.

The Wall Street Journal. 2000b. "Retired Kodak CEO Received $4.9 Million in Pay in 1999." March 14, A8.

The Wall Street Journal. 2000c. "Big Pay for Directors of Small Companies Comes to Light in a New Study." March 9, A1.

The Wall Street Journal. 2000d. "Retiring Plans." Jan. 25, B14.

The Wall Street Journal. 2000e. "CEO's Deal to Trade His Salary for Stock Begins to Pay Off Big." Sept. 13: B6.

Thomas, Randall S. and Kenneth J. Martin. 1999. "The Effect of Shareholder Proposals on Executive Compensation." *University of Cincinnati Law Review*, 67: 1,021-1,081.

Thomaselli, Rich. 2005. "Searching for Michael Jordan." *Advertising Age*, Sept. 5: 12.

Thurm, Scott. 2001. "No-Exit Strategies: Their Outlook Bright, Fiber-Optics Firms Put Job-Hoppers on Notice." *The Wall Street Journal*, Feb. 6: A1.

Tkacik, Maureen. 2003. "Hoops Phenom Signs $90 Million Nike Deal." *The Wall Street Journal.*

Tosi, Henry, Steve Werner, Jeffrey P. Katz and Luis R. Gomez-Mejia. 2000. "How Much Does Performance Matter? A Meta-Analysis of CEO Pay Studies." *Journal of Management*, 26(2): 301-339.

Towers Perrin. 2006. "Managing Global Pay and Benefits: Worldwide Total Remuneration."

Toyne, Michael F., James A. Millar and Bruce L. Dixon. 2000. "The Relation Between CEO Control and the Risk of CEO Compensation." *Journal of Corporate Finance*, 6: 291-306.

Unger, Harlow. 1984. "Life at the Top is Too Rich, U.S. Critics Say." *Industrial Management*, 8(6): 14.

Ungson, Gerardo Rivera and Richard M. Steers. 1984. "Motivation and Politics in Executive Compensation." *Academy of Management Review*, 9(2): 313-323.

Vafeas, Nikos. 2003. "Length of Board Tenure and Outside Director Independence." *Journal of Business Finance and Accounting*, 30(7-8): 1,043-1,065.

Wade, James, Charles A. O'Reilly and Ike Chandratat. 1990. "Golden Parachutes: CEOs and the Exercise of Social Influence." *Administrative Science Quarterly*, 35: 587-603.

Walkling, Ralph A. and Michael S. Long. 1984. "Agency Theory, Managerial Welfare and Takeover Bid Resistance." *RAND Journal of Economics*, 15: 54-68.

Walsh, James P. 1989. "Doing a Deal: Merger and Acquisition Negotiations and Their Impact Upon Target Company Top Management Turnover." *Strategic Management Journal*, 10: 307-322.

Walsh, James P. 1988. "Top Management Turnover Following Mergers and Acquisitions." *Strategic Management Journal*, 9(2): 173-183.

Warner, Jerold B., Ross L. Watts and Karen H. Wruck. 1988. "Stock Prices and Top Management Changes." *Journal of Financial Economics*, 20: 461-492.

Waters, Richard. 2005. "Microsoft Employee Can Work For Rival Google." *Financial Times*, Sept.14: 32.

Watson Wyatt Worldwide. 2004. "Report on Top Management Compensation in Privately Held Companies."

Watson Wyatt Worldwide and WorldatWork. 2006. "Strategic Rewards 2006/2007: Aligning Rewards With the Changing Employment Deal."

Watts, Ross L. and Jerold L. Zimmerman. 1986. *Positive Accounting Theory.* Englewood Cliffs, NJ: Prentice Hall.

Weinbach, Jon. 2005. "Petulance Pays as NFL Contracts Grow in Cost and Complexity." *The Wall Street Journal*, Sept. 9: W1.

Weisbach, Michael S. 1988. "Outside Directors and CEO Turnover." *Journal of Financial Economics*, 20:431-460.

Welles, Edward O. 1998. "Motherhood, Apple Pie & Stock Options." *Inc.*, February: 84-91.

Westphal and Zajac. 1994. "Substance and Symbolism in CEO's Long-Term Incentive Plans." *Administrative Science Quarterly*, 39: 367-390.

White, Erin. 2006. "Employers Increasingly Favor Bonuses to Raises." *The Wall Street Journal*, Aug. 28: B3.

White, Erin and Joann S. Lublin. 2007. "Full Disclosure: Companies Trim Executive Perks To Avoid Glare Jet Rides, Club Dues On Chopping Block As SEC Rules Kick In." *The Wall Street Journal*, Jan. 13: A1.

White, Lourdes Ferreira. 1996. "Executive Compensation and Dividend Policy." *Journal of Corporate Finance*, 2: 335-358.

Whitehouse, Mark. 2006. "How Wal-Mart's Price Cutting Influences Both Rivals and Inflation." *The Wall Street Journal*, Nov. 25: A4.

Whitford, David. 1999. "Consultants Chase the Internet Express: What the Departure of Andersen Consulting's Chief Really Means." *Fortune*, Oct. 25: 44.

Williams, Melissa A., Andrew K. Prevost and Ramesh P. Rao. 2000. "Institutional Shareholder Proposals and the Impact on Top-Management Compensation." Working paper, Georgia State, Cordia and Texas Tech universities.

Williams, Monci Jo. 1985. "Why Chief Executives' Pay Keeps Rising." *Fortune*, April 1: 66-76.

Willing, Richard. 2006. "Top Law Firms Rake in Bigger Buck." *USA Today*, May 1: B4.

Wiseman, Robert M. and Luis R. Gomez-Mejia. 1998. "A Behavioral Agency Model of Managerial Risk Taking." *Academy of Management Review*, 23(1): 133-153.

Woodruff, David. 2001. "Europe, a Latecomer, Embraces Options." *The Wall Street Journal*, May 15: A18.

Yeo, Gillian H. H., Sheng-Syan Chen, Kim Wai Ho and Cheng-few Lee. 1999. "Effects of Executive Share Option Plans on Shareholder Wealth and Firm Performance: The Singapore Evidence." *The Financial Review*, 34: 1-20.

Yermack, David. 1995. "Do Corporations Award CEO Stock Options Effectively?" *Journal of Financial Economics*, 39 (October-November): 237-269.

Yermack, David. 2006. "Golden Handshakes: Separation Pay for Retired and Dismissed CEOs." *Journal of Accounting and Economics*, 41 (3): 237-256.

Yermack, David. 1997. "Good Timing: CEO Stock Option Awards and Company News Announcements." *The Journal of Finance*, 52 (2): 449-476.

Yermack, David. 1996. "Higher Market Valuation of Companies with a Small Board of Directors." *Journal of Financial Economics*, 40: 185-211.

Yermack, D. 2004. "Remuneration, Retention and Reputation Incentives for Outside Directors." *Journal of Finance*, 59 (October): 2,281-2,308.

Zajac, Edward J. and James D. Westphal. 1995. "Accounting for the Explanations of CEO Compensation: Substance and Symbolism." *Administrative Science Quarterly*, 40: 283-308.

Zhou, Xianming. 1999. "Executive Compensation and Managerial Incentives: A Comparison Between Canada and the United States." *Journal of Corporate Finance*, 5: 277-301.

Zimmerman, Rachel. 2006. "Harvard Dropouts: Endowment's Chief to Leave with Others." *The Wall Street Journal*, Jan. 12: C1.

Zimmerman, Ann and Kris Hudson. 2005. "Wal-Mart Sues Ex-Vice Chairman: Complaint Accuses Coughlin Of Fraud, Seeks to Recoup Bonuses and Expenses." *The Wall Street Journal*, July 28: B2.

Zinser, Lynn and Sarah Lyall. 2007. "A Soccer Star Heads to U.S., Heeding Lure of Hollywood." *The New York Times*, Jan. 12, A1.

Zuckerman, Laurence. 1999. "Boeing Bets Faith and Money on Jetliner Executive." *The New York Times*, March 19, C4.

Index

About the Author

Steven Balsam, Professor of Accounting and Merves Research Fellow at the Fox School of Business at Temple University, obtained his Ph.D. from the City University of New York (Baruch College) in 1991. His research interests are executive compensation, earnings management and capital markets. He has published articles in academic journals including *The Accounting Review, Journal of Accounting Research, Journal of Accounting and Economics, Contemporary Accounting Research, Journal of the American Taxation Association, Journal of Accounting and Public Policy, Journal of Accounting, Auditing and Finance* and *Accounting Horizons*. He has been quoted, and his work cited, by *The Philadelphia Inquirer, the Philadelphia Business Journal* and the *Post-Gazette* (Pittsburgh). Prior to coming to Temple University, he taught at Baruch College and the University of Rochester. Before entering academia, he was a Certified Public Accountant working for the international accounting firm of Ernst & Young.